ENCYCLOPEDIA OF WORLD WAR II

VOLUME II

Alan Axelrod

Consulting Editor
Col. Jack A. Kingston, U.S. Army (Ret.)

Facts On File
An imprint of Infobase Publishing

Encyclopedia of World War II

Copyright © 2007 by Alan Axelrod

Facts On File, Inc.
An imprint of Infobase Publishing
132 West 31st Street
New York NY 10001

ISBN-10: 0-8160-6022-3
ISBN-13: 978-0-8160-6022-1

Library of Congress Cataloging-in-Publication Data

Axelrod, Alan, 1952–
Encyclopedia of World War II / Alan Axelrod; consulting editor, Jack A. Kingston.
p. cm.
Includes bibliographical references and index.
ISBN 0-8160-6022-3 (alk. paper)
1. World War, 1939–1945—Encyclopedias. I. Kingston, Jack A. II. Title. III. Title:
Encyclopedia of World War Two. IV. Title: Encyclopedia of World War 2.
D740.A94 2007
940.5303—dc22   2006026155

Facts On File books are available at special discounts when purchased in bulk quantities for
businesses, associations, institutions, or sales promotions. Please call our Special Sales Department
in New York at (212) 967-8800 or (800) 322-8755.

You can find Facts On File on the World Wide Web at http://www.factsonfile.com

Text design by Erika K. Arroyo
Cover design by Salvatore Luongo
Illustrations by Jeremy Eagle and Dale Williams

Printed in the United States of America

VB Hermitage 10 9 8 7 6 5 4 3 2 1

This book is printed on acid-free paper.

Contents

I

Iida Shojiro (1888–1980) *Japanese general*
Iida Shojiro was a skilled commander who proved highly effective during the BURMA CAMPAIGN. He commanded the 4th Imperial Guards Regiment during 1934–35 and was appointed 4th Division chief of staff in 1935, then head of the Military Administration Bureau in the Ministry of War. Named chief of staff of First Army in 1938, he was sent to Taiwan as commanding officer of the Formosa Mixed Brigade during 1938–39. From 1939 to 1941, Iida was in command of the 2nd Imperial Guards Division, then, later in the year, became commanding general of the Twenty-fifth Army in Indochina.

From 1941 to 1943, Iida was general officer commanding Fifteenth Army in Thailand and Burma. He planned and executed the invasion of Burma by his Fifteenth Army and the Southern Army in 1942. On March 10, Rangoon fell to his forces, and the Burma Road was closed, sealing off China from Allied communication, reinforcement, and supply.

During 1943–44, Iida was recalled to Japan and put in charge of the General Defense Command. He retired in 1944 but was recalled to active duty the following year to command the Thirtieth Army in Manchuria. It was his final assignment before the surrender of Japan.

Further reading: Astor, Gerald. *The Jungle War: Mavericks, Marauders and Madmen in the China-Burma-India Theater of World War II.* New York: Wiley, 2004; Dupuy, Trevor N. *Asiatic Land Battles: Allied Victories in China and Burma.* New York: Franklin Watts, 1963; Hogan, David W. *India-Burma (The U.S. Army Campaigns of World War II).* Carlisle, Pa.: Army Center of Military History, 1991; Webster, Donovan. *The Burma Road: The Epic Story of the China-Burma-India Theater in World War II.* New York: Farrar, Straus and Giroux, 2003.

Imamura Hitoshi (1886–1968) *Japanese general*
Before the war, during 1931–32, Imamura Hitoshi was chief of the Army General Staff Operations Section, then served as liaison to 9th Division in China. Promoted to regimental command after 1932, he became a major general and was named to command a brigade in 1935. The following year, Imamura was appointed deputy chief of staff of the Kwantung Army in occupied Manchuria, then was named commandant of the Infantry School in 1937.

Promoted to the rank of lieutenant general, Imamura was assigned to command the 5th Division in China, remaining in this position from 1938 to 1940, when he was named inspector general of military education. He held this very powerful post during 1940–41, his office exercising approval over all officer postings, up to and including the choice of army minister. This made him one of the most influential officers in the Imperial

Army. Imamura returned to a field command in November 1941, when he was named commanding general of the Sixteenth Japanese Army, which he led in the conquest of the Dutch East Indies during 1941–42. He personally landed with his troops on the island of Java. In November 1942, Imamura assumed command of the Eighth Area Army, a post that included responsibility for the Seventeenth Japanese Army in the Solomons and the Eighteenth Japanese Army in New Guinea. In 1943, he was promoted to full general.

After the war, Imamura Hitoshi was tried at the TOKYO WAR CRIMES TRIBUNAL for a variety of war crimes. Found guilty, he was imprisoned at Sugamo from 1946 to 1954.

Further reading: Astor, Gerald. *The Jungle War: Mavericks, Marauders and Madmen in the China-Burma-India Theater of World War II.* New York: Wiley, 2004; Slim, William. *Defeat Into Victory.* New York: Cooper Square, 2000.

Imphal Offensive

This was the key turning point in the BURMA CAMPAIGN. Lieutenant General Mutaguchi Renya led his Fifteenth Japanese Army in a high-stakes attack from Burma into India, targeting the Allied supply bases at Imphal in Manipur. His immediate objective in this action was to preempt an offensive by WILLIAM SLIM's Fourteenth British Army, but his longer-term goal was to gain a purchase for the Japanese-controlled INDIAN NATIONAL ARMY and thereby incite a revolt against the British raj (colonial government) in India. Had the Imphal Offensive succeeded, the British might well have lost control of India, and with India lost, China would have been doomed. Mutaguchi knew that he was outnumbered and lacked air superiority. His only hope, he decided, was to achieve complete tactical surprise and to move with great speed. To even the odds as best he could, Mutaguchi preceded the offensive by ordering Lieutenant General Kawabe Masakazu to attack Arakan in February, thereby drawing off some of Slim's reserves.

Mutaguchi formulated a plan intended to divide and dilute Slim's forces. On March 7, his 33rd Division attacked from the south, pushing Slim's 17th Division from its position at Tiddim and into a fighting retreat. Simultaneously, Mutaguchi's Yamamoto Force attacked the 20th Division near Tamu but was checked at Shenam Saddle. The following week, Mutaguchi sent his 15th and 31st Divisions across the Chindwin River in an attempt to catch Slim in a pincers action and create a decisive double envelopment of his forces. This might well have worked, had it not been for the defeat of the earlier Japanese Arakan offensive. With this attack neutralized, Slim airlifted his 5th and 7th Divisions to Imphal beginning on March 19.

By this time, the main body of the Japanese advance was a mere 30 miles away. But this was not the only cliff-hanger of the campaign. Although Slim had anticipated that Kohima, just northwest of Imphal, would be attacked, he relied on the rugged terrain here to impede such an action. He calculated that the Japanese would be unable to deploy more than a single regiment in the attack. This proved to be a nearly catastrophic assessment as, astoundingly, Lieutenant General Sato Kotuku was able to field his entire 31st Division, which engaged the vastly outnumbered 50th Indian Parachute Brigade at Sangshak and took Kohima on April 3. On April 12, Mutaguchi's 15th Division severed the road between Kohima and Imphal and positioned itself above Slim's 4th Corps.

The achievements of both Sato and Mutaguchi were extraordinary and certainly exploited the element of surprise to the utmost; however, travel and battle over the hostile terrain took a terrible toll on the attackers, victorious though they were, and Mutaguchi's men were simply too exhausted to press their hard-won advantages. In a counterattack that relied heavily on armor (against which the Japanese, lacking armor themselves, were powerless), Slim pushed back Mutaguchi but could not recover use of the Kohima-Imphal road. Therefore, Slim relied wholly on airlift to maintain supply of his now isolated forces. Desperate as this situation was, Slim knew that Mutaguchi was in an even tougher spot. Starved for supplies, Mutaguchi over-extended his forces in an attack on Dimapur. Slim checked this effort and forced Mutaguchi into a contest of attrition, which favored Slim. As the miserable monsoon encroached in May, Mutaguchi's men, starving and assailed by tropical diseases, melted away. At last, on July 18, Mutaguchi withdrew back across the Chindwin River. Although Slim's forces were subject to many of the same miseries, they were not in nearly as dire straits. Slim pursued the withdrawing Japanese and transformed the Japanese retreat into a rout. The result was disaster for the Japanese in Burma. Of 85,000 Japanese troops committed there, 53,000 became casualties. Some 30,000 were killed in combat, and thousands more died of disease and privation. Precious weapons and heavy equipment had to be abandoned. As for the Indian National Army, the reversal of the Imphal Offensive permanently removed it as a threat. Mutaguchi had gambled boldly and lost decisively.

Further reading: Astor, Gerald. *The Jungle War: Mavericks, Marauders and Madmen in the China-Burma-India Theater of World War II*. New York: Wiley, 2004; Dupuy, Trevor N. *Asiatic Land Battles: Allied Victories in China and Burma*. New York: Franklin Watts, 1963; Hogan, David W. *India-Burma (The U.S. Army Campaigns of World War II)*. Carlisle, Pa.: Army Center of Military History, 1991; Webster, Donovan. *The Burma Road: The Epic Story of the China-Burma-India Theater in World War II*. New York: Farrar, Straus and Giroux, 2003.

incendiary bombs

Incendiary bombs, aerial bombs intended to ignite fires, were used extensively for the first time in World War II, especially by the Americans against Japanese cities, which, because of their flammable building materials, were extremely vulnerable to incendiary attack. The most widely used incendiary bomb in the European theater was a 4-pound weapon filled with thermate, a mixture of thermite (iron oxide combined with powdered aluminum) and an oxidizing agent. Four-pound thermate bombs were dropped in a total quantity of 80 million units called "clusters." Against Japan, the Americans used another type of incendiary bomb, the six-pound M-69 "oil bomb," which was filled with napalm (jellied gasoline) and was designed to eject this flaming substance over many yards after being dropped in clusters. As it burned, the thick napalm, thus projected, tended to adhere to structures and people, thereby increasing damage and injury.

Napalm incendiaries proved highly effective, whereas the thermate incendiaries favored by the British tended to produce heat that dissipated too quickly for maximum effectiveness. German incendiaries improved on the thermite-only bombs by adding magnesium to the blend. The thermite ignited the magnesium, which provided a much longer-lasting source of ignition heat. Worse for those targeted, a magnesium fire cannot be extinguished with water. Instead of quenching a magnesium-fueled blaze, water both intensifies and spreads it.

The Japanese produced incendiary bombs of an entirely different design from those of the other combatants. The Japanese bomb was packed with some 700 open-ended iron cylinders filled with thermite. The bomb was fused so that it would detonate at 200 feet above the ground, broadcasting the flaming cylinders over a 500-foot radius. This made for a highly effective antipersonnel weapon.

Further reading: Javorek, Joseph. *Types of Incendiary Bombs, Composition and Method of Extinguishing*. Washington, D.C.: Civilian Defense, 1942.

India

At the outbreak of World War II, India, the "jewel in the crown" of the British Empire, had a population of some 318.7 million and represented for Great Britain an enormous military responsibility as well as resource. India was rich in a variety of strategic raw materials and was a potentially huge source of military manpower. Its location fronting both Africa and the Middle East was key in global warfare. Unfortunately for Great Britain, India was also in the throes of a long-standing independence movement and could not be counted on—as so much of the rest of the empire and commonwealth could be—to contribute to the war effort or, for that matter, to remain loyal.

The politically sensitive, even precarious, situation did not stop Lord Linlithgow, the British viceroy in India, from unilaterally declaring India to be at war with Germany. That he did not consult such rising Indian leaders as Mohandas Gandhi and Jawaharlal Nehru, let alone the Indian public, caused great outrage, resentment, and defiance. Most Indians and most Indian leaders were inclined to support the Allies and certainly abhorred the Nazis and fascists (although Gandhi and his followers advocated a policy of total nonviolence), but Linlithgow's high-handedness inextricably linked support for the war effort with support for continued imperial rule. Feeling betrayed and unwilling to be identified as puppets of the British, India's leaders withheld support from the British Raj (as the ruling government was called) and demanded that Britain plead its case for Indian support by stating its postwar "goals and ideals;" that is, the Indian leaders were looking for a pledge that Britain would progressively lead India toward full independence after the war. When Linlithgow refused to oblige the Indian Congress with such a declaration, Congress called on its provincial ministries to resign. This gave Muhammad Ali Jinnah, the most prominent leader of India's Muslims (and, later, founder of Pakistan), an opening to gain ground with the British. Jinnah pledged Linlithgow the support of India's Muslims, many of whom were members of the Anglo-Indian armed forces. Thus the course of the war saw a split between the Hindu-dominated Indian Congress, which drifted further and further from the British (espousing a doctrine of "active noncooperation"), and the Muslim League, which supported the British war effort.

Gandhi and Nehru both campaigned against the war on pacifist principles and were jailed for their protests. By June 1941, more than 20,000 protesters were in Indian prisons. Whereas Gandhi, Nehru, and their followers opposed war itself, SUBBAS CHANDRA BOSE actively seized on the war as a means of hastening Indian independence. He worked with the Germans and Japanese to create the INDIAN NATIONAL ARMY in 1943, which collaborated with the Japanese.

In March 1942, some four months after Japan had entered World War II, British prime minister WINSTON CHURCHILL sent Sir Stafford Cripps, a British Socialist and personal friend of Nehru, to India with a postwar proposal. Churchill's hope was to secure India as a bulwark against the rapid expansion of Japanese control in the East. Through Cripps, the government proposed to grant full dominion status to India after the war, with the proviso that any province could vote itself out of the dominion. Gandhi and Nehru rejected the proposal, and Gandhi repeated the demand of the movement he led, that the British summarily "quit India," leaving it to the Indians to deal with the Japanese through nonviolent means. In response, by August 1942, British authorities put another 60,000 Indians behind bars, and a major military effort was mounted to crush Indian resistance. By the middle of 1943, Field Marshal ARCHIBALD WAVELL replaced Linlithgow as viceroy and immediately put Indian under martial law for the rest of the war.

Despite resistance, India produced massive amounts of agricultural goods and other raw materials for the war effort. Manufacturing exploded in India during the war years, and the nation contributed guns, ammunition, machine tools, aircraft supplies, vehicles, and other goods. Airfields sprung up all across the subcontinent, and India's coastal cities became major ports as well as centers of ship repair. To some, the enormous surge in production brought substantial profit, but the war economy also created nearly ruinous inflation throughout India. Economic problems were compounded by the devastating Bengal famine of 1943, which brought severe food shortages. Another unanticipated consequence of the war economy was the transformation of India from a debtor nation to a creditor. By the end of the war, Great Britain alone owed India some £1.3 billion.

India's contribution to the Allied war effort also included its professional volunteer army, a service with a very long, distinguished record. At the outbreak of the war in 1939, the Indian army consisted of 205,000 Indian troops and 63,269 British troops, plus 83,706 troops from the "princely states"— Indian states not under direct British control but governed as British client states (representing about one-third of the subcontinent). Despite the preponderance of Indian soldiers in the Indian army, the officer corps was overwhelmingly British. At the outbreak of war, only 396 out of 4,424 officers were Indian. By the end of the war, the strength of the Indian army had risen to 2.5 million men, all volunteers and the largest all-volunteer army in history. This force was commanded by 34,500 British officers and 8,300 Indian officers. Casualties by war's end included 24,338 killed and more than 64,000 wounded. Some 12,000 went missing, and another 80,000 were taken prisoner.

While the Indian army was very large by the end of the war, the Royal Indian Navy, which had been established as recently as 1934, remained modest, although it did significantly expand during the war. In September 1939, its strength stood at 1,700 men. By the end of the war, its ranks numbered 30,478 men, furnishing the crews for 10 sloops, three frigates, four corvettes, 17 minesweepers, and various smaller vessels. The mission of the Royal Indian Navy was exclusively to patrol the coasts and see to all matters relating to coastal defense.

The Royal Indian Air Force came into being one year before the Royal Indian Navy and had 1,628 men in 1939 and 26,900 enlisted personnel, plus 1,638 officers, by 1945. At war's end, these personnel manned three fighter-reconnaissance squadrons, two ground-attack squadrons, two light bomber squadrons, and two fighter squadrons.

Further reading: Moser, Don. *China-Burma-India.* Alexandria, Va.: Time Life, 1978; Webster, Donovan. *The Burma Road: The Epic Story of the China-Burma-India Theater in World War II.* New York: Farrar, Straus & Giroux, 2003.

Indian National Army (INA)

The INA came into existence in February 1942, created from the Indian Independence League,
which was led by a Bangkok-based Sikh missionary named Giani Pritam Singh and F. Kikan, an Indian independence organization founded by Japanese army intelligence officer Fujiwara Iwaichi. The ranks of the INA were filled by Indian Army POWs captured after the FALL OF MALAYA and the FALL OF SINGAPORE. A women's auxiliary of the INA, the Rani of Jhansi Regiment, was also later created.

Mohan Singh, one of the Singapore POWs, was named commander of the INA and, with Fujiwara, set about recruiting members by advocating the organization as the quickest means of achieving independence for India. Some 20,000 of 60,000 POWs at Singapore joined, but by December 1942, Singh began to believe that the Japanese had little interest in actually allowing the creation of an independent India. When he began to voice his suspicions, he was arrested and the INA was temporarily disbanded. It was reconstituted in June 1943 under the nationalist leader SUBHAS CHANDRA BOSE, who planned to use the INA as the vanguard of a Japanese invasion of India, which, he believed, would trigger a massive popular rebellion against the British. The Japanese were not persuaded that such a rebellion would take place and instead wanted to use INA troops in piecemeal fashion as adjuncts to Japanese units for purposes of sabotage and propaganda. Bose continued to insist, however, and the Japanese agreed to use about 7,000 INA troops in their ill-fated IMPHAL OFFENSIVE, an abortive invasion of India.

The Imphal Offensive was a disaster, and the INA performed especially poorly in it. Large numbers deserted or surrendered. Subsequently, even more surrendered in Burma, and the 5,000-man INA garrison at Rangoon surrendered without offering resistance when that city was retaken by the British.

Although the INA was a total military failure, the British administration in India made the colossal error of putting many INA members on trial following the war. For independence-minded Indians, this cast them in a heroic light, and the INA thus became a political focal point of the postwar independence movement.

Further reading: Bakshi, Akhil. *The Road to Freedom: Travels Through Singapore, Malaysia, Burma, and India in the Footsteps of the Indian National Army.* Ajax, Ontario: Odyssey Books, 1998; Elsbree, Willard H. *Japan's Role in Southeast Asian Nationalist Movements, 1940 to 1945.* Cambridge, Mass.: Harvard University Press, 1953; Fujiwara, Iwaichi, and F. Kikan: *Japanese Army Intelligence Operations in Southeast Asia During World War II.* Hong Kong: Heinemann Asia, 1983; Jones, Francis Clifford. *Japan's New Order in East Asia: Its Rise and Fall, 1937–45.* London: Oxford University Press, 1954; Lebra, Joyce. *Japanese-trained Armies in Southeast Asia: Independence and Volunteer Forces in World War II.* Hong Kong: Heinemann Educational Books, 1977; Lebra-Chapman, Joyce. *Jungle Alliance: Japan and the Indian National Army.* Canberra, Australia: Donald Moore for Asia Pacific Press, 1971; Mangat, Gurbachan Singh. *Indian National Army: Role in India's Struggle for Freedom.* Columbia, Mo.: South Asia Books, 1992; Sareen, T. R. *The History of the Indian National Army.* New Delhi: Gyan Publishing House, 2003; Sareen, T. R. *Japan and the Indian National Army.* Columbia, Mo.: South Asia Books, 1986.

internment, Japanese-American

At the time of the BATTLE OF PEARL HARBOR, December 7, 1941, approximately 120,000 persons of immediate Japanese descent were resident in the continental United States, most of them living on the West Coast. Of these, some 80,000 had been born in this country and were citizens. Within four days after Pearl Harbor, the Federal Bureau of Investigation (FBI) arrested and detained 1,370 Japanese Americans as "dangerous enemy aliens," despite their American citizenship. On December 22, the Agriculture Committee of the Los Angeles Chamber of Commerce issued a public call to put Japanese Americans "under federal control." The source of this call was significant; for many years, Japanese-American farmers had been successfully farming in California, Oregon, and Washington, offering stiff competition to Caucasian farmers, who controlled the Agriculture Committee. The committee's probable special agenda notwithstanding, there can be no doubt that, following the "sneak attack" on U.S. territory, many Americans

genuinely feared that Japanese Americans would align themselves with their country of origin or ancestry and would commit acts of sabotage or worse.

On January 5, 1942, all U.S. draft boards automatically classified Japanese-American selective service registrants as enemy aliens, and many Japanese-Americans who were already serving were discharged or restricted to menial labor duties. On January 6, Leland Ford, congressman from the district encompassing Los Angeles, sent a telegram to Secretary of State Cordell Hull, asking that all Japanese Americans be physically relocated from the West Coast. Before the end of the month, the California State Personnel Board voted to bar from civil service positions all "descendants of natives with whom the United States [is] at war." As worded, the ban included descendants of Germans and Italians, but it was put into practice only against Japanese Americans.

On January 29, U.S. Attorney General Francis Biddle established "prohibited zones," areas forbidden to all enemy aliens. Accordingly, German and Italian as well as Japanese aliens were ordered to leave San Francisco waterfront areas. The next day, California attorney general Earl Warren (who would in the 1950s become nationally known as the civil libertarian chief justice of the U.S. Supreme Court) issued an urgent statement calling for preemptive action to prevent a repetition of Pearl Harbor. Early the next month, the U.S. Army designated 12 "restricted areas," in which enemy aliens were to be subject to a curfew from 9 P.M. to 6 A.M. and in which they were permitted to travel only to and from work, never going more than five miles from their homes.

On February 6, 1942, a Portland, Oregon, American Legion post published an appeal for the removal of Japanese Americans from the West Coast. This was followed a week later by an appeal from the entire West Coast congressional delegation to President FRANKLIN D. ROOSEVELT asking for an executive order for the removal. On February 16, the California Joint Immigration Committee urged that all Japanese Americans be removed from the Pacific Coast and other vital areas.

By February 19, the FBI held 2,192 Japanese Americans, and on that day, President Roosevelt signed Executive Order 9066, authorizing the secretary of war to define military areas "from which any or all persons may be excluded as deemed necessary or desirable." As interpreted and executed by Secretary of War Henry Stimson and the officer he put in charge of the operation, Lieutenant General John DeWitt, this meant that Japanese Americans, citizens (Nisei) and noncitizens (Issei), living within 200 miles of the Pacific Coast were ordered to be "evacuated." Pursuant to this order, more than 100,000 persons were moved to internment camps in California, Idaho, Utah, Arizona, Wyoming, Colorado, and Arkansas.

Conditions at the camps were neither inhuman nor inhumane and in no way merit comparison with Nazi CONCENTRATION AND EXTERMINATION CAMPS. Nevertheless, the camps were undeniably spartan, and it is true that many internees suffered significant to catastrophic financial loss as a result of their compulsory internment. The emotional trauma of forced dislocation is far more difficult to assess. In any case, the only significant opposition to the removal came from Quaker activists and the American Civil Liberties Union (ACLU). The ACLU funded lawsuits brought before the U.S. Supreme Court—most notably *Hirabayashi v. United States* and *Korematsu v. United States*—but in all cases, the high court upheld the constitutionality of the executive order in time of war.

During their internment, some 1,200 young Japanese men secured release from the camps by enlisting in the U.S. Army. They were segregated in the 442nd Regimental Combat Team, which also consisted of about 10,000 Japanese-Hawaiian volunteers. (Japanese-Hawaiians had not been subject to the removal order.) The 442nd was shipped out to Europe, where it compiled an extraordinary combat record in Italy, France, and Germany, emerging from the war as the most highly decorated unit of its size and length of service in American military history.

On December 17, 1944, Major General Henry C. Pratt issued Public Proclamation No. 21, which, effective January 2, 1945, permitted the "evacuees" to return to their homes. Congress passed a Japanese American Evacuation Claims Act of 1948, which paid out approximately $31 million in compensation, a tiny fraction of the actual financial losses incurred. All subsequent individual suits seeking compensation from the government failed until 1968, when a new act of Congress reimbursed some who had lost property because of their relocation. Twenty years after this, in 1988, Congress appropriated more funds to pay a lump sum of $20,000 to each of the 60,000 surviving Japanese-American internees.

Further reading: Irons, Peter H., ed. *Justice Delayed: The Record of the Japanese American Internment Cases.* Middletown, Conn.: Wesleyan University Press, 1989; Ng, Wendy L. *Japanese American Internment During World War II: A History and Reference Guide.* Westport, Conn.: Greenwood Publishing Group, 2002.

Iran

At the outbreak of World War II, Iran, which up to 1935 had been called Persia, was officially neutral; however, under its ruler, Reza Shah Pahlavi, the nation maintained warm relations with Germany, which was an important trading partner and source of foreign investment. The cordiality of this relationship was highly alarming to the Allies, particularly Great Britain, which saw Iran's tremendous oil reserves and oil production as vital to the war effort and a prize of inestimable value. Moreover, Iran, with its well-developed trans-Iranian rail system, was an important overland link to the Soviet Union, a means of conveying much-needed supplies to that ally.

On August 21, 1941, Britain and the Soviet Union jointly requested that Iran expel the 2,000–3,000 German nationals resident in the country. When the shah refused, Soviet and British forces invaded Iran on August 25, 1941. Two Indian divisions, the 8th and the 10th, invaded from the south and west, respectively, while the 47th Soviet Army and 44th Soviet Army invaded from the north, and the 53rd Soviet Army entered from the east. The multipoint invasion quickly overwhelmed Iranian resistance, which was scattered and uncoordinated, and Reza Shah Pahlavi, abdicating in favor of his son, Mohammad Reza Shah Pahlavi, fled to South Africa, where he died in exile in July 1944. In the meantime, the 22-year-old Mohammad Reza Shah quickly reversed the course set by his father. In return for a guarantee of territorial integrity and independence, he concluded a tripartite treaty of alliance with Great Britain and the USSR at Tehran on January 29, 1942. Soon after, he severed diplomatic relations with Germany, expelled all German nationals, and, on April 12, 1942, severed diplomatic relations with Japan as well.

The Allies pledged to leave Iran within six months after the end of hostilities with Germany, but later extended this to six months after the end of hostilities with Japan. At the Tehran Conference in November 1943, the United States affirmed its adherence to these terms as well. The Allies also pledged a strict policy of noninterference with the internal affairs of Iran during the war, but, in fact, they were very active within the country and exercised extensive control over roads, railways, waterways, ports, communications, and even food supplies and labor allotment, all to ensure a steady flow of oil to the Allies and the maintenance of a supply lifeline to the Soviet Union. About 4,159,117 tons of LEND LEASE goods were delivered to the USSR via Iran, representing 23.8 percent of the total wartime aid to that country. The Allies dubbed Iran "the bridge to victory."

Further reading: Andari, Ali. *A History of Modern Iran Since 1921: The Pahlavis and After.* London: Longman, 2003; Porch, Douglas. *The Path to Victory: The Mediterranean Theater in World War II.* New York: Farrar, Straus and Giroux, 2004.

Iraq

Iraq was part of the Ottoman Empire until after World War I, when the League of Nations made it a British mandate. In 1932, Iraq achieved full legal independence, except for certain provisions of the Anglo-Iraqi Treaty of 1930, which (among other things) gave Great Britain a special commercial interest in the oilfields of Mosul and Kirkuk, allowed free passage of British troops, and reserved land near Basra and Habbaniya for the maintenance of British air bases. The treaty never sat well with many factions in Iraq and, by the outbreak of World War II, generated sufficient anti-British sentiment to drive some in the government toward friendly relations with Germany. Emir Abdullah, as regent, was the titular head of the Iraqi state, but the government was actually led by Prime Minister Nuri es-Sa'id, who was pro-British. He favored a declaration of war against Germany but was blocked by strongly nationalist factions and, in the end, Nuri had to content himself with severing diplomatic relations with the Germans.

In March 1940, Nuri was replaced as prime minister by Rashid Ali, who was openly pro-Nazi and had ties to the Golden Square, an Iraqi military junta that favored the Axis. Under Rashid, the Iraqi government intrigued against British interests; however, British military successes in the Middle East turned Iraqi popular opinion against both Rashid and the Golden Square. He resigned in January 1941. A military coup soon followed the resignation, and Rashid Ali was returned to office as prime minister on April 3, 1941. The Axis governments dangled offers of aid to Rashid, who responded by refusing to honor the Anglo-Iraqi Treaty. British troops were barred from traversing Iraqi territory, and Iraqi troops were sent to surround the air base at Habbaniya. The Germans sent aircraft to assist the Iraqi army in resisting the British, and in May there were armed exchanges. The VICHY GOVERNMENT in Syria likewise furnished Iraqi forces with supplies and materiel.

Axis and Vichy support was insufficient to counter an invasion consisting of Indian, British, and Arab Legion (from Transjordan) troops. The Iraqi army dispersed before the invaders, the Iraqi air force, consisting of just 56 obsolescent aircraft, was destroyed, and Habbaniya was relieved in less than a month. The Anglo-Indian-Arab force surrounded Baghdad, forcing the conclusion of an armistice. The regent returned, and Nuri was reinstated as prime minister and head of an openly pro-British government. Iraq declared war on the Axis in January 1943.

Further reading: Marr, Phebe. *Modern History of Iraq.* Denver: Westview Press, 2003; Porch, Douglas. *The Path to Victory: The Mediterranean Theater in World War II.* New York: Farrar, Straus and Giroux, 2004; Shores, Christopher. *Dust Clouds in the Middle East: The Air War for East Africa, Iraq, Syria, Iran and Madagascar, 1940–1942.* London: Grub Street, 1996.

Iron Guard uprising in Romania

The *Garda de Fier,* or Iron Guard, grew out of the fascist Legion of the Archangel Michael, founded in 1927 by Corneliu Zelea Codreanu, a virulent anticommunist and anti-Semite. Codreanu created the Iron Guard in 1930 as the paramilitary arm of the legion, which was dedicated to the "Christian and racial" renewal of ROMANIA. Perceiving a threat from the Iron Guard, the Romanian government dissolved it in December 1933, but it quickly reappeared under the guise of the Everything for the Fatherland Party and even received some support from King Carol II. He suppressed the party once again in 1938, however, after proclaiming a personal dictatorship. By this time, Everything for the Fatherland was Romania's third-largest political party. Hoping to curb the party's influence, Carol imprisoned Codreanu in April 1938, and on November 30, 1938, while Codreanu was being transferred from one prison to another, he and 13 followers were garroted and shot. The government claimed they had tried to escape. Considering the manner of their deaths, this explanation is quite impossible to believe.

The Iron Guard was revived in 1940 after Carol abdicated, and Guardists were installed in the cabinets of General ION ANTONESCU during 1940–41. In January 1941, the Iron Guard mounted a revolt against Antonescu because they believed he was insufficiently pro-German. The government of ADOLF HITLER, however, disavowed the uprising, and the Iron Guard was again suppressed, this time permanently. The Guardists were purged from the government.

Further reading: Codreanu, Corneliu Zelea. *For My Legionaries: The Iron Guard.* Earlysville, Va.: Liberty Bell Publications, 2003; Giurescu, Dinu C., and Eugenia Elena Popescu. *Romania in World War II.* New York: Columbia University East European Monographs, 2000; Treptow, Kurt W., ed. *Romania and World War II.* Iasi, Romania: Center for Romanian Studies, 1996.

island-hopping strategy

Early in the Pacific war, U.S. admiral CHESTER NIMITZ proposed what was generally called the "island hopping strategy." It was an overall plan for the conduct of the amphibious war in the Pacific theater and consisted of developing a series of amphibious assaults on selected Japanese island fortresses while either entirely skipping over others or subjecting some islands to air attack only. What Nimitz recognized, with DOUGLAS MACARTHUR's concurrence, was that isolating some Japanese forces was as effective as attacking and destroying them—and, of course, far less costly. While the Japanese had control of many islands early in the war, the far-flung deployment of occupying forces rendered each of those forces vulnerable if communication with other occupied islands was severed.

As developed, the island-hopping campaign consisted of two prongs, a northern and a southern. The northern prong was projected from Midway into the central Pacific, reaching Iwo Jima in February 1945. The southern prong originated from Guadalcanal and moved out to the Solomon Islands and, finally, the Philippines in early 1945.

Further reading: Driskill, Frank A. *Chester W. Nimitz: Admiral of the Hills.* Austin, Tex.: Eakin Press, 1983; Hoyt, Edwin P. *How They Won the War in the Pacific: Nimitz and His Admirals.* New York: Lyons Press, 2000.

Italian Campaign

Costly and heartbreaking, the Allies' Italian Campaign had been conceived as an opportunity to make what seemed relatively easy inroads into the Nazi-held European mainland while also drawing off German military resources that would otherwise be committed to the Soviet front. British prime minister WINSTON CHURCHILL saw the invasion of Italy as a means of attacking "the soft underbelly of Europe," and following the successful completion of the NORTH AFRICAN CAMPAIGN, it certainly seemed like the next logical step. From North Africa, the Allies proceeded with the SICILY CAMPAIGN and, that completed, jumped off for Italy.

Opportunistic and logical, the Italian Campaign nevertheless did not receive unanimous Allied backing. In general, Churchill favored it, as he favored a concentration of force throughout the Mediterranean, but American military planners, including GEORGE C. MARSHALL and DWIGHT DAVID EISENHOWER, believed that devoting major forces to this theater unnecessarily diluted efforts that should be allocated to OPERATION OVERLORD, the NORMANDY LANDINGS (D-DAY). Soviet premier JOSEPH STALIN also objected to the concentration on the Italian Campaign, believing that it was an excuse to avoid a major invasion of Europe. Churchill and the British Imperial General Staff countered that the action in Italy would not only draw German strength away from the Soviet front, but also away from France, thereby facilitating the planned invasion. Ultimately, this logic carried the day. What none of the Allies had anticipated, however, was the fierceness of German resistance in Italy. The belief was that Allied forces would advance quickly up the Italian peninsula and would soon be positioned north of Florence, posing a grave menace to the highly vulnerable southern flank of the German army. In fact, progress up the peninsula was a deadly slog, and the southern flank of the German army was not reached until very nearly the end of the war.

One thing both the British and the Americans did agree on was the necessity for speed and surprise. Both of these elements were sacrificed, however, as the Allies held off invading the mainland while they debated whether the surrender terms offered by the provisional Italian government under Marshal PIETRO BADOGLIO were consistent with the agreement, reached at the CASABLANCA CONFERENCE, to accept nothing less than uncondi-

tional surrender. By the time this issue had been settled, the Germans had deployed 16 new divisions in Italy. On September 3 and 4, the Eighth British Army crossed the Strait of Messina from Sicily and landed on the toe of the Italian boot, at Reggio di Calabria. They were almost unopposed. The Italian surrender was announced on September 8, 1943, and, on the next day, the Fifth U.S. Army landed at Salerno and, in stark contrast to the British experience, were met by fierce German resistance in the very hard-fought BATTLE OF SALERNO, which nearly drove the invaders back into the sea. Although the Americans managed to hold the beachhead, ADOLF HITLER was highly impressed by the conduct of his principal commander in Italy, ALBERT KESSELRING, and he resolved with Kesselring to make the Allies pay dearly for every inch of an Italian advance.

The Allies had anticipated making a BLITZKRIEG-like advance up the peninsula. Instead, the entire Italian Campaign was a grinding war of attrition against extremely well-prepared and tenacious German defenses. If the German army had proved terrifying when it was on the attack early in the war, it showed itself to be equally formidable in the defensive role.

The BATTLES OF CASSINO, fought from January 12 to May 18, 1944, were all too typical of the Italian Campaign. The Germans were deployed expertly in the rugged terrain of central Italy, a defensive ground they exploited to full advantage. British general HAROLD ALEXANDER, in overall command of the Eighth British Army and the Fifth U.S. Army, consistently underestimated the Germans' ability to defend against the advance, and combat here came to resemble the deadly futility of World War I trench warfare far more than the mobile fighting typical of World War II elsewhere. The frustrating circumstances seemed to bring out the worst in Fifth U.S. Army commander MARK W. CLARK, who continually pounded the German line with frontal attacks that were doomed to fail. He was driven, in large part, by the need to break through the line in order to link up with and relieve the U.S. VI Corps, which was pinned down at Anzio. The ANZIO CAMPAIGN

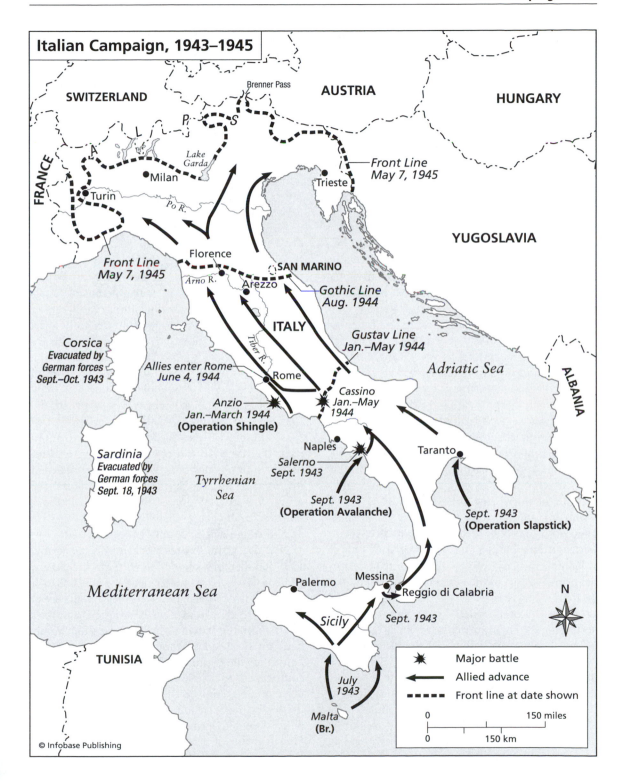

Italian Campaign, 1943–1945

SWITZERLAND
AUSTRIA
HUNGARY

Brenner Pass

A L P S

FRANCE

Lake Garda
Milan
Turin
Po R.

Trieste

Front Line May 7, 1945

YUGOSLAVIA

Florence
SAN MARINO
Front Line May 7, 1945
Arno R.
Arezzo
Gothic Line Aug. 1944

ITALY
Tiber R.

Gustav Line Jan.–May 1944

Adriatic Sea

ALBANIA

Corsica
Evacuated by German forces Sept.–Oct. 1943

Allies enter Rome June 4, 1944
Rome

Anzio
Jan.–March 1944
(Operation Shingle)

Cassino
Jan.–May 1944

Sardinia
Evacuated by German forces Sept. 18, 1943

Tyrrhenian Sea

Naples
Salerno Sept. 1943

Sept. 1943
(Operation Avalanche)

Taranto

Sept. 1943
(Operation Slapstick)

Mediterranean Sea

Palermo
Messina
Reggio di Calabria

Sept. 1943

N

Sicily

TUNISIA

July 1943

Malta (Br.)

✸	Major battle
←	Allied advance
▪▪▪▪	Front line at date shown

0   150 miles
0   150 km

© Infobase Publishing

had begun in January 1944 with an amphibious landing that depended on a rapid drive from the beach into the Alban hills. This would have relieved pressure on the Fifth U.S. Army. Sixth Corps commander JOHN LUCAS, however, frittered away much valuable time consolidating his position after the landing instead of moving on to an immediate advance, and thereby lost the initiative. The result was that his corps was cut off, isolated, and now in no position to offer relief. On the contrary, it was in desperate need of aid itself.

After the failure of the first Battle of Cassino, Alexander sent the Eighth British Army to make a new attempt to break through the so-called GUSTAV LINE. In the process, the ancient Benedictine monastery at Monte Cassino was reduced to rubble by artillery barrages and aerial bombardment. This tragic action was to no avail, as the Germans continued to fight, even more effectively, from the rubble. A third battle was launched, with equal futility. In the meantime, however, the U.S. Army Air Forces and the RAF had achieved air superiority over Italy, yet heartbreakingly, a campaign of bombing and close air support did little to aid the Allied advance on the ground.

Only with the fourth Battle of Cassino did Alexander and Clark achieve the level of coordination necessary to breach, at long last, the Gustav Line. This resulted in a general breakthrough and a massive offensive beginning on May 11, 1944. Monte Cassino fell, and the forces at Anzio could now commence their breakout as well. All elements were positioned for an attack on Kesselring's forces at Valmontine. Here was an opportunity to destroy the principal part of the German army in Italy. But on the very verge of victory, Clark decided instead to capture Rome rather than concentrate on destroying the enemy army. It was an all too familiar temptation, especially given the historical and even mythic significance of the Eternal City and the fact that here was an opportunity to retake the first of the Axis capitals. Rome fell on June 4 (ironically, the landings at Normandy on June 6 stole Clark's headlines as well as his thunder), but by diverting his forces to take Rome, Clark opened up a gap between the Allied armies and took the pressure off the rear of Kesselring's forces. The Germans were therefore able to withdraw intact, their army preserved. Rome had been gained, but the chance to end the Italian Campaign swiftly had been lost.

There was little doubt now among the Allies that the Germans would be defeated in Italy, but by succumbing to the seduction of Rome, Clark had relinquished the momentum of the campaign. As far as the Allies were concerned, Italy was now very much a secondary front and six entire divisions were withdrawn from the country to participate in landings in the south of France. A plan to supplement the remaining U.S. and British forces with Italian troops enjoyed little success, and the continued Allied advance was greatly impeded by the many rivers that cross the Italian peninsula, especially after abnormally heavy autumn rains caused extensive flooding. Progress continued, to be sure, but very slowly. The next great German defensive position, the GOTHIC LINE, was breached, but the British Eighth Army soon bogged down in mud during a very rainy September. Intending to press on into Austria, the army was delayed in the Romagna. At this point, Alexander was ordered by the Combined Chiefs, Allied high command, not to press the offensive, but to concentrate instead on merely pinning down in Italy as many German divisions as possible. This he did, and to substantial effect. As a culmination of the Italian Campaign, however, it was hardly the glorious blitzkrieg-style breakthrough originally anticipated.

The cost of the entire campaign was staggering: 188,746 killed or wounded in the Fifth U.S. Army, 123,254 killed or wounded in the Eighth British Army. German casualties were very high, some 434,646 killed, wounded, or missing. As a process of attrition, the Italian Campaign was punishingly hard on both sides—though, on balance, much harder on the Germans. The extent to which this contributed to the Allied victory in Europe is debatable. Certainly, the Germans could not afford the losses they sustained, but if the Italian Campaign drew off German forces from the Soviet and French fronts, it also drew off Allied forces from France. The best that can be concluded about the

Italian Campaign was that it produced mixed results, and while that assessment is true enough in a strategic sense, it in no way conveys the degree of destruction and misery the campaign also produced—on both sides.

Further reading: Blaxland, Gregory. *Alexander's Generals: The Italian campaign, 1944–45.* London: W. Kimber, 1979; Botjer, George F. *Sideshow War: The Italian Campaign, 1943–1945.* College Station: Texas A&M University Press, 1996; Shepperd, G. A. *The Italian Campaign 1943–45: A Political and Military Reassessment.* London: Barker, 1968; Strawson, John. *The Italian Campaign.* New York: Carroll & Graf, 1988; Wallace, Robert. *The Italian Campaign.* Alexandria, Va.: Time Life Education, 1978.

Italy

Italy fought on the side of the Allies during World War I and incurred heavy losses even as it failed to reap the territorial benefits it had anticipated from participation in the war. The nation emerged from the conflict in economic disarray and with a great deal of political instability as socialists, communists, anarchists, right-wing monarchists, and democrats competed for power. In this climate of chaos and malaise, Benito Mussolini rapidly rose to power with his seductive political philosophy of fascism. Although Italy remained, putatively, a constitutional monarchy under King Victor Emmanuel III, Mussolini, from 1922 to 1943, became absolute dictator.

Through a combination of personal charisma, national mythologizing, an oligarchical partnership with industrialists and financiers, police state tactics, and outright thuggery, Mussolini compelled his compatriots to trade liberty for a measure of prosperity and at least the appearance of efficiency of government. Mussolini and fascism were widely admired throughout Europe and even in the United States. Adolf Hitler looked to Mussolini as a role model for effective dictatorship. For many, however, the image of fascism was tarnished by Mussolini's aggression, naked and brutal, against Ethiopia (Abyssinia), which Italy invaded, conquered, and annexed in 1936, and by Italy's

support for the fascist Falange during the Spanish civil war. But among those committed to fascism, this aggressive expansionism was looked upon as a positive development, and Mussolini promised Italians that he would, in effect, restore Italy to the glory it had enjoyed in ancient times as the center of the Roman Empire.

As Hitler's Germany became increasingly powerful, the roles of Mussolini and Hitler were reversed. Mussolini, whom Hitler had admired in the 1920s and early 1930s, now increasingly came into the orbit of Hitler. Mussolini created an alliance with Germany (and, subsequently, with Japan as well) by concluding the Pact of Steel in 1939 and the Axis (Tripartite) Pact in 1940. Mussolini, however, failed to be an enthusiastic ally. After the outbreak of war, he hesitated to commit Italy to a full military alliance with Germany until the sweeping German victories of 1940 persuaded him that the alliance would bring Italy easy territorial expansion and profit, which would also greatly enhance his personal image as a leader and conqueror. But in the heat of combat the inadequacy of the Italian military quickly became apparent. As a military ally, Italy proved more of a liability than an asset to Germany, and Hitler made increasingly stringent demands on Italian forces and on the Italian economy. Mussolini not only became Hitler's puppet, but was widely perceived as such.

Mussolini promised the Italian people great things in return for the nation's participation in the war. Instead, even before Italy was invaded by the Allies, the war exacted great economic sacrifices, including shortages of everything from soap, to electric power, to gasoline, to clothing and food. The black market flourished. Corruption and inflation became serious problems, and national deficits skyrocketed.

German reversals in the Soviet Union by the end of 1941, coupled with the entry of the United States into the war following the Battle of Pearl Harbor, began to turn Italian public opinion sharply against Mussolini and the fascists, who were increasingly seen as leading Italy to ruin. Beginning in August 1942, Marshal Pietro Bado-

GLIO secretly schemed with Princess Maria José of Savoy, the daughter-in-law of King Victor Emmanuel III, to make overtures of a separate peace with the British and Americans. After the Germans, along with Italian forces, were defeated at the BATTLE OF STALINGRAD in 1942–43, Mussolini's tenure was clearly doomed. Life in Italy was made increasingly miserable by RAF bombing missions in the north. Finally, with the commencement of the SICILY CAMPAIGN, the Allied landings on Sicily on July 9, 1943, the Fascist Grand Council met and, on July 24, dismissed Mussolini from office. He was arrested the next day. Badoglio formed a new provisional government and immediately faced the problem of secretly negotiating with the Allies without provoking German retaliation. His plan was to coordinate an armistice with the landing of a large Anglo-American force. The armistice was announced on September 8, 1943, while the Allies landed at Salerno and commenced the bloody BATTLE OF SALERNO.

The ITALIAN CAMPAIGN proved to be prohibitively costly for the Allies, because German resistance was far more fierce and effective than they had anticipated. Italy became a battleground as the Allies gradually gained control of the south and slowly advanced northward. Mussolini, rescued from captivity by a German guerrilla operation under OTTO SKORZENY, was set up in far northern Italy as Hitler's marionette. The Italian army proved mainly ineffective in aiding the Allies, but Italian partisan activity was often most helpful. However, fighting in Italy did not end until the German surrender in May 1945.

See also ITALY, AIR FORCE OF; ITALY, ARMY OF; and ITALY, NAVY OF.

Further reading: Collier, Richard. *Duce! A Biography of Benito Mussolini.* New York: Viking Press, 1971; Hartenian, Larry. *Benito Mussolini* (World Leaders Past and Present). New York: Chelsea House, 1988; Hibbert, Christopher. *Il Duce: The Life of Benito Mussolini.* Boston: Little, Brown, 1962; Knox, MacGregor. *Mussolini Unleashed: Politics and Strategy in Italy's Last War.* New York: Cambridge University Press, 1982; Lyttle, Richard B. *Il Duce: The Rise and Fall of Benito Mussolini,* New York: Macmillan, 1987; Ridley, Jasper. *Mussolini: A Biography.* New York: Cooper Square Press, 2000; Smith, Denis Mack. *Mussolini.* New York: Vintage, 1983; Whittam, John. *Fascist Italy.* New York: St. Martin's Press, 1995.

Italy, air force of

BENITO MUSSOLINI promoted FASCISM as a political philosophy for the future, wedded to new technologies, especially those involving power and speed. Developing the Italian air force became a signature project for fascism, and Mussolini's air marshal, ITALO BALBO, a dashing figure and a daring aviator, made the perfect front man for the new air force. In the years before the outbreak of World War II, many foreign diplomats, politicians, and even some military figures were inordinately impressed by Italy's air arm. However, the facts were at odds with the image. At the outbreak of the war, Italy had 1,753 combat aircraft, of which approximately half, some 900 machines, were modern. The rest were obsolete or obsolescent. At that, even the modern aircraft were outclassed by the best Allied planes, and many airplanes lacked radios or the instrumentation to enable night flying. None of the Italian aircraft was radar equipped. Equally deficient were the Italian pilots; without question, they were brave but also poorly trained.

In early action, the Italian air force proved highly ineffective, especially against British warships in the Mediterranean during the summer of 1940. Performance significantly improved by the end of 1941, but by that time the heavy losses incurred by the service were not made up, and the strength of the air force rapidly dwindled. By the time Marshal PIETRO BADOGLIO concluded an armistice with the Allies in September 1943, Italy had only about 100 operational warplanes.

See also AIRCRAFT, ITALIAN.

Further reading: Apostolo, Giorgio, and Giovanni Massimello. *Italian Aces of World War II.* London: Osprey, 2000; Gunston, Bill. *An Illustrated Guide to German, Italian and Japanese Fighters of World War II: Major Fighters* *and Attack Aircraft of the Axis Powers.* London: Salamander, 1980; Gunston, Bill. *Japanese and Italian Aircraft.* London: Book Sales, 1985.

Italy, army of

During World War II, the Italian army, like the nation's other armed forces, was under the direct command of Benito Mussolini, who had appointed himself minister for war. He was assisted by Marshal Pietro Badoglio, who exercised no direct command authority but functioned as a personal military adviser to Mussolini. Below this top level, command of the army and the other armed forces was poorly defined. More often than not, Mussolini intervened directly in command decisions that should have been made on the staff or even field level. Like Adolf Hitler, Mussolini fancied himself a military genius, but, in fact, like Hitler, he had no experience in higher command and was an inept, even disastrous, military chief.

At the outbreak of World War II, the Italian army consisted of about 1.6 million men. The peak number of troops ultimately deployed approached 4 million. Throughout Italy's participation in the war, Mussolini frustrated and angered Hitler by insisting that a disproportionate number of these men—about 1 million—be retained within Italy. On the other hand, Mussolini also insisted on contributing forces to the Soviet front, even though the German commanders did not particularly want them to participate in the Soviet campaign, because they considered the Italian troops inferior.

The army consisted of 73 divisions at the outbreak of the war. There were 43 marching infantry divisions, five alpine divisions, three light divisions, two motorized divisions (consisting of 3 motorized regiments), three armored divisions, and 14 self-transportable divisions (capable of moving troops and one artillery regiment by truck). By 1942, one air-transportable division and one parachute division were added, along with 12 coastal divisions for defense. There were also militia and Libyan divisions. In addition, a Fascist Militia (Blackshirts) consisted of 177 legions, of which 39 were attached to the army. The Italian national police, or Cara-binieri, functioned as military police but also sometimes fought in combat. This force numbered about 156,000 men.

Besides defending Italy, the Italian army fought in the Balkans, France, North Africa, Italian East Africa, and, at the insistence of Mussolini, the Soviet Union. Leadership, equipment, training, and commitment to the mission were all uniformly poor throughout the army, and the Germans soon learned to look upon their ally as a military liability rather than an asset. After the Italian armistice with the Allies in September 1943, some army units actively opposed the German occupation. The commanders of the Anglo-American forces fighting in Italy, unimpressed with the quality of the Italian military, were not enthusiastic about allowing the Italians to participate in the Italian Campaign; however, a motorized group (the equivalent of single reinforced regiment) fought at the Battles of Monte Cassino, and the so-called Italian Corps of Liberation (with the strength of a conventional division) fought along the Adriatic. In August 1944, after significant numbers of Allied troops were transferred from Italy to the landings along the French Riviera, General Harold Alexander armed six Italian divisions and deployed four in combat. These men fought with a skill and passion not seen among Italian forces earlier in the war.

Fighting against the Allies, the Italian army suffered 380,000 military deaths (including 110,823 killed in combat) and 225,000 wounded in action. Many more were taken prisoner. In combat for the Allies, losses were 1,868 killed and 5,187 wounded.

See also Armor, Italian; Artillery, Italian; and Small Arms, Italian.

Further reading: Jowett, Philip S., and Stephen Andrew. *The Italian Army, 1940–45: Africa 1940–43.* London: Osprey, 2001; Jowett, Philip S. *Italian Army in World War II: Europe 1940–43.* London: Osprey, 2000.

Italy, navy of

At the outbreak of World War II, Italy had a formidable navy that included two modern battleships, four rebuilt older battleships, and 19 cruisers in addition to 100 smaller surface craft and 113 submarines. These vessels were manned by 168,614 officers and sailors at the beginning of the war, growing to 259,000 at peak strength in August 1943. Italian naval personnel were much better trained than either their army or air force counterparts, but while the roster of ships looked impressive on paper, the fleet was outclassed by the navies of the Allies. Italian vessels lacked RADAR, their guns were generally inferior to those of Allied vessels (of significantly shorter range), and, perhaps most serious of all, the navy suffered from a shortage of fuel oil. Another major shortcoming was the complete lack of aircraft carriers. Finally, there was a problem with command philosophy. Italian naval officers were extremely conservative and saw their principal objective as preserving the navy intact; they were, therefore, reluctant to put ships at risk and never deployed their naval assets aggressively or effectively.

Despite the conservative philosophy, the Italian navy suffered a severe blow early in the war at the BATTLE OF TARANTO on November 12, 1940, when British aircraft badly damaged one new battleship and two older ones, along with a cruiser and dock facilities. This disaster was followed on March 28, 1941, by the BATTLE OF MATAPAN, in which three cruisers and their escort vessels were sunk, and the battleship *Vittorio Veneto,* pride of the fleet, was badly damaged. More successful were Italian submarine operations against British convoys. Italian supply operations to troops in Libya were also quite successful, despite British efforts at interdiction.

At the time of Italy's armistice with the Allies in September 1943, the navy had six battleships and nine cruisers. Its fleet of smaller vessels and submarines had been decimated. In all, losses were a battleship, 12 cruisers, 44 destroyers, 41 torpedo boats, 75 submarines, and 171 smaller vessels.

Further reading: Bragadin, Marc'Antonio. *The Italian Navy in World War II.* New York: Arno, 1980; Sadkovich, James J. *The Italian Navy in World War II.* Westport, Conn.: Greenwood Press, 1994.

Iwo Jima, Battle of

Certainly the most celebrated battle of the war in the Pacific, the assault on Iwo Jima commenced on February 19, 1945, after 72 days of aerial and naval bombardment in which 12,600 tons of bombs had been dropped. In the three days immediately preceding the landings, a total of 6,800 tons of bombs were delivered, along with 21,926 naval artillery shells. On March 16, 36 days after the first landings, Iwo Jima was finally declared secure.

At stake in the Iwo Jima fight was a miserable volcanic island—"Iwo Jima" means sulfur island—just 4.5 miles long by 2.5 miles wide at its widest. The Japanese, however, had built three airstrips on the island and had fortified it by taking advantage of the island's natural network of caves and ravines, reinforcing these with concrete and steel. In all, there were some 1,500 fortified caves and 16 miles of tunnels. Perhaps no place on earth had ever been so formidably fortified. The Japanese regarded Iwo Jima as vital to the defense of their homeland. The Americans not only wanted to neutralize it, but to use the airstrips as an advance base for the emergency landing of B-29s raiding Japan.

U.S. Navy and marine planners knew that Iwo Jima would be an extremely difficult objective. However, they believed that, after the island had been softened up by extensive naval and aerial

U.S. Marines on Iwo Jima *(National Archives and Records Administration)*

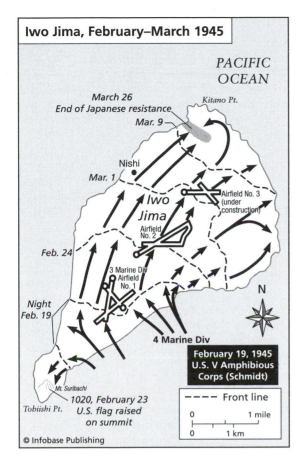

Iwo Jima, February–March 1945

PACIFIC OCEAN

Kitano Pt.

March 26
End of Japanese resistance

Mar. 9

Nishi

Mar. 1

Iwo Jima

Airfield No. 3 (under construction)

Airfield No. 2

Feb. 24

3 Marine Div
Airfield No. 1

Night
Feb. 19

4 Marine Div

N

**February 19, 1945
U.S. V Amphibious
Corps (Schmidt)**

Mt. Suribachi

Tobiishi Pt.

1020, February 23
U.S. flag raised
on summit

- - - - Front line

0 _____ 1 mile

0 _____ 1 km

© Infobase Publishing

would remain afloat offshore, manning some 800 warships.

The initial landing was met with little resistance. The marines advanced behind a rolling barrage supplied by the navy. The first wave progressed inland some 350 yards before it met with enemy fire, intense flanking fire from defenders thoroughly under cover. Despite this punishment, the marines took the first of three airstrips on the second day of the invasion. On the fifth day, the second airstrip was captured, along with the highest point on the island, MOUNT SURIBACHI. This was the scene of the flag raising, which, thanks to a very widely published Pulitzer Prize–winning photograph, became the single most famous image of World War II and seemed to symbolize the marines' indomitable will to gain victory.

The taking of Mount Suribachi was a severe blow to the Japanese defenders of the island, but the hardest, most costly fighting was yet to come. The Japanese still had two defensive lines intact, and they concentrated fire from a rise known as Hill 382. This objective was so formidable that it was dubbed "the Meat Grinder," and taking it resulted in heavy marine casualties as well as the

bombardment, a two-week ground battle would be required to take the objective. As it turned out, the ground phase of the battle consumed more than twice that time.

During the almost two and a half months of continual bombardment, the defenders of Iwo Jima dug deeper bunkers. The result was that the intensive preparation only hardened resistance by the Japanese garrison of 22,000 soldiers and Imperial naval troops, all under the command of Lieutenant General Kuribayashi Tadamichi. Against this force, on February 19, 1945, the 4th and 5th Marine Divisions were landed, with the 3rd Marine Division held in reserve. In all, 75,144 marines were initially committed to battle and 30,000 landed on the very first day. Before it ended, 110,000 men would be landed and some 220,000

This photograph of marines and a navy corpsman raising the Stars and Stripes on Mt. Suribachi became an emblem of the Marine Corps and of all U.S. service personnel in the Pacific. *(National Archives and Records Administration)*

award of five Medals of Honor in a single day of action.

The Japanese defended Iwo Jima with what might justly be described as fanatical heroism. Suicidal Japanese resistance was typical of the Pacific campaign, but Iwo Jima's status as a bastion protecting Japan itself motivated an even more exceptionally determined defense. At "Bloody Gorge," a 700-yard-long canyon, the defenders made their final stand, holding off the vastly superior force of marines for 10 days.

Marine casualties were 5,931 killed and 17,372 wounded, a 30 percent casualty rate. Japanese battle deaths numbered 20,703 out of the 22,000-man garrison. Among the dead was the commanding general, Kuribayashi, who almost certainly took his own life.

The taking of Iwo Jima deprived the Japanese of a key defensive base. It was also a tremendous blow to Japanese morale. Most important of all, however, it provided a landing strip for crippled B-29s. A total of 2,251 made emergency landings here before the war was over, and it is estimated that taking Iwo Jima saved the lives of as many as 24,761 U.S. Army Air Forces aircrew members.

Further reading: Bradley, James, with Ron Powers. *Flags of Our Fathers: Heroes of Iwo Jima.* New York: Bantam, 2000; Caruso, Patrick F. *Nightmare on Iwo.* Annapolis, Md.: Naval Institute Press, 2001; Kessler, Lynn, and Edmond B. Bart. *Never in Doubt: Remembering Iwo Jima.* Annapolis, Md.: Naval Institute Press, 1999; Ross, Bill D. *Iwo Jima: Legacy of Valor.* New York: Vintage, 1986; Newcomb, Richard F. *Iwo Jima.* New York: Owl, 2002.

J

Japan

At the outbreak of the war, Japan was a prosperous industrialized nation of about 70 million. Although Japan was a major manufacturer of consumer goods, by the early 1930s, the economy was increasingly militarized, and a strong central government set about replacing the market economy with such aspects of a totalitarian command economy as strict control and prescriptive planning. The electricity and oil industries were nationalized during 1934–36, and rice rationing was introduced in 1939. Heavy industries, suitable for war production, were emphasized, and by the end of the 1930s, Japan was effectively on a war footing with a wartime economy.

Japan was strategically located between Asia and the Pacific. This put the nation in an excellent position for launching a war of imperial conquest. Conversely, it also made the country vulnerable to attack and forced it to plan a prospective war on two fronts. The Japanese militarists who effectively controlled the country's government by the 1930s planned to conduct a rapid offensive war. The motives for conquest arose partly from a collective sense of racial superiority and national destiny, but also from a very real need to have access to large amounts of raw materials and foodstuffs not available on the overcrowded home islands.

Japan's offensive orientation created profound discontent in naval circles with the London Naval Treaty of 1930 (which had placed limits on the signatories' naval strength) and resulted in Japan's withdrawal from the treaty in 1936. The Imperial Navy embarked on an ambitious program of shipbuilding and developed what it called the "southern strategy," whereby Japan would aggressively expand into Southeast Asia.

As the Imperial Navy was gaining strength and political influence, so was the army. Concerned over Soviet threats to Japanese-held Manchukuo (Manchuria), junior officers attempted a coup d'état following the elections of 1936, assassinated the home secretary and the finance minister, and occupied government offices in Tokyo. In April the navy and the army agreed on the need for the southern strategy and secured from Emperor Hirohito approval of an offensively based "defense" policy. This evolved into a strategic policy calling for expansion on the continent as well as toward the south.

The attempted coup of 1936 and the competitive ascendancy of the Imperial Japanese Navy and Imperial Japanese Army reveal much about the nature of Japanese government in the years leading up to World War II. During the war, Japan's enemies portrayed the Japanese government simply as a totalitarian military dictatorship virtually identical to that of Nazi GERMANY. The reality, however, was more complex.

The Meiji Restoration and Constitution of 1889 created for Japan a constitutional monarchy in which sovereignty resided with the emperor, who enjoyed extensive executive, legislative, and military power and who, furthermore, was revered as a semidivinity. Yet the monarchy was far from absolute. The 1889 constitution also assigned the actual exercise of royal prerogatives variously to the emperor's cabinet, to the Diet (a bicameral parliament), and to the military. Emperor HIRO-HITO was no mere figurehead—as was, for example, the British king—but he was no unambiguous head of state either. He reigned, but did not rule. His true function, politically, was to ratify and sanction policy decisions created by the cabinet, Diet, and military. His most immediate advisers, the lord keeper of the privy seal and the grand chamberlain, both guided and insulated him. Their chief concern was to keep him elevated above quotidian politics, so that he was preserved as a national symbol of authority and collective destiny.

The ambiguity of Japanese government promoted a climate of cliques, cabals, secret dealings, personality clashes, and power struggles, all outside of the reach of law. Factions and individuals vied with one another to obtain the emperor's ratification of whatever policy they advocated. The result was often the imperial ratification of contradictory policies. Nevertheless, the broad contours of government were these: national policy was made by the cabinet, which reported to the emperor (who appointed a prime minister) rather than to the Diet. Yet the power of the cabinet was, in practice, inferior to that of the military. The power of the Diet was largely limited to budgetary review, and it was further vitiated by a division into a lower and upper house, the lower house consisting of popularly elected representatives and the upper house of hereditary nobles and appointed officials, who could (and did) check the actions of the lower house.

Japanese government was also strongly influenced by a welter of special civilian and military institutions, including business and labor interest groups, military organizations, and the Supreme War Council, to name only a few. The army's coup attempt of 1936 was an effort to replace the many ambiguous layers of government with a stream-lined right-wing military dictatorship. Although the coup was suppressed, it did give the military more leverage in government, enabling it to fashion Japan into what government leaders termed a "national defense state." This gave the military a high degree of control over foreign as well as domestic policy, which was ratified by the National Mobilization Law of March 1938. This legislation equipped the government (and the military especially) with an arsenal of wartime controls over labor power, resources, production, transportation, wages, and prices. Parallel with this legislation, Prime Minister Prince Fumimaro Konoe created a campaign of "spiritual mobilization," which was aimed at shaping mass public opinion in favor, first, of the SINO-JAPANESE WAR and then of the full-scale prosecution of World War II.

On October 12, 1940, army leaders, together with their civilian allies in government (the so-called revisionist bureaucrats) created the Imperial Rule Assistance Association (IRAA), with Prince Konoe as president. The IRAA was in some ways analogous to the Nazi Party in Germany in that it successfully exerted pressure on Japan's other political parties to dissolve themselves and join the IRAA. Moreover, the IRAA absorbed various labor unions and management organizations to merge into an IRAA-controlled Industrial Patriotic League.

Although the IRAA centralized government and gave the military more control over that government, it did not end the many personal rivalries and power contests. The result was that the central government continued to be a Byzantine structure. A Liaison Conference was created in an effort to coordinate military and civilian branches of government in decision making, but it soon developed into an extraconstitutional, military-dominated entity that usurped the role of the cabinet. Prince Konoe increasingly clashed with the military over basic questions of war or peace. He resigned as prime minister in October 1941 and was replaced by TOJO HIDEKI, a militarist and military officer whose task was to make final preparations for war with the British and Americans in the likely event that ongoing negotiations between Japan and the United States should break down.

Although he was by no means head of state, Tojo assumed virtually dictatorial powers within the narrow constraints of his mandate to prepare for war and, once war began, to prosecute war. He served not only as prime minister, but as army minister and home secretary, so that he had control over all the major bureaucracies. Even after the outbreak of war, Tojo did not abrogate the Diet but used it to enact needed wartime legislation. Tojo even called a general election in 1942, ensuring, however, that the majority slate of candidates all met with his approval. In contrast to the political situation in Nazi Germany, however, a minority of independent representatives—not members of the IRAA—were also elected. This minority occasionally criticized Tojo publicly, who sometimes suppressed such criticism with arrests and imprisonments.

Tojo saw the elected minority as less of a problem in Japanese government than other activist agitators, who were deemed "thought criminals." A secret police force, the Kempei, was dispatched to deal with these individuals under the Special Emergency Act of December 1942. While it is easy to find parallels between the Kempei and the Nazi GESTAPO, the Kempei never operated on the scale of its Nazi counterpart. Relatively few arrests were made.

While Japan's wartime enemies demonized Tojo as the equivalent of ADOLF HITLER, he was, in the final analysis, a master bureaucrat rather than a visionary political terrorist. With so much of the government under his direct command, he could rapidly rationalize the Japanese bureaucracies and regiment the Japanese civilian population to an unprecedented degree. What he failed to do successfully was end the rivalry between the army and the navy, a shortcoming that ultimately rendered him vulnerable, especially as the tide of war turned decisively against Japan in 1944. Tojo was forced out of office on July 18, 1944, and was replaced by another military officer, General Koiso Kuniaki. In an effort to reconcile the army and navy, Koiso created a Supreme Council for the Direction of the War in August 1944 to replace the former Liaison Conference as the principal decision-making body. This step was to no avail, however, and the two services continued a dispute that contributed significantly to the ultimate defeat of Japan.

In contrast to Germany and Italy, Japan was not motivated by anything truly equivalent to Nazi or fascist ideology. It was motivated instead by a hunger for imperial expansion and a desire to control and possess territories offering resources unavailable in the homeland. Japanese government was also motivated by a strong anti-Communist sentiment. The ANTI-COMINTERN PACT of 1936 was the basis of the first formal relationship between Germany (and in 1937, Italy) and Japan.

As for Japan's program of expansion, by the summer of 1941 the Japanese Empire consisted of Sakhalin island south of the 50th parallel; Korea (a colony since 1910); Formosa (acquired in 1895); and effective possession of Manchukuo, a Japanese puppet state created in 1932. In February 1939, Japan occupied the Chinese-owned island of Hainan and, as of March, the Spratly Islands. Japan established key air bases and naval stations in Thailand. In the summer of 1941, Japanese diplomats were negotiating with the U.S. government, which had insisted that Japan withdraw its military forces from China and French Indochina. The Japanese diplomats temporized and stalled as their nation's war preparations moved forward.

The Japanese negotiators well understood that the United States was Japan's principal supplier of oil, steel, and other strategic materials. On the one hand, there was fear that the aggressive Japanese policy in China would provoke an embargo; on the other hand, there was a desire to end the reliance on America by acquiring other sources of strategic materials. Thus the United States represented both an incentive to restrain aggression and an incentive to redouble it.

In the meantime, during the lead-up to the war, Japan was put on a wartime footing. Food and clothing were stringently rationed, and the population was "educated" by means of concerted propaganda campaigns. As in Nazi Germany, children and youth were targeted for special indoctrination and training through the Greater Japan Youth Corps and a revamped national school system called the People's Schools. Quasi-military training became a part of every school day. In universities, military training was made compulsory. Propaganda was directed at increasing nationalism and racial pride as well as creating the perception that Japan was being menaced by the ABCD (America, Britain, China, Dutch) League.

The indoctrination and propaganda were intended to harden the Japanese people and prepare them for sacrifice, which was extensive even before Japan began suffering military reversals. Despite rigorous rationing, virtually all staples quickly fell into critically short supply, and luxuries were unknown. These radical conservation measures notwithstanding, Japanese war production was disappointing during the first two years of war—a problem that surely contributed to the nation's defeat. As Japanese victory was increasingly replaced by defeat, the government's rationing edict and demands for production and military manpower became more draconian. Middle-school education was reduced from five to four years, and all limits on the working hours of women and minors were suspended. In September 1943 unmarried women under the age of 25 were summarily conscripted into a "volunteer" labor corps.

The domestic emergency measures did dramatically increase war production. Although Allied air and naval action greatly disrupted the flow of raw materials from conquered territories, Japan managed to increase production dramatically by usurping civilian raw material stockpiles, cutting production for all civilian purposes, and pressing women and children into the workforce. Increased employment did not bring any improvement in the standard of living, however, because of wartime rationing and shortages.

The greatest hardships on the Japanese people came with massive aerial bombardment of the cities by the United States. Initially, industrial targets were singled out, but raids on residential areas of the cities became frequent, culminating in the fire bombing of Tokyo on March 9, 1945, in which almost 15.5 square miles of the city were razed and some 100,000 civil-

ians killed. By the time of the atomic bombing of Hiroshima and Nagasaki, more than 10 million city dwellers (the majority women and children) had fled into the countryside. That American bombers attacked with near impunity testifies to the gross inadequacy of Japanese antiaircraft defenses. That civilian casualties were as high as they were also demonstrates the inadequacy of Japanese civil defense.

As horrific as the direct civilian casualties from bombing were, shortages during the final months of the war became desperate, and by the time of the atomic bombing attacks, acceptance of the Allied demand for unconditional surrender (with the single proviso that the emperor would remain in power, subject to the Supreme Allied Commander) was rapid, despite fanatical opposition from the army high command. In preparation for the occupation, Japanese authorities voluntarily and on their own initiative demobilized army forces that had been assembled for homeland defense. Civilians, who had been trained to fight the anticipated invasion to the death (using bamboo sticks and pikes), were now told to behave peaceably and to cooperate with the occupiers. The Americans met with virtually no resistance, as the Japanese people continued to obey the instructions of their government.

Further reading: Frank, Richard B. *Downfall: The End of the Imperial Japanese Empire.* New York: Penguin, 2001; Skates, John Ray. *The Invasion of Japan: Alternative to the Bomb.* Columbia: University of South Carolina Press, 2000; Toland, John. *The Rising Sun: The Decline and Fall of the Japanese Empire, 1936–1945.* New York: Modern Library, 2003.

Japan, air force of

Japan did not have a separate air arm in World War II. Its air forces were divided between the army and navy (see Japan, army of and Japan, navy of). This article discusses the forces operated by each of these services.

AIR FORCE OF THE IMPERIAL JAPANESE ARMY
By 1941 the air force of the Imperial Japanese Army (IJA) had about 1,500 aircraft ready to attack land

targets. Throughout the war, the army's aircraft were deployed mainly in Manchukuo and China and on other large land areas, including New Guinea. Nevertheless, symptomatic of the poor coordination between the Japanese army and navy, the army independently operated its own fleet of escort-class aircraft carriers, which launched army aircraft to protect troop convoys.

The army air force lacked long-range aircraft and was therefore poorly prepared to fight the Pacific war, which involved flying great distances over water. IJA pilots were trained mainly for short-range pursuit and ground-attack missions and were therefore also ill-prepared to fight in the vastness of the Pacific theater.

By the end of the war, the IJA Air Force consisted of six "air armies": the First through Third Air Armies created during June–July 1942, the Fourth in July 1943, the Fifth in February 1944, and the Sixth in August 1944. The basic operational air force unit was the Air Group (*sentai*), consisting of three squadrons (companies, *chitai*) of nine to 12 planes. An Air Brigade (*hikodan*) consisted of three fighter, light bomber, or heavy bomber Air Groups plus a reconnaissance unit. An Air Division (*hikoshidan*) was made up of two or three Air Brigades. An Air Army (*kokugun*) consisted of two or three Air Divisions.

AIR FORCE OF THE IMPERIAL JAPANESE NAVY

At the beginning of World War II, the Air Force of the Imperial Japanese Navy (IJN) had more aircraft than the IJA Air Force: about 1,750 fighters, torpedo bombers, and bombers, and 350 or more flying boats and float planes, used mainly for reconnaissance.

The organization of the naval air arm was complex, but its two major air units at the beginning of the war were the First Air Fleet, which operated aircraft carrier–launched airplanes, and the Eleventh Air Fleet, which operated land-based planes. Before the war was over, six more Air Fleets were formed: the Second, Third, Fifth, Tenth, Twelfth, and Thirteenth. Japan's Air Fleets were typically under the command of the commanders in chief of area naval fleets. Each Air Fleet was divided into at least two Air Flotillas, consisting of two or more Air Groups, each with 50 to 150 aircraft.

The naval air arm took the lead in aerial combat during the Pacific war. At the start of the war, its aircraft included some of the most advanced flown by any combatant, including the famed Zero fighter and the superb bombers, code named Nell, Betty, Jean, and Kate by the Allies. Admiral YAMAMOTO ISORUKU was a strong believer in naval air power and saw to it that not only was the navy equipped with excellent aircraft, but that the planes were manned by highly skilled and thoroughly trained pilots. As the war progressed, however, Allied aircraft increasingly outclassed the Japanese, and pilot losses were so heavy that undertrained pilots were rushed into combat. (A cardinal weakness of Japanese naval organization was its failure to use veteran pilots to train novices.)

The naval air arm enjoyed early triumphs, most notably against PEARL HARBOR on December 7, 1941. But the BATTLE OF THE CORAL SEA, although a tactical air victory for Japan, resulted in a strategic defeat and heralded much worse defeat in the BATTLE OF MIDWAY, in which four Japanese aircraft carriers were sunk, many planes destroyed, and many experienced pilots killed. Midway forced Japan to assume the defensive for the rest of the war, which became a struggle of attrition that the Japanese could not sustain. Not only were they unable to make up their ongoing aircraft losses, but, even worse, they could not replace their best pilots. The worst aerial defeat of all came in the BATTLE OF THE PHILIPPINE SEA in June 1944, when 243 Japanese carrier aircraft were lost in what American pilots dubbed the "Great Marianas Turkey Shoot."

As the situation of the naval air arm became desperate, a desperate measure was formulated: the KAMIKAZE, in which Japanese pilots deliberately used their aircraft as suicide weapons, human-guided missiles aimed at American ships.

See also AIRCRAFT, JAPANESE.

Further reading: Hata, Ikuhiko. *Japanese Army Air Force Units and Their Aces: 1931–1945.* New York: Grub Street, 2002; Hata, Ikuhiko, and Yasuho Izawa. *Japanese Naval*

Aces and Fighter Units in World War II. Annapolis, Md.: Naval Institute Press, 1989; Okumiya, Masatake. *Zero!: The story of the Japanese Navy Air Force, 1937–1945.* London: Cassell, 1957; Sakaida, Henry. *Japanese Army Air Force Aces 1937–1945.* London: Osprey, 1997; Tagaya, Osamu. *Imperial Japanese Naval Aviator 1937–45.* London: Osprey, 2003.

Japan, army of

The high command of the Imperial Japanese Army consisted of the Inspectorate General of Military Training, the War Ministry, and the General Staff. The Inspectorate General of Military Training administered the national military academy, war college, and various other service schools. The War Ministry had charge of political affairs related to military affairs, budget administration, personnel administration, mobilization procedures, and other areas. The General Staff was responsible for strategy, doctrine, tactics, and other functions of high command.

Just before the SINO-JAPANESE WAR, the army was composed of 17 divisions, and the Korean Army, the Formosan Army, and the Kwangtung Army in Manchukuo. Between 1937 and the outbreak of the Pacific war, the army was increased to 31 divisions, and the Kwangtung Army was expanded from five to 13 divisions. During the war, the regular Japanese army was augmented by the INDIAN NATIONAL ARMY and the Burma Independence Army. There were also various volunteer forces. Army command was structured this way: under the Imperial General Headquarters were general armies, area armies, and armies. Armies were formed from two or more divisions. The standard division (B-type) consisted of 20,000 men and had three infantry regiments and one engineer, one transport, and one artillery regiment in addition to a reconnaissance unit and service troops. There were two other, specialized divisions, the A-type and the C-type. A-type had 29,000 troops and operated mainly in China and Manchukuo. The C-type had 13,500 to 15,000 men and was used for garrison duty and antiguerrilla work.

In addition to divisions, the Japanese also fielded Independent Mixed Brigades, which had three to six infantry battalions (each with 750 to 900 men) with attached artillery, signals, and engineer units. Independent Mixed Regiments were smaller versions of the Independent Mixed Brigade used to defend certain Pacific islands. The army also employed Special Detachments (*shitai*), brigade-strength, combined-arms forces for special missions.

During the SINO-JAPANESE WAR and up to August 1939, Japanese armor doctrine subordinated tanks to the infantry. Armor was used strictly in support of infantry operations. Before the outbreak of World War II, however, the army began fielding discrete armored divisions, which were independent of infantry.

The army, like the navy, had AIRBORNE ASSAULT troops. In the army, these were organized into Raiding Regiments (*teishin rentai*) of 600 paratroops each, Two Raiding Regiments were organized into a Raiding Group (*teishin dan*), which also included two squadrons of transport aircraft to carry the paratroops, and also a glider regiment.

AMPHIBIOUS WARFARE capability was important to the Imperial Japanese Army, and two elite divisions were specially trained in amphibious operations. The army also operated an extensive supply service for its island garrisons. This included the Central Shipping Transportation Shipping and Transport Command, which operated three Water Transport Commands, Shipping Artillery Regiments, Shipping Regiments, and Shipping Communications detachments. The army even operated its own escort carriers to protect troop convoys. (Japan's air forces were divided between the army and the navy. See JAPAN, AIR FORCE OF.)

Japanese army doctrine was based on offensive operations. During the early phase of the Pacific war, the doctrine served land forces well. But the Allied counteroffensive that began in August 1942 with the GUADALCANAL CAMPAIGN forced a radical change of strategy and, increasingly, the adoption of a defensive posture. By the spring of 1944, with conditions in the Pacific deteriorating, Army High

Command had to reconfigure and redeploy its General Defense Command to build up defenses on mainland Japan and the Ryukyu Islands. After U.S. forces retook the PHILIPPINES and captured IWO JIMA and OKINAWA, troops were recalled to defend the mainland from an anticipated invasion. The remaining strength of the Imperial Japanese Army was impressive even at this stage of the war: 1,900,000 troops organized into 53 divisions, 23 independent mixed brigades, three security brigades, and two tank divisions. The atomic bombings of HIROSHIMA and NAGASAKI made the invasion unnecessary.

By the end of the war, August 1945, the Imperial Japanese Army had raised a total of 170 infantry, 13 air, four tank, and four antiaircraft divisions—2,343,483 men. Of this number, 1,439,101 were either killed in action or listed as missing in action. The exact number of wounded is unknown, but postwar statistics count 85,620 Japanese soldiers as permanently disabled due to war wounds.

Further reading: Drea, Edward J. *In the Service of the Emperor: Essays on Imperial Japanese Army.* Lincoln, Neb.: Bison Books, 2003; Harries, Meirion. *Soldiers of the Sun: The Rise and Fall of the Imperial Japanese Army.* New York: Random House, 1994; Rottman, Gordon. *Japanese Army in World War II: Conquest of the Pacific 1941–42.* London: Osprey, 2005.

Japan, navy of

After World War I, the Imperial Japanese Navy (IJN) was the world's third-greatest sea power. Although the Washington Naval Treaty of 1922 restricted Japanese tonnage to 60 percent of U.S. Navy tonnage, Japan flouted the restriction and, during the interwar period, embarked on a major shipbuilding program. Moreover, in 1936, Japan withdrew from the Washington Naval Treaty as well as the subsequent London Naval Treaty and no longer even pretended to adhere to tonnage restrictions.

Like Great Britain, Japan was a seagoing nation and, accordingly, followed the example of the British Royal Navy, giving the IJN precedence over the Army of Japan (*see* JAPAN, ARMY OF). The navy's officer corps, superbly trained at the Naval Academy (Etajima) and the Naval War College (Meguro), was socially and politically well connected. These connections proved a liability for some during the 1930s, when political instabilities resulted in the purge of many of Japan's senior naval officers—to the detriment of the service. Also during the 1930s, the influence of the army grew, and an intense and destructive army-navy rivalry crippled the strategic and tactical effectiveness of both services. Despite these problems, the IJN was a most formidable force at the commencement of World War II, not only because of the excellence of its crews and its advanced ships, but because of its advocacy of naval air power. (Japanese air forces were divided between the army and the navy; *see* JAPAN, AIR FORCE OF for discussion of Japan's naval air power.)

In planning for World War II, Japanese naval strategists correctly understood that the United States, an industrial giant, could and would maintain a larger fleet. Accordingly, the Japanese decided to exploit naval air power, advanced submarines, and advanced torpedo designs (Japan developed the most effective torpedoes of any World War II combatant), as well as forward naval bases on its mandate islands, including the Carolines, Marianas, and Marshalls, to enable a strategy of attrition intended fatally to degrade U.S. naval superiority. When the disparity in tonnage had been evened out through attrition, Japan, operating ultramodern ships from advance bases, would have a great tactical advantage over Americans who were operating far from sources of supply. At that point, the IJN would lure the U.S. Pacific Fleet into a final decisive battle, in which the U.S. fleet would be destroyed.

As of December 7, 1941, the IJN had 10 battleships (with two more under construction), 10 aircraft carriers (with four more under construction), 18 heavy cruisers, 20 light cruisers (plus four under construction), 112 destroyers (with another dozen under construction), 65 submarines (of which 21 were obsolete, but another 29 were under construction), and 156 other vessels (plus 37 under construction). Recognizing that oil supplies would be a critical issue, the IJN accumulated a two-year reserve before the war began. (This proved inadequate, and fuel became a critical problem for the navy during the late phases of the Pacific war.)

Despite its many strengths, the IJN also suffered from critical weaknesses. Its officer corps, though highly trained, was arrogant, believing that the navy was simply invincible. The spectacular Japanese tactical triumph at the BATTLE OF PEARL HARBOR intensified this attitude, prompting the IJN to push Japan's defensive perimeter in the Pacific far beyond the range of land-based air cover. This would prove to be a fatal error. Equally serious were the navy's failure to institute first-class training for replacement pilots, its scrimping on defensive armor plating in ships as well as naval aircraft to gain speed, its failing to develop adequate convoy tactics and commission escort vessels (armed escorts were little used, rendering convoys extremely vulnerable), and, despite the generally advanced design of Japanese ships, its choice almost totally to ignore RADAR technology. For their part, it should be pointed out, the Allies—especially the Americans and the British—grossly underestimated the fighting ability of the Japanese navy, an error in judgment that more than matched the Japanese in arrogance.

Japanese naval organization was complex during World War II. Generally speaking, however, most warships (except for the China Fleet) were organized into fleets that were part of the Combined Fleet, commanded by the most senior naval officer. At the start of the war, the fleets consisted of the First (Battle), Second (Scouting Force), Third (Blockade and Amphibious Force), Fourth (Mandates Fleet), Fifth (Northern Fleet), and Sixth (Submarine), plus two air fleets: the First (carrier aircraft) and Eleventh (land-based aircraft). There were also Home Naval Stations (at Kure, Sasebo, Maizuru, and Yokosuka), which patrolled home waters and were also assigned—on an ill-planned ad hoc basis—convoy escort duty. At Manchukuo, Korea, Formosa, and Hainan Island, Naval Guard Stations patrolled coastal waters.

The fleets were variously configured into task forces. At the outset of the war, these included the Main Body under Admiral YAMAMOTO ISORUKU (who also commanded the Combined Fleet); the Striking Force, the Southern Force, the South Seas Force, the Northern Force, and a Submarine Fleet. During the war, more fleets and task forces were formed, and, in November 1943, the IJN belatedly recognized the necessity of providing convoy protection and formed a General Escort Command (which, however, was never adequately supplied with ships or crews). In March 1944, naval high command extensively reorganized the IJN. The Combined Fleet was redesignated the First Mobile Fleet, which included almost all surface warships.

The navy's role in amphibious warfare was to support army ground operations. The IJN also had its own special naval ground troops, however, who were deployed in some amphibious operations and designated Special Naval Landing Forces. From one of these units, two battalions of paratroops were trained.

Admiral Yamamoto intended the BATTLE OF MIDWAY (June 4–7, 1942) to be the decisive battle that would permanently reduce the threat posed by the U.S. Pacific Fleet. Unknown to Yamamoto and other Japanese naval commanders, the Americans had broken Japanese naval codes and were therefore able to anticipate the IJN's moves at Midway. The result was, in fact, a decisive battle—but one that turned the tide of the Pacific war against Japan. From Midway onward, the IJN was on the defensive and suffered steady and catastrophic attrition. Of 451 surface warships and submarines the IJN operated during World War II, a staggering 332 had been sunk by the end of the war. A mere 37 vessels remained operational.

See also SHIPS, JAPANESE

Further reading: Atkinson, John. *Imperial Japanese Navy WWII.* Couldson, U.K.: Galago Books, 2003; Dull, Paul S. *A Battle History of the Imperial Japanese Navy, 1941–1945.* Annapolis, Md.: Naval Institute Press, 1978; Evans, David C. *Kaigun: Strategy, Tactics, and Technology in the Imperial Japanese Navy, 1887–1941.* Annapolis, Md.: Naval Institute Press, 1997.

Japanese-American soldiers in World War II

At the time of the BATTLE OF PEARL HARBOR, December 7, 1941, some 120,000 persons of immediate Japanese descent were resident in the continental United States. Of these, about 80,000 had been born in this country and were citizens. Within four days after Pearl Harbor, the Federal Bureau of Investigation (FBI) arrested and detained 1,370 Japanese Americans as "dangerous enemy aliens," despite their being American citizens. On January 5, 1942, U.S. draft boards summarily classified all Japanese-American selective service registrants as enemy aliens, and many Japanese Americans already serving were discharged or restricted to menial labor duties. On January 23, Japanese-American soldiers and sailors on the U.S. mainland were segregated out of their units. On February 19, 1942, President FRANKLIN D. ROOSEVELT signed Executive Order 9066, effectively authorizing the internment of Japanese-Americans living within 200 miles of the Pacific Coast.

In all, some 110,000 persons were moved to internment camps in California, Idaho, Utah, Arizona, Wyoming, Colorado, and Arkansas. During their confinement, some 1,200 young Japanese men secured release from the camps by enlisting in the army. The overwhelming majority of these young men were segregated in the 442nd Regimental Combat Team, which, activated on February 1, 1943, also included about 10,000 Japanese-Hawaiian volunteers. (Japanese Hawaiians had not been subject to Executive Order 9066.) The 442nd was sent to Europe and fought valiantly in Italy, France, and Germany, emerging from the war as the most highly decorated unit of its size and length of service in American military history.

In the meantime, on February 25, 1942, the all-Nisei Varsity Victory Volunteers (known as the "Triple V") was formed in Hawaii as part of the 34th Combat Engineers Regiment. On the west coast of the mainland, however, the War Department discontinued the induction of Japanese Americans as of March 30, 1942.

Shortly before Pearl Harbor, on November 1, 1941, the War Department had opened a secret language school under the control of the Fourth Army in San Francisco. The school was staffed by four Nisei instructors and had 60 students, of whom 58 were Nisei. These individuals would make up the first class of the Military Intelligence Language School. During the war, many of the school's graduates were sent to the Aleutian Islands and the South Pacific as Japanese linguists and as intelligence operatives. The language school was moved from San Francisco to Camp Savage, Minnesota, on May 25 in compliance with the order excluding all Japanese Americans from the West Coast.

On May 26, 1942, General GEORGE C. MARSHALL established the Hawaii Provisional Infantry Battalion, made up of Japanese Americans from the Hawaii National Guard. On June 5, the battalion left Honolulu for San Francisco and, on the June 12 it was activated in the Regular army as the 100th Infantry Battalion. Just five days later, the War Department announced that it would not accept for service any Japanese or persons of Japanese extraction, regardless of citizenship status. Before the end of the month, however, on June 26, army policymakers recommended the formation of a Board of Military Utilization of U.S. Citizens of Japanese Ancestry, to determine whether a Japanese-American unit should be sent to fight in Europe. In October, Elmer Davis, director of the Office of War Information, recommended to President Roosevelt that Japanese Americans be allowed to enlist.

While army policy shifted back and forth, 26 members of the 100th Infantry Battalion were sent to Ship Island and Cat Island off the Mississippi Gulf Coast to be used to train dogs, to recognize and attack Japanese. This assignment was based on what white officers believed was the unique scent of the Japanese.

On February 1, 1943, the army acted on the question of Japanese-American enlistment by activating the 442nd Regimental Combat Team (RCT), an all–Japanese-American force. The members of the Triple V unit formed the core of the 442nd, which began training in Mississippi in May.

Although the 442nd was destined to become the most celebrated Japanese-American unit, it was not the first to see action. On September 2, 1943, the 100th Infantry Battalion landed in Oran, Algeria, and was assigned to guard supply trains from Casablanca to Tunisia. Later, the unit was assigned to the 34th Infantry Division and, on September 22, 1943, landed on the beach at Salerno, Italy, as part of the 133rd Infantry Regiment, 34th Infantry Division. In November, the battalion participated in an offensive against the Germans crossing the Volturno River south of Naples, and, in January 1944, it fought in the BATTLES OF CASSINO. From this engagement, in March, the battalion landed at Anzio and fought in the ANZIO CAMPAIGN.

Generally, army policy was to use Japanese-American combat troops exclusively in the European theater; however, in late 1943, 14 Nisei were assigned to Merrill's Marauders, the famed commando unit operating in north Burma. In April 1944, the 1399th Engineering Construction Battalion, exclusively a Japanese-American unit, was formed to work on noncombat construction and maintenance projects in Hawaii. Throughout much of the Pacific and Asian war, Japanese-American graduates of the Military Intelligence Language School were deployed, typically in the front lines, as interpreters, translators, and intelligence operators.

The 442nd Regimental Combat Team finally shipped out of Hampton Roads, Virginia, bound for Europe on May 1, 1944, while the 100th continued to fight in Italy. Arriving in Italy on June 26, 1944, the 442nd RCT was assigned to the Fifth Army and attached to the 34th Division. At this point, the 100th Infantry Battalion was attached to the 442nd and, thus configured, the 442nd RCT was committed to battle near Belvedere, Italy. On July 27, 1944, General MARK W. CLARK, commanding the Fifth Army, personally presented the Distinguished Presidential Unit Citation to the 100th Infantry Battalion for action at Belvedere. The 442nd's Antitank Company was detached from the RCT and assigned to the 1st Airborne Task Force for glider training. On August 15, 1944, the unit participated in the invasion of southern France, then rejoined the 442nd on October 11.

The 442nd left Italy for France on September 26, 1944, and as part of the Seventh Army, fought in the Vosges Mountains. In March 1945, the 442nd left France to return to Italy, where it joined the all African-American 92nd Infantry Division. The following month, the 442nd made a spectacular surprise attack on Nazi mountainside positions, breaking through the infamous GOTHIC LINE in a single day. The unit then pursued the retreating Germans, driving them up the Italian coast to Genoa and Turin.

Detached from the 442nd, the 522nd Field Artillery Battalion participated in the liberation of Jewish prisoners of the Landsberg-Kaufering and Dachau concentration camps. After the German surrender on May 8, 1945, the 442nd participated in occupation duty, then returned to the United States in July 1946. On July 15, in Washington, D. C., President HARRY S. TRUMAN presented the 442nd RCT with a Presidential Unit Citation. "You fought not only the enemy," the president remarked, "but you fought prejudice—and you have won."

In addition to the Japanese-American men who rendered distinguished service in World War II, beginning in October 1943, Japanese-American women were accepted into the Women's Army Corps. Some 300 would serve during the war and immediately afterward.

See also INTERNMENT, JAPANESE-AMERICAN.

Further reading: Duus, Masayo. *Unlikely Liberators: The Men of the 100th and 442nd.* Honolulu: University of Hawaii Press, 1987; Moore, Brenda L. *Serving Our Country: Japanese American Women in the Military during World War II.* New Brunswick, N.J.: Rutgers University Press, 2003; Wakamatsu, Jack K. *Silent Warriors: A Memoir of America's 442nd Regimental Combat Team.* New York: Vantage Press, 1995.

jet aircraft

The basic constituents of the jet engine were patented in 1930 by the British aeronautical engineer Frank Whittle (1907–96). A British aircraft with a Whittle engine successfully flew in May 1941. German engineers patented an engine in 1935, but

A German Me-262, photographed just before delivery to the Luftwaffe *(National Archives and Records Administration)*

work on jets proceeded much more quickly in Germany than in Britain, and the first turbojet-powered aircraft, a Heinkel HE-178, flew in August 1939, a month before the start of World War II.

At first ADOLF HITLER was a strong supporter of developing jet technology, but during the course of the war, acting on the advice of Luftwaffe chief HERMANN GÖRING, he diverted production from jets to increasing the output of greater numbers of conventional aircraft. For this reason, Germany never produced jet aircraft in great quantity during the war. Nevertheless, both Germany and Britain recognized the jet as the wave of the future, at least for small fighter aircraft. In contrast, the American military and the aircraft industry were slow to develop jets, and the first American military jet fighter, the Shooting Star, did not become operational during the war. In Britain and Germany, the RAF and the Luftwaffe both flew jets in combat by 1944. Neither nation fielded a sufficient number to make a significant impact on the air war.

The British jet was the de Haviland Meteor. The principal German plane was the Messerschmidt Me262. The Me262 was extremely effective against U.S. bombers, since the aircraft easily outran even the best U.S. fighter escorts, such as the P-51 Mustang. The drawbacks of the Me262 were its short range and flight duration—it was extremely fuel hungry—and its relatively poor maneuverability

relative to piston fighters. Most important, it was introduced too late in the war and was produced in quantities too small to have a significant effect on the outcome of the struggle.

The Luftwaffe experimented with other jet designs, as well as the ultraradical tailless flying-wing, the Me163, which used a liquid-fueled rocket motor instead of an air-breathing jet engine. The Me163 could fly at nearly 600 miles per hour and quickly climb above bomber formations, then attack from above—the ideal approach against bombers. Fuel lasted a mere 12 minutes, however, making the aircraft highly impractical.

Had Germany devoted more development and production effort to jet aircraft, it is likely that both the United States and Britain would have been forced to curtail the strategic bombing of Germany, and the war might well have been prolonged.

See also AIRCRAFT, BRITISH; AIRCRAFT, GERMAN.

Further reading: Ethell, Jeffrey, and Alfred Price. *World War II Fighting Jets.* Annapolis, Md.: Naval Institute Press, 1994.

Jodl, Alfred (1890–1946) *chief of the Operations Staff of the German High Command*

As chief of the Operations Staff of the German High Command (OKW) during all of World War II, Jodl served as close military adviser to ADOLF HITLER.

Jodl was born in Würzburg, Bavaria, and served in World War I as an artillery officer. Between the wars, in 1932, he served as a major in the operations branch of the Truppenamt, a body created to circumvent the TREATY OF VERSAILLES proscription abolishing the German General Staff. Jodl advanced to leadership of the National Defense Branch of the Armed Forces Office, and in October 1938 took command of an artillery unit in Vienna, before returning to Berlin in August of the following year as chief of OKW's Operations Staff under WILHELM KEITEL, his father-in-law.

Jodl was a pliable military bureaucrat who had a talent for pleasing those above him, including

General Jodl signs the German surrender at SHAEF headquarters, Reims, France, on May 7, 1945. *(Library of Congress)*

Hitler. In July 1940, he was jumped from brigadier to lieutenant general, then to general in January 1944. Among many in the German high command, Jodl had a reputation for passivity and subservience. In fact, he was more loyal than subservient, but it is true that he took great pains to avoid direct confrontations with Hitler. Unlike many other high-ranking officers, he retained Hitler's confidence through the very end of the war. It was Jodl who signed the German surrender at Reims on May 7, 1945.

Jodl was tried by the NUREMBERG WAR CRIMES TRIBUNAL after the war and found guilty of war crimes. He was hanged. A German de-Nazification court posthumously exonerated him in 1953.

Further reading: Mellenthin, Friedrich Wilhelm von. *German Generals of World War II: As I Saw Them.* Norman: University of Oklahoma Press, 1977; Thomas, Nigel. *The German Army in World War II.* London: Osprey, 2002.

July Plot, 1944 (to assassinate Hitler)

The July Plot, or July 20 Plot, was a failed coup d'état and the most famous of some 17 attempts (before and during the war) to assassinate ADOLF HITLER.

The plot was formulated and led by Colonel Claus von Stauffenberg, a wounded war hero and the scion of old German nobility. Other principal plotters included General Ludwig Beck, Carl Goerdeler, Alfred Delp, Lieutenant Colonel Robert Bernardis, Carl Szokoll, Count Hans-Jürgen von Blumenthal, Adam von Trott zu Solz, Gottfried von Bismarck, and Princess Marie Vassiltchikov. All were of the same social class as Stauffenberg and had come to distrust, disdain, or hate Hitler as an incompetent man of the people who was not only leading Germany to defeat, but, even if victory were somehow achieved, was determined (they believed) ultimately to wipe out the old nobility. Peripherally involved in the plot were Field Marshal Erwin von Witzleben, GÜNTHER VON KLUGE, and, most important, Field Marshal ERWIN ROMMEL, Germany's most popular commander.

Stauffenberg's plan was to plant a time bomb near Hitler's place at the conference table of Wolfsschanze (Wolf's Lair), his military headquarters in Rastenburg, East Prussia. Once the bomb had been placed, Stauffenberg was to go to Berlin to take command of the troops who would be deployed to carry out the coup. The plotters had prepared a new government, to be led by General Beck with Goerdeler as chancellor. This was to be an interim government; the plotters planned ultimately to restore the Hohenzollern monarchy.

Stauffenberg designated the military aspect of the coup Operation Valkyrie. In essence, it was a deception by which the military would move on Berlin to "rescue" the capital from a purported takeover by slave laborers. This ruse was intended to cover extensive troop deployments designed to get troops in place for the main military coup d'état.

Stauffenberg succeeded in planting only one of the two time bombs he carried. The one he placed was hidden in a briefcase, which he took into Wolfsschanze. Stauffenberg then maneuvered himself close to Hitler, explaining that his war wound had impaired his hearing. He set the briefcase down on the floor, excused himself, and left the conference just before the bomb detonated. As fate would have it, after Stauffenberg left, someone pushed the briefcase farther under the heavy wooden conference table around which Hitler and his officers were gathered. The bomb detonated, killing four and injuring (in varying degrees) everyone else in the room; it had been repositioned behind a thick leg of the table, however, and the tabletop and leg shielded Hitler from most of the blast's force. Badly shaken, he escaped with minor injuries.

By this time, Stauffenberg was already on his way to Berlin and assumed Hitler was dead. He arrived in the capital to find that General Friedrich Olbricht had failed to launch Operation Valkyrie, so it began four hours behind schedule. Lacking momentum, the coup also failed to seize the radio stations (as planned), and these soon broadcast the news of the assassination attempt—as well as the fact that Hitler was alive and well. Indeed, later that very day, Hitler calmly and publicly welcomed to Berlin Benito Mussolini, who had just been rescued by German commandos from captivity in Italy.

As soon as it was clear that Hitler was still alive and in power, the Berlin-based reserve army troops, who had been carrying out Stauffenberg's orders, turned against him and the other plotters. The coup instantly collapsed, and Hitler dispatched various forces to round up the plotters and the plot organizers. Stauffenberg, Olbricht, Albrecht Mertz von Quirnheim, and Lieutenant Werner von Haeften were caught late in the evening and summarily executed by firing squad in the courtyard of the Bendler Block (the War Ministry building). Hitler ultimately oversaw the purge and execution (in some cases, accompanied by show trials) of some 5,000 persons he believed were implicated in the plot. All were known opponents of the Nazi regime. Many were tortured to death. Some were hanged by the neck using piano wire.

Stauffenberg and the other plotters are remembered in modern Germany as heroes of the anti-Nazi resistance.

Further reading: Fest, Joachim. *Plotting Hitler's Death: The Story of German Resistance.* New York: Owl, 1997; Galante, Pierre. *Operation Valkyrie: The German Generals' Plot Against Hitler.* New York: Cooper Square, 2002).

K

Kádár, János (1912–1989) *Hungarian underground leader*

Born in Fiume, Hungary, Kádár (whose original name was János Czermanik, or Csermanek) was a mechanic by trade and, at age 19, joined Hungary's then illegal Communist Party. Before the war, he became both accustomed to and skilled at covert operations. During the war, he was a member of the Hungarian underground, and in 1942 was admitted to the Central Committee of the Communist Party. He gained the status of popular hero in Hungary for his work in the resistance. Captured by the Germans, he managed to escape and continue his covert action.

At the end of World War II, in 1945, Kádár became a member of the powerful Politburo of the Hungarian Communist Party. He served as premier of Hungary twice—from 1956 to 1958 and again from 1961 to 1965—and, from 1956 until 1988, was first secretary of the party. He was instrumental in Hungary's transition from the anti-Soviet government of Imre Nagy in 1956 to a pro-Soviet orientation. Nevertheless, like Tito in Yugoslavia, Kádár achieved a significant degree of independence for Hungary from direct Soviet rule.

Further reading: Kádár, János. *On the Road to Socialism: Selected Speeches and Interviews, 1960–1964.* Budapest: Corvina Press, 1965; Kovrig, Bennett. *The Hungarian People's Republic.* Baltimore, Johns Hopkins University Press, 1970.

kamikaze

The Japanese word *kamikaze,* commonly translated as "divine wind," refers to a legendary typhoon that is believed to have saved Japan from a Mongol invasion fleet in 1281. During World War II (and in the present day as well) the word has been used in English to refer to suicide attacks made principally by Japanese pilots. The Japanese themselves reserved (and continue to reserve) *kamikaze* to describe only the 1281 typhoon. A World War II suicide attack unit was officially called *tokubetsu kōgeki tai,* "special attack unit," and was usually shortened to *tokkōtai.* The Imperial Japanese Navy called its suicide squads *shinpū tokubetsu kōgeki tai;* the word *shinpū* uses the same characters that form the word *kamikaze.*

American sailors became most terrifyingly familiar with airborne kamikazes, but the Japanese employed various modes of suicide attack, from soldiers who detonated explosives on their persons to explosive motorboats, to explosives-laden midget submarines, to human-guided torpedoes.

After the U.S. victory in the Battle of Saipan on July 15, 1944, which put American B-29 bombers in range for strikes against the Japanese mainland, and the subsequent commencement of the invasion of the Philippines on October 17, 1944, Japanese naval air commanders, whose forces were greatly diminished, faced the impossible task of stopping the Americans. In this desperate situation, First Air Fleet commandant Vice Admiral Takijiro

Deck-level view of a kamikaze strike on the aircraft carrier *Bunker Hill* *(National Archives and Records Administration)*

Onishi proposed the formation of a suicide attack unit, translated into English as the Kamikaze Special Attack Force. In October 1944, Commander Tamai Asaiki formed a group of 23 promising student pilots and one experienced lieutenant to join the special force. All were volunteers.

There is some controversy over what constituted the very first kamikaze attack. Late in 1944, the USS *Indiana* and USS *Reno* were hit by Japanese aircraft, but most authorities deem these to have been accidental collisions. Many believe that the first deliberate attack was led by Captain Masafumi Arima, commander of the 26th Air Flo-

tilla, on October 13, 1944. On that day, no fewer than 100 Yokosuka D4Y Suisei (Judy) dive bombers attacked the carrier *Franklin* near Leyte Gulf, and Arima's aircraft dived into the ship. Again, however, this might have been inadvertent. The attack on the heavy cruiser HMAS *Australia*, flagship of the Royal Australian Navy, on October 21, 1944, was unmistakably a kamikaze assault. The pilot and aircraft involved were apparently attached to the Imperial Japanese Army air force, not the navy.

On October 25, the Imperial Japanese Navy's Kamikaze Special Attack Force carried out its first mission, five Zeros targeting the USS *St. Lô* and other ships. The *St. Lô* was sunk. The October 25 attacks encouraged the Japanese to expand the kamikaze program, and over the next several months more than 2,500 planes and pilots made suicide attacks. The peak of the program came during April–June 1945, at the BATTLE OF OKINAWA. Suicide attacks by aircraft or boats sank or put out of action about 30 American warships and three American merchant vessels. Other Allied ships were also hit. The cost to the Japanese was a staggering 1,465 planes.

Planned as the most spectacular suicide mission was Operation Ten-Go on April 1, 1945. The *Yamoto*, pride of the Imperial Japanese Navy and the largest battleship of World War II, was sent on a suicide mission to attack the U.S. ships supporting landings on Okinawa. *Yamoto* was located before it got anywhere near the American invasion fleet and was attacked from the air on April 7. It sank with the loss of 2,475 sailors.

Most aircraft used in kamikaze attacks were ordinary fighters or dive bombers; very late in the war, however, the Japanese built the Nakajima Ki-115 Tsurugi, a cheap, simple, wooden airplane equipped with nonretractable landing gear jettisoned on takeoff (and reusable by other Ki-115s). Whereas the Ki-115 was a conventional piston design, the Yokosuka MXY7 Ohka was a rocket-powered aircraft—essentially a human-guided antiship missile. Also specially designed and manufactured for suicide missions were manned torpedoes, called Kaiten.

Defense against aerial kamikazes included anti-aircraft fire and fire from Allied fighters. Poorly trained and inexperienced, kamikaze pilots fell easy prey to Allied pilots. Nevertheless, kamikaze attacks were extremely demoralizing to Allied sailors. Official Japanese sources record that kamikazes sank 81 ships and damaged 195, accounting for about 80 percent of U.S. naval losses in the closing months of the Pacific war. U.S. sources differ from this, recording that about 2,800 kamikaze attacks sank 34 U.S. Navy ships and damaged 368 others. Some 4,900 sailors were killed in the attacks, and another 4,800 were wounded. About 14 percent of kamikazes managed to score hits, and about 8.5 percent of all ships hit by Kamikazes sank. As for Japanese losses, 2,525 kamikaze pilots died, along with 1,387 army pilots.

"Kamikaze" or more general suicide techniques were not exclusive to the Japanese. Late in World War II, OTTO SKORZENY, the daring German commando, and Hanna Reitsch, legendary German test pilot, proposed the *Selbstopfer* (self-sacrifice) program. Their idea was to convert V-1 BUZZ BOMBS for manned flight by installing a cockpit and controls. Approximately 100 pilots, from Skorzeny's commando group KG 200, were trained, and some 175 modified V-1s—renamed the Fieseler Fi 103 R Reichenberg—were manufactured. The mission was not 100 percent suicidal, since pilots were expected to bail out just before impact; however, this would have been a highly impractical maneuver: the cockpit was tiny, the aircraft would be in a steep dive, and the cockpit was located just below the pulsejet intake. It is not believed that *Selbstopfer* ever proceeded beyond the planning stage, and none of the modified V-1s was ever used in combat.

Further reading: Axell, Albert, and Hideaki Kase. *Kamikaze: Japan's Suicide Gods*. London: Longman, 2002; Inoguchi, Rikihei, Tadashi Nakajima, and Roger Pineau. *The Divine Wind: Japan's Kamikaze Force in World War II*. Annapolis, Md.: Naval Institute Press, 1994.

Kasserine Pass, Battle of

The first engagement between U.S. Army and German forces, the Battle of Kasserine Pass, Tunisia, during February 14–22, 1943, ended in humiliating defeat for the Americans.

In February 1943, ERWIN ROMMEL's German-Italian Panzer Army and JÜRGEN VON ARNIM's Fifth Panzer Army counterattacked DWIGHT DAVID EISENHOWER's Allied forces to block their advance to the central Tunisian coast, an advance that would have split the Axis forces. Rommel and Arnim pushed Allied forces back to the Western Dorsale and dealt U.S. II Corps, under Lieutenant General Lloyd Fredendall, a sound defeat. Fredendall's leadership was poor, and the inexperienced troops performed badly.

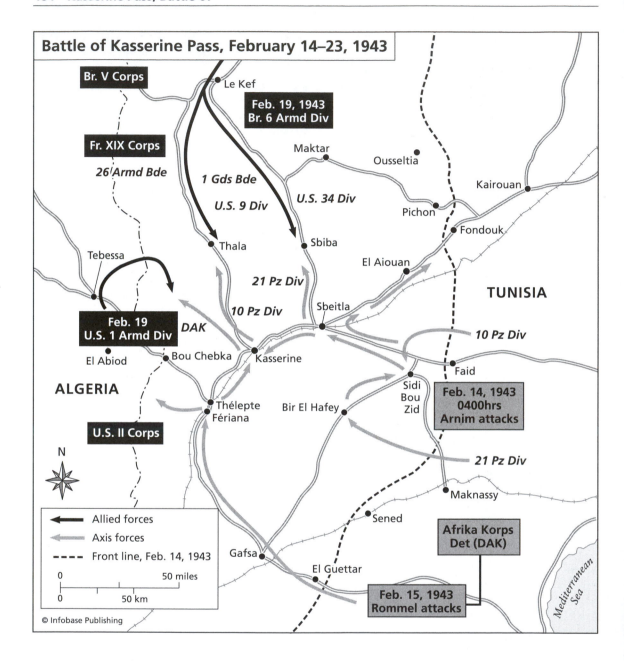

Battle of Kasserine Pass, February 14–23, 1943

The battle was also plagued by a misinterpretation of ULTRA intercepts, which prompted British commander Lieutenant General Kenneth Anderson to deploy the main body of Allied reserves too far north. This left the Kasserine Pass vulnerable to the AFRIKA KORPS steamroller. Fredendall ordered Colonel Robert Stark's mixed force to "pull a Stonewall Jackson" and make an immovable stand. Stark tried, and he did succeed in holding off the German advance on February 19, the first day of the battle, but Rommel pushed through by the next day. At this point, Fredendall's system of command seems to have broken down. Fortunately for the Allies, Rommel and Arnim also fell into some disarray, and this led them to exploit the breakthrough at Kasserine in a poorly coordinated manner. Fighting was heavy on February 21, but incessant rain crippled Rommel's armor in the difficult terrain of the Kasserine region, and on February 22, he called off the offensive.

Kasserine was highly demoralizing to the Americans, and their British allies were gravely disappointed in the performance of II Corps, derisively referring to the U.S. Army as "our Italians." Nevertheless, the defeat could have been far worse had Rommel and Arnim more successfully exploited it. Moreover, the battle came as a wake-up call to Eisenhower, who had placed blind trust in Fredendall. Eisenhower replaced that commander with GEORGE S. PATTON JR., who rapidly rehabilitated II Corps and transformed it into a highly effective unit before turning over the command to OMAR BRADLEY.

Further reading: Blumenson, Martin. *Kasserine Pass.* New York: Cooper Square Press, 2000; Zaloga, Steven J. *Kasserine Pass 1943: Rommel's Last Victory.* London: Osprey, 2005.

Keitel, Wilhelm (1882–1946) *top military adviser to Adolf Hitler*

Wilhelm Keitel was ADOLF HITLER's top military adviser throughout World War II. His loyalty to Hitler was fanatical, and he supported even the führer's most egregious military misjudgments. Others on the German General Staff secretly reviled Keitel with the derisive sobriquet of *Lackeitel,* a word suggesting "lackey" or "lickspittle."

Keitel was born in Helmscherode, Braunschweig, and served as an artillery officer during World War I. Seriously wounded in action, Keitel worked his way up to the General Staff. After the war, he became active in the FREIKORPS and in 1929 was named to head the Army Organization Department. Promoted to major general in 1934, Keitel was assigned to the War Ministry as head of the Armed Forces Office in 1935. He was promoted

to lieutenant general in 1936 and General der Artillerie in 1937. On February 4, 1938, he replaced General Werner von Blomberg as chief of staff of the Armed Forces High Command, becoming, in November, Generaloberst (colonel general). In July 1940, with victory in the BATTLE OF FRANCE, Keitel became a field marshal and was sent to Compiègne to negotiate the armistice with the French.

During the rest of the war, Keitel functioned as Hitler's conduit to the army. In contrast to many other senior German officers, his obedience to Hitler was unthinking. He approved mass murders in Poland, and he supported the creation and operations of the SS *Einsatzgrüppen,* the "Special Action Units" (see SCHUTZSTAFFEL [SS]), which perpetrated the mass murder of "undesirable" civilian populations throughout the Soviet Union and elsewhere. He was also responsible for the *Nacht und Nebel* (Night and Fog) order, which authorized the secret and summary arrest of any persons deemed to endanger German security. For all these actions, Keitel was ultimately tried by the NUREMBERG WAR CRIMES TRIBUNAL and found guilty of war crimes and crimes against humanity. He was hanged in the Nuremberg Prison on October 16, 1946.

Further reading: Gorlitz, Walter, ed. and trans. *The Memoirs of Field-Marshal Wilhelm Keitel.* New York:

German Field Marshal Wilhelm Keitel signs the German surrender in Berlin, May 8, 1945. *(National Archives and Records Administration)*

Cooper Square Press, 2000; Hart, Basil H. *German Generals Talk.* New York: Harper Perennial, 1971.

Kenney, George (1889–1977) *Allied air commander in the Southwest Pacific*

George Churchill Kenney was born in Nova Scotia, Canada, on August 6, 1889, while his family was vacationing there, and he grew up in Brookline, Massachusetts. He attended Massachusetts Institute of Technology for three years before leaving to work as an instrument technician with the Quebec Saguenay Railroad. When the United States entered World War I in 1917, Kenney enlisted as a Signal Corps private and was subsequently accepted for pilot training.

After the war, Kenney remained in the Army Air Corps and earned a reputation as a technical innovator. His most significant innovation was the introduction of machine guns in the wings of aircraft. An iconoclast, he advised, on the eve of the U.S. entry into World War II, a radical revision of the nation's military aviation program.

Kenney's first major assignment during World War II came in March 1942, when as a major general, he assumed command of the Fourth Air Force. In July 1942, he was assigned command of the Allied Air Forces in the Southwest Pacific as well as the Fifth U.S. Air Force. True to his reputation as an innovator, Kenney pioneered the use of parafrag (parachute fragmentation) bombs in the Pacific theater and developed low-altitude bombing techniques, including "skip bombing," by which a bomb was made to skip across the surface of the water, enabling below-the-waterline damage to enemy ships.

Kenney struggled in his corner of the Pacific, which was a much-neglected theater of the war. He organized his command to exploit every precious asset to the fullest and ruthlessly culled his officer corps, obtaining and retaining only the very best. Kenney also pioneered airlift techniques to support and transport troops in ground offensives.

Kenney was promoted to lieutenant general in October 1942 and then worked to improvise air-craft that could be used as "commerce destroyers" for high-speed, low-level attacks against cargo and transport vessels. A dozen B-25 bombers were modified with extra .50-caliber machine guns in their noses, and their crews were specially trained in skip bombing. The new squadron proved highly effective, especially in the Battle of the Bismarck Sea.

Kenney pioneered operations from crude forward airfields, always aiming to improve close air support and logistical support for ground offensives. General Douglas MacArthur learned to rely on him for highly imaginative and bold air operations under the most difficult and primitive conditions. He personally invited Kenney to accompany him on the deck of the battleship *Missouri* when he accepted the surrender of the Japanese on September 2, 1945.

After the war, Kenney went on to command the new Strategic Air Command and the Air University at Maxwell Field, Alabama.

Further reading: Griffith, Thomas E., Jr. *MacArthur's Airman: General George C. Kenney and the War in the Southwest Pacific.* Lawrence: University Press of Kansas, 1998; Kenney, George C. *General Kenney Reports: A Personal History of the Pacific War.* Colorado Springs, Colo.: Air Force History and Museums Program, 1997.

Kesselring, Albert von (1885–1960) *Germany's top commander in Italy*

Kesselring was a superb German general who showed himself in Italy to be a master of defensive strategy and tactics, which proved costly to the Allies.

Born in Marktsteft, Bavaria, Kesselring joined the Bavarian army as an artillery lieutenant in 1906. By the start of World War I, he had risen to become a staff officer and, after the war, remained in the army as an officer in the Reichswehr, the post-Versailles German military. He transferred from Wehrmacht (general military) staff assignments to the Luftwaffe in October 1933, when the branch, outlawed by the Treaty of Versailles, operated covertly. In 1936, Kesselring was pro-

General Albert Kesselring *(Library of Congress)*

moted to chief of the Luftwaffe general staff and promoted to lieutenant general. In 1937, promoted again, to general, he assumed command of Luftflotte I (Air Fleet 1).

In the opening action of World War II, the BLITZKRIEG invasion of Poland, Kesselring conducted devastating air operations. In January 1940, he transferred to command of Luftflotte 2 and assumed direction of air operations in the BATTLE OF FRANCE (May–June 1940). After victory was achieved there, Kesselring was promoted to field marshal on July 19, 1940. He now commanded his Luftflotte 2 in the BATTLE OF BRITAIN. During August 8–September 30, 1940, Kesselring concentrated on bombing RAF airfields in southern England. ADOLF HITLER ordered him to abandon this highly successful program and to commence attacks on London instead, beginning on September 7. That was the start of THE BLITZ, which, while highly destructive, ultimately spared the RAF and

led to the defeat and banishment of the Luftwaffe in the skies over England.

Despite what Hitler deemed the failure of the Luftwaffe, Kesselring was appointed Oberbefehlshaber (OB) Sud (commander in chief, south) in December 1941, an area of responsibility that encompassed the entire Mediterranean basin. With ERWIN ROMMEL, Kesselring shared responsibility for NORTH AFRICAN CAMPAIGNS.

By 1943, the Axis had lost the initiative in North Africa, and Kesselring's mission became one of defense. He proved a master at this form of warfare, which German planners had disdained and largely ignored. Thanks to Kesselring, much of the German army evacuated from Tunisia intact during May. He then directed the defense of Sicily from July 9–August 17, 1943. Although the island fell to the Allies, Kesselring's defense made their victory costly.

In November 1943, Kesselring was named to command Army Group C after Italian dictator BENITO MUSSOLINI had been overthrown (on July 24) and the Allies had commenced their invasion of the Italian mainland (during September 8–9). Kesselring's mission was a desperate one. Essentially, he fought a long retreat, which he made monumentally costly for the Allies, who were unable to capture all of Italy until the very end of the European war. Kesselring's defense spanned 1943 to March 1945, when he was rushed to the German western front and assigned to do all he could to arrest the Allied advance there. It was a hopeless mission, and in May 1945, Kesselring was captured.

Kesselring was tried by the NUREMBERG WAR CRIMES TRIBUNAL, charged with having authorized the massacre of 320 Italian prisoners in the Ardeatine Caves on August 24, 1944. Found guilty, he was sentenced to death in May 1947, but his sentence was commuted to life imprisonment in October 1947. Ill health prompted authorities to release him in October 1952, and he lived out the rest of his life in quiet retirement.

Further reading: Kesselring, Albert. *The Memoirs of Field-Marshal Kesselring.* Mechanicsburg, Pa.: Stackpole

Books, 1997; Macksey, Kenneth. *Kesselring: German Master Strategist of the Second World War.* London: Greenhill Books, 2000.

Kharkov, Battles of

An important administrative and railroad city in the eastern Ukraine, Kharkov was the scene of five battles during World War II and changed hands four times.

During the German INVASION OF THE SOVIET UNION, Kharkov fell to the Sixth German Army on October 24, 1941. From here, the Germans advanced 25 miles to the east, stopping at the Donets River. ADOLF HITLER decided this would be the rallying point for the 1942 summer offensive. Soviet Red Army planners called for five armies to cross the Donets 75 miles southwest of Kharkov, then form a salient that would retake the city.

On May 12, 1942, Marshal SemyonTimoshenko led his Southwest Front (a "front" is the Red Army equivalent of the Western allies' army group) in an advance on Kharkov. On May 17, the Sixth and First German Panzer armies counterattacked with converging advances along the Donets from the north and south. Timoshenko pulled up short, halting 15 miles outside the city on May 20. His timing was bad, and the German forces encircled his armies by May 23. When the battle was over, on May 28, Timoshenko had lost more than 250,000 troops and 1,200 tanks. It was a disastrous defeat.

On February 11, 1943, two armies of General N. F. Vatutin's Voronezh Front crossed the Donets east of Kharkov. Hitler ordered three SS panzer divisions to hold the city, which he wanted as a fortress. By February 16, however, the Soviet armies had enveloped Kharkov, prompting the panzers to abandon the city, which was also in the throes of a popular uprising. The panzers headed south for a distance of 115 miles, where they joined up with the Fourth Panzer Army, under General HERMANN HOTH. Then, on March 9, the SS divisions wheeled about, determined to restore their honor by retaking Kharkov. Realizing what was happening, Hoth ordered the SS to bypass the city, but on March 11, the divisions, defying him, entered it and fought a

three-day street battle, which ended in German victory on March 13. This prompted Hitler to issue orders for OPERATION CITADEL, with Kharkov as a staging area.

In early August, the Soviet victory in the great tank BATTLE OF KURSK enabled a massive offensive involving 14 Soviet armies and some 1.5 million troops. Kharkov was targeted by four armies of IVAN KONEV's Steppe Front. The German defenders were battered and repeatedly appealed to Hitler for permission to withdraw. It was not until August 22, 1943, that Hitler permitted the evacuation, and Kharkov remained in Soviet hands for the rest of the war.

Further reading: Bechtolsheim, Anton. *The Battle of Kharkov, 1942.* Leavenworth, Kans.: Historical Division, Headquarters, United States Army, Europe, Foreign Military Studies Branch, 1952; Glantz, David M. *Kharkov 1942: Anatomy of a Military Disaster.* Rockville Centre, N.Y.: Sarpedon Publishers, 1998; Nipe, George M. *Last Victory in Russia: The SS-Panzerkorps and Manstein's Kharkov Counteroffensive—February–March 1943.* Atglen, Pa.: Schiffer Publishing, 2000.

Khrushchev, Nikita (1894–1971) *Soviet war leader during World War II, Communist Party first secretary (1953–64), premier (1958–64)*

Nikita Khrushchev was born in Kalinovka, Ukraine, the son of a coal miner and the grandson of a serf. He had a rudimentary education then moved with his family to the mining town of Yuzovka (later named Stalino, now Donetsk) near the Donets River, where he went to work as a pipe fitter at age 15. His factory job allowed him to escape conscription in the tsar's army during World War I. In the course of the war, he became increasingly active in labor organizations and, by 1918, was a Bolshevik, a member of the Russian Communist Party. He joined the Red Army in January 1919 and served as a junior commissar, fighting the Whites as well as the invading Polish armies in 1920.

In 1922 Khrushchev enrolled in a Soviet worker's school in Yuzovka and received the equivalent of a high school education. He became secretary of the Communist Party Committee at the school and, in 1924, married his second wife, the schoolteacher Nina Petrovna, his first wife having died in a famine.

By 1925, Khrushchev was full-time party secretary of the Petrovsko-Mariinsk district of Yuzovka. Lazar M. Kaganovich, one of JOSEPH STALIN's lieutenants and secretary-general of the Ukrainian Party's Central Committee, took notice of Khrushchev and made him a nonvoting delegate to the 14th Party Congress in Moscow. After this, Khrushchev became an active party organizer in Yuzovka, Kharkov, and Kiev.

In 1929, Khrushchev enrolled at the Stalin Industrial Academy in Moscow to study metallurgy. He was quickly appointed secretary of the academy's Party Committee and, in 1931, returned to full-time party work in Moscow. In 1933, he was named second secretary of the Moscow Regional Committee and spent the rest of the decade solidifying his position in Moscow politics.

Khrushchev supervised the completion of the Moscow Metro (subway), for which he was decorated with the Order of Lenin in 1935, and he was elevated to first secretary of the Moscow city and regional party organization, becoming effectively the governor of Moscow. An ardent Stalinist, Khrushchev was one of the few close associates Stalin trusted. He became a member of the Constitutional Committee in 1936, an alternate member of the Politburo in 1937, and also a member of the Foreign Affairs Commission of the Supreme Soviet. In 1938, Khrushchev, as a candidate member of the Politburo, was sent to Kiev as first secretary of the Ukrainian party organization, and in 1939 he became a full member of the Politburo.

In 1940, after the commencement of World War II, when Red Army forces invaded and occupied eastern Poland, Khrushchev directed the annexation of the region to the Soviet Union. The German INVASION OF THE SOVIET UNION in June 1941 took Khrushchev away from this task, as he was rushed into position to oversee the emergency evacuation of Ukrainian industry to the east. This accomplished, he was commissioned a lieutenant

general in the Red Army and assigned to rouse and organize civilian resistance to the German invasion. Khrushchev served as political adviser to Marshal Andrey I. Yeremenko during the defense of STALINGRAD and to Lieutenant General Nikolay F. Vatutin at the BATTLE OF KURSK.

After the invaders had been ejected from the Ukraine in 1944, Khrushchev was restored to his position as first secretary of the Ukrainian party organization. He undertook the monumental task of recovery of the devastated region. A postwar famine in 1946 brought him into conflict with Stalin, who ruthlessly demanded that grain production from Ukraine be sent elsewhere. Despite friction with Stalin, the Soviet premier recalled him to Moscow in 1949 to resume his leadership of the Moscow City Party and to accept appointment as secretary of the Central Committee of the CPSU.

From 1949 until Stalin's death in 1953, Khrushchev moved gingerly to avoid being purged by the increasingly irrational dictator. During this period, Khrushchev became an innovator in centralized agriculture, but many of his innovations were rejected in 1951 by the new agriculture chief, Georgy M. Malenkov. After the death of Stalin and the execution of state security chief LAVRENTY BERIA (Khrushchev was instrumental in bringing about Beria's demise), Khrushchev outmaneuvered Malenkov, Stalin's heir apparent, and replaced him as first secretary. In 1955, Khrushchev removed Malenkov from the premiership and put in his place his own handpicked candidate, Marshal Nikolay A. Bulganin.

Khrushchev introduced an era of de-Stalinization and greater liberalization in Soviet government and society. Although a tough opponent of the Western democracies, he also advocated a policy of "peaceful coexistence" in the nuclear age. Yet Khrushchev never achieved the agricultural successes the Soviet Union badly needed, he broke with mainland China, and (as many saw it) he allowed the USSR to suffer humiliation in the Cuban missile crisis of 1962. On October 14, 1964, he fell victim to a bloodless coup by his deputy Leonid Brezhnev and went into forced retirement, living out the rest of his life in obscurity.

Further reading: Khrushchev, Nikita Sergeevich. *Memoirs of Nikita Khrushchev: Commissar (1918–1945)*. State College: Pennsylvania State University Press, 2005; Taubman, William. *Khrushchev: The Man and His Era*. New York: W. W. Norton, 2004.

Kimmel, Husband E. (1882–1968)
commander in chief, U.S. Pacific Command, during the Battle of Pearl Harbor

As commander in chief, U.S. Pacific Command (CINCPAC) at the outbreak of World War II, Admiral Kimmel, along with his army counterpart, General WALTER CAMPBELL SHORT, was assigned principal blame for America's unpreparedness at the BATTLE OF PEARL HARBOR.

Kimmel was born in Henderson, Kentucky, and graduated from the U.S. Naval Academy at Annapolis in 1904. He served on a number of battleships in the Caribbean during 1906–07, then was assigned to the USS *Georgia* (BE-15) during the around-the-world cruise of the Great White Fleet (under Admiral George Dewey) from December 16, 1907, to February 22, 1909. Kimmel was wounded in action during the U.S. occupation of Veracruz, Mexico, in April 1914.

In 1915, well before the United States entered World War I, Kimmel was appointed aide to assistant secretary of the navy FRANKLIN D. ROOSEVELT and then was detached to an advisory post with the British Grand Fleet, his assignment to teach British officers new gunnery techniques. In April 1917, when the United States entered World War I, Kimmel was recalled to serve as squadron gunnery officer with the U.S. Sixth Battle Squadron from 1917 to 1918. He was executive officer aboard USS *Arkansas* (BB-33) from 1918 to 1920, then served ashore as production officer at the Naval Gun Factory in Washington, D.C., from 1920 to 1923. His next assignment was as chief of the Cavite navy yard in the Philippines. During 1923–25, he also commanded Destroyer Divisions 45 and 38.

In 1926, Kimmel completed the senior course at the Naval War College and was promoted to captain in July. Assigned to the office of the chief of naval operations from 1926 to 1928, he then returned to sea as commander of Destroyer Squadron 12 in the Battle Fleet from 1928 to 1930. In 1930, he returned to shore as director of ships' movements in the office of the Chief of Naval Operations. His next sea assignment came in 1933, when he was given command of the USS *New York* (BB-34). Two years later, he was back on shore, attached to the Navy Budget Office. Promoted to rear admiral in November 1937, Kimmel was appointed commander of Cruiser Division 7 in July 1938. In June 1939, he was assigned command of Battle Force Cruisers, and of Cruiser Division 9.

Kimmel's career had attracted much attention, and he was chosen over 46 more senior admirals for the post of CINCPAC, with his flag aboard the USS *Pennsylvania* (BB-38) in Pearl Harbor, territory of Hawaii. He was promoted to admiral in February 1941 and made vigorous preparations for a Pacific war that most government and military officials believed likely. Incredibly, however, the single scenario neither he nor most other military planners foresaw was a first-strike surprise attack on Pearl Harbor itself. When the fleet was devastated in the attack of December 7, 1941, Kimmel and his army counterpart, General Walter Short, bore the brunt of direct blame for the disaster. On December 17, Kimmel was relieved as CINCPAC and recalled to Washington to testify in the initial

Admiral Husband E. Kimmel (center) confers with his aides. *(U.S. Navy History Center)*

Pearl Harbor inquiries. In the end—and unlike Short—he was never officially blamed for Pearl Harbor, but his career was smashed nevertheless. He retired from the navy with the reverted rank of rear admiral on March 1, 1942, and was periodically summoned to new Pearl Harbor inquiries through 1946.

During 1946–47, Kimmel worked for an engineering firm, then retired, later publishing *Admiral Kimmel's Story* as a defense of his actions.

Further reading: Brownlow, Donald Grey. *The Accused: The Ordeal of Rear Admiral Husband Edward Kimmel, U.S.N.* New York: Vantage Press, 1968; Kimmel, Husband E. *Admiral Kimmel's Story.* Chicago: H. Regnery, 1955.

Kimura Hyotaro (1888–1948) *Japanese vice minister of war*

Kimura was trained as an artillery officer and, from 1931 to 1932, then a lieutenant colonel, commanded the 22nd Artillery Regiment before being appointed an instructor at the Field Artillery School. In 1935, he was named chief of the Control Section in the Economic Mobilization Bureau at the Ministry of War. This brought him close to the policymaking center of the militaristic Japanese government. He achieved even greater influence in 1936, when he was appointed head of the Ordnance Bureau.

Kimura returned to the field in 1939, during the SINO-JAPANESE WAR, as a lieutenant general in command of the 32nd Division in China. In 1940, he was named chief of staff of the Kwantung Expeditionary Army in Manchuria. In effect, he now commanded the equivalent of what the Western allies would call an army group.

With the outbreak of World War II in 1941, Kimura returned to the Ministry of War as vice minister of war. He reported directly to TOJO HIDEKI and was a leading voice in strategy and policy until 1943.

As 1944 drew to a close, Kimura was named to command the Burma Area Army, charged with defending Burma against the Allies. It was a desperate assignment in a desperate situation and a measure of the esteem in which Kimura was held. The Japanese high command hoped that he could somehow make the beleaguered Burma Area Army logistically self-sufficient. In an attempt to achieve this, Kimura decided not to attempt the hopeless task of defending all of Burma. Instead, he pulled back to a position behind the Irrawaddy River. This unexpected strategic stroke took the Allies by surprise—but ultimately did nothing more than buy a little time for the Burma Area Army. The Allies refocused their offensive and took Meiktila and Mandalay. Kimura continued to fight delaying actions and, in contrast to many other Japanese officers, decided to preserve as much of his army as possible rather than throw lives away in a forlorn defense. He relinquished Rangoon, then set about regrouping for a fresh stand. Before he could accomplish this, Japan surrendered.

At the TOKYO WAR CRIMES TRIBUNAL, Kimura was tried for war crimes against Chinese civilians as well as Allied POWs. He was also tried for his role in formulating the Japanese policy of militaristic expansion early in the war. Found guilty on all charges, he was hanged in 1948.

Further reading: Pritchard, R. John, and Sonia Magbanua Zaide, eds. *The Tokyo War Crimes Trial: Proceedings of the Tribunal.* London: Taylor & Francis, 1981.

King, Ernest J. (1878–1956) *U.S. chief of naval operations*

King was born in Lorain, Ohio, and enrolled as a midshipman during the Spanish-American War. Serving aboard the USS *San Francisco,* he participated in patrols off the East Coast during April–December 1898. After the war, King returned to the Naval Academy at Annapolis, graduating near the top of the class of 1901. As an ensign in 1903, he served aboard the USS *Cincinnati,* from which he observed naval action during the Russo-Japanese War (February 1904–September 1905). Promoted to lieutenant in June 1906, he taught at the academy as an ordnance instructor. In 1909, he returned to seagoing duty on battleships of the Atlantic Fleet. Promoted to lieutenant commander in July

Admiral Ernest King (left) with Dwight D. Eisenhower in Europe at the end of the war *(National Archives and Records Administration)*

1913, he returned to shore as an officer in the Engineering Experimental Station, located at Annapolis. In 1914, King assumed command of the destroyer *Terry* (DD-25) and served in operations off Veracruz in the crisis with Mexico during April–November.

With U.S. entry into World War I, King was promoted to commander in 1917 and to the temporary rank of captain in September 1918. He was selected after the war to head the postgraduate department at the Naval Academy, but in 1921 he chose sea duty again, this time as commander of a refrigerator ship off the East Coast. In 1922, he enrolled in submarine training at New London, Connecticut, then took command of Submarine Division II, serving in this capacity until 1923, when he was named commandant of the submarine base at New London, Connecticut.

In 1926, King was named senior aide to Captain H. E. Yarnell, commander of Aircraft Squadrons Scouting Fleet. While serving in this post, King trained as a naval aviator, earning his wings in May 1927 at the advanced age of 48. He was named assistant chief of the Bureau of Aeronautics (1928–29), then was assigned as commander of the naval air base at Hampton Roads, Virginia.

From 1930 to 1932, King was skipper of the aircraft carrier *Lexington* (CV-3). He returned to shore in 1933 to take the Naval War College senior course and was promoted to rear admiral in April of that year. He was named chief of the Bureau of Aeronautics, a post he held until 1936, when he took command of the Aircraft Scouting Force. In 1938, after promotion to vice admiral, King was appointed to command the five-carrier Aircraft Battle Force, but he left to join the General Board in August 1939—a position that led to his receiving command of the Fleet Patrol Force (Atlantic) in December 1940. King was promoted on February 1, 1941, to admiral and was named commander in chief of the Atlantic Fleet. He was the first high-ranking officer to see action in World War II, directing the undeclared antisubmarine war with Germany off the U.S. East Coast.

Following the BATTLE OF PEARL HARBOR, King was named chief of naval operations (December 1941) and then commander in chief of the United States Fleet (March 13, 1942). In the latter post, he was a primary formulator of Allied naval strategy, and he participated in all of the major Allied war conferences. On December 17, 1944, King was promoted to fleet admiral, the rank he held upon his retirement in December 1945. Even after he formally retired, however, King continued to serve in an advisory capacity to secretaries of the navy and of defense, as well as to President HARRY S. TRUMAN.

King was a highly respected officer who nevertheless was notoriously irascible. His difficult personality notwithstanding, he was a brilliant strategist and an officer who ensured that operations were carried to victory.

Further reading: Buell, Thomas B. *Master of Sea Power: A Biography of Fleet Admiral Ernest J. King*. Annapolis, Md.: Naval Institute Press, 1995; King, Ernest J. *Fleet Admiral King,: A Naval Record*. New York: W. W. Norton, 1952.

King, William Lyon Mackenzie (1874–1950) *prime minister of Canada*

William Lyon Mackenzie King—universally known as Mackenzie King—was the wartime prime minister of Canada. He was born to John King and Isabel Grace Mackenzie, who was the daughter of William Lyon Mackenzie, one of the leaders of the 19th-century Upper Canada independence movement and the Rebellion of 1837. King was edu-cated at the universities of Toronto and Chicago and at Harvard University. While in Chicago, he became associated with Jane Addams's famed Hull House and developed a passion for the cause of social welfare.

A brilliant student, King was offered a professorship at Harvard in 1900, but declined it to become deputy minister of labor in the Canadian government. He resigned from the security of this civil service position in 1908 to run for Parliament on the Liberal ticket for his native county, North Waterloo, despite its being overwhelmingly Conservative. Elected, he was named in 1909 Canada's first full-time minister of labor. When the Liberal Party was defeated in 1911, King was out of government and, in 1914, worked with the Rockefeller Foundation in the field of industrial relations. King assumed the leadership of the Liberal Party in 1919 and, following the defeat of the Union Government in 1921, became prime minister—despite the minority status of the Liberal Party in Parliament. King proved skillful at forming a coalition government, which fell, however, to a customs department scandal in 1926. He dissolved Parliament and new elections were held, which finally gave him a majority in Parliament through a Liberal-Progressive alliance. He again became prime minister and was largely responsible for attaining Commonwealth status for Canada.

King's government was defeated in 1930, and he became the chief opposition leader during the first part of the Great Depression. Reelected in 1935, he remained prime minister until his retirement in 1948.

King's Canada was torn by many divisions, but, thanks to his leadership, the nation entered World War II in 1939 with great unity. King ensured that Canada not only served the interests of the British Commonwealth during the war, but was also a staunch ally of the United States. He was greatly admired by President FRANKLIN D. ROOSEVELT.

Further reading: Ferns, Henry, and Bernard Ostry. *The Age of Mackenzie King*. Halifax, NS: Lorimer, 1976; Stacey, C. P. *A Very Double Life: The Private World of Mackenzie King*. Halifax, NS: Goodread Biography, 1985.

Kinkaid, Thomas C. (1888–1972) *key U.S. Navy commander in the Pacific*

Kinkaid was born in Hanover, New Hampshire, and graduated from the U.S. Naval Academy in 1908. His first assignment was with Admiral George Dewey's Great White Fleet, aboard the USS *Nebraska* (BB-14) and the USS *Minnesota* (BB-22) during 1908–11. Kinkaid attended the ordnance course at the Naval Postgraduate School in Annapolis in 1913 and quickly became a respected authority on naval gunnery. Promoted to lieutenant (jg) in June 1916, he served patrol duty off the East Coast as the United States prepared to enter World War I. In November 1917, with America in the war, he was promoted to lieutenant and assigned as gunnery officer aboard the USS *Arizona* (BB-39) in April 1918.

After World War I, Kinkaid was called to Washington as an officer in the Bureau of Ordnance. Promoted to lieutenant commander in 1922, he was appointed aide to Admiral Mark Bristol. In 1924, Kinkaid was given his first sea command, of the destroyer *Isherwood* (DD-284), but returned to shore duty in 1925 as an officer at the Naval Gun Factory in Washington, D.C. During 1927–29, Kinkaid returned to sea as a commander and gunnery officer sailing with the U.S. Fleet. He then enrolled in the Naval War College, from which he graduated in 1930.

Kinkaid served as executive officer on the battleship *Colorado* (BB-45) from 1933 to 1934, then became director of the Bureau of Navigation's Officer Detail Section from 1934 to 1937. Promoted to captain, he was named to command the cruiser USS *Indianapolis* (CA-35) but left this command in 1938 to become naval attaché and naval air attaché in Rome (November 1938) and naval attaché in Belgrade, Yugoslavia. In March 1941, Kinkaid returned to the United States and was promoted to rear admiral.

Just one month before the Battle of Pearl Harbor, Kinkaid was assigned to command Cruiser Division 6. During March 1942, shortly after the war began, he led the division in support of action against Rabaul and in the early phases of the New Guinea Campaign. Kinkaid fought in the Battle of the Coral Sea (May 4–8, 1942) and at the Battle of Midway (June 2–5, 1942). He then took command of Task Force 16, which was built around the aircraft carrier *Enterprise* (CV-6), and he led the task force in support of the landings of the Guadalcanal Campaign (August 7, 1942) and then fought in the carrier battles of the Eastern Solomons during August 22–25, and off the Santa Cruz Islands (October 25–28). During November 12–15, he fought Japanese surface ships in the waters off Guadalcanal. Early in 1943, Kinkaid was assigned command of the North Pacific Task Force and directed the recapture of the Aleutian Islands in the Aleutian Islands Campaign. Fighting in this very difficult and little-heralded corner of the war, Kinkaid retook Amchitka Island on February 12, 1943, and Attu on May 11–30. He landed troops on Kiska on August 15, but was unopposed—the Japanese having earlier evacuated.

In June 1943, Kinkaid was promoted to vice admiral and transferred to command of Allied Naval Forces in the Southwest Pacific Area and on November 26, the U.S. Seventh Fleet was added to his portfolio as well. His chief assignment was to support General Douglas MacArthur's amphibious advance along the New Guinea coast toward the Philippines.

Coordinating operations with the Third Fleet under Admiral William F. "Bull" Halsey, Kinkaid led the Seventh Fleet in covering the American landings on Leyte (October 20, 1944). The great crisis of this battle came when Kinkaid, responding to intelligence of a massive Japanese counterattack, deployed his aged battleships under Admiral Jesse B. Oldendorf to pinch off the southern entrance to Leyte Gulf at Surigao Strait. Outgunned, Oldendorf nevertheless checked the advance of the Japanese southern force and, during a spectacular night battle on October 25, destroyed it. In the meantime, the principal Japanese attack force, which arrived off the east coast of Samar, was met by nothing more than a small group of escort carriers under Admiral Clifton E. Sprague. Sprague held off this vastly superior fleet until a detachment of Oldendorf's battleships arrived on October 25, forcing the Japanese (who were low on fuel) to withdraw.

Kinkaid directed more Philippine amphibious operations against Mindoro (December 15) and at Lingayen Gulf on Luzon (January 9, 1945). He was promoted to admiral in April 1945, then commanded the landing of U.S. occupation forces in China and Korea during September. This mission accomplished, he left the Seventh Fleet to take command of the Eastern Sea Frontier, headquartered at New York, from January to June 1946.

Kinkaid was named commander of the Atlantic Reserve Fleet in January 1947, in which post he served until his retirement on May 1, 1950.

See also Leyte, Battle of; New Guinea Campaign; and Philippines, fall and reconquest of.

Further reading: Wheeler, Gerald E. *Kinkaid of the Seventh Fleet: A Biography of Admiral Thomas C. Kinkaid, U.S. Navy.* Annapolis, Md.: Naval Historical Center, 1996.

Kleist, Paul Ludwig von (1881–1954)
commander of German Army Group A during the invasion of the Soviet Union

Kleist was born into an aristocratic family and had a military education. In World War I, he served as a lieutenant of hussars and a regimental commander, then commanded a cavalry division between the wars, from 1932 to 1935. Promoted to lieutenant general in August 1936, he retired in February 1938, but was recalled to active duty in August 1939. As commander of XXII Corps, he participated in the invasion of Poland.

In February 1940, Kleist was assigned to command three panzer corps during the Battle of France in May 1940. That summer, Kleist transferred to the eastern front, where he led the advance toward the Caucasus. The failure of this offensive prompted Adolf Hitler to relieve Siegmund List as commander of Army Group A. After briefly assuming personal control of the group, Hitler turned over command of it to Kleist on November 21.

Kleist took command at a point when Army Group A was cut off in the Caucasus. Despite the grave risk, he avoided encirclement, kept the army group intact, and, in February 1943, was promoted to field marshal in recognition of his skill as a general.

Kleist proved to be an independent-minded, pragmatic, and innovative commander. Whereas Hitler ordered that all Soviet citizens be treated mercilessly as subhuman Slavs, Kleist recognized that the survival of his army group depended on winning over the civilians in the occupied territories. Accordingly, he ignored Hitler's orders and worked hard to earn the cooperation of Soviet civilians. He exploited a strong anti-Stalinist sentiment in the region and gained considerable local support.

In September 1943, Kleist withdrew across the Kerch straits to the Crimea, thereby preserving his army. He repeatedly defied Hitler's orders for suicidal stands and the abuse or outright genocide of indigenous populations. Moreover, like some other distinguished German career officers, Kleist generally disdained the Nazis. At last, on March 30, 1944, Hitler dismissed Kleist, who sat out the remainder of the war. Tried for war crimes in 1946 in Yugoslavia, he was sentenced to 15 years imprisonment. After two years in a Yugoslav jail, he was extradited to the Soviet Union, where he was charged with alienating local Soviet populations—incredibly enough—"through mildness and kindness." He lived out the rest of his life in a Soviet prison camp.

Further reading: Davis, Clyde R. *Von Kleist: From Hussar to Panzer Marshal.* Mount Ida, Ark.: Lancer Militaria, 1979.

Kluge, Günther von (1882–1944) *anti-Hitler German general*

Scion of an aristocratic Prussian military family, Kluge was a staff officer during World War I, then fought in the Battle of Verdun in 1918, in which he was gravely wounded. Between the world wars, Kluge rose rapidly, gaining promotion to lieutenant general by 1936. In 1937, he was given command of Sixth Army Group (redesignated as Fourth Army after the outbreak of World War II).

Like a number of other military aristocrats, Kluge was anti-Nazi and participated in a plot, when ADOLF HITLER threatened to invade Czechoslovakia, to overthrow Hitler and create an anti-Nazi government. The plot died aborning, however, and, despite his involvement, Kluge escaped unscathed. When the INVASION OF POLAND came, he cast aside all doubt and brilliantly led the Fourth Army in the BLITZKRIEG. Nevertheless, when Hitler announced his plan to attack the West, Kluge again protested; yet when the call actually came, he and his Fourth Army were instrumental in the offensive that culminated in the BATTLE OF FRANCE. Kluge brought to the western front the same blitzkrieg tactics that had proved so devastating in the East. Despite his record of doubt and protest, he was promoted to field marshal in July 1940.

Kluge's Fourth Army was part of Army Group Center in the INVASION OF THE SOVIET UNION in June 1941 and reached the edge of Moscow by the fall. When, in December 1941, Field Marshal Fedor von Bock fell ill, Kluge took over as commander in charge Army Group Center. At this point, certain staff officers approached Kluge to participate in a planned coup d'état against Hitler. Once again, Kluge vacillated. His vacillation ended in October 1942 when he received 250,000 Reichsmarks from Hitler as a reward for his performance in the war. This essentially purchased his loyalty, and he blocked a scheme to arrest and assassinate the führer during a March 1943 tour of the eastern front. Moreover, against his own better judgment, Kluge followed Hitler's order to mount a desperate offensive during the BATTLE OF KURSK in July 1943.

In October 1943, Kluge suffered serious injuries in a car wreck at the front. He did not return to duty until June 30, 1944, when he replaced GERD VON RUNDSTEDT as overall commander in the West during the German defense against the NORMANDY LANDINGS (D-DAY). Yet again, Kluge turned against Hitler, as it became clear to him that defeat was inevitable. But when the JULY PLOT (TO ASSASSINATE HITLER) miscarried, he immediately withdrew from any attempt to overthrow the führer—although he

did attempt to make contact with Allied commanders on August 15, 1944. German intelligence intercepted an Allied wireless communication, which suggested to Hitler that Kluge intended to arrange a cease-fire. On August 17, Hitler relieved Kluge—replacing him with WALTHER MODEL—and recalled him to Germany. On August 18, 1945, Kluge shot himself.

Further reading: Barnett, Correlli. *Hitler's Generals.* New York: Grove Press, 2003; Heiber, Helmut, and David Glantz, eds. *Hitler and His Generals.* New York: Enigma Books, 2002; Mitcham, Samuel W. *Hitler's Field Marshals and Their Battles.* New York: Cooper Square, 2001.

Koga Mineichi (1885–1944) *Japanese officer who led operations in the fall of Hong Kong*

Koga was a career Japanese naval officer who served as a naval attaché in Paris before assuming command of the Yokosuka Naval Station. Appointed vice chief of the Naval Staff Board in December 1937, Koga served until October 1939. With the outbreak of the Pacific war, he was instrumental in operations leading to the FALL OF HONG KONG.

Koga was a competent officer, who worked effectively with other staff personnel, yet he was beset by two flaws: a tendency to be overcautious and a lack of tactical imagination, which prompted him to value battleships over aircraft carriers and air power. He replaced YAMAMOTO ISORUKU as commander in charge of the Combined Fleet in April 1943, by which time the reversal of Japanese fortunes was unstoppable. Koga directed the first Japanese withdrawals from the Gilbert Islands and the Philippines.

On March 31, 1944, Koga's aircraft disappeared in a dense fog, and he was reported missing, almost certainly having been killed in a crash at sea. His death, less than a year after Yamamoto's, was not announced until May, when he was replaced as commander in charge by TOYODA SOEMU.

Further reading: Toland, John. *The Rising Sun: The Decline and Fall of the Japanese Empire, 1936–1945.* New York: Modern Library, 2003.

Konev, Ivan (1897–1973) *Soviet Red Army marshal*

Born of peasant stock, Ivan Stepanovich Konev was drafted into the czar's army in 1916 during World War I, then joined the Communist Party and Red Army in 1918 after the Russian Revolution. With the outbreak of the Russian civil war, he became a military commissar, organizing guerrilla units and fighting the forces of the Whites. He was also instrumental in ending the 1921 Kronstadt Rebellion against the Bolshevik government.

In 1926, Konev graduated from the Frunze Military Academy and, during 1937–38, commanded Soviet special forces in Outer Mongolia. During the German INVASION OF THE SOVIET UNION, in October 1941, Konev was assigned command of a portion of the West Front (a Red Army "front" was equivalent to an Allied army group) and led the first significant counterattack against the invaders. He brilliantly employed what became known as the "Konev ambush"—drawing in German forces by means of tactical retreat, then enveloping them in the jaws of his army's flanks—to defeat HEINZ GUDERIAN's advance on Moscow in December 1941.

In the summer of 1942, Konev blocked the advance of German forces sent to reinforce STALINGRAD. When major combat shifted south during the winter, Konev was more or less idled until July 1943, when, commanding the Steppe Front, he collaborated with GEORGI KONSTANTINOVICH ZHUKOV in repelling and turning back the main German offensive. In February 1944, Konev was made a marshal of the Soviet Union and, in August, he brought the war beyond the Soviet border by crossing the Vistula River into Poland. After fighting rapidly through Poland, Konev led the Red Army advance into Germany. In coordination with forces under Zhukov, he fought the BATTLE OF BERLIN. Afterward, at Torgau, his army linked up with U.S. forces commanded by COURTNEY H. HODGES.

After the war, Konev was named supreme commissar for Austria and, in 1946, succeeded Zhukov as commander in charge of Soviet ground forces. He served in this capacity until 1950 and became commander in charge of the Warsaw Pact forces in 1955. He retired in 1960, but was recalled the following year to serve as commander in charge of Soviet forces in East Germany. He stepped down from this post in 1962, but remained in the Defense Ministry until his death.

Further reading: Konev, Ivan Stepanovich. *Marshal Konev's Reminiscences of 1945: USSR.* Washington, D.C.: U.S. Department of Commerce, Clearinghouse for Federal Scientific and Technical Information, Joint Publications Research Service, 1965; Konev, Ivan Stepanovich. *Year of Victory.* Honolulu: University Press of the Pacific, 2005.

Konoye Fumimaro (1891–1945) *prime minister of Japan during 1937–1939 and 1940–1941*

Konoye was born to one of the noble families from which regents and chancellors were traditionally chosen. Konoye was educated at Tokyo Imperial University and then Kyoto Imperial University, graduating with a degree in law. His education introduced him to Western philosophy, literature, and sociology, all of which he greatly admired. By the end of the 19th century, he even flirted with socialism.

Konoye entered politics as the protégé of elder statesman Saionji Kimmochi and served as an attendant to the Japanese delegation at the Paris Peace Conference, which produced the TREATY OF VERSAILLES ending World War I. He wrote an article criticizing the Wilsonian principle of pacifism not because it was pacifist as such, but because, Konoye argued, it was actually a cynical dodge designed to maintain the status quo, at the expense of Asia, in a world dominated by the Western nations.

As a Japanese prince, Konoye held a seat in the upper house of the Japanese Diet and here pressed for liberal reform. He was an opponent of rising fascism both abroad and in Japan, and he was deeply concerned over the growing influence of the military in Japanese government. He unsuccessfully advocated reform of the army general staff to remove it from any voice in foreign policy.

Konoye advocated the expansion of parliamentary politics and hoped to suppress militarism. Although his stance went against the dominant trend in Japan, Konoye served as vice president of the upper house and, in 1933, was appointed its president. In June 1937, as prime minister, he formed a nonparty cabinet and strove to make compromises with the military, accepting their more moderate demands while rejecting all that he considered extreme. He struggled to resolve the SINO-JAPANESE WAR, but was unsuccessful in this effort, and in January 1939 his cabinet fell. No longer prime minister, he served as head of the Privy Council and was given a post in the cabinet of Hiranuma Kiichiro. He resigned as head of the Privy Council in June 1940, hoping to develop a popular national movement that would prevent the military from seizing more power. This plan was forestalled by his elevation, for a second time, to the post of prime minister; however, the Imperial Rule Assistance Association, formed later in 1940, was conceived as the foundation of the national movement.

Konoye presided over a government that, against his wishes, continued to roll toward war. Although Konoye acquiesced in Japan's signing of the AXIS (TRIPARTITE) PACT with Germany and Italy, he continued to struggle against the expansion of the Sino-Japanese War in the hope of improving relations with Great Britain and the United States. As these relations nevertheless deteriorated, Konoye signed a nonaggression pact with the Soviet Union early in 1941. On the verge of opening personal talks with U.S. president FRANKLIN D. ROOSEVELT in the hope of ending the Sino-Japanese War, Konoye resigned in October 1941 as a result of unending disputes with the army minister TOJO HIDEKI.

After the commencement of the Pacific war, Konoye was pushed to the periphery of Japanese politics. He collaborated with other antimilitarists to bring about the end of the Tojo government in 1944, and he survived the war to become deputy minister of national affairs in 1945. Arrested by the U.S. Army of Occupation late in the year on charges of war crimes, he committed suicide by drinking poison rather than stand trial.

Further reading: Frank, Richard B. *Downfall: The End of the Imperial Japanese Empire.* New York: Penguin, 2001; Toland, John. *The Rising Sun: The Decline and Fall of the Japanese Empire, 1936–1945.* New York: Modern Library, 2003.

Korea, action in

Combat did not come to Korea until the very end of the war. The nation had unwillingly become a Japanese protectorate in 1905 and was annexed to Japan in 1910. Beginning about 1919, resistance to what was considered the Japanese occupation became increasingly organized. By the mid-1920s, this popular resistance movement was essentially communist in leadership and direction.

During the 1930s, Japanese militarists oversaw the conversion of a large sector of the Korean economy into industrial production. Moreover, in an effort to force the assimilation of the Korean people, the Korean language and literature were banned from schools, and Koreans were even ordered to adopt Japanese names. By the end of the 1930s, the Japanese began conscripting Korean labor, and in 1942 young Korean men were drafted into the Imperial Japanese Army. During the war, Korean nationalists, especially the communist factions, recruited young men for service in China against the Japanese.

During World War II, Japan pillaged Korea's agricultural output as well as its stock of raw materials, especially strategic metals. While such despoliation yielded important resources for the Japanese war effort, it raised the level of resistance in Korea, necessitating the deployment of large numbers of troops in the country to maintain order. In 1941, there were 46,000 Japanese troops in Korea; by the end of the war, there were 300,000—none involved in direct combat. Also by the end of the war, Korea represented a slave workforce of some 2.6 million. In effect, Japanese military administrators had transformed the country into a vast forced-labor camp, presided over by Japanese soldiers as well as by a large cadre of coopted Korean "police" in the employ of the Japanese. In addition to the Koreans forced to work in factories at home, approximately three-quarters of a million Korean workers were sent to work abroad, mostly in Japanese war industries. Perhaps the most notorious exploitation of the Korean population was the forced employment of tens of thousands of "comfort women," Korean girls and women forced into prostitution as sexual partners for Japanese soldiers.

The postwar disposition of Korea was the subject of the November 1943 Cairo Conference among the Allied leaders and the February 1945 YALTA CONFERENCE, which, unlike the earlier conference, included JOSEPH STALIN. It was agreed at both Cairo and Yalta that Korea would become an independent nation. Nevertheless, when the Soviet Union belatedly declared war on Japan in August 1945, Red Army forces made a number of amphibious landings in north Korea (north of the 38th Parallel), and an entire Soviet army invaded Korea overland via China. The United States and the USSR quickly agreed to divide occupation of Korea along the 38th parallel, with U.S. forces to the south and Soviet forces to the north. This line rapidly evolved into the hostile border between communist North Korea and Western-aligned South Korea, and the two nations would go to war during 1950–53.

Further reading: Dudden, Alexis. *Japan's Colonization of Korea: Discourse and Power.* Honolulu: University of Hawaii Press, 2004; Hicks, George L. *The Comfort Women: Japan's Brutal Regime of Enforced Prostitution in the Second World War.* New York: W. W. Norton, 1997; Myers, Ramon H., and Mark R. Peattie, eds. *The Japanese Colonial Empire, 1895–1945.* Princeton, N.J.: Princeton University Press, 1987.

Kowerski, Andrzej (1912–1988) *Polish resistance leader*

Born into the family of a large Polish landowner, Andrzej Kowerski had a promising future as an athlete but lost a leg as a result of a hunting accident. Despite his disability, he served in the sole mechanized brigade of the Polish army at the outbreak of World War II and was awarded the nation's highest decoration for bravery, the Virtute Militari.

Kowerski moved to Hungary after the Polish government went into Romanian exile on September 18, 1939. Working from Hungary, Kowerski created a covert network to aid Polish soldiers to escape from prison and internment camps. He oversaw their transportation via Yugoslavia to France and Britain.

Early in the war, Kowerski, adopting the name Andrew Kennedy, joined the British Special Operations Executive (SOE) and became that agency's only one-legged parachutist. He was air-dropped into Italy to aid in training a Polish legion there.

Kowerski survived his perilous SOE career and, after the war, started a chain of automobile dealerships in Germany. After the failure of his business, he returned to London, where he lived with Christine Granville, an SOE comrade.

Further reading: MacKenzie, William. *The Secret History of SOE: Special Operations Executive 1940–1945.* London: St. Ermin's Press, 2002; Matusak, Piotr. *Polish Resistance Movement, 1939–1945.* Warsaw: Presspol, 1985.

Kriegsmarine   *See* GERMANY, NAVY OF.

Kristallnacht (*Reichskristallnacht,* "Night of Broken Glass")

Kristallnacht or *Reichskristallnacht*—Crystal Night—the "Night of Broken Glass," occurred throughout Germany during the night of November 9–10, 1938. A nationwide pogrom instigated and led by Nazis and the Nazi leadership, *Kristallnacht* saw the burning or vandalism of more than 1,000 synagogues and the looting of some 7,500 Jewish businesses, the windows of which were smashed—hence the ironically poetic name *Kristallnacht.* At least 91 Jews are known to have been killed during the night of violence, which continued over the next two days. In addition, Jewish homes, hospitals, schools, and cemeteries were attacked.

Kristallnacht, a graphic symbol of Nazi-sponsored anti-Semitism, was triggered by the November 7 shooting, in Paris, of German diplomat Ernst von Rath by Herschel Grynszpan, a student who was a Jew from Poland. When news of the incident reached ADOLF HITLER and his minister of propaganda, JOSEPH GOEBBELS, the two apparently decided on a nationwide pogrom by way of reprisal. Goebbels rallied veteran members of the STURMAB-TEILUNG (SA), who organized an outbreak of violent "spontaneous demonstrations." The demonstrations were, in fact, carefully choreographed and coordinated from Munich, and the violence spread not only throughout Germany, but into Austria as well. GESTAPO chief Heinrich Müller issued telegrams to police units throughout the nation informing them of the demonstrations about to begin and instructing them not to interfere, except to arrest Jews—that is, the victims. Intervention was permitted only if the work of arsonists accidentally threatened "Aryan" lives or property.

In addition to property damage, loss, and desecration, as well as the 91 deaths, about 30,000 Jewish men and youths were arrested and sent to concentration camps, including DACHAU and BUCHENWALD, as well as Sachsenhausen. The name the Nazi authorities conferred on the pogrom, *Kristallnacht,* was intended to enshrine it in national memory as the night that shattered the Jewish presence in the Third Reich. In the aftermath of the violence, government officials moved to seize any insurance settlements that Jewish victims obtained, and they fined the Jewish community a total of perhaps 1 billion reichsmarks to defray the cost of cleaning up after the pogrom— although, in fact, it was the Jewish victims themselves who did the cleaning.

See also HOLOCAUST, THE.

Further reading: Pehle, Walter. *November 1938: From "Kristallnacht" to Genocide.* Oxford: Berg, 1990; Read, Anthony. *Kristallnacht: The Unleashing of the Holocaust.* New York: Viking Penguin, 1989.

Krueger, Walter (1881–1967) *key U.S. Army commander in the Pacific*

Born in Platow, West Prussia, Krueger came to the United States with his family in 1889 and was raised in Cincinnati, Ohio. He left high school to

Walter Krueger *(National Archives and Records Administration)*

enlist in the army during the Spanish-American War (1898), fighting in the Santiago de Cuba campaign of June 22–July 17. After returning to the United States, he joined the regular army and was dispatched to the Philippines during the Philippine Insurrection (1899–1903), which followed the war with Spain. He received a field commission as second lieutenant in the 30th Infantry in June 1901 and, on his return to the United States, attended the Infantry and Cavalry School. After graduating from the school in 1906, Krueger enrolled in the Command and General Staff School, from which he graduated in 1907.

Krueger was assigned a second tour in the Philippines during 1908–09, then served on the faculty of the Army Service School from 1909 to 1912. He was tasked during this assignment with translating German treatises on tactics and was recognized as an authority on the German army and its military practices.

Promoted to captain in 1916, Krueger served under John J. Pershing during the Punitive Expedition against Pancho Villa from March 1916 to February 1917. The United States entered World War I in April 1917, and Krueger was sent to France in February 1918. After attending the General Staff College at Langres, France, he was named assistant chief of operations for the 26th Division. He subsequently was transferred to the 84th Division and became chief of staff of the Tank Corps, serving in this capacity during the Meuse-Argonne offensive in October.

After the Armistice, Krueger remained in France as chief of staff for VI Corps, then became chief of staff for IV Corps in Germany with the temporary rank of colonel. After his return to the United States in 1919, he reverted to his Regular Army rank of captain and, in 1921, graduated from the Army War College. Assigned to the War Plans Division of the General Staff, he served there from 1923 to 1925, then graduated from the Naval War College in 1926. Krueger taught there from 1928 to 1932 and was promoted to Regular Army colonel. In 1936, he was promoted to brigadier general and appointed assistant chief of staff for War Plans. Krueger left this staff post in 1938 to command 16th Brigade at Fort Meade, Maryland, and was promoted to major general in February 1939, with command of the 2nd Division, followed by VIII Staff Corps in October 1940.

In May 1941, Krueger was promoted to temporary lieutenant general and named to command the Third U.S. Army and the Southern Defense Command. When the United States entered World War II, the Sixth U.S. Army was activated under his command, and he took it to Australia in January 1943, commanding it through a series of combat operations in the Southwest Pacific Theater under General Douglas MacArthur. Krueger led the landings on Kiriwina and Woodlark Islands on June 30, 1943, then directed the invasion of New Britain from December 15, 1943, to March 1944. He fought in the Battle of the Admiralty Islands and in operations along the northern coast of New Guinea during February–August 1944.

On October 20, 1944, Krueger directed the landings on Leyte, initiating the liberation of the Philippines. He commanded landings on Mindoro (December 15) and on Luzon (January 9, 1945); the Battle of Luzon stretched from February to August 1945. Krueger was promoted to general, just after the fall of Manila to U.S. forces on March 14. His troops mopped up Japanese resistance on Luzon, driving the diehards into the mountains of the northeast. By June 1945, the island was largely liberated.

Krueger remained in the Pacific after the surrender of Japan, commanding his Sixth Army in occupation duty on Honshu in September 1945. He retired in July 1946.

See also Leyte, Battle of; New Britain, Battle of; and New Guinea Campaign.

Further reading: Krueger, Walter. *From Down Under to Nippon.* Nashville, Tenn.: Battery Press, 1989; McDonald, John H. *General Walter Krueger: A Case Study in Operational Command.* Leavenworth, Kans.: School of Advanced Military Studies, U.S. Army Command and General Staff College, 1989.

Krupp munitions works

The storied firm of Krupp had been the leader of the German arms industry since the mid-19th century. During World War II, the firm, like a number of other war-production industries, entered into virtual partnership with the Nazi regime to ensure a steady and massive supply of the weapons of war.

Krupp was launched by Friedrich Krupp (1787–1826) as a modest steel foundry in Essen in 1811. Alfred (1812–87), his son, greatly expanded the firm, both in terms of finance and technology, transforming it into the foremost cannon foundry and locomotive manufacturer in Europe. For this, Alfred was dubbed "Alfred the Great" and the "Cannon King."

Under Alfred Krupp, the family firm became a significant power in Germany—not only as a supplier of arms, but as an owner of mines (in Germany as well as France) and as the creator of company towns and subsidized housing for a rapidly expanding workforce. By the 1840s, artillery had become a company specialty. Government subsidies aided the development of newer, bigger, and more powerful weapons. By the end of the 1880s, arms manufacture represented 50 percent of Krupp's output, and the firm, which employed just five workers when Alfred took it over, had some 20,000 by the time of his death in 1887, having become the largest industrial company in the world.

Despite government subsidies, the Krupp firm remained fiercely independent during World War I, manufacturing arms not only for Germany and the other Central Powers, but for the Allies as well; however, with the rise of ADOLF HITLER in 1933, the company's director, Gustav Krupp (1870–1950), son of Alfred, embraced Nazism and accepted the "patriotic" and profitable role as the very center of Germany's post-Versailles rearmament. A decree from Hitler in 1943 ensured Krupp's total reversion from a public stock company to a family-held firm, and Alfried Krupp von Bohlen und Halbach (1907–67), son of Gustav, assumed absolute control.

During the war, Krupp produced arms of all kinds for the German war machine, including tanks, artillery, and miscellaneous munitions; however, it was most celebrated for its gigantic guns, including those built shortly before the outbreak of the war: the 80-centimeter railway guns Schwerer Gustav and Dora, each weighting some 1,344 tons and capable of hurling a seven-ton projectile 37 kilometers.

After the war, the Allies wanted to try Gustav Krupp before the NUREMBERG WAR CRIMES TRIBUNAL, but, aged and infirm, he was judged incompetent to stand trial. Instead, in what became known as the "Krupp Trial," Alfried was convicted of war crimes relating to the firm's use of slave labor. He was sentenced to 12 years imprisonment and was ordered to divest himself of 75 percent of his holdings in the firm. But when no buyer materialized, and under Cold War pressures, Alfried was released, and he resumed control of Krupp in 1953.

As the Krupp Group, the company merged with its chief competitor, Thyssen AG, in 1999 to become ThyssenKrupp AG, today one of the world's great steel producers.

Further reading: Manchester, William. *The Arms of Krupp: The Rise and Fall of the Industrial Dynasty That Armed Germany at War.* Boston: Back Bay Books, 2003.

Kuribayashi Tadamichi (1891–1945)
commander of the Japanese garrison that fought to the death at the Battle of Iwo Jima

Kuribayashi was born into a samurai family and was marked from birth for a military career. From 1928 to 1930, he served as military attaché in Washington, D.C., and was greatly impressed by the industrial might of the United States. Like other top Japanese military leaders who came to know the United States, he believed war with the industrial giant would be all but unwinnable. This did not prevent his wholehearted commitment to the war, however, once it began.

In June 1944, Japanese emperor HIROHITO personally selected Kuribayashi Tadamichi to command the Iwo Jima garrison, which, Hirohito told him, was an absolutely critical prize that must be denied to U.S. forces at all costs. The general took his orders with absolute seriousness and deployed his defenders carefully, determined to conduct a grinding campaign of attrition against the invaders. He ordered each soldier to kill at least 10 Americans or destroy one tank.

In the end, it was the garrison that fell to attrition. Kuribayashi's last radio message was heard on March 22, 1945, when he signaled that he had only 400 troops left but was still fighting. He noted that he and his men had laughed at U.S. pleas, broadcast through loudspeakers, to surrender. Kuribayashi's body was never recovered.

Further reading: Bradley, James, with Ron Powers. *Flags of Our Fathers.* New York: Bantam, 2000; Newcomb, Richard F. *Iwo Jima.* New York: Owl Books, 2002.

Kurita Takeo (1889–1977) *Japanese admiral*

Kurita graduated from the Japanese naval academy in 1910 and became a torpedo specialist. By the outbreak of World War II, he had acquired extensive command experience, virtually all of it at sea. As a rear admiral, he commanded the 7th Cruiser Squadron, which played a key role in covering the Japanese invasion of Malaya and the INVASION OF THAILAND, both in December 1941. He next was instrumental in the ACTION IN THE NETHERLANDS EAST INDIES. As commander of the Western Attack Group, he successfully led the amphibious assault on Java on February 28, 1942, and he was commander of the Close Support Force in the BATTLE OF MIDWAY during June 1942.

Kurita fought with great skill at the BATTLE OF LEYTE in October 1944 as commander of the First Striking Force. His flagship was sunk under him, and, low on fuel, his remaining ships had to break off the battle against a significantly inferior U.S. force. Thus he was narrowly denied a victory that would have been disastrous for the U.S. forces landing on Leyte.

See also MALAYA, FALL OF.

Further reading: Fuchida, Mitsuo, and Masatake Okumiya. *Midway: The Battle That Doomed Japan, the Japanese Navy's Story.* Annapolis, Md.: Bluejacket Books, 2001; Parshall, Jonathan B., and Anthony Tully. *Shattered Sword: The Untold Story of the Battle of Midway.* Washington, D.C.: Potomac Books, 2005.

Kursk, Battle of

From the Soviet point of view, the Battle of Kursk, even more than Stalingrad, was the turning point of the war against the German INVASION OF THE SOVIET UNION. Victory at Kursk allowed the Red Army to seize the initiative, after which the German invaders were on the defensive for the remainder of the war.

The winter campaign of 1942–43 created a westward bulge in the front surrounding Kursk, a principal rail and road junction about 500 miles south of Moscow. Within this great bulge were five Soviet armies. Confronting them were the German Army Group Center (under GÜNTHER VON KLUGE) on the northern side of the bulge and, on the southern side, ERICH VON MANSTEIN's Army Group South. On April 15, 1943, ADOLF HITLER ordered Kluge and Manstein to prepare for the launch of OPERATION CITADEL on May 4, which was intended to pinch off the bulge and thereby envelop the Soviet armies. At the last minute, Hitler blinked, however, and postponed Operation Citadel.

The delay was fatal. JOSEPH STALIN and his top military commanders intended to expand the bulge into a wedge between the two German army groups and thereby seize the initiative in the war. Concerned that the Germans might be planning their own surprise attack, however, the Soviets reinforced the already vast forces holding the bulge. This put Hitler in position to make the first move, and Operation Citadel was launched on July 5 with Ninth German Army under WALTHER MODEL in the north and, in the south, the Fourth Panzer Army under General HERMANN HOTH and Army Detachment "Kempf" commanded by Lieutenant General Werner Kempf. In all, the Germans had nearly three-quarters of a million troops, 2,400 tanks and assault guns, and 1,800 aircraft. The Red Army fielded 1.3 million troops, 3,400 tanks and assault guns, and 2,100 aircraft. Moreover, the Soviets had prepared elaborate defenses around the bulge, including six trench lines of three to five trenches each. Additionally, six Soviet armies were held in reserve to the east.

Model's three panzer corps targeted the village of Olkhovatka, outside of Kursk, as their first objective. Red Army general Konstantin Rokossovsky assumed a blocking position and forced all three German corps into a fierce battle of attrition. On July 9, Model reported to Kluge that a breakthrough via Olkhovatka to Kursk was now doubtful. Accordingly, Hoth attacked northward west of the Donets River with two panzer corps while Kempf attacked east of the river. Hoth targeted Oboyan, halfway to Kursk and within the Soviets' last trench line. Hoth advanced steadily, crossing

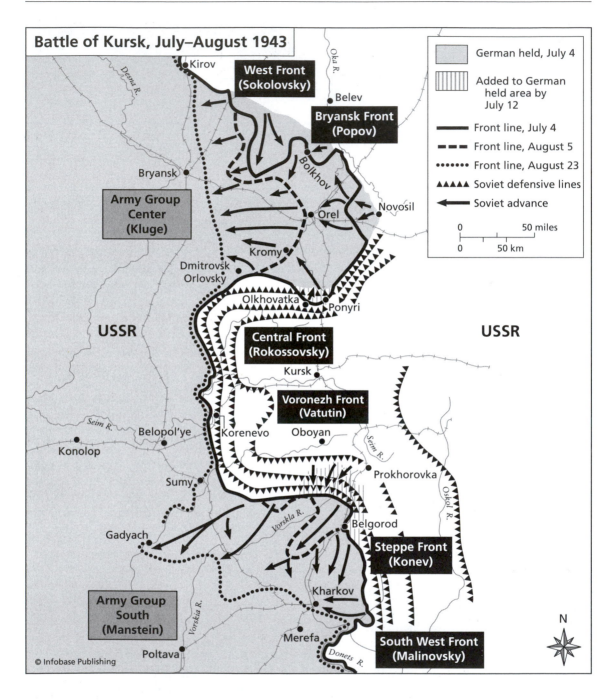

Battle of Kursk, July–August 1943

German held, July 4

Added to German held area by July 12

Front line, July 4

Front line, August 5

Front line, August 23

Soviet defensive lines

Soviet advance

0   50 miles

0   50 km

Kirov

West Front (Sokolovsky)

Belev

Bryansk Front (Popov)

Desna R.

Oka R.

Bryansk

Bolkhov

Army Group Center (Kluge)

Orel

Novosil

Kromy

Dmitrovsk Orlovsky

Olkhovatka

Ponyri

USSR

Central Front (Rokossovsky)

Kursk

USSR

Seim R.

Belopol'ye

Korenevo

Oboyan

Voronezh Front (Vatutin)

Konolop

Seim R.

Prokhorovka

Sumy

Vorskla R.

Oskol R.

Gadyach

Belgorod

Steppe Front (Konev)

Army Group South (Manstein)

Vorskla R.

Kharkov

N

Merefa

South West Front (Malinovsky)

Donets R.

Poltava

© Infobase Publishing

the last Soviet trench line on July 12. At Prokhorovka, 22 miles southeast of Oboyan, Hoth was confronted by the Fifth Guards Tank Army, which had been held in reserve. Now a titanic armored battle developed involving about 1,200 tanks (some 800 of them Soviet), which was the largest tank battle of the war. It is this exchange that is usually designated as *the* Battle of Kursk.

Tactically, the 2nd SS Panzer Corps dealt more destruction than it received, but the battle overall was a Soviet strategic victory, since Kluge was forced to take two panzer divisions from Model to check a Soviet attack against the rear of the Ninth German Army. Simultaneously, as an Anglo-American force carried out OPERATION HUSKY, the invasion of Sicily, Hitler aborted Operation Citadel on July 13, claiming that he needed the troops to deal with the Allied invasion of Italy. The Red Army was quick to seize the initiative, and the German army was forced to assume the defensive on its eastern front.

Further reading: Fowler, William. *Kursk: The Vital 24 Hours.* Fort Myers, Fla.: Amber, 2005; Glantz, David M., and Jonathan M. House. *The Battle of Kursk.* Lawrence: University Press of Kansas, 1999.

Marine raiders on Kwajalein Atoll *(National Archives and Records Administration)*

Kwajalein Atoll, Battle of

After the successful conclusion of operations on the Gilbert Islands in November 1943, U.S. admiral CHESTER A. NIMITZ launched the MARSHALL ISLANDS CAMPAIGN 600 miles to the northwest of the Gilberts. By February 1, 1944, the V Amphibious Corps, under marine general HOLLAND M. "HOWLIN' MAD" SMITH, poised to land at Kwajalein Atoll in the center of the Marshall archipelago. A massive air and naval bombardment was launched preparatory to a landing on the island of Kwajalein itself by the U.S. 7th Infantry Division under Charles Corlett. Simultaneously, the 4th Marine Division, Harry Schmidt commanding, landed on the twin islands of Roi-Namur, 45 miles to the north of Kwajalein Island. One marine regiment took Roi on the first day; another captured Namur by noon of the second day of the assault. The Japanese defenders of the twin islands lost 3,500 killed and a mere 264 captured, whereas marine losses were 190 dead and 547 wounded.

On Kwajalein, the 7th Infantry ground down the garrison, in three days killing more than 3,800 Japanese with a loss of 177 Americans killed and about 1,000 wounded. Kwajalein was declared secure on February 4.

The quick victories at the Kwajalein Atoll prompted Admiral Nimitz to initiate the BATTLE OF ENIWETOK ATOLL, 400 miles to the northwest, a full two months ahead of schedule.

Further reading: Marshall, S. L. A. *Island Victory: The Battle of Kwajalein Atoll.* Lincoln: University of Nebraska Press, 2001.

landing craft

Landing craft—shallow-draft vessels capable of transferring troops from troop transports to beachheads—were indispensable to amphibious operations during World War II, including many operations in the Pacific theater, the Mediterranean, and Europe; yet of all the combatant nations, only the United States developed and built landing craft in significant numbers. Even so, landing craft were regarded as a kind of stepchild by the principal U.S. military service arms—the navy was more interested in building large warships, and the army did not want to get involved in building ships at all; therefore, the availability of landing craft was always a critical issue. GEORGE S. PATTON JR. was forced to curtail some of his operations in Sicily for lack of adequate numbers of landing craft, and DWIGHT D. EISENHOWER was forced to delay landings in the south of France (Operation Anvil/Dragoon), which he had wanted to conduct simultaneously with the NORMANDY LANDINGS (D-DAY).

The most famous and most numerous landing craft was the LCVP (landing craft, vehicle, personnel), popularly known as the Higgins boat. These 36-foot wooden-hulled craft were designed and built by New Orleans boatbuilder Andrew Higgins, who modified a civilian craft, the Eureka, which his company manufactured. They were light and powerful, and later versions of the craft included the familiar ramp at the bow, which was raised during the trip to shore, then lowered for landing. After landing its troops, the Higgins boat went into reverse and withdrew from the shore. The LCVP could carry 36 combat troops or about 8,000 pounds of supplies. Displacement was about nine tons and, powered by a six-cylinder, water-cooled Gray Marine Diesel engine generating 225 horsepower through a single propeller, the vessel could make about 12 knots under load. Virtually every Allied soldier who landed at Normandy on D-day

LSTs (Landing Ships, Tank) disgorge men and equipment on a Pacific island. These large ships were intended to deliver men directly from sea to shore—without the dangers of transfer to and disembarkation from small landing craft. (U.S. Navy)

arrived on a Higgins boat. Another version of the Higgins boat, the LCM (landing craft, mechanized) was the same size, but was designed to carry heavier loads, including tanks.

Larger than the Higgins boats were the LCTs (landing craft, tank). There were various versions, but the average World War II LCT was about 114 feet long with a beam of nearly 33 feet. Displacement was 286 tons, and load capacity was 150 tons. Its three Gray Marine diesels produced 675 horsepower each, driving three props for a top speed under load of about 7 knots. Unlike the unarmed Higgins boats, the LCTs were fitted with antiaircraft and machine guns.

One other major category of landing craft were the LSUs (landing ship, utility). At 119 feet in length and with a 34-foot beam, they were slightly larger than the LCTs. They displaced 180 tons empty and 360 fully loaded. Although powered identically to the LCTs, their streamlined hull design allowed them to reach a top speed of 18 knots.

See also SICILY CAMPAIGN.

Further reading: Friedman, Norman. *U.S. Amphibious Ships and Craft: An Illustrated Design History.* Annapolis, Md.: Naval Institute Press, 2002; McGee, William L. *The Amphibians Are Coming!: Emergence of the 'Gator Navy and Its Revolutionary Landing Craft (Amphibious Operations in the South Pacific in World War II).* St. Helena, Calif.: BMC Publications, 2000; U.S. Navy Department. *Allied Landing Craft of World War Two.* Annapolis, Md.: Naval Institute Press, 1985.

Latvia

In 1939, at the outbreak of World War II, Latvia was an independent Baltic republic ruled by a dictator, Dr. K. Ulmanis, who had dissolved by fiat all political parties five years earlier. The nation had become independent of the Russian Empire following its breakup following World War I, and its independence was guaranteed by the Soviet Union through two treaties, a League of Nations agreement of August 1920 and a Treaty of Guarantee of March 1927. Despite this, the GERMAN-SOVIET NON-AGGRESSION PACT of August 1939 secretly assigned Latvia to the Soviet "sphere of influence." Armed with this agreement, JOSEPH STALIN compelled Ulmanis to sign a Treaty of Friendship and Cooperation on October 5, 1939, which permitted the stationing of Soviet troops in Latvia. Also pursuant to the treaty, most of the German population was deported to Germany or Poland.

In June 1940, the Soviets commenced the full-scale occupation of Latvia, claiming that the country had defaulted on conditions of the treaty. In addition to the outright occupation, Soviet agents subverted the Latvian government through programs of intimidation, arrest, and assassination, culminating in fraudulent elections that created the Latvian Soviet Socialist Republic, which was absorbed into the USSR on August 5, 1940. Through July 1941, when the first period of Soviet occupation ended (replaced by German occupation), Latvia was subject to a reign of terror intended to force the assimilation of Latvia into the Soviet Union by crushing and obliterating all vestiges of nationalism.

The German occupation of Latvia began in July 1941 and did not end until April 1945, a month before the end of the war in Europe. Latvia was effectively annexed to the Third Reich as part of Reich Commissariat Östland. Many young Latvian men served willingly in German-controlled police and military units, eager to fight the Soviets, who had destroyed their country. Latvia even contributed two elite WAFFEN SS divisions. As in other occupied or annexed territories, the nation's Jews were rounded up and deported to concentration camps or, as in the ghetto of Riga (Latvia's capital), murdered in place.

Latvia was subject to a second Soviet invasion beginning in 1944, although the German occupation was not completely ended until April 1945. Those parts of Latvia reoccupied by the Soviets were again subjected to a reign of terror, the population starved by the forced collectivization of agriculture. After the war, Latvia was thoroughly subjugated under Soviet rule. In August 1991, during the rapid decline of Soviet communism, the Latvian legislature declared independence, which the Soviet government recognized on September 6, 1991.

Further reading: Bilmanis, Alfred. *A History of Latvia.* Princeton, N.J.: Princeton University Press, 1951; Ezergailis, Andrew. *The Holocaust in Latvia, 1941–1944: The Missing Center.* Washington, D.C.: United States Holocaust Memorial Museum, 1996; Westermann, Edward B. *Hitler's Police Battalions: Enforcing Racial War in the East.* Lawrence: University Press of Kansas, 2005.

Laval, Pierre (1883–1945) *collaborationist Vichy minister*

Born in Châteldon, France, Pierre Laval became a member of the French Socialist Party in 1903. He began practicing law in Paris in 1909 and earned national renown for his brilliant defense work on behalf of trade unionists, socialists, and other leftists. He was elected deputy for Aubervilliers in 1914 and consistently called for a negotiated peace to end World War I.

Laval lost his bid for reelection to the Chamber of Deputies in 1919 and left the Socialist Party the following year. Elected mayor of Aubervilliers in 1923, he held this title through 1944, even as he served in the national government. Laval achieved reelection to the Chamber in 1924 but resigned in 1927 to accept election as a senator. He served as minister of public works (1925), undersecretary of state (1925), minister of justice (1926), and minister of labor (1930). He became premier in 1931, but was defeated the following year and accepted an appointment as minister of colonies and, subsequently in 1934, as minister of foreign affairs. He once again became premier in 1935, but did not relinquish the foreign affairs post to a separate minister.

Deeply alarmed by the growing instability of Europe during the mid-1930s, Laval sought to build a strong relationship between France and the fascist Italy of BENITO MUSSOLINI. This effort was destroyed, however, by Italy's brutal invasion of Ethiopia in 1936. That same year Laval's cabinet collapsed.

Laval reentered French government in 1940 after the fall of France, becoming minister of state (vice premier) under MARSHAL HENRI-PHILIPPE PÉTAIN. As the Germans swept through the nation during the BATTLE OF FRANCE, Laval dissuaded the government from going into exile and successfully counseled leaders to negotiate an armistice with Germany for the purpose of ensuring the existence of a legal government empowered to negotiate favorable terms with Nazi Germany. Laval additionally persuaded the National Assembly to dissolve itself, thereby bringing the Third Republic to an end on July 10, 1940.

Laval was an extreme defeatist who believed that German victory in World War II was inevitable. He therefore held that the best course for France was to collaborate fully with the German victors. This, he believed, was the nation's only hope for the future. Accordingly, acting on his own, he commenced negotiations with the Germans for a full and final treaty of peace. Outraged by this presumption, Pétain dismissed Laval in December 1940, replacing him with Admiral FRANÇOIS DARLAN. His colleagues did not mourn his leaving. In April 1942, however, the Germans forced Pétain to recall Laval as premier, and Pétain himself withdrew into the role of a powerless figurehead in the VICHY GOVERNMENT.

Laval realized that Germany by no means saw France as a political partner, and fearing that the nation would lose what little sovereignty remained to it, Laval decided to supply the German war machine with French laborers—in the hope that this would win the goodwill of ADOLF HITLER. He made a radio address calling for volunteers and announcing his hope for a German victory.

Laval's many historical critics argue that his policies were as craven as they were fruitless. His few apologists counter that he did what he thought would salvage as much of France as possible. Whatever his motives, his control over the country steadily melted away, as the Vichy government was caught between a growing RESISTANCE MOVEMENT, on the one hand, and an increasingly fanatical ring of German collaborators on the other.

Laval hung on until Germany surrendered to the Allies in May 1945. He then fled to Spain, which had been neutral during the war, and after preparing his defense, he returned to France to face trial in July 1945. Found guilty of treason, he was sentenced to death. He attempted suicide by poisoning, but was revived—only to be executed in Paris on October 15, 1945.

Further reading: Chambrun, René de. *Pierre Laval: Traitor or Patriot?* New York: Scribner, 1984; Laval, Pierre. *The Diary of Pierre Laval.* New York: AMS Press, 1978; Warner, Geoffrey. *Pierre Laval and the Eclipse of France.* New York: Macmillan, 1969.

Leahy, William (1875–1959) *close military adviser to Franklin Roosevelt*

Leahy graduated from the U.S. Naval Academy in 1897 and served during the Spanish-American War (1898), the Philippine Insurrection (1899–1901), and the Boxer Rebellion in China (1900). While he was commanding a navy transport during World War I, he met and was befriended by then Assistant Secretary of the Navy FRANKLIN D.

Admiral William Leahy in 1935 *(U.S. Navy History Center)*

ROOSEVELT. The two remained close for the rest of Roosevelt's life.

Leahy was promoted to admiral in 1936 and became chief of naval operations in 1937, serving in this capacity until his retirement (due to age) in 1939. Later that year, President Roosevelt appointed his old friend governor of Puerto Rico. In December 1940, he became ambassador to the VICHY GOVERNMENT of France, but was recalled to the United States in April 1942 and, in July, was named chief of staff to the president, a new position FDR had created. Reinstated from military retirement, he served as chairman of the Joint Chiefs of Staff throughout most of the war.

Leahy was one of the president's closest wartime advisers and accompanied FDR to all of the major Allied conferences. He was promoted to fleet admiral in December 1944, in time to accompany Roosevelt to the ailing president's final conference, at Yalta, the following year.

President HARRY S. TRUMAN retained Leahy, although he did not enjoy the same degree of influence as under FDR. Retiring in 1949, he wrote a memoir of World War II entitled *I Was There* (1950).

Further reading: Adams, Henry H. *Witness to Power: The Life of Fleet Admiral William D. Leahy.* Annapolis, Md.: Naval Institute Press, 1985; Leahy, William D. *I Was There.* 1950; reprint ed., New York: Arno, 1979.

Lebensraum

A German word meaning "living space," *Lebensraum* became a key part of the Nazi vocabulary as a motive and justification for aggressive German expansion—primarily to the east.

The word and concept may have been used first by RUDOLF HESS when he and ADOLF HITLER were in Landsberg prison together following the failure of the Beer Hall Putsch of 1924. Hitler incorporated it into official policy as early as November 1937. For Hitler, colonization was not a satisfactory means of obtaining *Lebensraum*. He asserted that the needed space must be in Europe and must be contiguous with Germany. This, he claimed, was also necessary for the security of Germany, and he repeatedly announced, in public, his intention to use whatever force was required to obtain *Lebensraum.*

Hitler's first explanation of the *Lebensraum* concept, in a secret meeting of November 1937, was recorded by his military adjutant, Colonel Friedrich Hossbach. Hossbach subsequently edited his notes of the meeting in what historians came to call the "Hossbach Memorandum." This document was offered at the NUREMBERG WAR CRIMES TRIBUNAL as proof of the Hitler regime's deliberate intention to wage offensive war.

Further reading: Shirer, William L. *The Rise and Fall of the Third Reich: A History of Nazi Germany.* New York: Ballantine, 1991; Spielvogel, Jackson J. *Hitler and Nazi Germany: A History.* Englewood Cliffs, N.J.: Prentice Hall, 2004.

Lebrun, Albert (1871–1950) *last president (1932–1940) of the French Third Republic when it fell to Germany*

Born at Mercy-le-Haut, France, Lebrun was trained as a mining engineer and was elected deputy for Lorraine in 1900. He became a senator in 1920 and president of the Senate in 1931. Lebrun also served as minister of colonies (1911–13 and 1913–14), minister of war (1913), and (during World War I), minister of blockade and of liberated regions (1917–19).

Lebrun was elected president of the republic in 1932 and was reelected in 1939. He was an agreeable man with no strong political convictions, and thus he made a pliable compromise candidate acceptable to all major French parties.

After the Germans defeated France in 1940, Lebrun acted without objection on his cabinet's decisions and thus concluded an armistice with Germany—although he did voice a preference for conducting a government-in-exile. In July, Lebrun voluntarily stepped aside to allow Marshal PHILIPPE PÉTAIN to assume leadership of the state. Retiring to Vizille near Grenoble, Lebrun was interned by the Germans at Itter in the Tirol during 1943–44.

Following the NORMANDY LANDINGS (D-DAY) and with the Allied liberation of France in progress, Lebrun endorsed General CHARLES DE GAULLE as head of the provisional French government. At the end of the war, Lebrun published a memoir in an attempt to justify his actions in the aftermath of the Battle of France. Although he was not indicted for treason, he was generally held in popular contempt as an ineffectual leader in a time of grave crisis.

Further reading: Jackson, Julian. *France: The Dark Years, 1940–1944.* New York: Oxford University Press, 2003; Paxton, Robert O. *Vichy France.* New York: Columbia University Press, 2001.

Leclerc, Jacques-Philippe (Jacques-Philippe Leclerc de Hauteclocque [from 1945])

(1902–1947) *Free French army general*

Born into wealth and privilege as Philippe-Marie, vicomte de Hauteclocque, Leclerc was a graduate of the French military academy, Saint-Cyr, and the cavalry school, Saumur. At the commencement of World War II in 1939, he was an infantry captain and was wounded in battle. Captured by the Germans, he escaped to England. There he joined General CHARLES DE GAULLE in London to take a command in the FREE FRENCH FORCES. He adopted the pseudonym Jacques-Philippe Leclerc to avert German reprisals against his prominent family still in France.

De Gaulle promoted Leclerc to colonel and sent him to French Equatorial Africa, where he proved to be a highly effective and dashing officer. He was quickly promoted to general, whereupon he led an extraordinary 1,000-mile march from Chad to Tripoli, Libya, so that he could join his forces to those of the British Eighth Army. En route, he engaged, defeated, and captured a number of Italian garrisons.

Leclerc participated in the NORMANDY LANDINGS (D-DAY) in command of a Free French armored division. It was to him, on August 25, 1944, that the German commander of the Paris garrison surrendered. In company with de Gaulle, he entered Paris in triumph on the following day.

Leclerc liberated Strasbourg on November 23, 1944, and subsequently, in Germany, captured Berchtesgaden, the town above which ADOLF HITLER had maintained his mountain retreat. After the surrender of Germany, Leclerc was assigned command of the French Expeditionary Force to the Far East in July 1945.

After the war, in March 1946, Leclerc was assigned duty in French Indochina. He judged the political situation there to be ultimately untenable, resigned, and, in July, assumed the post of inspector-general of French forces in North Africa. He died in an airplane crash and was posthumously promoted to marshal of France.

Further reading: Vézinet, Adolphe. *Le général Leclerc.* Paris: France-Empire, 1997.

Leeb, Wilhelm von (1876–1956) *German commander relieved by Hitler*

Leeb distinguished himself as a German officer in World War I and became a master theorist of defensive warfare. Between the wars, he rose rapidly, becoming a lieutenant general by 1934. Adamantly opposed to ADOLF HITLER and the Nazi regime, he was forced into retirement in January 1938—at the rank of general. Months later, during the Czech crisis of August 1938, Leeb was recalled to command the Twelfth Army, which occupied the SUDETENLAND pursuant to the terms of the MUNICH CONFERENCE AND AGREEMENT. The crisis passed and Leeb returned to retirement, only to be recalled yet again at the outbreak of World War II in September 1939. He was assigned to command Army Group C, which was deployed on Germany's western front opposite the MAGINOT LINE.

Leeb had strongly opposed "Fall Gelb," the German western offensive, arguing that violating Belgium's neutrality for the second time in the 20th century would turn the entire world against Germany. Accordingly, he supported General Franz Halder's proposed coup d'état against Hitler later in 1939. When the coup died aborning, Leeb went on to lead Army Group C with great success against the French, defeating them in Alsace-Lorraine during the BATTLE OF FRANCE and earning promotion to field marshal in July 1940.

After the fall of France, Leeb's Army Group C was redesignated Army Group North, and Leeb led it in the INVASION OF THE SOVIET UNION in June 1941. By September, Leeb was on the verge of taking LENINGRAD when Hitler ordered him to lay siege to the city instead of attacking. This was one of Hitler's great errors in the Russian campaign.

In January 1942, desperately defending against a Red Army counteroffensive, Leeb requested Hitler's permission to withdraw from the Leningrad front to make a more cohesive defensive stand. When Hitler refused, Leeb asked to be relieved of command, and he sat out the rest of the war. In October 1948, an Allied military court sentenced Leeb to three years' imprisonment for noncapital minor war crimes.

Further reading: Barnett, Correlli, ed. *Hitler's Generals.* New York: Grove Press, 2003; Heiber, Helmut, and David Glantz, eds. *Hitler and His Generals.* New York: Enigma Books, 2002; Mitcham, Samuel W. *Hitler's Field Marshals and Their Battles.* New York: Cooper Square, 2001.

Leigh-Mallory, Trafford (1892–1944) *commander in chief of the Allied Expeditionary Air Force during the Normandy Landings (D-day)*

Leigh-Mallory served in the British army as well as the Royal Flying Corps during World War I, then was among the first officers commissioned in the Royal Air Force (RAF), which was created in 1919. Leigh-Mallory rose rapidly in the interwar air arm, becoming an air vice marshal by 1938 with command of No. 12 Fighter Group. As commander of this unit, Leigh-Mallory participated in the BATTLE OF BRITAIN, with responsibility for the defense of the Midlands and, to some extent, support of No. 11 Fighter Group in southeast England.

Leigh-Mallory advocated what became known as "Big Wing" tactics. Whereas Air Vice Marshal Keith Park (commanding officer of No. 11 Fighter

Group) ordered German raids on Britain to be met by individual squadrons, which he considered the most flexible and effective means of response, Leigh-Mallory called for much larger formations, which would provide greater mutual protection and thereby reduce casualties. Leigh-Mallory and Park disputed this tactical point bitterly, and since the commander in charge of fighter command, Hugh Dowding, favored Park's approach, Leigh-Mallory's position became quite controversial. In November 1940 Dowding was replaced, and Park was transferred to a training command. This left Leigh-Mallory in position to promote his Big Wing tactics in offensives over France. Their effectiveness remains a subject of controversy to this day.

Leigh-Mallory was promoted to acting air marshal in July 1942 and, in August, commanded air operations in the ill-fated Dieppe raid. Named commander of Fighter Command in November 1942, he became commander in chief of the Allied Expeditionary Air Force for the Normandy Landings in December 1943. With this came promotion to air chief marshal.

His mission in Normandy accomplished by October 1944, Leigh-Mallory was transferred to the Southeast Asia Command as commander in charge of air operations. En route to his new command in November 1944, he was killed in an air crash.

Further reading: Bungay, Stephen. *The Most Dangerous Enemy: A History of the Battle of Britain.* London: Aurum Press, 2002; Grimley, Edmund. *The Big Six: Montgomery, Eisenhower, Tedder, Ramsay, Leigh-Mallory, Bradley.* London: Alliance Press, 1944.

LeMay, Curtis (1906–1990) *commander, U.S. Twentieth Air Force*

LeMay was born in Columbus, Ohio. After failing to obtain an appointment to West Point, he enrolled at Ohio State University, leaving it after he completed an ROTC program. He joined the army in 1928 and became a cadet in the Air Corps Flying School that September. Earning his wings on October 12, 1929, LeMay was commissioned a second

Curtis E. LeMay *(Library of Congress)*

lieutenant in January 1930. He served with the 27th Pursuit Squadron, based in Michigan, and, over the next three years, completed the civil engineering degree he had begun at Ohio State, earning his diploma in 1932.

During the Depression, LeMay worked with the Civilian Conservation Corps (CCC) and flew the air mails when President Franklin D. Roosevelt assigned army pilots to air mail operations in 1934. Promoted to first lieutenant in June 1935, LeMay attended an overwater navigation school in Hawaii. In 1937, he transferred from pursuit ships to bombers and was attached to the 305th Bombardment Group at Langley Field, Virginia. Here LeMay developed aerial techniques for locating ships at sea.

LeMay was among the first army pilots to fly the new B-17 bombers and led a flight of them on a goodwill tour to Latin America during 1937–38. He then enrolled in the Air Corps Tactical School during 1938–39 and was promoted to captain in

January 1940. Assigned to command of a squadron in 34th Bomb Group later that year, he was promoted to major in 1941.

After the United States entered World War II, LeMay rose rapidly, becoming a lieutenant colonel in January 1942 and a colonel just three months later. He assumed command of the 305th Bombardment Group in California in April and brought the unit to Britain as part of the Eighth Air Force. He worked to develop and perfect precision-bombing tactics by intense and comprehensive study of targets prior to missions and by employing the highly risky tactic of abandoning evasive maneuvering while over targets. Rigorous application of LeMay's techniques resulted in a doubling of the number of bombs placed on target.

In June 1943, LeMay became commander of the 3rd Bombardment Division, which he led in the famous "shuttle raid" against Regensburg, Germany, in August. In September, LeMay was promoted to temporary brigadier general, and in March 1944 to temporary major general. He was then sent to China to lead the 20th Bomber Command against the Japanese. LeMay transferred to command of the 21st Bomber Group, on Guam, in January 1945 and revolutionized bombing tactics using the B-29. He stripped the aircraft of defensive guns—as well as gun crews and ammunition—so that each ship could carry more bombs. Even more stunningly, he ordered these advanced high-altitude bombers to bomb from low altitudes for greater accuracy and to break formation. Air crews anticipated a slaughter, but, remarkably, survival rates actually increased—and bombing accuracy and effectiveness improved dramatically. Under LeMay, the 21st Bomber Group razed four major Japanese cities with incendiary bombs in attacks that proved far more destructive than the later atomic bombing of Hiroshima and Nagasaki, an operation also under LeMay's overall command.

In the late days of the war, in July 1945, LeMay was named commander of the Twentieth Air Force (20th and 21st Bomber Groups), then was appointed deputy chief of staff for research and development. He held this post through 1947, when he was promoted to temporary lieutenant general in the newly independent U.S. Air Force.

On October 1, 1947, LeMay took command of U.S. air forces in Europe and was a key planner of the great Berlin Airlift of 1948–49, the opening salvo of the cold war. In October 1948, LeMay returned to the United States as commander in charge of the newly created Strategic Air Command (SAC). He oversaw the entry of the USAF into the jet age with B-47 and B-52 bombers capable of virtually unlimited range by means of the in-air refueling techniques he was instrumental in developing. By the 1950s, LeMay oversaw the introduction of missiles into USAF's strategic arsenal.

Promoted to general in October 1951, LeMay was the youngest man to hold four-star rank since Ulysses S. Grant. He became vice chief of staff of the Air Force in 1957 and chief of staff in 1961. A right-wing conservative with an extremely prickly temperament, LeMay often found himself at odds with Presidents Kennedy and Johnson as well as with their secretary of defense, Robert S. McNamara. He retired from the USAF on February 1, 1965, and drew heavy criticism for becoming the running mate of segregationist third-party presidential candidate George Wallace in 1968.

Further reading: Coffey, Thomas M. *Iron Eagle: The Turbulent Life of General Curtis LeMay.* New York: Crown, 1986.

Lend-Lease Act

President Franklin Delano Roosevelt signed into law "An Act to Promote the Defense of the United States" on March 11, 1941, authorizing the president to aid any nation whose defense he deemed critical to that of the United States, despite U.S. neutrality. The act further authorized the acceptance of repayment "in kind or property, or any other direct or indirect benefit which the President deems satisfactory."

Well before the United States entered World War II, and while it was nominally neutral in that war, President Roosevelt committed the nation to aid the powers fighting Nazism and fascism. U.S.

law required that Great Britain, the first recipient of material war aid, acquire arms on a strictly cash-and-carry basis. By the summer of 1940, British prime minister WINSTON CHURCHILL warned the Roosevelt administration that Britain would soon be incapable of making such cash payments. On December 8, 1940, President Roosevelt responded by suggesting the concept of lend-lease as an alternative to cash for arms. In return for arms supplied under lend-lease, including the delivery of 50 World War I–era U.S. destroyers to the Royal Navy, Britain granted the United States 99-year leases on military and naval bases located on British possessions in the Caribbean.

On February 23, 1942, after the United States had entered the war, the British and American governments concluded "Agreement Relating to the Principles Applying to the Provision of Aid in the Prosecution of the War." The agreement codified and clarified the provisions of the Lend-Lease Act, including such details as arrangements for payment to patent holders of various weapons systems, and it incorporated a statement on measures to promote worldwide economic cooperation.

The USS *Black Hawk* tends destroyers at Chefoo, China, a few years before World War II. These and other World War I–vintage ships were transferred to the British in the destroyers-for-bases program that preceded the Lend-Lease Act. *(National Archives and Records Administration)*

Lend-lease was authorized in response to the needs of Great Britain, but it was soon extended to China and the Soviet Union. By the end of the war, more than 40 nations had participated in lend-lease, having received aid valued at a total of $49,100,000,000.

Further reading: Dougherty, James J. *The Politics of Wartime Aid: American Economic Assistance to France and French Northwest Africa, 1940–1946.* Westport, Conn.: Greenwood Press, 1978; Stettinius, Edward Reilly. *Lend-Lease, Weapon for Victory.* New York: Macmillan, 1944; Whidden, Howard Primrose. *Reaching a Lend-Lease Settlement.* New York: Foreign Policy Association, 1944.

Leningrad, siege and relief of

Leningrad (now St. Petersburg) was one of the prime objectives of the German INVASION OF THE SOVIET UNION. On July 8, 1941, the German Fourth Panzer Army severed the city's land contact with the Soviet interior by taking the fortress at Shlisselburg. The Finns, allied with the Germans, advanced to recover Karelia, which had been lost to the Soviets in the recent RUSSO-FINNISH WAR. Having recovered this territory, however, Finnish forces did not push on to the city itself. Had they done so, Leningrad would probably have fallen early in the campaign.

By the middle of July 1941, German Army Group North was within 60 miles of Leningrad and, by the middle of September—following intensive long-range artillery bombardment, which commenced on September 1—it had largely enveloped the city.

ADOLF HITLER was confident that the siege would quickly prove effective. The city had some 2.6 million inhabitants (of whom 100,000 were refugees from points west), but food stores were sufficient for only one, perhaps two months. It seemed a relatively easy matter to starve Leningrad into submission, but Hitler did not count on the endurance and resourcefulness of the Soviet people. Leningrad was the cultural and scientific center of the Soviet Union, and its proud citizens were determined to defend it. Scientists at the Leningrad Scientific

Institute rapidly developed a process for making flour out of shell-packing mixed with paste stripped from wallpaper. This significantly stretched meager food resources—as did the consumption of horses, dogs, cats, and rats. Additionally, small amounts of food and other provisions were brought across frozen Lake Ladoga—until November 9, 1941, when German forces captured Tikhvin, thereby cutting the route to the lake and rendering the German blockade apparently absolute.

After Tikhvin fell, the Soviets surreptitiously began cutting a road farther north, through forest lands. By the end of November, the road was partially ready, and supplies were once again transported via frozen Lake Ladoga. A relief convoy reached Leningrad on November 26 via this route, delivering 33 tons of food—a magnificent achievement but a supply that represented barely one-third of the city's daily requirement. When the forest road was completed on December 6, more food could be brought in, but by this time, Soviet forces had retaken Tikhvin, which once again opened the shorter route. Nevertheless, food rations remained barely above starvation level throughout the siege.

Soviet forces attempted to lift the siege with operations conducted during January–April 1942, but the Germans held. The Soviet Baltic fleet was the key military means of defending the city, supplemented by coastal artillery and aircraft. Despite all defensive efforts, however, the Germans landed some 150,000 artillery shells in Leningrad and dropped some 4,600 bombs.

On January 12, 1943, Red Army troops from within Leningrad (the Sixty-Seventh Army) and outside (the Second Shock Army) launched Operation Iskra (Spark) in a major effort to lift the siege. By January 18, 1943, advance units of these armies met just outside the city and forced a passage five to seven miles wide, through which the troops built a railroad and vehicle road in a mere 17 days. This was the first major break in the blockade. But it was not until February 1944 that the Red Army finally succeeded in driving out Army Group North, thereby ending the 900-day siege of Leningrad.

According to Soviet authorities, the total cost to the city was about 632,000 killed, almost all civil-

ians. Western historians believe the actual number of dead was closer to 1 million.

Further reading: Glantz, David M. *The Battle for Leningrad, 1941–1944.* Lawrence: University Press of Kansas, 2002; Salisbury, Harrison E. *The 900 Days: The Siege of Leningrad.* 1985; reprint ed., New York: Da Capo, 2000.

Leyte, Battle of

General Douglas MacArthur, supreme Allied commander in the Pacific, was eager to begin the campaign to retake the Philippines, which he had been forced to abandon at the beginning of the war. His forces had captured Morotai, between New Guinea and Mindanao, even as the III Marine Corps had conquered Peleliu and Angaur in the central Pacific. This put U.S. land forces in a position to begin the reconquest of the Philippines. However, after Admiral William "Bull" Halsey, in command of the Third U.S. Fleet, encountered little Japanese opposition at the Battle of Mindanao during September 9–10, 1944, MacArthur resolved to bypass the southern Philippines and make a direct assault on Leyte, in the center of the Philippine island group. Supporting the invasion was the spectacular naval Battle of Leyte Gulf.

The invasion was to be carried out by the Sixth U.S. Army under Walter Krueger with XXIV Corps (John Hodge) and X Corps (Franklin Sibert). Opposing Krueger was the Thirty-fifth Japanese Army (Suzuki Sosaku). The U.S. landings were carried out by the U.S. Seventh Fleet (Thomas Kinkaid) with air defense supplied by naval aviators as well as the Southwest Pacific Air Forces (George Kenney).

On October 17–18, army Rangers took the small islands guarding the eastern entrance to Leyte Gulf. The navy launched a two-hour bombardment on October 20, after which four infantry divisions landed on the east coast of Leyte between Tacloban and Dulag, 17 miles to the south. Two divisions of X Corps on the right and two divisions of XXIV Corps on the left fought inland from the beachheads in a four-day battle that secured operational airfields. It was November 2 before Sixth

Army gained control of the Leyte Valley, from Carigara on the north coast to Abuyog in the southeast. After this, on the left, the 7th Infantry crossed the island to Baybay on the west coast.

Progress had been slow but substantial. However, torrential rains and increased resistance from consolidated Japanese forces in the mountainous interior brought the American advance to a crawl. Determined to prevent the Americans from taking the Philippines, YAMASHITA TOMOYUKI, the Japanese commander in charge of the islands, funneled reinforcements to Leyte from surrounding islands. Between October 23 and December 11, about 45,000 Japanese troops landed at Ormoc on the island's west coast—even though the U.S. Navy had decimated Japanese sea forces.

Recognizing the urgent necessity of stopping the Japanese buildup, General Krueger launched a two-pronged offensive into the Ormoc Valley beginning in November. On the right, X Corps, reinforced by the 32nd Infantry Division, attacked the village of Limon, which was the northern entryway into the valley. Limon did not fall until December 10. On the left, the 11th Airborne Division joined XXIV Corps, as the 7th Infantry made a thrust across the island, at Balogo, on November 22. Two weeks after this, the main assault on Ormoc got under way when the 77th Infantry landed at Ipil. Ormoc was secured by December 10, and the 77th made contact with the 7th Division. The two units now advanced up both ends of the Ormoc Valley and converged at Libungao on December 20. Six days later, on Christmas Day, Palompon, the last Japanese-held port on Leyte, fell. On December 26, the Eighth U.S. Army (ROBERT EICHELBERGER) assumed command on the island (as XXIV Corps left for the OKINAWA CAMPAIGN) and spent the next four months in difficult mop-up operations.

Victory on Leyte cost the Americans 15,584 casualties, including 3,584 killed; Japanese losses totaled more than 70,000 men.

Further reading: Cutler, Thomas J. *The Battle of Leyte Gulf: 23–26 October 1944.* Annapolis, Md.: Naval Institute Press, 2001; Vego, Milan N. *Battle for Leyte, 1944: Allied and Japanese Plans, Preparations, and Execution.* Annapolis, Md.: Naval Institute Press, 2005; Willmott, H. P. *The Battle of Leyte Gulf: The Last Fleet Action.* Bloomington: Indiana University Press, 2005.

Leyte Gulf, Battle of

The Battle of Leyte Gulf was fought during October 23–26, 1944, in response to the attempt of Japanese naval forces to disrupt and destroy U.S. landings on the Philippine island of Leyte. The Battle of Leyte Gulf developed into the largest naval battle of any war and was also distinguished by the first KAMIKAZE attacks.

Learning where the American landings on Leyte were to take place, Admiral Toyoda Soemu, commander in charge of the Japanese Combined Fleet, launched Operation Sho-Go (Victory), by which he intended to draw the Third U.S. Fleet (under Admiral WILLIAM "BULL" HALSEY) into battle north of Leyte Gulf so that the Japanese naval forces could catch the landing forces as well as the smaller Seventh U.S. Fleet (under Vice Admiral THOMAS KINKAID), which was covering the landing, in a massive double envelopment, or pincers. Whereas in previous battles, U.S. Navy commanders had enjoyed the advantage of ULTRA decrypts, which gave them extensive knowledge of Japanese radio communications, the Japanese changed codes before Leyte Gulf and maintained a high degree of radio silence. Toyoda's trap very nearly succeeded.

Toyoda assigned Vice Admiral OZAWA JISABURO, commander in charge of the Mobile Force, tactical command of Operation Sho-Go. Ozawa divided his ships, including the two largest battleships ever built, *Yamato* and *Masashi,* five conventional battleships, and 16 cruisers, into two striking forces, under Vice Admirals KURITA TAKEO and Kiyohicle Shima. Ozawa himself led a decoy fleet, including four aircraft carriers, to lure Halsey to the north while Kurita and Shima closed the pincers. A portion of Shima's force, in company with a number of Kurita's ships (under Vice Admiral Shejo Nishimura), were detailed to sail into the Leyte Gulf via Surigao Strait, while Kurita approached the gulf by way of the San Bernardino

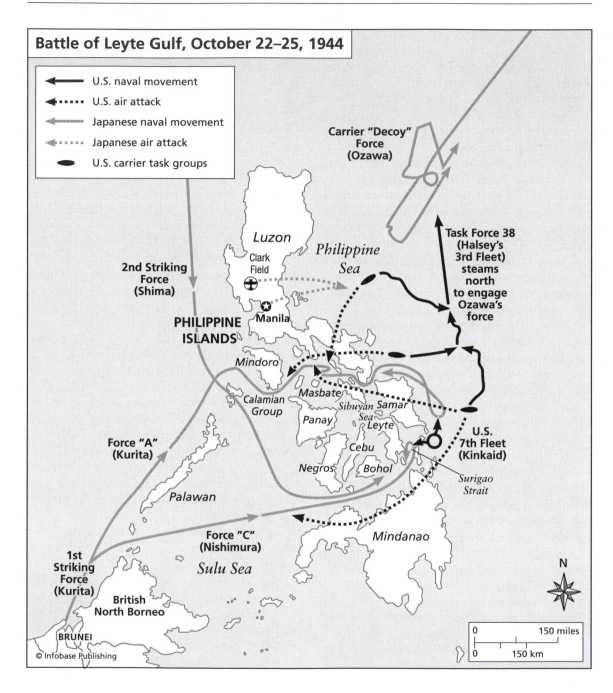

Battle of Leyte Gulf, October 22–25, 1944

Legend:
- ◄— U.S. naval movement
- ◄···· U.S. air attack
- ◄— Japanese naval movement
- ◄···· Japanese air attack
- ⬬ U.S. carrier task groups

Carrier "Decoy" Force (Ozawa)

Luzon

Clark Field

Philippine Sea

Task Force 38 (Halsey's 3rd Fleet) steams north to engage Ozawa's force

2nd Striking Force (Shima)

★ Manila

PHILIPPINE ISLANDS

Mindoro

Calamian Group

Masbate

Sibuyan Sea Samar

Panay   Leyte

U.S. 7th Fleet (Kinkaid)

Force "A" (Kurita)

Cebu

Negros   Bohol

Surigao Strait

Palawan

Force "C" (Nishimura)

Mindanao

1st Striking Force (Kurita)

Sulu Sea

British North Borneo

N

BRUNEI

© Infobase Publishing

| 0 | | 150 miles |
| 0 | | 150 km |

Strait. The rest of Shima's force escorted Japanese troop reinforcements to Leyte Island.

On October 24, Task Force 38, under Vice Admiral MARC MITSCHER, launched air strikes against Kurita as his ships crossed the Sibuyan Sea, sinking one battleship, damaging others, and prompting Kurita to reverse course for a time. Kurita's excess of caution put him behind schedule, but Halsey overestimated the damage that had been done to him and discounted Kurita as a threat. This played into the Sho-Go plan. With Kurita apparently out of the way, Halsey pursued Ozawa's decoy fleet.

The trap was set, but U.S. PT boats (followed by destroyers, then battleships and cruisers) attacked Nishimura as he entered Surigao Strait on the night of October 24. Nishimura was killed and all ships but a single destroyer of his force were sunk. Shima, who had been following Nishimura, withdrew without joining the fight. Thus one arm of the Japanese pincer was destroyed. Nevertheless, the other arm, Kurita's force, was still intact; Kurita sailed into the gulf via the San Bernardino Strait on the morning of October 25. A U.S. escort carrier group under Rear Admiral Clifton Sprague sighted the force off Samar Island. Both the American and the Japanese commanders were taken by surprise, but Kurita assumed that Sprague's ships were part of a much larger force and therefore ordered his ships to attack independently rather than risk committing his entire force. Had he used all that was available to him, he could easily have destroyed Sprague's outnumbered, outgunned escort carriers. As it turned out, however, in independent action Sprague's aircraft sunk two Japanese cruisers, and torpedo fire from a U.S. destroyer damaged a third cruiser. Sprague lost two of his escort carriers, one of them to a kamikaze attack. Two of his destroyers and a destroyer escort were also sunk, while a number of other ships sustained serious damage. It was perhaps the most desperate naval engagement of the Pacific war, but Kurita, presumably short on fuel—and doubtless still fearing the presence of a larger force—suddenly broke off the engagement and withdrew.

In the meantime, Admiral Kinkaid had radioed Halsey, who was in fighting pursuit of Ozawa, for aid. Halsey responded by sending one of Mitscher's task groups south to engage Kurita. Yet he apparently did not fully realize the desperate nature of the situation in Leyte Gulf and therefore retained some ships under Rear Admiral Willis A. Lee to continue the fight against Ozawa (who had already lost four carriers to Mitscher), rather than send them south to cut off Kurita's escape. Only after Lee was within range of what remained of Ozawa did Halsey, at last waking to the full danger to the Leyte landings and the U.S. Seventh Fleet, order Lee to break off and steam south as well. A smaller force continued to pursue Ozawa, and two more ships were sunk, but Ozawa nevertheless managed to escape complete annihilation. As for Lee, the delay imposed by Halsey meant that he arrived in the gulf too late to intercept Kurita.

The Battle of Leyte Gulf was a great American victory, albeit flawed by Halsey's misjudgment. The Japanese lost three battleships, four aircraft carriers, 10 cruisers, and nine destroyers as well as many aircraft. Most important, the Japanese failed to disrupt the Leyte landings, thereby virtually ensuring that the Americans would retake the PHILIPPINES.

Further reading: Cutler, Thomas J. *The Battle of Leyte Gulf: 23–26 October 1944.* Annapolis, Md.: Naval Institute Press, 2001; Willmott, H. P. *The Battle of Leyte Gulf: The Last Fleet Action.* Bloomington: Indiana University Press, 2005.

Liberty ships

From early in the Atlantic war, German U-boats took a terrible toll on Allied cargo transports plying the waters between the United States and Britain as well as between the United States and the Soviet Union. The ships were sunk faster than they could be built. In September 1940, well before the United States entered the war, Britain ordered 60 transports from the United States, supplying to the shipyards a radically simple design that lent itself to rapid construction. The single most important innovation was the use of welded rather than riveted plates. Welding greatly speeded construction but made for a far less durable ship. The British designers reasoned, however, that few vessels would survive the hazards of war long enough to create serious stress on the welded joints.

American designers, particularly those who worked for industrial giant Henry J. Kaiser, adapted and greatly modified the British plans, building ships at an even faster rate than the British had contemplated. In January 1941, the United States, girding for war, launched its own emergency construction program calling for 200 vessels. These were referred to as the "The Liberty Fleet," and the name "Liberty ship" was used to describe these cheap, ugly, slow transports—the first generation were 7,126-ton vessels, making no more than 11 knots—which were produced by mass-production factory methods to prefabricate large subassemblies put together at shipyards on the West and East Coasts. The ships were, sailors said, "built by the mile and chopped off by the yard." The first of the American vessels, *Patrick Henry,* was launched on September 27, 1941.

Although all were based on the same prefabricated structural plan, Liberty ships came in different lengths and were readily modified for different uses, including freight transportation (the most

Liberty ships under construction on Puget Sound (*Author's collection*)

common use), fuel transport, troop transport, tank transport (so-called "zipper ships"), and tender (floating repair) vessels. Some were even constructed as hospital ships. In all, 2,710 liberty ships were launched. Kaiser and other shipyard owners engaged in heated competitions to prove who could build ships the fastest. The record was an incredible four days, 15.5 hours from the laying of the keel to launch. The ships were customarily named for prominent Americans.

The Liberty ships were a tremendous success and served as a lifeline to Britain and, to a lesser extent, the Soviet Union. Two hundred of the vessels were given to Britain and 50 to the USSR as part of the LEND-LEASE program. Many of the other vessels were ultimately lost at sea, most of them victims of torpedo attack, but one in 30 succumbed to the inherent structural weakness of welded construction. The Liberty ships were lightly armed (and carried U.S. Navy gun crews). One, the *Stephen Hopkins,* earned the unique distinction of actually sinking an enemy combatant, a German auxiliary cruiser, with its single four-inch gun.

Further reading: Elphick, Peter. *Liberty: The Ships That Won the War.* Annapolis, Md.: Naval Institute Press, 2001; Hoehling, A. A. *The Fighting Liberty Ships: A Memoir.* Annapolis, Md.: Naval Institute Press, 1996; Jaffee, Walter W. *The Liberty Ships from A (A.B. Hammond) to Z (Zona Gale).* Palo Alto, Calif.: Glencannon Press, 2004.

The Liberty ship *Jeremiah Bryan* moored behind the submarine *Pampanito (U.S. Navy)*

Liddell Hart, Basil (1895–1970) *Allied adviser on armored warfare doctrine*

One of the most important writers on armored warfare doctrine before and during World War II, Basil Liddell Hart was the son of the Reverend Henry Hart and Clara Liddell, and was educated at St. Paul's School and Corpus Christi College, Cambridge. He left the university to join the British army in World War I, earning a commission as an officer in the King's Own Yorkshire Light Infantry. Twice wounded, he fought at Ypres and the Somme.

After the war, Liddell Hart wrote the *Infantry Training Manual* in 1920, was invalided out of the army in 1924, and became military correspondent for the *Daily Telegraph* (1925–35), *The Times* (1935–39), and the *Daily Mail* (1939–45). During these years, he was Britain's best-known writer on military topics and wrote extensively on the deployment of tanks as a striking force independent from the infantry. Whereas accepted British doctrine subordinated armor to an infantry support role, Liddell Hart advocated using tanks independently to make deep penetrations into enemy territory so as to cut off enemy troops from their supplies and higher command.

German generals and military planners read Liddell Hart avidly, using his ideas to develop their own devastatingly effective doctrine of the BLITZ-KRIEG. Ironically, British commanders largely ignored his ideas on armored warfare before World War II, although Liddell Hart did serve Britain's Secretary of State for War Leslie Hore-Belisha as military adviser from 1937 to 1940.

In addition to his doctrinal writing, Liddell Hart was an important military historian, specializing in the history of World War I. After World War II, he interviewed key German commanders for his provocative *The Other Side of the Hill* (1948).

Further reading: Corum, James S. *The Roots of Blitzkrieg.* Lawrence: University Press of Kansas, 1992; Liddell Hart, B. H. *Strategy,* second revised edition. New York: Plume, 1991.

List, Siegmund Wilhelm von (1880–1971) *important German commander*

List entered the German army in 1898 and served as a staff officer during World War I. He commanded the German forces sent into Austria following the ANSCHLUSS of March 1938. Promoted to general in April 1939, he commanded the Fourteenth Army during the INVASION OF POLAND, which started World War II during September–October 1939. On the western front, he led the Twelfth Army during the BATTLE OF FRANCE in June 1940.

List was given the baton of field marshal in July 1940 and, still in command of the Twelfth Army, fought in the Balkans from June to October 1941. In July 1942, List was succeeded by General Alexander Löhr as commander in charge of the Southeast, the Balkan theater commander. He then assumed command of Army Group A in the Soviet theater.

List was tasked with capturing Rostov-on-Don, then advancing to the Caucasus. His offensive faltered then failed, however, and ADOLF HITLER relieved him of command in September 1942, whereupon List retired. He was tried by the U.S. military for war crimes in 1948 and sentenced to life imprisonment for atrocities perpetrated in the Balkans and Greece. In 1952 he was pardoned and released.

Further reading: Barnett, Correlli. *Hitler's Generals.* New York: Grove Press, 2003; Mitcham, Samuel W. *Hitler's Field Marshals and Their Battles.* New York: Cooper Square, 2001.

Lithuania

At the start of World War II, Lithuania, the largest of the three Baltic states, was a republic ruled by the dictator Antanas Smetona. The Smetona government had cordial relations with the Soviets, the nation's independence guaranteed by a treaty signed with the Soviet Union in July 1920 and reaffirmed by a Soviet-Lithuanian nonaggression pact concluded in 1926 and extended in 1934 for a 10-year period. Prewar relations with Poland, in contrast, were tense. Lithuania sought the return of its historical capital, Wilno (Vilnius), which had been annexed by Poland in 1922. In January 1939, Poland issued an ultimatum forcing an end to the technical state of war that existed between it and Lithuania over the Wilno issue.

Lithuania's bow to Poland revealed just how precarious its claims to sovereignty were on the eve of World War II. On March 22, 1939, German forces annexed the Memel strip, to which Lithuania laid claim. Even more high-handedly, the GERMAN-SOVIET NON-AGRESSION PACT of August 1939 peremptorily assigned Lithuania to the German sphere of influence. When the Germans and Soviets invaded Poland in September 1939, however, it was Soviet troops that occupied Wilno. On September 28, the secret German-Soviet Treaty of Friendship and Demarcation transferred Lithuania to the Soviet sphere. The Soviets subsequently agreed to honor Lithuanian claims on Wilno in return for permission to station Soviet troops in Lithuania. Outwardly, this gave the appearance of most cordial relations between the USSR and Lithuania; in reality, Lithuania had become a Soviet puppet, and when the Soviet army entered the country in June 1940, Soviet agents undermined what remained of the Lithuanian government, arrested dissidents and nationalists, and conducted fraudulent elections. On August 5, 1940, Lithuania ceased to be an independent republic and was annexed to the USSR as the Lithuanian Soviet Socialist Republic.

The first period of Soviet occupation, from June 1940 to June 1941, saw mass terror, including the wholesale destruction of Lithuanian cultural and political institutions in an attempt to force assimilation into the Soviet state. All Germans living in the country were deported to Germany.

In June 1941, with Germany's invasion of the USSR, the German occupation of Lithuania began and did not end until July 1944. Lithuania was annexed to Germany as part of the Reich Commissariat Ostland. Lithuanian police and military units were formed under direct German command and were shipped to the Soviet front, and a Lithuanian Division was incorporated into the WAFFEN-SS. The HOLOCAUST came to Lithuania with ruthless speed, as Lithuanian police and the German mili-tary rounded up the country's large Jewish community and concentrated it for the most part in ghettos created in Wilno and Kaunas, the capital. They were then variously murdered.

The second Soviet occupation commenced in April 1944. While it liberated the nation from Nazi terror, it reintroduced Soviet terror, including a program of forced agricultural collectivization, which brought Lithuania to near starvation. Poles remaining in the country were deported, and the Catholic Church, a central feature of Lithuanian life, was mercilessly purged and persecuted.

World War II reduced the population of Lithuania by a quarter and probably even more, largely as a result of the loss of its German, Jewish, and Polish components. The nation remained a Soviet republic until March 11, 1990, when a newly elected parliament declared independence. Central authorities of the rapidly declining Soviet Union intervened militarily, but on September 6, 1991, the Soviet parliament acknowledged Lithuania's independence.

Further reading: Snyder, Timothy. *The Reconstruction of Nations: Poland, Ukraine, Lithuania, Belarus, 1569–1999.* New Haven, Conn.: Yale University Press, 2004.

Litvinov, Maxim (1876–1951) *Soviet minister to the United States, foreign minister*

Litvinov became a Marxist early in life, joining the Russian Social-Democratic Workers' Party in 1898. Arrested for subversive activity in 1901, he escaped and took refuge in Britain in 1902. He became a Bolshevik after 1903 and was a prominent Communist activist throughout Europe. After the Russian Revolutions of 1917 and the Bolshevik seizure of power, Litvinov was named the new regime's diplomatic representative in London. He was arrested by British authorities in October 1918, however, for engaging in illegal propaganda activities. In January 1919, he was exchanged for Robert Bruce Lockhart, a British journalist who led a special mission to the Soviet Union in 1918.

After this exchange, Litvinov returned to the USSR as a member of the Commissariat for Foreign Affairs. He became prominent in the international disarmament movement that followed World War I, and led the Soviet delegation to the preparatory commission for the League of Nations' World Disarmament Conference during 1927–30. The disarmament programs he advocated were the boldest and most extensive of any on the table.

In 1932, Litvinov was the principal Soviet delegate to the Geneva World Disarmament Conference, and he also headed the Soviet delegation to the 1933 World Economic Conference in London. He was the prime negotiator of the diplomatic relations that were established between the Soviet Union and the United States in 1934.

As ADOLF HITLER came to power in Germany, Litvinov attempted to move the League of Nations to mount an effective resistance to the rise of Nazism during 1934–38. At the same time, he negotiated anti-German treaties with France and Czechoslovakia during 1935. In the political climate created by the APPEASEMENT POLICY advocated by Britain and France, in which JOSEPH STALIN also sought rapprochement with Hitler, the Jewish and resolutely anti-German Litvinov was dismissed from the Soviet government on May 3, 1939. He was both vindicated and reinstated in 1941, however, following the German INVASION OF THE SOVIET UNION. Litvinov was appointed ambassador to the United States, serving from November 1941 to August 1943, then recalled to the Soviet Union to become deputy commissar for foreign affairs. He retired from government after the war, in August 1946.

Further reading: Phillips, Hugh D. *Between the Revolution and the West: A Political Biography of Maxim M. Litvinov.* Denver: Westview Press, 1992; Pope, Arthur Upham. *Maxim Litvinoff.* London: Secker & Warburg, 1943.

London Blitz   *See* BLITZ, THE.

Lucas, John Porter (1890–1949) *U.S. general replaced at Anzio*

Born in Kearneysville, West Virginia, Lucas graduated from West Point in 1911 and, as a second lieu-

John Lucas *(National Archives and Records Administration)*

tenant in the cavalry, was posted to the Philippines from December 1911 to August 1914. Back in the United States, he was assigned to the 13th Cavalry at Columbus, New Mexico, during the revolutionary violence in Mexico, which often spilled across the border. Lucas was a first lieutenant in 1916 and in command of the 13th Cavalry's machine-gun troop when the Mexican revolutionary Pancho Villa raided Columbus on March 9, 1916. Lucas and his unit played a major role in driving off Villa and his raiders. Lucas then served under John J. Pershing in the Punitive Expedition in pursuit of Villa (March 15, 1916–February 5, 1917).

After promotion to captain, Lucas was appointed aide-de-camp to Major General George Bell, headquartered at El Paso, Texas, during February–August 1917. When the United States entered World War I, Lucas, promoted to temporary major, was attached to the 33rd Infantry Division and, in January 1918, assigned command of the division's 108th Field Signals Battalion. By the time the division was shipped to France in May 1918, Lucas had been promoted to temporary lieutenant colonel. He fought with distinction and was so seriously wounded in combat near Amiens that he was forced to return to the States.

By the time of the armistice in November 1918, Lucas was sufficiently recovered to be assigned duty in Washington, D.C. He reverted to his Regular Army rank of captain and taught military science at the University of Michigan (1919–20). In 1920, he transferred to the field artillery and was promoted to major. After graduating from the Field Artillery School in June 1921, he served as an instructor there during 1921–23. In June 1924, Lucas graduated from the Command and General Staff School, then served as professor of military science and tactics at Colorado Agricultural College from 1924 to 1929, when he was assigned to command the 1st Battalion, 82nd Field Artillery, at Fort Bliss, Texas.

Lucas left Fort Bliss in June 1931 to enroll in the Army War College, from which he graduated in June 1932. Posted to the Personnel Division (G-1), of the War Department General Staff in 1932, he was promoted to lieutenant colonel in 1935, then, in 1936–37, commanded the 1st Field Artillery Regiment at Fort Bragg. From December 1937 to July 1940 he served on the Field Artillery Board.

After brief service as commander of the 4th Field Artillery in 1940, Lucas was promoted to brigadier general and assigned command of the 2nd Infantry Division. In July 1941, Lucas transferred to command of the 3rd Infantry Division and was promoted to temporary major general on August 5. After conducting successful amphibious maneuvers in Puget Sound, he was assigned command of III Corps, based in Georgia, during April 1942–May 1943.

In the spring of 1943, Lucas was sent to England as a staff officer to the supreme Allied commander, Europe, General DWIGHT D. EISENHOWER. In September, he was transferred to a field command as commander of VI Corps, Fifth Army, and led these troops in the ITALIAN CAMPAIGN through fighting at Campania and to the Venafro line. Lucas was next assigned to land his corps at Anzio (January 22, 1944) during the ANZIO CAMPAIGN in an effort to swing around the German defenses to take Rome. The methodical Lucas moved with an excess of caution (in large part because higher command had never made his objectives clear) and proved unable to do more than secure a beachhead before German forces blocked him. This brought intense criticism from the British Mediterranean Theater commander, General HAROLD ALEXANDER, and prompted Eisenhower to replace Lucas with the more aggressive LUCIAN K. TRUSCOTT. Lucas was returned to the United States, where he was assigned in March to command the Fourth Army in Texas.

Following the war, from June 1946 to January 1948, Lucas served as chief of the U.S. military advisory group to the Nationalist (Kuomintang—KMT) forces of Generalissimo CHIANG KAI-SHEK in his struggle against the Communists during the civil war in China. Promoted to the permanent rank of major general (retroactive to August 1944) at the end of his Chinese assignment, Lucas returned to the United States as deputy commander of the Fifth Army, headquartered in Chicago, and served in this capacity until his death.

Further reading: Blumenson, Martin. *Anzio.* New York: Cooper Square Press, 2001; Lamb, Richard. *War in Italy 1943–1945: A Brutal Story.* New York: Da Capo Press, 1996; Sassman, Roger W. *Operation SHINGLE and Major General John P. Lucas.* Carlisle, Pa.: U.S. Army War College, 1999.

Lumsden, Herbert (1894–1945) *British commander in France and North Africa*

Born in 1894, Lumsden did not join the British army until the outbreak of World War II in 1939. A colonel leading an armored car regiment, Lumsden was part of the British Expeditionary Force sent to fight the BATTLE OF FRANCE. He distinguished himself during the DUNKIRK EVACUATION.

In January 1942 Lumsden led the 1st British Armored Division in the NORTH AFRICAN CAM-

PAIGNS, but was severely wounded early in the fighting. He returned to duty in May 1942 and, after NEIL RICHIE, his commanding officer, was defeated at the BATTLE OF GAZALA (near Tobruk, Libya) in June, the new Eighth Army commander, BERNARD LAW MONTGOMERY, promoted him to command of the new X Corps. Although Lumsden incurred heavy losses in the battle at Kidney Hill during October 27–November 4 (see EL ALAMEIN, BATTLES OF), he achieved his objective, breaking through the Afrika Korps lines and taking El Agheila.

Lumsden and Montgomery were both strongly individualistic commanders, who, following El Alamein, fell to disputing over the conduct of the Desert War. At length, on December 13, 1942, Montgomery relieved Lumsden and replaced him with Brian Horrocks.

A tough fighter, Lumsden earned the admiration of Prime Minister WINSTON CHURCHILL, who sent him in 1944 to serve on the staff of DOUGLAS MACARTHUR in the Pacific theater. On January 6, 1945, while aboard the USS *New Mexico* observing the bombardment of Lingayen Gulf (see PHILIPPINES, FALL AND RECONQUEST OF), Lumsden was mortally wounded in a KAMIKAZE attack. He was buried at sea.

Further reading: Barnett, Correlli. *The Desert Generals.* New York: Sterling, 2000; Moorehead, Alan. *Desert War: The North African Campaign 1940–1943.* New York: Penguin, 2001.

Luzon, Battle of

Victory on land at the BATTLE OF LEYTE, in concert with the naval victory in the BATTLE OF LEYTE GULF, was the opening act in DOUGLAS MACARTHUR's promised return to the PHILIPPINES. These two battles allowed MacArthur to launch an amphibious invasion of Luzon, the principal island of the vast Philippine archipelago.

Preliminary to the invasion of Luzon was the landing by U.S. Eighth Army units under ROBERT EICHELBERGER on Mindoro, south of Luzon, on December 15, 1945. At San José, the infantry

secured a large beachhead and immediately scratched out two airfields to accommodate air support for the Luzon operation.

On Luzon, Japanese general YAMASHITA TOMOYUKI prepared his defenses by dividing the Fourteenth Japanese Army into three defensive groups: Shobu (140,000 men) in the north, Kembu (30,000) in the center, and Shimbu (80,000) in the south. The Japanese also unleashed a massive KAMIKAZE campaign against the ships of the Third Fleet (under WILLIAM HALSEY), which furnished carrier-launched air support, and the Seventh Fleet (THOMAS KINKAID), which provided principal transport for the U.S. Sixth Army invaders under WALTER KRUEGER. Kamikaze attacks sank 20 U.S. ships and severely damaged another 24.

Krueger landed at Lingayen Gulf on January 9, 1945—68,000 men in that first day—and immediately began a drive inland, penetrating 40 miles by January 20. I Corps, which pushed eastward, encountered the heaviest initial opposition from Yamashita's Shobu Group. Eichelberger kept pouring in reinforcements, including the 158th Regiment, the 25th Infantry Division, and the 32nd Infantry Division. (Notably, during this titanic battle, a detachment of army Rangers staged a raid behind Japanese lines to liberate several hundred Allied prisoners at Cabanatuan.)

While I Corps and its reinforcements slugged it out with Shobu group, XIV Corps, to the right of I Corps, advanced rapidly southward across the Central Plain of Luzon. It reached Clark Field—held by the Japanese since the beginning of the war—on January 23 and, within a week, secured this major base installation while also penetrating 25 miles farther south to Calumpit.

To the right of XIV Corps, XI Corps landed at San Antonio on January 29 and squared off against Kembu group. Fighting in concert with Filipino guerrillas, the 38th and 24th Infantry divisions of XI Corps sealed off the Bataan Peninsula after Bataan and Corregidor had been liberated. On February 2, Krueger sent XIV Corps on a rapid advance to Manila, the 1st Cavalry Division reaching the outskirts of the Filipino capital on the night of February 3–4, liberating 3,500 Allied prisoners held at Santo Tomas University. On the following night, the 37th Infantry advanced into northwestern Manila and liberated another 1,300 prisoners from Bilibid Prison.

The Japanese withdrew behind the Pasig River, where they mounted a desperate resistance, holding off the U.S. advance for a month and, in the process, razing most of Manila. In this combat of attrition, 16,000 Japanese defenders died before Manila fell to U.S. forces on March 4.

During the fight for Manila, I Corps, to the north, struggled against the Shobu group defenses in rugged mountainous terrain. The 6th Infantry broke through Bongabon to the east coast on February 14, 1945, then moved to the Manila front. Baguio, the Philippine summer capital, fell on April 27, followed by Santa Fe, a major Japanese communications center, on May 27. These two cities taken, the 37th Division advanced down Cagayan Valley, by June 26 splitting the Shobu group in two, rendering both fragments incapable of mounting any significant counterattack.

In the meantime, to the south—east of Manila—XI Corps confronted the Shimbu group's defensive line. The 6th and 43rd Infantry and the 1st Cavalry became all but stalled in the Sierra Madre, pushing back Japanese defenders by inches. Elements of XIV Corps also drove southeast toward and down the Bicol Peninsula, where resistance was not ended until June 1.

On July 1 the Eighth Army took over the campaign on Luzon, freeing up the Sixth Army for the planned invasion of Japan scheduled to begin in the fall. On July 4, General MacArthur declared Luzon secure.

Further reading: Morison, Samuel Eliot. *History of United States Naval Operations in World War II: The Liberation of the Philippines—Luzon, Mindanao, the Visayas, 1944–1945.* Urbana: University of Illinois Press, 2000.

M

MacArthur, Douglas (1880–1964) *supreme commander, Allied forces in the Southwest Pacific*

Douglas MacArthur was literally born into the United States Army, at Little Rock Barracks, Arkansas, the son of Arthur MacArthur, destined to earn the Medal of Honor and become the army's senior-ranking officer. MacArthur received an appointment to West Point, from which he graduated in 1903, first in his class. Commissioned a second lieutenant of engineers, he was sent to the Philippines, then served as aide-de-camp to his father during a military tour of Asia in 1905–06. In 1906, he was appointed aide to President Theodore Roosevelt and served until the following year, when he was given command of a company of the 3rd Engineers at Fort Leavenworth, Kansas, through 1909. He taught at the General Service and Cavalry Schools from 1909 to 1912, then was appointed to the General Staff, serving from 1913 to 1917. During this period, MacArthur fought in the military intervention at Veracruz, Mexico, during April–November 1914.

When the United States entered World War I in April 1917, MacArthur took a leading role in the creation of the 42nd "Rainbow" Division. He served as the division's chief of staff when it was sent to France in October 1917. MacArthur saw action at Aisne-Marne (July 25–August 2), then commanded a brigade during the assault on the Saint-Mihiel salient from September 12 to September 17. He also led a brigade at Meuse-Argonne (October 4–November 11, 1918) and commanded the entire Rainbow Division in the "race to Sedan" at the end of the war (November 6–11). MacArthur served with occupation forces in Germany after the armistice. On his return to the United States in April 1919, he was appointed superintendent of West Point.

MacArthur left West Point in 1922 to accept a command as major general in the Philippines. He

MacArthur observes Philippine operations with Vice Admiral Thomas Kinkaid, February 1944. *(National Archives and Records Administration)*

remained there until January 1925, returning to the United States until 1928, when he went back to the Philippines as commander of the Department of the Philippines through 1930. When he returned to the United States again in 1930, it was as chief of staff of the U.S. Army, the most senior post in the service.

In 1932, while serving as chief of staff, MacArthur personally led a detachment of troops to suppress the so-called Bonus Army (World War I veterans who demanded early payment of promised government moneys during the worst of the Great Depression) and drive them out of Washington, D.C. MacArthur exceeded his orders, acting not only against the Bonus marchers in the city, but raiding and razing an encampment just outside of town, at Anacostia Flats. Unseemly and brutal, the action brought upon MacArthur considerable negative publicity.

In October 1935, MacArthur stepped down as chief of staff to return to the Philippines to organize its military defenses in preparation for its assumption of full independence from the United States. When the new government of the Philippine Commonwealth bestowed on MacArthur the grandiose title of field marshal in August 1936, he resigned his U.S. Army commission to accept the appointment. Although he did not want to be transferred from the Philippines before completing preparations for its defense, MacArthur did accept recall to American service on the eve of war with Japan (July 26, 1941). He was promoted to lieutenant general and given overall command of U.S. Army Forces in the Far East (USAFFE), with his headquarters in Manila, Philippine Islands.

Like other senior American officers, MacArthur was stunned by the Japanese attack on PEARL HARBOR on December 7, 1941, and was unprepared for Japanese air attacks on Clark and Iba airfields in the Philippines, which followed on December 8. Nevertheless, hopelessly undermanned and underequipped, MacArthur mounted a skillful and determined defense of the islands, prudently withdrawing to fortified positions on Bataan during a long fighting retreat (December 23, 1941–January 1,

1942) that inflicted heavy casualties on Japanese ground forces.

MacArthur personally commanded the defense of Bataan and the Manila Bay forts until President FRANKLIN D. ROOSEVELT ordered his evacuation to Australia. He embarked on a harrowing escape aboard a PT boat on March 11, 1942, promising in a radio broadcast from Australia, "I shall return." They were three of the most famous words spoken during the war.

MacArthur was awarded the Medal of Honor for his defense of the Philippines and was named, in April, supreme commander of Allied forces in the Southwest Pacific Area. He assumed a leading role in laying out Allied Pacific strategy, beginning with the reconquest of NEW GUINEA as a first step in the liberation of the Pacific. During July–September 1942, MacArthur successfully planned and directed the repulse of a Japanese assault on Port Moresby—the loss of which would have doomed Australia to invasion (see PORT MORESBY, DEFENSE OF). Having defended that portion of New Guinea, he boldly assumed the offensive and advanced across the Owen Stanley Range during September–November, to attack and take the Buna-Gona fortifications during November 20, 1942–January 22, 1943 (see BUNA, BATTLE OF, and GONA, BATTLE OF).

With these victories achieved, MacArthur carried out an ISLAND HOPPING STRATEGY by which the Allied forces ultimately retook the Pacific islands in an inexorable advance against the Japanese homeland.

After campaigning along the north coast of New Guinea, MacArthur invaded western New Britain during December 15–30, 1943, cutting off the major Japanese base at RABAUL. Victories at Hollandia, Jayapura, and Aitape followed, cutting off and isolating the Japanese Eighteenth Army in April 1944. From here, MacArthur advanced west along the New Guinea coast, taking Sansapor on July 30, then, in September, coordinating a massive offensive with Admiral CHESTER NIMITZ in the central Pacific. While MacArthur's forces took Morotai in the Molucca islands, Nimitz first pounded and then invaded the Palau islands.

On October 20, 1944, MacArthur opened the reconquest of the PHILIPPINES by personally commanding landings at LEYTE, thereby redeeming his pledge to return to the islands. MacArthur concentrated on the expansion of Philippine operations to Mindoro on December 1, 1944, and LUZON on January 9, 1945. Following the successful conclusion of the Luzon campaign, MacArthur liberated the rest of the Philippines. While this effort was under way, his forces captured the coastal oil fields of Borneo, which fueled much of the Japanese war effort.

In April 1945, MacArthur was named commander of all U.S. ground forces in the Pacific and would therefore command the anticipated invasion of Japan. This operation was made unnecessary by the atomic bombing of HIROSHIMA and NAGASAKI in August, which moved the Japanese to surrender before the invasion was launched. MacArthur was promoted to the five-star rank of general of the army and given the honor of accepting the Japanese surrender, which took place aboard the U.S. battleship *Missouri* riding at anchor in Tokyo Bay on September 2, 1945.

Douglas MacArthur brilliantly made the transition from wartime commander to head of the U.S. occupation government in Japan. He administered the devastated nation with a strong hand tempered by a benevolence and good judgment that made him an enormously popular figure among the Japanese people and politicians alike. He promoted not only the physical and economic recovery of Japan, but oversaw its rapid transition to democratic government.

While administering the postwar Japanese government, MacArthur remained in command of U.S. Far Eastern forces, and when the Korean War began on June 25, 1950, with the North Korean invasion of South Korea, he was named supreme commander of United Nations forces in Korea by a UN Security Council resolution of July 8. He directed the defense of the Pusan perimeter during August 5–September 15, then planned and executed the most brilliant military operation of his career by landing an amphibious assault force at Inchon on September 15, thereby surprising and rapidly enveloping the North Koreans, pushing the invaders back into the north. After securing both UN and U.S. approval to invade North Korea in October, he drove the communist forces all the way to the Yalu River, North Korea's border with Manchuria.

Although MacArthur assured President HARRY S. TRUMAN that the Communist Chinese would not join in the war, massive numbers of Chinese troops crossed the Yalu during November 25–26, 1950, driving the United Nations and South Korean relentlessly southward. MacArthur conducted a fighting withdrawal, finally setting up a defensive front just south of the South Korean capital of Seoul. He now publicly advocated a dramatic expansion of the war, including bombing targets (even with nuclear weapons) in China itself. President Truman and others, fearing a new and cataclysmic world war, vetoed the proposal. When MacArthur persisted beyond the point of insubordination, Truman relieved him of command on April 11, 1951, even though he had recaptured Seoul on March 14.

Replaced by Lieutenant General MATTHEW RIDGWAY, MacArthur returned to the United States a national hero. On April 19, 1951, he delivered a memorable retirement address to Congress, which included the valediction, "old soldiers never die, they just fade away," and, amid talk of his running for president, he retired from public life.

Further reading: MacArthur, Douglas, *Reminiscences.* Annapolis, Md.: Naval Institute Press, 2001; Manchester, William. *American Caesar: Douglas MacArthur 1880–1964.* New York: Laurel, 1983; Perret, Geoffrey. *Old Soldiers Never Die: The Life of Douglas MacArthur.* Avon, Mass.: Adams Media, 1997.

machine gun

The machine gun was first used extensively in World War I, where it revealed itself to be perhaps the most important defensive weapon of the war, enabling one or two soldiers to defend a trench or other protected position against the onslaught of many times their number. In World War II, the weapon was also used extensively.

BRITISH AND COMMONWEALTH
MACHINE GUNS

Besa Marks 1-3. Originally licensed from a Czech manufacturer, the weapon was produced in Britain by the Birmingham Small Arms Company. It fired 7.62 mm rounds at 500–700 rounds per minute.

Mk 1 Bren Gun. A magazine-fed 7.62 mm weapon, the Bren fired 500 rounds per minute and was light enough to be issued to front-line combat troops, yet sufficiently potent to serve as an antiaircraft weapon.

Vickers .303. This water-cooled weapon fired .303-caliber rounds at 500 rounds per minute.

FRENCH MACHINE GUNS

Fusil Mitrailleur Modèles 1924/29U. Modeled after the American BROWNING AUTOMATIC RIFLE, this weapon fired a 7.5 mm round from a 25-round box.

Mitrailleuse MLE 1931. A modification of the Fusil Mitrailleur Modeles 1924/29U, this weapon was designed to be fired from tanks and other vehicles. It fired 750 rounds per minute from a 150-round drum magazine.

GERMAN MACHINE GUNS

MG34. This versatile standard-issue weapon fired 7.92 mm rounds at up to 900 rounds per minute. It could be fitted to tanks and other vehicles or carried into action by infantrymen.

MG42. An improvement on the MG34, this weapon fired at nearly twice the rate of the earlier gun.

JAPANESE MACHINE GUNS

Type 11. A light weapon, the "Nambu" (as soldiers called it) fired 6.4 mm rounds from a 30-round hopper at the rate of 500 rounds per minute.

Type 96. An improved version of the "Nambu," the weapon had a quick-change barrel (to prevent overheating), interchangeable sights, and a fixed bayonet.

SOVIET MACHINE GUNS

DSHK1938. A five-inch wheeled gun, the DSHK1938 fired 550 .5-inch rounds per minute and was belt-fed.

SG43. The standard-issue light machine gun of the Red Army, this weapon used 7.62 mm rounds, which it fired at 600 rounds per minute, fed from a belt.

UNITED STATES MACHINE GUNS

Browning Automatic Rifle. See BROWNING AUTOMATIC RIFLE (BAR).

M-1919A4. Air-cooled and belt-fed, this Browning weapon fired 400 to 500 rounds per minute and was used in a wide variety of settings, from vehicles to ships.

M-2HB. The Browning ".50 cal" attained iconic status by the end of World War II. It was used in every conceivable mount, including aircraft, antiaircraft, ships, and armored vehicles. The weapons fired a variety of ammunition, from standard machine gun ammo to armor-piercing rounds, to tracer bullets, to incendiary munitions. It was the workhorse machine gun of the U.S. armed forces.

Further reading: Walter, John. *Machine-Guns of Two World Wars.* London: Greenhill Books, 2005.

Mackesy, Pierse (1883–1956) *commanding officer, Allied Land Forces, Narvik Area, Norway*

Mackesy joined the British army's Royal Engineers in 1902 and served in Africa, surveying the Ashanti and Northern Territories of the Gold Coast (present-day Ghana) as Deputy Director of Surveys, Gold Coast, from 1911 to 1914. During World War I, he served in Togoland and Cameroons (1914), then was sent to France, where, from 1917 to 1919, he was staff officer to Chief Engineer, Army Corps, France. After the war he served on the Military Mission to South Russia (1919–20).

Mackesy was appointed instructor at the Staff College, Quetta, India (present-day Pakistan), serving here from 1927 to 1930. He served on the staff of the War Office from 1932 to 1935 in London, then was assigned command of 3rd Infantry Brigade, with service in Britain and Palestine during 1935–38. On his return to Britain in 1938, he was assigned as commander of the West Riding Division and Area of the Territorial Army, serving in this capacity until 1940.

Mackesy was the commanding officer of Allied Land Forces, Narvik Area, Norway, in 1940 (*see* NARVIK, BATTLES OF). He retired later in the year but returned to serve in the War Office through part of 1941 before leaving the army to become military correspondent for the *Daily Telegraph* (1941–42). After the war, Mackesy served as councilor, Southwold Borough Council (1946–53), and as mayor of Southwold, from 1949 to 1952.

Further reading: Kersaudy, François. *Norway 1940.* Lincoln: University of Nebraska Press, 1998.

Macmillan, Harold (1894–1986) *British minister resident, Mediterranean Command, postwar prime minister*

Born in London, the son of an American-born mother and grandson of the founder of the famed British publishing house that bears his surname, Harold Macmillan graduated from Balliol College, Oxford, and fought with distinction in World War I. He was a member of Parliament from 1924 to 1929 and from 1931 to 1964.

Macmillan was an outspoken opponent of the APPEASEMENT POLICY of Prime Minister NEVILLE CHAMBERLAIN, a stance that gained the attention of WINSTON CHURCHILL, who, after he became prime minister, appointed Macmillan parliamentary secretary to the Ministry of Supply. He next served as colonial undersecretary before being sent, on December 30, 1942, to northwest Africa as the British minister resident in Allied Forces Headquarters, Mediterranean Command. Macmillan dealt with DWIGHT D. EISENHOWER on a daily basis, and also with other top Allied leaders.

Immediately after the conclusion of the war in Europe, Macmillan was named secretary of state for air, serving in this capacity from May to July 1945, when Churchill was defeated in his bid for reelection. With the return of the Conservative government in 1951, Macmillan served as minister of housing and local government (October 1951) and minister of defense (October 1954),

under Churchill, then as foreign secretary (April–December 1955) and chancellor of the exchequer (1955–57) under ANTHONY EDEN. Appointed prime minister on January 10, 1957, after Eden resigned amid the Suez crisis, Macmillan was elected leader of the Conservative Party on January 22. Macmillan resigned office on October 18, 1963, due to illness, and left the House of Commons in September 1964. He devoted the rest of his long life to writing a distinguished series of memoirs.

Further reading: Macmillan, Harold. *Winds of Change, 1914–1939.* New York: Harper and Row, 1966; Macmillan, Harold. *The Blast of War, 1939–1945* New York: Harper and Row, 1967; Macmillan, Harold. *Tides of Fortune, 1945–1955* New York: Harper and Row, 1969.

Madagascar, Battle of

At the outbreak of World War II, Madagascar was a French colonial island off the coast of East Africa. After the fall of France in the BATTLE OF FRANCE, the governor of Madagascar rallied to the cause of Free France at the call of CHARLES DE GAULLE, but then resigned after the British attack on the French fleet at the BATTLE OF MERS-EL-KEBIR in July 1940. He was replaced by an official of the VICHY GOVERNMENT.

When British intercepts of Japanese coded messages revealed that Germany had asked Japan to occupy Madagascar, Major General Robert Sturges was ordered to capture the naval base of Diégo Suarez on the northern end of the island. The landing, using a mixed force of British, British East African, and South African troops, was carried out on May 5, 1942, and was the first major British AMPHIBIOUS WARFARE of World War II.

The landing achieved total surprise, followed by stout resistance from the French. Sturges ordered an attack on the night of May 6–7, and the French troops surrendered by morning. The Vichy governor, however, refused to capitulate and instead withdrew to the south of the island with the forces that remained loyal to him. At this point, the British, at the urging of South Africa's Marshal JAN CHRISTIAAN SMUTS, revised and expanded their original plan beyond the capture of Diégo Suarez. More landings were made on September 10 and afterward, which resulted in an armistice on November 5. Control of Madagascar thus passed to the Free French.

See also MAGIC (JAPANESE CODE).

Further reading: Osborne, Richard. *World War II in Colonial Africa.* Indianapolis: Riebel-Roque, 2001.

MAGIC (Japanese code)

The term "MAGIC" was often used by the Allies in World War II to refer to all Japanese military and diplomatic communications, but it was officially intended more narrowly to refer to the U.S. decrypts of secret Japanese diplomatic (not military) communications.

The most important MAGIC decrypts were of codes encrypted by a machine codenamed by the Allies PURPLE. U.S. intelligence was able to read most of the PURPLE ciphers well before the outbreak of World War II and thus had a unique over-the-shoulder perspective on prewar Japanese diplomatic communications. Despite this, MAGIC provided no specific information warning of the attack on PEARL HARBOR. Throughout the war, MAGIC not only yielded insight into Japanese diplomacy, but, indirectly, it provided a picture of German diplomacy as well—via comments relayed by the Japanese using the PURPLE cipher machine. Decrypts of MAGIC communications continued until the end of the war; the Japanese apparently never suspected that their principal diplomatic ciphers had been thoroughly compromised.

See also ULTRA.

Further reading: Lewin, Ronald. *The American Magic: Codes, Ciphers, and the Defeat of Japan.* New York: Penguin, 1983.

Maginot Line

Named for André Maginot, the French minister of war who began its construction between World War I and World War II, the Maginot Line was a series of fortifications running from Switzerland to the Luxembourg and Belgian borders, as well as in southern France. Its sole purpose was to deter a German invasion.

The Maginot Line fortifications were state-of-the-art, and the entire complex was a marvel of military engineering. The installation was also symptomatic of the myopic French focus on defensive warfare, which did not adequately anticipate the effectiveness of highly mobile offensive warfare (BLITZKRIEG). Nor did the French anticipate an invasion via neutral Belgium, which allowed the Germans merely to outflank the Maginot Line during the initial stages of the BATTLE OF FRANCE in May 1940.

The Maginot Line did hold against an Italian attempt to breach it in the south of France in June 1940, and where the Germans actually challenged the line, it also held well—the 400,000 French troops who garrisoned the line refusing to surrender. By the same token, the manpower requirements of the Maginot Line served to keep those 400,000 men from participating in the main battle, where they might have been used to greater effect.

The Maginot Line dramatically demonstrated the failure of defensive thinking and fixed fortifications in an age of high explosives, total war, and highly mobile combat.

Further reading: Allcorn, William. *The Maginot Line 1928–45.* London: Osprey, 2003; Kaufmann, J. E., H. W. Kaufmann, and Tomasz Idzikowski. *Fortress France: The Maginot Line and French Defenses in World War II.* New York: Praeger, 2005; Kaufmann, J. E., and H. W. Kaufmann. *The Maginot Line.* New York: Praeger, 1997.

Makin Island Raid

In August 1942, Carlson's Raiders, led by EVANS CARLSON, mounted a raid against the Japanese garrison on this northernmost atoll of the Gilbert Islands. The purpose of the raid was to decoy the garrison during the landings at GUADALCANAL.

Operationally, the raid was innovative and successful. A force of 222 USMC raiders (2nd Raider Battalion) was transported 2,000 miles by submarine, then landed without detection. Strategically, the effect of the raid was counterproductive. It did relatively little damage, yet it prompted the Japanese to reinforce and fortify the adjacent island of Tarawa, which made the subsequent BATTLE OF TARAWA ATOLL very costly for the U.S. Marines who landed there in November 1943.

Further reading: Smith, George H. *Carlson's Raid: The Daring Marine Assault on Makin.* New York: Berkley, 2003.

Malaya, fall of

During the night of December 7–8, 1941, elements of the Twenty-Fifth Japanese Army (YAMASHITA TOMOYUKI) under naval cover from ships of the Japanese Southern Force, invaded northern Malaya and southern Thailand preparatory to an assault on SINGAPORE.

The Malayan Campaign began early on the morning of December 7, even before the BATTLE OF PEARL HARBOR, and was therefore the first Japanese act of aggression in the Pacific. Yamashita deployed 60,000 men, supported by 158 naval aircraft and 459 aircraft of 3rd Air Division to attack Malaya. The Anglo-Indian garrison on the island was taken by surprise, quickly lost the ability to maneuver, and was unable to defend its handful of air bases.

Yamashita's first landings, at Singora and Patani in southern Thailand, were unopposed. His next landings, on the northern Malayan coast, were inadequately met. Although the British commander in chief, Far East, Air Chief Marshal Robert Brooke-Popham, had a superior force of 88,600 Australian, British, Indian, and Malay troops under the direct command of Lieutenant General ARTHUR PERCIVAL, they were inadequately equipped with just 158 obsolete or obsolescent aircraft and no tanks.

Before the war, British planners had clearly recognized the importance of adequately defending Malaya because of its position with regard to Singapore. An enemy who took Malaya would possess the means of invading Singapore from the rear. Accordingly, a plan (known as MATADOR) was drawn up before the war to occupy Singora-Patani in Thailand, thereby interdicting any Japanese landing there. Political considerations, however, prevented implementation, and orders were not given to occupy defensive positions around Jitra until a full 10 hours after the Japanese had landed. The delay enabled the Japanese to seize control of the airfields at Singora and Patani. They were thus able to hit Anglo-Indian installations freely and frequently.

While the ground battle was rapidly developing into a British disaster, at sea the Japanese sank the *Prince of Wales* and the *Repulse,* two major Royal Navy ships.

Yamashita moved with great speed, quickly occupying Bangkok and sweeping aside all resistance at Jitra. The Japanese invaders also secured the cooperation of the Malayan civilian population and were thereby enabled to advance to the south with extraordinary rapidity, so that the Anglo-Indian defenders were repeatedly outflanked.

On January 11, 1942, Yamashita took Kuala Lumpur, forcing the British III Corps to retreat to Johore. A new force, designated Westforce and made up of the 8th Australian and 9th Indian Divisions, was quickly assembled to check the main Japanese advance in the west. Shortly after this, "Eastforce," consisting of the 22nd Australian Brigade and other units, was created with the intention of blocking the Japanese advance down the east coast. Both of these units were readily defeated, and by January 31, 1942, all British, Indian, and Australian forces had withdrawn to Singapore, which was now rendered highly vulnerable and ripe for invasion.

Further reading: Bayly, Christopher, and Tim Harper. *Forgotten Armies: The Fall of British Asia, 1941–1945.* Cambridge, Mass.: Belknap Press, 2005; Farrell, Brian P. *The Defence and Fall of Singapore 1940–1942.* Stroud, U.K.: Tempus, 2005; Glover, Edwin M. *In 70 Days: The Story of the Japanese Campaign in British Malaya.* London: F. Muller, 1946.

Malayan Campaign, December 1941–January 1942

KRA ISTHMUS

from Bangkok
IG

Singora

THAILAND

Patani

25th Army (Yamashita)

Jitra

11 Indian

Georgetown

Kroh

Khota Bharu

9 Indian

Penang

Taiping

Ipoh

MALAYA

Legend:
- → Japanese advance
- IG Imperial Guards
- ✈ British airfield
- ✸ Sunken British ship
- ⊠ Allied infantry division
- ▦ Allied corps

9 Indian
Type and size of military unit   Name of military unit

0 — 100 miles
0 — 100 km

South China Sea

N

Kuala Selangor

Kuala Lumpur
Jan. 11

Kuantan

Port Swettenham

Strait of Malacca

3 Perceval

Malacca

Endau

8 Australian

Repulse *sunk* December 10

Prince of Wales *sunk* December 10

Sumatra
(DUTCH EAST INDIES)

Johore Bharu

Singapore

© Infobase Publishing

Malinovsky, Rodion (1898–1967) *Soviet Red Army commander*

A Ukrainian, born in Odessa, Malinovsky was conscripted into the tsar's army at the outbreak of World War I. He joined the revolutionary Red Army in 1919 and fought in the Russian civil war, rising in rank to command a battalion. Malinovsky joined the Communist Party in 1926 and attended the Frunze Military Academy, graduating in 1930. During the Spanish civil war (1936–39), he served as an adviser to the Republicans.

During the German INVASION OF THE SOVIET UNION, Malinovsky commanded the 48th Rifle Corps, rose rapidly to command of the Sixth Army, then was put in charge of the South Front (army group). He led the Second Guards Army during the BATTLE OF STALINGRAD in December 1942 and took charge of offensives in Romania (late 1944) and Austria (spring of 1945).

After the war ended, during 1945–55, Malinovsky served in Soviet-held Manchuria and the Soviet Far East. He was named first deputy minister of defense and commander in chief of ground forces in 1956 and was elevated to full membership in the Central Committee of the Communist Party. During the height of the cold war, from 1957 to 1967, Malinovsky guided the expansion of the Soviet military.

Further reading: Beevor, Antony. *Stalingrad: The Fateful Siege, 1942–1943.* New York: Penguin, 1999; Beevor, Antony. *The Spanish Civil War.* New York: Penguin, 2001; Seaton, Albert. *Russo-German War, 1941–45.* Novato, Calif.: Presidio Press, 1993.

Malmédy massacre

During the BATTLE OF THE ARDENNES (BATTLE OF THE BULGE), at Baugnez near Malmédy, Belgium, on December 17, 1944, SS Standartenführer (colonel) JOACHIM PEIPER's special Kampfgruppe (battle group) summarily executed 86 U.S. prisoners of war in an atrocity that became infamous as the Malmédy Massacre. During World War II, the killing of enemy combatants who had surrendered and had been disarmed was forbidden by the GENEVA CONVENTIONS and was universally considered a war crime.

After the war, the commander of Sixth SS Panzer Army, General SEPP DIETRICH, along with Peiper and two other commanding officers, were found guilty of having issued illegal orders. Sixty-nine other German soldiers were also tried for complicity in the executions in a trial that began in May 1946. All were found guilty; Peiper and 42 others were sentenced to death, and 22 others, including Dietrich, were sentenced to life imprisonment.

Subsequently, U.S. prosecutors admitted to having coerced confessions by threatening execution, introducing false witnesses, and even staging

Discovery of the Malmédy massacre *(Army Medical Department)*

mock trials. The cases were appealed and reviewed, and all were initially reduced, then reduced even further after it was determined that all the suspects had been variously abused.

In March 1949, the Senate Armed Services Committee investigated the prosecution and concluded that the army had acted improperly. Senator Joseph McCarthy of Wisconsin, who would soon become infamous himself for his anti-Communist "witch hunts," accused the army of employing the tactics of the Nazi GESTAPO and then engaging in a cover-up. In the end, all of the death sentences were vacated. Dietrich was paroled in 1955, and Peiper released in 1956.

Further reading: Bauserman, John M. *The Malmédy Massacre.* Shippensburg, Pa.: White Mane, 2002; Weingartner, James. *A Peculiar Crusade: Willis M. Everett and the Malmédy Massacre Trial.* New York: New York University Press, 2000.

Malta, siege of

Malta, a British Mediterranean island colony (World War II–era population, 270,000), was subjected to severe aerial bombardment by Germany but refused to surrender, thereby continuing to play a key role in Allied MEDITERRANEAN OPERATIONS.

Until May 1942, Malta's governor, Lieutenant General WILLIAM DOBBIE, served as commander in charge of the island's defenses. Afterward General Lord Gort held this post. Malta's military significance lay in its airfields and harbor—the only British harbor between Gibraltar and Alexandria, Egypt. British offensive operations against Axis convoys supplying forces in North Africa were launched from Malta. The strategic location of Malta also made it highly vulnerable to attack. It was close to Sicily, yet far from any other British base. British commanders feared an invasion, and, indeed, the Axis leaders contemplated just that; however, they restricted their assault against the island to aerial bombardment.

Malta first fell under attack, from Italian bombers, on June 11, 1940. The Luftwaffe, flying from Sicilian bases, carried out more raids from January through April 1941. In July 1941, Italy's Tenth Light Flotilla attacked Valetta Harbor but failed either to destroy or take it. By this time, the Germans had diverted most of their Luftwaffe effort to the INVASION OF THE SOVIET UNION, thereby giving the islanders a reprieve. Beginning in December, however, the raids were resumed and picked up in intensity. From January 1 to July 24, 1942, air raids were a daily event, and the people of Malta took to living in underground shelters. Held under siege from the air, the population suffered severe privation, including malnutrition and epidemic disease. Civilian bombing casualties were 1,493 dead and 3,764 wounded.

British high command sent fighter squadrons to help protect the island, and fast convoys kept up a flow of supplies, despite Axis attacks on the ships. Of 86 vessels sent to the island between August 1940 and August 1942, 31 were sunk and others were damaged. The Axis also laid mines so thickly that by the spring of 1942, resupply had become all but impossible. With uncharacteristic optimism, German general ALBERT KESSELRING reported Malta "neutralized" on May 10, 1942. This led to another respite for the island, and bought time for the arrival of fighter reinforcements. By the middle of July, the Luftwaffe raids had decreased, and mine-clearing operations had made a path for resupply—although food shortages remained critical.

In October 1942, Kesselring resumed air raids, but Axis losses in the NORTH AFRICAN CAMPAIGNS, especially at the BATTLE OF EL ALAMEIN, deprived him of airfields, and the air raids were called off. With the Axis withdrawal from Africa in May 1943, the siege of Malta, the most thoroughly bombed island in World War II, ended. The courage and fortitude of the entire island was recognized by the British Crown by the award of the George Cross.

Further reading: Bradford, Ernle. *Siege: Malta 1940–1943*. London: Pen & Sword Military Classics, 2003; Holland, James. *Fortress Malta: An Island Under Siege 1940–43*. New York: Miramax Books, 2003.

Mandalay, Battle of

Fought between the Fourteenth British Army (WILLIAM SLIM) and the Fifteenth Japanese Army (Shihachi Katamura) in March 1945 during the BURMA CAMPAIGN, the Battle of Mandalay resulted in a British victory.

Japanese bombers virtually destroyed Mandalay in April 1942, leaving it to occupation by the anti-British nationalist forces known as the Burma Independence Army, which collaborated with the Japanese. Slim recaptured Mandalay, routing Shihachi and thereby opening the way to the capture of Rangoon.

Further reading: Astor, Gerald. *The Jungle War: Mavericks, Marauders and Madmen in the China-Burma-India Theater of World War II*. New York: Wiley, 2004; Dupuy, Trevor N. *Asiatic Land Battles: Allied Victories in China and Burma*. New York: Franklin Watts, 1963; Hogan, David W. *India-Burma (The U.S. Army Campaigns of World War II)*. Carlisle, Pa.: Army Center of Military History, 1991; Webster, Donovan. *The Burma Road: The Epic Story of the China-Burma-India Theater in World War II*. New York: Farrar, Straus and Giroux, 2003.

Manhattan Project

Officially begun in 1942, the Manhattan Project was the largest wartime scientific and industrial project ever undertaken by the United States. Its object was to create and produce a practical atomic weapon.

The origin of the project may be traced to 1939, when a group of American scientists, including recent refugees from European fascist and Nazi regimes, became alarmed by what they knew to be work ongoing in Germany (led primarily by Werner Heisenberg) into nuclear fission, a process by which the energy of the binding force within the nucleus of the uranium or plutonium atom might be liberated to produce an explosion of unprecedented magnitude. These scientists decided to prevail upon the U.S. government to launch a project to develop fission for military purposes—before the German researchers could do so.

G. B. Pegram, a Columbia University physicist, brokered a meeting between the eminent Italian expatriate physicist Enrico Fermi and the U.S. Department of the Navy in March 1939. Leo Szilard, a Hungarian expatriate physicist, and other scientists prevailed on the nation's most celebrated refugee scientist, Albert Einstein, to write a letter to Franklin D. Roosevelt on August 2, 1939, advising the president of the urgent necessity of beginning work on a military fission project in light of the dangers posed by Germany. FDR responded, and in February 1940, the modest sum of $6,000 was authorized to begin research directed by a committee under the chairmanship of L. J. Briggs, head of the National Bureau of Standards. Direction of the research project was transferred on December 6, 1941, to the Office of Scientific Research and Development, headed by Vannevar Bush, another prominent scientist. The next day, the Battle of Pearl Harbor thrust the United States into World War II, and shortly after this, the War Department was given joint responsibility for the project. By the middle of 1942, project researchers had concluded that the military application of fission was feasible, but that many facilities, including laboratories and industrial plants, would be required; therefore, the War Department assigned the U.S. Army Corps of Engineers to manage the necessary construction work on an accelerated basis. Because most of the early research was being conducted at Columbia University, in Manhattan,

responsibility was assigned to the Corps's Manhattan Engineer District in June 1942. The army's direction quickly expanded beyond construction, and in September 1942 Brigadier General Leslie R. Groves, an army engineer who had directed design and construction of the brand-new Pentagon outside of Washington, D.C., was put in charge of all military and engineering aspects of what was now being called, after the Manhattan Engineer District, the Manhattan Project. Work and facilities would extend across the country, yet the project would remain top secret until the end of the war.

Beginning in autumn 1941 Pegram and fellow physicist Harold C. Urey were authorized by the U.S. government to travel to Britain, where fission research was ongoing, to establish cooperation between scientists in the two countries. By 1943, the United States established a joint policy committee with Great Britain and Canada, and a number of leading British and Canadian nuclear researchers came to the United States to work on the Manhattan Project. Thus, the work became an international effort among allies.

The Manhattan Project was a unique, superaccelerated program of scientific, military, and industrial collaboration and coordination on a vast scale. An entirely new and hitherto theoretical field had to be researched, the research rapidly transformed into practical demonstrations, and those demonstrations quickly prototyped into a workable fission weapon. The unknowns were staggering, and success was far from assured. Moreover, because of the necessity for speed, various research programs had to be conducted simultaneously in the full knowledge that some might prove costly dead ends. Even before research was completed, design and construction of critical production plants would have to get under way.

The first problem to be solved was how to separate uranium 235, the fissionable material that would be the heart of the bomb, from its companion isotope, uranium 238. A massive amount of U238 was required to obtain a minute amount of U235, which, however, could not even be separated from U238 by any known chemical means. An entirely novel physical process had to be invented.

Two major processes were identified: an electromagnetic process developed at the University of California, Berkeley, under Ernest Lawrence, and the diffusion process Urey developed at Columbia University. Both processes required huge, highly complex plants with access to very large amounts of electric power. Under normal circumstances, pilot plants would have been developed to determine which process was superior, after which major facilities would be constructed. Groves decided to save time by taking the bold—and costly—step of creating production facilities to implement both methods. Construction was begun at Oak Ridge, a 70-square-mile tract near Knoxville, Tennessee. Additionally, a third method, thermal diffusion, was employed to produce initial separation.

To complicate matters further, there was another candidate element suitable for fission, plutonium 239. Groves also authorized full-scale production of this material. Developed at the metallurgical laboratory of the University of Chicago under the direction of Arthur Compton, it could be produced only by transmuting U238 via a fission chain reaction. In December 1942, Fermi produced the world's first controlled fission chain reaction in a U238 reactor pile constructed beneath the stands of the University of Chicago's Stagg Field. If the so-called atomic age may be said to have had a specific birth, this was it. But to produce sufficient quantities of P239 a massive reactor had to be built, requiring the development of chemical extraction processes that were entirely without precedent. To develop these procedures, a medium-sized reactor was built at Oak Ridge, chemical engineering work was quickly conducted using it, then large-scale production reactors were built on a remote 1,000-square-mile tract along the Columbia River north of Pasco, Washington. The facility was called the Hanford Engineer Works and, with Tennessee's Oak Ridge, it became the major production plant of the Manhattan Project.

While the work of creating fissionable materials was under way, a central laboratory capable of translating bomb theory into a working bomb had to be established. In 1943, J. Robert Oppenheimer, a leading American physicist, was chosen

to create and direct the laboratory. Whereas General Groves directed the engineering and military aspects of the Manhattan Project, Oppenheimer was responsible for managing the scientific research. Groves and Oppenheimer were polar opposites in terms of background, intellectual interests, political beliefs, and overall personality; yet they learned to respect each other, and they formed a highly effective partnership.

For construction of the required laboratory, Oppenheimer chose a site on a remote mesa at Los Alamos, New Mexico, north of Santa Fe. This isolated and austerely beautiful location became a magnet that drew the nation's greatest physicists and chemists. A combination top-secret military installation and research laboratory, Los Alamos required a unique compromise between the creative freedom and openness necessary for scientific research and the high degree of discipline and security required in weapons production. Groves and Oppenheimer managed to create and maintain the compromise.

The task at Los Alamos was to invent methods of reducing the fissionable materials that emerged from the production plants to pure metal that could be fabricated into the precisely machined shapes that would enable and facilitate an explosive chain reaction. The goal was to bring together a sufficient quantity of fissionable material rapidly enough to achieve a supercritical mass. Critical mass would result in explosive release of energy: an atomic blast. Moreover, this exquisitely difficult feat of materials engineering had to be carried out within a device that could be carried in a bomber, dropped over a target, and detonated at precisely the proper moment above the target; explosion on impact was not desirable, because much of the explosive force would be absorbed by the earth and therefore dissipated. To complicate the task further, these problems had to be solved well before much fissionable material was available. The idea was to conserve as much of what could be produced for use in the finished bombs.

By the summer of 1945, when enough P239 had emerged from Hanford to produce a nuclear explosion, the Los Alamos scientists had created a weapon they believed was ready to field-test. The scientists assembled observation and monitoring equipment to ensure that they would have accurate data on the performance—or failure—of the bomb. At Alamogordo, 120 miles south of Albuquerque, a special tower was constructed, from which the test bomb—the scientists dubbed it "the gadget"—was suspended. Although the site was remote from population centers, the scientists were far from certain as to the "yield" (the force and extent) of the explosion that would be produced. There was even a chance, some believed, that the detonation of the bomb could set off a chain reaction in the atoms of the air itself, perhaps destroying a vast area. Theoretically, it was possible the blast would ignite the very atmosphere of the earth.

The test bomb was detonated at 5:30 A.M. on July 16, 1945. Scientists and a handful of VIPs observed from bunkers and trenches 10,000 yards distant. All who witnessed the explosion were awed. A blinding flash was followed by a heat wave and, finally (since sound travels much more slowly than radiated energy), by a roar and a shock wave. The blast produced a great fireball, followed by the mushroom-shaped cloud (rising to an altitude of 40,000 feet) that would become a dreaded emblem of the "atomic age." This first bomb was calculated to have produced an explosion equivalent in energy to 15,000–20,000 tons of TNT.

In August, two more bombs, one using U235 and the other using P239, were dropped on the Japanese cities of HIROSHIMA and NAGASAKI.

Further reading: Groves, Leslie M. *Now It Can Be Told: The Story of the Manhattan Project.* New York: Harper, 1962; Rhodes, Richard. *The Making of the Atomic Bomb.* New York: Simon and Schuster, 1986.

Mannerheim, Carl Gustav Emil von
(1867–1951) *Finnish army commander in chief*

Born in Villnäs, Finland, Mannerheim attended various military schools and, in 1889, was commissioned a lieutenant of cavalry in the Russian army. (Finland belonged to Russia at the time.) He was a charismatic officer and a brilliant horseman popular with his troops. He was chosen in 1895 as one of the honor guard at the coronation of Russian czar Nicholas II and the czarina Alexandra.

Mannerheim's first combat experience came during the Russo-Japanese War of 1904–05. He emerged with the rank of colonel, then during World War I rose even more swiftly, becoming a lieutenant general in command of a corps by the middle of 1917. But with the collapse of much of the army and the Russian Revolution, Mannerheim resigned his commission, returned to Finland, and answered his nation's call after it declared independence from Russia on December 6, 1917.

A conservative, Mannerheim was not an enthusiastic supporter of Finland's revolutionary government, but he was a strong opponent of communism, and he therefore accepted command of the anti-Communist White forces in Finland on January 18, 1918. Operating from a base at Vasa, in western Finland, he engaged the Red Guard on March 16 outside of Tampere. Mannerheim captured the Karelian isthmus on April 29 and successfully contained Communist attempts at a breakout. On December 12, 1918, Mannerheim was named regent of Finland, serving in this capacity until a republic was established on June 17, 1919. He continued to serve in the Finnish military, quelling minor outbreaks along the Russian-Finnish border until the Treaty of Dorpat, signed on October 14, 1920, formally ended the war with Russia.

After the conclusion of peace, Mannerheim retired briefly then returned to public service as chairman of the Finnish defense council. Increasingly concerned over the Soviet threat to Finland's fragile independence, he lobbied for increased military funding and directed construction of border fortifications on the Karelian isthmus. Upon their completion in 1939, these defensive forts became known as the MANNERHEIM LINE. After the conclusion of the GERMAN-SOVIET NON-AGGRESSION PACT in August 1939, at the beginning of World War II, Mannerheim was appointed commander in chief of all Finnish forces just in time to meet the crisis of the Soviet invasion of Finland on

November 30, 1939, which started the RUSSO-FINNISH WAR.

Initially, Mannerheim enjoyed considerable success, but he could not withstand indefinitely the Soviets' vast numerical superiority. What he did succeed in doing was making the Red Army's eventual victory very costly by the time he capitulated on March 12, 1940. When the war against the Soviet Union resumed on June 25, 1941, Mannerheim was again commander in chief, directing operations on the Karelian isthmus and in eastern Karelia. He was promoted to field marshal on June 4, 1942.

After the successful Soviet summer offensive of 1944, Finland's president, Risto Ryti, resigned. Mannerheim stepped in, offered himself as a candidate, and won, taking office on August 4, 1944. He concluded an armistice with the Soviets in September, agreeing to aid the Red Army in clearing Lapland of German troops during September-December 1944.

Mannerheim continued in office until shortly after the war. Illness forced his resignation in 1946.

Further reading: Jagerskiold, Stig Axel Fridolf. *Mannerheim, Marshal of Finland.* Minneapolis: University of Minnesota Press, 1987; Mannerheim, Carl Gustav Emil von. *The Memoirs of Marshal Mannerheim.* New York: E. P. Dutton, 1954; Screen, J. E. O. *Mannerheim: The Finnish Years.* London: Hurst & Company, 2001; Screen, J. E. O. *Mannerheim: The Years of Preparation.* Vancouver: University of British Columbia Press, 1993; Warner, Oliver. *Marshal Mannerheim and the Finns.* London: Weidenfeld & Nicolson, 1967.

Mannerheim Line

A line of defensive fortifications extending across the Karelian isthmus from the Gulf of Finland to Lake Ladoga, the Mannerheim Line was named for CARL GUSTAV EMIL VON MANNERHEIM, the Finnish military commander and president who, as chairman of the Finnish defense council, advocated construction of the line and oversaw its construction.

The Mannerheim Line was intended to defend against a Soviet invasion of Finland, and it was here that the most intense fighting of the RUSSO-FINNISH WAR (WINTER WAR) took place in 1939.

The Mannerheim Line was first planned after the Finnish civil war, which followed the conclusion of World War I. Construction began in the 1920s and continued throughout the 1930s. When completed, the fortification line consisted of approximately 200 machine-gun emplacements encased in concrete bunkers. The Mannerheim Line was incomplete by the outbreak of the Russo-Finnish War but proved effective nonetheless.

The great advantage of the Mannerheim Line over the more extensive and more famous MAGINOT LINE built by the French along their border with Germany was in its use of the natural terrain to leverage the effectiveness of its defenses. Whereas the Maginot Line and other traditional line fortifications used massive bunkers and other artificial structures, the Mannerheim Line exploited such landscape features as boulders and fallen trees. Whereas the Maginot Line was exceedingly conspicuous, the Mannerheim Line was skillfully camouflaged and thus a far more effective defensive position.

Although superior Red Army numbers eventually forced the surrender of Finland, the Mannerheim Line defenses stalled the Soviet advance for two very bloody months. Embarrassed by the cost of the invasion of Finland, Soviet commanders and politicians greatly exaggerated the extent and construction of the Mannerheim Line, as if to suggest that it was virtually impregnable. It was, in fact, for the most part a series of trenches and common field fortifications punctuated at considerable intervals by more substantial bunkers. Machine guns were the weapon of choice. The Mannerheim Line had virtually no artillery positions. Skillful defense by Finnish troops, not impregnable military architecture, was responsible for the effectiveness of the Mannerheim Line.

Further reading: Chew, Allen F. *The White Death: The Epic of the Soviet-Finnish Winter War.* East Lansing: Michigan State University Press, 2002; Engle, Eloise, and Lauri Paananen. *The Winter War: The Soviet Attack on Finland 1939–1940.* Mechanicsburg, Pa.: Stackpole,

1992; Trotter, William R. *The Winter War, the Russo-Finnish War of 1939–40.* London: Aurum Press, 2003.

Manstein, Erich von (1887–1973) *German commander*

Manstein was born Erich von Lewinski in Berlin, the son of General Eduard von Lewinski. When his father died, his mother was unable to support her 10 children, Erich was adopted by a childless aunt married to General George von Manstein, from whom the child took the name by which he would become known.

Manstein graduated from cadet school in 1906 and was commissioned lieutenant in the 3rd Foot Guards Regiment, an elite unit under the command of Paul von Hindenburg, Manstein's uncle. Manstein was soon enrolled in the Kriegsakademie, the highest German military college, but withdrew to enter active service at the outbreak of World War I in 1914. Wounded in November of the first year of the war, Manstein convalesced in a staff assignment. Excelling in this duty, he served out the rest of the war as a staff officer.

After the armistice of 1918, Manstein served in the Reichswehr, the post–TREATY OF VERSAILLES German army, and in 1929 was appointed to the General Staff. In 1936, he was appointed deputy to the chief of the General Staff, General Ludwig Beck, but was removed two years later when Defense Minister General Werner von Blomberg and army commander in chief WERNER VON FRITSCH, outspoken opponents of ADOLF HITLER's plans for conquest, were relieved of their offices. Manstein was transferred to command of an infantry division in Silesia, and then became chief of staff of the German occupation army in Czechoslovakia.

In August 1939, the month before war began, Manstein was appointed chief of staff of the Eastern Army Group under GERD VON RUNDSTEDT. He participated in the BLITZKRIEG invasion of Poland in September 1939. Reviewing the General Staff's plan for the invasion of France, Manstein objected to the simple head-on approach and called instead for the main part of the invasion to go through the Ardennes. The French assumed that this approach was too thickly wooded for an invading army, so they defended it only lightly. The MANSTEIN PLAN was adopted and enabled a rapid penetration across the French border, which stunned the defenders and was chiefly responsible for the German victory in the BATTLE OF FRANCE.

During the culminating stages of the Battle of France, in May 1940 Manstein was given a field command. In March 1941, he was transferred to the eastern front in command of LVI Panzer Corps, which he led with breathtaking success in the INVASION OF THE SOVIET UNION during June 1941. Promoted to field marshal in July, Manstein was assigned command of the Eleventh German Army in the Crimea, then took over Army Group Don in November 1942. This force was sent to the relief of the German Sixth Army at the BATTLE OF STALINGRAD. Manstein openly protested Hitler's order

Erich von Manstein *(National Archives and Records Administration)*

that the Sixth German Army not break out of Stalingrad to link up with Army Group Don. Nevertheless, the order stood, and, thus hobbled, Manstein was unable to stem the tide of battle at Stalingrad.

Transferred to command of Army Group South, Manstein worked feverishly to salvage the German campaign in southern Russia. He staged a surprise attack in March 1943 and recaptured KHARKOV, then commanded the right wing of the doomed German assault on the KURSK salient in July 1943. After this, he commanded the fighting withdrawal from southern Russia.

Relieved of command in March 1944 because of what Hitler deemed his poor performance on the Eastern Front, Manstein was inactive during the rest of World War II. He surrendered himself to British forces in May 1945 and was indicted for war crimes during the later phases of the NUREMBERG WAR CRIMES TRIBUNAL in August 1949. The Western Allies declined to prosecute, but the Soviets insisted on a trial. Found guilty of war crimes, Manstein was sentenced to 18 years' imprisonment. His sentence was subsequently reduced, however, and he was released in 1953.

During 1955–56, Manstein chaired the West German parliament's military subcommittee. During this cold war period, he reorganized West Germany's military and developed its operating doctrine.

Further reading: Manstein, Erich von. *Lost Victories: The War Memoirs of Hitler's Most Brilliant General.* Osceola, Wis.: Zenith Press, 2004.

Manstein Plan

Proposed by senior German army commanders led by ERICH VON MANSTEIN and Franz Halder, the so-called Manstein Plan was the overall plan the Germans followed in the BATTLE OF FRANCE. Its major feature was an attack through the Ardennes in southern Belgium, which allowed the invaders to bypass the MAGINOT LINE. This sector was very thinly defended because the French assumed that no major invading army would attempt to march through the thickly wooded region. The culmination of the Manstein Plan was an advance all the way to the English Channel to bring about the surrender of France.

ADOLF HITLER approved the Manstein Plan on February 17, 1940, but it was May 10 before it was implemented. On this day, the Luftwaffe bombed Dutch and Belgian airfields while German ground forces took Moerdijk and Rotterdam. The 9th Panzer Division under Fedor von Bock used BLITZKRIEG tactics to pass through the Netherlands and Belgium, while the 7th Panzer Division (ERWIN ROMMEL), the IXX Corps (HEINZ GUDERIAN), and the 6th and 8th Panzers (GERD VON RUNDSTEDT) advanced through the Ardennes north of the Maginot Line. Seven panzer divisions reached the Meuse River at Dinant on by May 12. On May 13, the French government fled Paris.

The speed of the invasion under the Manstein Plan stunned the French, who offered little effective resistance. The British Expeditionary Force and elements of the French army were narrowly saved from complete annihilation by Operation Dynamo, the DUNKIRK EVACUATION, carried out from May 27 to June 4, 1940. Almost 2 million French soldiers were taken prisoner during the invasion, and some 390,000 soldiers were killed. The cost to the invaders was about 35,000 killed in action.

Further reading: Bloch, Marc. *Strange Defeat.* New York: W.W. Norton, 1999; Deighton, Len. *Blitzkrieg: From the Rise of Hitler to the Fall of Denmark.* London: Book Sales, 2000; Gordon, Bertram M., ed. *Historical Dictionary of World War II: France.* Westport, Conn.: Greenwood Press, 1998; Jackson, Julian. *The Fall of France: The Nazi Invasion of 1940.* New York: Oxford University Press, 2003; Pallud, Jean-Paul. *Blitzkrieg in the West.* London: After the Battle, 1991.

Manteuffel, Hasso-Eccard Freiherr von
(1897–1978) *German commander*

Born in Potsdam to an aristocratic Prussian family, Manteuffel enrolled in cadet school in 1908 and joined the army in 1916 as an officer of hussars. In

April, he entered World War I with the 3rd Hussar Regiment and was wounded on October 12. He convalesced as a staff officer assigned to the Divisional General Staff.

After the German army was dissolved by the TREATY OF VERSAILLES, Manteuffel joined the FREIKORPS in January 1919, then joined the Reichswehr, the small army permitted under the Treaty of Versailles. By the late 1930s, Manteuffel was an armored warfare expert, who served as an adviser to the Panzer Troop Command of the General Headquarters (OKH) and a professor at Panzer Troop School II.

On May 1, 1941, Manteuffel assumed command of the 1st Battalion, 7th Rifle Regiment, 7th Panzer Division and saw his first action in World War II during the INVASION OF THE SOVIET UNION. On August 25, 1941, he took over command of the 6th Rifle Regiment, 7th Panzer Division, and fought in the BATTLE OF MOSCOW during the winter of 1941–42. In the spring, he returned with the 7th Panzer Division to France and there was named commander of the 7th Panzer Grenadier Brigade of the 7th Panzer Division.

Manteuffel was sent to North Africa at the beginning of 1943 and, on February 5, was given command of Division von Manteuffel, attached to the 5th Panzer Army of ERWIN ROMMEL's Army Group Afrika (Afrika Corps). Manteuffel participated in defensive operations during the TUNISIA CAMPAIGN, conducting highly effective counteroffensives against the Allies. On March 31, 1943, however, he collapsed from exhaustion and was evacuated to Germany. While convalescing, on May 1, 1943, he was promoted to major general, then, on August 22, he was elevated to command of the 7th Panzer Division on the Soviet front. Severely wounded in an air attack on August 26, 1943, he refused evacuation and fought at the BATTLES OF KHARKOV and at Belgorod, and along the Dnieper River, bringing a Red Army offensive to a halt. Late in November, he retook Zhitomir to relieve the enveloped 8th Panzer Division, which his efforts rescued.

In recognition of his achievements, Manteuffel was made commander of the elite Grenadier Division Grossdeutschland on February 1, 1944. He led this unit in intense fighting west of Kirovograd as part of the German army's fighting withdrawal from the Soviet Union. Entering Romania in late March 1944, he regrouped his forces and fought a series of effective defensives in the northern part of the country through June. By that time the Grossdeutschland Division, exhausted, was withdrawn for refitting. Late in July, it was moved to East Prussia to defend against Soviet invasion. Manteuffel led a bold counterattack against the advancing Red Army in Lithuania, which stalled the Soviet advance.

Promoted to General of Panzer Troops on September 1, 1944, Manteuffel assumed command of the 5th Panzer Army on the Western Front and deeply penetrated Allied lines during the BATTLE OF THE ARDENNES (BATTLE OF THE BULGE), nearly reaching the Meuse River in December 1944.

On March 10, 1945, Manteuffel was given command of the 3rd Panzer Army on the eastern front and led a desperate defense against the Red Army's advance into western Pomerania and Berlin. When he judged the situation to be hopeless, Manteuffel retreated to Mecklenburg, where, rather than fall into Soviet hands, he surrendered his forces to the Western Allies on May 3, 1945.

Held as a POW until September 1947, he was released and entered politics, becoming a representative in the Bundestag, the West German parliament, from 1953 to 1957. He later lectured at the U.S. Military Academy at West Point.

Further reading: Brownlow, Donald G. *Panzer Baron: The Military Exploits of General Hasso von Manteuffel.* North Quincy, Mass.: Christopher Publishing House, 1975; Manteuffel, Hasso von. *The 7th Panzer Division: An Illustrated History of Rommel's "Ghost Division," 1938–1945.* Atglen, Pa.: Schiffer, 2000.

Mao Zedong (1893–1976) *Chinese Communist leader*

Best known as one of the founders of the Chinese Communist Party (CCP, 1921) and the founder of the People's Republic of China (1949), Mao was also a grassroots military leader of great tactical and strategic skill, and he was a charismatic leader of troops.

He was born to a prosperous family of Hunan peasant landowners and was educated at the local elementary school, where the curriculum emphasized classical Chinese Confucian thought. In October 1911, Mao left school after forces under the revolutionary leader Sun Yat-sen, (Sun Yixian) overthrew the Qing (Ch'ing, or Manchu) dynasty. Mao fought in the revolution of 1911–12 as an orderly in a militia unit until he was summoned home by his father, who sent the youth to a trade school, which he attended during 1912–13. In 1913, Mao moved to the provincial capital of Changsha and enrolled in the normal school, intending to become a teacher. In 1918, however, he moved to Beijing (Peking), supporting himself as a clerk in the library of Beijing University. In 1919, he returned to Hunan and secured an appointment as a teacher at the Changsha Normal School, having by this time acquired a reputation as a political intellectual.

After marrying Yang Kaihui (K'ai-hui), daughter of one of his teachers, Mao served as Hunan's chief delegate to the founding congress of the Chinese Communist Party (CCP) in 1921. With the rest of the CCP, he joined the Nationalist Party—the Kuomintang (Guomindang, KMT)—in 1923 and was elected as an alternate member of the KMT Shanghai Executive Committee in 1924. A bout of illness forced his return to Hunan, and as he convalesced, he drifted inexorably to the left. Mao organized unauthorized unions of laborers and peasants, provoking authorities to issue a warrant for his arrest. He fled to Canton in 1925, where he worked as a radical journalist. His journalism helped gain him entry into the inner circle of KMT leader CHIANG KAI-SHEK (Jiang Jieshi), who appointed Mao head of the KMT's propaganda section.

Mao and Chiang soon came into conflict, and in May 1926 Mao was removed from the propaganda post. He joined the Peasant Movement Training Institute, a radical, far-left CCP cell, and by April 1927, the divide between the KMT and the CCP had become too great to bridge. Chiang repudiated the KMT alliance with the CCP and launched his Northern Campaign against CCP units. Mao retreated underground and, acting independently even of the CCP, put together a revolutionary army. He led it in the Autumn Harvest Uprising in Hunan during September 8–19. After the uprising failed, Mao was ejected from the CCP. Instead of giving up, however, he regrouped the remnants of his army—his most loyal followers—and retreated with them into the mountains, where he made an alliance with another CCP outcast, Zhu De (Chu Teh). Together, in 1928, they formed a peasant army called the Mass Line, with which they boldly set about creating their own republic, the Jiangxi (Kiangsi) Soviet. By 1934, the Soviet numbered some 15 million people.

The existence of the Jiangxi Soviet was an affront not only to Chiang's KMT, but also to the Moscow-dominated International Communist Party, which directed revolutionaries to concentrate their efforts on urban areas (in accordance with orthodox Marxist doctrine), rather than work among the rural peasantry. Mao and Zhu De did their organizing among the peasantry and, between 1929 and 1934, skillfully employed guerrilla tactics to repulse four KMT attempts to wipe out the Soviet.

In 1930, the KMT executed Mao's first wife, Yang Kaihui, and, after a fifth KMT assault on the Jiangxi Soviet in 1934, Mao fled with some 86,000 men and women. This began the celebrated Long March over a distance of some 6,000 miles to the province of Sha'anxi (Shensi). By October 1935, now with a mere 4,000 followers, Mao established a new party headquarters at Yenan.

Japanese aggression against China prompted the KMT to suspend further attacks on the CCP, and Mao made peace with Chiang in December 1936 so that they could present a united front against the Japanese.

During August 20–November 30, 1940, Mao launched the Hundred Regiments offensive against the Japanese invaders. It had negligible effect, and Mao did little else to fight the Japanese during World War II. Instead, he used the war years to consolidate the CCP position in northern China as well as his own leadership of the party. In April 1945, he was elected chairman of the party's central committee.

During the war, Mao wrote and published a series of essays promulgating the basis for Chinese communism. His efforts to grow the party succeeded remarkably well. The CCP had 40,000 members in 1937. By the end of World War II, it had grown to 1.2 million.

The end of World War II—and, with it, the end of the Japanese threat—brought an end to the uneasy alliance between the CCP and KMT. Civil war broke out, in which Mao repeatedly defeated the armies of Chiang Kai-shek during 1946–49. After Chiang and his Nationalists fled to the island of Taiwan in 1949, Mao proclaimed the People's Republic of China.

The United States remained loyal to its wartime ally Chiang and rejected Mao's attempts to establish diplomatic relations. Mao carried out sweeping party purges during 1949–54 and instituted agricultural collectivization on a vast scale. He intervened militarily in the Korean War, then from 1956 to 1957, initiated the Hundred Flowers movement (named for his famous slogan, "Let a hundred flowers bloom, let a thousand schools of thought contend"), encouraging intellectuals to criticize the party and its methods of government and administration. This done, he suddenly turned the Hundred Flowers movement against the critics and dissidents in a remarkably successful effort to create a cult of personality around himself. He called for the total elimination of private property and the formation of people's agricultural communes. Simultaneously, he promulgated the Great Leap Forward, an attempt to accelerate industrialization on a massive scale.

China descended into chaos, and late in 1958, Mao stepped down as head of state and was replaced by Liu Shao-chi. He returned to the public stage in the mid-1960s, displaced Liu, and provoked the Cultural Revolution, which ushered in his reentry as party chairman and head of state. The Cultural Revolution produced a mass army of radical Maoist students, known as the Red Guard, who wrought havoc on China. Mao managed to suppress the Red Guard by the early 1970s. During this period, he moderated his views and approach to government and reached a remarkable rapprochement with the United States, initiated by a conference in Beijing with President Richard M. Nixon in 1972.

See also SINO-JAPANESE WAR.

Further reading: Chang, Jung, and Jon Halliday. *Mao: The Unknown Story.* New York: Knopf, 2005; Short, Philip. *Mao: A Life.* New York: Owl Books, 2001; Spence, Jonathan D. *Mao Zedong.* New York: Penguin, 1999.

Mariana Islands campaign

U.S. victories in the Gilbert Islands and the MARSHALL ISLANDS CAMPAIGN penetrated Japan's outermost defensive ring in the central Pacific, which cleared the way for an attack on the Mariana Islands, a group of 15 islands stretching in a 500-mile arc halfway between Japan and New Guinea. The biggest islands of the group, Saipan, Tinian, Rota, and Guam, were U.S. possessions (having been ceded by Spain in 1898). The other islands had been purchased by Germany, but were captured by Japan during World War I and mandated to Japan by the League of Nations after that war.

The strategic location of the Mariana islands made them ideal for use as U.S. B-29 bomber bases because, from here, the long-range bombers could reach the Japanese homeland as well as the Philippines. They also figured as key military objectives because they were the headquarters of Japan's Central Pacific fleet, under command by Admiral NAGUMO CHUICHI, who had been in command at the BATTLE OF PEARL HARBOR. The islands were garrisoned by the Japanese Thirty-first Army, under General Obata Hideyoshi. Admiral CHESTER A. NIMITZ, U.S. commander in chief in the central Pacific, believed that a battle in the Marianas would be decisive for the entire course of the Pacific war.

On June 15, 1944, the marines of HOLLAND "HOWLIN' MAD" SMITH's V Amphibious Corps invaded Saipan, the northernmost of the three major islands. The 2nd and 4th Marine Divisions

Japanese aircraft shot down in the "Marianas Turkey Shoot" *(National Archives and Records Administration)*

landed on the western side of the island, fighting their way nearly a mile inland by nightfall. During the night of June 16–17, the U.S. Army's 27th Infantry Division landed, capturing Aslito (Isely) Airfield on the 18th. (U.S. Army Air Forces fighters began using the field on June 23.)

After four more days of intense combat, V Corps cleared most of the southern portion of Saipan, then turned left to push the attack northward on June 23. The 2nd Marine Division advanced along the west coast, the 27th Infantry advanced up the center, and the 4th Marine Division took responsibility for the east coast. When the 27th Infantry fell behind the other two divisions, Smith relieved its commander, General Ralph Smith, and replaced him with General Sanderford Jarman and, subsequently, General George Griner. Under these commanders, the army unit caught up with the marines by July 1. With the invasion force now abreast, the 2nd Marine Division went on to take Garapan, while the other two divisions advanced toward Marpi Point, at the northern tip of the island. Resistance throughout was fierce, but, faced with the certainty of defeat, the Japanese commanders Nagumo and Saito committed suicide on July 6. Leaderless now, the Japanese troops staged fierce and suicidal *banzai* attacks. On July 9, all resistance on Saipan ended with a mass suicide of Japanese

soldiers and civilians off Marpi Point. U.S. forces took just 1,000 prisoners. U.S. casualties were 10,347 (marines) and 3,674 (army), including a total of 3,426 marines and soldiers killed in action.

With Saipan secure, the attack on Guam, at the southern end of the Marianas chain, was launched on July 21. Marine general ROY GEIGER, in command of the newly created III Amphibious Corps, landed 3rd Marine Division (Allen Turnage) north of Apra Harbor while 1st Brigade (Lemuel Shepherd) and 77th Infantry Division (Andrew Bruce) attacked south of Apra. The island was garrisoned by 19,000 Japanese troops under General Takashina Takeshi.

Good progress was made inland from the southern beachhead by nightfall, but the 3rd Marine Division, to the north, had a much harder fight. Whereas in the south, the advance was a mile by night, it took four days for the 3rd Marine Division to advance the same distance and link up the two advances. No sooner was this accomplished than, during the night of July 25–26, the garrison counterattacked, nearly overwhelming the marines before the Japanese were beaten back. This accomplished, 1st Brigade undertook mop-up operations between the two landing beaches.

While the 1st Brigade mopped up, the 3rd Marine and the 77th Infantry divisions attacked northeast on July 31. These two units were joined by the 1st Brigade a week later, and by August 10 the augmented assault had reached the northern tip of the island, and Guam was declared to be secure. U.S. casualties included 6,716 marines, 839 soldiers, and 245 sailors (of which total 1,023 were killed in action).

Three days after the Guam invasion stepped off, V Amphibious Corps marines under Harry Schmidt (replacing Holland Smith, who had been promoted to command of the General Fleet Marine Force Pacific), landed on Tinian, an island ideal for the construction of a B-29 air base. On July 24 the 2nd Marine Division made a decoy landing near Tinian Town on the southwest coast of the island, while the 4th Marine Division (now commanded by Clifton Cates) made the principal landing in the northwest. Tinian was defended by a garrison of

9,000 Japanese soldiers and sailors, but by early evening the 4th Marines had penetrated a full mile inland.

On July 25, the 2nd Marine Division landed and swept through the northern end of the island before turning right to attack down the east coast in concert with the 4th Marine Division. The entire island was secure by July 31, at the relatively light cost of 327 marines killed and 1,771 wounded. Almost the entire Japanese garrison was killed in action or committed suicide.

In all, the Marianas Campaign killed more than 40,000 Japanese troops, and on November 24 the first B-29 raid on Japan was launched from Saipan.

See also SAIPAN, BATTLE OF, and GUAM, BATTLE OF.

Further reading: Crowl, Phillip A. *The War in the Pacific: Campaign in the Marianas.* Washington, D.C.: Center of Military History, 1985; Denfeld, D. Colt. *Hold the Marianas: The Japanese Defense of the Mariana Islands.* Shippensburg, Pa.: White Mane, 1997; Hoyt, Edwin Palmer. *To the Marianas: War in the Central Pacific, 1944.* New York: Van Nostrand Reinhold, 1980; Rottman, Gordon. *Guam 1941–1944: Loss and Reconquest.* Osceola, Wis.: Motorbooks International, 2004; Rottman, Gordon. *Saipan and Tinian 1944: Piercing the Japanese Empire.* Osceola, Wis.: Motorbooks International, 2004.

Marshall, George Catlett (1880–1959) *U.S. Army chief of staff*

Born in Uniontown, Pennsylvania, Marshall graduated from Virginia Military Institute (VMI) in 1901 and was commissioned a second lieutenant of infantry on February 3, 1902. He served in the Philippines and saw action during the insurrection on Mindoro during 1902–03. On his return to the United States, he attended Infantry and Cavalry School at Fort Leavenworth, graduating at the top of the class of 1907 and staying on at the Staff College during 1907–08. After promotion to first lieutenant in 1907, he taught at the service schools from 1908 to 1910.

Marshall was variously posted during 1910–13, then returned to the Philippines as aide to General Hunter Liggett. He was promoted to captain in 1916, returned to the United States, and was assigned as aide to General James F. Bell in 1917. In June 1917, Marshall shipped out to France as operations officer with the 1st Division. He was among the planners of the first U.S. offensive of World War I in May 1918.

Marshall was promoted to temporary colonel in July and, the next month, attached to General John J. Pershing's General Headquarters at Chaumont. Here he participated in the planning of the Saint-Mihiel offensive of September 12–16. When this offensive was completed successfully, he took charge of the transfer of 500,000 troops from Saint-Mihiel to the Meuse-Argonne front. The swift efficiency of this mass movement on a battlefront earned Marshall praise as a brilliant logistician, and he was appointed chief of operations for the First Army in October. In November, he became chief of staff of VIII Corps.

George C. Marshall *(National Archives and Records Administration)*

After the armistice of 1918, Marshall served with the army of occupation in Germany, returning to the United States in September 1919. He reverted to his prewar rank of captain and was appointed aide to Pershing, who was now army chief of staff. Marshall served as Pershing's aide through 1924 and worked with him on many aspects of the National Defense Act.

In July 1920, Marshall was promoted to major, then lieutenant colonel three years later. After he left Pershing's staff, he served in Tientsin, China, as executive officer of the 15th Infantry, then returned to the United States in 1927 to become assistant commandant of the Infantry School at Fort Benning, a post he held through 1932. He was promoted to colonel and worked with the Civilian Conservation Corps (CCC) in 1933, then was assigned as senior instructor to the Illinois National Guard from 1933 to 1936, when he was promoted to brigadier general and given command of 5th Infantry Brigade at Vancouver Barracks, Washington.

In 1938, Marshall came to Washington, D.C., as head of the War Plans Division of the Army General Staff. He was promoted to major general in July and was appointed deputy chief of staff. On September 1, he was made a temporary general and appointed chief of staff. From this position, he directed the rapid expansion of the army preparatory to war. It was under his direction that the army would grow from its prewar, predraft strength of 200,000 to 8 million by 1945.

After the BATTLE OF PEARL HARBOR and U.S. entry into World War II, Marshall reorganized the General Staff and, by March 1942, restructured the army itself into three major commands: Army Ground Forces, Army Service Forces, and Army Air Forces. As a member of the Joint Chiefs of Staff, he was a principal military adviser to President FRANKLIN D. ROOSEVELT and was present at all the Allied conferences, first in company with Roosevelt and then with President HARRY S. TRUMAN.

As chief of staff, Marshall was one of the principal architects of American and Allied military strategy. In December 1944, he was promoted to general of the army (five-star rank). He ended his service as chief of staff on November 20, 1945. But five days later, President Truman sent him to China as his special envoy. For the next year, Marshall unsuccessfully attempted to mediate a peace between CHIANG KAI-SHEK (and his Nationalists) and MAO ZEDONG (and the Chinese Communist Party). He then returned to the United States to replace James F. Byrnes as secretary of state in Truman's cabinet on January 1947.

In June 1947, in a speech at Harvard University, Marshall broadly outlined a sweeping program of economic aid to rebuild war-ravaged Europe, thus rendering aid to stricken humanity while also forestalling the spread of communism in economically devastated areas. The European Recovery Program was soon universally dubbed the MARSHALL PLAN and was a great success, both in rebuilding Europe and in helping the United States to win the cold war.

Marshall resigned as secretary of state in January 1949, but returned to the Truman cabinet in September of the next year as secretary of defense. He served in that post during the opening phase of the Korean War. Marshall fell under attack by red-baiting Senator Joseph McCarthy during the early 1950s. Suffering from ill health, he resigned as secretary of defense and retired from public life in September 1951. In December 1953, Marshall was awarded the Nobel Peace Prize, largely in recognition of his advocacy of the Marshall Plan.

Further reading: Cray, Ed. *General of the Army*. New York: Cooper Square Press, 2000; Stoler, Mark A. *George C. Marshall: Soldier-Statesman of the American Century*. New York: Twayne, 1989.

Marshall Islands campaign

The Marshall Islands are a group of 36 Micronesian atolls in the Pacific, which includes the world's largest atoll, Kwajalein, where the BATTLE OF KWAJALEIN ATOLL was fought.

As a result of World War I, the Marshalls had been mandated to Japan, and, during World War II, the islands were an important constituent of Japan's outermost defensive perimeter. The U.S. invasion of the islands began on January 30, 1944, when a marine and army amphibious assault force of 85,000 men, escorted by some 300 warships and landing craft, landed. The first contingent to land consisted of reconnaissance patrols, which hit the beach on Majuro Atoll. This was the first American occupation of Japanese soil.

Following the reconnaissance landings, the 4th Marine Division and 7th Infantry (Army) Division landed on the inner islands of Kwajalein Atoll, Kwajalein and Roi-Namur. These inner islands were targeted because ULTRA intercepts and decrypts had revealed that the Japanese had transferred the bulk of their forces to the outer atolls, where they expected landings. In accordance with the U.S. ISLAND HOPPING STRATEGY, the outer atolls were merely subjected to intensive air raids but were bypassed by troops, who simply cut the garrisons off by occupying the other islands. The outer atolls did not surrender until the very end of the war, although after victory in the BATTLE OF ENIWETOK ATOLL, the Marshalls came firmly under U.S. control.

The conquest of the Marshalls forced the withdrawal of the Japanese fleet from this area and cleared the way for the MARIANA ISLANDS CAMPAIGN, which resulted in the severe contraction of the Japanese defensive perimeter.

Further reading: Marshall, S. L. A. *Island Victory.* New York: Penguin, 1944; Nalty, Bernard C. *The United States Marines in the Marshalls Campaign.* Washington, D.C: Historical Branch, G-3 Division, Headquarters, U.S. Marine Corps, 1962; Rottman, Gordon L. *The Marshall Islands 1944: Operation Flintlock, the Capture of Kwajalein and Eniwetok.* London: Osprey, 2004.

Marshall Plan

After six years of war, Europe lay devastated, with two crises especially urgent: a shortage of food and a shortage of coal for heating. During 1946–47, the average German lived on a semistarvation died of just 1,800 calories daily, and if the German people were slowly starving, some were quickly freezing as well. During the brutal winters of 1945, 1946, and 1947, hundreds, perhaps thousands died in homes unheated for lack of fuel.

Although the United States had begun sending aid and relief to all of Europe even before the end of the war (amounting to approximately $9 billion by early 1947), these efforts were not sufficient, and the hope that Britain and France would recover sufficiently and quickly enough to care for their own populations as well as extend aid to others proved illusory. The economies even of the European victors were shattered, and recovery was slow. The cycle of the entire European economy was stalled. Although farmers could still produce food, urban populations had no way to pay for it. Even if industrial plants were rebuilt, neither urbanites nor farmers could pay for the goods produced.

Among the various plans proposed to aid European recovery was that favored by GEORGE C. MARSHALL, army chief of staff throughout World War II and, in the administration of HARRY S. TRUMAN, secretary of state. He understood the intense humanitarian crisis gripping Europe, and he also well understood how the punitive terms of the TREATY OF VERSAILLES, which had ended World War I, created a general desperation that made the rise of a new dictator and another world war virtually inevitable. Marshall also believed that because Germany had been the most powerful industrial force in Europe before World War II, its current state of economic prostration was holding back the recovery of all Europe. Moreover, the universal devastation across the continent rendered even the Western nations vulnerable to intimidation and takeover by the Soviet Union. Truman, Marshall, and others believed that only a massive infusion of capital, intended to relieve the humanitarian crisis while also jump-starting the collective European economy, could help Europe recover and remain free of Soviet influence.

The program that the press dubbed the Marshall Plan was no giveaway. Marshall and Truman believed that the political, social, and economic fate of Europe hinged on overcoming motives of rivalry, vengeance, and nationalistic passions. To recover, they believed, Europeans would have to act

Nations in the Marshall Plan, 1949

Legend: Nations in the Marshall Plan, 1949

0   300 miles
0   300 km

ICELAND

Faeroe Is. (Denmark)

Shetland Is. (U.K.)

NORWAY

SWEDEN

FINLAND

USSR

UNITED KINGDOM

IRELAND

DENMARK

NETHER-LANDS

EAST GERMANY

POLAND

BELGIUM   WEST GERMANY

LUXEMBOURG

CZECHOSLOVAKIA

FRANCE   SWITZ.   AUSTRIA   HUNGARY

LIECHTENSTEIN

ROMANIA

YUGOSLAVIA

PORTUGAL

SPAIN

Corsica (France)

ITALY

BULGARIA

ALBANIA

Balearic Is. (Spain)

Sardinia (Italy)

TURKEY

GREECE

Sicily (Italy)

Cyprus (U.K.)

Malta   Crete

© Infobase Publishing

with a unity they had never known before. Marshall believed that it was essential to make all of Europe, in collective agreement, responsible for determining just how the funds would be used. He proposed that the nations of Europe meet to formulate a unified plan for the disbursement and use of funds. No funds would be released until the plan had been made and presented.

On June 5, 1947, in a commencement address delivered at Harvard University, Marshall announced the broad outline of the plan for European recovery. His speech was based on studies and reports he had commissioned from State Department officials George F. Kennan and Charles Bohlen, but in the speech, Marshall avoided all mention of precise figures. Instead, he spoke only of a "U.S. proposal . . . aimed at hunger, poverty, and chaos and not against any group" or ideology. Kennan wanted Marshall to direct the speech against Soviet aggression, but Marshall refused, arguing that the message should be universal, and he offered aid to "all Europe including the Soviet Union and her satellites." Disavowing, then, any political or ideological agenda, Marshall called on Europeans to create a plan for European recovery, which the United States would fund. That was the sum and substance of the speech that launched the Marshall Plan, a program unprecedented in the history of the world.

The plan, signed into law on April 3, 1948, provided funding to Austria, Belgium, Denmark, France, Greece, Iceland, Ireland, Italy, Luxembourg, the Netherlands, Norway, Portugal, Turkey, the United Kingdom, western Germany, and even to neutral Sweden and Switzerland. Over four years, some $13 billion in economic aid was distributed, most of it in the form of direct grants and a lesser amount in loans. Thanks to the Marshall Plan, the countries involved experienced a rise in their gross national products of 15 to 25 percent over four years. President Truman extended the plan to less-developed countries throughout the world under the "Point Four Program," launched in 1949.

Further reading: Dulles, Allen W. *Marshall Plan*. Oxford: Berg, 1993; Hogan, Michael J. *The Marshall Plan: America, Britain and the Reconstruction of Western Europe, 1947–1952*. New York: Cambridge University Press, 1989.

Masaryk, Jan (1886–1948) *Voice of Czech freedom fighters*

Born in Prague, Bohemia (modern Czech Republic), the son of the Czech statesman Tomáš Masaryk, Jan Masaryk saw military service with the Hungarian army during World War I. After CZECHOSLOVAKIA became independent following World War I in 1919, Masaryk joined the foreign office and was dispatched to Washington, D.C., and London. In 1921, he became secretary to Czech foreign minister EDVARD BENEŠ.

In 1925, Masaryk was appointed ambassador to Great Britain and served until 1938, when he stepped down to become foreign minister of the Czech government in exile, headquartered in London, following the German invasion of Czechoslovakia in the aftermath of the MUNICH CONFERENCE AND AGREEMENT.

During World War II, Masaryk was the voice of Czech exiles and freedom fighters. He regularly broadcasted to occupied Czechoslovakia, but his patriotic message was heard worldwide, and he emerged as a much-admired and popular figure. His speeches were collected, translated into English, and published in 1944 as *Speaking to My Country*. For many, the spirit of Czech freedom was kept alive during the war in the person of Jan Masaryk.

After the war, Masaryk resumed his role as foreign minister and accompanied Beneš to a conference with the Soviets in Moscow. Persuaded that Czechoslovakia had no choice but to remain on friendly terms with the USSR, he nevertheless tried to retain strong connections with the West. The Soviets soon proved overbearing, however, as when they vetoed Czech acceptance of the MARSHALL PLAN. Increasingly dismayed by the growing influence of Soviet communism, Masaryk nonetheless complied with President Beneš's request that he continue in his post as foreign minister after the Communist regime was installed on February 25, 1948. A short time after this, however, Masaryk died under suspicious circumstances. The public story was that he had committed suicide by leaping out of a foreign office window. Certainly, he was heartbroken enough to have contemplated taking his own life; however, many believe that he was a victim of assassination—that he had been thrown out of the window.

Further reading: Zeman, Z. A. B. *The Masaryks: The Making of Czechoslovakia*. London: Weidenfeld and Nicolson, 1976.

Matapan, Battle of

This battle took place during the Italian INVASION OF GREECE, on March 28, 1941. A British flotilla under Admiral Henry Pridham-Whippell intercepted an Italian force under Admiral Arturo Riccardi off Cape Matapan in the Greek Peloponnese. The battle, which lasted all day and stretched into the night, pitted three British battleships, four British cruisers, and a British aircraft carrier against the Italians, who lost three larger cruisers, one (possibly two) light cruisers, and two destroyers. An Italian battleship was also badly damaged. The British lost just two naval aircraft. Two thousand four hundred Italian sailors were killed in the battle. British crews rescued about 900 survivors.

The Battle of Matapan was crucial to the Allies in maintaining supremacy in the eastern Mediterranean.

See also MEDITERRANEAN OPERATIONS.

Further reading: Pack, S. W. C. *The Battle of Matapan.* London: Macmillan, 1961.

Matsuoka Yosuke (1880–1946) *Japanese foreign minister*

Matsuoka Yosuke was Japanese ambassador to the League of Nations in 1933 when Japan left the League rather than bow to its demands that it end its occupation of Manchuria.

From July 1940 to July 1941, Matsuoka served as Japan's foreign minister. He had extensive experience of the United States, having been raised there from age 13 and having attended an American university. Nevertheless, he had little affection for either the United States or Great Britain, both of which he deeply mistrusted. This mindset was critical in leading Japan on the road to war during Matsuoka's fateful year as foreign minister.

Matsuoka supported and abetted the aggressive, expansionist policies of Japan's militarists. In 1940, he obtained military bases in French Indochina and successfully pressured Britain into temporarily closing the Burma Road from July to October 1940 to suppress the Chinese nationalist movement. Also in 1940, Matsuoka negotiated the AXIS (TRIPARTITE) PACT with Germany and Italy. In April 1941, in a move that stunned many in the Japanese government, he also concluded a nonaggression pact with the Soviet Union, a longtime rival. This pact prevented Japan from collaborating with Germany in the INVASION OF THE SOVIET UNION, yet it did not stop JOSEPH STALIN from declaring war on Japan shortly before Japan surrendered.

On the eve of the Pacific war, Matsuoka was widely regarded as a liability in the Japanese government. The only way to shed him was to dissolve the entire government, which the prime minister, Prince KONOYE FUMIMARO, did. The government was then reorganized without Matsuoka, who was without office and powerless throughout the war itself. This did not prevent his being arrested after the war on charges of war crimes. By that time, Matsuoka was broken in spirit and health. He died before he was brought before the TOKYO WAR CRIMES TRIBUNAL.

See also SINO-JAPANESE WAR.

Further reading: Beasley, W. G. *Japanese Imperialism 1894–1945.* Oxford and London: Oxford University Press, 1991; Iriye, Akira. *Power and Culture: The Japanese-American War, 1941–1945.* Cambridge, Mass.: Harvard University Press, 2004; Utley, Jonathan G. *Going to War with Japan, 1937–1941.* New York: Fordham University Press, 2005.

Mauthausen concentration camp

Opened in August 1938 near Linz, Austria, Mauthausen grew from a single camp to a facility consisting of the original main camp and 60 satellites. Some 206,000 inmates, mostly Jews from all over Europe, were held here. Although Mauthausen was not ostensibly a death (extermination) camp in the service of the FINAL SOLUTION, it was a forced-labor camp, and it is believed that some 71,000 inmates died of starvation, disease, and overwork.

In addition to the Jews incarcerated at Mauthausen, the camp received victims of the so-called Bullet Decree of March 1944, by which all escaped and recaptured prisoners of war (excluding U.S. and

British nationals) were condemned to be shot. Mauthausen was chosen as the site of these executions.

The camp was liberated by U.S. Army forces on May 5, 1945. A mass grave discovered by the liberating troops contained at least 10,000 bodies.

See also HOLOCAUST, THE.

Further reading: Allen, Michael Thad. *The Business of Genocide: The SS, Slave Labor, and the Concentration Camps.* Chapel Hill: University of North Carolina Press, 2002; LeCheìne, Evelyn. *Mauthausen: The History of a Death Camp.* London: Corgi Books, 1973.

McAuliffe, Anthony (1898–1975) *U.S. hero of Bastogne*

McAuliffe earned lasting fame as the U.S. Army general who commanded the 101st Airborne Division in the desperate defense of Bastogne during the BATTLE OF THE ARDENNES (BATTLE OF THE BULGE) and replied to a German surrender demand with the monosyllabic expletive, "Nuts!"

Born in Washington, D.C., McAuliffe graduated from West Point in 1919 and was posted to the field artillery. During the NORMANDY LANDINGS (D-DAY), he was the artillery commander of the 101st Airborne Division, but a brigadier general, he was acting commander of the entire division during the defense against the Ardennes offensive. Led by McAuliffe, the 101st stalled the offensive long enough for the Third U.S. Army under GEORGE S. PATTON JR. to counterattack.

McAuliffe's reply to the German surrender demand became news worldwide and symbolized for many the offhanded, wisecracking courage and determination of the American approach to World War II.

McAuliffe retired from the army in May 1956 and worked in the industrial private sector.

Further reading: Eisenhower, John S. D. *The Bitter Woods: The Battle of the Bulge.* New York: Da Capo Press, 1995; Parker, Danny S. *The Battle of the Bulge: Hitler's Ardennes Offensive, 1944–1945.* New York: Da Capo Press, 2004; Toland, John. *Battle: The Story of the Bulge.* Lincoln: University of Nebraska Press, 1999.

McNair, Lesley James (1883–1944) *chief of U.S. Army ground forces*

Leslie McNair was born in Verndale, Minnesota, and graduated from West Point near the top of his class in 1904. As a second lieutenant of artillery, he served variously in the United States and was promoted to first lieutenant in June 1905 and to captain in May 1907. From 1909 to 1913, he served with the 4th Artillery Regiment in the American West, then was sent to France to observe artillery training techniques. He returned to the United States in time to serve in the Veracruz Expedition (April 30–November 23, 1914), then under John J. Pershing in the Punitive Expedition in pursuit of Pancho Villa, the Mexican revolutionary leader who had raided a New Mexico town (March 1916–February 1917).

Promoted to major in May 1917, the month after the United States entered World War I, McNair served on the General Staff, then shipped out to France with 1st Division, only to be transferred in August to General Headquarters, American Expeditionary Force, with the rank of lieutenant colonel. Promoted to colonel in June 1918, he became a brigadier general in October, at the time the youngest general officer in the army.

At the end of World War I, McNair was serving as senior artillery officer in the General Staff's Training Section and reverted to his permanent Regular Army rank of major. He taught at the General Service School (1919–21), then transferred to a staff post in Hawaii, serving there from 1921 to 1924, when he returned to the mainland as a professor of military science at Purdue University. Promoted to lieutenant colonel in 1928, he left Purdue to attend the Army War College. After graduating in 1929, he was appointed assistant commandant of the Field Artillery School and also worked with the Depression-era Civilian Conservation Corps (CCC).

McNair was promoted to colonel in May 1935 and assigned command of the 2nd Field Artillery Brigade in Texas two years later, when he was also promoted to brigadier general in the Regular Army. McNair was named to command the Command and General Staff School at Fort Leavenworth in April 1939 and served there until October 1940.

McNair was promoted to major general in September 1940, then to temporary lieutenant general, in June 1941. In March 1942, he was named chief of Army Ground Forces (AGF). From his headquarters at Army War College, McNair directed the expansion of AGF from 780,000 men to its maximum wartime strength of 2.2 million in July 1943. He traveled extensively throughout the country and to the various theaters of the war in a tireless effort to ensure that the troops he had trained were combat ready. During one of these trips in Tunisia in 1943, he was seriously wounded by a shell fragment.

In June 1944, McNair was sent to Great Britain to replace General George S. Patton Jr. as commander of the fictitious "First U.S. Army Group," which had been contrived to deceive the Germans prior to the Normandy landings (D-day). In July, with the Normandy invasion well under way, McNair was in France observing the invasion. On July 25, 1944, Eighth U.S. Air Force bombers, assigned to soften up German positions, dropped some of their bombs short. McNair became a victim of this friendly-fire incident.

The death of McNair deprived the army of a much respected and highly able organizer, planner, and trainer of troops. He had been instrumental in building the wartime U.S. Army and in streamlining its tactical structure in brilliant ways, most notably in the transformation of the two-brigade, four-regiment "square" division into a three-regiment "triangular" division, which proved much more flexible in combat operations.

Further reading: Kahn, E. J. *McNair, Educator of an Army*. Washington, D.C. Infantry Journal, 1945; McNair, Lesley James. *Raids*. Fort Leavenworth, Kans.: Command and General Staff School, 1920.

Meiktila, Battle of

For four weeks during the Burma Campaign, in February–March 1945, Japanese and British forces sparred with each other near and in Meiktila, which was a key Japanese communications and supply center.

Under William Slim, the Fourteenth Army (Anglo-Indian) crossed the Irrawaddy River in central Burma on the trail of Lieutenant General Shihachi Katamura's Fifteenth Japanese Army. Determined to trap the Fifteenth Army, Slim staged a magnificent deception, broadcasting misleading radio signals from a decoy headquarters, which persuaded Shihachi that Slim was about to attack Mandalay. To reinforce this impression, Slim made a feint toward Mandalay while secretly moving his main striking force (the 17th Indian Division and 255th Tank Brigade) down the Myittha Valley, across the Irrawaddy, and toward Meiktila.

The striking force encountered resistance from the Indian National Army, which, however, was no match for Slim's hardened veterans. At Meiktila, Japanese transportation troops and a small contingent of combat infantry put up a determined defense, but were soon defeated. Meiktila fell on March 3.

Lieutenant General Masaaki Honda led the Japanese 49th Division and elements of four other divisions in a counteroffensive to retake the Meiktila nerve center. Honda managed to cut off the 17th Indian Division, but Slim responded with air drops that kept the division supplied. He also flew in a full brigade to reinforce the 17th. This was sufficient to repulse Honda, who withdrew on March 28, 1945.

Further reading: Young, Edward. *Meiktila 1945: The Battle to Liberate Burma*. London: Osprey, 2004.

Mein Kampf

Perhaps the most infamous book of the 20th century, *Mein Kampf (My Struggle)* was a combination autobiography and political manifesto by Adolf Hitler. In it, he expressed the core concepts of Nazi ideology.

Hitler began composing the book, dictating it to his henchman Rudolf Hess, while both were serving terms at Landsberg Prison following the collapse of the Munich "Beer Hall" Putsch of November 1923—Hitler's premature and abortive coup d'état against the government of the Weimar

Republic. The first volume of *Mein Kampf* was published in the summer of 1925. A second volume was published in December 1926 and then was added to the first volume in 1930, which became the standard edition.

Twenty-three thousand copies of the first volume sold between 1925 and 1930, and 13,000 of the second volume sold from the end of 1926 to 1930. With Hitler's meteoric rise to power after he was named chancellor of Germany in 1933, sales of *Mein Kampf* exploded. By the end of 1933, the combined "standard" edition had sold 1.5 million copies. It is believed that at least 10 million copies were sold during the author's lifetime.

Mein Kampf is a historically important book, but, as literature it is undistinguished and nearly unreadable. Stylistically, it is repetitive and turgid. Although it was required reading throughout Germany during the Third Reich, Hitler himself was not pleased with the work. He recognized its defects of expression. Nevertheless, he repeatedly affirmed its substance, declaring that he would change nothing in it.

See also NAZI PARTY (NSDAP).

Further reading: Hitler, Adolf. *Mein Kampf.* New York: Mariner Books, 1998.

Memel (Lithuania)

Memel, the Memel Strip, or Memelland was a region along the Baltic Sea north of the Neman River that had belonged to East Prussia before World War I. As a result of the TREATY OF VERSAILLES, Memel—most of whose population were Lithuanian—was severed from Germany and made a French protectorate. The French proposed that the region be declared a free state, but in January 1923, Lithuanian military forces seized it, and Memel was annexed to Lithuania as Klaipeda. It was held by Lithuania as an autonomous region until, on March 23, 1939, the German government issued an ultimatum that forced the return of Memel to Germany. The ultimatum was the result of months of agitation by ADOLF HITLER, who demanded the return of "the Memel Strip."

Memel was restored to Lithuania in 1945, after the German surrender. By then, Lithuania itself had been swallowed up by the Soviet Union.

Further reading: Robbins, Keith. *Appeasement.* London: Blackwell, 1997.

Mengele, Josef (1911–1979) *SS physician*

Born in Günzburg, Germany, Josef Mengele was the son of a manufacturer of farm machinery in Bavaria. Raised in privilege, Mengele was a philosophy student at the University of Munich during the 1920s and fell under the spell of the racial ideology of Alfred Rosenberg. After graduating, he went on to earn a degree in medicine at the University of Frankfurt am Main.

Propelled by Rosenberg's racist philosophy, he was naturally attracted to the STURMABTEILUNG (SA), the Storm Troopers, which he joined in 1933. Mengele became a dedicated Nazi who went to work as a researcher at the newly founded Institute for Hereditary Biology and Racial Hygiene in 1934.

With the outbreak of World War II, Mengele became a medical officer with the WAFFEN SS and served in France and the USSR until May 1943, when HEINRICH HIMMLER appointed him chief physician at Birkenau, an extermination camp attached to the AUSCHWITZ EXTERMINATION CAMP.

Mengele and his staff were responsible for "selection," choosing which of the prisoners coming into the camp would be immediately murdered and which would be used as slave laborers. He also selected certain prisoners as the involuntary subjects of bizarre, grotesque, and horrific medical experiments, including experiments intended to devise means of increasing fertility to accelerate the growth of the German "race." Mengele's particular interest was in twins. Ostensibly, his experiments on twins were related to his search for the means of multiplying the German nation, although most of the experiments appear to have been nothing more or less than exercises in extreme sadism. He injected many twins with varying concentrations of poisons and pathogens to study their effects. He even oversaw a surgical operation in which two gypsy children were sutured together in an effort to create conjoined twins. Thousands died by his hand, and many others suffered permanent injury or disfigurement.

Mengele was always impeccably attired in a white lab coat and was dubbed by inmates "the White Angel" or the "Angel of Death." Despite his high profile at Birkenau-Auschwitz, Mengele managed to evade capture by the Allies after the war and lived in obscurity for four years near Rosenheim in Bavaria, working as a stable hand. In 1949, it is believed that he slipped out of Germany, traveling via Genoa, Italy, to South America. He married—it was his second marriage—under his own name in Uruguay in 1958; calling himself "José Mengele," he applied for and was granted citizenship in Paraguay the following year. It is believed that he moved to Brazil in 1961, apparently assuming the identity of Wolfgang Gerhard, a former Nazi who had also found refuge in Brazil.

Mengele was never brought to justice, and his final whereabouts remained a mystery until 1985, when a team of Brazilian, West German, and American forensic specialists determined that Mengele had died of a stroke in 1979 while swimming and was buried under Gerhard's name. This conclusion was confirmed by dental records.

Further reading: Lagnado, Lucette Matalon, and Sheila Cohn Dekel. *Children of the Flames: Dr. Josef Mengele and the Untold Story of the Twins of Auschwitz.* New York: Penguin, 1992; Lifton, Robert Jay. *The Nazi Doctors: Medical Killing and the Psychology of Genocide.* New York: Basic Books, 2000; Posner, Gerald L. *Mengele: The Complete Story.* New York: Cooper Square Press, 2000.

Merrill, Frank Dow (1903–1955) *leader of "Merrill's Marauders"*

Merrill was born in Hopkinton, Massachusetts, and enlisted in the army in 1922, serving in Panama through 1925. He received an appointment to West Point, from which he graduated in 1929 and was commissioned a second lieutenant of cavalry. During 1931–32, he attended Ordnance School,

then, from 1934 to 1935, Cavalry School, in which he became an instructor during 1935–38.

In 1938, Merrill was attached to the U.S. embassy in Tokyo and took the opportunity to study both the Japanese language and the imperial military organization. Promoted to captain in 1939, he left the embassy assignment the following year to join the intelligence staff of General Douglas MacArthur's Philippine Command. In 1941, he was promoted to temporary major and was on a mission in Rangoon when the United States entered World War II on December 8, 1941. Remaining there, he joined the command of Lieutenant General Joseph W. "Vinegar Joe" Stilwell when Stilwell reached Burma with Chinese forces in March 1942.

Merrill served with Stilwell during the first Burma Campaign and accompanied his retreat to India in May. He was promoted to temporary lieutenant colonel at that time and then to full colonel early the following year. Stilwell appointed him to command a provisional U.S. infantry regiment, which he sent into combat in northern Burma as part of the joint American-Chinese offensive to reopen the Burma Road in February 1944. Merrill's all-volunteer Ranger unit, dubbed "Merrill's Marauders," marched 100 miles into Burma and spearheaded a broad Chinese-American envelopment action. Merrill and his Marauders were celebrated as masters of quasi-guerrilla jungle warfare tactics.

During this arduous jungle campaign, Merrill suffered from heart trouble and had to be hospitalized twice. At last, in mid-August, he was transferred to lead a liaison group of the Allied Southwest Asia Command in Ceylon and was promoted to major general in September. He was then appointed chief of staff of General Simon B. Buckner's Tenth Army in the Okinawa campaign from April 1 to June 22, 1945. After Buckner's death, Merrill served as chief of staff to Stilwell, who replaced him.

After the war, Merrill served as chief of staff of the Sixth U.S. Army, headquartered in San Francisco. He was appointed chief of the American Advisory Military Mission to the Philippines in 1947, but retired from the army the following year and served the state of New Hampshire as commissioner of roads and public highways.

Further reading: Baker, Alan D. *Merrill's Marauders.* New York, Ballantine Books, 1972; Ogburn, Charlton. *The Marauders.* New York: Quill, 1982.

Mers-el-Kebir, Battle of

Mers-el-Kebir was the Algerian port, near Oran, where the French fleet, now under the control of the VICHY GOVERNMENT, was anchored when, on July 3, 1940, it came under attack by the British Royal Navy. After France's defeat in the BATTLE OF FRANCE, the British were anxious to ensure that the ships of the French fleet would not fall into German hands. The French warships anchored at Mers included the advanced battle cruisers *Dunkerque* and *Strasbourg,* magnificent vessels that outclassed German ships of the same type, as well as two older battleships and six large destroyers. Another seven destroyers and four submarines were anchored nearby, at Oran.

By the terms of the armistice signed by the defeated French, neither the Germans nor the Italians were to make use of the French fleet, which would be held, immobilized, under German and Italian control. Despite the armistice agreement, Admiral FRANÇOIS DARLAN, the navy minister under the Vichy regime, sent messages to his captains that they were not to allow their ships to fall into German hands. The British were unaware of this message and acted independently to ensure that the French ships would not be taken by Germany. On July 3, 1940, all French ships in British ports were seized. On that same day, Force H (the fleet responsible for the Mediterranean) sailed to Mers-el-Kebir. British admiral JAMES SOMERVILLE presented to Admiral Marcel Gensoul, the local French naval commander, four options:

1. To sail and join forces with the Royal Navy
2. To sail with reduced crews to any British port, where the ships would be interned and the crews repatriated

3. To sail with reduced crews to a French port in the West Indies, where the ships would be immobilized for the duration of the war
4. To scuttle the ships immediately—that is, within six hours

Although Somerville did not present the option to Gensoul, he was also authorized to offer a fifth choice: immobilization of the fleet at Mers.

Somerville warned Gensoul that if he refused to accept one of the four options he presented, his fleet would be sunk by British fire. When Gensoul reported to the French Admiralty, he mentioned only the fourth option: scuttling. The admiralty replied with instructions to resist.

Somerville was profoundly uneasy about firing on French ships, and he continued negotiations. Yet even while he and Gensoul conferred aboard the *Dunkerque,* the British intercepted a French Admiralty communication ordering all French naval forces in the Mediterranean to sail to Oran to defend the fleet there. Somerville now had no choice but to act quickly, before ships got under way.

At 5:54 in the afternoon, the British opened fire, destroying the battleship *Bretagne* and severely damaging a number of other ships, killing in the process 1,297 French sailors. *Dunkerque* was lightly damaged in the initial attack, but was entirely disabled in a subsequent air attack on July 6. *Strasbourg* and six other ships escaped, along with some cruisers that had been stationed at Algiers.

On July 5, the battleship *Richelieu,* anchored at Dakar, was hit by torpedo bombers, but intervention by Admiral ANDREW CUNNINGHAM persuaded the French commander at Dakar to surrender and disarm all of his ships. In this way, further bloodshed was avoided.

The Battle of Mers-el-Kebir came close to propelling Vichy France into an outright military alliance with Germany. At the height of the crisis created by the battle, Vichy severed diplomatic relations with Great Britain, and French torpedo bombers attacked Gibraltar in a gesture of retaliation. In the end, however, the crisis subsided, the ships stayed out of ADOLF HITLER's hands, and Vichy France essentially stayed out of the war.

See also MEDITERRANEAN OPERATIONS.

Further reading: Kettle, Michael. *De Gaulle and Algeria 1940–1960: From Mers El-Kebir to the Algiers Barricades.* London: Quartet Books, 1993; Tute, Warren. *The Deadly Stroke.* London: Collins, 1973.

Messe, Giovanni (1883–1968) *commander of Italian Expeditionary Force during invasion of the Soviet Union*

Messe commanded the Italian Expeditionary Force, which was Italy's contribution to the Axis INVASION OF THE SOVIET UNION. The force, which was ordered into action by BENITO MUSSOLINI, had not been requested by ADOLF HITLER, who, from very early in the war, had a low regard for the Italian military. The Italian Expeditionary Force made little impact on the Russian front and suffered heavy casualties before it was withdrawn in October 1942.

In February 1943, Messe was given command of what had been the German-Italian Panzer Army (formerly commanded by ERWIN ROMMEL). Renamed the First Italian Army, it fought in Tunisia during the NORTH AFRICAN CAMPAIGN and managed to pin down the Eighth British Army at Enfidaville before it was defeated and surrendered along with the rest of the Axis forces—Italian and German—remaining in North Africa.

Despite Messe's record of defeat, he was promoted to marshal later in 1943 but saw no more action. In November 1943, after Italy's surrender to the Allies, Messe was named to head the Italian High Command.

Further reading: Corti, Eugenio. *Few Returned: Twenty-Eight Days on the Russian Front, Winter 1942–1943.* Columbia: University of Missouri Press, 1997; McClure, W. K. *Italy in North Africa.* New York: Hyperion, 1990.

Messervy, Frank (1893–1973) *commander of British "Desert Rats"*

Messervy was a dashing and popular British commander in World War II who led a brigade in East Africa and then, in the WESTERN DESERT CAMPAIGN, the 7th Armored Division—better known as the "Desert Rats"—which was pitted against elements of ERWIN ROMMEL's Afrika Korps.

During the BURMA CAMPAIGN, Messervy commanded the 7th Indian Division. From December 1944 to July 1945, he commanded 4th Corps against the Japanese at the BATTLE OF MEIKTILA, as a result of which he became the liberator of Rangoon.

Messervy ended the war as commander in chief, Malaya command.

Further reading: Forty, George. *7th Armoured Division: The Desert Rats.* Hersham, U.K.: Ian Allan Publishing, 2003; Verney, G. L. *The Desert Rats: The 7th Armored Division in World War II.* London: Greenhill, 2002; Young, Edward. *Meiktila 1945: The Battle to Liberate Burma.* London: Osprey, 2004.

Metaxas, Ioannis (1871–1941) *Greek dictator*

Ioannis Metaxis was born in Ithaca, Greece, and enlisted in the Greek military. He saw action in the Greco-Turkish War of 1897, then went to Germany to further his military education. Returning to Greece, he rose through the officer ranks, gaining appointment to the general staff during the Balkan Wars of 1912–13 and becoming chief of staff in 1913. He was promoted to general in 1916.

In 1914, at the outbreak of World War I, Metaxas served as military adviser to King Constantine I, but his outspoken counsel that Greece maintain neutrality brought him into conflict with the premier, Eleutherios Venizelos, who favored alliance with the Allies. When Constantine abdicated in 1917, Metaxas, opposed to the pro-Allied military policies of Venizelos, resigned. After Constantine returned to the throne in 1920, Metaxas was restored as well and used his position to oppose Venizelos; however, when Constantine's son and successor George II was forced to abdicate in 1923, Metaxas again stepped down and, this time, left the country. He returned after a brief interval to accept a ministry-level position in the government of the new republic. During this period, he founded a small royalist party, which he employed as a platform from which to voice his opposition to the very government he was serving.

With the restoration of George II in 1935, Metaxas was named minister of war and then, in April 1936, premier. Backed by the king, he imposed a dictatorship on August 4, 1936, modeling himself on BENITO MUSSOLINI and the fascist example. Despite this, however, he carefully maintained diplomatic ties with both Britain and France. Using his near-absolute authority, Metaxas carried through a limited but badly needed program of economic and social reform. As for opposition, he suppressed it with summary brutality.

When Italy invaded Greece in 1940, Metaxas made limited use of his good relations with the West. Although he did not want overt aid from Britain—lest he antagonize Germany—he accepted covert military assistance and drove the Italian invaders back into Albania.

Metaxas died on January 21, 1941, just three months before the Germans invaded Greece with far greater success than the Italians.

See also GREECE, INVASION OF.

Further reading: Bitzes, John G. *Greece in World War II: To April 1941.* Manhattan, Kans.: Sunflower University Press, 1989; Petrakis, Marina. *The Metaxas Myth: Dictatorship and Propaganda in Greece.* London and New York: Tauris Academic Studies, 2005.

MI5 (British Military Intelligence)

During World War II, the British security service MI5 shared with MI6 (BRITISH MILITARY INTELLIGENCE) and the Special Branch of the Metropolitan Police authority for evaluating and advising the government on intelligence relating to national security. MI5 provided intelligence to aid in defense against espionage, sabotage, and political subversion.

The personnel of MI5 and MI6 often came into conflict over matters of jurisdiction. Originally, when the two agencies were established under the War Office before World War I, MI5 (created in 1909 by Sir Vernon Kell) was responsible for intelligence within the United Kingdom to a limit of three miles off the coastline. Additionally, MI5 could cooperate in intelligence work in countries of the British Empire, including Egypt. MI6, in contrast, was concerned primarily with collecting intelligence abroad and was also responsible for national security beyond the geographical limits imposed on MI5.

Between the wars, MI5 handled security related to the British armed forces, whereas the Special Branch was responsible for security relating to the civilian population. In 1931, MI5 (now officially called the Security Service, but still familiarly referred to by its original name) took over from Special Branch intelligence work relating to all subversion, military or civilian. Throughout World War II, there was considerable dispute over whether MI5 should be incorporated into MI6 or assume responsibility for all counterespionage, at home and abroad. Despite this clash, the traditional division of responsibility remained more or less in force, with MI5 concentrating on domestic counterintelligence and MI6 focusing on espionage and counterespionage abroad.

During the war, MI5 monitored the activities of outspoken British fascists and fascist sympathizers, such as OSWALD MOSLEY, as well as anyone who had, before the war, advocated close ties with Germany. Early in the war, panic over the existence of a vast domestic fifth column threatened to overwhelm the meager resources of MI5.

At the outbreak of the war, MI5 was headed by its superannuated founder, Kell. Prime Minister WINSTON CHURCHILL effectively forced Kell's retirement, replacing him briefly with Brigadier General Jasper Harker until Kell's permanent replacement, Sir David Petrie, arrived from India. Petrie had worked for 36 years with the Indian police and was a thoroughgoing expert in counterespionage and countersubversion tactics. Under Petrie, MI5 rapidly developed into a highly competent agency and a fitting adversary of the German espionage unit known as the Abwehr. MI5 infiltrated the Abwehr in Britain by introducing double agents. This infiltration, combined with efficient interception and decryption of coded German radio messages, allowed MI5 to defeat the first major Abwehr operation against Britain in November 1940. All 21 German agents active in Britain at this time were either captured or surrendered. One committed suicide. Through 1943, MI5 intercepted Abwehr agents trying to infiltrate into Britain at the rate of about 20 a year. Some of these MI5 turned into double agents. The agency's success was such that the Abwehr essentially presented no real threat to Britain by the middle of the war. Worse for the Germans, MI5 used its double-agent network to generate disinformation and deception, which proved especially important during the lead-up to the NORMANDY LANDINGS (D-DAY).

Further reading: Burnes, John. *MI5.* London: Pocket Essentials, 2006; West, Nigel. *MI5: British Security Service Operations, 1909–1945.* London: Bodley Head, 1981.

MI6 (British Military Intelligence)

MI6 was created before World War I along with MI5. Whereas MI5 had responsibility for domestic and colonial counterespionage, MI6 worked abroad to gather foreign intelligence relating to national security. (Despite this geographical division of jurisdiction, disputes between the two agencies were common during World War II.) MI6 was put under the control of the British Foreign Office in 1921 and officially redesignated Secret Intelligence Service; however, it continued to be far more familiarly known as MI6.

In addition to managing a network of agents abroad, MI6 also administered the British Code and Cypher School at Bletchley Park, which was responsible for intercepting and deciphering coded messages produced by the German ENIGMA CIPHER AND MACHINE and producing ULTRA intelligence. It was in this work that MI6 made its greatest impact in World War II, although its fieldwork was also important and effective.

Like MI5, MI6 had a staff inadequate for its mission on the eve of war; however, in 1938, funding was provided to build up the agency under the leadership of Admiral Hugh Sinclair (codenamed "C"), who augmented the existing counterespionage section and created a new section—desig-

nated Section D—for sabotage and subversion. On Sinclair's death late in 1939, Stewart Menzies took over. He immediately faced a crisis when two of his top officers were abducted, compromising much of MI6's European network. Another blow came in May 1940, when the new prime minister, WINSTON CHURCHILL, transferred Section D from MI6 to the Special Operation Executive (SOE). This created an ongoing competition between MI6 and SOE for a variety of scarce resources.

Despite various handicaps, parts of MI6 worked well in conjunction with MI5 and SOE, especially in the management and coordination of double agents. Very early in the war, breakthroughs in reading encrypted communications to and from German Abwehr agents yielded extremely valuable intelligence and counterintelligence.

At the outbreak of the war MI6 created a special scientific section that was responsible for conducting and analyzing aerial photographic reconnaissance. Although this work was taken over by the RAF early on, the advances developed by the scientific section of MI6 were invaluable.

MI6 truly came into its own beginning in 1942, as the Allies gradually seized the initiative and began offensive operations. MI6 became a key provider of tactical intelligence and served as liaison among and coordinator of the intelligence services of the various Allied governments in exile, including, most important, the Poles, Czechs, Free French, and Resistance operatives in occupied France. Covert activity in France steadily gained in importance as the war progressed. MI6 also established and maintained important contacts with the German internal resistance (*see* RESISTANCE MOVEMENTS).

Perhaps the most spectacular work of MI6 came during preparations for the NORMANDY LANDINGS (D-DAY). An MI6 agent managed to steal plans of the Atlantic Wall, the massive fixed defenses along the coast that the Germans had built with slave labor. Other agents working under MI6 provided detailed sketches of some 50 miles of Norman coastline. After the invasion, MI6 created Special Counter-Intelligence Units to accompany the Allied armies into France, Belgium, and the

Netherlands. Their mission was to prevent enemy infiltration of the invading forces. By the end of the war, the reputation of MI6 had not only been rehabilitated but even mythologized. It came to be regarded as among the most effective intelligence organizations of World War II.

Further reading: Fraser-Smith, Charles. *Secret Warriors: Hidden Heroes of MI6, OSS, MI9, SOE, and SAS.* Bletchley, U.K.: Paternoster Press, 1984; West, Nigel. *MI6: British Secret Intelligence Service Operations, 1909–45.* New York: HarperCollins, 1985.

Midway, Battle of

Japan's Admiral Yamamoto Isoroku conceived a grand plan to lure the U.S. Pacific fleet into a single decisive battle that would finish the work of the Battle of Pearl Harbor, destroying or at least crippling the fleet so severely that the United States would be forced to seek a negotiated peace in the Pacific theater. Midway Island, just 1,000 miles west of Hawaii, was a strategically located piece of land from which either side could launch major attacks against the other. Yamamoto believed that he could trap the U.S. fleet here and administer a coup de grâce.

He sent a diversionary force to the Aleutian Islands, U.S. territory in the northern Pacific, while Admiral Nagumo Chuichi, the very man who had led the attack on Pearl Harbor, took a four-carrier striking force followed by an invasion fleet—a total of about 88 ships—to Midway. Thanks to Ultra intelligence, the U.S. Pacific commander, Admiral Chester A. Nimitz anticipated Yamamoto's move and intended to oblige him by providing the decisive battle he wanted—with, however, a very different outcome: an American victory.

Nimitz hurriedly assembled two task forces east of Midway: Number 16, under Admiral Raymond Spruance, and Number 18, commanded by Admiral Frank Fletcher. In addition to the aircraft

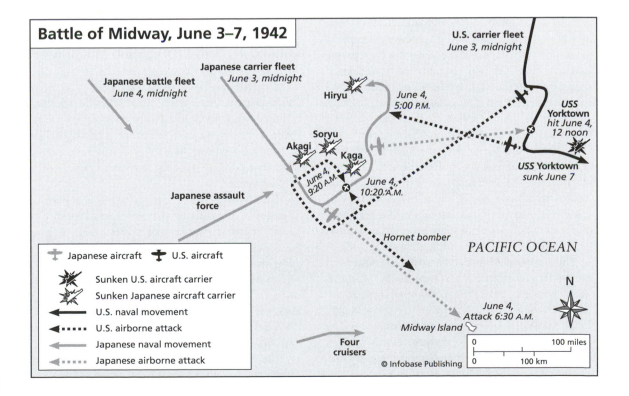

Battle of Midway, June 3–7, 1942

U.S. carrier fleet
June 3, midnight

Japanese battle fleet
June 4, midnight

Japanese carrier fleet
June 3, midnight

Hiryu

June 4, 5:00 P.M.

USS **Yorktown**
hit June 4,
12 noon

Soryu

Akagi

Kaga

June 4, 9:20 A.M.

June 4, 10:20 A.M.

USS **Yorktown**
sunk June 7

Japanese assault force

Hornet bomber

PACIFIC OCEAN

✠ Japanese aircraft   ✠ U.S. aircraft

Sunken U.S. aircraft carrier

Sunken Japanese aircraft carrier

U.S. naval movement

U.S. airborne attack

Japanese naval movement

Japanese airborne attack

Four cruisers

June 4, Attack 6:30 A.M.

Midway Island

N

0   100 miles

0   100 km

© Infobase Publishing

launched from the large carriers *Enterprise, Hornet,* and *Yorktown,* land-based planes would operate from Midway itself.

Midway-based planes attacked a portion of the Japanese fleet more than 500 miles west of Midway on June 3, 1942. The attack failed to do significant damage, and American losses were heavy. On the morning of June 4, the Japanese seized the initiative, sending 108 planes against Midway, causing heavy damage, including the loss on the ground of 15 of the 25 USMC fighter planes defending the island. At the same time, U.S. torpedo bombers made a second air attack against the Japanese fleet. They hit no ships and lost seven aircraft. In a second strike this day, eight of 27 USMC dive bombers were lost, again having inflicted no damage. At last, 15 heavy B-17 bombers flying out of Midway attacked, but, again, the Japanese carriers escaped unscathed. However, American torpedo bombers launched from all three carriers made yet another attack on the Japanese fleet. They inflicted little damage, and, worst of all, 35 of the 41 bombers engaged were shot down. But this costly attack forced the Japanese carriers to launch all of their aircraft in defense, leaving the carriers vulnerable to an attack. As the Japanese crews were still preparing their aircraft, which had just returned from defending against the latest torpedo bomber attacks, 54 dive bombers from the *Enterprise* and *Yorktown* (the *Hornet*'s planes failed to find their targets) descended on three of the great Japanese carriers—*Akagi, Kaga,* and *Soryu.* All were loaded with just-recovered aircraft not yet ready to take off. In a mere five minutes, all three ships were sent to the bottom, along with crews, aircraft, and pilots. A fourth carrier, *Hiryu,* was sunk in a second attack later in the afternoon—although not before the *Hiryu*'s planes had savaged the *Yorktown,* ultimately sinking it.

The Battle of Midway was costly for American pilots and sailors, but it was fatal to the Japanese. Losing four aircraft carriers, many aircraft, and—perhaps worst of all—many of its most highly skilled pilots, the Japanese withdrew on June 5. The U.S. forces in the area were themselves too battered to give chase—although they did subsequently sink a heavy cruiser, the *Mikuma,* on June 6.

The Battle of Midway is universally regarded as the turning point of the Pacific war. Up to this point, Japan had been on the offensive, a veritable juggernaut. After Midway, it could fight only a defensive war, and its hold on the vast Pacific was steadily eroded. The cost to the United States for this momentous strategic triumph was 150 planes, 307 men, a destroyer, and the carrier *Yorktown.* Japanese losses were 275 planes, four carriers, a heavy cruiser, and nearly 5,000 sailors and airmen—the latter an irreplaceable loss.

See also ALEUTIAN ISLANDS CAMPAIGN.

Further reading: Fuchida, Misuo, and Masatake Okumiya. *Midway: The Battle That Doomed Japan, the Japanese Navy's Story.* Annapolis, Md.: Bluejacket Books, 2001; Lord, Walter. *Incredible Victory: The Battle of Midway.* Springfield, N.J.: Burford Books, 1998; Parshall, Jonathan B., and Anthony Tully. *Shattered Sword: The Untold Story of the Battle of Midway.* Dulles, Va.: Potomac Books, 2005; Prange, Gordon W., Donald M. Goldstein, and Katherine V. Dillon. *Miracle at Midway.* New York: Penguin, 1983.

Mihailović, Draža (Dragoljub Mihailović) (1893–1946) *commander of the Chetniks—Serbian guerrillas*

Draža Mihailović entered the Belgrade (Serbia) Military Academy at age 15 and saw his first combat in 1912 during the Serbian war against Turkey. Mihailović next fought in World War I, emerging from that conflict with the rank of captain in the Serbian army.

After World War I, Serbia became a part of Yugoslavia, and, during the run-up to World War II, the Yugoslav government under Prince Regent Paul aligned itself with the Axis; however, Paul's government was toppled by a military coup on March 27, 1941, which established a government more or less aligned with the Allies. Just ten days after the coup, however, German aircraft devastated Belgrade, an attack that was followed by the INVASION OF YUGOSLAVIA.

After the German occupation of Yugoslavia, Mihailović became head of the Chetniks (Četniks), a mountain guerrilla movement that took its name from the anti-Turkish fighters of 1912–18. Aided by the Allies, Mihailović and his Chetniks fought alongside the partisans of Marshall Tito—at least for a time. The two leaders and their partisan armies came to blows over a basic political and ideological conflict. Whereas Mihailović was a staunch monarchist, Tito was a committed communist.

Ultimately, the ideological differences between Mihailović and Tito overwhelmed Mihailović's opposition to the Germans. He began to collaborate with the Germans and Italians against Tito and his partisans. Pursuant to a decision at the Teheran (Tehran) Conference of November 28–December 1, 1943, the Allies abruptly ended all aid to Mihailović and funneled everything to Tito.

After the war, on March 13, 1946, Tito loyalists captured Mihailović, who was tried and convicted as a collaborator. He was executed on July 17, 1946.

Further reading: Djilas, Milovan. *Tito: The Story from Inside.* Charleston, S.C.: Phoenix Press, 2001; Hehn, Paul N. *The German Struggle against Yugoslav Guerrillas in World War II: German Counter-Insurgency in Yugoslavia, 1941–1943.* New York: Columbia University Press, 1979.

Mikołajczyk, Stanisław (1901–1967) *prime minister of Polish government in exile*

Stanisław Mikołajczyk launched his political career as an activist in rural Polish youth organizations and in agricultural special-interest organizations. He joined the Polish Peasants Party (PIAST) in 1922 and in 1927 became cofounder of the Wielkopolska Union of Rural Youth, based in Pozna . He earned national fame and became a prominent Polish politician. In 1933, he was elected to the Polish parliament (Sejm) and rose in the ranks of the Polish Peasants Party.

During the INVASION OF POLAND in September 1939, Mikołajczyk escaped to London, where he joined with WŁADYSŁAW SIKORSKI and Władysław Raczkiewicz to establish a Polish government in exile, the National Council. Mikołajczyk served as deputy prime minister in the National Council under Sikorski. When Sikorkski was killed in an air crash in July 1943, Mikołajczyk was appointed prime minister.

Mikołajczyk returned to Poland in June 1945 and assumed the post of deputy prime minister and minister of agriculture and agricultural reforms in the postwar Provisional Government of National Unity. He also took up leadership of the re-formed Polish Peasants Party in July 1945. He struggled against domination by Moscow and, in October 1947, was forced by the Soviets to flee the country. He spent the rest of his life in exile in the United States, working as an activist against Soviet totalitarian communism.

Further reading: Kacewicz, G. V. *Great Britain, the Soviet Union and the Polish Government in Exile (1939–1945).* Berlin: Springer, 1989; Mikolajczyk, Stanislaw. *The Rape of Poland.* Westport, Conn.: Greenwood Press, 1972.

mines, land

Land mines in World War II were of two major types, antitank mines and antipersonnel mines. The latter were developed chiefly to foil attempts to detect and remove the antitank mines.

The first antitank mines deployed in World War II were laid by the Italians in 1940 during the WESTERN DESERT CAMPAIGNS. These devices were activated by pressure on the top of the mine. The Italians also deployed antipersonnel mines—chiefly to protect the antitank mines—which were nothing more than stick hand grenades triggered by trip wires or pressure fuses.

The British were the second belligerent to develop antitank mines, but these were not deployed until after the conclusion of the BATTLE OF FRANCE. Fearing invasion, the British began to mass-produce the mines to defend against Panzer attack. The devices were manufactured from modified cake tins, which were filled with eight pounds of TNT and fitted with a primitive pressure fuse. The first model, designated Mark IV, was easily cleared by explosive blasts detonated nearby, so the mine was redesigned with a new fuse that could not be so easily triggered by a blast; this was designated Mark V. The British did not produce antipersonnel mines, instead defending their minefields by gunfire.

The German Tellermine was first used in the Western Desert Campaigns in 1941. Like the British mines, it was circular. The mine was packed with 11 pounds of TNT and was activated by a pressure fuse. In addition to this antitank mine, the Germans deployed the S-Mine (*Springenmine*), an antipersonnel device that was buried just below the surface of the topsoil. Small prongs remained above ground; when triggered, these set off a shrapnel-filled canister, which sprayed the deadly metal shards upward to chest height.

The Soviets produced few mines at the outbreak of the war, largely because, as defensive rather than offensive weapons, they were frowned on by JOSEPH STALIN and other Communist Party members. It was not until 1941 that production of antitank mines began in earnest in the USSR. Before the end of the war, however, the Soviets produced mines in massive quantities, laying perhaps as many as 200 million.

Mines were laid principally wherever armor was extensively employed in combat. For that reason, the Pacific war, which made relatively little use of tanks, did not see a large quantity of mines.

As a weapon, mines were not only destructive in and of themselves, but required an extensive commitment of manpower to clear, so beyond their direct effect, their use tended to tie down significant numbers of troops and generally to delay the advance of armor. They were often a menace to the mine-laying side however, as well as the enemy. It was all too easy to blunder into one's own minefield.

As the war progressed, the technology of mine detection advanced. Initially, mines could be detected only by dangerous and time-consuming prodding with bayonets or special metal probes. Once found, they had to be carefully lifted by hand—a hazardous undertaking not just because of the mines themselves, but because of the necessity to expose oneself to enemy fire. In 1942, all sides had small, hand-held electromagnetic mine detectors intended to take the place of manual probing, but these did not prove wholly reliable.

The British developed and deployed several devices designed to clear mines quickly and with less danger. Tanks were fitted with special rollers and mine plows, but the most successful device was the mine flail—also called a "Crab" or "Scorpion." A large rotating drum was fitted to the front of a tank, the rotation of the drum driven by the tank's transmission. As the drum rotated, weighted chains flailed out from it, beating the earth and detonating the mines. Vehicles that followed directly behind the flail could reliably traverse a tankwide path cleared of mines.

Another mine-clearing device was a modification of the Bangalore torpedo. Explosive-filled steel pipes (called Snakes) were pushed through minefields by tanks. The explosives set off most antipersonnel mines, clearing a wide path, but the method was less effective for clearing antitank mines, which were less susceptible to detonation by blast.

In 1943, the Axis began laying wooden mines with plastic pressure fuses. Because they were nonmetallic, these mines could not be detected by Allied electromagnetic mine detectors. In addition to nonmetallic antitank mines, the Germans also laid many *Schuhmines,* which consisted of a wooden box filled with just enough explosive to blow off the foot of anyone unfortunate enough to step on one. The maimed soldier was thus rendered unfit for battle, and at least one or two other troops had to come to his aid.

Land mines did not defeat the tank as a weapon, but they surely made an impact and significantly reduced their mobility. It is estimated that between 20 and 30 percent of all tank casualties in World War II were caused by mines

Further reading: Bull, Stephen, and Mike Chappell. *World War II Infantry Tactics (1): Squad and Platoon (Elite).* London: Osprey, 2004; Bull, Stephen, and Mike Chappell. *World War II Infantry Tactics (2): Company and Battalion (Elite).* London: Osprey, 2005.

mines, naval

The history of naval mines is longer than that of LAND MINES, dating to before the middle of the

19th century. It is estimated that the belligerents laid approximately a half million naval mines during World War II. The direct effect of this weapon was not as great as one might expect. Mines were responsible for sinking about 6.5 percent of all Allied merchant shipping during the war; aircraft, submarines, and surface ships accounted for the vast majority of sinkings. Nevertheless, the presence of mines had a profound effect on naval strategy. By laying mines, the Germans could prompt the closing of British and U.S. ports for days at a time. Mines were important in the siege of MALTA, and the British made effective use of mines against German surface raiders in February 1942. The United States used naval mines—laid from the air—most effectively in the blockade of Japan. This heavy mine barrage greatly disrupted merchant supply traffic into the Japanese homeland.

All combatants deployed primarily moored contact mines. These were ball-shaped mines from which horns projected. When the hull of a ship broke one of the horns, a chemical was released, which triggered a firing mechanism that touched off approximately 600 pounds of explosive material. Contact mines were generally laid in moderately shallow waters, no more than 600 feet deep (although the Japanese developed mines that could be laid in water as deep as 3,500 feet). They were moored to the sea bottom by a weighted cable. Contact mines were laid by specialized minelaying ships as well as by other warships modified to carry minelaying equipment.

During World War I, both the British and the Germans developed more sophisticated magnetic mines, which were also called influence mines. Whereas contact mines were detonated by actual contact with a ship's hull, magnetic mines were detonated by the proximity ("influence") of the steel hull of a passing ship. This significantly increased the chance that a mine would be detonated.

At the beginning of the war, the Germans deployed many influence mines to great effect; however, a hiatus in the German minelaying program from early December 1939 until the end of March 1940 proved strategically damaging to the Germans, who were never able thereafter to lay sufficient quantities of influence mines to disrupt British shipping significantly. Moreover, by mid-1940 the British had developed effective minesweeping countermeasures. The British Minesweeping Service recovered an intact German magnetic mine in November 1939, analyzed it, and by mid-1940 developed and deployed a magnetic sweep. The Germans then began deploying another type of influence mine, the acoustic mine, which was detonated by the sound of a passing ship's screw. The British quickly developed effective sweeps for these as well.

Whereas contact mines were generally laid by ships, influence mines, which were cylindrical rather than spherical, were usually air-dropped. Early in the war, this required flying at extremely low altitudes, which exposed aircraft to enemy fire, but by the beginning of 1944, the use of airborne RADAR enabled Allied aircraft to deploy mines from as high as 15,000 feet. Influence mines could pack as many as 775 pounds of explosives.

Of the combatant nations, the Soviet Union developed influence mines late in the war (after 1943), and Japan never developed them.

The German Luftwaffe dropped 2,200-pound naval magnetic mines by parachute on British cities. Called Luftmines by the Germans, they were classified as "G" mines by the British Bomb Disposal Service. These attacks provoked British retaliation in the form of Operation Royal Marine, which, in May 1940, air-dropped small, buoyant mines so that they would float down the Rhine River, greatly disrupting river traffic between Karlsruhe and Mainz.

In 1944, at the time of the NORMANDY LANDINGS (D-DAY), the Germans introduced yet another kind of influence mine, the pressure mine, which the Allies referred to by the code name "Oyster." This mine was detonated by changes in ambient water pressure caused by a vessel passing overhead. Some 400 were laid off the Norman coast and caused significant losses until one was recovered intact and analyzed. The British then calculated the maximum speed at which a vessel could move in various depths without triggering the mine. If a captain were very careful, this countermeasure worked well, but it required scrupulous calculation.

See also MINESWEEPER.

Further reading: Hartmann, Gregory Kemenyi. *Weapons That Wait: Mine Warfare in the U.S. Navy.* Annapolis, Md.: Naval Institute Press, 1991; Levie, Howard. *Mine Warfare at Sea.* Berlin: Springer, 1992; Morison, Samuel L. *Guide to Naval Mine Warfare.* Arlington, Va.: Pasha, 1995.

minesweeper

During World War II, minesweeping—the removal of NAVAL MINES—was carried out by specially built minesweepers and destroyer-minesweepers as well as an array of converted civilian craft, including trawlers and even paddle steamers. Some of the specialized vessels had wooden hulls, so that they would not detonate magnetic mines. But most World War II–era minesweepers were conventional steel-hulled ships, of which the U.S. Navy YMS Class was typical. The YMS ships displaced 270 tons, were 136 feet in length, and were crewed by 32 men. They carried a single three-inch antiaircraft gun and a pair of 20 mm antiaircraft guns. Driven by a pair of diesels making about 2,000 horsepower, the YMS-class ships had a top speed of 15 knots.

Most commonly, Allied minesweepers were equipped with Oropesa sweeps (named after the first ship to use this equipment in 1919). Designed to sweep contact mines, the Oropesa sweep was towed behind the minesweeper. It severed the mine's mooring cable by means of a weighted wire equipped with sharp cutters and a small explosive charge. When the released mine bobbed to the surface, it was detonated by gunfire.

Magnetic mines were swept using the LL, or magnetic sweep. This consisted of two long buoyant electrical cables towed behind a wooden-hulled sweeper. An electric current was passed through the cables, creating a magnetic field that detonated the mines. Magnetic mines could also be swept using coils mounted on wooden barges and towed by a tug. Low-altitude aircraft fitted with magnetic coils could also be employed to clear magnetic mines. The Allies experimented less successfully with ships that had massive electromagnets installed in their bows. The sweeping of magnetic mines became less important after degaussing technology advanced, by which the magnetic field of a steel hull could be effectively neutralized.

Further reading: Brookes, Ewart. *Glory Passed Them By.* London: Jarrolds, 1958; Lott, Arnold S. *Most Dangerous Sea: A History of Mine Warfare and an Account of U.S. Navy Mine Warfare Operations in World War II and Korea.* Annapolis, Md.: U.S. Naval Institute, 1959; Lund, Paul, and Harry Ludlam. *Out Sweeps!: The Story of the Minesweepers in World War II.* London and New York: Foulsham, 1978; Morison, Samuel L. *Guide to Naval Mine Warfare.* Arlington, Va.: Pasha, 1995.

Mitscher, Marc (1887–1947) *U.S. Pacific commander*

Marc Mitscher was born in Hillsboro, Wisconsin, and raised in Oklahoma City, but his landlocked birthplace and early home notwithstanding, he gained admission to the U.S. Naval Academy, from which he graduated in 1910. While serving on the USS *California* during 1913–15, he participated in the landings at Veracruz, Mexico, in April 1914. In 1915, he enrolled in flight training at Pensacola Naval Air Station, earning his wings in June 1916. After advanced flight training at Pensacola, he served aboard the attack cruiser *Huntington* and performed balloon and aircraft catapult experiments during April 1917.

During World War I, Mitscher served aboard vessels on Atlantic convoy escort duty, then was posted to Montauk Point Naval Air Station on Long Island, New York, then given command of the Rockaway, Long Island, Naval Air Station in February 1918.

In 1919, Mitscher assumed command of the Miami NAS and in May of that year attempted a transatlantic flight, but made it only as far as the Azores—a feat for which he nevertheless received the Navy Cross.

In the winter of 1920, Mitscher transferred to the Pacific as commander of the Pacific Fleet's air unit based in San Diego, California. In 1922, he returned to the East Coast as commander of the Anacostia NAS in Washington, D.C., and also served in the Plans Division of the Bureau of Aeronautics from 1922 to 1926. In 1922, he led the navy team at the international air race at Detroit and, in 1923, at St. Louis.

From July to December 1926, Mitscher served aboard the USS *Langley,* the navy's first aircraft carrier, in the Pacific. He transferred to another carrier, the USS *Saratoga,* and was appointed the ship's air officer when it entered the fleet in November 1927. Promoted to commander in October 1930, Mitscher returned to shore duty in Washington at the Bureau of Aeronautics, serving until 1933, when he was named chief of staff to Base Force commander Admiral Alfred W. Johnson. He served aboard the seaplane tender *Wright* for a year before being appointed executive officer of the *Saratoga* in 1934. Mitscher returned to the Bureau of Aeronautics as leader of the Flight Division from 1935 to 1937.

Late in 1937, Mitscher assumed command of the USS *Wright* and was promoted to captain the following year. As captain, he took command of Patrol Wing 1, operating out of San Diego, serving until June 1939, when he was named assistant chief of the Bureau of Aeronautics. In July 1941, Mitscher

Marc Mitscher *(U.S. Navy History Center)*

was given command of the new aircraft carrier USS *Hornet.* He was skipper of this carrier when Army Air Corps colonel JIMMY DOOLITTLE flew the DOOLITTLE TOKYO RAID from its deck. Mitscher also commanded the *Hornet* during the BATTLE OF MIDWAY (June 1942), after which he was promoted to rear admiral and assigned command of Patrol Wing 2. In December 1942, he became commandant of Fleet Air, based at Noumea, capital of New Caledonia. After the U.S. victory in the BATTLE OF GUADALCANAL, he moved his base to that island in April 1943.

During the Solomon Islands campaigns, Mitscher directed combined operations of army, navy, marine, and New Zealand air units, then returned to sea as commander of the Fast Carrier Task Force during the MARSHALL ISLANDS CAMPAIGN, the BATTLE OF TRUK ISLAND, and in the NEW GUINEA CAMPAIGN.

Promoted to vice admiral in March 1944, Mitscher took command of carrier operations at the BATTLE OF THE PHILIPPINE SEA and was in command during the destruction of the Japanese carrier force in the celebrated "Marianas Turkey Shoot" of June 19–21. During August and September, he supported amphibious landings at the Bonins and Palau, then commanded air cover operations for the landings at the BATTLE OF LEYTE in October. During the BATTLE OF LEYTE GULF (October 24–26), he directed carrier operations that destroyed most of the remaining Japanese carrier fleet.

Mitscher next played a supporting role at the BATTLE OF IWO JIMA in February 1945 and the BATTLE OF OKINAWA in April. During the Battle of the East China Sea (April 7), Mitscher's carriers sank the great Japanese battleship *Yamato* along with most of its escorts.

Mitscher returned to Washington, D.C., in July 1945 as deputy chief of Naval Operations (Air) and, in March 1946, he was promoted to admiral. He commanded the Eighth Fleet briefly before his death, at age 60, from illness.

Further reading: Coletta, Paolo Enrico. *Admiral Marc A. Mitscher and U.S. Naval Aviation: Bald Eagle.* Lewiston,

Pa.: Edwin Mellen Press, 1997; Taylor, Theodore. *The Magnificent Mitscher*. Annapolis, Md.: Naval Institute Press, 1991.

Model, Walther (1891–1945) *German commander, "Führer's Fireman"*

Model was born in Genthin near Magdeburg, the son of a music teacher. He joined the army in 1909 and, by the outbreak of World War I, had risen to service in several staff and adjutant positions. He received the Iron Cross in October 1915. After the armistice, Model was one of the small cadre of 4,000 officers retained for service in the Reichswehr, the diminutive army Germany was permitted under the TREATY OF VERSAILLES.

An early follower of ADOLF HITLER, Model joined the Nazi Party and was rewarded in 1935 with command of the Technical Department of the Army General Staff. On March 1, 1938, Model was promoted to major general, and the following year was given command of IV Corps in the INVASION OF POLAND (September–October 1939). Promoted to lieutenant general on April 1, 1940, he led the 3rd Panzer Division through Flanders and France during the BATTLE OF FRANCE (May–June 1940).

Elevated to *General der Panzergruppen* (panzer group general), Model was sent to the Russian front on October 1, 1941, where he briefly commanded the XXXI Panzer Corps before promotion to *Generaloberst* (colonel general) on February 28, 1942. He was given command of the Ninth German Army, which he led from January 1942 to January 1944. After leading the northern arm of the failed offensive against KURSK during July 5–12, 1943, he was assigned command of Army Group North in January 1944. In March, after promotion to field marshal, he took command of Army Group North Ukraine. On June 28, Model assumed command of what remained of Army Group Center on the eastern front.

After the JULY PLOT (TO ASSASSINATE HITLER)—July 20, 1944—Model reaffirmed his loyalty to Hitler, whereupon he was named commander of Army Group B and commander in chief (OB) West on August 17, 1944. Days later, however, on Sep-

tember 5, his authority reverted to command of Army Group B only.

Model led a highly effective defense against the Allied advance at Arnhem during OPERATION MARKET-GARDEN (September 17–26, 1944), and he was in overall command of the daring Ardennes offensive from December 16, 1944, to January 15, 1945. By April 1945, however, Model's forces were surrounded in the Ruhr Pocket Campaign. He conducted a hopeless though valiant resistance for 18 days before finally surrendering his 300,000 remaining troops. As for himself, rather than surrender, he committed suicide at Lintorf on April 21, 1945.

The majority of Germany's best military commanders were often contemptuous of Hitler as a strategist, and they harbored deep ideological and moral objections to Nazism. In contrast to these, Model was a zealous follower of Hitler and a thoroughgoing Nazi. His military philosophy was unceasingly aggressive, and his talent for intervening productively in desperate situations earned him the nickname "Führer's Fireman."

See also ARDENNES, BATTLE OF THE (BATTLE OF THE BULGE), and KURSK, BATTLE OF.

Further reading: Newton, Steven H. *Hitler's Commander: Field Marshal Walter Model—Hitler's Favorite General*. New York: Da Capo, 2005.

Moelders, Werner (1913–1941) *German air ace*

Born in Gelsenkirchen, Germany, Moelders graduated from the Dresden Military Academy and joined the Luftwaffe in 1935. He served as a flight instructor until 1938, then as a squadron commander, fought during the Spanish civil war. He emerged from this conflict an ace, credited with 14 victories, more than any other German pilot.

When World War II began, Moelders assumed command of Jagdgeschwader 53, then, during the BATTLE OF FRANCE, commanded Jagdgeschwader 51, narrowly escaping death on June 5, 1940, when his Messerschmitt Bf109 was shot down over Chantilly. Moelders flew next in the BATTLE OF BRITAIN and in the INVASION OF THE SOVIET UNION. In these two campaigns, he quickly became Germany's ace of aces, scoring an incredible 115 kills. He was not only the first Luftwaffe flier to be decorated with the Knight's Cross with Oak Leaves, Swords, and Diamonds, but Germany's most highly decorated soldier.

When Ernst Udet, German air ace of World War I, committed suicide on November 17, 1941, Moelders was summoned from the Russian front to attend the hero's funeral. He was killed when his Heinkel He111 crashed in fog at Breslau on November 21, 1941.

Further reading: Kurowski, Franz. *Luftwaffe Aces: German Combat Pilots of World War II.* Mechanicsburg, Pa.: Stackpole Books, 2004.

Molotov, Vyacheslav (1890–1986) *Soviet foreign minister*

Born Vyacheslav Mikhaylovich Skryabin in Kukarka (modern Sovetsk), Russia, Molotov was one of the founders of the Bolshevik Party in 1906. He was arrested by tsarist police in 1909 and again in 1915 for revolutionary agitation, and when the Bolsheviks seized power in the Russian Revolution of 1917, he was active in a number of provincial party organizations. In 1921, he was elevated to the Central Committee of the Communist Party, both as a member and as a secretary. He also became a candidate member of the Politburo.

Following the death of Vladimir Ilich Lenin in 1924, Molotov was an ardent supporter of JOSEPH STALIN and quickly entered Stalin's inner circle, becoming a full Politburo member in 1926. This put him in a position to control the Moscow Party Committee, which, during 1928–30, he purged of all anti-Stalinists. Stalin rewarded him in 1930 with appointment as chairman of the Council of People's Commissars, effectively making him the equivalent of prime minister of the Soviet Union. He held this post until 1941.

On the eve of World War II, in May 1939, Stalin selected Molotov to replace MAXIM LITVINOV as the commissar of foreign affairs. Molotov negoti-

ated the GERMAN-SOVIET NON-AGGRESSION PACT in August 1939. In May 1941, Stalin personally assumed the post of chairman of the Council of Ministers (the new name for the Council of People's Commissars), but Molotov remained its first deputy chairman.

After the INVASION OF THE SOVIET UNION in June 1941, Molotov was appointed to the State Defense Committee, Stalin's war cabinet, a post he held simultaneously with the first deputy chairmanship of the Council of Ministers. While he was on the Defense Committee, Molotov negotiated Soviet alliances with Great Britain and the United States. He was in attendance at three key Allied conferences, the 1943 Teheran Conference, the Yalta Conference of 1945, and the POTSDAM CONFERENCE, also in 1945. Molotov was the chief representative of the Soviet Union at the 1945 San Francisco Conference, which created the United Nations.

The Western Allied leaders, especially WINSTON CHURCHILL, FRANKLIN D. ROOSEVELT, and HARRY S. TRUMAN, found Molotov difficult to deal with since he did nothing to disguise his extreme hostility to the West. During the war, his name was memorialized by association with the improvised incendiary device, the so-called Molotov cocktail, a glass bottle partly filled with gasoline or alcohol, its mouth stoppered airtight with a cork, and a cloth rag tied around the mouth. Before use, the rag was soaked with gasoline or alcohol and lit. The bottle was thrown at the target and shattered on impact, disgorging its flammable contents, which ignited explosively. Cheap, quick, and easy to make, the Molotov cocktail was used extensively by the Red Army as well as by partisans. Molotov ordered its mass production.

Molotov remained in high office after the war but, in March 1949, resigned as foreign minister only to resume this post after the death of Stalin in March 1953. He fell to disputing with NIKITA KHRUSHCHEV and was dismissed in June 1956, but was named minister of state control in November of that year. In June 1957, he made an unsuccessful attempt to overthrow Khrushchev and was subsequently stripped of all of his offices, but was appointed ambassador to Mongolia and then served as Soviet delegate to the International Atomic Energy Agency in Vienna (1960–61). He persisted in criticizing Khrushchev, and was expelled from the Communist Party in 1962. From that time on, he lived out the rest of his long life in obscure retirement in Moscow.

See also YALTA AGREEMENT.

Further reading: Molotov, Vyacheslav M. *Molotov Remembers: Inside Kremlin Politics.* Chicago: Ivan R. Dee, 1993; Watson, Derek. *Molotov: A Biography.* London and New York: Palgrave Macmillan, 2005.

Monckton, Walter (1891–1965) *British propaganda director*

Walter Monckton was born in Plaxtol, Kent, and was educated at Harrow and at Balliol College, Oxford. During World War I, he served in the army, was decorated with the Military Cross, and mustered out with the rank of captain. After the war, he practiced law, earning appointment as attorney general to the Duchy of Cornwall in 1932. He was Edward VIII's legal adviser during the abdication crisis of 1936.

When World War II began, Prime Minister NEVILLE CHAMBERLAIN appointed Monckton director general of the Press and Censorship Bureau. In 1940, when WINSTON CHURCHILL became prime minister, he appointed Monckton director general of the Ministry of Information and undersecretary of state for foreign affairs. In July 1941, Brendan Bracken replaced Duff Cooper as minister of information and sent Monckton on a propaganda mission to the Soviet Union in an effort to smooth relations between the two mutually suspicious and hostile allies.

Monckton became director general of British Propaganda and Information Services in Egypt in 1942 and served in this capacity throughout most of the rest of the war, repeatedly declining Churchill's invitation to join his government until May 1945, when he accepted the post of solicitor general. He attended the Potsdam Conference in July 1945 as the British delegate on the Reparations Commission.

Following the war, Monckton joined the Conservative Party and, in 1951, was elected to the House of Commons. After Churchill was reelected as prime minister later in the year, he appointed Monckton minister of labor. In 1955, ANTHONY EDEN appointed Monckton minister of defense. Monckton disagreed with Eden during the Suez crisis (1956) and agreed to step down as defense minister to accept the far lesser position of paymaster general.

Monckton became a viscount in 1957, left the House of Commons, and served as chairman of Midland Bank through 1964. He held several other distinguished posts concurrently, including that of chancellor of the University of Sussex from 1961 until his death in 1965.

See also POTSDAM AGREEMENT.

Further reading: Winston Furneaux Smith Birkenhead, Frederick. *Walter Monckton: The Life of Viscount Monckton of Brenchley.* London: Weidenfeld & Nicolson, 1969; Hyde, H. Montgomery. *Walter Monckton.* London: Trafalgar Square, 1992.

Montgomery, Sir Bernard Law (first viscount Montgomery of El Alamein) (1887–1976) *British commander of World War II*

Born in London to the family of a clergyman, Montgomery was raised in Tasmania until he returned to London as a youth to attend St. Paul's School. In 1906, he enrolled at Sandhurst, the British military academy, graduating in 1908 with a commission in the Royal Warwickshire Regiment. He saw action with this regiment during World War I and fought with distinction at the first Battle of Ypres in October–November 1914, suffering a severe wound and earning the Distinguished Service Order (DSO). He was invalided back to Britain and assigned training duties during 1915. At the beginning of 1916, Montgomery was sufficiently recovered to return to France, where he served as brigade major of the 104th Brigade at the Somme from June 24 to November 13, 1916. Promoted to staff officer for the 33rd Division at Arras during

April 9–15, 1917, and then for IX Corps at Passchendaele from July 31 to November 10, he ended the war as a staff officer with the 47th Division.

Montgomery saw service in the army of occupation in Germany after the armistice, then enrolled in the staff college at Camberley in 1921. He served in various home posts until 1926, when he was appointed an instructor at Camberley. In 1929, he rewrote the army's *Infantry Training Manual,* then was posted for three years in Jerusalem, Alexandria, and Poona (India), where he commanded a regiment from 1930 to 1933. Appointed chief instructor at Quetta Staff College (in India; now Pakistan), he served there from 1934 to 1937. Back in Britain, Montgomery assumed command of the 9th Brigade at Portsmouth until October 1938, when he was named commander of the 8th Division in Palestine. Through August 1939, he was involved in suppressing anti-British Arab insurrection.

Montgomery was recalled to Europe at the outbreak of World War II in September 1939 and assigned command of 3rd Division, II Corps, during the failed British offensive in Flanders. He won distinction for his role in managing the DUNKIRK EVACUATION, in which he led a brilliant rearguard action during May–June 1940. He was knighted for this action and named to replace Sir CLAUDE AUCHINLECK as commander of V Corps in July, then transferred to command of XII Corps in April 1941. By November, he was in command of the entire Southeastern Army.

Montgomery played a role in planning the ill-fated DIEPPE RAID of August 1942, but (fortunately for his reputation) he was transferred to OPERATION TORCH, the Allied landings in North Africa, before the Dieppe raid was executed. Originally Montgomery was to command the First British Army, but, after General W. H. E. Gott died in August, he took over the Eighth British Army in Egypt. With this body he would make his greatest contribution to the war.

Montgomery immediately came under attack by the vaunted Afrika Korps of ERWIN ROMMEL, whose August 31–September 7 offensive at Alam Halfa Montgomery successfully repulsed. Seizing the initiative created by this defense, Montgomery

Bernard Law Montgomery *(National Archives and Records Administration)*

attacked at El Alamein during October 23–November 4 and achieved a victory. He was subsequently promoted to general and continued to pursue the Afrika Korps, driving it to the border of Tunisia by January 1943. Rommel eluded Montgomery and turned the tables on him at Medenine on March 6, 1943, then at Mareth, on March 20. Montgomery quickly recovered, however, and outflanked the German position during March 27–April 7.

Montgomery led the Eighth British Army through the rest of the Tunisia campaign, which ended on May 13, 1943. Victory achieved, he participated next in OPERATION HUSKY and the subsequent SICILY CAMPAIGN. Montgomery drove the Germans out of their positions around Mount

Etna during July 9–August 17. In the subsequent invasion of the Italian mainland, he captured the critical airfields at Foggia during September 3–27, but his advance was stalled at the Sangro River at the end of the year, and he was grateful for his recall to Britain, where he was assigned command of the Twenty-First Army Group in preparation for the invasion of France, the NORMANDY LANDINGS (D-DAY).

In the Normandy invasion, Montgomery was assigned overall command of ground forces, reporting directly to the supreme Allied commander, DWIGHT D. EISENHOWER. On September 1, 1944, he was promoted to field marshal.

After the Allied breakout from Normandy and the advance of the Allied armies across France, Montgomery conceived OPERATION MARKET-GARDEN (BATTLE OF ARNHEM) as a quick means of invading Germany and hastening the conclusion of the war. The operation failed, however, when the British component of the force was defeated at Arnhem during September 17–26. Montgomery was temporarily shifted to a secondary role in the final months of the war in Europe, but at least partially redeemed himself when he took command of the northern end of the American line during the ARDENNES OFFENSIVE (BATTLE OF THE BULGE) during December 16, 1944–January 15, 1945. Although Montgomery did much to prevent disaster in this battle, he offended American commanders by publicly proclaiming that he had saved the American army.

Montgomery was assigned to plan and direct the British crossing of the Rhine at Wesel on March 23, 1945, and from here he pushed into northern Germany. It was Montgomery who accepted the surrender of German forces in the Netherlands and Denmark, and then, on May 4, in northwestern Germany as well.

Montgomery was assigned command of British occupation forces in Germany in May 1945 and was created Viscount Montgomery of Alamein in January of the following year. In June 1946, he became successor to Lord Alanbrooke as chief of the Imperial General Staff, but was highly unpopular in this post, which he soon relinquished to become chairman of the Western European Union commanders in chief in 1948. This organization evolved into the military arm of NATO and led to Montgomery's appointment as first commander of NATO forces in Europe. Montgomery served in this post from March 1951 until his retirement from the army in September 1958.

See also EL ALAMEIN, BATTLES OF.

Further reading: Hamilton, Nigel. *Monty: The Battles of Field Marshal Bernard Montgomery.* New York: Random House, 1994; Hamilton, Nigel. *Monty: The Making of a General: 1887–1942.* New York: McGraw-Hill, 1981; Montgomery, Bernard Law. *The Memoirs of Field-Marshal the Viscount Montgomery of Alamein, K.G.* New York: Tab Books, 1990.

Morgenthau, Henry, Jr. (1891–1967)
Franklin Roosevelt's secretary of the Treasury

Born in New York, Morgenthau entered public life as the editor of *American Agriculturist,* a leading farm journal, from 1922 to 1933. During this period, he became a good friend of FRANKLIN D. ROOSEVELT, whose family's estate at Hyde Park was not far from Morgenthau's farm in Dutchess County, New York. When FDR became governor of New York (1929–33), Morgenthau was appointed state conservation commissioner and chaired the governor's Agricultural Advisory Committee. He also became a vigorous campaign worker, both in FDR's bid for reelection as governor in 1928 and for election as president in 1932.

FDR nominated Morgenthau as secretary of the Treasury. He proved to be a dynamic leader, serving all 12 years of FDR's four terms. It was his responsibility to administer the disbursement of some $370 billion during the Great Depression and World War II. This sum was a staggering three times the amount of money that had been administered by all previous secretaries—combined.

Morgenthau's most controversial position during World War II was as the formulator and champion of what was called the Morgenthau Plan. This was a proposal that Germany be made responsible for paying all the costs of World War II, thereby effectively hobbling the German economy permanently and reducing this industrial nation to a level of subsistence agriculture. In this way, Morgenthau hoped to prevent Germany from ever posing a threat to world peace again.

Although FDR initially endorsed the Morgenthau Plan, the president died before it was put into effect. FDR's successor, HARRY S. TRUMAN, with others, objected to the Morgenthau Plan on the grounds that it would repeat the great error of the TREATY OF VERSAILLES, which had imposed punitive reparations on Germany after World War I and thereby created an economic and cultural desperation that provided the fertile soil from which ADOLF HITLER rose to power. Moreover, Truman and others regarded Germany's economic and industrial recovery as vital to the postwar recovery of all Europe as a whole. With Truman's rejection of the plan, Morgenthau resigned as secretary of the Treasury in April 1945, very shortly after FDR's death. In retirement, he became a farmer and a philanthropist.

Further reading: Dietrich, John. *The Morgenthau Plan: Soviet Influence on American Postwar Policy.* New York: Algora, 2002; Kimball, Warren F. *Swords or Ploughshares? The Morgenthau Plan for Defeated Nazi Germany, 1943–1946.* Philadelphia: Lippincott, 1976; Morgenthau, Henry, III. *Mostly Morgenthaus: A Family History.* New York: Ticknor & Fields, 1991.

Morocco

During World War II the French protectorate of Morocco was a country of 6.25 million inhabitants, including 187,000 Europeans, nominally governed by a sultan, Mohammed Ben Youssef, who sided with France at the outbreak of war in September 1939. Local French authority was represented by General AUGUSTE NOGUÈS, who resisted the U.S. landings of OPERATION TORCH in November 1942. Even after General GEORGE S. PATTON JR. took Casablanca and occupied Morocco, Noguès retained his position until he was relieved by the pro-Allied French Committee for National Liberation in June 1943. Gabriel Puaux took over the

administration of the government at that time and successfully resisted Mohammed Ben Youssef's efforts to achieve independence.

Under Puaux, Morocco contributed troops to the Allied cause. Elite *Tirailleurs* fought in the BATTLE OF FRANCE in June 1940, and, with soldiers known as *Goums,* fought in the NORTH AFRICAN CAMPAIGN, again on the side of the Allies. Moroccan units were also dispatched to fight in the ITALIAN CAMPAIGN, and some participated in the landings on the French Riviera (Operation Anvil/Dragoon), which followed the NORMANDY LANDINGS (D-DAY) in August 1944.

Further reading: Anderson, Charles R. *Algeria-French Morocco (U.S. Army Campaigns of World War II).* Washington, D.C.: Department of the Army, 1993.

Morrison shelter

Named for Herbert Morrison, the British wartime home secretary and minister of home security in the administration of WINSTON CHURCHILL, the Morrison shelter was introduced in the fall of 1941. It was a home shelter that consisted of a steel plate mounted on legs with wire mesh forming the sides. Intended for indoor use, it was, in effect, little more than a heavily reinforced table—which is what many families used it for. The Morrison unit sold for £7 but was issued free of charge to families whose annual income was less than £350.

See also ANDERSON SHELTER.

Further reading: Bungay, Stephen. *The Most Dangerous Enemy: A History of the Battle of Britain.* London: Aurum Press, 2002; Cross, Arthur, Fred Tibbs, and Mike Seaborne. *The London Blitz.* London: Dirk Nishen, 1987; Johnson, David. *The London Blitz: The City Ablaze, December 29, 1940.* New York: Stein and Day, 1982; Nixon, Barbara Marion. *Raiders Overhead: A Diary of the London Blitz.* London: Scolar Gulliver, 1980.

mortar

The World War II–era mortar was a weapon that fired at angles greater than 45 degrees. Mortars were primarily light, smoothbore weapons used by infantry for their own close support; however, the term *mortar* was also applied to heavy rifled HOWITZER weapons sometimes mounted on special rail cars or used for coastal defense (although in practice the coastal weapons were rarely fired in anger during World War II).

World War II infantry mortars were chiefly derived from two prototypes developed in World War I: the British Stokes mortar and the French Brandt mortar. Between the wars, the manufacturers of these weapons licensed them worldwide, so that during World War II, there was a remarkable similarity among the mortars used by the belligerents.

Infantry mortars were of three classes: light mortars were 50–60 mm in caliber, medium mortars were 81–82 mm, and heavy mortars were 100 mm (or greater) in caliber. A simple weapon, virtually all mortars consisted of a smooth-bore barrel, its butt end resting on a steel base plate that transmitted and spread the recoil shock to the ground. A bipod or tripod held the barrel at the desired elevation. Depending on the model, adjustments were provided to facilitate more accurate elevation and traversal.

The mortar fired a projectile typically referred to as a bomb. It was generally of a teardrop shape and was fitted with tail fins for stability. The projectile was propelled by a two-part charge. The primary charge was a shotgun cartridge fitted in the center of the tail and packed with smokeless powder; secondary charges were placed around or between the tail fins in cloth bags or celluloid containers, retained in place by clips or springs.

Loading was simple. The bomb dropped down the barrel from the barrel's front end. When the primary cartridge at the tail struck a firing pin at the base of the weapon, the charge detonated, thereby igniting the secondary charge, which propelled the bomb out of the barrel. (Some mortars incorporated a more complex design with firing pins actuated by a trigger.)

The U.S. Army developed a rifled mortar, which used a specially designed bomb that permitted drop loading while still accepting the rifling when fired. Despite the added complexity, the American

rifled mortar achieved enhanced accuracy and could fire a heavy 107 mm projectile.

Early in the war, the German army used an 81 mm. mortar, but later developed a 120 mm weapon after engaging the Soviets, who used the heaviest infantry mortars of the war. Soviet mortars included 160 mm and 240 mm weapons—the latter attached to artillery units. The 160 mm Soviet mortar was a muzzle loader, but the 240 mm weapon loaded at the breech.

British mortars came in two-inch (51 mm), three-inch (76 mm), and 4.2-inch (107 mm) models—the 4.2-inchers attached to artillery regiments for use in the BURMA CAMPAIGN, where dense jungle made most conventional field artillery useless.

Japanese mortars were based mostly on the French Brandt designs. The Allies were particularly fascinated by one variety they called the "knee mortar," which was carried strapped to an infantryman's leg. Some Allied soldiers also believed that the "knee mortar" could be fired from the bent knee. This was a mistaken belief, as such use would surely have broken the soldier's leg.

Both the United States and Italy also made use of 60 mm and 81 mm Brandt mortar designs licensed from the French.

Further reading: Engelmann, Joachim. *German Heavy Mortars.* Atglen, Pa.: Schiffer, 1991; Fleischer, Wolfgang. *German Trench Mortars and Infantry Mortars 1914–1945.* Atglen, Pa.: Schiffer, 1996; Norris, John. *Infantry Mortars of World War II.* London: Osprey, 2002.

Moscow, Battle of

ADOLF HITLER targeted Moscow, the capital of the Soviet Union, in the initial drive of the INVASION OF THE SOVIET UNION in 1941. In September of that year, however, the German advance on Moscow was halted at Smolensk because the German Army Group Center (under Field Marshal Fedor von Bock) had to send two armies southward to form a great pincers against Kiev with Army Group South. Not until October 2 could the forces initially massed against Moscow be reassembled. At this time, 60 divisions resumed the advance on Mos-

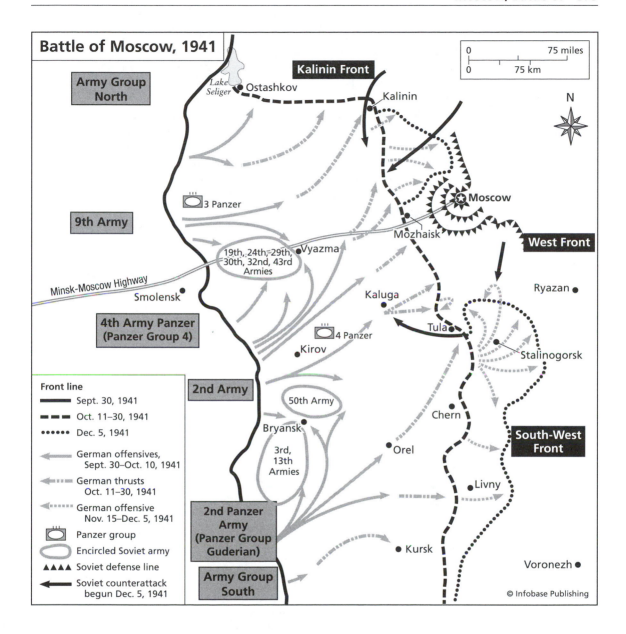

Battle of Moscow, 1941

Front line	
——	Sept. 30, 1941
– – –	Oct. 11–30, 1941
••••	Dec. 5, 1941

German offensives,
Sept. 30–Oct. 10, 1941

German thrusts
Oct. 11–30, 1941

German offensive
Nov. 15–Dec. 5, 1941

Panzer group

Encircled Soviet army

Soviet defense line

Soviet counterattack
begun Dec. 5, 1941

Army Group North

Kalinin Front

9th Army

4th Army Panzer (Panzer Group 4)

2nd Army

2nd Panzer Army (Panzer Group Guderian)

Army Group South

West Front

South-West Front

© Infobase Publishing

cow, racing against time to move the final 200 miles to the capital before the onset of winter.

Forming the right of this advance was HEINZ GUDERIAN's Second Panzer Group, which thrust through Orel on October 8 and Chern on October 24, then moved forward toward Tula, just 100 miles due south of the capital. The center of the advance consisted of the Third and Fourth Panzer groups under HERMANN HOTH and ERICH HOEPPNER, respectively, which worked in pincers fashion against the Soviet position at Vyazma during October 2–13. The cost to the Soviets in this portion of the offensive was approximately 600,000 killed or captured.

The Third Panzer Army, under Hans Reinhardt, supported by the Ninth German Army, wheeled north and west of Moscow, taking Kalinin on October 15. In the meantime, in the center, GÜN-THER VON KLUGE's Fourth German Army made a drive directly for the capital, which was just 40 miles away. Almost certain that Moscow would fall, the Soviet government—except for JOSEPH STALIN himself—evacuated 550 miles southeast to Kuibyshev on the Volga.

With the prize in view, the Germans suddenly found that Soviet resistance was becoming increasingly fierce and increasingly effective. Worse, late fall rains churned roads into mud, greatly hindering the advance of heavy German armor. Mid-November brought the first hard freeze, which enabled Kluge to speed up his advance and intensify his attack. But this advantageous change in the weather soon turned deadly. On November 20, a severe winter storm stopped the German advance—quite literally—cold.

On December 2, the 2nd Panzer Division made a do-or-die drive toward the city and actually sighted the Kremlin, which they had been ordered to level with explosives as a blow against communism. Yet even with the objective in sight, the unit, under heavy counterattack, could move no farther.

The 258th Infantry Division, Fourth German Army, slugged its way into the Moscow suburbs, only to be driven back by bands of armed factory workers during two days of intense fighting. Casualties were heavy on both sides.

Like Napoleon before him, Hitler was largely unprepared for the Russian winter. His troops had not been issued cold-weather clothing and equipment. Nevertheless, Hitler gave explicit orders forbidding withdrawal. As a result, the weather began to take its deadly toll.

On December 6, GEORGI KONSTANTINOVICH ZHUKOV, now in command of the Moscow front (he had relieved SEMYON TIMOSHENKO, who took over the southern front), launched a counteroffensive with 100 brand-new divisions. On December 9, Soviet ski troops led a massive attack on Guderian's Tula salient south of Moscow, killing 30,000 Germans in five days and prompting the replacement of Guderian by General Rudolf Schmidt.

Having gained the initiative, the Red Army advanced westward, taking Kaluga on December 26. The Germans briefly recaptured the city, but soon lost it again. On January 18, Zhukov took Mozhaisk, 60 miles west of Moscow. To the north, Kalinin was retaken on December 15.

Kluge, who now commanded the German forces in the center, retreated to Vyazma in the south and Rzhev in the north. Both of these positions were about 125 miles from Moscow. Kluge dug in here and held off further Soviet advances, but also bore the full brunt of the ongoing winter. It was the weather that now claimed more lives than the enemy, and the Germans were never able to mount another assault on the Soviet capital. The Battle of Moscow was the first major defeat the Nazis suffered on land in World War II. The German army held in place throughout the rest of 1942 and into early 1943, before beginning to fall back in March 1943, reeling under one Soviet thrust after another.

Further reading: Haupt, Werner. *Assault on Moscow 1941: The Offensive, the Battle, the Set-Back*. Atglen, Pa.: Schiffer, 2000; Seaton, Albert. *The Battle for Moscow*. London: Book Sales, 2002; Zhukov, Georgi Konstantin. *From Moscow to Berlin: Marshal Zhukov's Greatest Battles*. Newport Beach, Calif.: Noontide Press, 1991.

Mosley, Oswald (1896–1980) *leader of British fascism*

Oswald Mosley was born in London and served as a member of Parliament from 1918 to 1931. He began his political career as a Conservative, became an independent, then joined the Labour Party, serving in a Labour ministry during 1929–30. He married Lady Cynthia Blanche Curzon in 1920; she died in 1933, and, three years later, he married Diana Guinness (née Freeman-Mitford), whose father, the 2nd Baron Redesdale, was a prewar supporter of the rise of ADOLF HITLER and the Nazi regime in Germany. Like many right-wing Europeans, he saw the Nazis and fascists as desirable alternatives to the Communists.

Mosley also became increasingly attracted to the extreme right wing of European politics. In 1932, he founded the British Union of Fascists after unsuccessfully trying to form a socialist party the year before. He led this group until 1940, then founded its successor, the Union Movement, in 1948 and led that until his death. British Union members wore Nazi-style uniforms and insignia and adopted paramilitary discipline. They were enthusiastically pro-Hitler and pro-BENITO MUSSOLINI, and they were virulently anti-Semitic, sponsoring the publication and distribution of anti-Semitic literature and conducting hostile marches through the Jewish neighborhoods of east London.

Mosley was a powerful demagogue whose oratory attracted a considerable following. He was promoted, too, by friendship with Viscount Rothermere, a prominent newspaper publisher.

WINSTON CHURCHILL and others considered Mosley dangerous in the years leading up to the war. At the outbreak of hostilities, Mosley, unrepentant, was ordered interned. He fell ill in prison and was released in 1943, but remained aloof from public life until February 7, 1948, when he founded the Union Movement, a politically irrelevant fascist fringe organization consisting mostly of far-right book clubs.

Further reading: Mosely, Nicholas. *Rules of the Game/ Beyond the Pale: Memoirs of Sir Oswald Mosley and Family.* Normal, Ill.: Dalkey Archive Press, 1991; Mosley, Oswald. *Revolution by Reason and Other Essays.* Lewiston, N.Y.: Edwin Mellen Press, 1997; Skidelsky, Robert. *Oswald Mosley.* London: Pan Macmillan, 1980.

Moulin, Jean (1899–1943) *French resistance leader*

Born in Bézier, France, the son of a history professor, Jean Moulin was drafted into the French army during the last year of World War I, but was mustered out at the end of the war without seeing action. Following the armistice, Moulin entered the civil service, rising to become the youngest prefect in France. Between the wars, Moulin became a radical leftist and used his civil service connections during the Spanish civil war to smuggle at least one French airplane to the Republicans.

After the fall of France following the BATTLE OF FRANCE in 1940, Moulin refused to cooperate with officials of the German occupation. For this, he was arrested and tortured by the GESTAPO. He sought escape by means of a suicide attempt, cutting his throat with a piece of broken glass, but was treated, recovered, and released. He returned to his post as prefect, but, in November 1940, when VICHY GOVERNMENT officials ordered all prefects to dismiss leftist town and city mayors, Moulin refused and was himself dismissed.

Moulin began to organize other French men and women who wanted to overthrow the Vichy government and rise up against the German occupiers. He made contact with the leaders of disparate French RESISTANCE MOVEMENTS, then slipped out to London in September 1941, where he met with CHARLES DE GAULLE and other leaders in exile of the Free France movement. In October 1941, Moulin wrote *The Activities, Plans and Requirements of the Groups Formed in France,* a comprehensive summary of the state of resistance in France. Impressed with Moulin's command of the French situation, De Gaulle anointed him as the principal leader of the French resistance. Accordingly, Moulin was returned to France, dropped by parachute on January 1, 1942.

Moulin's first assignment was to use money he carried into the country to establish an underground press to recruit resistance members and coordinate their activities. This was a crucial step in his effort to unite the various resistance groups. Following weeks of dangerous meetings, Moulin succeeded in persuading all eight major groups to form the Conseil National de la Résistance (CNR), the closest the movement ever came to being governed by a single central body. The first meeting of the group, chaired by Moulin, was held in Paris on May 27, 1943. The following month, however, on June 7, René Hardy, a key resistance operative, was arrested and tortured by Gestapo agents under the command of the infamous KLAUS BARBIE. He revealed the identity of Moulin, who was then arrested at Caluire on June 21. Moulin died under torture on July 8, 1943.

Further reading: Clinton, Alan. *Jean Moulin, 1899–1943: The French Resistance and the Republic.* London and

New York: Palgrave Macmillan, 2002; Marnham, Patrick. *Resistance and Betrayal: The Death and Life of the Greatest Hero of the French Resistance.* New York: Random House, 2002.

Mountbatten, Louis (first earl Mountbatten of Burma) (1900–1979)
supreme allied commander, China-Burma-India theater

Louis Francis Albert Victor Nicholas Mountbatten, Earl Mountbatten of Burma, was born at Frogmore House, Windsor, to Prince Louis of Battenberg (later first marquess of Milford Haven) and Princess Victoria of Hesse-Darmstadt, who was a granddaughter of Queen Victoria. Battenberg changed the family name to Mountbatten during World War I because of public hostility toward all things German or German-sounding.

Mountbatten enrolled as a cadet at the Osbourne Naval Training College in 1913. After graduating in November 1914, he enrolled at the Royal Naval College, from which he graduated at the top of his class in June 1916. He served as a midshipman in World War I aboard Admiral David Beatty's flagship HMS *Lion* (July 1916–January 1917) and HMS *Queen Elizabeth* (February–July

Lord Louis Mountbatten (left) with an unidentified officer *(National Archives and Records Administration)*

1918). Promoted to lieutenant, he transferred to P-boat (coastal torpedo boat) service in August and served aboard these craft through the end of the war.

After the armistice, Mountbatten studied for a year at Cambridge University, then toured Australia, Japan, and India with the Prince of Wales (later Edward VIII) beginning in 1920. He returned to Britain and married Edwina Ashley in 1922, then, the following year, served aboard HMS *Revenge* (1923). He completed an advanced signals course in July 1925 and was assigned as assistant fleet wireless officer in the Mediterranean during 1927–28, becoming fleet wireless officer in 1931. Promoted to captain in 1932, he continued to serve as Mediterranean Fleet wireless officer through 1933, when he briefly commanded the destroyer HMS *Daring.* From 1936 to 1938, Mountbatten served as naval aide-de-camp to Edward VIII and then George VI. On the eve of World War II, in June 1939, he was assigned to command the destroyer HMS *Kelly,* then under construction. After overseeing the completion of the vessel, Mountbatten sailed aboard it as commander of the 5th Destroyer Flotilla, consisting of *Kelly* and *Kingston,* on September 20, 1939. Mountbatten performed with great distinction in the evacuation of Namsos following the ill-fated offensive in Norway during June 1940 (*see* NARVIK, BATTLES OF). During the evacuation of CRETE on May 23, 1941, HMS *Kelly* was sunk by German dive bombers.

After the loss of *Kelly,* Mountbatten was given command of the aircraft carrier HMS *Illustrious,* which was being repaired in the United States during October 1941. While overseeing the repair work, Mountbatten made many valuable American contacts and favorably impressed U.S. naval leaders.

In April 1942, Prime Minister WINSTON CHURCHILL recalled Mountbatten to Britain to serve as director of Combined Operations. Eager to take offensive action in the war, Mountbatten was among the chief advocates and planners of the DIEPPE RAID (August 18, 1942), which resulted in disastrous defeat. Characteristically of Mountbatten, the loss at Dieppe did not shake his resolve. On the contrary, it persuaded him that Britain's amphibious capabilities required development, and he set about building an amphibious-capable force, so that by April 1943, Combined Operations consisted of some 2,600 landing craft and 50,000 personnel. He also turned his attention to creating technological improvements to facilitate amphibious operations, including "mulberries" (towed harbors) and the PLUTO system (Pipe-Line Under the Ocean), both of which were of crucial logistical importance in the NORMANDY LANDINGS (D-DAY).

As a result of the August 1943 Quebec Conference, Mountbatten was advanced above other more senior officers to become supreme Allied commander for Southeast Asia, which proved to be a very difficult assignment in a theater of the war that was chronically undermanned, poorly supplied, and generally neglected. Mountbatten accepted these challenges and was highly innovative and resourceful in his direction of Allied operations in the BURMA CAMPAIGN and the Indian Ocean.

Following the surrender of Japan in August–September 1945, Mountbatten had the difficult task of accepting the surrender of various Japanese forces and then reestablishing British colonial authority in places that had been occupied by the Japanese and were now increasingly nationalistic in spirit. He became personally convinced that the era of colonial rule had come to an end, and he committed himself to working toward a peaceful transition to independence for many of the British possessions. He also oversaw the speedy and humane liberation of Allied POWs throughout the Southeast Asian theater.

Mountbatten's immediate postwar authority extended over Indochina and Indonesia during September 1945–46. From March 24 to August 15, 1947, he was the last British viceroy of India and directed the difficult and delicate British withdrawal from India and the inauguration of independence for India and Pakistan.

In 1946, Mountbatten was created a viscount, then made an earl in 1947. In 1950, he was appointed fourth sea lord, serving until 1952, when he became commander in chief of the Mediterranean Fleet. In 1954, he was made first sea lord and served in this post until 1959. Promoted to admiral

of the fleet in 1956, he was named chief of the United Kingdom Defence Staff and chairman of the Chiefs of Staff Committee in July 1959. He served in these posts until July 1965, when he became governor—and, in 1974, lord lieutenant—of the Isle of Wight.

In 1979, Mountbatten, his teenaged grandson Nicholas, and a local Irish boy were killed when an Irish Republican Army bomb exploded aboard Mountbatten's yacht.

Further reading: McGeoch, Ian. *The Princely Sailor: Mountbatten of Burma.* Dulles, Va.: Potomac Books, 1996; Ziegler, Philip. *Mountbatten: The Official Biography.* Charleston, S.C.: Phoenix Press, 2001.

Mount Suribachi

The highest point on the Pacific island of Iwo Jima, Mount Suribachi was a key objective of the U.S. Marines who landed on the Japanese-held island during the BATTLE OF IWO JIMA. Suribachi was taken on February 23, 1945, and the American flag was ordered to be raised—largely as a means of enhancing the morale of the marines who were still heavily engaged in combat on the island. When the first flag raised was judged too small for troops scattered across the island to see, a second, much larger flag was ordered to be raised about two hours later. This second raising was photographed by Joe Rosenthal of the Associated Press, and the Pulitzer Prize–winning photograph became perhaps the single most pervasive image of the U.S. role in World War II. It was reprinted endlessly in newspapers, magazines, and books, and was reproduced on a U.S. postage stamp in 1945.

Most famously, the Rosenthal photograph served as the model for a heroic bronze sculpture group in Arlington, Virginia (near Arlington National Cemetery), officially called the U.S. Marine Corps War Memorial, but more familiarly known as the Iwo Jima Memorial. Like the photograph, the monument depicts five marines and a U.S. Navy hospital corpsman—Sergeant Michael Strank, Corporal Harlon H. Block, Private First Class Franklin R. Sousley, Private First Class Rene

A. Gagnon, Private First Class Ira Hayes, and Pharmacist's Mate Second Class John H. Bradley—raising the Stars and Stripes.

Further reading: Bradley, James, and Ron Powers. *Flags of Our Fathers.* New York: Bantam, 2001.

Mulberry harbor

"Mulberry" was the code name for a type of artificial harbor, two of which were constructed for use in the NORMANDY LANDINGS (D-DAY).

The mulberries were conceived as a means of supplying troops during a massive invasion. The disastrous DIEPPE RAID had vividly demonstrated the futility of attempting to capture a French port by a head-on attack. Yet a port was necessary to sustain a major invasion. Charged by Prime Minister WINSTON CHURCHILL in May 1942 with investigating the potential of floating piers as logistical components for an invasion, LOUIS MOUNTBATTEN, chief of Combined Operations Headquarters, authorized intensive research into floating piers (known as "whales") with adjustable legs (codenamed "spuds"). The spuds were protected by hollow concrete caissons (called "phoenixes"). This entire assembly became the mulberry.

Two mulberries were prefabricated for transportation and emplacement at Normandy. They had 213 "spuds," and some of the "phoenixes" were 200 feet in length and 60 feet high. As an additional guard against severe weather, 200-foot-long floating tanks ("bombardons") were also built to provide secure anchorages along the whales.

Before the mulberries were put into place, five smaller floating harbors—called "gooseberries"—were formed from 74 blockships (or "corncobs"). These would provide shelter for the multitude of small craft involved in the early phases of the landing operations while the phoenixes were being readied. Once the mulberries were in place, two of the gooseberries were integrated into them, and the rest provided boat shelters closer to shore.

The components for the mulberries—400 discrete units with a total weight of 1.5 million tons—were built at various locations in Britain. All the components were towed to the south coast, then temporarily submerged to prevent their being spotted by German aerial reconnaissance. After the first Normandy landings on June 6, 1944, the mulberry components were towed across the English Channel and, in a monumental operation employing 10,000 men and 132 tugboats, they were assembled.

The mulberries—at St. Laurent (to accommodate the Americans) and at Arromanches (for the British and Canadians)—were nearly completed when, on June 19, a fierce storm so severely damaged the St. Laurent mulberry that it had to be abandoned. The single Arromanches mulberry thereafter accommodated all supplies—an influx of some 11,000 tons per day. Intended as a temporary expedient to last through the summer of 1944 only, the Arromanches mulberry continued to operate through December.

Further reading: Ambrose, Stephen E. *D-day: June 6, 1944—The Climactic Battle of World War II.* New York: Simon & Schuster, 1994; Messenger, Charles. *The D-day Atlas: Anatomy of the Normandy Campaign.* London and New York: Thames & Hudson, 2004; Penrose, Jane, ed. *The D-day Companion.* London: Osprey, 2004.

Munich Conference and Agreement

Pursuant to the APPEASEMENT POLICY advocated by British prime minister NEVILLE CHAMBERLAIN after the German annexation of Austria (ANSCHLUSS) in March 1938 and ADOLF HITLER's demand for the annexation of the Czech SUDETENLAND, Chamberlain agreed to a four-power conference proposed by Italy's BENITO MUSSOLINI. The conference took place in Munich on September 29–30, 1938, and included Hitler, Mussolini, Chamberlain, and French prime minister EDOUARD DALADIER. President FRANKLIN D. ROOSEVELT did nothing more than send a message to the principals on September 26, rather lamely reminding them that, by virtue of having signed the Kellogg-Briand Pact of 1928, they had agreed to refrain from going to war with each other. No representative from the Soviet Union was invited to the conference, and while two Czech diplomats were called to Munich, they were not permitted to attend the conference, but were held under guard by the GESTAPO until the morning of September 30, when they were summoned to hear what the four powers in attendance had decided in their absence.

They had decided that the German army was to take over the Sudetenland—the largely German-speaking frontier areas of Czechoslovakia—by the beginning of October, including the military and industrial installations in this region. The sovereignty of the rest of Czechoslovakia would be guaranteed in some manner not specified by the four conference principals.

At the conclusion of the Munich Conference, on the morning of September 30, Hitler and Chamberlain signed a joint declaration (the so-called Munich Agreement), pledging that Germany and Britain would peacefully consult whenever problems should arise between them. It was a copy of this declaration that Chamberlain held aloft on his return to London, claiming to have secured "peace with honour" and "peace for our time."

Further reading: Adams, R. J. Q. *British Politics and Foreign Policy in the Age of Appeasement, 1935–39.* Palo Alto, Calif.: Stanford University Press, 1994; McDonough, Frank. *Hitler, Chamberlain and Appeasement.* Cambridge: Cambridge University Press, 2002; Schmitz, David F., and Richard D. Challener, eds. *Appeasement in Europe: A Reassessment of U.S. Policies.* Westport, Conn.: Greenwood Press, 1990.

Murphy, Audie (1924–1971) *most-decorated U.S soldier in World War II*

Audie Leon Murphy was born near Kingston, Texas, one of 12 children in the family of a sharecropper. During World War II, in June 1942, about the time of his 18th birthday, he enlisted in the U.S. Army and first saw combat in the NORTH AFRICAN CAMPAIGN as a private in Company B, Fifteenth Infantry Regiment, Third Infantry Division. This was the beginning of a remarkable military career in which Murphy received 33 awards, citations, and decorations, as well as a battlefield commission as second lieutenant. Murphy received every decora-

tion presented by the United States for valor—two of them awarded twice—and on January 26, 1945, he was awarded the Medal of Honor for his actions near Holtzwhir, France. There he killed or wounded some 50 Germans and stopped a tank attack. Murphy was the most decorated U.S. soldier in history. In addition to his American decorations, he received medals from France and Belgium.

Murphy participated in eight World War II campaigns, in Sicily, Italy, France, and Germany, as well as two amphibious assaults, in Sicily and southern France. He was wounded in action three times.

After his discharge from the army on August 17, 1945, Murphy became a successful (if critically undistinguished) film actor, a top-selling country-and-western lyricist, a best-selling author, and a poet. He appeared in 45 films, starring in 39, including the motion picture version of his 1949 World War II memoir, *To Hell and Back* (1955). Murphy's greatest film popularity came not in war stories, however, but in westerns.

Murphy joined the Texas National Guard in 1950, as a captain, in the hope of fighting in the Korean War. His division was never called to active duty, however. Before he was assigned to inactive status in the Guard in 1957, he was promoted to major. He transferred to the United States Army Reserve in 1966, remaining a reservist until his death in an airplane crash on May 28, 1971, near Christiansburg, Virginia. Murphy was buried with full military honors near the Tomb of the Unknown Soldier at Arlington National Cemetery.

Further reading: Graham, Don. *No Name on the Bullet: A Biography of Audie Murphy* (New York: Viking Penguin, 1989); Murphy, Audie. *To Hell and Back.* 1949; reprint ed., New York: Owl Books, 2002; Simpson, Harold B. *Audie Murphy, American Soldier* (Hillsboro, Texas: Hill Junior College Press, 1975).

Mussolini, Benito (1883–1945) *dictator of Italy, founder of fascism*

Born in Verano di Costa, near Forli, Italy, to a blacksmith father (a radical socialist) and school-teacher mother, Benito Mussolini was a violent

Benito Mussolini *(Author's collection)*

bully as a child, but was also highly intelligent, his romantic imagination stimulated by his indulgent mother, who repeatedly told him that he was destined for great things. A voracious reader as a youth, Mussolini devoured the works of such political philosophers as Louis Auguste Blanqui, Friedrich Nietzsche, Georges Sorel, and, perhaps most significantly, Machiavelli.

Mussolini received his formal education in the Salesian college of Faenza and then at the normal school there, from which he obtained a teaching certificate. By 18, he had obtained a post as a provincial schoolteacher and also traveled, living essentially as a vagabond for several years in Switzerland and the Austrian Trentino. He soon gave up teaching for socialist journalism, becoming editor of the Milan Socialist Party newspaper *Avanti!* in 1912.

Mussolini's political development was astonishingly inconsistent, even mercurial. During his early Socialist phase, he was a committed pacifist and wrote many articles arguing against Italy's entry into World War I. Suddenly, however, he abandoned the Socialist Party line and just as vehemently urged Italy's entry into the war on the side of the Allies. The Socialist Party accordingly expelled Mussolini, who quickly founded a rival newspaper in Milan, *Il popolo d'Italia.* He used the new magazine to develop and disseminate the doctrine of what became the fascist movement, but he

broke off publication to enlist in the Italian army as a private in 1915. He served until he was wounded in the buttocks by trench mortar fragments early in 1917. After convalescing, he resumed publication of *Il popolo.*

On March 23, 1919, encouraged and inspired by the grandiloquent poet, novelist, patriot, and adventurer Gabriele d'Annunzio, Mussolini founded in Milan with other war veterans a revolutionary hypernationalistic group called the Fasci di Combattimento. The name was derived from the Italian word *fascio,* "bundle," or "bunch," which in itself suggested unity but was also directly derived from the Latin word *fasces,* the bundle of rods bound together around an ax with the blade protruding that was the ancient Roman emblem of government power and authority.

Fascism soon abandoned its left-wing socialist origins to become a radical right-wing nationalism founded on ideas of brute force. Although many of Mussolini's early speeches were radically pro-labor and anti-church (in effect, left even of socialism and verging on anarchy), what captured the public's imagination was a nationalist message that evoked visions of a return to imperial Roman glory. This message was popular not only with the average Italian, but resonated with the likes of d'Annunzio and the wealthy landowners in the lower Po Valley, leading industrialists, and senior army officers.

As the fascists became increasingly influential, Mussolini created squads of thugs, the Blackshirts, who waged a street-level civil war against all opposing parties and interests, including socialists, communists, Catholics, and liberals. By 1922, Mussolini enjoyed the support of the rich and powerful, as well as many among the masses. On October 28, he authorized his Blackshirts to march on Rome (to which he journeyed by train), with the object of intimidating King Victor Emmanuel III into forming a coalition government with the Fascist Party. The king yielded, and, in the manner of the dictators of the classical Roman republic, Mussolini was granted absolute dictatorial powers set to last one year.

Mussolini used what became the inaugural year of his dictatorship to refashion Italy's economic structure, slashing government expenses for public services, reducing taxes on industry to encourage production, and centralizing as well as consolidating government bureaucracy. Backed by big finance, business, and industry, Mussolini was indeed able to revitalize the nation's foundering economy.

Mussolini also used his first year to replace the royal guard with his own Fascist armed coterie and the Orva, a secret police force that reported directly to him. He greatly increased Italy's prestige in foreign affairs when he responded to the murder of Italian officials at the hands of bandits on the Greek-Albanian border by demanding a huge indemnity from the Greek government, then bombarded and seized the Greek island of Corfu. He next negotiated an agreement with Yugoslavia to obtain Italian possession of the long-contested Fiume.

In the beginning, Mussolini carefully avoided attacking labor, and in 1924 he even relinquished his dictatorial powers and called for new elections. This was a deception, however, since he had taken care to secure legislation guaranteeing a two-thirds' parliamentary majority for his party regardless of the outcome of the popular vote. Among the handful of Socialists elected that year despite fascist domination was Giacomo Matteotti, who made a series of antifascist speeches, exposing such political outrages as acts of intimidation and violence, misuse of public funds, and even political murder. Shortly after one of these speeches, Matteotti's own murdered body was found, and a protracted parliamentary crisis ensued. Emboldened, the opposition press attacked Mussolini and his followers. This prompted Mussolini to end all pretext of democracy. He imposed by fiat a single-party dictatorship and a policy of strict censorship. He sent his Blackshirts to bully and terrorize all opponents. And he now moved openly against labor, solidifying his power base among Italian capitalists by abolishing free trade unions. At the same time, in 1929, he secured the backing of the Catholic Church by negotiating the Lateran Treaty, by which the Vatican was established under the absolute temporal sovereignty of the pope.

An absolute dictator, Mussolini was now called Il Duce, the Leader, and during the 1930s he pros-

ecuted a blustering and aggressive foreign policy. Seizing as a pretext a clash over a disputed zone on the Italian Somaliland border, he invaded Ethiopia during 1935–36 without a declaration of war, unleashing aerial bombardment and poison gas on the civilian population. On May 9, 1936, Italy annexed the now prostrate African nation. At this time, Mussolini also gave military assistance to Generalissimo Francisco Franco in the Spanish civil war. During 1936–39, Mussolini forged a fateful alliance with Adolf Hitler's Germany.

In April 1939, Mussolini sent his armies to occupy Albania, but Hitler's entreaties notwithstanding, he kept Italy out of World War II until June 1940, during the Battle of France, when the fall of France was assured. Initially, Hitler embraced Mussolini as an inspiration and mentor, but he soon had reason to regret the alliance. Mussolini's military suffered one humiliation after another in Greece and North Africa, and by the middle of World War II, the popular tide in Italy rapidly turned against Il Duce.

Mussolini was deposed by vote of the Fascist Grand Council on July 25, 1943, and he was immediately dismissed as premier by King Victor Emmanuel. Held under a kind of house arrest, Mussolini, on Hitler's orders, was rescued on September 12 by German commandos led by the brilliant Otto Skorzeny. Hitler then installed Mussolini as his puppet in northern Italy, territory that had yet to be taken by the inexorably advancing Allies.

By the spring of 1945, Allied forces were closing in on Mussolini. In April, he and his mistress, Clara Petacci, fled, only to be captured by Italian partisans at Lake Como. The couple was executed by a partisan firing squad on April 28, and their half-naked bodies were strung up by the heels in a public square in Milan, where they were exposed to public shame and desecration.

Further reading: Axelrod, Alan. *Benito Mussolini.* New York: Alpha, 2002; Gregor, James. *Young Mussolini and the Intellectual Origins of Fascism.* Berkeley: University of California Press, 1979; Hartenian, Larry. *Benito Mussolini* (World Leaders Past and Present). New York: Chelsea

House, 1988; Hibbert, Christopher. *Il Duce: The Life of Benito Mussolini.* Boston: Little, Brown, 1962; Lyttle, Richard B. *Il Duce: The Rise and Fall of Benito Mussolini,* New York: Macmillan, 1987; Mussolini, Benito. *My Rise and Fall.* Reprints *My Autobiography* (1928) and *History of a Year* (1945). New York: Da Capo, 1998; Ridley, Jasper. *Mussolini: A Biography.* New York: Cooper Square Press, 2000.

Mykikyina, Battle of

U.S. general JOSEPH "VINEGAR JOE" STILWELL led the First Chinese Army in a campaign to clear a supply route to China via BURMA before the onset of monsoon season in May 1944. With the support of Merrill's Marauders and CHINDITS, the First Chinese Army attacked and seized the airfield at Mykikyina on May 17, 1944. The next objective was the town itself, which, however, the Japanese rushed to reinforce. The Japanese garrison, led by Major General Genzu Mizukami, held out for an incredi-ble 79 days against the vastly superior numbers Stilwell threw against it. At last, the few survivors among the defenders retreated across the Irrawaddy River, having lost 790 killed and 1,180 wounded. Stilwell took the town on August 3, having lost 972 Chinese killed and 3,184 wounded, in addition to 272 Americans killed and 955 wounded. Some 980 men from all of Stilwell's forces succumbed to tropical disease during the siege. Rather than join the retreat or surrender, Genzu committed suicide.

Further reading: Astor, Gerald. *The Jungle War: Mavericks, Marauders and Madmen in the China-Burma-India Theater of World War II.* New York: Wiley, 2004; Dupuy, Trevor N. *Asiatic Land Battles: Allied Victories in China and Burma.* New York: Franklin Watts, 1963; Hogan, David W. *India-Burma (The U.S. Army Campaigns of World War II).* Carlisle, Pa.: Army Center of Military History, 1991; Webster, Donovan. *The Burma Road: The Epic Story of the China-Burma-India Theater in World War II.* New York: Farrar, Straus and Giroux, 2003.

N

Nagasaki, atomic bombing of

At 11:02 (local time) on August 9, 1945, Nagasaki became the second Japanese city to suffer nuclear attack, after HIROSHIMA, which had been bombed on August 6.

Like the Hiroshima weapon, the Nagasaki bomb was the product of the MANHATTAN PROJECT; however, in contrast to "Little Boy," the uranium 235 Hiroshima weapon, the fissionable component of "Fat Man," as the Nagasaki bomb was called, was plutonium 239. Like the earlier bomb, it was dropped by parachute so that it would detonate at a preset altitude (1,625 feet) to ensure the maximum destructive effect of the blast (if detonated at ground level, much of the explosive force would be absorbed by the earth). Fat Man weighed almost 9,000 pounds, was 11 feet, 4 inches long, and packed the explosive equivalent of 22 kilotons of TNT.

The B-29 from which Fat Man was dropped, *Bock's Car,* piloted by Major Charles W. Sweeney, had as its first-choice target the city of Kokura, now part of Kitakyushu. Heavy cloud cover prompted diversion to the second-choice target, Nagasaki.

Although Fat Man was more powerful than Little Boy, the topographical situation of Nagasaki, within narrow valleys bordered by mountains, resulted in less destruction. Approximately 2.6 square miles of Nagasaki were razed as compared with 5 square miles of Hiroshima. Nearly 23 percent of the city's 51,000 buildings were destroyed or badly burned; just over 36 percent were left essentially undamaged. Of the 270,000 people in the city that morning (a number that included some 2,500 Korean slave laborers and 350 Allied prisoners of war), at least 73,884 were killed and 74,909 injured. Over the years, many others suffered the long-term effects of exposure to high levels of radiation—although, as at Hiroshima, the very high rates of cancer anticipated did not occur. Within days of the bombing, Japan's emperor HIROHITO broadcast his surrender message.

Further reading: Goldstein, Donald K., J. Michael Wenger, and Katherine V. Dillon. *Rain of Ruin: A Photographic History of Hiroshima and Nagasaki.* Dulles, Va.: Potomac Books, 1999; Grant, R. G. *Hiroshima and Nagasaki (New Perspectives).* Chicago: Raintree, 1998.

Nagumo Chuichi (1887–1944) *commander of Japanese elite carrier striking force at the Battle of Pearl Harbor, December 7, 1941*

Vice Admiral Nagumo Chuichi achieved remarkable tactical success in the Pearl Harbor attack, but, worried that U.S. submarines would soon pursue the force, he failed to launch a third-wave attack, which, had he targeted more of Pearl Harbor's permanent installations, might have crippled the base for a very long period. His decision to withdraw after the second wave gave the lie to his peacetime reputation for boldness. He was, in fact, a cautious

Nagumo Chuichi *(U.S. Navy History Center)*

commander. (Indeed, he was a somewhat curious choice as commander of an aircraft carrier force, since he was a torpedo specialist and not a naval air commander.)

After Pearl Harbor, Nagumo fought during early 1942 in the invasion of the Netherlands East Indies and led raids against the northern Australian port of Darwin, as well as against objectives in the Indian Ocean. He played a key role in the BATTLE OF MIDWAY in June 1942, at which he suffered a disastrous strategic defeat, despite tactical triumphs off Guadalcanal.

Midway shook Nagumo's confidence and the confidence of others in him. He was relieved of his principal command in 1943 and sent to the Mariana Islands, where he was given the responsibility for preparing the defenses of SAIPAN. In July 1944, on the eve of the U.S. invasion of the island, Nagumo committed suicide.

See also GUADALCANAL CAMPAIGN and NETHERLANDS EAST INDIES, ACTION IN.

Further reading: Fuchida, Misuo, and Masatake Okumiya. *Midway: The Battle That Doomed Japan, the Japanese Navy's Story.* Annapolis, Md.: Bluejacket Books, 2001; Goldstein, Donald M., and Katherine V. Dillon, eds. *The Pearl Harbor Papers: Inside the Japanese Plans.* Dulles, Va.: Potomac Books, 1999.

Nanking, Rape of

Also called the Nanking Massacre and (in Japan), the Nanking Incident, the Rape of Nanking describes the atrocities committed by the Imperial Japanese Army in and around Nanking (Nanjing), which was the capital of China at the time of the city's fall to the Japanese on December 13, 1937, during the SINO-JAPANESE WAR.

Japanese soldiers entered Nanking on December 13 and over at least the next six weeks committed atrocities including looting, rape, arson, and the wanton slaughter of noncombatant civilians and prisoners of war. Modern Chinese historians adhere to the Chinese Communist Party estimates that some 300,000 civilians were killed in Nanking. Some of these victims may in fact have been Nationalist Chinese soldiers masquerading as civilians, but it is indisputable that massive numbers of women and children were killed. During the TOKYO WAR CRIMES TRIBUNAL after the war, officials of the Imperial Japanese Army claimed that all the deaths in Nanking were military in nature and denied that massacres and atrocities took place. The tribunal, in sentencing to death the commander of the Japanese army in Nanking, General Iwane Matsui, fixed the number of civilian dead at 100,000. Even today, Japanese and Chinese authorities dispute both the toll and the nature of the Rape of Nanking—although no one now denies that something terrible occurred there.

The occupation of Nanking followed the Battle of Shanghai, which was very costly to the victorious Japanese. Many historians believe that the Rape of Nanking was vengeance taken by the Japanese soldiers. Eyewitness accounts of six weeks of mayhem abound, including what most historians judge as the reliable accounts of foreigners (chiefly missionaries and businessmen) living in the city.

An American missionary, John Magee, took still photographs as well as motion-picture footage of scenes of atrocity. Indeed, a German businessman resident in Nanking, John Rabe, organized a 15-man International Committee on November 22, 1937, and proclaimed a Nanking Safety Zone in an effort to protect civilians. Many believe that but for the Rabe committee's efforts, the death toll would have been even higher.

Atrocities reported and (in many cases) documented include a rampage through the Nanking Hospital, during which soldiers tore bandages from the flesh of the wounded, smashed casts with clubs, and raped nurses. Throughout the Nanking area, 20,000 to 80,000 girls and women were raped. Victims ranged from seven-year-old girls to very elderly women. The rapes were often public and frequently in the presence of spouses, children, and other family members. In many cases, victims were gang raped then murdered, often by mutilation. Many women were compelled to serve as so-called comfort women—military prostitutes for the pleasure of Japanese soldiers. Reports also exist of various instances of forced sexual exhibition: troops compelling families to commit grotesque acts of incest, celibate monks forced to commit rape, and even instances of forced necrophilia (sex acts with corpses). Those who refused to comply were instantly shot.

In addition to rape and rape-murder were thousands of instances of especially brutal murder, usually with the bayonet or, en masse, by machine gun. Those machine gunned were typically shot beside the Yangtze River, so that their corpses would fall into the river and be carried down to Shanghai. Others were subjected to mass execution in trenches dubbed "Ten-Thousand Corpse Ditches." Decapitation was another common method of killing, while some individuals were immolated, nailed to trees, or hanged by their tongues. Others were simply beaten to death.

Arson caused the destruction of two-thirds of Nanking, as well as buildings outside of the city. No attempt was made to suppress looting and burglary, which apparently was condoned or even encouraged among the troops. Soldiers were also instructed to strip the city of metal, for use as scrap metal for Japanese war production purposes.

At present, although the historiography of the Rape of Nanking remains controversial, no reputable Chinese or Japanese group or individual denies that atrocities were committed in Nanking. Yet there is widespread disagreement over the numbers involved.

Further reading: Brook, Timothy, ed. *Documents on the Rape of Nanjing.* Ann Arbor: University of Michigan Press, 1999; Chang, Iris. *The Rape of Nanking: The Forgotten Holocaust of World War II.* New York: Penguin, 1998; Fogel, Joshua, ed. *The Nanjing Massacre in History and Historiography.* Berkeley: University of California Press, 2000; Honda, Katsuichi. *The Nanjing Massacre: A Japanese Journalist Confronts Japan's National Shame.* London: M. E. Sharpe, 1999; Lu, Suping. *They Were in Nanjing: The Nanjing Massacre Witnessed by American and British Nationals.* Hong Kong: Hong Kong University Press, 2004; Rabe, John. *The Good Man of Nanking: The Diaries of John Rabe.* New York: Vintage, 2000; Yamamoto, Masahiro. *Nanking: Anatomy of an Atrocity.* New York: Praeger, 2000.

Narvik, Battles of

Narvik, Norway, was an ice-free port strategically vital to Germany as a point of embarkation for Swedish-export iron ore, which was essential to the German war effort. Recognizing this, the British Royal Navy laid mines off West Fjord, the entrance to the port, on April 8, 1940, but the Germans checked any Allied attempt to occupy Narvik by preemptively landing 2,000 German troops at the port on April 9. A five-destroyer British flotilla under Captain Bernard Warburton-Lee arrived too late to prevent the German landing, but Warburton-Lee sank two German destroyers and damaged another on April 10 and also sank six German merchantmen.

Unaware that five more German destroyers were in neighboring fjords, Warburton-Lee came under attack himself. He was killed, his flagship was run aground, one destroyer was sunk, and two others damaged. The German ships were also damaged in the battle, however, and could not pursue the remaining British destroyers to finish them off.

On April 13, the British battleship *Warspite* and nine destroyers attacked and sank the remaining eight German destroyers, which were stranded at Narvik for lack of fuel. The *Warspite* group also sank a U-boat and successfully set up a naval blockade, which cut off the German troops who had landed on Narvik.

Further reading: Dickens, Peter. *Narvik: Battles in the Fjords.* Annapolis, Md.: Naval Institute Press, 1996; Waage, Johan. *The Narvik Campaign.* Edinburgh: Harrap, 1964.

Navajo code talkers

Philip Johnston, the son of a missionary to the Navajo and one of very few non-Navajo who spoke the Navajo language, was a veteran of World War I who knew that Native American languages, especially Choctaw, had been used during that war to encode messages. He believed that the Navajo language would be ideal for secure communications in World War II. The language was unwritten and extremely complex. Its syntax, qualities of intonation, and dialectical variety rendered it wholly unintelligible to those who lacked either lifelong exposure or extensive training. At the time of World War II, it was estimated that fewer than 30 non-Navajos—none of them Japanese—could understand Navajo.

With all of this in mind, Johnston met with Major General Clayton B. Vogel, commanding general of Amphibious Corps, Pacific Fleet, early in 1942 and presented his idea. Johnston agreed to conduct tests under simulated combat conditions. The tests demonstrated that Navajo could encrypt, transmit, and decrypt a three-line message in 20 seconds. Conventional cipher machines of the period required a half-hour to perform the same task. Impressed, Vogel recommended to the commandant of the Marine Corps that the USMC immediately recruit 200 Navajo.

The first 29 recruits reported for basic training in May 1942. Working at Camp Pendleton, this first contingent created the Navajo code, quickly accomplishing the task of developing a dictionary and inventing many words for military and technological terms. This dictionary, including all code words, had to be committed to memory during the training of the so-called code talkers. After completing their training, the code talkers were sent to a marine unit in the Pacific. Their principal mission was to transmit orders and information relating to tactics and troop movements over field telephones and radios. Secondarily, the code talkers served as messengers. They participated in every assault and campaign the marines conducted in the Pacific from 1942 to 1945, including the BATTLE OF GUADALCANAL, the BATTLE OF TARAWA, the BATTLE OF PELELIU, and the BATTLE OF IWO JIMA, and they served in all six marine divisions as well as in USMC Raider battalions and parachute units. The Japanese never succeeded in breaking the code.

As of 1945, some 540 Navajos had enlisted in the Marine Corps, of whom 375 to 420 were trained as code talkers. Their contribution to World War II in the Pacific went largely unheralded until September 17, 1992, when the code talkers were officially recognized by a special permanent exhibition at the Pentagon.

Further reading: Bixler, Margaret T. *Winds of Freedom: The Story of the Navajo Code Talkers of World War II.* Darien, Conn.: Two Bytes, 1992; Kawano, Kenji. *Warriors: The Navajo Code Talkers.* Flagstaff, Ariz.: Northland, 1990; McClain, Sally. *Navajo Weapon: The Navajo Code Talkers.* Tucson: Rio Nuevo, 2002; Paul, Doris A. *The Navajo Code Talkers.* Pittsburgh: Dorrance, 1998.

naval war with Germany, undeclared (1940–1941)

Officially, the United States remained neutral in World War II until the U.S. declaration of war on Japan, on December 8, 1941, following the BATTLE OF PEARL HARBOR; however, in October 1939, a month after World War II began in Europe with the INVASION OF POLAND, the United States and 21 Latin American countries jointly issued the Declaration of Panama, creating in the waters of the Americas a 300-mile neutrality zone off limits to all belligerents. In June 1940, the Declaration of Havana reasserted and expanded the Monroe Doctrine. Whereas the 1823 doctrine warned that the United States would regard any attack against any state in the Americas as an attack against itself, the Declaration of Havana stipulated that *each* signatory would regard an attack against *any* nation in the hemisphere as an attack on itself. The chief enforcer of the Havana document was the United States, of course, and President Franklin D. Roosevelt ordered U.S. Navy ships to patrol the neutrality zone.

On March 11, 1941, Roosevelt signed into law Lend Lease, which authorized the president to provide material aid to any nation whose defense he deemed vital to the safety and security of the United States. The U.S. Navy presented Great Britain with 50 World War I–era destroyers (valuable as convoy escorts) in return for 99-year leases on British naval bases located on British possessions in the Caribbean. Also early in the year, the U.S. Navy's neutrality patrol was extended to 2,000 miles from the U.S. coast.

On August 14, 1941, President Roosevelt concluded with British prime minister Winston Churchill the Atlantic Charter, which effectively divided the world into spheres of strategic control for the common defense. At this point, American warships began escorting fast convoys partway to Britain, taking escort responsibility in the sea lanes of the western Atlantic, including in the vicinity of Iceland. By mid-September, navy vessels were escorting convoys between the Grand Banks and Iceland. While U.S. ships escorted fast convoys, ships of the Royal Canadian Navy escorted slow convoys.

Escort operations resulted in an undeclared naval war between the United States and Germany, especially in conjunction with the Canadians and the highly vulnerable slow convoys. On September 4, 1941, the destroyer USS *Greer* was attacked by a German submarine. On October 15, the USS *Kearny* was attacked, and on October 31, the *Reuben James* was sunk. The sinking of the *Reuben James* and other armed exchanges prompted Congress, on November 17, 1941, to amend the latest in a series of Neutrality Acts to permit the arming of merchant vessels and to allow merchant vessels to carry cargoes into belligerent ports.

Further reading: Bailey, Thomas A., and Paul B. Ryan, *Hitler vs. Roosevelt: The Undeclared Naval War.* New York: Free Press, 1979; Kemp, Peter. *Decision at Sea: The Convoy Escorts.* New York: Dutton, 1978; Morison, Samuel Eliot. *History of United States Naval Operations in World War II,* 15 vols. Boston: Little, Brown, 1947–1962.

Nazi Party (NSDAP)

"Nazi" was the familiar name for the Nationalsozialistische Deutsche Arbeiterpartei (NSDAP), the National Socialist German Workers' Party, which was born of a post–World War I political movement called National Socialism. Contrary to popular belief, the Nazi Party was not founded by Adolf Hitler, but by an obscure Munich locksmith named Anton Drexler, as the German Workers' Party, in 1919. Hitler, at the time a political agent for the German army, joined Drexler's party in September 1919 and began a rapid rise within it. In 1920, he took charge of the party's propaganda operations and resigned from the army to devote himself full-time to the party. Hitler proved to be a popular orator of extraordinary power, and during 1920–21, he took over leadership of the party, pushing out the original leaders and renaming it the National Socialist German Workers' Party.

In many respects, Hitler was typical of the thousands of Germans outraged by the humiliating and economically ruinous terms imposed by the Treaty of Versailles. The general discontent and desperation made fertile soil for the rise of the Nazis and, within Germany, no place was more promising for the rapid growth of the party than Bavaria, which had always harbored separatist sentiments with regard to the rest of the nation and which particularly despised the Berlin-based republican government imposed by the Versailles treaty. The principal Bavarian city, Munich, birthplace of the Nazi Party, was a magnet for disaffected veterans, including those who had joined the Freikorps, the extralegal paramilitary organization founded in 1918–19 and made up of German army units that, in effect, simply refused to demobilize. It was from the Freikorps ranks that many of the early members of the Nazi Party were recruited; this gave the party a strong paramilitary slant. The most prominent of the early Freikorps Nazi recruits was Ernst Röhm, who became closely associated with Hitler and raised and organized the uniformed thugs whom Hitler used early on to protect party meetings and to engage in street brawls with socialists and communists. Most of all, Röhm's thugs projected the organized strength of the party, much as BENITO MUSSOLINI's Blackshirts projected the strength of the Fascist Party in Italy. In 1921, Röhm organized his thugs—now known as Brownshirts—into a kind of palace guard called the STURMABTEILUNG (SA). Increasingly, Röhm obtained the cooperation and protection of the Bavarian government, which relied on him—at the time he was also a staff member of the official district army command—to employ the local army to maintain order. Thus Bavarian officials were often complicit in the tactics of terrorism and intimidation the SA used to suppress opposition to the Nazi Party.

Early in his rise within the party, in 1920, Hitler promulgated a 25-point program that became the foundation of Nazism. The chief provisions of the program were the abrogation of the Treaty of Versailles and the expansion of German territory. Always driving this basic message was an appeal to nationalism on the basis of a racial definition of it—the idea of a German race—whose destiny was to dominate the world. The chief enemies of the German race were the Bolsheviks and their natural allies, the Jews. From the beginning, the Nazi Party was steeped in anti-Semitism. That was hardly a new strain in European political movements, but Hitler and the Nazis made it a focus of their demonizing demagoguery, which was aimed at radicalizing the disaffected German working class.

The Nazi Party quickly developed as a projection of a cult of personality centered on Adolf Hitler. It became sufficiently strong in Bavaria that, in 1923, Hitler and his followers staged the coup d'état in Munich known as the Beer Hall Putsch, an attempt to seize control of the Bavarian state government in the expectation that this would in turn set off a national uprising against the Weimar Republic. The coup, premature, instantly collapsed, the Nazi Party was temporarily outlawed, and Hitler was imprisoned for most of 1924.

Hitler used the period of his incarceration to write a combination political memoir and party manifesto, *MEIN KAMPF,* and, on his release, resurrected the Nazi Party. He decided that he would not again attempt a coup, but would instead build power through at least ostensibly legal political means. In 1925, the party had some 25,000 members. Four years later, the membership had grown to 180,000. Hitler instituted a system of district leaders, called Gauleiters, to nationalize the party, which began to make its presence increasingly felt in municipal and state as well as federal elections. The party also benefited from the growing economic desperation of the Great Depression. The immediate postwar years had been bad for Germany, but the worldwide economic Depression that began in 1929 made conditions even worse. Unemployment spiked during 1929–30 and gave the Nazis millions of jobless voters to whom they could appeal. In a remarkably brief period, from 1929 to 1932, party membership exploded. In the elections of July 1932, the Nazi Party received some 14,000,000 votes, making it the single largest voting bloc in the Reichstag (German Parliament), with 230 members, or 38 percent of the total vote.

As the popular power of the Nazi Party grew, it also drew important support from German financiers and industrialists, who saw the Nazis as a bulwark against communist and socialist workers' movements and as a means of gaining important business advantages (such as government-sanctioned cartels) by controlling aspects of the government. Thus the party became increasingly well financed. Moreover, the legal, political, and financial rise of the party was always augmented by the paramilitary intimidation provided by the SA.

A significant decline in unemployment during late 1932 reduced the Nazi Party's vote to about 33 percent in the November 1932 elections; however, by this time, Hitler had become an individual to reckon with, and he commanded a sufficient bloc to compel Paul von Hindenburg, the superannuated president of the Weimar Republic, to name him chancellor on January 30, 1933, thereby elevating him and the Nazi Party to the very highest level of government.

Hitler now moved with lightning speed to consolidate his power and that of his party. In the elections of March 5, 1933, the Nazis skyrocketed to 44 percent of the vote, which Hitler used to usurp control of the Reichstag. On March 23, he pushed through that body the Enabling Act, by which the government Hitler now controlled was "enabled" to issue decrees independently of the Reichstag and of President Hindenburg. Adolf Hitler was now Germany's dictator. Among the first uses he made of his new absolute power was to declare the Nazi Party the only political party in Germany on July 14, 1933. When Hindenburg died the following year, Hitler extended his cult of personality beyond the party and to the nation by officially adopting the title of Führer (Leader). He also retained the roles of chancellor and commander in chief of the army. Additionally, he remained the head of the Nazi Party.

Although legally distinct from the German government, the Nazi Party became the core of the German nation. All significant government and civil service posts were occupied by party members. Gauleiters became potent figures in state governments. Having outgrown his need for Ernst Röhm, who was now perceived as a rival (because he led the socialist-oriented left wing of the party), Hitler turned against him and other top-level SA leaders. In 1934, they were executed, with Röhm. This left Hitler unopposed within the party, and the party, in turn, controlled every aspect of German government and German life, from German society to the German economy to German culture. The Nazi ideology was compounded of the thoroughgoing exploitation of propaganda, of national and racial mythologies, of a concept of national and racial destiny, of the hatred of all things "non-Aryan" (non-racially German)—especially Jews—and of the indissoluble marriage of government, industry, and the military toward the goal of world domination.

Adolf Hitler promised the German people that National Socialism would bequeath to them ultimate prosperous stability in a "Thousand Year Reich." The Nazi government lasted, in fact, a dozen years, half of them consumed in world war. Following Germany's defeat and the suicide of Hitler and many other Nazi leaders, the Nazi Party was outlawed by the Allied occupiers, who also subjected the surviving leaders to trials for war crimes and crimes against humanity. Although Nazi and quasi-Nazi movements and parties have appeared in various countries since World War II, including the United States (mainly in the form of white supremacist movements), National Socialism has reemerged nowhere as a significant political force, let alone a mass movement.

See also Fascism and Nuremberg War Crimes Tribunal.

Further reading: Brustein, William. *The Logic of Evil: The Social Origins of the Nazi Party, 1925–1933*. New Haven, Conn.: Yale University Press, 1996; Kater, Michael H. *The Nazi Party: A Social Profile of Members and Leaders, 1919–1945*. Cambridge, Mass.: Harvard University Press, 1983; McDonough, Frank. *Hitler and the Rise of the Nazi Party*. London: Longman, 2003.

Netherlands

At the outbreak of World War II, the Netherlands, also called Holland, was a constitutional European monarchy—a democratic kingdom—with about nine million people. The Dutch Empire at the time also included two major colonies, the Dutch West Indies and the Netherlands East Indies.

The Netherlands had a long-standing tradition of absolute neutrality and had even managed to remain neutral during World War I. The outbreak of World War II found the nation without war plans of any kind. Adolf Hitler sent Queen Wilhelmina his personal guarantee that Germany would respect Dutch neutrality. It was a pledge he immediately violated. Before the war was over, 220,000 Dutch citizens were dead, and the nation suffered an economic loss of approximately one-third of its gross national product.

The last general election held before the war, in 1937, gave 4 percent of the vote to the Dutch Nazi Party, which had at the time only 30,000 members. Even during the German occupation, this grew only to 50,000 members. Hitler never worked closely with the Dutch party and seems not to have taken it very seriously. More than 5,000 Dutchmen joined the WAFFEN SS; however, the vast majority of the Dutch population was hostile to the occupation, and the Dutch resistance was highly active. Although the occupiers kept the established Dutch police force in operation, it generally adopted an attitude of passive noncooperation with German authorities.

The German army invaded the Netherlands on May 10, 1940, during the BATTLE OF FRANCE. Three days later, Queen Wilhelmina was evacuated by a British destroyer. Her intention had been to take refuge in Zeeland, in southwest Holland, but the German advance proceeded so rapidly that she was transported to London instead, to which the Dutch cabinet (after conferring its legal powers upon General H. G. Winkelman, commander in charge of Dutch armed forces) followed her. A government in exile was established, as was a small Dutch military force, consisting of a handful of airmen (who became part of Squadron 320 of the RAF) and an army brigade, called the Irene Brigade, which fought in the NORMANDY LANDINGS (D-DAY) and in northwestern Europe. Those Dutch warships that had managed to evade German capture fought under the control of the British Royal Navy. Throughout the war, Wilhelmina made broadcasts to her people via Radio Orange and acquitted herself nobly as a symbol of Dutch freedom and nationalism.

Within the Netherlands, the German invaders set up a government to administer the nation as a province of the Third Reich. ARTHUR SEYSS-INQUART, as head of Reichskommissariat Niederlanden, was the chief Nazi administrator of the Netherlands. His top lieutenant was H. A. Ranter, commander of the SCHUTZSTAFFEL (SS) and security police. As usual, the policy of the occupiers was to loot the country for the purpose of prosecuting the war. Most food production and virtu-ally all manufacturing capacity was siphoned off. Forced Dutch food exports significantly undermined the effectiveness of the British blockade against Germany.

The German occupiers sternly regulated all aspects of Dutch life. Dutch Jews, who had for centuries enjoyed the benefits of a tolerant government and society, were removed from virtually all professions. When non-Jewish faculty members of the University of Leyden objected, the institution was closed. Gentile professionals, including doctors, architects, lawyers, and so on, were compelled to join Nazi-sanctioned professional organizations. Many refused and resigned from their positions in protest. Some went underground. Although Nazi philosophy regarded the Dutch as fellow Aryans, the vast majority of Dutch citizens were revolted by Nazism on moral as well as religious grounds. As the German occupation developed, approximately 104,000 Dutch Jews, including ANNE FRANK were deported to CONCENTRATION AND EXTERMINATION CAMPS. At least 36,000 escaped this fate, however, many of them by hiding among and with the aid of their gentile neighbors. Popular outrage over the Nazi roundup of Amsterdam Jews triggered a general labor strike in February 1941, which affected much of the country. When the occupiers responded by executing 17 Dutchmen (including 15 who were already being held on charges of sabotage), Dutch citizens responded with even more outrage, since the nation had abolished the death penalty during the previous century.

Three major RESISTANCE MOVEMENTS developed in the Netherlands during the occupation. The Orde Dienst (OD), specially sanctioned by the government in exile, worked in close cooperation with the British SPECIAL OPERATIONS EXECUTIVE. The Raad van Verzet (Resistance Council) operated independently, as did the so-called *knokploegen* (combat groups). Both of these groups gave assistance to citizens (including Jews) who had gone underground (and were collectively known as *onderduikers*). They also performed acts of sabotage. Beginning in 1942, Dutch operatives supplied the Allies with a good deal of useful intelligence.

The Dutch resistance maintained a clandestine news service, circulating underground papers to a surprisingly large readership. The Nazi policy of forcing many in conquered populations into slave labor prompted large numbers of young Dutchmen to become *onderduikers*. These men, combined with the active resistance movement, formed a ready body to assist the Allies when they entered the Netherlands in 1944.

Active resistance brought brutal German retaliation. At the start of the ill-fated OPERATION MARKET-GARDEN, an attempt to invade Germany via Holland, P. J. Gerbrandy, prime minister of the Dutch government in exile, broadcasted from London in September 17, 1944, an order for the Dutch railways to strike. They did precisely that, whereupon the Germans cut off all movement of food by canal as well. This brought on mass hunger and the death by starvation of some 16,000 Dutch citizens.

THE DUTCH MILITARY IN WORLD WAR II

Dutch neutrality dictated a strictly defensive military policy at the outbreak of World War II. The Dutch government placed inordinate reliance on the ability to flood vast portions of the low-lying country as a sovereign means of halting any invasion. German BLITZKRIEG tactics readily overwhelmed Dutch defenses, however, which were powerless against heavy aerial assault. On May 14, 1940, the Luftwaffe carried out the massive ROTTERDAM AIR RAID, which prompted the Netherlands to capitulate.

In 1940, the Dutch army consisted of about 400,000 men, but it totally lacked armor and had a mere 656 obsolete artillery pieces. It could offer no credible resistance to invasion.

The Dutch navy was small but modern, and was deployed principally to defend the Netherlands East Indies. It consisted of five cruisers, eight destroyers, 24 submarines, 16 minesweepers, and a number of torpedo boats and small auxiliary craft. The navy also operated about 50 obsolete aircraft. Many of the vessels stationed in the Netherlands escaped to Britain during the invasion and operated with the Royal Navy in the Mediterranean theater. Virtually all Dutch ships in the Netherlands East Indies were lost to the Japanese.

The Dutch air force, called the Luchtvaart Afdeling (Military Aviation Division), was administered by the army. At the time of the invasion, it consisted of just 175 planes, of which 132 were operational and 72 sufficiently modern not to be classed as obsolete. Sixty-two of these modern, serviceable aircraft were lost on the first day of the invasion.

Perhaps the most significant of the Netherlands' military assets was its merchant marine, which was for the most part overseas during the invasion and therefore escaped capture, destruction, or internment. The merchant marine gallantly served the government in exile throughout the war.

See also FINAL SOLUTION; HOLOCAUST; and NETHERLANDS EAST INDIES, ACTION IN.

Further reading: De Jong, L. *The Allies and Dutch Resistance, 1940–1945: Report Prepared for the Second International Conference on the History of European Resistance, 1939–1945*. Amsterdam: Rijksinstituut voor oorlogsdocumentatie, 1961; Remmerden, Hendrik van. *In the Shadow of the Swastika: The Double Life of a Resistance Leader in World War II Occupied Holland*. Privately printed, 1996; Woodruff, John H. *Relations between the Netherlands Government-in-Exile and Occupied Holland during World War II*. Boston: Boston University Press, 1964.

Netherlands East Indies, action in

At the outbreak of World War II, the Netherlands East Indies was a Dutch colony in Southeast Asia. It encompassed Java, Sumatra, Dutch Borneo, Dutch New Guinea, Celebes, western Timor, and the Moluccas. It was a key resource for raw materials vital to war, including oil (mostly from Sumatra), tin, bauxite (aluminum ore), and coal. Also produced here were rubber, copper, nickel, timber, quinine, sugar, rice, tea, and coffee. The population of the vast colony was about 70.5 million at the outbreak of the war; it included 1 million Chinese and 250,000 Dutch nationals.

After the Germans occupied the NETHERLANDS in May 1940, the People's Council in Batavia, the colonial legislative body in Java, declared loyalty to the Dutch government in exile, although the Council governed the colony with near autonomy. In January 1941, the Japanese foreign minister called the Netherlands East Indies part of the Greater East Asia Co-prosperity Sphere—in effect laying claim to its bounty. In response, the People's Council protested and refused many (but not all) Japanese demands for its products. The Council also declined to grant Japan large-scale fishing and prospecting rights and denied unrestricted access to its ports. Nevertheless, the colony did increase its general exports to Japan. In August 1941, however, the Council obeyed orders from the Dutch government in exile to stop shipping oil to Japan. With this, relations between the Netherlands East Indies and Japan deteriorated precipitously.

The Japanese saw the Netherlands East Indies as a major prize. Although they were confident that they could conquer the region, they were fearful that the Allies would first destroy many of the mines and plantations rather than let them fall into Japanese hands; speed of conquest was therefore of the essence. On December 20, 1941, Lieutenant General Hitoshi Imamura dispatched elements of his Sixteenth Army from Mindanao Philippines, to assault Dutch Borneo, Celebes, and the Moluccas. Paratroops were deployed on north Celebes on January 11, 1942.

Japanese units seized the oilfields of Dutch Borneo, as well as airfields at Kendari (southern Celebes) and Amboina (Moluccas). On February 16, 1942, a paratroop assault spearheaded an invasion by the Sixteenth Army at Palembang, southern Sumatra. A major oil refinery was captured. Next to fall was Dutch Timor, which was occupied on February 19. Resistance to the invasion was offered by small and poorly equipped colonial forces with modest assistance from Australian, and British forces commanded by British general ARCHIBALD WAVELL. Wavell was severely handicapped, however, by an almost total lack of an air force, which was mostly destroyed in Japanese raids on February 19 and 27. Allied naval forces fared somewhat better, as American destroyers managed to sink four Japanese transports and a patrol boat off

Balikpapan, which delayed the advance—albeit not for long. Japanese forces ultimately overwhelmed all defenders.

On February 25, 1942, the Allies dissolved Wavell's American-British-Dutch-Australian Command and left the Dutch governor-general on Java to assume command of the remaining forces. This represented a considerable number of troops, but by this time the Japanese were so firmly established everywhere that the situation was hopeless. Japanese forces landed on Java on March 1 and marched on Bandung. On March 8, the governor-general surrendered some 93,000 men of the Royal Netherlands East Indies Army. Other Allied units in the region also capitulated. At the same time, more Japanese troops landed in northern Sumatra. By the end of March, Sumatra fell, and the Japanese assaulted Dutch New Guinea. Here resistance persisted until October 1942, and the Japanese never succeeded in taking quite all of the Netherlands East Indies, as portions of Dutch New Guinea held out throughout the war.

The Japanese occupiers put Sumatra under the military administration that also controlled Malaya from headquarters in Singapore. The army also administered Java and some other islands directly, but two other major administrative areas, centered on Borneo (British and Dutch) and on Celebes, the Moluccas, and Dutch New Guinea, were governed by the Imperial Japanese Navy. Administration was harsh, and Dutch internees were subjected to particular brutality.

The Japanese did not eliminate resistance during the occupation. Guerrilla operations were widespread, but such was the hostility bred by years of colonial administration that the indigenous people often failed to cooperate with or support operations by the British SPECIAL OPERATIONS EXECUTIVE, Special Operations Australia, and the Netherlands Forces Intelligence Service.

Further reading: Krancher, Jan A., ed. *The Defining Years of the Dutch East Indies, 1942–1949: Survivors Accounts of Japanese Invasion and Enslavement of Europeans and the Revolution That Created Free Indonesia.* Jefferson, N.C.: McFarland, 2003; Rees, Laurence. *Horror in the East:*

Japan and the Atrocities of World War II. New York: Da Capo, 2002; Rottman, Gordon. *Japanese Army in World War II: Conquest of the Pacific 1941–42.* London: Osprey, 2005.

neutral nations

Few major nations chose or were able to remain neutral during World War II. BELGIUM proclaimed neutrality, but was brutally invaded during Germany's initial assault on the West. The NETHERLANDS had received assurances from ADOLF HITLER that its neutrality would be respected, but it, too, was invaded during the BATTLE OF FRANCE. The UNITED STATES adhered to its NEUTRALITY ACTS, although increasingly close cooperation with the British marked an unmistakable drift toward war until the BATTLE OF PEARL HARBOR forced FRANKLIN D. ROOSEVELT's hand.

The Republic of Ireland remained neutral throughout the war, largely because of its long history of hostility toward Great Britain. It was the only British Commonwealth nation to declare neutrality. Despite this, some 60,000 Irishmen voluntarily joined the British armed forces, others worked in the British merchant marine, and untold thousands went to Britain to work in war industries. In 1920, Ireland had been divided into the Irish Free States (which later became the Republic of Ireland) and Northern Ireland, which remained legally unified with Great Britain. During World War II, the population of Northern Ireland was exempted from conscription; nevertheless, some 30,000 Northern Irishmen voluntarily enlisted in the British armed forces.

Portugal had fought on the side of the Allies during World War I, but at the outbreak of World War II, its dictator, Oliveira Salazar, had sympathies with the fascist regime of Spain's FRANCISCO FRANCO and Italy's BENITO MUSSOLINI as well as the Nazi government of ADOLF HITLER. His ties with Franco had been formalized by the 1939 Friendship and Non-Aggression Pact between Portugal and Spain. At the same time, like Franco, he chose neutrality in preference to alliance with the Axis. Salazar was instrumental in persuading Franco to maintain neutrality. Salazar quite correctly feared that an alliance with the Axis would bring occupation of Portugal.

Unlike Franco, Salazar became increasingly sympathetic to the Allied cause as the war progressed and, in October 1943, he allowed the Allies to base aircraft and ships in the Azores, which Portugal controlled. Throughout the war, Lisbon was a hotbed of international intrigue carried out by Allied and Axis agents.

In Spain, Franco owed his power to the military aid proffered by fascist Italy and Nazi Germany during the Spanish civil war of 1936–39. Hitler assumed that Franco would join the Axis, and Franco repeatedly asserted his intention to do so "when the time was right." Although that time apparently never came, Spain, which had declared itself neutral at the outbreak of the war, changed its status from "neutral" to "nonbelligerent" after Italy entered the war. This meant that the Spanish government supported the Axis, but was not actively fighting in a military alliance. Nevertheless, Spain allowed German ships to refuel and refit in Spanish harbors, condoned various German espionage operations, and sanctioned the formation of the Blue Division, Spanish volunteers who served on the Russian front alongside German troops.

The Allies were long unwilling to take any action that might drive Spain wholly into the German camp; however, in 1944, they instituted an oil embargo against Spain, to which Franco responded by ending the export to Germany of wolfram (necessary for the production of tungsten and tungsten steel), expelled a number of German spies, recalled the Blue Division from the East, and released to the Allies three Italian warships that had been interned in Spanish ports. In April 1945, as Allied victory in Europe was assured, Franco severed diplomatic relations with Germany as well as Japan.

Sweden declared neutrality in both world wars and, in contrast to its neighbors Finland and Norway, was able to resist invasion and maintain its neutrality throughout the war. Its stance toward Germany was one of defiance, and it persuaded Hitler that Swedish resistance would be so fierce that German troops would be tied down indefinitely.

Unwilling to take this risk, Hitler abstained from invasion. For its part, however, Sweden met heavy German demands for export of iron ore, and German troops were permitted to transit Swedish territory via Swedish railroads. When the war turned inexorably against Germany by 1943, however, Sweden cut off iron exports and barred German troop movement across Sweden. By the end of the war, Sweden was not so much a neutral nation as a pro-Allied nonbelligerent. Yet only on the very last day of the European war did Sweden formally sever diplomatic relations with the Nazi regime.

The best-known neutral during World War II was Switzerland, a historically neutral state. The Axis respected Swiss neutrality largely because the small nation had a formidable military, which could readily defend its extremely mountainous territory. Switzerland would have been a daunting objective for any invader. Moreover, the Swiss made many accommodations to Axis demands, allowing both German and Italian troops to transit the country and to use Swiss railroads. Swiss banks, food producers, and industry traded extensively with the Germans and Italians. Only long after the war did the full extent of Swiss war profiteering emerge, especially with regard to dealings between Swiss banks and the German government. Swiss banks have been especially recalcitrant in refusing claims by HOLOCAUST survivors and their heirs to return money the Nazi regime had looted from them and deposited in Swiss accounts.

Switzerland did serve as a refuge for escaped POWs and political prisoners, and the Swiss government often granted political asylum to victims of the Axis. But early in 1942, it closed its borders to some 170,000 French Jews seeking asylum.

Further reading: Chevallaz, Georges-André. *The Challenge of Neutrality: Diplomacy and the Defense of Switzerland.* Lanham, Md.: Lexington Books, 2002; Cull, Nicholas John. *Selling War: The British Propaganda Campaign Against American "Neutrality" in World War II.* New York: Oxford University Press, 1996; Halbrook, Stephen P. *Target Switzerland: Swiss Armed Neutrality in World War II.* New York: Perseus Books Group, 2003.

Neutrality Acts, U.S.

Italy's first attack on Ethiopia prompted the U.S. Congress to pass the first of four prewar Neutrality Acts in August 1935. The act empowered the president to embargo arms shipments to belligerents in the Ethiopian conflict and to issue official warning to U.S. citizens traveling on the ships of belligerents that they did so at their own risk. A second act, passed in February 1936, added to these provisions a prohibition on extending loans or credit to belligerents. As if to certify U.S. neutrality, neither act distinguished between aggressor and victim, although it was abundantly clear to the world that Italy was the former and Ethiopia the latter.

In July 1936, the outbreak of the Spanish civil war posed a legislative problem because the two existing acts applied only to wars between nations, not civil conflicts. A joint resolution of Congress on January 6, 1937, forbade supplying any party involved in the war with arms, and when the 1936 Neutrality Act expired, the resolution was incorporated into a new law, which not only included civil wars, but also authorized the president to expand the embargo list to include "strategic materials" (for example, steel and oil) in addition to weapons. Even more significantly, the 1937 act expressly outlawed travel by U.S. nationals aboard ships of the belligerents.

As President FRANKLIN D. ROOSEVELT increasingly saw the nation's interests as aligned with the opponents of fascism and Nazism, he found that the Neutrality Act of 1937 was becoming an obstacle to the foreign policy he wanted to develop. Therefore, FDR enforced it selectively, most specifically in favor of China and against Japan, which had invaded China in the ongoing SINO-JAPANESE WAR. The 1937 act made additional important provisions:

Section 4 excepted from the act "an American republic or republics engaged in war against a non-American state or states, provided the American republic is not cooperating with a non-American state or states in such a war." This upheld the Monroe Doctrine of 1823, which held that an attack by a European state against any American state would be considered a direct attack against the United States.

Section 5 created a National Munitions Control Board, charged with carrying out the provisions of the act.

Section 6 prohibited American vessels from carrying arms to belligerent states.

Section 7: Whenever, during any war in which the United States is neutral, the President, or any person thereunto authorized by him, shall have cause to believe that nay vessel, domestic or foreign, whether requiring clearance or not, is about to carry out of a port of the Untied States, fuel, men, arms, ammunition, implements of war, or other supplies to any warship, tender, or supply ship of a belligerent state, but the evidence is not deemed sufficient to justify forbidding the departure of the vessel as provided for by section 1, title V, chapter 30, of the act approved June 15, 1917, and if, in the president's judgment, such action will serve to maintain peace between the United States and foreign states, or to protect the commercial interests of the United States and its citizens, or to promote the security or neutrality of the United States, he shall have the power and it shall be his duty to require the owner, master, or person in command thereof, before departing from a port of the United States, to give a bond to the United States, with sufficient sureties, in such amount as he shall deem proper, conditioned that the vessel will not deliver the men, or any part of the cargo, to any warship, tender, or supply ship of the belligerent state. (b) If the president, or any person thereunto authorized by him, shall find that a vessel, domestic or foreign, in a port of the United States, has previously cleared from a port of the United States during such war and delivered its cargo or any part thereof to a warship, tender, or supply ship of a belligerent state, he may prohibit the departure of such vessel during the duration of the war.

Section 8: Whenever, during any war in which the United States is neutral, the President shall find that special restrictions placed on the use of the ports and territorial waters of the United States by the submarines or armed merchant vessels of a foreign state, will serve to maintain peace between the United States and foreign states, or to protect the commercial interests of the United States and its citizens, or to promote the security of the United States, and shall make proclamation therefore, it shall thereafter be unlawful for any such submarine or armed merchant vessel to enter a port or the territorial waters of the United States or to depart therefrom, except under such conditions and subject to such limitations as the President may prescribe. Whenever, in his judgment, the conditions which have caused him to issue his proclamation have ceased to exist, he shall revoke his proclamation and the provisions of this section shall thereupon cease to apply.

Section 9 prohibited the arming of American merchant vessels.

On November 4, 1939, two months after the German invasion of POLAND started World War II in Europe, President Roosevelt signed into law a new neutrality act. Although it substantially recapitulated the Neutrality Act of 1937, the Neutrality Act of 1939 permitted sales of arms and strategic materials to belligerents, except as might be prohibited by presidential proclamation. Most important, all sales were to be on a cash-and-carry basis only. This was to prevent the United States from being drawn into a war because it held the debt of some belligerent country; nor would a U.S. vessel be permitted to risk running a blockade for the delivery of goods. (The cash-and-carry provision created an obstacle to the concept of LEND LEASE, which would be overcome by the Lend-Lease Act of 1940.)

The 1939 act also gave the president the authority to designate "combat areas," through which travel by U.S. nationals and vessels would be prohibited. As originally passed, the act retained the earlier prohibition against the arming of merchant vessels; however, on November 17, 1941, after incidents with German submarines and the torpedoing of the U.S. destroyer *Reuben James,* Congress amended the act to permit the arming of merchant vessels and additionally permitted those vessels to carry cargoes into belligerent ports. This amendment is traditionally considered the fourth Neutrality Act; it was, however, short-lived, since the entry of the United States into World War II on December 8, 1941, ended neutrality.

See also NAVAL WAR WITH GERMANY, UNDECLARED (1940–1941).

Further reading: Drummond, Donald Francis. *The Passing of American Neutrality, 1937–1941.* 1955. Reprint, New York: Greenwood Press, 1968; United States Congress. *Neutrality Act of 1937.* Washington, D.C.: U.S. Government Printing Office, 1937; United States Congress. *American Neutrality: Comparative Print of H. J. Res. 306, the Neutrality Act of 1939; Present Neutrality Law Approved May 1, 1937; Proposed Neutrality Act 1939 (H. J. Res. 306) as Passed by the House of Representatives, June 30, 1939; Proposed Substitute Neutrality Act of 1939 (H. J. Res. 306) as Reported to the Senate by the Senate Foreign Relations Committee, September 29, 1939.* Washington, D.C.: U.S. Government Printing Office, 1939.

New Britain, Battle of   *See* RABAUL, BATTLES OF.

New Georgia Campaign

A phase of the Solomon Islands campaign, the New Georgia Campaign was fought as part of the U.S. effort to capture Rabaul, which was the principal base in Japan's southeast Pacific area of operations.

The New Georgia campaign commenced in June 20, 1943, when a U.S. Army Raider battalion landed at Segi Point on the main island of the group, New Georgia. Over the next two weeks, marines as well as troops of the U.S. Army 43rd Division landed on Rendova and Vangunu islands and on western New Georgia, where they seized a Japanese airfield at Munda point. The U.S. Navy coordinated with these assaults, fighting the naval battles of Kula Gulf and Kolombangara, yet the

combined operations were unable to interdict some 4,000 Japanese reinforcements, which augmented the 10,500-man New Georgia garrison under Major General Noboru Sasaki.

Most of the reinforcements took up positions on Munda, which became the center of the Japanese defense. The Japanese troops did not content themselves with passive defense, but practiced night infiltration, which was extremely effective against the U.S. troops, many of whom were inexperienced. Japanese infiltration tactics took an enormous toll on U.S. morale, greatly increasing the incidence of battle fatigue and prompting the replacement of many troops by those of the 37th Division. The reinvigorated U.S. forces were ordered to go on the offensive, and an entire corps attacked on July 25. By August 1, the overwhelmingly outnumbered Japanese withdrew inland. Augmented naval forces prevented more Japanese reinforcements from reaching Munda; the Battle of Vella Gulf on August 6–7 sank three Japanese troop transports.

Munda was declared secure and became a base from which the marines launched an amphibious assault on Vella Lavella on August 15, bypassing—and isolating—the Japanese garrison on Kolombangara. Most of these men were able to withdraw on September 15, as were the Japanese survivors on Vella Lavella. Although the Americans prevailed at New Georgia, the campaign proved costly.

See also RABAUL, BATTLES OF.

Further reading: Miller, John. *War in the Pacific: Cartwheel—The Reduction of Rabaul.* Washington, D.C.: Department of the Army, 2000.

New Guinea Campaign

New Guinea, in the southwestern Pacific, was the focus of military action from 1942 to 1944. The Japanese well understood that by controlling New Guinea, they could readily invade Australia. The Allies understood this as well.

The Japanese captured Lae and Salamaua on New Guinea's Huon Gulf coast on March 8, 1942. This served as a springboard to the conquest of the

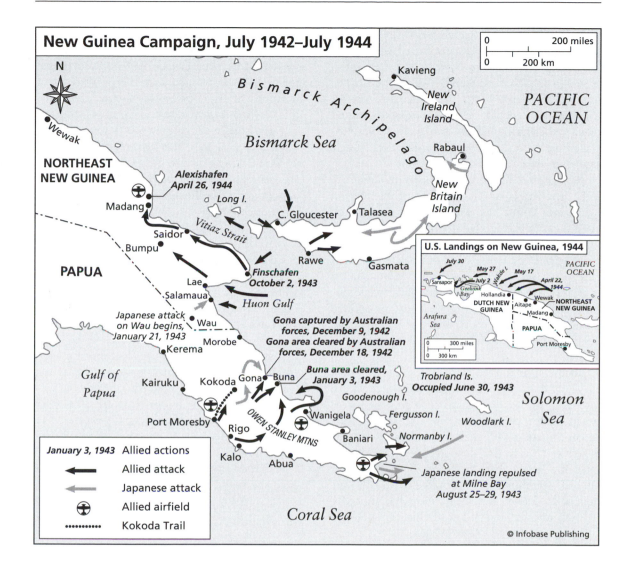

New Guinea Campaign, July 1942–July 1944

Dutch East Indies and put the Japanese in position for an assault on the key base of Port Moresby, in southeastern New Guinea, the final position defending Australia. The U.S. Navy intercepted the Japanese fleet in the BATTLE OF THE CORAL SEA on May 7–8, suffering a tactical defeat but achieving a strategic victory in that the Japanese were forced to withdraw their Port Moresby–bound invasion convoy.

The next major Japanese assault on New Guinea came on July 21–22, 1942, when elements

of the Eighteenth Japanese Army (under Adachi Matazo) landed at Gona and Buna. From here, the Japanese launched a new offensive against Port Moresby. On August 26, 1,900 Japanese troops landed at Milne Bay but were repulsed by combined Australian and American engineer troops, who were building airstrips.

On July 22, two Japanese regiments left Gona-Buna on a treacherous march along the Kokoda Trail over the 13,000-foot Owen Stanley Range. They occupied Kokoda village on August 12 and reached Ioribaiwa on September 17, putting the advance guard of the Japanese force just 32 miles from Port Moresby. Here, however, they were intercepted by the 7th Australian Division, which counterattacked, driving the Japanese out of the mountains and down into the swamplands around Gona and Buna. Joined now by U.S. and other Australian units, the 7th Division fought a fierce jungle campaign that drove the Japanese out of Gona on December 10, 1942, and out of Buna on January 3, 1943. The last Japanese resistance in this area, at Sanananda Point, was neutralized on January 23. With this, Papua was liberated. U.S. and Australian forces had suffered 8,546 combat casualties in this phase of the New Guinea Campaign, whereas Japanese losses were estimated at 12,000 killed and 350 captured; some 4,000 Japanese withdrew successfully. Victory in this phase of the campaign allowed Douglas MacArthur to seize the initiative and begin the Allied counteroffensive in the Southwest Pacific.

In the spring of 1943, the U.S. I Corps, under Robert Eichelberger (which would be expanded into the Sixth U.S. Army under Walter Krueger) began the next phase of the New Guinea Campaign. In coordination with Admiral Thomas Kinkaid's Seventh U.S. Fleet, Eichelberger led the fight to push the Japanese from the north coast of New Guinea. Beginning at Gona, on the coast, and Wau, inland, U.S. and Australian troops conducted a fighting advance west and north toward the Salamaua-Lae area. On the night of June 29–30, a regiment of the U.S. 41st Infantry landed at Nassau Bay, near Salamaua. In concert with the 5th Australian Infantry, the 41st captured Salamaua on September 12. Simultaneously, the 9th Australian Division landed 10 miles east of Lae while the U.S. 503rd Parachute Regiment and the 7th Australian Infantry Regiment were air dropped into the Markham Valley to the west of the village. This enveloped the Japanese position, and on September 16, Lae fell.

On September 22, a brigade of the 9th Australian Infantry landed at Finschhafen, 50 miles from Lae. Finschhafen fell to the Allies on October 2, which enabled the conquest of the entire Huon Gulf region.

On January 2, 1944, the U.S. 32nd Infantry landed at Saidor, 100 miles to the west of Finschhafen. The troops, who had simply bypassed 12,000 Japanese defenders on the north coast of the Huon Peninsula, seized an airstrip, giving the Allies control of the region and cutting off the Japanese garrison, of which only one-third survived.

On March 5, the 32nd Infantry advanced farther west, taking Mindiri. Elements of the 5th and 11th Australian divisions advanced to the Astrolabe Bay area and took Bogadjim, Madang, and Alexishafen during April 24–26. While the Australians conducted these operations, Krueger's Sixth U.S. Army made an amphibious advance 400 miles to the west, landing near Hollandia on April 22, the U.S. 24th Infantry landing at Tanahmerah Bay, and part of the 41st Infantry landing at Humboldt Bay, 25 miles to the east of the 24th's position. The divisions linked up on April 26 while the U.S. 163rd Regiment captured Aitape, 125 miles farther east. These spectacular three-pronged landings bypassed and cut off no fewer than 50,000 soldiers of the Eighteenth Japanese Army in the Wewak area. U.S. troops of XI Corps (Charles Hall) repulsed every Japanese attempt to break out. Japanese losses were heavy—8,800 killed, for U.S. losses of 450 dead and 2,500 wounded.

With many of the Japanese on New Guinea contained, the Sixth U.S. Army leapfrogged 125 miles to the west on May 17, 1944, landing at Arara and, on May 18, at Wakde Island, both in the Maffin Bay area. Japanese resistance on Wakde was very heavy, and the island was taken only after four arduous days of combat. All of Maffin Bay was declared secure by the end of June. While the Wakde battle raged, however, the U.S. 41st Infantry jumped 200 miles on May 27 to Biak Island, which controlled the entrance to Geelvink Bay, near the western end of New Guinea. Ten thousand Japanese held the island. They resisted the initial assaults and, early in June, were reinforced by an additional 1,000 troops; but air and sea attacks interdicted the remaining Japanese transports in the troop convoy. Two Japanese destroyers were sunk and some 50 planes shot down. Hopelessly cut off on Biak, the Japanese gradually yielded; nevertheless, Biak was not declared completely secure until August. The Biak operation cost the 474 U.S. troops killed and 2,400 wounded. Japanese losses were in excess of 6,100 killed and 450 captured.

Seventy miles southwest of Biak, Noemfoor Island fell to the 503rd Parachute Regiment during July 1–6. For 70 U.S. killed and 350 wounded, the Japanese lost 2,000 killed and 250 captured.

The U.S. 6th Infantry took Sansapor (on the Vogelkop Peninsula at the northwestern end of New Guinea) on July 30–31, thereby completing MacArthur's titanic 1,500-mile operation across the northern coast of New Guinea cut off and thus neutralized. This extraordinary combination of fighting and bypassing the Japanese cut off and thus neutralized some 135,000 Japanese troops.

The New Guinea Campaign had one final action. While the main Japanese forces suffered one defeat after another on New Guinea, another Japanese force established a base to the northwest of New Guinea proper, on Halmahera Island in the Moluccas. The U.S. XI Corps (Charles Hall) was dispatched to the area. It bypassed the Japanese on Halmahera and landed on Morotai on September 15. Airfields were built so that the Allies would have a base midway between western New Guinea and Mindanao (in the southern Philippines). All that was left after Morotai was taken were mop-up operations on Asia and Mapia (Saint David) islands, 150 miles north of the Vogelkop Peninsula, during November 15–20.

See also BUNA, BATTLE OF; DUTCH EAST INDIES, ACTION IN; and GONA, BATTLE OF.

Further reading: Drea, Edward J. *New Guinea (The U.S. Army campaigns of World War II).* Washington, D.C.: U.S. Government Printing Office, 1993; Gailey, Harry. *MacArthur's Victory: The War in New Guinea, 1943–1944.* New York: Presidio, 2004; Taaffe, Stephen. *MacArthur's Jungle War: The 1944 New Guinea Campaign.* Lawrence: University Press of Kansas, 1998.

New Zealand, air force of

During World War II, the Royal New Zealand Air Force (RNZAF) operated two reconnaissance squadrons in New Zealand and two in Fiji. Under the British Empire Air Training Scheme (BEATS), it also provided trained air crews for the British RAF—some 10,000 men by the end of the war. New Zealanders served in RAF units as well as New Zealand squadrons. The major concentration of RNZAF personnel was in the Pacific, where New Zealand squadrons participated in the Solomon Islands campaigns and in the BATTLE OF RABAUL. The peak wartime strength of the RNZAF was 45,000 men—and women; the RNZAF was the first Allied air force to recruit women when its Women's Auxiliary Air Force was created in January 1941. Peak female enlistment was 4,000 in August 1943.

See also GREAT BRITAIN, AIR FORCE OF.

Further reading: Francillon, Rene J. *Royal Australian Air Force and Royal New Zealand Air Force in the Pacific.* New York: T A B-Aero, 1970; Ross, John Macaulay Sunderland. *Royal New Zealand Air Force (Official History of New Zealand in the Second World War, 1939–1945).* Auckland: War History Branch, Department of Internal Affairs, 1955.

New Zealand, army of

At its peak, the army of New Zealand consisted of approximately 150,000 men and women. The first major force was the expeditionary force, initially designated the New Zealand Division and, from June 1942, the 2nd Division. In proportion to population, the size of the New Zealand army was the equivalent of 25 British divisions.

The commander in charge of the 2nd Division was Major General Bernard Freyberg, who was instructed to treat the army as a national force and to act under the orders of the British theater commander subject to the "requirements of His Majesty's government in New Zealand." The 4th Brigade was the first New Zealand unit to see action in the war, arriving in Egypt on February 12, 1940. A second echelon, consisting of the 5th Brigade, was sent to Britain as part of the force assembled to defend against an anticipated German invasion during the second half of 1940.

From March 1941 to September 1942, New Zealanders fought as part of the Eighth British

Army under BERNARD LAW MONTGOMERY. In 1941, a Women's Army Auxiliary Corps was formed, reaching its peak strength of 4,600 in July 1943. In addition to fighting in the WESTERN DESERT CAMPAIGN, New Zealand army forces took over some British responsibilities in the Pacific Islands. The 2nd Division also fought in the ITALIAN CAMPAIGN from October 1943 until it was involved in the occupation of Trieste in May 1945. In September 1944, pursuant to a decision by the Combined Chiefs of Staff in Washington and after the Quebec Conference, the 2nd Division was reduced and the 3rd Division disbanded, so that its men could be held in reserve as reinforcements or returned to New Zealand, where they were employed in much-needed agricultural and other labor.

Further reading: Clayton, C. J. *The New Zealand Army: A History from the 1840's to the 1990's.* Auckland: Public Relations of the New Zealand Army, 1990; Wigzell, Francis Alexander. *New Zealand Army Involvement: Special Operations Australia, South West Pacific, World War II.* Lancaster, U.K.: Carnegie Publishing, 2001.

New Zealand, navy of

At the outbreak of World War II, the New Zealand navy was called the New Zealand Division of the British Royal Navy. It consisted of the light cruisers *Leander* and *Achilles,* two British escort vessels, and one minesweeping trawler.

Achilles participated in the BATTLE OF THE RIVER PLATE in December 1939, and *Leander* sank an Italian auxiliary cruiser in the Indian Ocean in February 1941. In September 1941, the New Zealand Division was given autonomous status as the Royal New Zealand Navy (RNZN), which included a New Zealand section of the Women's Royal Naval Service. The British cruisers of the RNZN were augmented by the addition of two corvettes, 16 mine sweepers, 12 anti-submarine patrol boats, and more than 100 harbor defense launches and other small craft.

See also GREAT BRITAIN, NAVY OF.

Further reading: Harker, Jack S. *The Birth and Growth of the Royal New Zealand Navy.* Lancaster, U.K.: Carnegie

Publishing, 2001; Waters, S. D. *The Royal New Zealand Navy.* Auckland: War History Branch, Department of Internal Affairs, 1956.

Nimitz, Chester William (1885–1966) *U.S. commander of the Pacific Fleet*

A native of Fredericksburg, Texas, Nimitz enrolled in the U.S. Naval Academy in 1901 and graduated in 1905. He was commissioned an ensign while serving on the China station in 1907 and then served on the submarine *Plunger.* Promoted to lieutenant in 1910, he was given command of the submarine *Skipjack* as well as the Atlantic Submarine Flotilla in 1912. During 1913, he toured Germany and Belgium, studying diesel engines and subsequently supervised construction of the U.S. Navy's first diesel ship engine.

Nimitz was promoted to lieutenant commander in 1916. After U.S. entry into World War I in April 1917, he was appointed chief of staff to the commander of the Atlantic Fleet's submarine division. He served in various posts immediately after the war, then promoted to commander in 1921, attended the Naval War College, graduating in 1923. From 1923 to 1925, he was attached to the staff of the commander in chief, Battle Fleet. During 1925–26, he served on the staff of the commander in chief, U.S. Fleet. After this assignment, he organized the first training division for naval reserve officers at the University of California and administered this program from 1926 to 1929. He was promoted to captain in 1927 and, in 1929, was assigned command of Submarine Division 20, serving in this capacity through 1931.

Nimitz was given his first surface command, of the cruiser USS *Augusta* (CA-31) in 1933. In 1935, he was named assistant chief of the Bureau of Navigation, and in 1938 was promoted to rear admiral. He left the bureau to command a cruiser division and then a battleship division, returning to the Bureau of Navigation in June 1939 as its chief.

After Admiral HUSBAND E. KIMMEL resigned on December 17, 1941, following the BATTLE OF PEARL HARBOR, Nimitz, promoted to admiral, was named on December 31 to replace him as commander in charge of the Pacific fleet. Nimitz extensively reorganized Hawaiian defenses and directed the rebuilding of the shattered Pacific fleet. On March 30, 1942, he took unified command of all U.S. naval, sea, and air forces in the Pacific Ocean Area.

Acting on superb naval intelligence, Nimitz had overall command of operations that checked Japanese operations against Port Moresby at the BATTLE OF THE CORAL SEA on May 7–8, 1942. He was instrumental in the great victory at the BATTLE OF MIDWAY (June 2–6, 1942), which turned the tide of the Pacific war. With DOUGLAS MACARTHUR, Nimitz formulated the Allied ISLAND-HOPPING STRATEGY, which played a key role in Pacific victory.

Nimitz personally directed strategy in the Gilbert Islands (November 20–23, 1943) and the MARSHALL ISLANDS CAMPAIGN (January 31–February 23, 1944), delegating tactical authority to key subordinates, with whom he worked brilliantly. Nimitz presided over the advance into the MARIANA ISLANDS CAMPAIGN (June 14–August 10, 1944) and the Paulay Islands campaign (September 15–November 25). With MacArthur, Nimitz planned and executed the invasion of Leyte in the U.S. return to the Philippines on October 20, 1944.

On December 15, 1944, Nimitz was promoted to the newly created rank of fleet admiral (five-star), then went on to direct naval operations in the BATTLE OF IWO JIMA (February 19–March 24, 1945) and the OKINAWA CAMPAIGN (April 1–June 21, 1945), followed by operations against the Japanese homeland itself during January 1945 until the surrender of Japan—in a ceremony aboard Nimitz's flagship, USS *Missouri,* on September 2, 1945.

After the war, Nimitz served as chief of naval operations from December 15, 1945, to December 15, 1947, when he was appointed special assistant to the secretary of the navy during 1948–49. Nimitz served as a U.N. commissioner for Kashmir from 1949 to 1951 and wrote (with E. B. Potter) an important history of warfare at sea, *Sea Power: a Naval History,* published in 1960.

See also LEYTE, BATTLE OF; and LEYTE GULF, BATTLE OF.

Further reading: Hoyt, Edwin P. *How They Won the War in the Pacific: Nimitz and His Admirals.* Guilford, Conn.: Lyons Press, 2000; Potter, E. B. *Nimitz.* Annapolis, Md.: Naval Institute Press, 1976.

Admiral Chester Nimitz *(National Archives and Records Administration)*

Noguès, Auguste (1876–1971) *Vichy French commander of forces in North Africa*

At the outbreak of World War II, in September 1939, Noguès was the French commander in charge of forces in North Africa. Under the VICHY GOVERNMENT, he served as French resident-general of

Auguste Noguès with U.S. general Mark Clark
(National Archives and Records Administration)

French Morocco. On the one hand, he defied Germany by maintaining his irregular mountain troops, the Goums, in an armed and ready status, thereby purposely violating the terms of the armistice that ended the Battle of France; yet on the other hand, his forces resisted the U.S. landings in Morocco during Operation Torch in November 1942. With the invasion an established fact, however, he agreed to cooperate with the Allies. His proclivity for changing allegiance was such that the Allies punned on his name, dubbing him "General No-yes."

General Charles de Gaulle forced Noguès to resign in June 1943, whereupon he took refuge in neutral Portugal. After the war, in 1947 a French court sentenced Noguès in absentia to 20 years imprisonment as a collaborator. In 1956, he was duly arrested when he returned to France, but he was subsequently released, and he served no time for the collaboration conviction.

Further reading: Jackson, Julian. *France: The Dark Years, 1940–1944.* New York: Oxford University Press, 2003; Kelly, Orr. *Meeting the Fox: The Allied Invasion of Africa, from Operation Torch to Kasserine Pass to Victory in Tunisia.* New York: Wiley, 2002; Paxton, Robert O. *Vichy France.* New York: Columbia University Press, 2001.

Norden bombsight

The Norden bombsight was one of the legendary secret weapons of World War II—so secret that the device was always loaded onto the bomber, under armed guard, just prior to takeoff, and it was removed, again under armed escort, immediately after landing. All crewmembers—especially bombardiers—who flew on aircraft equipped with the Norden bombsight were required to swear an oath to protect the bombsight and its secrets with their lives.

Although the Norden bombsight was a remarkable piece of engineering and a significant advance in bombsight technology, much of the super-secrecy surrounding it was hype and propaganda, engendered both by the U.S. government and by the sight's inventor, Carl Norden, a Swiss-educated Dutch engineer who had immigrated to the United States in 1904 and originally worked with Elmer Sperry's gyroscope firm. Norden began designing the bombsight for the U.S. Navy in 1920. Simultaneously, his former boss, Sperry, developed a bombsight for the Army Air Corps. Norden's sight was delivered to the navy in 1928. In 1932, the army studied the navy's device and, finding it superior to the Sperry bombsight, purchased it from the navy. It was in service with U.S. Army Air Forces heavy bombers that the Norden bombsight earned its primary wartime fame.

The function of a bombsight is to allow a bomb to be dropped precisely at the right time to hit the target. The Norden bombsight did this so well that it enabled U.S. bomber crews to carry out their assigned mission of precision daylight strategic bombing. Norden's device was really an advanced analog computer, which used a system of gyros, motors, gears, mirrors, levels, and a telescope to factor in the data provided by the bombardier, including air speed, wind speed and direction, altitude, and angle of drift. The Norden would then calculate the correct trajectory of the bomb. Early versions of the Norden bombsight merely determined the exact moment bombs had to be dropped to hit the target accurately. Later versions—those employed beginning with the B-17G Flying Fortress—were actually coupled to the aircraft's flight controls. As the plane neared its target, the pilot would relinquish control to the Norden, which, via autopilot, would fly the aircraft through the bomb run and even automatically release the bombs. In an aircraft flying at some 300 feet per second, human reaction time was simply too slow.

Norden claimed that the sight was sufficiently accurate to hit a 100-foot circle from an altitude of 21,000 feet. As a practical matter, in combat, accuracy was typically much lower.

The Norden bombsight was used on the *Enola Gay* on August 6, 1945, to drop the atomic bomb on HIROSHIMA.

Further reading: Pardini, Albert L. *The Legendary Norden Bombsight.* Atglen, Pa.: Schiffer, 1999.

Normandy landings (D-day)

The Allied invasion of western Europe, launched on June 6, 1944, was the implementation of OPERATION OVERLORD (and the phase of Overlord devoted specifically to the initial assault, Operation Neptune), the product of some two years of planning, training, and buildup of personnel, equipment, and supplies.

By May 1944, 47 divisions—about 800,000 combat troops—had been assembled at embarkation points in Britain, ready to cross the English Channel to designated beaches in Normandy, France. The operation was under the overall command of U.S. general DWIGHT DAVID EISENHOWER, supreme Allied commander, Europe, whose headquarters was designated Supreme Headquarters, Allied Expeditionary Forces (SHAEF). Directly under Eisenhower was British general BERNARD LAW MONTGOMERY, who had field command of all Allied ground forces.

The Allies had chosen to land along a 50-mile expanse of Norman coast, from Caen west to the base of the Cotentin Peninsula. Tactically, this area was divided into five beaches, code-named, from east to west, Sword (to be assaulted by the British 3rd Division), Juno (Canadian 3rd Division), Gold (British 50th Division), Omaha (U.S. 1st Division and part of the 29th), and Utah (U.S. 4th Division). These initial landings represented about 156,000 troops.

The Atlantic coast was formidably guarded and fortified by the Germans, who had built the so-called Atlantic Wall, consisting of mammoth hardened fortresses and gun emplacements in addition to all manner of beach and sea obstacles, as well as explosive mines. Behind the Atlantic Wall were the German Seventh Army (FRIEDRICH DOLLMAN) and a portion of Army Group B, commanded by the legendary Field Marshal ERWIN ROMMEL. Another of Rommel's armies, the Fifteenth, was commanded by Hans von Salmuth and was held north of the Seine River. Overall German command in the west was under Field Marshal GERD VON RUNDSTEDT, who had 36 infantry and six Panzer divisions in the coastal area. The Allies understood that the success of the initial assault would depend heavily on surprise. Geographically, the most logical place for the assault was at the Pas de Calais, at the shortest distance between the English and French coasts; it provided a direct line of advance inland. Precisely because it was the most logical point of assault, the Allies decided to land at Normandy instead. In the months preceding the operation, they staged an extraordinary campaign of deception, which included disinformation disseminated through double agents, phony radio traffic, and elaborate decoys, all designed to deceive the Germans into believing the landings would come at Pas-de-Calais. The deception worked extremely well, and the German command placed the bulk of its forces opposite the Pas-de-Calais instead of Normandy. Even well after the initial breakout from the beachheads, the German high command continued to believe that the Normandy landings were merely a feint and that landings by much larger forces were imminent at the Pas-de-

D-day and Normandy Campaign, June–July 1944

Calais. For this reason, the entire Fifteenth German Army was retained north of the Seine and did not participate in resisting the initial breakout.

The cross-Channel invasion required precisely the right combination of tidal conditions, moonlight, and weather to succeed. This meant that timing was critical. A severe storm forced a one-day delay in the launch, but a narrow window of marginally acceptable weather permitted the invasion to proceed on June 6, 1944. It was the biggest amphibious landing in history. The first-wave force of 156,000 men sailed in a fleet of more than 4,000 ships commanded by British admiral Sir Bertram

Ramsay. The landings were preceded the night before with an AIRBORNE ASSAULT by paratroopers of the U.S. 82nd and 101st Airborne divisions behind Utah Beach. Their mission was to capture exits into the Cotentin Peninsula. At the same time, the British 6th Airborne parachuted onto the eastern margin of Sword Beach to take bridges over the Orne River and the Caen Canal, which would be vital to the protection of the invasion's left flank. The air component of the invasion also included operations by 4,900 fighter planes and 5,800 bombers, all under the British air chief marshal TRAFFORD LEIGH-MALLORY. During the first 24 hours of the operation, these aircraft flew some 14,600 sorties against German coastal defenses.

The actual landings began at dawn on June 6 supported by massive naval bombardment and close air support. By the evening of the first day, four of the five beachheads had been completely secured. These included, on the left (the east end of the assault), the three landings of the Second British Army (MILES DEMPSEY). The First U.S. Army (OMAR BRADLEY) had advanced five miles inland at Utah Beach, but at Omaha Beach, which was much more heavily defended, the U.S. 1st Division ended June 6, 1944, with a most precarious hold on the beachhead. Nevertheless, Allied casualties in the first 24 hours were about 11,000 (including 2,500 killed in action), costly, yet far less than had been anticipated.

Over the next six days, the invaders successfully joined together their five beachheads into an 80-mile-broad lodgment with an average depth of 10 miles. During this period, eight additional combat divisions landed. There was now no chance that the invasion would be repelled; nevertheless, the breakout into France would not be easy. On the left flank of the invasion, panzers kept the British Second Army out of strategically vital Caen for weeks after the landings. On the right, three corps of the First U.S. Army defended the perimeter from Caumont to Carentan. North of Carentan, the U.S. VII Corps attacked to the west across the base of the Cotentin Peninsula. Progress was greatly impeded by the *bocage*, or hedgerows, of the Norman coastal farmlands. On June 18, the Americans were able to turn north, and, on June 20, the 9th, 79th, and 4th Infantry divisions reached the outer defenses of Cherbourg. From June 22 to June 27, the Americans battered Cherbourg's defenses. This port, once secured, became a major avenue of supply for the growing forces of the invasion.

Elsewhere, the battle of Normandy developed with great violence. The Allies raced to build up forces behind their lodgment preparatory to a major breakout. For their part, the Germans brought up reinforcements in a bid to contain the beachhead. On June 28, Seventh German Army commander Dollman was killed and replaced by SS

General Paul Hausser. ADOLF HITLER, in panic, relieved the highly capable Rundstedt on July 3 and replaced him with Field Marshal GÜNTHER VON KLUGE, who was transferred from the eastern front. On this same day, the First U.S. Army attacked to the south but met fierce resistance and at first made little progress. The First Army took Lessay as an anchor for the invasion's right flank. The important village of Saint-Lô, at the approximate center of the American sector, was captured on July 18 at great cost. In the meantime, on the left flank of the invasion, the Second British Army at long last took at least part of Caen (west of the Orne River) on July 8. It was not until July 20 that a second attack took the rest of the town. Although the landing phase of the Normandy invasion had gone remarkably well, by July 20 the invading forces held little more than 20 percent of the area that had been assigned to them. Nevertheless, by July 24 they were poised to attempt a breakthrough in OPERATION COBRA.

Total casualties to this point were 122,000 for the Allies and 117,000 for the German defenders.

Further reading: Ambrose, Stephen E. *D-day June 6, 1944: The Climactic Battle of World War II.* New York: Simon and Schuster, 1994; Carell, Paul. *Invasion—They're Coming: The German Account of the Allied Landings and the 80 Days' Battle for France.* New York: Dutton, 1963; D'Este, Carlo. *Decision at Normandy.* London: Collins, 1983; Eisenhower, Dwight D. *Crusade in Europe.* Garden City, N.Y.: Doubleday, 1948; Keegan, John. *Six Armies in Normandy: From D-day to the Liberation of Paris.* New York: Penguin, 1983; Ryan, Cornelius. *The Longest Day: June 6, 1944.* New York: Popular Library, 1959.

North African Campaign

The North African Campaign commenced after the Allied landings on French Morocco and Algeria, November 8, 1942, in OPERATION TORCH. The campaign concluded in May 1943 with the surrender of Axis forces in Tunisia.

British prime minister WINSTON CHURCHILL and U.S. president FRANKLIN D. ROOSEVELT agreed that the Allies' first joint offensive in World War II

Shell burst by night somewhere in North Africa
(Library of Congress)

would be an attack on North Africa and its liberation from Axis control. The defeat of France in the BATTLE OF FRANCE in June 1940 left that nation's North African colonies under the control of VICHY GOVERNMENT forces, which were supposed to defend the colonies against any invader, Allied or Axis. The initial British plan for the occupation of Tunisia and Algeria (Operation Gymnast) was nevertheless based on the assumption that Axis support was soft among the colonial French administration and that, ultimately, the French in North Africa would cooperate with (or at least not resist) an Allied invasion. When the United States entered the war after the BATTLE OF PEARL HARBOR, Operation Gymnnast was revised as Operation Super-Gymnast, which included an American component. Still, it was based on an assumption of French cooperation. But when the Eighth British Army suffered defeat at the Battle of Gazala in June 1942 and was forced to withdraw from Libya, Super-Gymnast was shelved—only to be resurrected when an invasion of North Africa was settled upon (over objections from U.S. high commanders GEORGE C. MARSHALL and DWIGHT D. EISENHOWER) as a more feasible alternative to an immediate joint invasion of France. This time, the Allies did not simply assume French cooperation; nevertheless, they gambled on this as a probability. French general Henri Giraud, resolutely opposed to collaboration with Germany, was spirited out of

Vichy France in the hope that he would become the nucleus around which pro-Allied colonial French forces would rally. This quickly became a forlorn hope, as Giraud initially failed to cooperate with the Allied leaders, then simply proved ineffectual.

Now assuming that the French might offer at least some degree of resistance, Allied leaders reformulated Super-Gymnast as Operation Torch, which would be primarily an American operation under Eisenhower (as commander in charge of the Allied Expeditionary Force). American major general MARK CLARK was named Eisenhower's deputy, and another American, Brigadier General JAMES DOOLITTLE, took charge of the Western Air Command (Twelfth USAAF). The rest of Eisenhower's top commanders were British: Lieutenant General Kenneth Anderson, Admiral ANDREW CUNNINGHAM, and Air Marshal William Welsh (Eastern Air Commander). Eisenhower set as his task the goal of achieving perfectly unified command between the Allies; although he was never able to remove all friction, he succeeded, after some stumbling, to a remarkable degree.

The Combined Chiefs of Staff—the joint Allied high command—assigned Eisenhower to take all of North Africa, from the Atlantic to the Red Sea. He was to land in Algeria and French Morocco, conquer these, then attack to the east to destroy ERWIN ROMMEL's German-Italian panzer force in Libya. Eisenhower assigned Clark to make a clandestine landing near Algiers on October 22, 1942, to meet with Major General Charles Mast, chief of staff of the French IXX Corps and known to be a supporter of Giraud. As a result of the meeting, Mast pledged that, given four days' notice of the invasion, he would order the French army and air force to offer no more than token resistance to the Allied landings (sufficient to satisfy French honor), especially in the vicinity of Algiers. He warned, however, that he could not speak for the French navy—which, in fact, resisted more stoutly.

Three landings were planned. Major General GEORGE S. PATTON JR. would lead the Western Force in an assault on Casablanca, Major General Lloyd Fredendall would land at Oran with the Central Force, and Major General Charles Ryder would assault Algiers with the Eastern Force. Western Air Command would provide close air support for the two western landings, and Eastern Air Command would support the Algiers landings. The Western and Central land forces, consisting of American troops, would become the U.S. II Corps. Because it was believed that the French would fiercely oppose a British landing—as retribution for the destruction of the French fleet in the BATTLE OF MERS-EL-KEBIR—the Eastern Force consisted initially of a modest American assault force, which would be reinforced by British troops only after the landings had been secured. This would then become the First British Army. In all, 65,000 Allied troops would land—about half the number of French forces in North Africa.

The landings were made on November 8, 1942, and achieved complete surprise. Patton's Western Force encountered the stiffest opposition near Casablanca, but Algiers fell on the very day of the landing and Oran just two days later. Eisenhower exercised his own initiative to negotiate with Admiral FRANÇOIS DARLAN, the highest Vichy authority

in Algiers, and negotiated a general cease-fire by November 10. All fighting in French Morocco and Algeria ceased, and no attempt was made to retake Casablanca. The Vichy government in France, however, severed diplomatic relations with the United States and accepted the offer of German air support, which led to the German occupation of Tunisian airfields. Moreover, the Vichy government repudiated Darlan's cease-fire, prompting the admiral to attempt to rescind it, whereupon American authorities arrested him.

The Allied invasion of North Africa and Darlan's cease-fire caused the Germans to occupy Vichy France. Italian forces moved into Corsica, and Axis troops invaded Tunisia. But Darlan resolved that the German occupation of Vichy France released him from any obligations to the Vichy government, and he now agreed to give full cooperation to the Allies in return for Eisenhower's appointing him high commissioner for French North Africa. This caused great consternation among some Allied leaders, but both Roosevelt and Churchill backed Eisenhower's decision. Darlan's

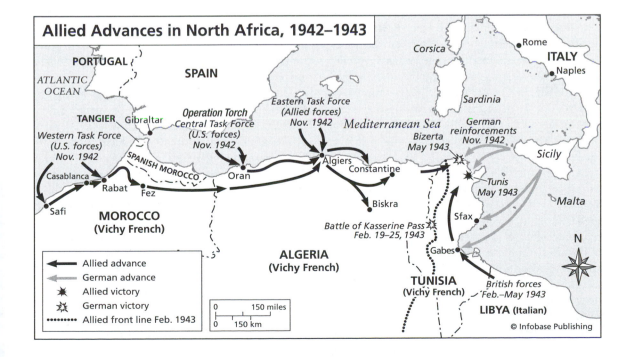

cooption in this manner doubtless saved Allied lives, although Darlan failed to persuade the French fleet at Toulon to join him in the Allied cause (the fleet was scuttled), and he himself proved short-lived, falling victim to an assassin's bullet on December 24, 1942. Giraud replaced Darlan as high commissioner.

Although the French were neutralized as a threat by the end of November 1942, the Luftwaffe and Axis ground forces offered fierce resistance. By December, the ground forces were consolidated as the Fifth Panzer Army, with the 10th Panzer Division as its principal striking force, under JÜRGEN VON ARNIM. His assignment was to prevent the capture of Tunis and to block the Allied advance to the central Tunisian coast (and thereby prevent the Allies from driving a wedge between Arnim's forces and those of Rommel). Initially, Arnim succeeded against the Allies. In mid-January 1943, the U.S. 1st Armored Division and part of the U.S. 1st Infantry gathered to mount a new assault, but before this could be launched, Arnim counterattacked on January 18, rolling up the French forces that were now fighting alongside the Allies. By the end of January, the Germans controlled all Eastern Dorsale mountain passes, and in mid-February they launched a new offensive. Arnim captured Sidi Bou Zid and Sbeitla, while Rommel took Gafsa as the Allies withdrew to the mountains of the Western Dorsale. Although the withdrawal was completed on February 19, 1943, Fredendall's U.S. II Corps was badly mauled, first by Arnim and then by Rommel at the BATTLE OF KASSERINE PASS—which was the first major engagement between U.S. and German forces.

The defeat of II Corps gave Rommel an opportunity to outflank the Allied forces in northern Tunisia, but he was compelled to yield to the Italian high command, which ordered him to attack Allied reinforcements at Le Kef instead. This lost the opportunity for a major blow.

In the meantime, the Allies reorganized their forces into the Eighteenth Army Group and a unified air command. British air chief marshal ARTHUR TEDDER now assumed overall command of the Mediterranean Air Command, and Alexander became Eisenhower's deputy as well as commander in charge of the army group (which included the U.S. First and the British Eighth armies) in Tunisia. On February 21, the Allies returned to Kasserine, but the disgraced Fredendall was replaced the following month by Patton, whose orders from Eisenhower were to rehabilitate II Corps.

Alexander oversaw an extensive reorganization of the front, and by April 1, the Allies retook Kasserine and the other lost ground. In the meantime, on March 6, the Eighth British Army defeated Rommel at Medenine in southern Tunisia, and Rommel, sick with diphtheria, was evacuated to Germany on March 9. Montgomery went on to lead the Eighth British Army against the forces of GIOVANNI MESSE at the Mareth Line. Montgomery's first assault, on March 19, failed, but a flanking maneuver in conjunction with Patton's II Corps and coupled with an Allied naval blockade forced Messe to withdraw. The Allies now pushed the Axis forces into an ever contracting pocket around Tunis. On April 22, 1943, Alexander launched Operation Vulcan, a major offensive in which the First U.S. Army attacked toward Tunis, with OMAR BRADLEY (who had taken over command of II Corps from Patton) striking at Bizerta and the French IXX Corps advancing toward Pont du Fahs. Montgomery proved unable to break through Messe's new positions at Enfidaville, however. Nevertheless, the Allies quickly recovered by mounting a new assault—Operation Strike—by the U.S. IX Corps along the Medjez-Tunis road. Augmented by artillery and close air support, this offensive rolled up Arnim's defenses, bringing about the sudden collapse of Tunis, Bizerta, and Pont du Fahs. On May 13, the Axis forces, essentially disorganized, surrendered, and the North Africa Campaign ended.

The Allies suffered 76,000 casualties during the campaign, but took more than 238,000 Axis prisoners of war. Despite its success, the wisdom of the North African Campaign was debated by contemporary strategists and has been further debated by military historians ever since. Some argue that it distracted the Allies from the "real" task of invading France; others, however, counter that the mixed performance record of the Allied armies in North

Africa proves that they were hardly ready to invade Europe and that the North African Campaign was, in fact, an appropriately less ambitious alternative at the time.

Further reading: Haupt, Werner. *North African Campaign, 1940–1943.* London: Macdonald, 1969; Jackson, W. G. F. *The North African Campaign, 1940–43.* London: Batsford, 1975; Kelly, Orr. *Meeting the Fox: The Allied Invasion of Africa, from Operation Torch to Kasserine Pass to Victory in Tunisia.* New York: Wiley, 2002; Moorehead, Alan. *Desert War: The North African Campaign 1940–1943, Comprising Mediterranean Front, a Year of Battle, the End in Africa.* New York: Penguin, 2001; Porch, Douglas. *Hitler's Mediterranean Gamble: The North African and the Mediterranean Campaigns in World War II.* London: Orion, 2004.

Norwegian Campaign

Initially, ADOLF HITLER showed little interest in Norway, but about six months after the conclusion of the INVASION OF POLAND, which started World War II, he decided to launch a combined arms operation against neutral Norway with the object of ensuring that the Allies would not interdict the free passage of Swedish iron ore to the Reich's war machine.

On April 9, 1941, the German army occupied Denmark and, on the same day, invaded six major ports along a thousand miles of neutral Norway's coast. The attack consisted of AIRBORNE ASSAULT as well as troops clandestinely transported into the harbors in the holds of merchant ships. Altogether, the invasion force of 25,000 achieved total surprise, which was further facilitated by a Norwegian pro-Nazi underground and turncoats, chief among whom was VIDKUN QUISLING, whose very name would become a byword for treason. Control of Narvik, Trondheim, Bergen, Stavanger, Kristiansand, and Oslo—all key ports—was accomplished within a mere 48 hours. Oslo, the nation's capital, was taken by just 1,500 parachutists. Much of the Norwegian army, apparently stunned into inaction, surrendered without offering resistance. A minority of the forces rallied around King Haa-

kon VII, retreated inland, and organized a gallant but largely ineffective resistance from headquarters in forests and mountains.

At the behest of WINSTON CHURCHILL, the Allies attempted a counterinvasion between April 14 and 19, landing primarily at Namsos and Andalsnes, on either side of Trondheim, on the central coast. Simultaneously, they attacked in the far north, in and around Narvik. Inadequately supported logistically, most of the hastily conceived operation soon collapsed, and 30,000 Allied troops withdrew. By May 3 all of central Norway was under firm German control.

The Allies enjoyed more success in the far north, at Narvik, but, here, too, they were ultimately forced to withdraw—not because of the situation in Norway, but because of the collapse of France in the BATTLE OF FRANCE. The last Allied troops left Narvik on June 9, taking with them King Haakan VII, who presided over a government in exile in London.

At sea, the Germans did not fare nearly so well. To begin with, Norway's large merchant fleet—perhaps 1,000 vessels—joined the Allies. British warships sank a heavy German cruiser, two light cruisers, 10 destroyers, 11 troop transports, eight submarines, and 11 auxiliary vessels for the loss of the aircraft carrier *Glorious,* the cruisers *Effingham* and *Curlew,* nine destroyers, and six submarines. The German navy would never make up the losses among its surface fleet, without which the prospect for an invasion of Britain dimmed significantly. Nevertheless, the German conquest of Norway and Denmark secured the northern flank of the German armies and assured the Reich access to iron ore as well as agricultural produce—the latter an important hedge that significantly reduced the stranglehold of the British naval blockade. Militarily, Germany gained submarine and air bases from which to attack Allied convoys in the North Atlantic.

See also NARVIK, BATTLES OF.

Further reading: Kersaudy, François. *Norway 1940.* Lincoln: University of Nebraska Press, 1998; Lindbaek, Lise. *Norway's New Saga of the Sea: The story of Her Merchant Marine in World War II.* Hicksville, N.Y.: Exposition Press, 1969.

Nuclear Weapons Program, United States   *See* MANHATTAN PROJECT.

Nuremberg Laws

The Congress of the Nazi Party convened in Nuremberg, Germany, on September 10, 1935, to discuss passage of laws to clarify the requirements of citizenship in the Third Reich, to promote and protect the "purity of German blood and honor," and to define the position of Jews in the Reich. Two principal laws were enacted by the Reichstag (parliament) on September 15, 1935, which, along with various ancillary laws that followed them, were collectively called the Nuremberg Laws or, in full, the Nuremberg Laws on Citizenship and Race.

The laws actually grew out of a debate over the economic effects of Nazi Party actions against Jews. It was decided that the party would cease such actions once the Reich had formulated a firm official policy against the Jews. The policy, embodied in the Nuremberg Laws, was hastily drawn up—so hastily that, because there was a shortage of regular stationery, some portions of the text of the laws were drafted on menu cards.

The first major law, called the Law for the Protection of German Blood and German Honor, prohibited marriage as well as extramarital sexual intercourse between Jews and Germans. The law also barred the employment of German females under 45 years of age in Jewish households.

The second major law, the Reich Citizenship Law, summarily stripped Jews of German citizenship, introducing a new distinction between "Reich citizens" and "Reich nationals"—the Jewish Germans to be included in the latter category.

The Nuremberg Laws codified what had been the general but unofficial measures taken against Jews in Germany to 1935.

Further reading: Burrin, Philippe. *Nazi Anti-Semitism: From Prejudice to the Holocaust.* New York: New Press, 2005; Hecht, Ingeborg. *Invisible Walls: A German Family Under the Nuremberg Laws.* Orlando, Fla.: Harcourt, 1985.

Nuremberg War Crimes Tribunal

After the war in Europe, during 1945–46, a series of trials were conducted by an International Military Tribunal convened in Nuremberg, Germany, to call to account former Nazi leaders on charges of war crimes. The indictments lodged against each defendant consisted of a possible four counts: crimes against peace (the planning, instigation, and waging of wars of aggression in violation of international treaties and agreements), crimes against humanity (exterminations, deportations, and genocide), war crimes (violations of the accepted laws and international conventions of war), and conspiracy to commit any or all of the criminal acts listed in the first three counts.

The International Military Tribunal at Nuremberg was convened pursuant to the London Agreement of August 8, 1945, which included a charter, signed by representatives from the United States, Great Britain, the Soviet Union, and the provisional government of France, for a military tribunal to try major Axis war criminals whose offenses had no particular or specific geographic location. Subsequently, 19 other nations accepted the tribunal provisions of the agreement. The tribunal was authorized to find any individual guilty of the commission of war crimes (as specified in the three enumerated counts) and also to find any group or organization to be criminal in character. In the case of an organization determined to be criminal, tribunal prosecutors had the option of bringing individuals to trial for having been members. The defense would be barred from challenging the criminal nature of the group or organization.

The tribunal was made up of a member (plus an alternate member) selected by each of the four principal signatory countries. The first session was convened under the presidency of General I. T. Nikitchenko, the Soviet member, on October 18, 1945, in Berlin. At this session, 24 former Nazi leaders were charged with war crimes, and various groups (including the GESTAPO) were charged as being criminal in character. After this first session, all others, beginning on November 20, 1945, were held in Nuremberg under the presidency of Lord Justice Geoffrey Lawrence, the British member.

Defendants had the right to receive a copy of the indictment, to offer an explanation or defense, to be represented by legal counsel, and to confront and cross-examine all witnesses brought against them.

At the conclusion of 216 court sessions, on October 1, 1946, the verdicts on 22 of the original 24 defendants were handed down. One defendant, Robert Ley, had committed suicide while in prison, and the aged Gustav Krupp von Bohlen und Halbach, the great German arms manufacturer, was judged mentally and physically unfit to stand trial. Of the 22 tried, three, Hjalmar Schacht, Franz von Papen, and Hans Fritzsche, were acquitted; four, Karl Dönitz, Baldur von Schirach, Albert Speer, and Konstantin von Neurath, were sentenced to 10 to 20 years in prison; three, Rudolf Hess, Walther Funk, and Erich Raeder, were sentenced to life imprisonment; and 12 were sentenced to be hanged. Of these, ten—Hans Frank, Wilhelm Frick, Julius Streicher, Alfred Rosenberg, Ernst Kaltenbrunner, Joachim von Ribbentrop, Fritz Sauckel, Alfred Jodl, Wilhelm Keitel, and Arthur Seyss-Inquart—were executed on October 16, 1946. Martin Bormann was tried and condemned to death in absentia, and Hermann Göring committed suicide before sentence could be carried out.

The tribunal established certain enduring principles of international law, including those embodied in the rejection of the chief defenses offered by the defendants. The tribunal rejected the contention that only a state, and not individuals, could be found guilty of war crimes. The court concluded that crimes of international law are committed by men and women and that only by holding individuals to account for committing such crimes could international law be enforced. The tribunal also rejected the defense that the trial as well as its adjudication were ex post facto. All acts of which the defendants were found guilty, the tribunal held, had been universally regarded as criminal prior to World War II. These principles and others created a precedent for subsequent war crimes trials relating to World War II as well as subsequent conflicts.

See also Tokyo War Crimes Tribunal.

Further reading: Davidson, Eugene, ed. *The Trial of the Germans: An Account of the Twenty-Two Defendants Before the International Military Tribunal at Nuremberg.* Columbia: University of Missouri Press, 1997; Harris, Whitney R. *Tyranny on Trial: The Trial of the Major German War Criminals at the End of the World War II at Nuremberg Germany 1945–1946.* Dallas: Southern Methodist University Press, 1999; Marrus, Michael R. *The Nuremberg War Crimes Trial, 1945–46: A Documentary History.* New York: Bedford/St. Martin's, 1997; Persico, Joseph E. *Nuremberg: Infamy on Trial.* New York: Penguin, 1995.

O

Oberth, Hermann (1894–1989) German rocket pioneer

Born in Nagyszeben, Austria-Hungary (modern Sibiu, Romania), Hermann Oberth was the son of a physician. He studied medicine in Munich, but his education was interrupted by service in the Austro-Hungarian army during World War I. Wounded, he spent his convalescence pursuing his true scientific passion, the infant field of astronautics and rocketry. A visionary, Oberth created experiments to simulate weightlessness and designed a long-range, liquid-propellant rocket that impressed his commanding officer sufficiently to prompt him to send it on to the War Ministry, where it was summarily rejected as the stuff of science fiction.

After the war, Oberth wrote a doctoral dissertation devoted to his rocket design. When the text was rejected by the University of Heidelberg, Oberth privately subsidized its publication as *The Rocket into Interplanetary Space* (1923). The book presented the mathematical formulation of the speed and thrust required to achieve escape velocity to reach beyond the gravitational pull of the earth. Oberth became famous in scientific circles as a result of the book. He began a correspondence with U.S. rocket pioneer Robert Goddard and Soviet rocket theorist Konstantin Tsiolkovsky, then wrote *Ways to Spaceflight* (1929), which won the first annual Robert Esnault-Pelterie-André Hirsch Prize of 10,000 francs, which he use to finance practical research on liquid-propellant rocket motors. In 1931, Oberth was awarded a patent for a liquid-propellant rocket by the Romanian Patent Office and launched his first rocket on May 7, 1931, near Berlin.

Widely acclaimed, Oberth joined the faculty of the Technical University of Vienna in 1938, became a German citizen in 1940, and began working on German military rocket development at Peenemünde under WERNHER VON BRAUN, whom he had earlier mentored.

In 1943, Oberth left Peenemünde to work on solid-propellant antiaircraft rockets. Unlike von Braun and many other German rocket scientists, Oberth, after the war, worked neither for the Americans nor the Soviets, but lived in Switzerland for a year, working as a rocket consultant, before moving to Italy in 1950 and designed solid-propellant antiaircraft rockets for the Italian navy. It was not until 1955 that Oberth came to the United States, where he worked in space research for the U.S. Army. In 1958, he retired and returned to live in West Germany. His "retirement" was absorbed in theoretical and philosophical studies unrelated to rocket science.

See also V-1 BUZZ BOMB and V-2 ROCKET.

Further reading: Walters, Helen B. *Hermann Oberth: Father of Space Travel.* London: Macmillan, 1962.

Oboe

"Oboe" was one of the key advances in RADAR during World War II. It was introduced early in 1943 by the RAF as the first radar precision-bombing system. The nickname was derived from the simple fact that the radar pulses were translated into sounds that called to mind the pure, high pitch of an oboe.

The oboe system exploited radar's ability to measure the range of an aircraft with a high degree of accuracy. Two ground stations were at the heart of the system. One tracked the aircraft as it flew along an arc of constant range running through the target. It transmitted to the aircraft correction signals whenever the plane drifted from this arc. Simultaneously, the second ground station measured the range along the arc, broadcasting a release signal when the bomber aircraft reached the bomb release point that had been previously calculated and programmed into the system. The third component of the oboe system was a pair of repeater-transmitters on board the bomber itself. These amplified both the range and the track signals, then returned them to the ground stations.

Oboe proved to be remarkably accurate, but it was a line-of-sight system limited in range by the curvature of the earth to 280 miles between ground transmitters. These had to be erected in friendly territory, of course, which meant that bombers could not rely on oboe for distant penetration into enemy territory; nevertheless, the England-based system was within range of the industrial Ruhr Valley. The other serious limitation of oboe was that each pair of ground stations could control only one bomber at a time. This limitation could be compensated for by equipping a light bomber, such as the Mosquito, with the oboe device and assigning it to serve as a pathfinder for a formation of heavy bombers.

Oboe had a great advantage over other radio guidance systems (including those used by the Germans) in that it was difficult to jam.

Further reading: Brown, L. *A Radar History of World War II: Technical and Military Imperatives.* New York: Taylor & Francis, 1999; Fisher, David E. *A Race on the Edge of Time: Radar-The Decisive Weapon of World War II.* New York: McGraw-Hill, 1987.

O'Connor, Richard (1889–1981) *British general in the Western Desert Campaign*

Born in Srinagar, Kashmir, India, Richard O'Connor was the son of a major in the Royal Irish Fusiliers. He was educated in British public schools, then enrolled in the Royal Military Academy Sandhurst in 1908. Before World War I, O'Connor received signals and rifle training; stationed in Malta from 1911 to 1912, he served as regimental signals officer. With the outbreak of World War I in 1914, he served as signals officer of the 22nd Brigade, 7th Division and saw distinguished action, earning in brevets from captain to major and lieutenant colonel. He was also highly decorated.

Between the wars, O'Connor served during 1921–24 as brigade major of the Experimental Brigade, which was created to test methods for using tanks and aircraft in coordination with infantry and artillery. He then served in various posts, including as an instructor at the Staff College at Camberley from 1927 to 1929. In 1935, he attended the Imperial Defence College, London, and, promoted to brigadier general, assumed command of the Peshawar Brigade in northwest India. Here he learned valuable lessons in mobile warfare, which he applied in Libya during the WESTERN DESERT CAMPAIGN of World War II.

In September 1938, O'Connor was promoted to major general and named to command the 7th Division in Palestine while also serving as military governor of Jerusalem. In August 1939, his division was transferred to the fortress at Mersa Matruh, Egypt, and was assigned to defend against a potential attack from the Italian Tenth Army across the Libyan border. When Italy declared war on Britain and France on June 10, 1940, O'Connor was named to command the Western Desert Force, his chief mission to defend Egypt and the Suez Canal from Italian attack. Greatly outnumbered—with 36,000 men opposing some 150,000 Italians—O'Connor led a brilliant defense, which included the Long Range Desert Group that became the famed DESERT RATS. After disrupting the Italians, O'Connor conducted a counteroffensive that cut a broad swath through the Italian rear areas, driving the Italians out of Egypt by December 1940.

After a brief interval of rest, O'Connor led his Desert Force into Italian Libya and, on January 22, 1941, captured Tobruk. O'Connor swept through Italian Libya, ultimately destroying an entire 10-division Italian army and taking some 130,000 prisoners.

By March 1941, ERWIN ROMMEL and the German Afrika Korps arrived to bolster the Italians. During a night reconnaissance mission on April 7, 1941, O'Connor and General Philip Neame were captured by a German patrol. O'Connor spent the next two and a half years as a prisoner of war, mainly in Florence, Italy, and made repeated escape attempts before finally succeeding, with the aid of the Italian resistance, in September 1943.

O'Connor was given command of VIII Corps for the NORMANDY LANDINGS (D-DAY) and the breakout that followed, plus OPERATION MARKET-GARDEN. On November 27, 1944, he was transferred to India as commander in charge of the Eastern Army.

After the war, in November 1945, O'Connor was promoted to general and appointed commander in charge of the North Western Army. In July 1946, he became adjutant general to the Forces and aide-de-camp general to King George VI. Following a dispute over the cancellation of demobilization of troops stationed in the Far East, O'Connor retired in 1948. He served as commandant of the Army Cadet Force, Scotland, from 1948 to 1959 and in other largely honorific posts.

See also TOBRUK, BATTLES OF.

Further reading: Barclay, Cyril Nelson. *Against All Odds: The Story of the First Offensive in Libya, 1940–41.* London: Sifton Praed, 1955; Baynes, John. *The Forgotten Victor: General Sir Richard O'Connor, KT, GCB, DSO, MC.* London: Brassey's, 1989; Barnett, Corelli. *The Desert Generals.* London: Allen and Unwin, 1960.

Office of Strategic Services (OSS)

The OSS was the principal American intelligence organization in World War II. Its origin may be found in the work of WILLIAM DONOVAN, who, in July 1940, at the personal request of FRANKLIN D. ROOSEVELT, undertook a series of study missions abroad to appraise the state of U.S. intelligence and to make recommendations for creating an efficient, centralized intelligence-gathering apparatus. With war looming, the United States had no central intelligence agency. The army's G-2, the navy's N-2, the Department of State, and individual diplomats and departments gathered intelligence on a catch-as-catch-can basis. In his presidential, "Memorandum of Establishment of Service of Strategic Information," Donovan called for a centralized channel for acquiring and processing strategic information, noting that political as well as psychological factors would be critical in World War II. In July 1941, responding to the memorandum, FDR appointed Donovan, a U.S. Army general, to the civilian position of Coordinator of Information (COI), with responsibility and authority for consolidating intelligence-gathering and analytical tasks and reporting the results to the Joint Chiefs of Staff and to the president himself.

Donovan was an aggressive administrator who rapidly expanded his agency, assuming the functions of information gathering, propaganda, espionage, subversion, and even postwar planning. Donovan was soon seen by others as an empire builder, and interagency friction developed between his organization and the existing intelligence units. On June 13, 1942, propaganda functions were removed from the COI and turned over to a newly created Office of War Information (OWI). It was at this time that COI received its new designation as the Office of Strategic Services.

The OSS brief was now to collect and analyze such "strategic information" as required by the Joint Chiefs of Staff. Working directly under Donovan was Brigadier General John Magruder, who directed the four major intelligence branches of OSS: Secret Intelligence (SI), which obtained—by whatever means necessary—information about Axis and Axis-occupied countries; Counter-Intelligence (X-2), which monitored the intelligence and espionage operations of other nations, fielded double agents, and vetted the reliability of foreign nationals who offered their services to the United States; and the Foreign Nationalities Branch (FN), which interviewed refugees and foreign citizens living in the United States. The fourth branch, Research and Analysis (R&A), was the largest. Directed by William L. Langer, a Harvard University historian, this branch employed academic scholars (including many recent European refugees) to create analytical reports on economic, political, geographical, and cultural topics relevant to all theaters, as well as the Soviet Union and Latin America.

In addition to the intelligence branches, the OSS included operational branches under the leadership of a deputy director for strategic services and operations. Special Operations Branch (SO) conducted subversion, including sabotage, support of resistance movements, raiding, and other irregular combat missions. Morale Operations (MO) conducted psychological warfare, including the dissemination of rumor, disinformation, leaflets, and covert radio broadcasts to the people of the Axis nations and those occupied by the Axis.

The OSS also had an extensive technical service, including a Research and Development group, which developed and built advanced communications equipment and weapons; a Field Photographic Unit, which produced materials for informational and foreign propaganda purposes; the Interdepartmental Committee for the Acquisition of Foreign Periodicals, which collected published documents from the Axis countries; the Presentation Branch, which prepared data and other exhibits for presentation to the president and other top officials. (This branch designed the chambers in which the NUREMBERG WAR CRIMES TRIBUNAL sessions were conducted.)

Headquartered in Washington, D.C., OSS also had many offices abroad, the most important of which was maintained in London. Additionally, offices were established in neutral Sweden (Stockholm) and Switzerland (Berne) and, as the war progressed, elsewhere as well.

The guiding principle of the OSS was its freedom from politics and policymaking. It was subordinated not to politicians but to military theater commanders. While this imposed severe limitations on the agency's ability to influence diplomatic policy, it endowed the OSS with a reputation for objectivity that won for it a high degree of confidence in military as well as civilian government circles.

OSS worked extensively during the NORTH AFRICAN CAMPAIGN, gathering much valuable intelligence, identifying informants, drumming up popular political support, and establishing a communications network. At the same time, the agency developed the Enemy Objectives Unit (EOU), which consisted of economists who played a key role in formulating the objectives of the Allied STRATEGIC BOMBING campaign, focusing on the industrial targets the EOU determined to be the most important.

When Allied operations moved into Sicily and mainland Italy, OSS conducted missions throughout central and northern Italy to support local resistance, often coordinating with British SPECIAL OPERATIONS EXECUTIVE (SOE) as well as MI6. By mid-1943, OSS teams attached to SOE missions entered Yugoslavia in support of partisans there.

The OSS played an important role in conjunction with British intelligence before and after the NORMANDY LANDINGS (D-DAY). So-called Jedburgh teams—each of which included an OSS man, a British SOE representative, and an agent of FREE FRENCH FORCES—were parachuted into France to coordinate resistance during the early phases of the Normandy operations.

One of the most important OSS operations was Operation Sunrise, led by ALLEN DULLES beginning in November 1942. Dulles worked out of the OSS mission in Berne under cover as Special Legal Assistant to the U.S. ambassador. Charged with conducting espionage operations against Germany as well as neutralizing Soviet influence during the immediate postwar period, Dulles created and managed a remarkable network of agents and informants, including those active in the anti-Nazi resistance in Germany.

By the end of 1944, OSS agents began to penetrate Germany itself. Germans and Austrians who had slipped into the West were trained and equipped for missions inside the Reich. Some operatives penetrated the very highest levels of government and the military, but most agents were assigned merely to report on general conditions within Germany, to evaluate the changing status of German forces, to identify important targets, and to facilitate or commit acts of sabotage and subversion.

As the European war neared its conclusion, OSS personnel participated in the planning for the occupation government of Germany and the German-occupied territories. As early as 1943, OSS researchers had begun compiling and composing handbooks and guides for the eventual use of occupation authorities. The OSS also planned—and in large measure executed—programs of postwar de-Nazification. These programs employed political and legal theorists who worked in cooperation with the War Department as well as the U. S. Department of Justice and were instrumental in creating the guidelines used by American prosecutors at the Nuremberg War Crimes Tribunal.

In the Pacific and Asian theaters, the OSS encountered resistance from both General DOUGLAS MACARTHUR and Admiral CHESTER NIMITZ, who were reluctant to give the agents free rein. Nevertheless, the OSS was especially important in the China-Burma-India theater, especially in coordinating Chinese resistance against the Japanese, as well as organizing guerrilla operations against the Japanese occupiers of Thailand and Burma.

Immediately after the war, President HARRY S. TRUMAN terminated the Office of Strategic Services as of September 30, 1945 by Executive Order 9620, signed 10 days earlier. The many intelligence functions of the OSS were widely dispersed until the Central Intelligence Agency (CIA) was created by the National Security Act of 1947.

See also RESISTANCE MOVEMENTS.

Further reading: O'Donnell, Patrick K. *Operatives, Spies, and Saboteurs: The Unknown Story of the Men and Women of World War II's OSS.* New York: Free Press, 2004; Smith, Richard H. *OSS: The Secret History of America's First Central Intelligence Agency.* Guilford, Conn.: Lyons Press, 2005.

Okinawa Campaign

Okinawa was the culminating campaign of the Pacific war. The island, 794 square miles, was located some 400 miles below southern Kyushu, on the threshold of the Japanese homeland. U.S. planners intended to use Okinawa as the principal base from which the invasion of the home islands (beginning with Kyushu in November 1945) would be launched.

The Japanese recognized the last-ditch importance of Okinawa and defended it with more than 100,000 troops belonging to the Thirty-second Japanese Army under General USHIJIMA MITSURU. The bulk of these forces were deployed behind the Naha-Shuri-Yonabaru Line, a well-fortified entrenchment extending across the island's southern fifth. Here Ushijima intended to make an absolute stand, holding the invaders while KAMIKAZE forces destroyed the Fifth U.S. Fleet under RAYMOND SPRUANCE, which was assigned to cover the invasion.

The invasion was under the overall command of Admiral CHESTER NIMITZ, and the assault troops—the Tenth U.S. Army under SIMON BUCKNER JR.—were transported under the command of Admiral RICHMOND TURNER.

The initial assault came on March 26, 1945, when the 77th Infantry Division (Andrew Bruce) captured the Kerama and Keise Islands, off the southwestern coast of Okinawa. Six days after this, on April 1, the U.S. Marines, III Amphibious Corps (ROY GEIGER), landed on Okinawa's western shore. The 6th Marine Division (Lemuel Shepherd) was on the left of the assault and the 1st Marine Division (Pedro del Valle) on the right, while the 2nd Marine Division (Thomas Watson) made a decoy landing on the southern tip of Okinawa. Simultaneously, Tenth Army formed the right (south) wing of the initial assault, with XXIV Corps (JOHN HODGE), 7th Infantry Division (Archibald Arnold), and 96th Infantry Division (James Bradley) deployed left to right.

Okinawa, April–June 1945

Legend:

- April 19, 1945 U.S. Tenth Army
- U.S. Assaults ("ICEBERG")
- May 4–5, 1945 Japanese counterattacks
- Japanese defense line ("Shuri Line")
- ▲ Mountain

0   10 miles
0   10 km

Hedo Point

Hedo
April 13

April 20
Taken by U.S.
Sixth Marine Div.

U.S. Sixth Marine Div.

Aha
April 19

le Shima

Bise
Motobu
Pen.
Yagachi
Tako
April 8
Taira
April 11

April 16–21
Seventy-Seventh Infantry Div.

Yae Take   Nago

**Twenty-Seventh Infantry Div.
Floating Reserve
(Griner)**

East China Sea

Atsuta
April 8

Onna
Kushi

**"ICEBERG," April 1, 1945
U.S. Tenth Army
(Buckner)**

April 4
Ishikawa
Isthmus
Kin

Okinawa

PACIFIC OCEAN

Chimu Bay

U.S. Sixth Marine Div.

├ U.S. III Amph Corps → **U.S. First Marine Div.**
(Geiger)

U.S. Seventh Infantry Div.

├ U.S. XXIV Corps → **U.S. Ninety-Sixth Infantry Div.**
(Hodge)

Yontan

Hagushi

Kadena

Katchin
Pen.

Takabanare
April 10–11
Twenty-Seventh Div.

Heanna

Kuba
April 4

Tsugen Shima

**JP Thirty-Second
Army (Ushijima)**

Hagushi Bay
April 19

Nakagusuku Bay

June 21
End of Japanese
Resistance

March 26
Invasion by
Seventy-Seventh
Infantry Division

Keise Is.

U.S. Sixth Marine Div.

Oruku
Pen.

Shuri

Yonabaru

May 21
Japanese withdraw
from "Shuri Line"

Itoman   Minatoga

Kiyamu   Mabuni

April 1–2
Demonstrations by U.S. Second Marine Div.

Kerama Is.

© Infobase Publishing

By nightfall of April 1, 50,000, U.S. troops were deployed along a beachhead eight miles long and three to four miles deep. By April 3, the 1st Marine Division established a passage clear through to the east coast across the island's 2.5-mile width. To the left of the 1st Marines, the 6th Marine Division moved north in an arc that swept up both coasts. It reached the Motobu Peninsula on April 8. This rugged area was strongly defended by well-dug-in Japanese forces and held out for a dozen days. Nevertheless, by April 20 the northern fourth-fifths of Okinawa were

declared secure. That left the last-ditch troops to contend with.

While the northern component of the campaign proceeded apace, resistance was much fiercer on the southern end of the island. After moving east for the first two days, XXIV Corps turned 90 degrees to the south, the 7th Infantry Division on the left flank, the 96th on the right. On April 8, Japanese resistance sharply increased, and XXIV Corps was stalled at the periphery of the Naha-Shuri-Yonabaru Line. To break the deadlock, Hodge sent in the 27th Infantry Division (George

Griner) along the west coast to the right of the 96th. With this unit in place, XXIV Corps launched a major assault on April 19 across a five-mile front. Progress was heartbreakingly slow. In 12 days, fewer than two miles had been gained. The Marine III Amphibious Corps was called up on the right—the 6th Marine Division on the west coast, the 1st inland. On the left flank, the 7th Infantry held the east coast, while the 77th moved in on its right to relieve the beleaguered and exhausted 27th and 96th divisions.

Fighting continued and, on May 4–5, the Japanese launched a massive counterattack against the Tenth Army's left. This proved to be a catastrophic tactical error. Once out of their hardened entrenchments, the Japanese were exposed to the full force of the re-formed American forces. Some 6,227 Japanese troops were killed versus 714 battle deaths among members of the U.S. XXIV Corps.

The onset of monsoonal rains interfered with the rest of the U.S. offensive, but General Buckner resumed the assault, despite the rains, on May 11. The two sides pounded each other until, on May 23, the 6th Marine Division broke through into Naha and turned the Japanese west flank. On May 29, the 1st Marine Division, occupying the center position in the attack, captured Shuri Castle. With the Japanese lines crumbling, XXIV Corps, on the right, drove southward and outflanked the line on the east.

On June 4, the 6th Marine Division made a shore-to-shore amphibious assault against Oroku Peninsula, in the southwest. After 10 days of continuous fighting, the peninsula was cleared. At the same time, the 8th Regiment of the 2nd Marine Division reinforced the main body of attackers advancing to the southern tip of Okinawa. During this culminating phase of the campaign, General Buckner was killed in an artillery barrage on June 18. Geiger then assumed command of both the marine and the army forces (the only time in World War II that a marine officer commanded army forces), and, on June 21, the Tenth Army attained the southern coast of Okinawa. Elements of the army wheeled about to conduct mop-up operations before the island was declared secure on July 2, 1945.

Virtually the entire Thirty-second Japanese Army was dead: 100,000 killed and about 10,000 captured. U.S. casualties were 2,938 marines killed or missing and 13,708 wounded. Army dead or missing numbered 4,675, with 18,099 wounded.

While the land battle raged, combat was under way at sea and in the air. On April 7, *Yamato,* pride of the Japanese Imperial Navy and the world's biggest battleship, was sunk by air attack in the East China Sea. Navy aircraft also sank a Japanese light cruiser, four destroyers, and nine other Japanese ships, essentially finishing off the Imperial Japanese Navy. Kamikaze attacks were heavy. Some 1,900 sorties sank 36 U.S. ships and damaged 368, killing 4,907 sailors and wounding another 4,824. However, the cost to the Japanese was much higher. In the space of three months, about 7,800 Japanese aircraft were destroyed—versus 763 U.S. planes. Japanese air power, like its naval force, was virtually at an end.

Further reading: Astor, Gerald. *Operation Iceberg: The Invasion and Conquest of Okinawa in World War II.* New York: Dell, 1996; Feifer, George. *The Battle of Okinawa: The Blood and the Bomb.* Guilford, Conn.: Lyons Press, 2001; Leckie, Robert. *Okinawa: The Last Battle of World War II.* New York: Penguin, 1996; Yahara, Hiromichi. *The Battle for Okinawa.* New York: Wiley, 1997.

Operation Anvil/Dragoon

Operation Anvil was planned as a nearly simultaneous complement to Operation Hammer. The former was the code name for Allied landings on the French Riviera, and the latter for the invasion of Normandy. Dwight D. Eisenhower and other American military planners saw the two operations as necessarily complementary—the means of invading Europe while crushing the enemy between two major forces. Operation Hammer was subsequently renamed Operation Overlord, however, and Operation Anvil was put on hold—delayed until after the Normandy landings had been completed and the advance across France (Operation Cobra) under way—in part because of a shortage of Landing craft and in part because British prime minister WINSTON S. CHURCHILL believe that Operation Anvil represented a diversion of resources that would be better used invading the oil-producing Balkans. Churchill and top British commanders also feared that the operation would divert resources from the ongoing ITALIAN CAMPAIGN. Ultimately, the Balkan operation did not materialize, and Churchill was persuaded to allow the authorization of Operation Anvil, which, when it took place on August 15, 1944, between Toulon and Cannes, was renamed Operation Dragoon (because, it was said, Churchill claimed that he had been "dragooned" into agreeing to it).

As originally conceived, Operation Anvil/Dragoon was to land Free French and American troops in the south of France. Initially, the objective was Toulon, to which Marseille was soon added. Later, Saint Tropez became a third objective. These were to be captured simultaneously with the Normandy landings. The postponement of the operation threatened to become permanent, but the capture of Rome and the excellent progress made with Operation Cobra finally convinced the British to agree to the renamed Operation Dragoon.

On August 1, 1944, the U.S. 6th Army Group ("Southern Group of Armies" or "Dragoon Force") was activated in Corsica under Lieutenant General JACOB L. DEVERS. The army group included American and FREE FRENCH FORCES. The assault was carried out by three U.S. divisions of VI Corps, reinforced with a Free French armored division. The 3rd Infantry Division landed on the left at Cavalaire-sur-Mer (designated Alpha Beach), the 45th Infantry Division on the center at Saint-Tropez (Delta Beach), and the 36th Infantry Division on the right at Saint-Raphaël (Camel Beach). French commandos demolished German artillery emplacements at Cap Negre, west of the main invasion (this suboperation was code-named Operation Romeo). The commandos were supported by additional French commando units and by British and American airborne troops (in Operation Dove). In Operation Sitka, the U.S. 1st Special Service Force captured two small islands offshore to ensure the security of the beachhead. All of Opera-

tion Dragoon was covered by a deception and decoy operation (code-named Span). A large naval fleet provided heavy gunfire, and seven escort carriers launched close air support.

On the first day, more than 94,000 troops with 11,000 vehicles were landed. Because many German troops that had been in the area were sent north to resist the Normandy invasion, the landings met with light resistance, and the Allies penetrated inland 20 miles in just 24 hours. This remarkable movement inspired French resistance units to lead an uprising in occupied Paris—an event that made Paris an early priority target for liberation.

After the first day's landings, follow-on units landed, and the German Nineteenth Army rapidly retreated from the Riviera. Progress was much faster than the Allied planners had anticipated, so that the advance was limited not so much by German resistance as by Allied logistics: a shortage of gasoline. The Dragoon troops linked up with elements of Operation Overlord by mid-September, near Dijon.

Operation Dragoon liberated Marseille and the southern network of French railways. These became key to Allied logistics during the rest of the advance across France and into Germany.

Further reading: Breuer, William. *Operation Dragoon: The Allied Invasion of the South of France.* Novato, Calif.: Presidio Press, 1996; Gaujaz, Paul. *Dragoon.* Paris: Histoire and Collections, 2004.

Operation Barbarossa

Operation Barbarossa was the German code name for the invasion of the Soviet Union, which began on June 22, 1941. The operation was named after the 12th-century German king and Holy Roman emperor who, for modern Germans, was a symbol of German conquest and unity.

Operation Barbarossa stunningly abrogated the GERMAN-SOVIET NON-AGGRESSION PACT, but this should have come as no surprise to JOSEPH STALIN because ADOLF HITLER had, as early as his *MEIN KAMPF* (1924), advocated conquest of the Soviet

Union, both to wipe out communism and to acquire LEBENSRAUM.

The operational origin of Barbarossa may be traced to the summer of 1940, when, on Hitler's orders, the German military undertook a study of the prospects for invasion. The leading issue to decide was whether the principal thrust of the invasion should be against Moscow or divided between north and south flanks. Hitler favored a wheel north and south from the center, after breaking through the Soviet defensive line, whereas the army wanted to attack Moscow first and foremost. In the end, Directive No. 21, which described Operation Barbarossa (December 18, 1940), together with the Army High Command Deployment Directive (January 31, 1941), specified a "swift campaign" to crush the Soviet Union by means of offensive operations to destroy forces in the western part of the country. Army high command believed it would quickly defeat the Red Army west of the Dvina and Dnieper Rivers, then capture the industrialized Donets basin as well as Moscow.

Hitler gave the go order—in the form of the single code word "Dortmund"—on June 20, 1941, and the surprise attack was launched on a broad front between 3 and 3:30 A.M. on June 22. Barbarossa mounted a force of nearly 3.6 million German and other Axis soldiers, with some 3,600 tanks and more than 2,700 aircraft. It was the greatest invasion force ever assembled in European military history.

The border crossing was between the Baltic and the Black Seas under the overall command of Field Marshal WALTHER VON BRAUCHITSCH, who had three army groups. The North Army Group was commanded by Field Marshal WILHELM VON LEEB, the Center Army Group by Field Marshal Fedor von Bock, and the South Army Group by Field Marshal GERD VON RUNDSTEDT. The air component was divided into three tactical air forces under General Alfred Keller, Field Marshal ALBERT KESSELRING, and General Alexander Löhr.

Red Army formations in the west included 140 divisions and 40 brigades—some 2.9 million men, with as many as 15,000 tanks (many obsolescent)

and 8,000 aircraft (again, many of them obsolescent). The invaders quickly defeated the ground forces, and the German air force achieved air supremacy in a matter of days.

See also SOVIET UNION, INVASION OF THE.

Further reading: Bergstrom, Christer, and Andrey Mikhailov. *Black Cross/Red Star: Operation Barbarossa 1941*. Pacifica, Calif.: Pacifica Press, 2000; Clark, Alan. *Barbarossa*. New York: Harper Perennial, 1985; Fugate, Bryan I. *Operation Barbarossa: Strategy and Tactics on the Eastern Front, 1941*. Novato, Calif.: Presidio Press, 1984; Glantz, David M. *Before Stalingrad: Barbarossa—Hitler's Invasion of Russia 1941*. Stroud, U.K.: Tempus, 2003.

Operation Cobra

The NORMANDY LANDINGS (D-DAY) proceeded even better than expected, with all beachheads established at a lower cost than predicted. However, the subsequent progress inland was unexpectedly slowed by increasingly heavy German resistance and the nature of the terrain in the *bocage,* the landscape of ancient hedgerows that crisscrossed pastoral Normandy, forming obstacles both to visibility and to advance. The key to the Allied invasion of Europe was speed, and now, after so promising a beginning, First U.S. Army Group commander OMAR BRADLEY found himself confronting the possibility of a deadly war of attrition through France. Each initial attempt to break out of the *bocage* was checked by the Germans. After a month of frustration, Bradley then revived a plan originally proposed by Third U.S. Army general GEORGE S. PATTON JR. As Bradley reformulated it, Operation Cobra was intended as nothing more than a limited attack to punch through the German defenses west of Saint-Lô. If this succeeded, Bradley planned to make a deeper penetration using a large armored force as a follow-up on the initial advance. It would be Bradley's third attempt in a month to move out of the Cotentin Peninsula.

Operation Cobra had been planned to step off on July 24, 1944, but bad weather forced delay until July 25. Some of the bombers, however, did not get the postponement order and were launched on the

24th. The result was catastrophic, as bombs were rained down on American infantry. To compound the friendly-fire tragedy, more bombs were dropped on American infantry on the actual day of the attack because targets were poorly marked. Refusing to be disheartened, however, Bradley and Patton pressed on with the operation, even though the premature bomb drop had sacrificed the element of surprise.

Despite the bombing errors, the massive carpet bombing raids, followed by a two-thousand-bomber attack on German troops outside of Saint-Lô, was a stunning success. It weakened the German front so badly that the enemy was unable to counterattack the breakthrough. Bradley managed to mass his 15 divisions and 750 tanks against all the Germans could muster, nine divisions, with 150 tanks. Early on the morning of July 26, U.S. medium bombers attacked German lines, then the 1st Armored Division advanced, the advance protected on its flanks by tanks positioned to the east of the columns during the night of the 25th.

The Allies pushed through Saint-Lô, routing the Germans, whose retreat—uncharacteristically—was disordered. This hacked out a base from which the First and Third Armies drove out in opposite directions, toward Brest and toward Paris.

By the end of the day on July 27, the German lines had fallen back 15 miles. This was the victory

George S. Patton Jr. (center) confers with General Hugh J. Gaffey (seated) and Colonel M. C. Helfers of the 5th Division, August 26, 1944, during Operation Cobra, which Patton's Third U.S. Army spearheaded. *(Virginia Military Institute Archives)*

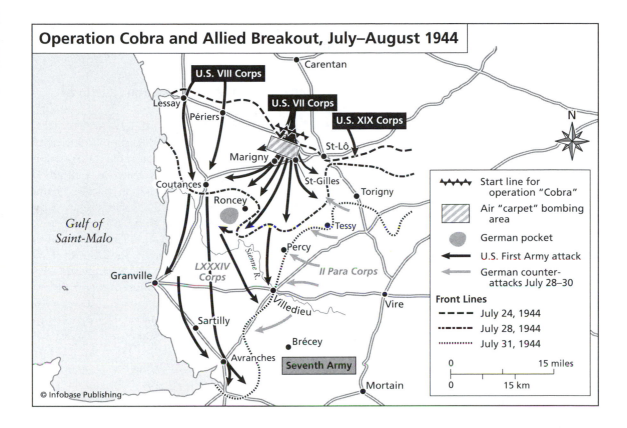

Operation Cobra and Allied Breakout, July–August 1944

Carenton

U.S. VIII Corps

Lessay

Périers

U.S. VII Corps

U.S. XIX Corps

St-Lô

Marigny

Coutances

St-Gilles

Torigny

Roncey

Tessy

Gulf of Saint-Malo

Percy

LXXXIV Corps

Sienne R.

II Para Corps

Granville

Villedieu

Vire

Sartilly

Brécey

Avranches

Seventh Army

Mortain

Legend:

⋀⋀⋀⋀	Start line for operation "Cobra"
▨	Air "carpet" bombing area
●	German pocket
◄━	U.S. First Army attack
◄━	German counter-attacks July 28–30

Front Lines

- - - - July 24, 1944

-·-·- July 28, 1944

······· July 31, 1944

0 — 15 miles

0 — 15 km

© Infobase Publishing

Bradley had hoped for with Operation Cobra. But Patton and his Third U.S. Army amplified the original intention of Cobra by exploiting the breach in German defenses with a violent, high-speed march. On July 30, the 6th Armored Division (of Patton's Third Army) crossed Bréhal and drove past Granville. Simultaneously, Avranches fell to Third Army infantry, which advanced on July 31 to secure a bridgehead over the Sélune River at Pontaubault, thereby putting the U.S. Army in Brittany.

After a month of costly heartbreak in the *bocage*, Bradley and Patton had, in the space of a week, broken through a distance of nearly 40 miles, capturing 18,000 prisoners in the process. There was no longer the danger of stalemate and attrition. Now the Allied armies—Patton's Third in particular—were poised to transform the invasion of Europe into a war of remarkably rapid movement.

Further reading: Pugsley, Christopher. *Operation Cobra: Battle Zone Normandy.* Stroud, U.K.: Sutton, 2005; Yenne, Bill. *Operation Cobra and the Great Offensive: Sixty Days That Changed the Course of World War II.* New York: Pocket, 2004; Zaloga, Steven. *Operation Cobra 1944: Breakout from Normandy.* London: Osprey, 2001.

Operation Dragoon   *See* Operation Anvil/Dragoon.

Operation Husky

Operation Husky was the code name for the Allied invasion of Sicily from North Africa, following the successful completion of the North African campaign. The operation grew out of a decision made at the Casablanca Conference in January 1943.

Overall command of the invasion was the responsibility of General Dwight D. Eisenhower, with operational command under British general HAROLD ALEXANDER, heading the newly created Fifteenth Army Group, which consisted of the Eighth British Army (BERNARD LAW MONTGOMERY) and the U.S. I Armored Corps (GEORGE S. PATTON JR.), which, after landing on Sicily, was redesignated the Seventh U.S. Army. The Fifteenth Army Group fielded a total of eight divisions, including airborne, commando, and Ranger units. Naval support was under the command of British admiral ANDREW CUNNINGHAM and air support under British air marshal ARTHUR TEDDER.

Planning Operation Husky was hampered by inter-Allied squabbling, despite Eisenhower's best efforts to compel the British and American planners to work together harmoniously. As originally conceived, Husky had Montgomery and Patton landing on opposite sides of the island with the object of making a large-scale pincer attack. Fearing this would fatally divide the invading forces, however, Montgomery insisted on changing the plan, so that Patton's Seventh U.S. Army was to do no more than protect the coastwise advance of Montgomery's Eighth British Army to Messina, stepping-off place to mainland Italy. As the campaign played out, however, Montgomery became bogged down, leaving Patton to make the spectacular advance that took both Palermo (the Sicilian capital) and Messina and that proclaimed to the British, the Germans, and the rest of the world that the U.S. Army was a force to be reckoned with.

The landings were launched before dawn on July 10, 1943, and would be eclipsed in size and scope only by OPERATION OVERLORD, the NORMANDY LANDINGS (D-DAY). The Sicilian landings involved 180,000 Allied troops and 2,590 ships. Although the landings succeeded, inadequate air support (coupled with unfavorable winds) seriously jeopardized that success. Fortunately, a program of Allied deception and decoy (Operation Mincemeat), which preceded the invasion, worked so well that German strength at the points of landing was weak.

See also SICILY CAMPAIGN.

Further reading: Pack, S. W. C. *Operation, Husky: The Allied invasion of Sicily.* Newton Abbot, U.K.: David &

Charles, 1977; Swanson, Jon M. *Operation Husky: A Case Study.* Carlisle, Pa.: U.S. Army War College, 1992.

Operation Market-Garden (Battle of Arnhem)

British commander BERNARD LAW MONTGOMERY, commander in charge of Allied ground forces following the NORMANDY LANDINGS (D-DAY), conceived Operation Market-Garden as a means of hastening the end of the war in Europe by outflanking the "West Wall" German defensive line and establishing a bridgehead across the lower Rhine at Arnhem, Netherlands. This would put the Allied armies at the doorstep of the Ruhr River Valley, thereby gaining early and expeditious entry into the German industrial heartland.

The supreme Allied commander, DWIGHT D. EISENHOWER, approved Market-Garden on September 10, adding to Montgomery's Twenty-first Army Group the First Allied Airborne Army (LEWIS BRERETON) and then diverting much-needed supplies to the operation. It was a bold gamble.

Under the tactical command of British lieutenant general Frederick Browning, Market-Garden was a twofold operation. The "Market" portion was an AIRBORNE ASSAULT to capture bridges across eight key waterways; "Garden" was the ground advance of the British XXX Corps (Brian Horrocks) across those bridgeheads.

Market-Garden depended wholly on speed, and this was both its great boldness and terrible vulnerability. XXX Corps was expected to advance nearly 60 miles in three days, from the Meuse-Escaut Canal to Arnhem. The Dutch government in exile, broadcasting from London, called for a railway strike to impede the Germans' ability to resist this movement. The strike was effective in interdicting the flow of German military supplies, but it triggered reprisals in the form of a stoppage of all canal traffic, which created acute food shortages that brought on a winter famine throughout the Netherlands.

Operation Market-Garden was launched on September 17, 1944, when the U.S. 101st Airborne Division landed between Eindhoven and Veghel, the U.S. 82nd Airborne Division landed around Grave and Groesbeek, and the British 1st Airborne Division dropped near Arnhem. The first drops, 16,500 paratroopers and 3,500 glider troops, were accomplished with great accuracy, and the two American divisions landed quite near their bridgehead objectives. The British airborne troops, however, did not land near enough Arnhem to take the vital bridges there—and on this failure turned the failure of the entire operation. Portions of two SS Panzer Divisions, the 9th and 10th, were being refitted near Arnhem. During the four hours it took the British troopers to reach the Arnhem bridges on foot, German resistance was built up in the area. The Germans quickly blew up the railway bridge and pinned down the British paratroops. Reinforcement from the Polish Parachute Brigade might have enabled a breakout, but a siege of bad weather delayed their arrival, then forced them to drop at Driel, where the Germans bottled them up.

In the meantime, gathering German resistance slowed the land assault as well. British XXX Corps was late linking up with 101st Airborne Division near Eindhoven. The delay was compounded by the necessity of erecting a temporary bridge (Bailey bridge) at Zon to replace the bridge the Germans had destroyed. This put Horrocks nearly a day and a half behind schedule. The delay menaced the 101st Airborne, which was exposed to flank attacks that cut the Eindhoven-Nijmegen road so frequently that the troopers dubbed it "Hell's Highway." At first, the 82nd Airborne Division fared better, taking the Groesbeek bridge, thereby blocking German counterattacks. On September 20, after elements of the British corps finally began arriving, a battalion of the 82nd embarked across the Waal River in assault boats and took both Nijmegen bridges. After this, however, like the 101st, the 82nd was forced to wait for the arrival of the main body of XXX Corps, which was unable to commence its march to Arnhem for 24 hours after the 82nd had secured the bridges. This final delay proved fatal to Operation Market-Garden.

By the time the main body of XXX Corps was on the move, the Germans had driven the British airborne troops from the Arnhem bridgehead.

German artillery then crossed the bridge and checked the advance of XXX Corps at Ressen. Despite last-minute maneuvering, it was no longer possible to organize sufficient strength to overcome the German defenses.

On September 25, a retreat was ordered. Nearly 2,300 British and Polish paratroops were able to withdraw from the Arnhem area, but more than 6,000 were captured—about half of them wounded. The U.S. 101st and 82nd airborne divisions, loath to relinquish ground gained, remained in contact with the enemy for another two months and suffered a combined total of 3,532 casualties, killed and wounded. This action allowed the Allies to hold on to a salient from which a later advance into Germany (Operation Veritable) was launched in February 1945. In all other respects, Operation Market-Garden was a costly and heartbreaking failure.

See also NETHERLANDS.

Further reading: Badsey, Stephen. *A Bridge Too Far: Operation Market Garden.* London: Osprey, 2000; Badsey, Stephen. *Arnhem 1944: Operation Market Garden.* New York: Praeger, 2004; Farrar-Hockley, Anthony H. *Airborne Carpet: Operation Market Garden.* New York: Ballantine Books, 1969.

Operation Overlord

Operation Overlord was the code name for the Allied invasion of German-occupied northwest Europe. The NORMANDY LANDINGS (D-DAY)—the first critical stage of Overlord—were code-named Operation Neptune, a suboperation of Overlord.

The Overlord concept was a product of the CASABLANCA CONFERENCE of January 1943, which authorized the creation of an invasion planning staff (called COSSAC, after the acronym for Chief of Staff to the Supreme Allied Commander) and also authorized a buildup of American troops in Great Britain for use in a cross-Channel invasion (this buildup phase was code-named Operation Bolero).

The first task of planning was to determine an appropriate landing area either in the Low Countries or France. Requirements were severely limiting: the landing place had to be within the range of Allied fighters, had to be defended by German positions that could feasibly be knocked out, and had to offer logistics that would enable a rapid and massive buildup of landing troops that would outpace the Germans' ability to move in defenders. Ultimately, COSSAC planners decided that the chief requirement was the proximity of a major port and the ability to supply troops on an adequate beachhead for a 90-day interim period, which was considered sufficient time to capture and repair the required port. Moreover, the troops would need to land in a place well served by a road network, lest they become trapped between the sea and the interior. After much study, COSSAC determined that the Baie de la Seine, between Le Havre and the Cherbourg peninsula, met the necessary criteria better than any other place: Cherbourg offered a major port, which (it was mistakenly believed) could be captured quickly, and supplies could be landed in the interim by means of unique artificial MULBERRY HARBORS while fuel was pumped all the way across the English Channel via a pipeline system dubbed "Pluto" (*Pipe Line Under the Ocean*).

The initial COSSAC plan was presented at the Allies' Quebec Conference in August 1943. WINSTON CHURCHILL, burdened by memories of the catastrophic Dunkirk and the harrowing DIEPPE RAID, called for a 25 percent increase in the initial assault force. Ultimately, in January 1944, the decision was made to expand the assault force even further, from three to eight divisions, including three AIRBORNE ASSAULT divisions. The problem with this expansion was not manpower but a chronic shortage of LANDING CRAFT.

One month after the decision to expand the force was taken, Supreme Headquarters Allied Expeditionary Force was created under DWIGHT D. EISENHOWER as supreme Allied commander, Europe. Under Eisenhower's direction, BERNARD LAW MONTGOMERY (as commander in charge of the invasion's ground component), TRAFFORD LEIGH-MALLORY (commander in charge of air forces), and Sir Bertam Ramsay (commander in

charge of the naval component) drew up the initial plans for Operation Neptune, the actual landing and assault phase of the invasion. At this point, the landing craft shortage became the critical factor, and proposed simultaneous landings on the French Riviera (Operation Anvil, later called Operation Dragoon) had to be delayed until after Operation Neptune—which was itself delayed.

Scheduling, timing, and coordinating the Neptune phase of Operation Overlord proved to be extraordinarily intricate. Despite the advantages of operating under cover of darkness, so many ships and aircraft were involved that it was decided to make the landing assault after dawn. Moreover, the actual landings had to be carried out no more than about one hour after low tide, so that German coastal obstacles (including mines) would be visible and accessible to engineers. To complicate matters further, airborne troops who were to be dropped just prior to the landings required a full moon. All of these prerequisites narrowed the window of the invasion to June 5–7. June 5 was chosen, but the landings had to be delayed for a day because of severe storms. At that, June 6 offered only marginally acceptable weather.

Operation Overlord and Operation Neptune were cloaked in the most stringent secrecy of the war. Extreme restrictions were placed on military movements as well as civilian travel, and all diplomatic travel was temporarily frozen. An elaborate program of deception was launched before the invasion, including the dissemination of disinformation through a network of double agents, the creation of phony radio traffic, and the erection of decoy camps and equipment, all intended to suggest to the Germans that an invasion was set to land not in Normandy but at the Pas de Calais, which, geographically, was the most logical invasion point.

Also preparatory to the invasion, between April 1 and June 5, 1944, more than 11,000 Allied aircraft flew in excess of 200,000 sorties, dropping 195,000 tons of bombs on rail and road networks, on airfields and other military facilities, on factories, and on coastal batteries and radar outposts, all to weaken the so-called Atlantic Wall, by which ADOLF HITLER defended what he called Fortress Europe

(*Festung Europa*). These missions were carried out at great cost (almost 2,000 Allied aircraft were lost), but they proved highly effective not only in damaging the military infrastructure in occupied France, but also in winning air supremacy against the Luftwaffe before the invasion. Additionally, many of the bombing missions were deliberately diverted to the area near Pas de Calais in a bold effort to enhance the impression that this is where the landings would be made.

Operation Overlord and Operation Neptune also relied heavily on preparatory work done by the French resistance, which operated in conjunction with the British SPECIAL OPERATIONS EXECUTIVE and the American OFFICE OF STRATEGIC SERVICES to supply on-the-ground intelligence, to undermine German defenses, and to commit acts of sabotage, especially against rail lines.

The course and outcome of Operation Neptune is discussed in NORMANDY LANDINGS (D-DAY) and those of Operation Overlord are discussed in that entry and other entries devoted to operations and leaders in the European theater.

See also DUNKIRK EVACUATION; RESISTANCE MOVEMENTS.

Further reading: Ambrose, Stephen E. *D-day June 6, 1944: The Climactic Battle of World War II.* New York: Simon and Schuster, 1994; Carell, Paul. *Invasion—They're Coming: The German Account of the Allied Landings and the 80 Days' Battle for France.* New York: Dutton, 1963; D'Este, Carlo. *Decision at Normandy.* London: Collins, 1983; Eisenhower, Dwight D. *Crusade in Europe.* Garden City, N.Y.: Doubleday, 1948; Keegan, John. *Six Armies in Normandy: From D-day to the Liberation of Paris.* New York: Penguin, 1983; Ryan, Cornelius. *The Longest Day: June 6, 1944.* New York: Popular Library, 1959; Schofield, Brian Betham. *Operation Neptune.* Annapolis: Naval Institute Press, 1974.

Operation Sealion

Called *Seeltiwe* in German, Operation Sealion was the code name for one of the most consequential operations of World War II that never happened: the planned German invasion of England.

Very early in the war, ADOLF HITLER was confident that Great Britain would come to favorable terms with Germany. When it did not, he decided that invasion would force a negotiated peace. On July 16, 1940, Hitler issued Directive No. 16, relating to preparations for landings against England. Hitler's number-one priority preparatory to invasion was the neutralization of the RAF. This concern reflected only one of many doubts Hitler had about the feasibility of an invasion—doubts that were echoed by his top army and navy commanders. Hitler seems never to have had the unambivalent will to drive the invasion. He told his commanders that if invasion preparations could not be completed by the start of September 1940, other operations would have to be undertaken, most notably an attack on the Soviet Union. Admiral ERICH RAEDER, commander in chief of the German navy, voiced grave doubts as to the feasibility of landing—citing difficulties in attaining air supremacy, carrying out adequate minesweeping operations, and deploying so large a transport fleet—and told Hitler that navy preparations could not be completed before September 15. Hitler decided that this would be the deadline for all preparations and that, furthermore, the final decision to invade would depend on victory in the BATTLE OF BRITAIN—the contest for supremacy in the skies above the British Isles. Thus, it was on the outcome of this campaign that the question of invasion—at least in 1940—would hang.

The defeat of France in the BATTLE OF FRANCE in June 1940 positioned the Luftwaffe perfectly for operations against England. Had Hitler wholeheartedly pushed for an invasion, preparations would have proceeded apace; however, he continued to vacillate. Nevertheless, air supremacy continued to be a goal for the German air force, and certain other invasion preparations were made, including a survey of all available sea and river craft in Germany and the occupied countries, training and exercises in embarkation and disembarkation, and the creation of occupation authorities. Yet German air marshal HERMANN GÖRING delayed *Aldertag* (Eagle Day)—the commencement of the air campaign against England—until August 13, 1940, a full seven weeks after the fall of France. This hiatus gave the British valuable time to prepare and strengthen air defenses, which were already extensive, and to marshal all RAF assets. Despite its geographical advantages, the Luftwaffe found itself going up against a very strongly and skillfully defended target. Thus, on September 14, when Hitler met with his commanders to tell them that the navy had completed its preparations for Operation Sealion, he still could not order the invasion to proceed because the Luftwaffe was far from having achieved air supremacy.

Yet even as Hitler temporized, he refused to cancel Sealion outright. He believed that the continued threat of invasion, combined with the unremitting air raids on English cities, would in and of themselves drive the British to seek a negotiated peace.

In the meantime, Admiral Raeder proposed October 8 as a new date for a landing. Hitler countered by ordering preparations for September 27, noting that September 17 would be the decision date. If conditions were judged unfavorable at that time, he would accept the October 8 alternative.

In the end, all of this proved to be empty posturing on Hitler's part. Göring refused to cooperate fully with the demands of preparing for Operation Sealion, and on September 19, the German high command ordered the assembled transport fleet to disperse, because it had become too vulnerable to British air attacks. On October 2, recognizing the toll taken by British air attacks, Hitler himself ordered that Sealion be shelved, perhaps to be rescheduled for the spring of 1941. In December 1940, Hitler redirected the German war effort to planning for the INVASION OF THE SOVIET UNION.

See also OPERATION BARBAROSSA.

Further reading: Assmann, Kurt. *German Plans for the Invasion of England in 1940: Operation "Sealion."* London: Naval Intelligence Division, 1947; Schenk, Peter. *Invasion of England, 1940: The Planning of Operation Sealion.* London: Conway Maritime Press, 1990.

Operation Torch

Operation Torch was the code name for the Anglo-American landings in French Morocco and Algeria that began the NORTH AFRICAN CAMPAIGN on November 8, 1942.

Operation Torch was strongly endorsed by British prime minister WINSTON CHURCHILL and his high command, but only grudgingly accepted by the U.S. military, whose high command wanted to concentrate on immediate operations against the European continent. Although JOSEPH STALIN continually pressured the Western Allies into opening a second European front, Churchill and other British planners believed that an invasion of the Continent would be premature and that first invading North Africa was far more feasible—especially inasmuch as it would provide the American troops, who had just joined the war, with an easier baptism of fire.

Despite the lukewarm attitude of the U.S. high command, Operation Torch was primarily a U.S. operation directed by DWIGHT D. EISENHOWER, who was named commander in charge of the Allied Expeditionary Force. Eisenhower and his British colleagues hoped that the VICHY GOVERNMENT administrators of French North Africa would side with the Allies or, at least, offer no substantial resistance. Germany and Italy were sufficiently formidable adversaries without having to face the French as well.

Operating directly under Eisenhower were U.S. major general MARK CLARK, deputy commander of Torch, and U.S. brigadier general JAMES DOOLITTLE, Western air commander. The other operational commanders were British, including Lieutenant General KENNETH ANDERSON (operational ground commander), Admiral ANDREW CUNNINGHAM (commander in chief of naval support), and the Eastern Air Commander, Air Marshal William Welsh. Operation Torch was thus the Allies' first great experiment in the concept of unified or single command: the command and coordination of an Anglo-American force under one supreme commander. Despite many problems created by this concept, unified command would become the model for every other phase of Allied operations in World War II, and it would prove far more successful than the approach taken by the Germans and Italians, who were often at bitter odds in the conduct of the war.

Operation Torch was the first step in carrying out the mission assigned to Eisenhower: to conquer all of Axis-occupied North Africa, beginning with Algeria and French Morocco. The Torch landings were preceded by the covert landing of General Clark near Algiers on October 22, 1942, to meet the French Major General Charles Mast, chief of staff of the French IXX Corps and known to have pro-Allied sympathies. Clark negotiated Mast's promise that, given four days' notice of the landings, he would ensure that the French army and air force would offer no more than token resistance—a demonstration sufficient to satisfy French military honor. As for the French navy, Mast could make no guarantees.

Operation Torch consisted of three landings: at Casablanca (the Western Force, under U.S. major general GEORGE S. PATTON JR.), at Oran (the Central Force, under U.S. major general Lloyd Fredendall), and at Algiers (the Eastern Force, under U.S. major general Charles Ryder). Air support would be provided for the two western landings by the Western Air Command, while the Eastern Air Command would cover the vicinity of Algiers.

The total Allied troop strength of the landings, 65,000, represented only a bit more than half the strength of the French forces in North Africa. About 650 warships supported the landings, which took place early on November 8, 1942. Algiers fell immediately and Oran just two days later. French resistance at Casablanca was stiffer, but on November 10, the principal French authority in North Africa, Admiral JEAN-FRANÇOIS DARLAN, agreed to order a general cease-fire, and Casablanca accordingly capitulated.

With the success of the landings and the attainment of the major objectives in French North Africa, Operation Torch gave way to the rest of the North African Campaign.

Further reading: Haupt, Werner. *North African Campaign, 1940–1943.* London: Macdonald, 1969; Jackson, W. G. F. *The North African Campaign, 1940–43.* London: Batsford, 1975; Kelly, Orr. *Meeting the Fox: The Allied Invasion of Africa, from Operation Torch to Kasserine Pass to Victory in Tunisia.* New York: Wiley, 2002.

Oppenheimer, J. Robert (1904–1967)
director of the Los Alamos laboratory (1943–1945), which developed atomic weapons

Born in New York to the family of a German immigrant who built a fortune as a textile importer, Oppenheimer early on showed evidence of genius. During a brilliant undergraduate career at Harvard University, he studied Greek and Latin as well as Asian philosophy and published poetry, in addition to pursuing the study of physics and chemistry. In 1925, after graduation, he was awarded a research grant to study in England at the famed Cavendish Laboratory of Cambridge University. There he worked with the legendary physicist Lord Ernest Rutherford. In England, Oppenheimer became increasingly interested in advanced atomic research.

At the invitation of another great physicist, Max Born, Oppenheimer studied in Germany at Göttingen University with the likes of Niels Bohr

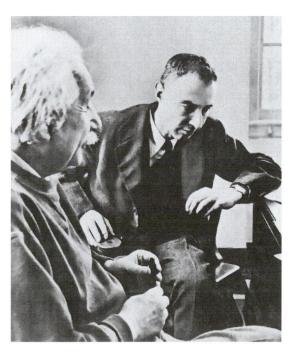

J. Robert Oppenheimer with Albert Einstein *(U.S. Department of Energy)*

and Paul Dirac. It was from Göttingen, in 1927, that Oppenheimer earned a doctorate, after which he returned to the United States, where he joined the faculties of the University of California at Berkeley and the California Institute of Technology. There he conducted advanced theoretical work based on the implications of quantum mechanics and relativity theory. Oppenheimer was especially interested in the energy processes of subatomic particles, including electrons, positrons, and cosmic rays.

Like many American intellectuals in the 1930s, Oppenheimer was deeply disturbed by the ascension in Germany of ADOLF HITLER and became active in various antifascist and anti-Nazi organizations. The inheritance into which Oppenheimer came following the death of his father in 1937 allowed him to contribute generously to these organizations, and although Oppenheimer drifted toward the Communist Party, he did not join it, nor was he ever seduced into overlooking the enormity of the oppression perpetrated by JOSEPH STALIN. Ultimately, in protest against Stalinism, he severed all ties with the Communists.

Oppenheimer was one of a group of scientists—including, most prominently LEO SZILARD and ALBERT EINSTEIN—who were alarmed by the probability that German physicists were at work developing nuclear weapons for Hitler. After the INVASION OF POLAND began World War II in September 1939, Oppenheimer commenced research to find a process for the separation of fissionable uranium 235 from natural uranium and to determine just how much fissionable U-235 was required to make an atomic bomb. In August 1942, the U.S. Army inaugurated the MANHATTAN PROJECT, the massive government effort to create nuclear weapons, and Oppenheimer, recruited for the project, was charged with creating and administering a laboratory to carry out the major research. As a boy, he had spent time in a boarding school near Santa Fe, New Mexico, and he now chose the remote Los Alamos plateau near that school as the location for the laboratory.

Oppenheimer drew to Los Alamos a team of scientists that was unprecedented in scope and depth. Working in an often tense and difficult collaboration with Major General LESLIE R. GROVES, the military director of the Manhattan Project, Oppenheimer oversaw the research that produced the first nuclear device, which was successfully tested at the so-called Trinity Site, near Alamogordo, New Mexico, on July 16, 1945. The following month, two bombs were used against Japan, prompting that nation to surrender, thereby ending World War II.

In October 1945, Oppenheimer resigned as director of Los Alamos and, in 1947, was appointed to head the Institute for Advanced Study at Princeton University. Concurrently, from 1947 to 1952, he also served as chairman of the General Advisory Committee of the Atomic Energy Commission, which under his leadership announced its opposition in October 1949 to the development of the hydrogen bomb. Oppenheimer had profound reservations about nuclear weapons and regarded thermonuclear—or hydrogen—weapons, which were far more powerful, as immoral and certainly capable of ending civilization.

At the height of the cold war, Oppenheimer's opposition to the hydrogen bomb created enormous controversy, and on December 21, 1953, he learned of a military security report that accused him of having had Communist ties in the past, of having interfered with the investigation of Soviet espionage agents, and of opposing the building of the hydrogen bomb not on moral grounds but in a deliberate effort to undermine national security. Although a subsequent hearing cleared him of treason, it ruled that his access to military secrets should be terminated, and he was removed as adviser to the Atomic Energy Commission. Oppenheimer became a cause célèbre and an icon of the fate of the scientist in the modern age: the man whose work creates a weapon with profound moral consequences and who is subsequently condemned when he makes his moral convictions public. Oppenheimer was widely regarded as a haunted genius, a modern Prometheus punished for the great force he brought into the world, the wizard who liberated the atomic genie then struggled futilely and tragically to put that genie back into the bottle.

Oppenheimer spent his later years immersed less in theoretical physics than in the moral and philosophical questions relating to the place of science in society. He received the Enrico Fermi Award of the Atomic Energy Commission in 1963, retired from Princeton in 1966, and succumbed in 1967 to cancer of the throat.

Further reading: Bernstein, Jeremy. *Oppenheimer: Portrait of an Enigma.* Chicago: Ivan R. Dee, 2004; Bird, Kai, and Martin J. Sherwin. *American Prometheus: The Triumph and Tragedy of J. Robert Oppenheimer.* New York: Knopf, 2005.

ORANGE (Japanese code)

In 1930, the Japanese Foreign Office began using a rotor-based cipher machine similar to Germany's famous Enigma, which American cryptanalysts code-named RED. A U.S. Army Signals Intelligence Service cryptanalyst team broke the RED ciphers before World War II; however, in 1939, the Japanese began using a new cipher machine, code-named by U.S. analysts PURPLE. The advanced device employed telephone stepping switches in place of mechanical rotors. The Japanese believed that the PURPLE machine was essentially immune from cryptanalysis. But as Polish and British cryptanalysts cracked the Enigma ciphers, U.S. cryptanalysis succeeded in cracking the PURPLE ciphers and the even more important ORANGE ciphers. The latter were essential to the Allied conduct of the Pacific war because the ORANGE ciphers were extensively used by the Imperial Japanese Navy as well as the Japanese merchant marine.

U.S. analysts recognized five major ORANGE naval cryptographic systems, including an Administrative Code system, which employed a cipher that changed every 10 days; the Merchant Ship Code system; the Materiel Code system, which had cipher changes at irregular intervals of from 10 to 30 days and was vital in signaling the movement of war matériel; the Operations Code system, which was used to transmit fleet operational commands; and the Intelligence Code system, which was considered of relatively minor importance.

ORANGE decrypts provided vital tactical and strategic information to the Allies, especially the U.S. Navy, throughout World War II. The Japanese never discovered that their "unbreakable" ciphered messages were being read regularly.

See also ENIGMA CIPHER AND MACHINE and ULTRA.

Further reading: Aldrich, Richard J. *Intelligence and the War against Japan: Britain, America and the Politics of Secret Service.* New York: Cambridge University Press, 2000; Winton, John. *Ultra in the Pacific: How Breaking Japanese Codes and Ciphers Affected Naval Operations against Japan 1941–45.* London: Leo Cooper, 1993.

Ozawa Jisaburo (1886–1963) *last commander in charge of the Combined Fleet of the Japanese Imperial Navy*

Ozawa had commanded the Malaya Force (Southern Expeditionary Fleet) during the Malayan Campaign and was a brilliant advocate and practitioner of naval air power. On December 10, 1941, aircraft of his command sank Britain's Force Z (the *Prince of Wales* and *Repulse*) off the coast of Malaya. Ozawa was also in command during the invasion of the Netherlands East Indies and was instrumental in action on the Indian Ocean.

During the BATTLE OF THE PHILIPPINE SEA in June 1944, Ozawa played a key role and also fought in the BATTLE OF LEYTE GULF in October 1944. It was the carriers under his command that drew Admiral WILLIAM "BULL" HALSEY's Third Fleet away from the U.S. invasion forces, thereby imperiling the invasion of the Philippines.

Ozawa was one Japan's ablest sea commanders and one of the great admirals of World War II.

See also MALAYA, FALL OF; NETHERLANDS EAST INDIES, ACTION IN.

Further reading: Cutler, Thomas J. *The Battle of Leyte Gulf: 23–26 October 1944.* Annapolis, Md.: Naval Institute Press, 2001; Evans, David C. *The Japanese Navy in World War II: In the Words of Former Japanese Naval Officers.* Annapolis, Md.: Naval Institute Press, 1993; Willmott, H. P. *The Battle of Leyte Gulf: The Last Fleet Action.* Bloomington: Indiana University Press, 2005.

P

"Pact of Steel"

The "Pact of Steel" was the familiar name ADOLF HITLER and BENITO MUSSOLINI applied to the treaty concluded by their representatives, German foreign minister JOACHIM VON RIBBENTROP and his Italian counterpart, Count GALEAZZO CIANO, at Berlin on May 22, 1939, formalizing the Rome-Berlin Axis, the ideologically based military alliance between Germany and Italy.

The Pact of Steel acknowledged Italy's hegemony over Ethiopia, which it had annexed in 1935, and cited the "close relationship of friendship and homogeneity ... between National Socialist Germany and Fascist Italy" as the basis for the alliance outlined in "this solemn pact." The pact spoke of the "inner affinity between ... [the] ideologies" of the two nations and of their joint resolution to "act side by side and with united forces to secure their living space and to maintain peace." In contrast to most military alliances, which typically specify that one nation will come to the other's aid if it is attacked, the Pact of Steel stipulated that the military alliance would become active if a signatory "became involved in warlike complications with another Power or Powers." Thus, the alliance covered not merely defensive action, but military aggression as well. In this, the Pact of Steel proclaimed to the world that Germany and Italy were poised to conquer—and intended to do so.

See also LEBENSRAUM.

Further reading: Phillips, Charles, and Alan Axelrod, *Encyclopedia of Historical Treaties and Alliances,* 2d ed. New York: Facts on File, 2005; Toscano, Mario. *The Origins of the Pact of Steel.* Baltimore: Johns Hopkins University Press, 1968.

Palestine

At the outbreak of World War II, Palestine was a British mandate on which about 1 million Arabs and nearly a half million Jews—the former indigenous, the latter predominantly immigrants—lived in chronic conflict. The British were obligated by the Balfour Declaration of 1917 to acknowledge Palestine as the rightful homeland of the stateless Jews. Shortly before the beginning of World War II, in July 1937, the British Peel Commission divided Palestine among the Arabs, the British, and the Jews, thereby provoking the Arab Revolt led by Hadj Amin el-Husseini, the mufti of Jerusalem. The revolt was crushed before the outbreak of World War II, Husseini fled, and the British administrators interned the other Arab leaders. This essentially forced the Palestinian Arabs to suspend political agitation for years, including the war years. Nevertheless, seeking to appease the Arabs as the war approached—and wanting above all to ensure access to oil in the region—Britain rescinded the partition of Palestine in May 1939, announcing its intention to create within a decade a single independent nation-state, which would include Arabs and Jews. Preparatory to the creation of the new state, Britain barred the sale of Palestinian land to Jews and capped Jewish immigration at 75,000 over the next five years. At the end of this period, no more Jewish immigration would be permitted without Arab agreement.

The new British policy did appease Arabs in Palestine even as it put the Jews in a corner. If they objected and opposed the British, they would be giving aid to the Nazis. Having little choice, therefore, the Jewish Agency—the political organization that worked toward the establishment of a Jewish homeland in Palestine—chose to cooperate with the new British policy and even mobilized agricultural and industrial resources to help Britain in its war effort. Jewish-owned war-production factories in Palestine became very important, and the rapid growth of this industry extended Jewish settlement, including irrigated and cultivated land, throughout the region. Although the British had sought to limit Jewish growth and influence in Palestine for the coming decade, its encouragement of Jewish war industries actually promoted the permanent establishment of Jews throughout the area.

At the outbreak of the war, some 136,000 Jewish men and women volunteered to join the British armed forces, and some even agreed to serve with Arabs in mixed companies. Jews fought in British units during the WESTERN DESERT CAMPAIGN and served with the Eighth British Army, primarily against the Italians. During March through September 1944, 32 Jewish parachutists from Palestine were dropped behind enemy lines in Europe to assist Jews in escaping the reach of the FINAL SOLUTION.

Despite the large number of Jewish volunteers, it is estimated that only 30,000 Palestinian Jews actually served in the British armed forces, along with about 9,000 Palestinian Arabs. Palestine itself had little tactical or strategic significance in the war.

Further reading: Shepherd, Naomi. *Ploughing Sand: British Rule in Palestine, 1917–1948.* New Brunswick, N.J.: Rutgers University Press, 2000.

Papagos, Alexandros (1883–1955) *Greek minister of war and chief of staff*

Born in Athens, Alexandros Papagos was commissioned an officer in the Greek army in 1906 and fought in the Balkan Wars during 1912–13, then against Turkey during 1919–22. Promoted to major general in 1927, he rose to become minister of war in 1935 and chief of staff in 1936.

In response to the Italian INVASION OF GREECE in October 1940, Papagos led an uninspired, highly conventional defense. Despite this pedestrian approach, his forces drove the Italians back into Albania, from which they had launched the invasion. Against the Germans, however, who invaded in April 1941, Papagos did not stand a chance. Greece was quickly overrun and occupied. Papagos himself was interned in Germany as a hostage.

Papagos was liberated by the Allies in 1945 and assumed leadership of Greek government forces operating against communist guerrillas and insurgents. In 1949, he was promoted to field marshal. He retired from the army in May 1951 to found a new political party, the Greek Rally, which rapidly became a powerful force in Greek politics. Papagos was elected Greek premier in November 1952 and died in office three years later.

Further reading: Papagos, Alexandros. *The Battle of Greece, 1940–1941.* Athens: J.M. Scazikis "Alpha" Editions, 1949.

Papen, Franz von (1879–1969) *engineer of the* Anschluss—*the German annexation of Austria*

Papen was born in Wirl, Germany, to a prosperous, land-rich Catholic family. He set his sights on a career in the military and, at the outbreak of World War I, was serving as German military attaché in Washington, D.C. His involvement in espionage and sabotage prompted the U.S. government to demand his recall in 1915, whereupon Papen served as chief of staff of the German-administered Fourth Turkish Army in Palestine.

At the end of World War I, Papen returned to Germany, where he entered politics as a monarchist in opposition to the Weimar Republic. Elected to the Reichstag (parliament) as a candidate of the extreme rightist Catholic Center Party, Papen served as a deputy for 11 years, from 1921 to 1932, when, acting on the advice of General Kurt von Schleicher, his adviser, President Paul von Hindenburg elevated Papen to the chancellorship. Papen put in place a rightist government and sought to placate the Nazis (who formed the second-largest party in the Reichstag) by lifting a ban earlier imposed on the Storm Troopers, or STURMABTEILUNG (SA), and by removing the Social Democratic government of Prussia. Papen also engineered what amounted to the cancellation of Germany's catastrophic war reparations obligations imposed by the TREATY OF VERSAILLES.

Despite Papen's efforts to appease him, ADOLF HITLER opposed him. Moreover, Papen's extreme reactionary bias soon alienated Schleicher as well, who believed him incapable of creating a genuinely broad national front. Thanks to Schleicher, several cabinet ministers rejected Papen's policies, forcing him to step down on December 4, 1932. He was succeeded as chancellor by Schleicher.

Papen's ouster drove him into the arms of Hitler, and, on January 4, 1933, Papen persuaded German president Paul von Hindenburg to remove Schleicher and replace him with Hitler as chancellor. Papen assumed the post of vice chancellor. Because he managed to place his political allies—all nationalists but not Nazis—in most of the ministerial positions, Papen assumed that he would be able to control Hitler as well as keep a tight rein on the Nazi Party. It did not take long for Papen to realize his error, but by that time, he had apparently decided to remain loyal to Hitler.

Papen was nearly purged (murdered) during the "Night of the Long Knives," Hitler's action against the SA on June 30, 1934. Three days after this event, Papen prudently stepped down as vice chancellor and accepted an ambassadorship to Austria. He served in this post from 1934 to 1938, and was instrumental in engineering the ANSCHLUSS, or annexation of Austria to the German Reich.

In 1939, Papen was appointed ambassador to Turkey. He served in that post until 1944, working vigorously to prevent the Turks from entering into an alliance with the Allies.

At the end of the war in Europe, the Allies arrested Papen, who was tried by the NUREMBERG WAR CRIMES TRIBUNAL as a war criminal. He was one of a handful of defendants acquitted by the tribunal (on a count of engaging in conspiracy to prepare aggressive war), but a German court subsequently tried him for his major role in the Nazi Party. Sentenced by the German court to eight years in prison, he was released on appeal in 1949, but was compelled to pay a fine. He retired from public life and published his memoirs in 1952.

Further reading: Adams, Henry M., and Robin K. Adams. *Rebel Patriot: A Biography of Franz von Papen.* Santa Barbara, Calif.: McNally & Loftin, 1987; Dutch, Oswald. *Errant Diplomat: The Life of Franz Von Papen.* New York: AMS Press, 1982; Koeves, Tibor. *Satan in Top Hat: The Biography of Franz von Papen.* New York: Alliance Book Corporation, 1941.

Paris, occupation and liberation of

In the culmination of the BATTLE OF FRANCE, Paris fell on June 14, 1940. In contrast to the heroic defense of the capital during the early weeks of World War I, in which the Germans and French fought it out on the nearby Marne, Paris in World War II was undefended and was proclaimed an open city, thereby avoiding artillery and aerial bombardment.

Although Paris became a center for French resistance activity, it was not the hotbed of subversion and sabotage often portrayed in postwar romantic fiction. Despite the heroism of a few notable individuals—especially JEAN MOULIN and his circle—recent scholarship suggests that relatively few Parisians were members of the Resistance. For the great majority of the city's inhabitants, life went on under German occupation much as it had before the war—albeit with many wartime shortages. Most Parisians cooperated with the Germans politically and also did profitable business with the occupiers. In contrast to the people of Danish, Dutch, and even Italian cities, they rarely took a stand against the arrest of Jewish citizens, and the French police often collaborated openly in the round-ups and deportations that were part of the FINAL SOLUTION and the HOLOCAUST.

In Paris, the Germans refrained from the pillage, rape, and murder often associated with conquest and rampant in German actions in the east. The Paris press was even complimentary in many of its remarks concerning the soldiers of the occupation, whom papers routinely described as decent and even polite. Although newsreels carried footage of a German column marching under the Arc de Triomphe, ADOLF HITLER issued personal orders forbidding large-scale victory parades for fear that such displays would alienate the Parisians and make them less cooperative. After the initial shock of the German entry into the capital had passed, schools, cafés, theaters, newspapers, trains, and most other public services were operating on a virtually normal basis. The Paris police force, an armed body that outnumbered the German occupation troops, remained cooperatively on duty throughout the entire occupation and generally did the bidding of the German occupation authorities. Even among the intellectual elite and other high-profile cultural figures, life under German occupation went on. The likes of Jean-Paul Sartre, Coco Chanel, Louis-Ferdinand Céline, Christian Dior, Yves Montand, Maurice Chevalier, Pablo Picasso, and Albert Camus lived and worked in Paris quite openly and quite productively during the occupation. To be sure, there were arrests—but relatively few. The occupation of Paris was by no means characterized by the barbarism of the Warsaw occupation.

In one important sense, the relatively easy relations between the German occupiers and the citizens of Paris did have a positive effect on the Allied war effort. Instead of rapidly consolidating their remarkably swift victory in the fall of France, the German occupiers reveled in the comforts and distractions of Paris, and this led to nearly two months of complacency in which the British prepared superb air defenses to resist German invasion. The

seductions of Paris were far more effective in undermining the German war effort than any organized resistance movement.

If most Parisians did not actively resist the occupation, many actively protested Resistance and other partisan activity, fearing reprisals. Many of the Communist partisans, who became active after the INVASION OF THE SOVIET UNION in June 1941, were not native Frenchmen, and the majority of Parisians did not sympathize with them or with their motives—which included the deliberate provocation of German reprisals in the hope and expectation that these would alienate and rally the French populace against the occupiers.

Only after the war turned decidedly against the Germans did large numbers of Parisians begin to be stirred by the London-based broadcasts of CHARLES DE GAULLE, urging active resistance. In the lead-up to the NORMANDY LANDINGS (D-DAY), the work of the U.S. OFFICE OF STRATEGIC SERVICES, British SPECIAL OPERATIONS EXECUTIVE, and French Resistance teams began to organize indigenous resistance groups for truly effective military service. After D-day, as the Allies drew near Paris, resistance to the occupiers intensified. French rail workers went on strike on August 10, 1944, and, on August 15, so did the police. French postal workers walked off their jobs on August 16. The object of these strikes was to make the movement and communication of German troops difficult and thereby encourage the Allies to liberate the city.

At this point in the war, Paris was occupied by just 20,000 troops, mostly second-line garrison soldiers (albeit stiffened somewhat by the inclusion of a few armored WAFFEN SS units) under the command of General Dietrich von Choltitz, who had earlier overseen the outright destruction of Rotterdam (May 1940) and Sevastopol (1942). As the Allies approached, the still deeply divided French Resistance differed sharply on the question of what to do next. The Communists wanted an all-out uprising, whereas those aligned with de Gaulle called for caution. The latter group was in contact with the Allies, who made it known that they did not intend to enter Paris before the second week in September. DWIGHT D. EISENHOWER, the supreme Allied commander, was far more intent on destroying the German armies in the field than on diverting forces to liberate Paris. Despite this, the Communists, who had majorities on the local Paris Resistance committees, decided to take immediate action.

Henri Rol-Tanguy, Communist leader of the Parisian liberation committee, announced that the time for action had come. No sooner did he make this proclamation, however, than he was shocked to discover, as he bicycled past *police headquarters* in Paris on the morning of August 19, that the Tricolor had been raised above the building and the "Marseillaise" was being sung inside. Learning that the Communists were about to act, de Gaulle had suddenly ordered preemptive action by the Resistance members loyal to him. Thus it was a threat from the Communists, not the Nazis, that initiated the liberation of Paris.

For the first time during the occupation, large-scale if sporadic fighting broke out in the streets of Paris. A truce was arranged on the evening of the 19th, so that both sides could collect their wounded, but by the evening of the 20th, the truce had broken down. Although the police continued officially to collaborate with the Germans, most Parisian officers now defected to the Resistance. Barricades went up on many streets throughout the city, but the uprising was most intense on the east side of Paris, which was working class and dominated by the Communists. Resistance members continually sniped at German soldiers, who had long been accustomed to easy duty in the capital.

Choltitz received Hitler's orders to defend Paris at all costs and ultimately to demolish the city—using explosive charges against key landmarks and the Seine bridges—rather than relinquish it. Believing the war to be lost, the German general was reluctant to carry out the order of destruction, and his reluctance was encouraged by Raoul Nordling, the Swedish consul-general, who appealed to Choltitz's sense of duty as a European and a Christian to preserve a city that was a monument both to European civilization and to Christian culture. The desire to preserve Paris, especially at this late stage in the war, was shared by the more moderate members of the Resistance as well. They well knew of the devastation that was even then being visited upon Warsaw by its occupiers. In the meantime, however, Eisenhower still declined to issue the liberation order. At last, the British forced his hand. On August 23, 1944, the BBC broadcasted that Paris had already been liberated. Understanding that the failure to liberate the capital *in fact* would now create a potentially disastrous collapse in Allied morale—and would give aid and comfort to the enemy—Eisenhower and Third U.S. Army commander George S. Patton Jr. released the 2nd French Armored Division from Third Army control. The division's commander, Jacques-Philippe Leclerc, sent a small number of tanks into Paris, then followed up with rest of the division. Under Captain Raymond Dronne, the first tanks—a token liberation force—reached the Place de l'Hôtel de Ville after sunset on August 24. He met with no significant resistance, and the rest of the division arrived on the next morning, along with elements of the U.S. forces. With Paris jubilant, Choltitz signed a surrender document. On the French side, significantly, Rol-Tanguy signed first, Leclerc second.

Outwardly, there was much joy and celebration on the streets of Paris, and all supporters of the Allied cause were greatly heartened by the liberation. As the Germans began to withdraw from France, however, retribution against collaborators and suspected collaborators brought a new reign of terror throughout the country including Paris, in the immediate aftermath of the liberation. Between June 1944 and February 1945, it is believed that Frenchmen executed some 105,000 of their own countrymen, either in summary fashion or after one-sided tribunal proceedings. This number almost certainly exceeded the number of French citizens who died at the hands of the German occupiers as hostages, deportees, and slave laborers.

See also resistance movements and Operation Sealion.

Further reading: Aron, Robert. *De Gaulle before Paris: The Liberation of France, June–August, 1944.* New York: Putnam, 1962; Beevor, Antony, and Artemis Cooper.

Paris after the Liberation, 1944–1949. New York: Penguin Books, 2004; Perrault, Gilles. *Paris Under the Occupation.* New York: Vendome Press, 1990; Pryce-Jones, David. *Paris in the Third Reich: A History of the German Occupation, 1940–1944.* New York: Holt, Rinehart & Winston, 1981.

Patch, Alexander McCarrell, Jr. (1889–1945) *American general in both the Pacific and in Europe*

Patch, the son of an army captain, was born at Fort Huachuca, Arizona Territory, and raised in Pennsylvania, where he attended a year of Lehigh University before entering West Point in 1909. After graduating in 1913, Second Lieutenant Patch served on the Mexican border during 1916–17. Promoted to captain on May 15, 1917, he shipped out to France during World War I and commanded the Army Machine Gun School there from April to October 1918. While in France, Patch also fought at Aisne-Marne (July 18–August 5), at the Saint-Mihiel salient (September 12–16), and in the Meuse-Argonne offensive (September 26–November 11). After the armistice, he served in Germany with the army of occupation through 1919. During his war service, he was promoted to temporary lieutenant colonel, but like many other officers, he reverted to his peacetime rank—captain—on his return to the United States.

Promoted to major on July 1, 1920, Patch served in training positions through 1924. He graduated with distinction from the Command and General Staff School in 1925 and from the Army War College in 1932. During 1925–28 and 1932–36, he taught as professor of military science and tactics at Staunton Military Academy, Virginia.

Promoted to lieutenant colonel on August 1, 1935, Patch was appointed to the Infantry Board at Fort Benning, Georgia, the following year. In this post, he tested the new three-regiment "triangular" division the army had adopted in an effort to make movement and command more efficient. Thanks in part to Patch's work, the streamlined triangular division would become the foundation of army organization during World War II.

In August 1939, Patch was promoted to colonel and assigned command of the 47th Infantry. On August 4, 1941, he was promoted to brigadier general and given command of the Infantry Replacement Center at Camp Croft, South Carolina. After the United States declared war on Japan on December 8, 1941, Patch, in January 1942, was sent to New Caledonia in the Pacific with the remnants of units left over after the "triangularization" of the 26th and 33rd Divisions. After his promotion to major general on March 10, his units became the core of the Americal Division—"American troops on New Caledonia"—activated on May 27, 1942. Patch led the Americal Division in the GUADALCANAL CAMPAIGN, relieving the 1st Marine Division there on December 9. He commanded mop-up operations on Guadalcanal from December 1942 to February 7, 1943, then, from January to April 1943, served as commander of XIV Corps. In April 1943, Patch was called back to the United States to assume command of the IV Corps area. He was responsible for troop training from April 1943 to March 1944, when he was sent to Sicily in command of the Seventh U.S. Army there. He then led the Seventh Army in OPERATION ANVIL-DRAGOON, the invasion of southern France (the French Riviera), beginning on August 15. Three days into the operation, Patch was promoted to lieutenant general.

Patch led the Riviera invasion with efficiency and rapidity, so that on September 11, 1944, he was able to link up with the Third U.S. Army under GEORGE S. PATTON JR. at Dijon. His Seventh Army next became part of the Sixth Army Group and advanced into Alsace. Patch took Strasbourg in November, then participated in the defense against a German counteroffensive in January 1945 and the reduction of the COLMAR POCKET in February. From Colmar, Patch led the Seventh U.S. Army through southern Germany and into Austria, where he linked up with elements of MARK W. CLARK's Fifth U.S. Army at the Brenner Pass on May 4.

After the German surrender, Patch returned to the United States in June to command the Fourth Army at Fort Sam Houston, Texas, again taking responsibility for troop training. In October, he was assigned to a special group formed to study postwar defense reorganization, but succumbed to pneumonia shortly after completing this assignment.

Further reading: Wyant, William K. *Sandy Patch: A Biography of Lt. Gen. Alexander M. Patch.* New York: Praeger Publishers, 1991.

Patton, George Smith, Jr. (1885–1945) *U.S. field commander in Europe*

Although he never attained top strategic command, Patton may well be the most famous American general of World War II, and, because of his abrasive leadership style, flamboyance, and almost atavistic ferocity, perhaps the most controversial as well. Beyond question is what he achieved with his Third U.S. Army, breaking out of the *bocage* at Normandy and sweeping through France and Germany and into Czechoslovakia. He spearheaded the advance of the Allied western front.

Born in San Gabriel, California, George S. Patton Jr. was the son of a family with a strong military tradition. Longing to gain admission to West Point, Patton decided to hone his weak academic skills (he suffered lifelong from dyslexia) by enrolling for a year at Virginia Military Institute (1904). He then entered West Point and graduated in 1909. A superb horseman, Patton was commissioned a second lieutenant in the cavalry and served with distinction in a number of army posts. A fine athlete, he was selected to represent the U.S. Army on the U.S. pentathlon team at the 1912 Stockholm Olympics.

Young Patton was honored by an appointment to study at Saumur, the prestigious French cavalry school. On his return to the States, he attended the Mounted Service School at Fort Riley, Kansas (1913), then served as an instructor at the school from 1914 to 1916. In addition to his equestrian prowess, Patton was an expert swordsman and earned appointment as the army's Master of the Sword—a title specially created for him. He also composed the official saber manual for the service and designed the "Patton saber" still worn by army officers. In 1916, Patton was assigned to General

George S. Patton Jr. strikes a well-deserved pose as conqueror of Sicily, August 1943. *(Virginia Military Institute Archives)*

John J. Pershing's Punitive Expedition against the Mexican revolutionary Pancho Villa and was promoted to captain at the conclusion of the assignment in 1917. Patton greatly admired Pershing, whom he regarded as *the* model military officer, and was thrilled to be appointed to his staff when Pershing led the American Expeditionary Force (AEF) to France in May 1917 after the United States entered World War I.

In Europe, Patton became the first American officer to receive tank training. He became an enthusiastic convert to the potential of armor and mechanized warfare generally. He learned all that he could from French and British armor commanders, then established the AEF Tank School at Langres, France, in November 1917. Promoted to temporary lieutenant colonel, then temporary colonel, he organized the 1st Tank Brigade, which he led in the assault on the Saint-Mihiel salient during September 12–17, 1918. In this critical engagement, Patton was seriously wounded, but he recovered quickly and fought at Meuse-Argonne (September 26–November 11). Like most other U.S. Army officers, Patton reverted to his prewar rank on his return to the United States after the Armistice, but was soon promoted to major (1919) and given command of the grandiosely misnamed 304th Tank Brigade (it was really only a battalion), based at Fort Meade, Maryland. Here he did much to formulate, hone, and perfect the tactics of mechanized war during 1919–21.

Patton was posted to Fort Myer, Virginia, during 1921–22 and served with the 3rd Cavalry Regiment. In 1923, he graduated at the top of his class from the Command and General Staff School, then served on the Army General Staff from 1923 to 1927. From 1928 to 1931, Patton was chief of cavalry. After attending the Army War College, he was appointed executive officer of the 3rd Cavalry and promoted to lieutenant colonel in 1934. Returning to the general staff in 1935, he was promoted to colonel in 1937.

After commanding 3rd Cavalry from December 1938 to July 1940, Patton took over the 2nd Armored Brigade during July–November 1940. Promoted to temporary brigadier general on October 2, 1940, he moved up to acting commanding general of the 2nd Armored Division in November, an appointment that was made permanent on April 4, 1941, when Patton was promoted to temporary major general.

In command of the 2nd Armored Division, Patton distinguished himself in the massive war maneuvers conducted in Louisiana and Texas during the summer and fall of 1941, and, soon after U.S. entry into World War II, he was named commander of I Armored Corps (January 15, 1942). Patton was assigned to create and command the Desert Training Center at Indio, California, during March 26–July 30, 1942 in preparation for the NORTH AFRICAN CAMPAIGN. Patton played a leading role in the final planning for OPERATION TORCH (July 30–August 21), the Allied landing and invasion of North Africa, and he commanded the Western Task Force in landings there on November 8, 1942. Patton was named to replace Major General Lloyd R. Fredendall as commander of U.S. II

Corps on March 3, 1943, after Fredendall encountered disaster against Panzer general ERWIN ROMMEL at the BATTLE OF KASSERINE PASS. The American defeat there had greatly demoralized the army, and it was largely thanks to Patton that II Corps was transformed from a gun-shy and inefficient unit into a victorious force.

Patton was promoted to temporary lieutenant general on March 12, 1943, then days later, he turned over II Corps command to OMAR N. BRADLEY. Patton next assumed command of I Armored Corps, which became the Seventh U.S. Army on July 10, 1943. He led this army with great boldness in OPERATION HUSKY and the rest of the SICILY CAMPAIGN from July 10 through August 17, beating British commander BERNARD LAW MONTGOMERY by taking both Palermo and Messina.

Twice during his command in Sicily, Patton slapped and verbally abused soldiers suffering from battle fatigue. After these incidents were publicized, the American public as well as Patton's superiors were scandalized, and Patton, heretofore recognized as the most dashing, brilliant, and effective of American tacticians, was effectively banished from the front on January 22, 1944, and sent to England in disgrace, where he was temporarily sidelined. The planners of the upcoming NORMANDY LANDINGS (D-DAY) decided to use Patton's presence in England in a campaign of disinformation to mislead the Germans into thinking that he was going to lead an invading army to Pas de Calais (the most logical point of departure for an invasion) and not Normandy. Only after the initial landings was Patton given a new command, that of the Third U.S. Army, which had been created especially for him. Patton arrived in France with it on July 6, 1944.

It is for his leadership of the Third Army that Patton is remembered as one of the great heroes of World War II. He led the Third Army during OPERATION COBRA, the breakout from Normandy, and drove this force of nearly half a million men in a lightning advance across France through the summer of 1944, collecting retroactive promotions to brigadier general and to major general in the process. During a period of nine months and eight days, beginning on July 6, 1944, and ending with the surrender of Germany, Patton's Third Army liberated or gained 81,522 square miles of France, 1,010 square miles of Luxembourg, 156 square miles of Belgium, 29,940 square miles of Germany, 3,485 square miles of Czechoslovakia, and 2,103 square miles of Austria. Some 112,000 cities, towns, and villages were liberated or captured, and 1,280,688 prisoners of war taken. At a cost of 160,692 casualties, killed or wounded, Patton's Third Army inflicted a total of 1,443,888 enemy casualties, including killed, wounded, and captured. As if this were not achievement enough, when the Germans launched their desperate surprise offensive in the ARDENNES (December 16, 1944–January 1945), Patton performed a tactical miracle by wheeling the entire Third Army, exhausted from months of forced marching and battle, 90 degrees north and launching a bold counterattack into the southern flank of the German penetration. By this action, he relieved Bastogne on December 26, 1944, ended the Battle of the Bulge, rescued the besieged 101st Airborne Division, then positioned his army for its final push into Germany.

After encountering stiff resistance during January–March 1945, the Third Army crossed the Rhine at Oppenheim on March 22 and advanced into central Germany and northern Bavaria by April. Units reached Linz, Austria, on May 5 and Pilsen, Czechoslovakia, on May 6—even before the Germans surrendered.

With the war in Europe won, Patton's absence of political tact once again became a major issue. While serving as military governor of Bavaria, he acted in defiance of official denazification policies by retaining former Nazis in certain civil service and administrative positions. He did this, he explained, because no other qualified personnel were available. Allied authorities, however, yielded to public and diplomatic pressure and relieved Patton from command of the Third Army and from the governorship of Bavaria.

Although he desperately wanted to be sent to the Pacific to fight in the war against Japan, Patton was assigned to command the Fifteenth Army, which was essentially a "paper army," an adminis-

trative unit set up to collect records and compile a history of the war. On December 9, 1945, in a relatively trivial automobile accident near Mannheim, Patton sustained a severe injury. His neck broken, the general was paralyzed from the neck down. Pulmonary edema and congestive heart failure developed, and George S. Patton Jr. died on December 21, 1945.

Further reading: Axelrod, Alan. *Patton: A Biography.* New York: Palgrave Macmillan, 2006; Hirshson, Stanley. *General Patton: A Soldier's Life.* New York: Perennial, 2003; D'Este, Carlo. *Patton: A Genius for War.* New York: HarperCollins, 1995.

Paulus, Friedrich von (1890–1957)
commander of the German Sixth Army in the invasion of the Soviet Union

Paulus was born at Breitenau in Hesse, Germany, the son of a school administrator. His first military ambition was to become an officer in the Imperial German Navy, but when he was unable to secure a cadetship, he turned to the law instead, which he studied at Marburg University. In February 1910, he left the university to enter the 111th ("Markgraf Ludwig's 3rd Baden") Infantry Regiment as an officer-cadet. At the outbreak of World War I in August 1914, Paulus fought through September with his regiment (as part of the Seventh German Army) in the Battle of the Frontiers on the western front. He also served at Arras, France, following the Battle of the Marne during September-October. In November, illness sent him back home until 1915, when he returned to active duty with an assignment in the Alpenkorps—the mountain troops—as a staff officer. He fought in Macedonia during 1915. Promoted to Oberleutnant, he went with the Alpenkorps to the western front, fighting during June 23–30, 1916, at Fleury, and, from February to November 1916, in the Battle of Verdun. During April 9–17, 1918, Paulus fought in Erich Ludendorff's attack on the Lys and in the defense against the British Somme-Lys offensive as well as the Battle of Saint-Quentin during August 22–September 4.

By the armistice, Paulus was a captain in the Alpenkorps. He served between the wars in the Reichswehr, the small German military force authorized under the terms of the TREATY OF VERSAILLES, as a company commander in the 13th Infantry Regiment at Stuttgart from 1919 to 1921. Through 1934, he served in staff posts, then was assigned command of a motorized battalion. In 1935, he was assigned as chief of staff for the new Panzer headquarters, and in 1939, promoted to major general, he was named chief of staff for the Tenth German Army under General WALTHER VON REICHENAU. He was with the Tenth Army during the BLITZKRIEG INVASION OF POLAND (September 1–October 5, 1939) and remained with this army after it was redesignated the Sixth German Army in Holland and Belgium during May 10–28, 1940.

Paulus was one of the principal planners of OPERATION SEALION, the contemplated but never executed invasion of Britain. He was elevated to deputy chief of staff of the Operations Section of the German High Command (Oberkommando des Heeres, or OKH), a post in which he played an important role in planning OPERATION BARBAROSSA, the INVASION OF THE SOVIET UNION.

In January 1942, Paulus replaced Reichenau as commander of the Sixth German Army and repulsed a Soviet offensive at the First Battle of KHARKOV in February. He next led the Sixth German Army toward the Volga during June 28–August 23 and approached Stalingrad in late August. Uniting with elements of the Fourth Panzer Army, he began to slog out the battle for the city. But it was here that the Red Army decided to make its most resolute stand, and Paulus was unable to advance. He was plagued by tenuous and overlong supply lines—and by the worst Russian winter in decades. In November, the Red Army initiated a counteroffensive, which encircled the battered Sixth Army during November 19–23. Paulus became wholly dependent on HERMANN GÖRING's promise to supply the isolated and starving Sixth Army by air. The promised support never materialized, and on January 15, 1945, when ADOLF HITLER promoted Paulus to field marshal, awarding him the Oak Leaves grade of the Knights Cross, he and his army were clearly doomed. Nine days later, the last of the German wounded were evacuated by air. On February 2, Field Marshal Paulus surrendered the 91,000 survivors of his army to the Soviets.

Paulus was held under house arrest in Moscow until 1953, when he was released with 6,000 other long-incarcerated survivors of the Battle of Stalingrad. The Soviets permitted him to reside exclusively in East Germany. He developed a degenerative neuromuscular disorder soon after his release and died at a Dresden clinic two years later.

Further reading: Beevor, Antony. *Stalingrad: The Fateful Siege, 1942–1943.* New York: Penguin Books, 1999; Heiber, Helmut, and David Glantz, eds. *Hitler and His Generals.* New York: Enigma Books, 2002; Hoyt, Edwin P. *199 Days: The Battle for Stalingrad.* New York: Forge Books, 1999; Walsh, Stephen. *Stalingrad: The Infernal Cauldron, 1942–1943.* New York: Thomas Dunne Books, 2001.

Pearl Harbor, Battle of

At 6 A.M., local time, air forces of the Japanese Imperial Navy were launched in a preemptive surprise attack on the U.S. Navy's Pacific Fleet at Pearl Harbor, Hawaii. The attack was planned by Admiral YAMAMOTO ISORUKO, despite his personal belief that it would provoke the United States to an all-out war against Japan. The Japanese intention was to begin the actual bombardment of Pearl Harbor immediately after a severance of diplomatic relations, to follow the anticipated collapse of negotiations with the United States over (among other things) a U.S. trade embargo against Japan and Japanese aggression in China; however, delays in communication between the Japanese government and its representatives in Washington, D.C., and time consumed in the laborious process of decrypting diplomatic communications meant that the attack began before the severance of diplomatic relations, let alone a declaration of war. This fact alone—an unprovoked "sneak" attack—did more than any other aspect of the Pearl Harbor operation to galvanize American political and popular resolve to strike back at Japan and bring about its total defeat.

Gun crew of the U.S. destroyer *Ward,* which sunk a Japanese midget submarine just before the Battle of Pearl Harbor *(National Archives and Records Administration)*

The Japanese striking force, led by Vice Admiral Nagumo Chuichi, consisted of two fleet carriers, two light carriers, a carrier that had been converted from a battleship, a carrier converted from a cruiser, two battleships, two cruisers, a screen of destroyers, and eight support vessels. This fleet departed the Kure naval base during November 10–18, observing throughout its voyage strict radio silence, which, in conjunction with decoy radio messages ("signals deception"), effectively prevented U.S. forces (in particular, Pacific Fleet commander Husband E. Kimmel) from determining the location of the Japanese striking force. Compounding the absence of intelligence was the failure of U.S. planners to anticipate a first strike against Pearl Harbor from Japan. They assumed that any Japanese attack would have to originate from the Japanese-governed Marshall Islands, the Japanese territory closest to Hawaii. With limited numbers of reconnaissance aircraft, Kimmel concentrated on patrolling the Marshalls, whereas Nagumo's striking force approached from the opposite direction, the north. Even more egregious was the American tendency to discount the likelihood of an attack on Pearl Harbor—from *any* direction. It was simply assumed that a Japanese first strike would be against the Philippines. There was, however, a fear that Japanese nationals and/or Americans of Japanese descent living in Hawaii would perpetrate acts of sabotage against the air and naval facilities at Pearl Harbor or that the harbor would fall prey to submarine attack. It seemed highly unlikely that the Japanese would mount an air assault—not only because of the distances involved, but because it was believed that the waters of the harbor were too shallow for torpedoes dropped by torpedo bombers. So confident were American planners that torpedoes could not be used at Pearl Harbor, that they neglected to employ torpedo nets to protect the fleet. Indeed, Pearl Harbor was too shallow for conventional torpedoes; however, after observing the successful British raid against the Italian fleet at the Battle of Taranto in 1940, the Japanese created a new type of torpedo designed to operate in shallow water. Another consequence of discounting an air attack was Kimmel's transfer of many of his P-40 fighters from Hawaii to Wake and Midway islands to provide cover for bombers being flown to reinforce the Philippines.

If an air attack seemed highly unlikely, sabotage loomed as a high-priority probability. For this reason, when Kimmel and his army counterpart, Lieutenant General Walter Short, received (along with all other major U.S. commanders) a war warning on November 27, Short put his troops on high alert—for sabotage. He communicated this to Washington and, receiving no reply, assumed that high command concurred with his understanding that the only likely threat was sabotage. This persuaded him not to stock his antiaircraft batteries with ready ammunition, and it further prompted him to order all U.S. Army Air Forces planes to be grouped together, wingtip-to-wingtip, so that they could be more easily guarded. This, of course, rendered them all the more vulnerable to air attack. For his part, Kimmel also made preparations chiefly to thwart saboteurs. Only every fourth navy machine gun was manned, and all ammunition was locked up to secure it from saboteurs. Antiaircraft batteries were unmanned, and no special air reconnaissance was ordered. About one-third of the fleet's captains were ashore, along with many other officers, rather than standing by on their ships.

In the aftermath of the battle, most of the blame for the lack of vigilance and preparation at Pearl Harbor was directed at Kimmel and Short. To a significant degree, they were indeed culpable. But the failure at Pearl Harbor was also a symptom of failures at higher levels of command. Interservice rivalry, a lack of initiative and imagination, as well as general incompetence prevented key intelligence from being disseminated to the commanders in Hawaii.

The Japanese striking force rallied at Etorofu in the Kurile Islands on November 22. From here, on November 26, it sailed toward Pearl Harbor, taking advantage of the cover provided by a weather front,

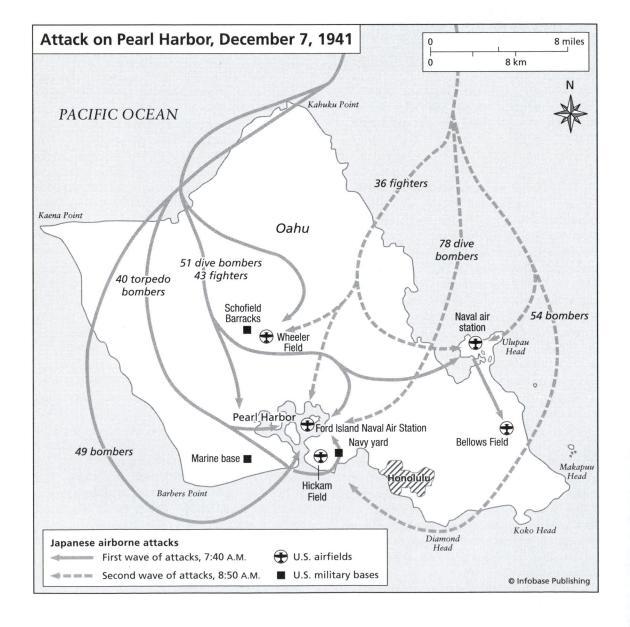

Attack on Pearl Harbor, December 7, 1941

0   8 miles
0   8 km

N

PACIFIC OCEAN

Kahuku Point

36 fighters

Kaena Point

Oahu

78 dive bombers

51 dive bombers
43 fighters

40 torpedo bombers

Schofield Barracks

Wheeler Field

Naval air station

54 bombers

Ulupau Head

Pearl Harbor

Ford Island Naval Air Station

Navy yard

Bellows Field

49 bombers

Marine base

Hickam Field

Honolulu

Makapuu Head

Barbers Point

Diamond Head

Koko Head

Japanese airborne attacks

⟵ First wave of attacks, 7:40 A.M. ⊕ U.S. airfields

◀--- Second wave of attacks, 8:50 A.M. ■ U.S. military bases

© Infobase Publishing

Destroyer USS *Shaw* explodes during the Battle of Pearl Harbor. *(National Archives and Records Administration)*

which moved at approximately the speed of the fleet. The fleet took up its attack position just 275 miles north of Hawaii without being detected. From here, Nagumo launched his aircraft on December 7, 1941.

Nagumo's first wave consisted of 49 bombers, 40 torpedo bombers, 51 dive-bombers, and 43 fighters. This was followed by a second wave, made up of 54 bombers, 78 dive-bombers, and 36 fighters. As the weather had served the attackers for cover, so the clouds that shrouded Hawaii that morning suddenly parted to reveal the target with perfect clarity. To the Japanese, this seemed nothing less than evidence of divine intervention.

At 6:45 that morning, a U.S. destroyer on patrol attacked and sank a Japanese midget submarine as it tried to enter Pearl Harbor. As it turned out, this was one of several midget submarines (which had been deployed by larger I-type submarines) that Yamamoto intended to use to sink any ships that escaped the air attack. Although the submarine had been sighted three hours before its sinking, the U.S. destroyer skipper did not report its presence until it was sunk. Worse, the navy never passed on this report to the army. Thus a valuable opportunity for advance warning of the attack was lost. (In the end, the submarines—there were 16 I Types in all and numerous midget subs—failed to sink any American ships at Pearl Harbor.)

Between 6:45 and 7:00 A.M., the newly installed Opana Mobile Radar Unit made contact with a Japanese reconnaissance float plane and duly reported its presence. No action was taken on the report. Of three operating radar, two were shut down at 7:00 A.M. so that the operators could eat breakfast. The truck delivering breakfast to the third set of operators was late, so they continued operating their single radar, which detected the approach of the carrier aircraft of the first wave. The operators reported this but did not specify the number of aircraft detected. As a result, the duty officer who received the report assumed the targets were a flight of USAAF B-17 bombers, whose approach was expected. Yet again, advance warning of the impending attack was ignored.

The first wave of Japanese aircraft initially homed in on Pearl Harbor by following the signal of commercial radio broadcasts from Honolulu, then, as they neared their target, the pilots followed a bombing grid drawn up by the Japanese consul general stationed in Honolulu. Moored in the harbor that sleepy Sunday morning were 70 U.S. warships, including eight battleships and 24 auxiliaries. As luck would have it, the heavy cruisers and fleet carriers were at sea.

The first wave of torpedo and dive-bombers attacked the battle fleet and bombed and strafed the airfields from 7:55 to 8:25. Fifteen minutes after this, high-level bombers attacked. At 9:15, the dive-bombers of the second wave attacked, withdrawing at 9:45. In all, some 360 Japanese planes were involved in the operation. The toll they took was terrible: the battleship *Arizona* was completely destroyed and the *Oklahoma* capsized; the battleships *California, Nevada,* and *West Virginia* sank in shallow water. Three cruisers, three destroyers, and four other vessels were damaged or sunk. One hundred sixty-four aircraft were destroyed on the ground and another 128 were damaged. Casualties included 2,403 service personnel and civilians killed and 1,178 wounded. Japanese losses amounted to 29 aircraft and 6 submarines—one I-Type and five midget subs.

Except for the unanticipated absence of the U.S. carriers and heavy cruisers, the attack succeeded beyond Japanese expectations, but Nagumo, an overly cautious commander, decided against launching a third wave of aircraft, because he feared a counterattack. If the third wave had concentrated on the base's repair facilities and fuel installations, Pearl Harbor could have been knocked out of the war for a long time, if not permanently. As it was, the base returned to service quickly. As for the fleet's losses, they were severe but not fatal. The damaged battleships were repaired, and those that had sunk in shallow water were later refloated, so that six of the eight battleships attacked at Pearl Harbor eventually returned to service, along with all but one of the other ships sunk or damaged. There was, however, no salvaging the careers of Kimmel and Short, both of whom soon resigned.

Many commentators have described the attack on Pearl Harbor as a spectacular tactical victory for Japan, even as it was a monumental strategic blunder that, in provoking a great industrial power to a massive and united war effort, ensured Japan's ultimate defeat.

Further reading: Goldstein, Donald M., and Katherine V. Dillon, eds. *The Pearl Harbor Papers: Inside the Japanese Plans.* Dulles, Va.: Potomac Books, 1999; Lord, Walter. *Day of Infamy: Sixtieth-Anniversary Edition.* New York: Owl Books, 2001; Prange, Gordon W. *At Dawn We Slept: The Untold Story of Pearl Harbor,* revised edition. New York: Penguin, 1991; Prange, Gordon W., with Donald M. Goldstein and Katherine V. Dillon. *Dec. 7, 1941: The Day the Japanese Attacked Pearl Harbor.* New York: Warner Books, 1989; Prange, Gordon W., with Donald M. Goldstein and Katherine V. Dillon. *Pearl Harbor: The Verdict of History.* New York: Penguin, 2001.

Peenemünde (V-1 and V-2 base)

Peenemünde is a village on the Baltic island of Usedom in northeastern Germany. During World War II, it was the site of German rocket research on the so-called V-weapons, the V-1 BUZZ BOMB and the V-2 ROCKET, conducted by the Heeresversuchsanstalt, the organization created in 1937 to study and imple-

ment rocket development. Before 1937, the lead German rocket scientist, WERNHER VON BRAUN, had been working at Kummersdorf, near Berlin, but facilities there proved too small for test-firing.

At Peenemünde, both before and during the war, the foundations of practical rocketry were laid and two weapons produced, the V-1 and the V-2. The V-1 was test-fired early in 1942, and the V-2 test-fired on October 3, 1942. Peenemünde scientists also developed advanced night-navigation and radar systems.

Peenemünde was the target of a number of Allied bombing raids, the biggest of which was a night attack by nearly 500 RAF heavy bombers during August 16–17, 1943. The raid prompted the Germans to move V weapons production into hardened underground bunkers.

Further reading: Neufeld, Michael. *The Rocket and the Reich: Peenemünde and the Coming of the Ballistic Missile Era.* Cambridge, Mass.: Harvard University Press, 1996; Huzel, Dieter K. *Peenemünde to Canaveral.* Englewood Cliffs, N.J.: Prentice Hall, 1965.

Peiper, Joachim (1915–1976) *German SS commander associated with the Malmédy Massacre*

Joachim Peiper was recruited out of college by the WAFFEN SS and was soon serving in the elite Liebstandarte-SS ADOLF HITLER division. Peiper was a born military leader who achieved the rank of colonel before he turned 30. He was a very able armor tactician.

During the Soviet campaign, Peiper's command was dubbed the "Blowtorch Battalion" because it compiled a record of great savagery, including against civilians. During the BATTLE OF THE ARDENNES (BATTLE OF THE BULGE), all German units were explicitly ordered to fight with the utmost brutality. In particular, they were instructed to take no prisoners, lest this slow the German advance. Peiper was singled out even among the general horror for the MALMÉDY MASSACRE, the machine-gun murder of 86 U.S. POWs. Although this was the most notorious of the atrocities committed by Peiper's SS unit, it was hardly an isolated incident. These same troops had cut down 19 disarmed American prisoners at Honsfeld. After Malmédy, the unit executed 50 Americans at Büllingen.

After the war, Peiper was tried with others for the Malmédy Massacre. Found guilty, he was sentenced to death. The sentence was later commuted to life imprisonment, then reduced. After serving 11 years in prison, Peiper was paroled in December 1956. He spent the rest of his life in France as a translator and was killed when his home was firebombed in July 1976. No one was ever apprehended for the fire bombing, and no individual or group claimed responsibility for it; however, it is generally believed that the attack was in retaliation for the atrocities committed under Peiper's command.

Further reading: Bauserman, John M. *The Malmédy Massacre.* Shippensburg, Pa.: White Mane, 2002; Weingartner, James. *A Peculiar Crusade: Willis M. Everett and the Malmédy Massacre Trial.* New York: New York University Press, 2000.

Peirse, Richard (1892–1970) *British air marshal*

Richard Peirse was born in Croydon, England, the son of a Royal Navy admiral. From King's College, London, he enlisted in the Royal Flying Corps during World War I and was decorated with the Distinguished Service Order in 1915. He flew on the western front as well as at Gallipoli and in Italy.

After World War I, Peirse joined the newly created Royal Air Force (RAF) and rose to command British forces in Palestine and Transjordan (modern Jordan) from 1933 to 1936. In 1937, he was promoted to vice air marshal and named director of Operations and Intelligence in the Air Ministry. Concurrently, he also served as deputy chief of Air Staff. Peirse was elevated to command of Bomber Command in October 1940, but failed to produce results sufficient to satisfy CHARLES PORTAL, air chief of staff. In January 1942, Portal replaced Peirse with J. E. A. Baldwin. Peirse was given command of the Allied air forces in Southeast Asia. Friction with LOUIS MOUNTBATTEN, supreme commander of the

theater, resulted in his resignation in November 1944. With the end of the war, Peirse retired from the RAF, holding the rank of air marshal.

Further reading: Philpott, Brian. *RAF Bomber Units 1939–1942.* London: Osprey, 1977; Richards, Denis. *The Hardest Victory: RAF Bomber Command in the Second World War.* New York: W. W. Norton, 1995.

Peleliu, Battle of

In the U.S. Pacific campaign, military planners saw the Japanese-held islands as so many stepping stones leading toward the Philippines and Japan. Following American triumphs in the MARIANA ISLANDS CAMPAIGN and the BATTLE OF THE PHILIPPINE SEA, Admiral CHESTER NIMITZ targeted the Palau Islands in the western Carolines. Take these, and U.S. forces would be ready to launch against the Philippines.

The U.S. Marines' III Amphibious Corps (under the temporary command of Julian Smith) was poised by September 1944 to invade Peleliu and the smaller island of Angaur just to the south. Peleliu was only six miles long and two miles wide, but it was garrisoned by more than 10,000 Japanese troops (under Inoue Sadae), who were lodged in some 800 highly fortified caves and other strong points. Their defenses were largely interconnected by tunnels.

Marines at Peleliu *(National Archives and Records Administration)*

The 1st Marine Division (William Rupertus) landed in southwest Peleliu on the morning of September 15 following an intensive air and naval bombardment. The dug-in Japanese held on for four days before this corner of the island, which included the airfield, was taken. Having accomplished this, the marines directed their attack to the north and began an advance up the island. From Japanese positions on Umurbrogol Mountain (dubbed Bloody Nose Ridge by the marines) came heavy artillery fire as well as intense small-arms fire. This was sufficient to arrest the marines' advance.

While the marines were thus engaged, the army's 81st Infantry Division (Paul Mueller) landed at Angaur Island on September 17. This smaller island was garrisoned by about 1,400 Japanese soldiers, who resisted for three days before most of the Angaur was secured—even at that, some resistance continued through October 13.

In the meantime, ROY GEIGER, permanent commander of III Corps, resumed his command and sent the 321st Regiment to Peleliu, while the 323rd occupied Ulithi unopposed. On September 24, the 321st augmented the ongoing marine attack by hitting Bloody Nose Ridge from the west, so that, within three days, the Japanese position here had been encircled. On October 15, General Mueller assumed command of operations on Peleliu as the 321st reduced resistance at Bloody Nose Ridge practically on an inch-by-inch basis. Later, the 323rd Regiment joined the 321st, but, even thus augmented, it was November 25 before the Japanese defenders were wiped out here.

Peleliu and the associated battles exacted the highest casualty rate of any AMPHIBIOUS ASSAULT in American history: a staggering 40 percent.

Further reading: Falk, Stanley L. *Bloodiest Victory: Palaus.* New York: Ballantine Books, 1974.

Percival, Arthur (1887–1966) *British general who surrendered Singapore*

Percival was born in Aspenden Lodge, Aspenden near Buntingford, Hertfordshire, England. His father was the land agent of the Hamel's Park estate, and his mother belonged to a prosperous Lancashire cotton family. Educated locally and at Rugby, Percival enlisted as a private during World War I. He rose to the rank of captain by October 1916 and compiled a superb combat record. By the beginning of World War II, he was a brigadier general. After the DUNKIRK EVACUATION, he was assigned to protect the English coast in anticipation of a German invasion, then in the spring of 1941, he was promoted to acting lieutenant general and named general officer commanding British forces in Malaya.

Percival had fewer than three divisions in Malaya. He called for six more to be sent to him, but no additional forces could be spared. During the night of December 7, 1941, Japanese forces landed at Kota Bharu—a feint to draw attention from the main assault landings at Singora and Patani on the northeast coast of the Malay Peninsula on December 8. Two days later, the *Prince of Wales* and *Repulse* were sunk by Japanese aircraft off the Malayan coast, thereby giving the Imperial Japanese Navy control of the sea, enabling it to supply an invading force.

Percival ordered a general retreat across the Johore Strait to the island of Singapore on January 25, 1942. On February 8, 13,000 Japanese troops landed in northwest Singapore. On the 9th, 17,000 more landed on the west. Percival retreated to the southern tip of the island, but surrendered on February 15. He turned over 138,000 soldiers to the much smaller but better equipped and better supported Japanese force. It was a staggering humiliation for British arms. Percival and his troops were held as prisoners throughout virtually the entire war. As far as Prime Minister WINSTON CHURCHILL and many other Allied officials were concerned, Percival was chiefly to blame for the ignominious defeat; however, he suffered no official censure and was present at the Japanese surrender aboard the USS *Missouri* on September 2, 1945. In 1949, he published his memoir, *The War in Malaya.*

Further reading: Percival, Arthur. *The War in Malaya.* London: Eyre & Spottiswoode, 1949.

Pétain, Henri-Philippe (1856–1951) *French hero of World War I who headed the Vichy government after the fall of France*

Pétain was born in Cauchy-à-la-Tour, Pas-de-Calais, France. Although his background was that of a peasant, he showed such early promise that he was enrolled at Saint-Cyr, the French military academy, where he excelled. In 1876, he was commissioned an officer of the *chasseurs alpines* (mountain troops) and began a slow rise through the ranks. In 1906, he was appointed to the faculty of the École de Guerre, where his conservative and methodical approach to strategy and tactics, which emphasized the importance of defense and the exploitation of artillery firepower, put him at odds with prevailing war policy, which advocated a vigorous offensive. This was sufficient to retard Pétain's career, and at the outbreak of World War I in August 1914, he was no more than a colonel, commanding the 33rd Regiment.

In combat, Pétain quickly distinguished himself, achieving promotion to brigadier general within the first month of the war. His performance at the Battle of the Marne (September 4–10) earned him promotion to general of division, and by October 25 he was in command of XXXIII Corps in Artois. In June, he rose to command of the Second Army, and in February 1916, when the physically and symbolically crucial fortress of Verdun was under heavy attack, it was upon Pétain that France called. In response, he pronounced the phrase that made him a popular hero of the war: *"Ils ne passeront pas!"*—"They shall not pass!"

Pétain's fierce defense against the long siege of Verdun was costly to the French as well as to the Germans, but it was a victory. Nevertheless, it was a victory of defense—and that did not sit well with high command. The aggressive Robert Nivelle was effectively jumped ahead of Pétain, but when Nivelle failed disastrously in his Chemin-des-Dames offensive, Pétain was called in to relieve him and to assume supreme command of all the French armies.

Pétain's first crisis was a mass mutiny of the war-weary ranks. He vigorously prosecuted the ringleaders of the mutiny, even as he sought to act swiftly to address the soldiers' grievances, enacting reforms to humanize the French army and improve the treatment of the common soldier. By the end of the war, Pétain was elevated to marshal of France and in 1920 was appointed vice president of the Supreme War Council. In 1922, Pétain was made inspector general of the army, then, after retiring from the army, he served as minister of war during the brief government of Gaston Doumergue in February–November 1934.

Through the 1930s, Pétain became increasingly disdainful of liberalism and turned to advocacy of autocratic government. He was appointed ambassador to Spain in March 1939, but was recalled to France in May 1940 during the BATTLE OF FRANCE. By this time, Marshal Pétain was an old and tired man, perhaps verging on senility. Nevertheless, French President ALBERT LEBRUN decided to call on the hero of Verdun to save France once again. He asked Pétain to form a new government, and on June 22, 1940, as titular head of that government, Pétain negotiated an armistice with Germany.

Pétain was given emergency powers that made him, in effect, a dictator. He resolved to retain for himself and for France as much independence from German domination as possible, and in December 1940 he went so far as to dismiss PIERRE LAVAL, the unabashedly collaborationist foreign minister who had been instrumental in bringing Pétain to power in the first place. Yet it was a losing battle. Increasingly, Pétain was forced to be little more than a puppet of the Reich, and he was well on his way to being remembered as the man who sold out his nation to the Nazis.

Under unrelenting German pressure, Pétain repeatedly yielded, even recalling Laval to office in 1942. In November of that year, the Germans occupied Vichy, the seat of the Pétain government, and in August 1943, they arrested Pétain himself, eventually interning him in Germany.

Pétain was returned to France in April 1945, just before the German surrender. Tried for treason, he was found guilty and sentenced to death. CHARLES DE GAULLE, as provisional president of the republic, chose to remember the heroic Pétain under whom he had served during World War I. De Gaulle commuted the sentence to life imprisonment, and Pétain was incarcerated in a fortress on Île d'Yeu. After he fell ill, he was transferred to a villa at Port-Joinville, where he died on July 23, 1951.

Further reading: Griffiths, Richard. *Pétain: A Biography of Marshal Philippe Pétain of Vichy.* Garden City, N.Y.: 1972; Lottman, Herbert R. *Pétain, Hero or Traitor? The Untold Story.* New York: Morrow, 1985; Williams, Charles. *Petain: How the Hero of France Became a Convicted Traitor and Changed the Course of History.* New York and London: Palgrave Macmillan, 2005.

Philippine Constabulary

The Philippine Constabulary was created in 1901 by U.S. administrative authorities as one of the Philippines' two national police forces. In 1935, under the Philippine National Defense Act promulgated by DOUGLAS MACARTHUR, who was serving as head of the Philippine military, the Philippine Constabulary was reconstituted as the core of the Philippine Regular Army, which MacArthur was in the process of organizing.

As MacArthur shaped it, the Philippine Constabulary was modeled after the U.S. Army as a small, professional force of about 10,000 regulars who, in time of war, were to function as the nucleus around which a reserve force would be mustered. MacArthur planned for a total strength, as augmented by mobilized reserves, of about 400,000 men. The constabulary was nowhere near this size at the outbreak of World War II; however, it functioned well and in close cooperation with the U.S. Army when the Japanese invaded. After U.S. forces withdrew or were captured, constabulary troops retreated into the jungles and hills, from which they fought a continuous guerrilla action against the Japanese invaders until the Philippines were liberated in 1945.

See also PHILIPPINES, FALL AND RECONQUEST OF.

Further reading: Hurley, Victor. *Jungle Patrol: The Story of the Philippine Constabulary.* New York: Dutton, 1938; Steinberg, David Joel. *Philippine Collaboration in World War II.* Ann Arbor: University of Michigan Press, 1967.

Philippine Sea, Battle of the

The U.S. invasion of the Marianas in the MARIANA ISLANDS CAMPAIGN, beginning on June 15, 1944, lured the Japanese fleet into a fight for the first time since the naval battles that had accompanied the GUADALCANAL CAMPAIGN during the autumn of 1942.

Japanese admiral TOYODA SOEMU was desperate to force a make-or-break battle and therefore committed a force of nine aircraft carriers and 18 battleships and cruisers against the American ships covering the landings during the BATTLE OF SAIPAN. To counter Toyoda, U.S. admiral RAYMOND SPRUANCE, commanding the Fifth Fleet, dispatched 15 fast carriers of Task Force 58 (under MARC MITSCHER) to meet and intercept the Japanese attack fleet when it was still some 90 miles distant from Saipan. The result was the Battle of the Philippine Sea, between the Marianas and the Philippines.

The battle commenced on June 19, 1944, when Japanese land-based planes launched from Guam and Truk hit Task Force 58. Mitscher launched his carrier-based Hellcats, which shot down 35 Japanese fighters and bombers. The air battle continued, pitting some 430 Japanese carrier-based planes against 450 U.S. aircraft over the course of eight hours. In the end, all but 100 of the Japanese aircraft were lost. U.S. aviators dubbed their victory the "Great Marianas Turkey Shoot," and it is considered the most decisive air combat of World War II—perhaps even in the entire history of aerial combat. Only 30 U.S. aircraft were lost, and damage to the ships of the Fifth Fleet was inconsequential. During the air combat, a pair of American submarines managed to slip through the screen protecting the Japanese carriers. Firing a single torpedo, the USS *Albacore* sank the 33,000-ton *Taiho*, Japan's largest aircraft carrier, with the loss of 1,650 Japanese sailors and airmen. USS *Cavalla* fired three torpedoes into the 22,000-ton carrier *Shokaku*, sinking it.

During the night of June 19, the surviving ships of the Japanese fleet withdrew to the northwest as U.S. carriers gave chase. After nightfall on June 20, Mitscher launched a new attack of 209 aircraft against the fleeing Japanese some 300 miles away.

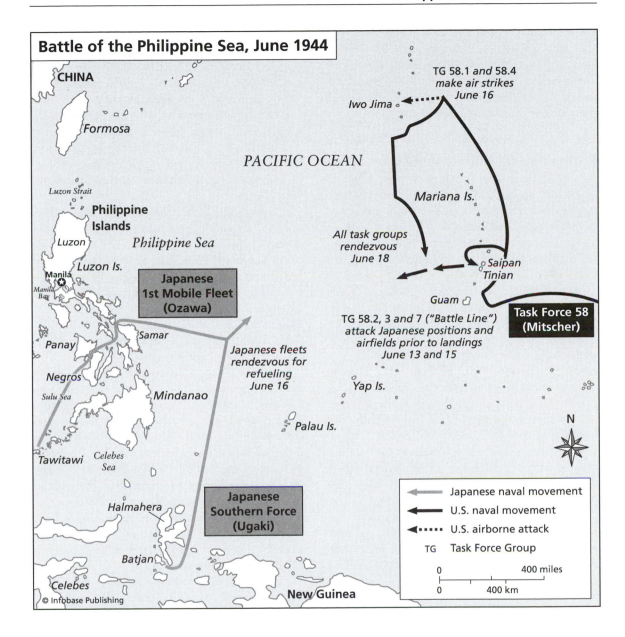

Battle of the Philippine Sea, June 1944

CHINA

Formosa

PACIFIC OCEAN

TG 58.1 *and* 58.4
make air strikes
June 16

Iwo Jima

Luzon Strait

**Philippine
Islands**

Luzon

Philippine Sea

Mariana Is.

Luzon Is.

Manila

Manila
Bay

**Japanese
1st Mobile Fleet
(Ozawa)**

All task groups
rendezvous
June 18

Saipan
Tinian

Samar

Panay

*Japanese fleets
rendezvous for
refueling
June 16*

Guam

**Task Force 58
(Mitscher)**

Negros

Sulu Sea

Mindanao

TG 58.2, 3 and 7 ("Battle Line")
attack Japanese positions and
airfields prior to landings
June 13 and 15

Yap Is.

Palau Is.

Tawitawi   Celebes
Sea

N

Halmahera

**Japanese
Southern Force
(Ugaki)**

Batjan

Celebes
© Infobase Publishing

New Guinea

	Japanese naval movement
	U.S. naval movement
	U.S. airborne attack
TG	Task Force Group

0   400 miles
0   400 km

This attack sank the aircraft carrier *Hiyo* and shot down 40 of the 75 Japanese planes launched against the attackers. The cost to U.S. fliers was 20 aircraft shot down and another 80 lost while attempting to return to their aircraft carriers in the dark. Although, then 100 aircraft were lost, 51 pilots were rescued.

The Battle of the Philippine Sea ended on the night of June 20. The cost to the Japanese was staggering and irrecoverable. Although six aircraft carriers escaped destruction, the vast majority of Japan's veteran aviators had been killed and their aircraft lost. As for the U.S. landings at Saipan, they continued unhindered.

Further reading: Grove, Eric. *Fleet to Fleet Encounters: Tsushima, Jutland, Philippine Sea.* London: Arms & Armour Press, 1991; Lockwood, Charles A. *Battles of the Philippine Sea.* New York: Crowell, 1967; Y'Blood, William T. *Red Sun Setting: The Battle of the Philippine Sea.* Annapolis, Md.: Naval Institute Press, 2003.

Philippines, fall and reconquest of

No objective in the Pacific was more hotly or intensively contested than the Philippine Islands. At the outbreak of the war, the Japanese targeted the Philippines, beginning with Luzon, the largest and most important island in the Philippine archipelago, in an invasion assault launched on December 8, 1941.

On Luzon, U.S. general Douglas MacArthur commanded the bulk of the U.S. Far East forces: about 11,000 U.S. soldiers and marines, 8,000 U.S. Army Air Force personnel, 12,000 Filipino Scouts (who were incorporated into the regular U.S. Army), and more than 100,000 other Filipino troops—most of whom were untrained and either poorly equipped or altogether without arms. Manila Bay was a major U.S. Navy facility and home to the U.S. Asiatic Fleet under Admiral Thomas Hart. Army Air Forces assets on the Philippines were not extensive. Major General Lewis Brereton had about 275 aircraft, but many were obsolete—except for 35 B-17s and 107 P-40s.

Although MacArthur and his command had received a war warning from Washington and were on a war footing, they were taken by surprise when the Japanese aircraft raided the principal air base, Clark Field, about noon on December 8. The attack was devastating, destroying on the ground 15 of 17 B-17s parked here. Under cover of darkness, Admiral Hart steamed out of Manila Bay and sailed south to Borneo to protect his ships from the Japanese bombers. This saved the fleet, but left the Philippines largely without naval assets.

The invasion proper began on December 10, two days after the initial raids, when 4,000 men landed at Aparri and Vigan, at the northern end of Luzon. A second landing was made on December 14, at Legaspi, on the southern end of the island.

These were pilot or probing attacks intended to assess U.S. defenses. The principal invasion assault came on December 22, when 43,000 men of General Homma Masaharu's Fourteenth Japanese Army landed at Lingayen Gulf on Luzon's west coast, 125 miles north of Manila. Thanks to the early raids, Homma enjoyed total air superiority and quickly linked up with the first invaders who had landed at Aparri and Vigan. The link-up completed, he advanced southward toward Manila, the islands' capital.

Overwhelmed by the assault, MacArthur ordered U.S. and Filipino forces to withdraw to the Bataan Peninsula on December 23, on Luzon's west coast, between Manila Bay and the South China Sea. Under the circumstances, it was the only viable move. On December 24, another 9,500 Japanese troops landed at Lamon Bay, 60 miles southeast of Manila, which, with Homma's massive force pushing in from the north, placed Manila in a vise from which there would be no escape.

Japanese planners believed that the conquest of the Philippines would be rapid and relatively easy; however, MacArthur's troops made a fighting withdrawal, which proved very costly to the invaders and bought time for the general withdrawal, largely intact, to Bataan. In the meantime, from December 24 to December 26, Manila was subject to intensive air raids, prompting MacArthur to abandon its defense and declare it an open city in the hope that it would be spared further destruction. That hope proved forlorn—as the Japanese, who occupied Manila on January 2, 1942, treated the city and its citizens with utmost brutality.

The principal U.S.-Filipino force, under Lieutenant General Jonathan Wainwright, and the smaller southern force unit (under George Parker, later replaced by Albert Jones) completed their withdrawal to Bataan by January 1, 1942. MacArthur saw to the destruction of the bridges over the Pampanga River, to slow the Japanese advance, and he and Philippine president Manuel Quezon set up their headquarters on Corregidor Island, a hardened natural fortress known as "the Rock," off the southern coast of Bataan. Although many would criticize MacArthur's poor preparation for the invasion, the massive withdrawal was a brilliant feat, which greatly frustrated the Japanese and substantially delayed all their offensive operations. With combat losses and desertions (mainly from the Philippine army), casualties amounted to 13,000, leaving MacArthur about 80,000 troops, whose most immediate problem, besides holding out against incessant Japanese bombardment and shelling, was a shortage of food, ammunition, and equipment.

In the meantime, the invasion continued. During the initial phase of the Luzon assault, 5,000 Japanese troops were diverted to landings on Mindanao, at the southern end of the archipelago, on December 20. These invaders took the important port of Davao, then advanced south to Jolo Island and North Borneo. This action severed communication between the Philippines and the Allied base in Australia. Aside from this, however, the Luzon defenders repeatedly frustrated further conquest.

MacArthur held out hope that major reinforcements would be dispatched to the Philippines. This was deemed impossible by U.S. military planners, however, and President FRANKLIN D. ROOSEVELT personally ordered MacArthur to evacuate with his family to Australia. This he did on March 11, 1942, leaving Wainwright in overall command and instructing him not to surrender. Wainwright stayed on Bataan for another month, but on April 10, he deemed the U.S.-Filipino position to be untenable and evacuated his remaining troops to Corregidor. The invaders now overran and occupied all of the strategic coastal positions throughout the Visayan Island group in the central Philippines.

Under continual bombardment and with his troops near starvation, Wainwright held out on Corregidor until May 6, when he finally surrendered. Four days later, on May 10, Major General William Sharp surrendered his troops on Mindanao. A guerrilla force under Colonel John Horan, which had withdrawn to the mountains of northern Luzon, gave up on May 18. With this, the Philippines was turned over to the Japanese.

The Japanese occupiers never had an easy time of it. Continuous Filipino and American guerrilla activity—from units that had refused to heed the order to surrender—harassed the occupation forces, tying down large numbers of troops. These guerrillas also served important intelligence functions, continually supplying information to Allied commanders operating in the region.

When MacArthur, having left the islands, reached the safety of Australia, he broadcast the famous pledge, "I shall return." While various resistance groups continued to fight, the occupiers treated the Philippine population with the utmost brutality. When, in July 1944, as the Allies steadily closed in on the Japanese homeland, Admiral ERNEST J. KING, chief of naval operations, proposed accelerating the campaign by bypassing the Philippines to attack Formosa directly. MacArthur, aching to make good on his pledge of 1942, objected, arguing not only that the Philippines were strategically critical, but that the United States was morally obligated to liberate the Filipino people. Roosevelt agreed, and the recapture of the Philippines became a major objective of the Pacific war.

In September, U.S. aircraft launched from aircraft carriers bombed Japanese airfields in central Luzon, damaging or destroying some 400 Japanese aircraft. Within a short time, the Americans claimed air superiority—although not air supremacy. By the middle of the following month, MacArthur supervised the assembly of a massive amphibious force east of the Visayan Islands to invade Leyte. Ultimately, the force consisted of more than 700 ships, hundreds of aircraft, and about 160,000 men. A naval barrage commenced at dawn on October 20, 1944, followed at 10 A.M. by the landing of four divisions. Initial resistance was light, and the troops secured both a beachhead and an airstrip by nightfall. This allowed for the landing of more troops and equipment and for the expansion of the beachhead.

In the meantime, on October 24, U.S. and Japanese ships fought the BATTLE OF LEYTE GULF, the biggest naval battle in history. It was a desperate Japanese bid to destroy the U.S. fleet covering the invasion and thereby cut off the landed troops; however, the Japanese were decisively defeated, all but ensuring the success of the U.S. liberation effort.

As usual, despite suffering major reversals, the Japanese refused to give up. General YAMASHITA TOMOYUKI, who had recently assumed command of the Japanese forces in the Philippines, reinforced Leyte with 50,000 troops and summoned aircraft from Japan and Formosa. With these fresh forces, he attacked U.S. positions throughout Leyte. Instead of responding with mere defense, MacArthur landed more troops, at Ormoc, on the west coast of the island. This unexpected move outflanked Yamashita's newly arrived forces, splitting them in two. For all intents and purposes defeated, the Japanese nevertheless fought to the death. Some 80,000 Japanese died within the space of weeks. U.S. forces took fewer than 1,000 prisoners.

Leyte was secured by the end of December. The next objective was Luzon, across the San Bernardino Strait. MacArthur first dispatched a task force to Mindoro, quickly capturing it, along with airfields that would be invaluable for operations against Luzon. MacArthur planned to surprise Yamashita by circling to the north rather than attacking directly from the south, as he assumed Yamashita expected. In fact, brilliant Japanese reconnaissance detected MacArthur's maneuver, but, outgunned by the U.S. fleet, the Japanese were unable to interdict the advance, and the U.S. landings proceeded.

Essentially, MacArthur's forces recapitulated what the Japanese had done in 1941–42. Whereas the Americans had given up Manila, however, Yamashita defended it fiercely in a month-long battle, which razed much of the city. It was March 3, 1945, before Manila was liberated—a city largely reduced to ashes. The Battle of Manila cost about 1,000 American lives and 16,000 Japanese. Filipino casualties—mostly civilian—amounted to at least 100,000.

Simultaneously with the Battle of Manila, U.S. forces carried out the grim work of eradicating Japanese resistance on Bataan and Corregidor, a bloody slog that was not completed until the end of February 1945. Sporadic fighting continued through the very end of the war. Although the islands were declared secure by June, holdouts continued to resist through August.

Further reading: Astor, Gerald. *Crisis in the Pacific: The Battles for the Philippine Islands by the Men Who Fought Them.* New York: Dell, 2002; Bailey, Jennifer. *Philippine Islands: The United States Army Campaigns of World War II.* Carlisle, Pa.: Army Center of Military History, 1992; Connaughton, Richard. *MacArthur and Defeat in the Philippines.* New York: Overlook, 2001; Connaughton, Richard, John Pimlott, and Duncan Anderson. *Battle for Manila.* Novato, Calif.: Presidio Press, 2002; Falk, Stanley L. *Liberation of the Philippines.* New York: Ballantine Books, 1971; Rutherford, Ward. *Fall of the Philippines.* New York: Ballantine Books, 1971; Smith, Robert Ross. *Triumph in the Philippines.* Carlisle, Pa.: Army Center of Military History, 1984.

Phony War

"Phony War" was a term coined by U.S. newspapers to describe the period of relative military inactivity that followed the Anglo-French declaration of war against Germany on September 3, 1939, after Nazi Germany's INVASION OF POLAND. British Prime Minister WINSTON CHURCHILL called it the "Twilight War," and the British man in the street often referred to it as the "Bore War." The French referred to the period as *la drôle de guerre,* and the Germans as *Sitzkrieg,* a play on "blitzkrieg."

The Phony War was essentially a period of Allied timidity and inactivity, during which Hitler completed his BLITZKRIEG campaign against Poland, which Britain and France had been obligated by treaty to defend (but did not). Only the BATTLE OF THE ATLANTIC, destined to span almost the entire war, was hot during the balance of 1939. Most historians deem the German NORWEGIAN CAMPAIGN, which began on April 9, 1940, as the end of the Phony War.

Further reading: Shachtman, Tom. *The Phony War, 1939–1940.* New York: Harper & Row, 1982; Smart, Nick. *British Strategy and Politics during the Phony War: Before the Balloon Went Up.* New York: Praeger, 2003.

pillbox

In World War II, a pillbox was a small, low fortification housing antitank weapons, machine guns, and the like. The pillbox was usually made of concrete or steel or of steel-reinforced concrete; however, improvised pillboxes might be made of nothing more than filled sandbags. Pillboxes were intended to provide cover and blast protection; they were not intended for long-term occupation—they were not miniature forts—and offered no living accommodations.

The term "pill-box" (the word was often hyphenated in World War II), first used in World War I, referred to the shape of the typical pillbox structure: circular or octagonal and always low and flat, suggesting the shape of a tin box commonly used to contain pills.

Pillboxes were employed extensively in the European theater of the war as well as by the Japanese on some Pacific islands. A network of pillboxes was rapidly constructed in England in anticipation of a German invasion.

Further reading: Sanders, Ian J. *Pillboxes—Images of an Unfought Battle*. Napa, Calif.: Lulu Press, 2005; Wills, Henry. *Pillboxes: A Study of UK Defences, 1940*. London: Leo Cooper, 1985.

Pius XI (1857–1939) *pope who made controversial prewar agreements with Benito Mussolini and Adolf Hitler*

Born Ambrogio Damiano Achille Ratti in Desio, Lombardy, Pius XI was pope from 1922 to 1939. His pontificate coincided with the rise to power of BENITO MUSSOLINI, with whom Pius XI concluded the Lateran Treaty on February 11, 1929, by which the Italian government recognized the sovereign existence of Vatican City in return for the papacy's recognition of the kingdom of Italy and its pledge that the pope and the Vatican would remain neutral in all military and diplomatic conflicts of the world. Further, by the Lateran Treaty, Pius agreed that no pope would intervene in Italian foreign affairs as a head of state—although he might voice an opinion as head of the church. Pius also concluded a concordat at this time, acknowledging the validity of church marriage in Italy, providing for compulsory religious instruction for Catholic schoolchildren, and declaring Roman Catholicism Italy's exclusive state religion. In 1933, Pius XI concluded an agreement with the Nazi German government of ADOLF HITLER, seeking to protect the rights of German Catholics.

Although some historians have viewed Pius XI's agreements with Mussolini and Hitler as improper and even craven, his intentions clearly seem to have been to preserve peace and promote tolerance. During 1933–36, Pius repeatedly protested Third Reich ethnic and racial policies, and beginning in 1938, when Mussolini also introduced policies of racial supremacy into fascist life, Pius protested.

Further reading: Anderson, Robin. *Between Two Wars: The Story of Pope Pius XI*. Quincy, Ill.: Franciscan Press, 1978; Aradi, Zsolt. *Pius XI: The Pope and the Man*. New York: Hanover House, 1958; Teeling, William. *Pope Pius XI and World Affairs*. New York: Frederick A. Stokes, 1937.

Pius XII (1876–1958) *pope during World War II*

Born Eugenio Maria Giuseppe Giovanni Pacelli in Rome, Pius XII reigned as pope from 1939 to 1958, leaving behind a heritage of controversy over his conduct of church policy during the war.

Ordained in 1899, Pacelli rose rapidly through the Church hierarchy and was an archbishop by 1917, when he was sent as a papal nuncio to Bavaria to negotiate a concordat with the Bavarian government, recognizing certain rights of the Church. From 1925 to 1929, he served as nuncio in Berlin, then returned to the Vatican, where he served as papal secretary of state until his elevation to the papacy. Clearly, Pius XII came to the throne with a background as a papal diplomat, his business having been the negotiation of concordats, which guaranteed the Church its traditional rights even in nations ruled by regimes whose policies and actions ran counter to Christian principles.

Under Pius XI, Pacelli's brother, an attorney, was instrumental in hammering out the concordat and Lateran Treaty with Benito Mussolini. Pius XII believed he could come to similar accommodations with Adolf Hitler's Germany. Indeed, Pius XII was not only a fluent German speaker, but a great admirer of the German people and German culture. He was eager to come to terms with Hitler, not just to protect the Church, but out of his admiration for Germany.

As secretary of state under Pius XI, he fashioned the 1933 concordat with Hitler's regime, which, he later said, was a compromise intended to preserve some modicum of Catholic life in what had become a hostile society. While many have seen the concordat as an unacceptable bargain with the devil, it is also true that, again as secretary of state, he was instrumental in composing the anti-Nazi encyclical *Mit brennender Sorge* ("With Burning Sorrow") issued by Pius XI in 1937. Also as secretary of state, he wrote frequent protests to the German government and openly reproached the Austrian cardinal Theodor Innitzer for his passivity during the Anschluss. It must also be observed that Pacelli voiced disapproval of the Appeasement Policy in general and of the Munich Conference and Agreement in particular. He exercised his influence in an attempt to keep Italy neutral as war came to seem increasingly inevitable.

Once war broke out, Pacelli—now Pius XII—cleaved to the neutrality pledged in several concordats. He largely refrained from protesting Nazi and fascist persecution, and—critics have pointed out—was most profoundly silent on the subject of the Holocaust. While apologists claim that Pius XII covertly aided Catholic activists who attempted to shield Jews or aided in their evacuation and further point out that any overt protest would merely have resulted in the persecution of Catholics, the most severe critics of Pope Pius XII suggest a degree of complicity in Nazi persecution and even excoriate Pius as "Hitler's pope."

Pius XII and the Catholic Church survived World War II, Pius reigning until his death in 1958. While most of the world mourned respectfully on that occasion, there was little enthusiasm associated with this pope's memory, his papacy forever clouded by compromises (for better or worse) with absolute evil.

Further reading: Blet, Pierre. *Pius XII and the Second World War: According to the Archives of the Vatican.* Mahwah, N.J.: Paulist Press, 1999; Bottum, Joseph, and David G. Dalin, eds. *The Pius War: Responses to the Critics of Pius XII.* Lanham, Md.: Lexington Books, 2004; Cornwell, John. *Hitler's Pope: The Secret History of Pius XII.* New York: Penguin, 2000; Dalin, David G. *The Myth of Hitler's Pope: How Pope Pius XII Rescued Jews from the Nazis.* Chicago: Regnery, 2005; Sanchez, José M. *Pius XII and the Holocaust: Understanding the Controversy.* Washington, D.C.: Catholic University of America Press, 2002.

Ploeşti raid

Located north of Bucharest, Romania, Ploeşti supplied perhaps 60 percent of Germany's crude oil during World War II. Additionally, the city's 40 refineries turned out about 400,000 tons of gasoline yearly. Its strategic importance was not lost on the Allies.

On June 23, 1941, Soviet bombers attacked Ploeşti. A year later, on June 12, 1942, a dozen U.S. bombers raided it. A year after that, on August 1, 1943, came the largest and most famous raid, by 178 B-24 Liberators of the Ninth U.S. Army Air Force.

By the time of the 1943 raid, Ploeşti was among the most heavily defended targets in Europe. The mission depended on the element of surprise, which was compromised because the Germans had intercepted Ninth Air Force radio traffic and had cracked the cipher used. Worse, the two principal pathfinder navigators were shot down en route to the target, and this created great confusion. Despite all the setbacks, the raid was pushed forward and destroyed 42 percent of Ploeşti's production capacity. The cost, however, was staggering: 54 bombers were lost, 41 of them shot down. Among the crews, 532 men became casualties, killed, wounded, or taken prisoner. The raid occasioned the award of no fewer than five Medals of Honor—a record for a single action.

Within weeks, Ploești had recovered and was producing at a rate even higher than that before the raid. Nevertheless, it continued to loom as a target, and in April 1944, the Italian-based Fifteenth USAAF began a full-scale campaign against it. By the end of the war, all of the Ploești facilities had been destroyed.

Further reading: Dugan, James, and Carroll Stewart. *Ploești: The Great Ground-Air Battle of 1 August 1943.* Dulles, Va.: Potomac Books, 2002; Stout, Jay A. *Fortress Ploești: The Campaign to Destroy Hitler's Oil.* Havertown, Pa.: Casemate, 2003; Ward, Ray. *Those Brave Crews: The Epic Raid to Destroy Hitler's Ploești Oil Fields.* Waverly, N.Y.: Weldon, 2003.

pocket battleship

"Pocket battleship" was the British and American term for the Panzerschiff (armored ship) class of warships built by the German navy between the wars in accordance with the restrictions on German naval building stipulated in the Treaty of Versailles.

Smaller than standard battleships, pocket battleships displaced a tonnage equivalent to that of a heavy cruiser—but they carried guns significantly larger than those carried on the heavy cruisers of other nations. *Deutschland,* launched in 1931, was the first of the class (it was renamed *Lützow* in 1939 because Adolf Hitler did not want to risk the loss of a ship bearing the name of Germany) and was followed by *Admiral Scheer* and *Admiral Graf Spee* by 1934.

The pocket battleships were marvels of innovative engineering. To enable ships of this size to carry armament suited to a battleship, the Germans developed techniques of large-scale welding rather than riveting to join hull components. The ships also refined the use of triple-gun main armament turrets and employed modern diesel engines. The 11-inch guns of the pocket battleships easily outgunned enemy cruisers and outran enemy battleships of the post–World War I era; by the beginning of World War II, however, the top speed of the class—28.5 knots—was no longer fast enough to outrun adversaries capable of matching the ships gun for gun.

The Panzerschiff-class ships were built mainly as commerce raiders, and they performed this duty early in the war. *Admiral Graf Spee,* the most famous of the pocket battleships, sank nine British merchant ships before it was scuttled to avoid capture on December 17, 1939. *Admiral Scheer* and *Deutschland* survived through the war, but after the opening months of the conflict, neither ship was exposed to the high seas.

Further reading: Chesneau, Roger. *German Pocket Battleships.* London: Chatham, 2004; Krancke, Theodore. *Pocket Battleship: The Story of Admiral Scheer.* New York: Berkley, 1958; Williamson, Gordon. *German Pocket Battleships 1939–45.* London: Osprey, 2003.

Poland

World War II began with the German invasion of Poland on September 1, 1939. Poland fell quickly and remained occupied throughout the war. In proportion to its population of 35 million at the outbreak of hostilities, it suffered the highest rate of casualties among all combatants: 6 million killed—about 17 percent of the population. In addition to deaths, many hundreds of thousands of Poles were made refugees, and it is estimated that 500,000 homes were destroyed.

The invasion of Poland was part of Adolf Hitler's aggressive expansion of Germany in search of Lebensraum, living space, for the German people. After annexing Czechoslovakia, Germany demanded the incorporation of Danzig (Gdańsk) into the Third Reich, along with a road and rail link to East Prussia. As Hitler expected, Poland rejected these incursions into Polish sovereignty. What Hitler did not expect was that the British government would guarantee Poland's independence and conclude a Mutual Assistance Pact with Poland. This prompted Hitler to denounce Germany's 1934 Non-Aggression Pact with Poland and to conclude the German-Soviet Non-Aggression Pact with Joseph Stalin on August 23, 1939. The pact made certain territorial concessions to the Soviet Union in return for Stalin's pledge that he would not ally the Soviet Union with Poland to resist Hitler's expansion there; indeed, he would participate in and benefit from the invasion. With the way prepared—and despite the British guarantee—Hitler ordered the invasion to proceed.

The BLITZKRIEG advance was a one-sided battle between a highly mobile modern army and a gallant but outnumbered and outgunned force of defenders. To make a desperate situation utterly hopeless, on September 17, the Red Army also invaded Polish territory; however, Hitler quickly altered the terms of his original agreement with Stalin, which had divided Poland along the Vistula River, putting the western portion under German control and making the eastern portion a puppet of the Soviets. Now that the invasion was an accomplished fact, Stalin was compelled to cede a large portion of Poland to Hitler, and the dividing line was placed at the Bug River.

During the period before the outbreak of war, the Polish government was ostensibly a democracy, although it was dominated by followers of Marshal Jósef Piłsudski, the strongman-cum-dictator who had governed the nation since its independence in 1918 until his death in 1935. The president in 1939, Ignacy Mokicki (1867–1946), who had been a close associate of Piłsudski, maintained an authoritarian government with a strong military air. Dissent was not tolerated, and the government moved steadily toward a monolithic one-party system. The repressive climate gave rise to various rebellious undercurrents; however, once the invasion began, Poles universally rallied to the defense of their nation. The resulting unity was short-lived. With the rapid collapse of the Polish military, recriminations against the Mokicki government came in abundance.

The government fled south to Romania on September 18, and was interned there. Marshal Edward Smigly-Rydz, commander in chief of the Polish armed forces, interned with other officials, ordered all military personnel to seek sanctuary in neutral states and then move on to France, where the Polish army would be re-formed.

With the government interned, leadership of Polish resistance to the invasion was temporarily suspended. On September 30, Mokicki officially transferred his powers to Władysław Raczkiewicz, former interior minister and marshal of the Senate who happened to be in France at the outbreak of the war. Raczkiewicz turned immediately to General WŁADYSŁAW SIKORSKI and charged him with forming a government in Paris. Sikorski had been a close associate of Piłsudski, but had fallen from grace and lived mainly in the French capital. His distance from the late regime gave him a certain credibility that enabled him to create a coalition government in exile that included representatives of the parties that had been suppressed by Mokicki. France recognized the new government instantly, and the Polish cause was thereafter identified with Sikorski.

Although Sikorski assumed a great deal of authority, he also authorized the creation of a National Council (Rada Narodowa) in December 1939, which functioned as a kind of parliament in exile. Members were not elected, however, but chosen from 20 prominent Polish politicians who happened to be in France. The council was advisory in nature and had no legislative authority. Nevertheless, thanks to its first president, the charismatic Ignacy Paderewski, a world-famous pianist and composer as well as a Polish nationalist and patriot, the council wielded considerable moral force. This did not mean that Poland enjoyed much practical influence in the conduct of the war. Sikorski understood that his exile government existed at the sufferance of France and, after the fall of France in June 1940, of Britain and (later) the United States and the Soviet Union as well. Unfortunately, most of the Polish army in France was lost in the Battle of FRANCE before it could be evacuated to England. Indeed, Sikorski fell under heavy criticism for his inept handling of the crisis attendant on the fall of France, especially his acquiescence in the deportation of Poles to the Soviet Union. President Raczkiewicz called for the dismissal of Sikorski, but the British stood by him, and Poland, weak as it was, stood as Britain's only ally against Hitler's Germany after the fall of France and until the German invasion of the SOVIET UNION on June 22, 1941, which propelled the USSR into the fight against the Germans.

The entry of the Soviets into the war against Germany motivated the Polish government in exile to sign a treaty with the USSR on July 30, providing for full military cooperation against Germany. Despite the treaty, Poland's military (except for forces that had fled to England) was under virtually total control by the Soviet Union during the rest of the war.

On July 4, 1943, Sikorski was killed in an aircraft accident. The result was a division within the ranks of the Polish government in exile that greatly diminished Poland's voice in its own postwar fate and ensured that its future would be dominated by the Soviets.

Further reading: Chodakiewicz, Marek Jan. *Between Nazis and Soviets: Occupation Politics in Poland, 1939–1947.* New York: Lexington Books, 2004; Hempel, Andrew. *Poland in World War II: An Illustrated Military History.* New York: Hippocrene Books, 2005; Kacewicz, G.V. *Great Britain, the Soviet Union and the Polish Government in Exile (1939–1945).* New York: Springer, 1899.

Poland, air force of

At the time of the German invasion of POLAND in September 1939, the Polish air force had 400 operational aircraft. In terms of numbers and types, the Polish air force was no match for the German Luftwaffe.

After the invasion, the Polish air force consisted of several squadrons formed in France and Britain. Poland operated two fighter squadrons, two reconnaissance squadrons, and one bomber squadron in France. After the Battle of FRANCE, Polish air units expanded in Britain under the command of the Royal Air Force (RAF). The RAF used Polish pilots against German air attack in the Battle of BRITAIN, in which Polish airmen compiled a superb record. Of 1,733 German aircraft downed in that campaign between July 10 and the end of October 1940, 203 were shot down by Poles. By the end of the war 15 Polish squadrons were operational under RAF command, with a total of 19,400 personnel.

Further reading: Fiedler, Arkady. *Squadron 303: The Story of the Polish Fighter Squadron with the R.A.F.* Letchworth, U.K.: Letchworth Printers, 1944; Olson, Lynne, and Stanley Cloud. *A Question of Honor: The Kosciuszko Squadron: Forgotten Heroes of World War II.* New York: Knopf, 2003.

Poland, army of

At the time of the German invasion of POLAND in September 1939, the regular Polish army consisted of 280,000 men divided into 30 infantry divisions, 11 cavalry brigades, and two mechanized brigades. Reservists accounted for another 3 million men.

The Polish army was quickly defeated, but by the end of September 1939, about 90,000 Polish troops fled Poland to escape capture and to re-form elsewhere to continue the war. About 70,000 troops crossed the southeastern border into Hungary and Romania; most of the rest made it into Lithuania and Latvia. Ultimately, during 1939–40, 43,000 troops reached France from Hungary or Romania. Here the French government formed them into Polish military units. They were based in Brittany at Coetquidan. Command headquarters was in Paris, at the Hotel Regina. Tragically for the Poles, during the Battle of FRANCE virtually all of the Polish forces in the country were dispersed among French defensive units and about half were lost in battle, piecemeal; some 20,000 were removed during the DUNKIRK EVACUATION and were taken to Scottish ports, from which they were sent to camps on the east coast of Scotland, where they were used in coastal defense.

During the Battle of NARVIK in Norway, troops of the Polish Highland (Podhale) Brigade were landed, but were soon ordered to return to Brittany because of the grave situation in France. The brigade was captured by the Germans.

On August 5, 1940, an Anglo-Polish Military Agreement was concluded to regulate Polish forces stationed in Britain as well as Polish formations outside of Britain, the most important of which were the Carpathian Brigade (which fought in the WESTERN DESERT CAMPAIGNS) and Władysław Anders's Army, which, designated as II Polish Corps, fought alongside the Eighth British Army in the ITALIAN CAMPAIGN.

Further reading: Zaloga, Steven. *Poland 1939: The Birth of Blitzkrieg.* London: Osprey, 2002; Zaloga, Steven. *The Polish Army 1939–1945.* London: Osprey, 1982.

Poland, invasion of

World War II began at 4:30 in the morning (local time) on September 1, 1939, when purportedly responding to a Polish attack on a German border radio station (the attack was fabricated by the Germans), the German Luftwaffe began bombing Polish airfields even as ground forces began to surge across the border and a German battleship "visiting" the Polish port of Danzig (Gdańsk) opened fire on Polish fortifications there.

Germany—and the Soviet Union, which cooperated in the invasion—had far greater military strength than Poland: more than 100 active and reserve divisions and a cavalry brigade (in all, some 2,500,000 active and reserve troops) versus 30 infantry divisions, 11 cavalry brigades, two mechanized brigades, and supporting units in the Polish army (about 280,000 men—with a potential semitrained but virtually unequipped reserve pool of 3,000,000). Even more significant than mere numbers was the fact that the German military was a very modern force, whereas the Polish military relied on largely obsolete or obsolescent equipment. For instance, whereas the Luftwaffe had more than 3,600 operational aircraft available, the Polish Air Force had about 1,900, all of which were outclassed by the German aircraft. On the ground, the German army was equipped with the most advanced tanks of the era, while the Poles still relied on cavalry for mobility. On the sea, the German Baltic fleet included two modern battle cruisers, three POCKET BATTLESHIPS, two heavy cruisers, six light cruisers, 22 destroyers, 43 U-boats, and two older Dreadnought battleships, whereas the Polish navy had four destroyers and five submarines.

As overwhelming as German superiority of arms was in September 1939, the German military went into the invasion with something equally important: the BLITZKRIEG, a combined-arms approach to highly mobile, very swift, very violent combat intended to overwhelm enemy defenses, then disrupt the rear echelons, especially logistics.

The overall German invasion plan was known as "Fall Weiss" (Operation White) and called for the complete destruction of the Polish army west of the Vistula-Narew-San River line with an attack via Silesia in the south and Pomerania–East Prussia from the north. Army Group South contained the bulk of the German forces deployed in the Polish campaign. Under the command of General GERD VON RUNDSTEDT, it comprised Eighth Army, Tenth Army, and Fourteenth Army. Tenth Army advanced on Warsaw while the Eighth and Fourteenth Armies protected its flanks.

Fall Weiss was an ambitious maximum-effort operation, which committed more than 60 divisions—nearly two-thirds of the entire German army—to the Polish campaign. All that was left in the west was a screening force. Success depended on a very rapid victory against Poland, so that forces could be speedily transferred to the western front. ADOLF HITLER gambled that neither France nor Britain would be able to mobilize rapidly enough to come to the defense of Poland or to menace Germany's western frontier. He was right.

Whereas the Germans planned Fall Weiss thoroughly, the Polish high command did relatively little to plan an effective defense against invasion. Plan Z called for a cordon defense concentrated in the west and assuming the timely aid of allies—namely, France and Britain. Entirely unanticipated was the complicity of the Soviet Union in the invasion. Per Plan Z, defensive units were parceled out thinly along the entire length of the Polish frontier with Germany and Slovakia.

The air attacks that opened the invasion achieved almost instant air superiority. German aircraft were quickly able to penetrate deep into Polish territory, disrupting rear areas even before the front echelons became fully engaged on the ground. The German army broke through Polish

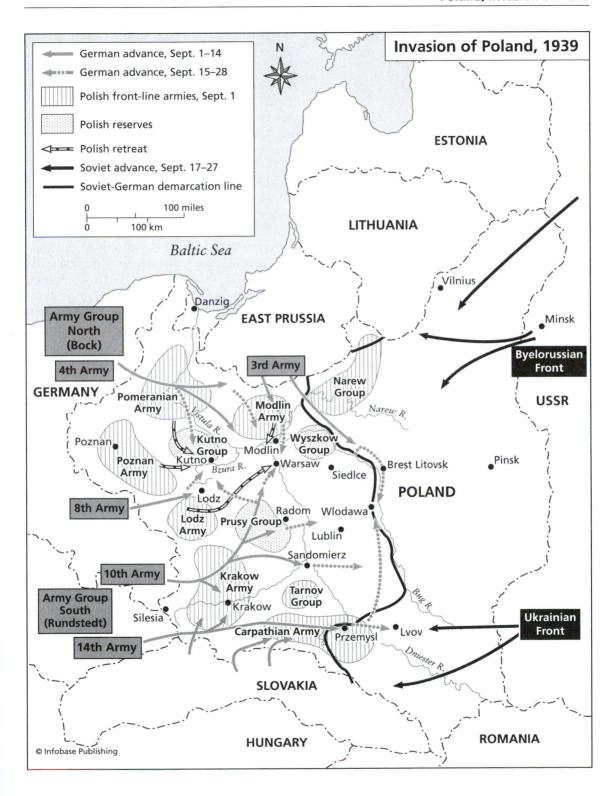

Invasion of Poland, 1939

German advance, Sept. 1–14
German advance, Sept. 15–28
Polish front-line armies, Sept. 1
Polish reserves
Polish retreat
Soviet advance, Sept. 17–27
Soviet-German demarcation line

0   100 miles
0   100 km

Baltic Sea

ESTONIA

LITHUANIA

Vilnius

Minsk

Danzig

EAST PRUSSIA

Byelorussian
Front

Army Group
North
(Bock)

USSR

4th Army

3rd Army

Narew
Group

GERMANY

Pomeranian
Army

Modlin
Army

Narew R.

Poznan

Kutno
Group

Wyszkow
Group

Pinsk

Poznan
Army

Kutno

Modlin

Vistula R.

Bzura R.

Warsaw

Brest Litovsk

POLAND

Siedlce

8th Army

Lodz

Radom

Wlodawa

Lodz
Army

Prusy Group

Lublin

Sandomierz

10th Army

Krakow
Army

Tarnov
Group

Army Group
South
(Rundstedt)

Silesia

Krakow

Bug R.

Ukrainian
Front

14th Army

Carpathian Army

Przemysl

Lvov

Dniester R.

SLOVAKIA

HUNGARY

ROMANIA

© Infobase Publishing

defenses in the initial battles, progressing with great rapidity through three phases: the battles on the frontier, the advance to Warsaw, and the mop-up of remaining pockets of resistance.

As early as September 3, the German Third and Fourth Armies in the north linked up, thereby cutting the Polish corridor at its base. The Polish Pomorze Army was destroyed, and the Modlin Army was forced to withdraw. In the meantime, advancing from Silesia, German Army Group South broke through against the Łodz and Kraków armies, so that the Polish position was virtually hopeless by September 5.

During September 6 through 10, the Third and Fourth German Armies pressed in from the north while Army Group South moved up from the south against Warsaw. The Fourth Army and the Tenth (which was part of Army Group South) were the most thoroughly equipped with motorized and panzer divisions, and it was these that carried out the full force of blitzkrieg.

Polish forces mounted only one significant counterattack when the retreating Poznan Army launched an assault on September 9 against the flank of the advancing German Eighth Army. In the ensuing three-day battle of Kutno, the Poznan Army annihilated an entire German division before air attacks and elements of the German Tenth Army ended the counterattack. Elsewhere, the blitzkrieg came so fast and so overwhelmingly that no adequate defense could be mounted. As the rear echelons fell into confusion, the entire Polish command structure disintegrated, and by the middle of September, elements of Army Groups North and South linked up near Brest-Litovsk, thereby surrounding Warsaw, along with most of the surviving Polish army. This brought on the final phase of the campaign and the collapse of Polish resistance, which was hastened by the invasion of the Red Army into eastern Poland on September 17.

Surviving Polish forces continued stubbornly to defend Warsaw and the fortress of Modlin north of the capital; however, Warsaw surrendered on September 27, and Modlin on the 28th. The very last organized resistance was mopped up by October 5.

German forces lost 8,082 killed, 27,278 wounded, and 5,029 missing, whereas Polish losses included 70,000 killed and some 130,000 wounded. About 90,000 Polish troops escaped to Hungary, Latvia, Lithuania, and Romania, and about half this number made their way west to France and Britain to fight on behalf of the Polish government in exile.

The German invasion was followed by nearly six years of brutal occupation founded on terror. *Einsatzgruppen* units of the SCHUTZSTAFFEL (SS) quickly followed the invasion troops and made mass arrests and executions of political activists and others, including Jews. All acts of resistance were crushed by means of overwhelmingly disproportionate reprisals. In some parts of Poland, notably Wartheland, the population was ordered to be "Germanized." All traces of Polish culture were eradicated. A million Poles deemed unsuitable for Germanification were expelled in the depths of the winter of 1939–40, and ethnic Germans were moved in. Many of those expelled were sentenced to slave labor, whereas many Poles who remained in areas annexed to the Third Reich were typically forced into German military service. Some 200,000 children deemed to have "Aryan" characteristics were forcibly removed to the Reich in the Lebensborn program, in which such children were adopted by the families of SS men and raised as Germans. The object was to increase rapidly the Aryan population.

Throughout Poland, privation and semistarvation became universal. The Warsaw food ration as early as 1941 was cut to a mere 669 calories per day. Jews were starved, allotted no more than 184 daily calories. Additionally, German authorities raised the minimum age for marriage in an effort to lower the birthrate, even as they stepped up the rate of deportation of men and women to the Reich for forced labor.

The German occupation authority established some 300 forced-labor and CONCENTRATION AND EXTERMINATION CAMPS throughout Poland, including (most notoriously) the AUSCHWITZ EXTERMINATION CAMP. Housed in these camps were Jews, Poles, and prisoners from all over Europe; however, it was in Poland that among the worst crimes of the HOLOCAUST were perpetrated. Among the first regulations introduced by the German occupiers was compulsory labor for Jews between 14 and 60 years of age. This was followed by the restriction and then elimination of Jewish property rights and the confiscation of Jewish property. Beginning in January 1940, Jews were increasingly confined to ghettos in principal Polish cities, where overcrowding, starvation, and disease rapidly reduced the Jewish population.

Almost immediately after the German invasion of the SOVIET UNION in June 1941, all of Poland fell under direct German rule. About 30.8 percent of Poland was absorbed into the Reich, 38.8 percent was designated as part of the General Government (essentially a Polish reservation), and 30.3 percent as part of the eastern Reichskommissariats. Before 1941 ended, Hitler decreed that the General Government would become a German region, which meant that 80 percent of the Polish population would be expelled. As for the Jews, they were condemned to extermination, mostly in death camps.

Polish resistance to the German occupation developed rapidly. In Warsaw, the leading underground organization was called Service for the Victory of Poland and was led by General Michal Tokarzewski-Karasiewicz, who maintained communications with the government in exile based in France. In January 1940, General WŁADYSŁAW SIKORSKI, head of the exile government, ordered the creation of an underground army, the Union for Armed Struggle (Związek Walki Zbrojnej, or ZWZ), which absorbed Service for the Victory of Poland. Many Polish officers were involved in the ZWZ, which mounted acts of sabotage against the Germans. ZWZ operatives also played a crucial role in gathering intelligence for the Western allies. The underground also created a Committee for Aid to Jews, and it was active in preserving the Polish educational and cultural activities the Germans had sought to eradicate. On February 14, 1942, the ZWZ became the Armia Krajowa, the POLISH HOME ARMY, its activities increasingly coordinated by the Polish government in exile in cooperation with British SPECIAL OPERATIONS EXECUTIVE.

See also POLAND; WARSAW GHETTO UPRISING; WARSAW RISING.

Further reading: Chodakiewicz, Marek Jan. *Between Nazis and Soviets: Occupation Politics in Poland, 1939–1947.* New York: Lexington Books, 2004; Hempel, Andrew. *Poland in World War II: An Illustrated Military History.* New York: Hippocrene Books, 2005; Kacewicz, G.V. *Great Britain, the Soviet Union and the Polish Government in Exile (1939–1945).* New York: Springer, 1899; Matusak, Piotr. *Polish Resistance Movement, 1939–1945.* Warsaw: Presspol, 1985.

Poland, navy of

At the outbreak of World War II, the Polish navy, commanded by Rear Admiral Józef Swirski, consisted of four modern destroyers, five modern submarines, and 23 naval aircraft in addition to a diminutive coastal defense force.

During the German invasion of POLAND, naval ships and personnel (as well as ships and personnel of the Polish merchant marine) were highly successful in avoiding capture by the Germans. Many ships, pursuant to agreements with the British, actually left port before the outbreak of war and sailed for Britain.

By the Anglo-Polish Naval Accord, the escaped Polish warships and personnel agreed to submit to British admiralty control. Most Polish warships performed convoy escort duties during the war or patrolled the British coastline, although the Polish destroyer *Piorun* participated in the sinking of the BISMARCK in May 1941.

After the Battle of FRANCE, the Polish navy and merchant marine were merged under British admiralty control. The service actually grew during the war through recruitment. Some 1,500 Polish naval personnel made their way to Britain at the outbreak of the war. By 1945, the service had expanded to some 4,000.

Further reading: Peszke, Michael Alfred. *The Polish Navy in the Second World War: A Historical Sketch.* London: Polish Naval Association, 1989.

Polish Home Army

General WŁADYSŁAW SIKORSKI, commander of the Polish army in exile, assumed command of the Związek Walki Zbrojnej (ZWZ), the "Union for Armed Struggle," the Polish underground resistance network that had been created from Służba Zwycięstwu Polski (SZP), "Service for Poland's Victory," which had come into being immediately after the collapse of the Polish army during the German invasion of POLAND. On February 14, 1942, Sikorski changed the name of the ZWZ to Armia Krajowa (AK), or "Home Army," under the leadership of its commander in chief, General Tadeusz Komorowski. During World War II it was heavily involved in the resistance to German occupation.

During 1942–43, various resistance groups were unified under the Home Army, which by 1943 claimed 300,000 members or more. The Home Army planned for an uprising and set up secret training schools as well as secret factories for the manufacture of weapons and ammunition. Working in conjunction with Britain's SPECIAL OPERATIONS EXECUTIVE, the Home Army operated an extensive intelligence network that reported on German troop and supply movements. Of especially great significance was intelligence concerning German rocket research at PEENEMÜNDE (V-1 AND V-2 BASE), which led to successful air raids on the site. The Home Army also planned and executed various sabotage operations and, by the end of 1942, guerrilla operations, which increased in scope as the Soviet Red Army turned the tide against the Germans on the eastern front. This phase of Home Army operations was dubbed Operation Tempest and involved units as large as battalion and regimental size.

By the summer of 1944, the Soviet Union began operations preparatory to the occupation of Poland. The Red Army now turned against the Home Army and set about dismantling it. When at the end of July 1944, the arrival of Soviet troops in Warsaw seemed imminent, the Home Army decided to liberate the capital before the Red Army reached the city. The resulting WARSAW RISING, which began on August 1, ended in defeat on October 2, 1944, with the surrender of some 20,000 Home Army soldiers. The Red Army had deliberately refused to come to the aid of the Home Army. Surviving Home Army units continued fighting elsewhere in Poland until January 1945, when Soviet armies occupied most of the country. The order to disband the Home Army came from the government in exile on January 19, 1945.

Further reading: Davies, Norman. *Rising '44: The Battle for Warsaw.* New York: Viking, 2004; Maslany, Z. W. *The Lonely Soldier: The Memoirs of a Polish Partisan.* London: Caliban Books, 1989; Mayevski, Florian, with Spencer Bright. *Fire Without Smoke: Memoirs of a Polish Partisan.* Portland, Ore.: Vallentine-Mitchell, 2003.

Portal, Charles (1893–1971) *British air marshal and Air Staff chief*

Born in Chichester, Sussex, Portal was educated at Winchester School and at Christ Church College, Oxford. He joined the Royal Engineers during World War I and was commissioned in the Royal Flying Corps in 1915. Portal rapidly distinguished himself as a pursuit pilot, earning the Distinguished Service Order and Bar as well as the Military Cross.

He was variously posted with the Royal Air Force (RAF) between the wars, and in 1940 briefly served as air officer commander in chief, Bomber Command, before being elevated to chief of the Air Staff, the most senior RAF post, which he held throughout the war. As the leader of RAF policy and operations, Portal was present at all of the major Allied conferences as a member of the Chiefs of Staffs Committee.

After the war, from 1946 to 1951, Portal directed the British atomic research facilities at Harwell. In 1945, he was created a baron, and then a viscount the following year.

Further reading: Philpott, Ian M. *The Royal Air Force History.* London: Pen and Sword Books, 2006; Terraine, John. *The Right of the Line: The Royal Air Force in the European War 1939–1945.* London: Wordsworth Editions, 1998.

Portugal

A traditional ally of Great Britain, Portugal remained neutral throughout World War II. Its wartime president, General Antonio Carmona, appointed Antonio Salazar as prime minister. Both men were rightists who admired ADOLF HITLER and the Nazis; however, the Portuguese working class tended to favor the Allies.

In March 1939, Portugal and Spain signed a Treaty of Friendship and Non-Aggression (Pacto Iberico); nevertheless, despite Salazar's right-wing orientation, he did not approve of the Nazis and was instrumental in dissuading Spain's FRANCISCO FRANCO from joining the Axis. At the outbreak of the war on September 1, 1939, both Portugal and Spain declared their neutrality. Whereas Spain frequently aided Germany, Portugal maintained very strict neutrality—until October 1943, when it permitted the Allies to establish air bases in the Azores and therefore became a cobelligerent of the Allies. Even this, however, was tinged with ambivalence. After Hitler's suicide, Salazar ordered flags to be flown at half-staff as a sign of respect.

Portugal's Atlantic possessions—the Azores, Cape Verde Islands, and Madeira—were strategically situated, and Portugal was also a key producer of tungsten, an important strategic metal. As a neutral, Portugal traded with the Allies as well as the Axis, and only after intense pressure was applied in June 1944 did Salazar agree to end exports of tungsten to Germany.

Lisbon, the Portuguese capital, was an international city in World War II, which served as the distribution port for International Red Cross Committee relief supplies to prisoner-of-war and internment camps and also as a center of espionage for both the Allies and the Axis.

Further reading: Anderson, James M. *The History of Portugal.* Westport, Conn.: Greenwood Press, 2000; Lewis, Paul H. *Latin Fascist Elites: The Mussolini, Franco, and Salazar Regimes.* New York: Praeger, 2002; Costa Pinto, Antonio. *Salazar's Dictatorship and European Fascism.* Boulder, Colo.: East European Monographs, 1996.

Potsdam Conference

This was the last of the major Allied conferences of World War II. Held from July 17 to August 2, 1945, in the Berlin suburb of Potsdam, its principal participants were President HARRY S. TRUMAN, Soviet premier JOSEPH STALIN, and (at the beginning of the conference) British prime minister WINSTON CHURCHILL, whose place was later taken by CLEMENT ATTLEE, when he replaced Churchill as prime minister.

The major subjects of the conference were the European peace settlements; the urgently pressing issue of administering a defeated and substantially destroyed Germany; the determination of Polish boundaries; the terms of the occupation of Austria; the Soviet role in Eastern Europe; reparations; and, not least, the continued prosecution of the war against Japan.

The conference produced the Potsdam Declaration. With regard to Germany, the declaration asserted the Allies' intention to give the "German people . . . the opportunity to prepare for the eventual reconstruction of their life on a democratic and peaceful basis." Four zones of occupation were demarcated in Germany, each to be administered by military governments under the commanders in chief of the U.S., British, Soviet, and French armies of occupation. Austria was also divided into four zones of occupation, as were the capital cities of Berlin and Vienna. Coordination among the occupation zones was to be handled by an Allied Control Council. The conference agreed that occupation policy would embody the principles stated in the YALTA AGREEMENT, including demilitarization, denazification, democratization, decentralization, and deindustrialization.

Regarding the issue of reparations, each Allied power was to recover reparations from its own zone of occupation, with the proviso that the Soviet Union was entitled to recover 10 to 15 percent of the industrial equipment in the western zones of Germany in exchange for agricultural produce and other natural products from its zone.

With regard to the settlement of the Polish border, this was fixed at the Oder and Neisse Rivers in the west, and the country absorbed a portion of what had been East Prussia. This settlement required relocating millions of Germans from these areas.

The settlement of the Soviet role in Eastern Europe was highly contentious, as Stalin refused to permit Western intervention in those Eastern governments already controlled by communists.

At Potsdam President Truman revealed to Stalin the existence of the atomic bomb and that he intended to use it against Japan. Stalin hardly reacted to this revelation—because (as it turned out) his espionage network had already informed him of the existence of the bomb. However, because of the weapon, the conferees were emboldened to issue an ultimatum to Japan on July 26 demanding unconditional surrender. After Japan rejected the ultimatum the United States dropped atomic bombs on HIROSHIMA and NAGASAKI.

Further reading: Feis, Herbert. *Between War and Peace: The Potsdam Conference.* Princeton, N.J.: Princeton University Press, 1960; Mee, Charles L. *Meeting at Potsdam.* New York: M. Evans, 1975; Noble, G. Bernard, ed. *Foreign Relations of the United States 1945: Conference of Berlin (Potsdam), 1945.* Washington, D.C.: U.S. Department of State, 1960.

prisoners of war

All of the major combatants in World War II were parties to the Hague Conventions of 1899 and 1907, and all but two—Japan (signed but did not ratify) and the Soviet Union (neither signed nor ratified)—were parties to the GENEVA CONVENTIONS. The Hague documents laid down the principle that prisoners of war were to be treated humanely. The subsequent Geneva Conventions specified standards of humane treatment, including speedy removal of POWs from the combat zone, adequate medical care for the wounded, and the provision of shelter and food equal to that received by garrison troops of the captor's side. The conventions also governed the rules of interrogation, specifying that prisoners had the right to refuse to give any information except for their name, rank, and service number. Prisoners were to be permitted to practice their religion and to cor-

respond with family and friends. Attempted escape was to be punished by nothing more severe than a month's solitary confinement. The Geneva Conventions provided for inspection of permanent POW camps by the Committee of the International Red Cross.

Even with the best of intentions, it would have been difficult if not impossible for some combatants to observe the Hague and Geneva rules. The number of prisoners was often so great that POW facilities were overwhelmed. At the beginning of the war, for example, the Germans very quickly acquired some 2 million Polish and French prisoners. In any event, intentions were not always of the best, and poor treatment, including deliberate abuse, was not uncommon. On the eastern front of the European war, the WAFFEN SS was notorious for taking no prisoners; those who surrendered were shot. For the most part, the regular German army (Wehrmacht) and the German air force (Luftwaffe) treated British and American prisoners decently, but were deliberately abusive to Red Army prisoners, of whom only one in six survived incarceration. Soviet prisoners were given little in the way of food and shelter and were often shot after

This Japanese submarine crew member is on his way to a POW camp. *(National Archives and Records Administration)*

U.S. POWs celebrate the Fourth of July—in captivity. *(National Archives and Records Administration)*

interrogation. Disease, especially typhus and dysentery, were common causes of death.

Of all combatants, the Japanese were the most notorious for ill treatment of prisoners. The Japanese warrior code (*bushido*) held that surrender was dishonorable and that a dishonored soldier did not deserve to be treated honorably. Neglect, beatings, and torture were the rule in Japanese prisoner of war camps. The Allied death rate in Japanese prison camps was 27 percent versus 4 percent for Allies held by the Germans or Italians.

Further reading: Bird, Tom. *American POWs of World War II: Forgotten Men Tell Their Stories.* New York: Praeger, 1992; Dwas, Gavan. *Prisoners of the Japanese: POWS of World War II in the Pacific.* New York: William Morrow, 1994; Strau, Ulrich. *The Anguish of Surrender: Japanese POWs of World War II.* Bellingham: University of Washington Press, 2005; Westheimer, David. *Sitting It Out: A World War II POW Memoir.* Houston, Tex.: Rice University Press, 1992.

propaganda

Propaganda—which may be broadly defined as the dissemination of ideas and points of view that promote one's cause or damage that of one's enemies—was widely employed by virtually all combatants in World War II. Propaganda was directed against enemies and also used to shape the sentiment of a combatant nation's own population, as well as the population of its allies.

Most authorities distinguish two types of propaganda. "White propaganda" is based on fact, which is portrayed to best advantage to report and enhance one side's victories and the other side's defeats. "Black propaganda" is essentially fabrication used to undermine enemy morale or in some other way to hamper enemy military operations.

During World War II, mass media—including magazines, newspapers, radio, and movies—were exploited as the vehicles for disseminating propaganda. Internally, commercial radio networks, newspapers, and movie studios often produced propaganda for domestic consumption, whereas government-controlled media outlets—most notably the British Broadcasting Company (BBC) in Britain and the Voice of America (VOA) in the United States—transmitted propaganda to enemy nations with the purpose of countering enemy "lies," undermining the morale of the civilian population, and in some cases broadcasting instructions to members of RESISTANCE MOVEMENTS.

ALLIED PROPAGANDA AGENCIES AND PROGRAMS

Great Britain

British Broadcasting Corporation (BBC). This government-controlled radio broadcasting entity broadcast war information to Europeans living under Nazi German occupation. The BBC sought to counter Nazi propaganda, and millions relied on it (listening surreptitiously and often at great risk) for accurate news—as well as for entertainment. During the NORMANDY LANDING (D-DAY), the BBC broadcast coded instructions to Resistance operatives in France to coordinate their activities with the needs of the invasion force.

Department of Propaganda to Enemy Countries. The straightforward name of this agency accurately described its mission, which was to disseminate propaganda to Europeans in German-occupied countries. Radio broadcast and airborne leaflet drops were used.

Ministry of Information (MOI). MOI had responsibility for the production and dissemination of domestic propaganda. Led by Duff Cooper and Brendan Bracken, MOI was essentially an educational effort that sought to explain and keep uppermost in the public mind the reasons "why we fight." A large part of MOI's task was to justify the many sacrifices the civilian population was required to make. MOI operated through all media, including popular films.

United States

Bureau of Motion Pictures (BMP). The BMP advised commercial Hollywood film studios on how they should portray the war to promote the war effort. The agency had no enforcement authority.

Hollywood. Long the world capital of movie-making, Hollywood eagerly contributed to the war effort by making films that portrayed the war—both at the front lines and on the home front—in a favorable light.

Office of War Information (OWI). This was the central U.S. agency responsible for propaganda, both for domestic distribution and for distribution abroad. Modes of dissemination ranged from aerial leaflets to radio broadcast to propaganda films.

Psychological Warfare Division (PWD). Operating under the OWI, the PWD focused on propaganda directed at the populations of Germany and Japan.

Voice of America (VOA). Another OWI agency, the VOA broadcasted to occupied Europe in an effort to counter Nazi propaganda and provide reliable war information.

AXIS PROPAGANDA AGENCIES AND PROGRAMS

Germany

General entertainment. Nazi Germany developed propaganda to a very high state, so that it pervaded all aspects of German popular culture beginning in the 1930s and extending throughout the war years. The evil genius behind the German propaganda effort was JOSEPH GOEBBELS, the Third Reich's official propaganda minister and a member of ADOLF HITLER's innermost circle.

Radio broadcast and film production were the leading media, which Goebbels strictly controlled. LENI RIEFENSTAHL was preeminent among German filmmakers in creating effective propaganda films for popular consumption. Goebbels was also a master at staging live spectacles, including massive torchlight parades and rallies, and at directing the creation of graphically powerful posters and symbols.

German-American Bund. Various pro-Nazi organizations came into existence in Britain, France, the United States, and elsewhere during the years leading up to the war. The German-American Bund was never large (it may have had 8,000 members during its 1930s peak), but it staged numerous highly visible rallies before the war. U.S. authorities outlawed and disbanded the organization during the war.

HITLER YOUTH. This organization is covered in a separate entry.

Ministry of Public Enlightenment and Propaganda. Headed by Goebbels, this agency controlled all news and public information. Through the ministry, Goebbels did not so much manipulate facts as he created them to suit the purposes of the Reich's war effort. It was standard practice for the ministry to present even the worst military defeats as victories, and when the war had clearly become a lost cause, Goebbels disseminated rumors of "wonder weapons," about to be introduced, which would instantly reverse the course of defeat.

Ministry of Science, Education, and Popular Culture. This agency ensured that propaganda was thoroughly integrated into every aspect of German life. It controlled the educational system of the nation, introducing Nazi ideology (especially anti-Semitism and Aryan racial theory) into virtually every subject. The ministry also oversaw civilian military training.

Reich Chamber of Culture. Another of Goebbels's agencies, the chamber oversaw virtually all cultural activity in the Reich, including the fine arts, music, theater, literature, the press, radio, and film. All creative artists in these fields had to register with the chamber, the approval of which was required before any work could be published or exhibited. Works by Jews were banned, as was, generally, all art classified as "modern," largely because Hitler considered it degenerate.

Reich Press Law. Promulgated on October 4, 1933, this law was the chief vehicle by which the German press was subordinated to the will of the government. Newspaper editors met daily with Goebbels or his designated lieutenants to receive their marching orders, all aimed at promoting the Nazi party line.

Lord Haw-Haw. William Joyce was a pro-Nazi British subject who collaborated with the enemy by broadcasting anti-Allied propaganda aimed especially at undermining the morale of Allied troops. British listeners christened him Lord Haw-Haw, because of his aristocratic accent and as an expression of the skepticism with which they received everything he said. Born in 1906, Joyce was hanged as a traitor by the British on January 3, 1946.

Italy

BENITO MUSSOLINI. A journalist by trade, the dictator of Italy was a master at the creation and dissemination of propaganda and took a personal hand in crafting the ongoing image of fascist Italy. As Hitler often evoked a mythic Aryan past as the foundation on which the present glories of the Third Reich were founded, so Mussolini built upon the bygone glories of the ancient Roman Empire to enhance the prestige of Fascist Italy.

Ministry of Popular Culture. Created in 1937, the ministry ensured that all entertainment produced in Italy promoted fascist ideals.

Undersecretariat for Press and Propaganda. Established in 1933, this ministry controlled the reporting of news in Italy.

Italian educational system. Before he became a politician, Mussolini had been a journalist; before this, he was a schoolteacher. After he became dictator of Italy, he personally oversaw the redesign of the Italian educational system, including the parochial system run by the Catholic Church, so that its curriculum would embody fascist doctrine and ideals.

Japan

Greater East Asia Co-Prosperity Sphere. Perhaps the boldest stroke of Japanese propaganda was the invention of the Greater East Asia Co-Prosperity Sphere, the concept that the nations of Asia and the southwestern Pacific were united by a common interest both racially and economically. In reality, the concept was a fiction created to justify Japanese conquest and subjugation of the region.

Militarist propaganda. Beginning in the 1920s and intensifying through the 1930s, the Japanese government was increasingly controlled by militarists who sought to indoctrinate the entire country with military values based, ultimately, in myths of a Japanese warrior tradition, which included *bushido,* the warrior code of the Samurai that exalted conquest and self-sacrifice.

Tonarigumi. In addition to large-scale propaganda efforts controlled through the central government and including extensive press censorship, the Japanese government encouraged the creation of neighborhood groups, or *tonarigumi,* consisting of 10 to a dozen households united behind the war effort and dedicated to domestic surveillance. Each of these cells was pledged to live by seven virtues—early rising, thankfulness for what you have (however little), cooperation with the government in everything, public service, punctuality, frugality, and the development of physical and spiritual strength—and to be vigilant against any evidence of disloyalty, noncooperation, or defeatism. It was on this micro level that the Japanese central government made itself most thoroughly felt.

Tokyo Rose. Born in Los Angeles in 1916, Iva Toguri was in Japan visiting relatives when the United States entered World War II. As "Tokyo Rose," she made broadcasts beamed at American G.I.s intended to undermine their morale. Tokyo Rose broadcast classic "black propaganda," ranging from false news of catastrophic American defeats to stories about the mass infidelity of girlfriends and wives while their "soldier boys" were away. Her program featured popular American music and was widely listened to as entertainment. In reality, several English-speaking women assumed the identity of Tokyo Rose to make propaganda broadcasts, but Toguri was the only U.S. citizen to do so. After the war, she claimed that she had been forced to make the broadcasts. Nevertheless, she was convicted of undermining the morale of American troops and sentenced to 10 years imprisonment and a $10,000 fine. After her release, she labored for vindication and to prove her innocence. President Gerald R. Ford pardoned her in 1977.

Further reading: Fyne, Robert. *The Hollywood Propaganda of World War II.* Lanham, Md.: Scarecrow Press, 1994; Horten, Gerd. *Radio Goes to War: The Cultural Politics of Propaganda during World War II.* Berkeley: University of California Press, 2002; Kallis, Aristotle A. *Nazi Propaganda and World War II.* London and New York: Palgrave Macmillan, 2006; Koppes, Clayton R., and Gregory D. Black. *Hollywood Goes to War: How Politics, Profits, and Propaganda Shaped World War II Movies.* Berkeley: University of California Press, 1990; Rhodes, Anthony. *Propaganda: The Art of Persuasion World War II.* London: Book Sales, 1988.

PT boats

The PT (Patrol Torpedo) boat was a small, fast, plywood-hulled craft used by the U.S. Navy against larger surface ships. The U.S. Navy PTs were modeled after the British Motor Torpedo Boats and were manufactured mainly by Elco (Electric

PT 333 under way off New York, August 20, 1943
(National Archives and Records Administration)

Launch Company) of Athens, New York. Elco built 399 80-foot PT boats during the war.

Prior to U.S. entry into the war, Elco built 70-foot PT Boats that were found to be too light for the open sea. Elco then built 24 77-foot boats for the navy. After a design competition in 1944 (nicknamed "The Plywood Derby"), the navy let more contracts for the 77-foot Elco boats, but also commissioned the Higgins company to build a number of its 76-foot designs and the Huckins firm to build some 72-foot boats. Fairly early in the war, an Elco 80-foot design and the Higgins 78-foot design became the standard U.S. Navy PT boats.

The Elco boats were plywood-hulled, 80 feet long with a beam of 20 feet 8 inches. They were powered by three 12-cylinder gasoline engines, which were built by Packard, based on the company's 3A-2500 V-12 liquid-cooled aircraft engine. PT boats cruised at a brisk 23 knots and had a top speed of 41+ knots. At top speed, their endurance was severely limited to about six hours of sailing time. The boats were crewed by three officers and 12 to 14 sailors and displaced 56 tons fully loaded.

Elco boats were variously armed. Early models carried a single 20 mm Oerlikon cannon, four M-2 .50-caliber machine guns or four .30-caliber Lewis guns, and two or four 21-inch torpedo tubes launching Mark 8 torpedoes. Some also carried two or four Mark 6 depth charges in roll-off racks. Later in the war, boats mounted a 40 mm Bofors gun aft and four 22.5-inch Mark 13 torpedo launching racks, two along each side. A few boats were equipped with rocket launchers capable of launching 16 rockets. The PTs operated chiefly at night and relied heavily on radar for navigation and target detection.

The New Orleans–based Higgins company produced 199 78-foot boats, many of which were sent to the Soviet Union and Great Britain. Those used by the U.S. Navy were employed in the north Pacific and in the Mediterranean, whereas the Elco boats were most extensively used in the south and central Pacific.

The primary mission of PT boats was to attack larger surface ships, but they were also used to lay mines and generate smoke screens for convoys. PTs often did rescue patrol, recovering downed aviators, and they carried out intelligence and raider operations. It was a PT boat that evacuated DOUGLAS MACARTHUR and his family from the Philippines in 1942, but certainly the most famous PT boat of the war was PT-109, commanded by Lieutenant (junior grade) John F. Kennedy, who performed heroically after his boat was run down and cut in two by the Japanese destroyer *Amagiri* on August 2, 1943, in the Solomon Islands. Kennedy led the survivors to deserted Plum Pudding Island, from which they were later rescued, and received the Navy and Marine Corps Medal. The story of this exploit helped win Kennedy victory in his first congressional campaign and was also publicized during his successful campaign for the White House in 1960.

Further reading: Bulkley, Robert J., Jr. *At Close Quarters: PT Boats in the United States Navy.* Washington: Naval Historical Division, 1962; Chun, Victor. *American PT Boats in World War II: A Pictorial History.* Atglen, Pa.: Schiffer, 1997; Johnson, Frank D. *United States PT Boats of World War II in Action.* Poole, U.K.: Blandford Press, 1980; Nelson, Curtis L. *Hunters in the Shallows: A History of the PT Boat.* Washington: Brassey's, 1998.

Puller, Lewis B. "Chesty" (1898–1972)
one of the great U.S. Marine heroes of World War II

Born in West Point, Virginia, Puller enlisted in the Marine Corps during World War I in August 1918. He earned a reserve commission as second lieutenant in 1919, but was almost immediately inactivated when the corps was reduced in size during the rush to demobilize following the Armistice. Undaunted, Puller reenlisted as a noncommissioned officer. He served in Haiti with the ambiguous rank of USMC sergeant but as *captain* of the Haitian Gendarmerie. Puller served for five years in the turbulent island nation.

In 1924, Puller returned to the United States and received an officer's commission. After service at Norfolk and Quantico (both in Virginia), he took flight training at Pensacola Naval Air Station

"Chesty" Puller, USMC *(U.S. Marine Corps)*

in 1926, then shipped out to Nicaragua in 1928 as an instructor assigned to train the U.S.-supported Nicaraguan National Guard in its fight against rebels led by Augusto Sandino. During his tour in Nicaragua, Puller was awarded the Navy Cross.

After returning to the United States in 1931, Puller attended a company officers' course, then returned to Nicaragua to resume work with the National Guard. During this second tour, he received a second Navy Cross.

After leaving Nicaragua, Puller was assigned to the Marine Corps legation detachment (embassy guard) in Peking (Beijing) in 1933, then served a stint at sea. In 1936, he became an instructor at the basic school in Philadelphia, returned to sea duty in 1939, and was attached to the 4th Marines in 1940, soon becoming commanding officer of this unit.

At the outbreak of World War II, Puller was assigned command of 1st Battalion, 7th Marines, which he led to Samoa and then in the BATTLE OF

GUADALCANAL. Seriously wounded in this engagement, he refused evacuation until the defense of Henderson Field was complete. For this, he was awarded his third Navy Cross.

While convalescing from his wounds, Puller toured U.S. posts, then rejoined the 7th Marines as executive officer of the division. He participated in the landings at Cape Gloucester and led a 1,000-man patrol on New Britain Island, for which he earned a fourth Navy Cross. He commanded a regiment in the BATTLE OF PELELIU, sustaining 50 percent casualties.

Following World War II, Puller commanded the training regiment at Camp Lejeune, then was assigned as director of the 8th Reserve District. In 1950, he once again assumed command of the 1st Marines and led this regiment in the Inchon landing during the Korean War. During action in Korea, he was awarded a fifth Navy Cross and in January 1951 was promoted to brigadier general and assigned as assistant division commander.

Returned to the United States, Puller was given command of the 3d Brigade and became assistant commander after the unit was upgraded to a division. Assigned to direct marine training at Coronado, California, Puller was promoted to major general in 1953 and was assigned to command the 2d Division, headquartered at Camp Lejeune. He retired on November 1, 1955, with the rank of lieutenant general and is celebrated as one of history's greatest marines.

Further reading: Hoffman, Jon T. *Chesty: The Story of Lieutenant General Lewis B. Puller, Marine Corps.* New York: Random House, 2001.

PURPLE (Japanese diplomatic cipher)

"PURPLE" was the code name U.S. cryptanalysts assigned to the Japanese diplomatic cipher, which was used on messages encrypted on a cipher machine known as Alphabetical Typewriter 97. This machine consisted of two typewriter keyboards connected by circuits, a plugboard, and switches. The machine encrypted messages through stepping switches (similar to telephone stepping switches). When the operator pressed a plain-text letter on one keyboard, an electric current passed through the plugboard, which provided letter substitutions that served as the code's key for the day. From the plugboard, the current passed through the stepping switches, which continually changed the substitution for each plain-text letter pressed. A combination of four stepping switches was used, which ultimately passed the current to the second typewriter keyboard, depressing a key, which printed out the substituted letter. Because of the multiplicity of stepping switches, the encryption was quite deep and very difficult to decipher. However, the Japanese diplomatic departments often repeated certain formulaic words and phrases, which gave U.S. cryptanalysts clues to the cipher. Moreover, cipher keys, although they were changed every 10 days, were changed in a predictable manner. The PURPLE cipher was broken by September 25, 1940, and the flow of U.S. decrypts of PURPLE messages continued through the end of the war. The Japanese never discovered that their diplomatic cipher had been compromised.

See also ENIGMA CIPHER AND MACHINE; MAGIC (JAPANESE CODE); ORANGE (JAPANESE CODE); and ULTRA.

Further reading: Lewin, Ronald. *The American Magic: Codes, Ciphers, and the Defeat of Japan.* New York: Penguin, 1983.

pursuit aircraft *See* FIGHTER AIRCRAFT.

Pyle, Ernie (1900–1945) *most famous of U.S. war correspondents*

Ernest Taylor Pyle was born near Dana, Indiana, and enrolled at Indiana University to study journalism. He left without a degree when he was hired by a small-town newspaper. After working for various papers, he found his niche as a columnist-at-large for the Scripps-Howard newspaper chain, writing stories based on his daily encounters and experiences, which were syndicated in some 200 newspapers.

Pyle truly came into his own as a journalist during World War II, when he served as a correspondent covering campaigns in North Africa,

Ernie Pyle in a 1945 news clipping, which appeared shortly after his death *(Author's collection)*

Sicily, Italy, and France. He became famous for his upfront, uncompromising portraits of the day-to-day life of the ordinary GI, the American infantry rifleman. Pyle was the voice of the "dogface" soldier, sharing his dangers, hardships, terror, loneliness, boredom, and, ultimately, indomitable spirit. There was never a trace of propaganda or cant about Pyle's reporting, which earned him a Pulitzer Prize in 1944, among other awards.

Pyle's enormously popular columns were collected during World War II in *Pyle in England* (1941), *Here Is Your War: The Story of G.I. Joe* (1943), and *Brave Men* (1944). Hollywood depicted Pyle's coverage of the Italian campaign in a 1945 film, *G.I. Joe* (1945).

After the end of the European war, Ernie Pyle covered the Battle of Iwo Jima and the Okinawa Campaign. He was killed on April 18, 1945, on the island of Ie Shima by Japanese machine-gun fire.

Further reading: Miller, Lee Graham. *The Story of Ernie Pyle.* New York, Viking Press, 1950; Pyle, Ernie. *Brave Men.* New York: H. Holt, 1945; Pyle, Ernie. *Here Is Your War: The Story of G. I. Joe.* New York, H. Holt, 1943; Pyle, Ernie. *Last Chapter.* New York: H. Holt, 1946.

Q

Q-ship

Q-ships were armed U.S. merchant vessels disguised as unarmed ships and intended to lure German U-boats into surfacing for an attack. Once surfaced, the Q-ship would open fire with its hidden guns.

Q-ships were debuted in World War I and had a degree of success. They were deployed again during World War II in 1942, but did not sink any U-boats. One Q-ship was torpedoed and sunk with the loss of 141 crew members. British Q-ships were called decoy ships. The Royal Navy deployed eight in 1939–40 without successfully attacking any enemy vessel. Two were hit by torpedoes. The decoy ships were withdrawn from service in December 1940.

Further reading: Beyer, Kenneth M. *Q-Ships Versus U-Boats: America's Secret Project.* Annapolis, Md.: Naval Institute Press, 1999.

Quisling, Vidkun (1887–1945) *Nazi collaborator who aided the German invasion of Norway in 1940*

Born on July 18, 1887, in Fryesdal, Norway, Vidkun Quisling served as an officer in the Norwegian military, passing the War College examination in 1911 and gaining promotion to assistant to the general staff in 1916. Commissioned a captain in 1917, Quisling served as military attaché in Petro-grad (modern St. Petersburg), Russia, and later, from 1918 to 1921, in Helsinki, Finland.

In 1931, Quisling was promoted to major of field artillery and also served on many international committees in the League of Nations. The same year in which he advanced in military rank, he became minister of defense in the Karlstad cabinet. An arch-conservative, he was virulently anticommunist and believed that the labor wing in Norway was under the influence of the Bolsheviks and was plotting revolution. This extreme position put him at odds with the rest of the cabinet. Finally disgusted with what he deemed his colleagues' liberalism, Quisling founded his own political party, the National Union Party—essentially the Norwegian Nazis—on the platform of

Vidkun Quisling *(Mailhuagen Museum, Oslo)*

suppressing "revolutionary" parties and "freeing" labor from union control.

The National Union Party was badly defeated in the 1933 elections, garnering only 2 percent of the vote. In the next two elections, the party's power base was successively halved, so that by 1939 it was virtually extinct.

Publicly rebuked, Quisling became an associate of Alfred Rosenberg, a leading German ideologue of National Socialism. Through this connection he attracted the attention of Adolf Hitler, who was especially interested in the defenses of Oslo Fjord and the inner harbor areas of the capital city. On the night of April 5, 1940, Quisling was in Berlin at the Reich Chancellery; three days later, German war ships, led by U-boat wolfpacks, steamed into Oslo and, armed with the necessary intelligence concerning coastal and harbor defenses, easily penetrated them and quickly overran Norway.

With neither the consent nor official support of the Nazis, Quisling proclaimed himself premier of Norway simply by announcing it over the air. The Nazis were engaged in trying to compel the abdication of King Haakon, who also refused to recognize Quisling. Reasoning that if they forced Quisling on Norway, the people would likely rally to the side of their king in opposition to the Nazis, the Germans continued to withhold support from Quisling, who was at last compelled to resign after a week in office. Nevertheless, the invaders put him in charge of Norwegian demobilization, and he traveled to Berlin. After his return to Norway on August 20, 1940, he made another attempt to build a following. He enjoyed no success until the Norwegian parliament refused to bow to German demands to set up a puppet government. When Nazi patience wore sufficiently thin, Hitler simply installed Quisling as premier and outlawed all political parties except for his National Union Party.

Propped up by Germany, Quisling remained in office throughout the war. After the German surrender and withdrawal from Norway, Quisling was arrested on May 9, 1945. Convicted of treason on September 10, he was executed on October 24, 1945. His name survived him as a synonym for *traitor:* quisling.

Further reading: Dahl, Hans Fredrik. *Quisling: A Study in Treachery.* New York: Cambridge University Press, 1999; Hayes, Paul M. *Quisling: The Career and Political Ideas of Vidkun Quisling, 1887–1945.* London: David and Charles, 1971.

R

Rabaul, Battles of

The Japanese attacked the Australian base of Rabaul on northern New Britain Island early in 1942, during Japan's initial sweeping advance across the Pacific. After launching air attacks from Truk (in the Caroline Islands) and from aircraft carriers under the command of Admiral NAGUMO CHU-ICHI (whose fleet had just returned from the BATTLE OF PEARL HARBOR), Japanese troops landed at Rabaul and at Kavieng on New Ireland Island on January 23, 1942. The outnumbered Australian garrisons were quickly defeated and the Japanese built Rabaul (and, on a smaller scale, Kavieng) into its principal naval and air bases in the southwest Pacific.

Rabaul loomed large in Allied plans for a Pacific counteroffensive; however, as part of the U.S. ISLAND-HOPPING STRATEGY, Rabaul was initially bypassed to isolate it from other Japanese-held objectives.

During June 22–30, 1943, the U.S. 112th Cavalry and 158th Infantry regiments landed on and seized the Woodlark and Trobriand islands in the Solomon Sea, south of Rabaul. These toeholds, plus airfields acquired elsewhere in the course of the Solomon Islands campaign, served as bases from which air attacks were finally—and repeatedly—launched against Rabaul. Naval aircraft from the U.S. Third Fleet (WILLIAM H. "BULL" HALSEY) supplemented the land-based air attacks over a period that extended through most of 1943.

On December 15, 1943, the U.S. 112th Combat Team landed on the southwest coast of New Britain as a preliminary attack in preparation for a major amphibious assault by the 1st Marine Division (William Rupertus) at Cape Gloucester, on December 26, 75 miles to the northwest of the December 15 landings. On December 30, the Cape Gloucester airstrip was in marine hands, and by January 16, 1944, the marines had created a strong defensive perimeter around the field, so that it was ready to accommodate U.S. aircraft for further operations against Rabaul.

From Cape Gloucester, the 1st Marine Division leapfrogged to Talasea, which fell during March 6–8. Half of the 10,000-man Japanese garrison on New Britain was killed in this operation, which gave General DOUGLAS MACARTHUR's Southwest Pacific Command access to the straits separating New Britain and New Guinea, completing the isolation of Rabaul and rendering it vulnerable to further assault. In the meantime, the 3rd New Zealand Division took the Green Islands, 115 miles east of Rabaul, on February 15. Early in March, the U.S. 1st Cavalry Division landed at Los Negros in the Admiralties to the west, then advanced to Manus and occupied it, thereby gaining control of the Admiralty Islands and severing Japanese communications with Rabaul to the southeast. In this way, the Japanese base was entirely surrounded.

On March 20 the U.S. 4th Marine Regiment invaded Emirau Island in the Bismarcks, 70 miles north of Kavieng. An airstrip was built here, which, with those already constructed on the other captured islands, completely neutralized Rabaul and Kavieng as military bases. At this point, Rabaul still had some 100,000 Japanese troops manning the bases. Cut off now, they were useless in the war, and the Allies simply moved on to more objectives in the west and the north. The battles of Rabaul embodied the essence of the island-hopping strategy, by which even very large numbers of the enemy could be disposed of without direct confrontation.

The battles of Rabaul were also notable because of the exploits of Marine Corps aviator Major GREGORY (PAPPY) BOYINGTON, who downed 28 enemy planes, becoming the top marine air ace of World War II. His streak ended on January 2, when he was shot down and captured near Rabaul.

Further reading: Aplin, Douglas A. *Rabaul 1942.* Melbourne: 2/22nd Battalion A.I.F. Lark Force Association, 1980; Miller, John. *Cartwheel: The Reduction of Rabaul.* Washington, D.C.: Office of the Chief of Military History, Department of the Army, 1959; Sakaida, Henry. *The Siege of Rabaul.* Osceola, Wis.: Voyageur Press, 1997; Shaw, Henry I. *Isolation of Rabaul.* Washington, D.C.: Historical Branch, G-3 Division, Headquarters, U.S. Marine Corps, 1963.

Raczkiewicz, Władysław (1885–1947)
president of the Polish government in exile during World War II

Born in Russia into the family of a judge, Władysław Raczkiewicz studied in St. Petersburg, became active in the Polish Youth Organization, then graduated with a law degree from the University of Dorpat. He practiced law in Minsk and joined the underground Polish independence movement during World War I. He enlisted in the private army of Józef Piłsudski and, in 1914, fought alongside the Austrians against the Russian army. The onset of the Russian Revolution of 1917 resulted in Raczkiewicz's arrest and imprisonment in July 1917. He was released the following year, after Piłsudski became provisional head of the Polish state and commander in chief of the Polish army. In 1921,

Piłsudski appointed Raczkiewicz his minister of internal affairs. Subsequently, he rose to become Speaker of the Senate.

During the German INVASION OF POLAND in September 1939, Raczkiewicz fled with other government officials to London, where he joined with WŁADYSŁAW SIKORSKI and Stanislaw Mikołajczyk to establish the Polish government in exile. Raczkiewicz served as the president of the London-based government. In February 1945, pursuant to the YALTA CONFERENCE, the Western Allies, yielding to JOSEPH STALIN's claim that only a pro-Communist Polish government could guarantee the security of the Soviet Union, withdrew recognition of the Polish government in exile. Raczkiewicz effectively ceased to exercise presidential authority at this point; however, he retained his title until his death in 1947.

Further reading: Chodakiewicz, Marek Jan. *Between Nazis and Soviets: Occupation Politics in Poland, 1939–1947.* New York: Lexington Books, 2004; Kacewicz, G.V. *Great Britain, the Soviet Union and the Polish Government in Exile (1939–1945).* New York: Springer, 1979.

radar

"Radar" is an acronym for r*adio* d*etection* a*nd* r*anging.* As the name suggests, it is a system that uses radio waves to detect the presence of remote objects and to measure their location (range). As an adjunct to weapons systems, radar came into its own during World War II and figured as a crucial technology.

Radar emerged independently in France, Germany, the Netherlands, Italy, Japan, Great Britain, and the United States between 1934 and 1936 and continued to develop in the lead-up to the war and during the war. The single most important center of the development of radar as a military technology was the Radiation Laboratory of the Massachusetts Institute of Technology, especially beginning in November 1940. The United States, Britain, and Germany were the leaders in the development of military radar, with Japan (among the major combatants) somewhat lagging in the field and the Soviet Union quite far behind.

UNITED STATES

The earliest experiments in radar technology took place in 1930 at the Naval Research Laboratory, which led to the development, in 1934, of a pulse radar set—a radar system in which a brief radar signal pulse (about a millionth of a second) is broadcast, followed by silence for some thousandths of a second, during which time the radar receiver "listens" for a return echo of the pulse. By 1939, a practical military version of the system was ready, and 20 sets were installed on battleships, aircraft carriers, and cruisers by 1940.

The U.S. Army developed radar systems independently of the navy beginning in 1933. A prototype radar set was ready by May 1937, and a long-range radar system was completed and in service by 1940. The army maintained radar warning systems to protect the U.S. coast throughout the war. Relatively early in the war, the United States also developed radar sets small enough to be carried on board aircraft.

GREAT BRITAIN

Motivated by a desire to improve its antiaircraft defenses, British scientists developed Radar Direction Finding, a primitive radar system, by May 1935. Later in the year, a chain of radar stations (code named Chain Home, or "CH") was designed; 18 of the CH stations were operational on September 3, 1939, when Britain entered the war. Chain Home was expanded and improved between 1940 and 1943.

The British developed airborne radar as early as 1937, and the Royal Navy began shipboard experimentation in 1935, deploying Air Warning Set Type 79 in its larger ships in 1939. The army also worked intensively on radar, beginning in 1936.

GERMANY

Radar research got under way in Germany in 1934, with ship-borne radar prototypes emerging by 1936. Although antiaircraft radar was being used in Germany by 1939, the German radar program as a whole was not as well organized as programs in the United States and Britain. During the summer of 1940, radar was incorporated into what the Allies called the Kammhuber Line, the German air defense system created by General J. Kammhuber, consisting of overlapping defensive zones equipped with searchlights and radar.

OTHER COMBATANTS

France. Radar chains were operational at naval bases along the English Channel, the Atlantic, the Mediterranean, and the northeastern approach to Paris by 1939. During the BATTLE OF FRANCE, mobile radar sets were used for early warning and for gun laying (artillery direction).

Japan. Radar research began in Japan in 1933, but the first practical military radar sets were not put into operation until 1941. The army and navy worked on radar independently, and so intense was the rivalry between these two services that the development as well as the deployment of the technology was significantly retarded, much to the detriment of the Japanese war effort.

Netherlands. The Phillips Physics Laboratory and the physics laboratory of the Dutch armed forces worked on radar independently during 1936. Only a few prototypes had been built and deployed by the outbreak of the war.

Italy. Radio inventor and pioneer Guglielmo Marconi built a radar system in 1933 and demonstrated it two years later to BENITO MUSSOLINI and members of the Italian general staff. Development of a military model was turned over to Ugo Tiberio, who produced the EC-3 in 1941. About 100 radar sets were deployed before Italy surrendered to the Allies in September 1943.

Soviet Union. The Soviets developed an air-defense radar system by August 1934, but the Soviet government failed to promote the further development of radar, and it was not in general usage until 1942.

Further reading: Brown, L. *A Radar History of World War II: Technical and Military Imperatives.* London: Taylor & Francis, 1999; Fisher, David E. *A Race on the Edge of Time: Radar—The Decisive Weapon of World War II.* New York: McGraw-Hill, 1987; Guerlac, Henry E. *Radar in World War II.* Melville, N.Y.: AIP Press, 1987.

Raeder, Erich (1876–1960) *admiral instrumental in creating Germany's World War II navy*

Born in Wandsbek, a suburb of Hamburg, Raeder enlisted in the navy in 1894 and was commissioned an ensign in 1897. After service during World War I at the fleet and staff level and in mine-laying operations and raids along the British coast, Raeder remained with the navy after the armistice and was promoted to vice admiral in 1925. In 1928, promoted to admiral, he was appointed chief of the Naval Command.

Raeder directed the expansion and modernization of the German navy, transforming it from the coastal defense fleet it had become following the TREATY OF VERSAILLES into a major blue-water force. ADOLF HITLER personally promoted Raeder to a rank created expressly for him, Generaladmiral, in 1935, ratifying his position as commander in chief of the navy. Raeder now drew up a grand plan for naval expansion, Plan Z, which called for the construction of a fleet of six battleships, three battle cruisers, two aircraft carriers, and a massive force of cruisers and destroyers, all to be completed by 1944 or 1945. Raeder was promoted to Grossadmiral on April 1, 1939.

Hitler's haste in committing Germany to war prompted Raeder to shelve his plans for a large surface fleet and embark instead on a crash program of submarine construction and a naval strategy that relied almost totally on submarine warfare.

As World War II developed, Raeder experienced sharp strategic differences with his colleagues and with the Nazi leadership. Personally, he remained loyal to Hitler, but he disapproved of prosecuting a two-front war. As this was added to other differences, he was ultimately pressured to resign on January 30, 1943. He was replaced by KARL DÖNITZ.

Even though he was out of the war by early 1943, Raeder was tried after the German surrender by the NUREMBERG WAR CRIMES TRIBUNAL and was convicted of war crimes by reason of his endorsement of unrestricted submarine warfare. On October 1, 1946, the tribunal sentenced Raeder to life imprisonment, but he was paroled on September 26, 1955.

Further reading: Bird, Keith W. *Erich Raeder: Admiral of the Third Reich.* Annapolis, Md.: Naval Institute Press, 2006; Raeder, Erich. *Grand Admiral.* New York: Da Capo Press, 2001; Raeder, Erich. *My Life.* Manchester, N.H.: Ayer Company, 1980.

Rangers, U.S. Army

In World War II, the U.S. Army's special forces were the Rangers. The first battalion of Rangers was created by Brigadier General LUCIAN TRUSCOTT, who modeled the unit on the British commandos. Truscott raised the unit in mid-1942 from troops already stationed in Northern Ireland. Fifty of these soldiers participated in the ill-fated DIEPPE RAID.

In December 1942, the 29th Ranger Battalion (Provisional) was formed in Britain, and other Ranger battalions (the 3rd and 4th Battalions) were created in Morocco during the NORTH AFRICAN CAMPAIGN in May 1943. Rangers fought in the SICILY CAMPAIGN, in the BATTLE OF SALERNO, and in the ANZIO CAMPAIGN. In these Italian operations, the Rangers were used as conventional infantry—despite their special forces training.

Two Ranger battalions, the 2nd and 5th, were raised in the United States and took part in the NORMANDY LANDINGS (D-DAY). One Ranger battalion, the 6th, was formed in the Pacific theater, in New Guinea in September 1944. This unit was employed in special forces operations, including raids on the Philippines.

Further reading: Black, Robert W. *Rangers in World War II.* Novato, Calif.: Presidio Press, 2001; Ross, Robert Thomas. *U.S. Army Rangers and Special Forces of World War II: Their War in Photographs.* Atglen, Pa.: Schiffer, 2002.

Rashid Ali el-Ghailani (Rashid Ali al[el]-Kaylani, Rashid Ali al[el]-Gillani) (1882–1965) *Iraqi prime minister who cooperated with the Axis against the British*

Rashid Ali el-Ghailani was an Iraqi lawyer and nationalist who cofounded the Muslim Brotherhood, a political party that opposed the 1930

Anglo-Iraqi Treaty, protesting that it compromised Iraqi sovereignty after Iraq became nominally independent in 1932. After briefly serving as prime minister in 1933, he was reappointed to the post in 1940. Early in World War II, Rashid Ali made common cause with four colonels in the Iraqi army, who, aligning themselves with the Axis, were known as the Golden Square. Wishing to block the election of pro-British candidate Nuri al-Said as prime minister, the Golden Square backed the third-term reelection of Rashid Ali in April 1941. In return for this support Rashid Ali abrogated the 1930 treaty by refusing the British permission to transit Iraqi territory. After this, it became increasingly clear that Rashid Ali was receiving material support from Germany via the VICHY GOVERNMENT that held sway over colonial Syria. Indeed, in May 1941, partisans of Ali Rashid attacked a British air base at Habbaniya. These troops were repulsed and suffered a decisive defeat, which prompted Rashid Ali himself to flee to Persia (Iran). From here, he journeyed to Germany, where he set up as the most important pro-Nazi voice from the Arab world. After the war, he remained in European exile until 1958.

Further reading: Raghid El-Solh. *Britain's Two Wars With Iraq: 1941, 1991*. Ithaca, N.Y. Cornell University Press, 1997; Simons, Geoff. *Iraq: From Sumer to Saddam*, 3d ed. London: Palgrave Macmillan, 2004.

refugees

No one knows for certain how many refugees World War II produced, but the most widely accepted estimate is approximately 30,000,000—more than any other war in history. The refugee crisis was primarily a European phenomenon. In the years leading up to the war and during the early part of it, tens of thousands of Jews and other ethnic and political refugees fled Germany and, later, German-occupied countries before escape was cut off. During the war, invasion sent many people into flight, and the effects of total war, especially the devastation created by STRATEGIC BOMBING, left hundreds of thousands homeless.

The first major refugee exodus came during the BATTLE OF FRANCE, as the people of such cities as Brussels, Lille, and Paris fled southwest, so clogging the roads as to make the movement of French and British troops all but impossible. The German INVASION OF POLAND also created many refugees, and, as a result of ADOLF HITLER's political realignment of Poland during the German occupation of that country, massive numbers of Poles were forced to move from western to eastern Poland. By the winter of 1944–45, it was the turn of massive numbers of German citizens to flee. Very large numbers sought to escape the onslaught of the Soviet counterinvasion by escaping to the West, even into the arms of the Western allies.

As the war in Europe approached its end, the newly founded UNITED NATIONS created UNRRA, the United Nations Relief and Rehabilitation Administration, which sought to provide resettlement and relief for the refuges, who were officially designated "Displaced Persons," or DPs. UNRRA created DP camps throughout western and central Europe and worked to reunite families torn apart by the war. In the Soviet Union, most DPs were held out of the reach of UNRRA and were typically forced to subsist and work in labor camps.

Further reading: Genizi, Haim. *America's Fair Share: The Admission and Resettlement of Displaced Persons, 1945–1952*. Detroit: Wayne State University Press, 1993; Klemme, Marvin. *The Inside Story of the UNRRA, an Experience in Internationalism: A First Hand Report on the Displaced People of Europe*. New York: Lifetime Editions, 1949; Wyman, Mark. DPs: *Europe's Displaced Persons, 1945–1951*. Ithaca, N.Y.: Cornell University Press, 1998.

Reichenau, Walther von (1884–1942) *field marshal in command during the early German conquests of World War II*

Born in Karlsruhe, Germany, to the family of an artillery general, Reichenau was commissioned in an artillery unit in 1903, and by the time of World War I he was an officer on the general staff. In January 1933, he headed the Wehrmachtamt (armed forces office) of the German Ministry of Defense and enjoyed rapid promotion, becoming a lieutenant general by 1935. He emerged as one of ADOLF HITLER's most trusted military commanders and led the Tenth Army (subsequently renamed the Sixth Army) in the INVASION OF POLAND in September 1939. He was then transferred to the western front, where he took a leading role in the BATTLE OF FRANCE, personally accepting the surrender of Belgium's King Leopold in May 1940.

In July 1940, he was promoted to field marshal and was again sent to the east with his Sixth Army, where he was initially successful in the UKRAINE CAMPAIGN during the fall of 1941, taking Kiev in September. However, in November, he was defeated by forces under Marshal SEMYON TIMOSHENKO and was forced to withdraw from Rostov. On January 17, 1942, while being evacuated from the front after having suffered a heart attack or stroke, Reichenau died.

Further reading: Barnett, Correlli, ed. *Hitler's Generals.* New York: Grove Press, 2003; Heiber, Helmut, and David Glantz, eds. *Hitler and His Generals.* New York: Enigma Books, 2002; Mitcham, Samuel. *Hitler's Field Marshals and Their Battles.* New York: Cooper Square Press, 2001.

Remagen Bridge

The Ludendorff Railway Bridge over the Rhine River at Remagen, near Bonn, was captured on March 7, 1945, by an armored unit of the First U.S. Army (COURTNEY HODGES). It was one of the few Rhine bridges that the retreating Germans had failed to destroy.

The taking of the Remagen bridge gave the Americans their first passage across the Rhine and was, therefore, a milestone in the war against Germany and a great boost to Allied morale. About 8,000 troops, together with tanks and self-propelled guns, crossed the bridge in the space of 24 hours.

Although the capture of the bridge at Remagen figured as a psychological triumph, the bridgehead was not exploited into a general breakthrough. As for the bridge itself, it collapsed on March 17, after

five divisions had crossed, killing 26 G.I.s. By this time, however, army engineers had built pontoon bridges at this crossing.

Whatever the U.S. shortcomings in exploiting the capture of the bridge, it made a deep impression on ADOLF HITLER, who relieved GERD VON RUNDSTEDT and replaced him with ALBERT KESSELRING. One officer and four German soldiers who had been assigned to destroy the bridge were summarily executed. Desperate to bring the bridge down—after the U.S. crossings had already begun—German commanders unsuccessfully attempted to destroy it with V-2 ROCKETS; this was the only instance in which these strategic weapons were employed tactically.

Further reading: Hechler, Ken. *The Bridge at Remagen.* Novato, Calif.: Presidio Press, 2005; Rawson, Andrew. *Bridge at Remagen: 27th Armoured Infantry Division.* London: Pen and Sword, 2004.

resistance movements

Every Axis-occupied country responded to occupation with some degree and some form of resistance. Although such Allied governmental and military organizations as Britain's SPECIAL OPERATIONS EXECUTIVE (SOE) and the U.S. OFFICE OF STRATEGIC SERVICES (OSS) attempted with varying degrees of success to organize and coordinate foreign resistance activity, there was never a unified European continental resistance movement (as was frequently rumored to exist during the war), and throughout the conflict resistance movements remained primarily local and indigenous. The one characteristic all resistance movements shared was that their membership tended to become larger as the approach of liberation became increasingly likely.

Resistance may be classed into two broad categories: active and passive. Active resistance encompasses three principal activities—espionage and intelligence gathering; assisting in escape (helping POWs and downed fliers to get across hostile borders, rescuing Jews and other "enemies of the Reich," and so on); and sabotage, which ranged from isolated acts (the proverbial monkey wrench covertly cast into a vital machine at a war plant), to the ambush of occupying troops, to full-scale partisan military action. Another form of sabotage widely practiced by resistance movements might be called moral sabotage and included the circulation of PROPAGANDA, disinformation, demoralizing rumors, and news furnished by Allied sources.

Passive resistance was nonviolent and more civilian in nature. It included labor strikes, organized slowdowns of war production assembly lines, general noncooperation, the maintenance of underground information networks, and escape assistance.

Resistance work could be very lonely, the activity of a few individuals operating in isolation; however, in some places, such as France, resistance organizations, such as the Maquis, were quite large. Resistance organizations were typically motivated by patriotism and other idealistic impulses, but these organizations were not above collaborating with criminal elements in a city, town, or village. After all, resistance work often required the services of forgers, thieves, murderers, and black marketers.

NORWAY

Following the German invasion of April 1940, the Norwegian resistance was led by two organizations: Milorg, which focused on obtaining military supplies, training operatives, and cooperating with Allied military forces; and Sivorg, which focused on passive resistance—clergy, teachers, and others of influence in the community led noncooperation movements to undermine the occupation administration.

DENMARK

After it was occupied beginning in April 1940, Denmark was often swept by strikes and other anti-occupation demonstrations. Resistance operatives engaged in many acts of sabotage. Danish resisters focused much attention on protecting Jews from the HOLOCAUST, most famously in October 1943, when the resistance managed to send most of Denmark's Jewish population to Sweden.

NETHERLANDS

Most Dutch resistance was passive, and there was little sabotage or armed action. Workers engaged in mass strikes: in February 1941, to protest the arrests of Jews; in spring 1943, to protest the use of former prisoners of war as forced labor; and in September 1944, to disrupt railroad transportation to prevent the Germans from rushing reinforcements to meet the NORMANDY LANDINGS (D-DAY). The German occupiers typically made disproportionately harsh reprisals for resistance activity. In the Netherlands, after the 1944 rail strikes, the occupation government cut off the shipment of food to the civilian population, creating a severe famine.

FRANCE

France saw a combination of active and passive resistance. While the Maquis and other active resistance organizations are best known—especially for their activity in association with the liberation of Paris—ordinary French railway workers were extremely successful in disrupting rail service used by the German military before and during the Normandy landings.

NOTABLE ACTS OF RESISTANCE

Resistance movements are discussed in more detail in entries devoted to the major combatant nations of World War II. The following is a survey of some of the most notable acts of resistance during the war:

- August 1941: Resistance gunmen shoot and wound Vichy foreign minister PIERRE LAVAL and a German newspaper editor near Versailles. The assassination fails, but demonstrates the vulnerability of the Vichy government to attack.
- October 1941: Maquis members assassinate the German commander in Nantes. In reprisal, German authorities execute 50 French hostages.
- May 1942: The SOE infiltrates Czech resistance operatives into Prague, who assassinate the Reich's Protector REINHARD HEYDRICH (the "Butcher of Prague"). The Nazi reprisal is

horrific: the total destruction of the village of Lidice and the murder of all its male residents, the "deportation" of women to the Ravensbrück concentration camp, and the dispersal of most of the children into Germany, where they were raised as Germans.

November 1942: Greek resistance operatives, coordinated by the SOE, demolish a viaduct on the Athens–Salonika railroad at Gorgopotamus, thereby cutting the main German supply line to North Africa.

February 1943: Norwegian resistance paratroops are flown in from England to sabotage the Norsk hydro power station near Ryukan, a source of "heavy water" (deuterium) vital to German nuclear weapons research.

June 1943: French Maquis and SOE agents sabotage the Michelin tire plant at Clermont-Ferrand.

July 1943: French resistance fighters destroy six locomotives and damage another six in a roundhouse at Troyes.

September 1943: Neapolitan resisters fight their German occupiers for three days as the Allied army approaches.

November 1943: French resistance fighters bomb the Peugeot factory at Sochaux, where tank turrets and aircraft engine assemblies are made. The Germans quickly replace the machinery, which is almost immediately sabotaged again.

January 1944: French Maquis and SOE agents blow up the Ratier aircraft plant near Figeac, France, temporarily halting production of propellers for the Luftwaffe.

June 1944: French resistance fighters destroy a train carrying tanks through Toulouse. By way of reprisal, the WAFFEN SS kills 800 residents of Oradour-sur-Glane.

June 1944: In coordination with the Normandy invasion, French resistance agents cut telephone lines, block roads, blow up bridges, destroy canal locks, set fire to fuel dumps, and sabotage railroad lines in a successful effort to slow the German response to the invasion.

August 1944: In Paris, resistance fighters begin full-scale street warfare against the occupying garrison as the Allied armies approach.

See also BELGIUM; CZECHOSLOVAKIA; FRANCE; FRENCH RESISTANCE AND UNDERGROUND MOVEMENTS; GERMAN RESISTANCE TO NAZISM; GERMANY; GREECE; HUNGARY; ITALY; MOULIN, JEAN; NETHERLANDS; NORWEGIAN CAMPAIGN; POLAND, INVASION OF; and SOVIET UNION, INVASION OF.

Further reading: Dupuy, Trevor N. *European Resistance Movements.* New York: Franklin Watts, 1965; Files, Yvonne de Ridder. *The Quest for Freedom: Belgian Resistance in World War II.* McKinelyville, Calif.: Fithian Press, 1991; Miller, Russell. *The Resistance.* Alexandria, Va.: Time-Life, 1979; Werner, Harold D. *Fighting Back: A Memoir of Jewish Resistance in World War II.* New York: Columbia University Press, 1992; Wilhelm, Maria De Blasio. *Other Italy: The Italian Resistance in World War II.* New York: Norton, 1988.

Reynaud, Paul (1878–1966) *French premier whose attempt to avert German occupation failed*

Reynaud was born in Barcelonnette, France, became a lawyer, then served in the army during World War I. Following the war, he entered politics in the Chamber of Deputies representing his home district during 1919–24 and, from 1928, a Paris constituency. He was appointed minister of finance, of colonies, and of justice, serving in these posts from 1930 to 1932, when he lost his seat in the government.

During most of the 1930s, as a private citizen, he campaigned for French resistance to German expansionist aggression and backed Colonel CHARLES DE GAULLE's recommendations for military preparedness to defend against a mechanized, air-supported attack (BLITZKRIEG). His calls fell on deaf ears, but Reynaud was appointed minister of justice in April 1938 and used his position to protest the French government's approval of the APPEASEMENT POLICY introduced by British prime minister NEVILLE CHAMBERLAIN. After the leader of his parliamentary bloc went so far as to congratulate ADOLF HITLER after the MUNICH CON-

FERENCE AND AGREEMENT, Reynaud resigned in protest. He was subsequently appointed minister of finance in November 1938 and served until March 1940, leading France in the direction of austerity in an effort to gear up the economy for war.

Once World War II began, Reynaud became premier on March 21, 1940, and appointed de Gaulle his undersecretary of state for war. As France collapsed in the Battle of FRANCE, Reynaud did his best to rally resistance, but Marshal HENRI-PHILIPPE PÉTAIN—whom Reynaud had named vice premier in a bid to strengthen his cabinet—led other ministers in a call for capitulation to and an armistice with Germany. Unable to block the armistice and unwilling to be a party to it, Reynaud resigned as premier on June 16, 1940. He was promptly arrested and held in custody throughout the war.

After the liberation Reynaud was elected to the Chamber of Deputies, in which he served from 1946 to 1962. He broke with de Gaulle in 1962 over a constitutional issue.

Further reading: Graud, André. *The Gravediggers of France: Gamelin, Daladier, Reynaud, Pétain, and Laval: Military Defeat, Armistice, Counter-revolution.* New York: Doubleday, Doran, 1944.

Rhine crossings

The Rhine River figured as the final natural obstacle the Allies had to overcome in their advance into Germany in 1945. It was also an objective of great symbolic and psychological importance, both for the Allies and for the Germans, for whom it was a powerful national symbol.

DWIGHT D. EISENHOWER, supreme Allied commander, decided on crossing the Rhine along a broad front—over the objection of one of his two principal field commanders, BERNARD LAW MONTGOMERY, who favored a sharp, concentrated thrust. As Eisenhower planned it, the Twenty-First Army Group (Montgomery) would cross in the north, the Twelfth Army Group (OMAR N. BRADLEY) in the center, and the Sixth Army Group (Jacob Devers) in the south. Preparatory to these cross-

ings, Twenty-first Army Group had to implement Operation Veritable and Operation Grenade, and the First U.S. Army had to complete Operation Lumberjack, all of which were intended to clear the Rhine approaches. These operations were under way by February; however, progress was slower in the south, where the Third and Seventh U.S. Armies had not yet closed in on the Rhine region.

Elements of the Ninth U.S. Army were the first to reach the west bank of the Rhine, opposite Düsseldorf, on March 2. Their crossing was delayed, however, because the Germans had destroyed all the bridges. Elements of COURTNEY HODGES's First US Army discovered the REMAGEN BRIDGE intact on March 7, seized it, and began crossing.

On March 10, Montgomery's Twenty-First Army Group reached the Rhine and prepared to cross it at Wesel, north of the Ruhr. In the meantime, the Third U.S. Army (GEORGE S. PATTON JR.) and the Seventh U.S. Army (ALEXANDER McCARRELL PATCH JR.) cleared the region between the Moselle and the Rhine. Simultaneously, the First French Army (Jean-Marie de Lattre de Tassigny) addressed resistance in the COLMAR POCKET.

Eisenhower held back on a full-scale crossing of the Rhine until several bridgeheads had been established in addition to that at Remagen. On March 22–23, Patton established one at Oppenheim, south of Mainz, and Montgomery crossed at Emmerich, Rees, Wesel, and Rheinberg on the 24th. Over the following days, Patton made additional crossings at Boppard and near St. Goar between Koblenz and Mainz. The Seventh U.S. Army crossed near Worms on March 26, and the French at Germersheim and Speyer, between Mannheim and Karlsruhe, on March 31, followed by another crossing at Leumersheim on April 2. Combined, these crossings gave the Allies a 200-mile front across the Rhine.

Further reading: Allen, Peter. *One More River: The Rhine Crossings of 1945.* New York: Scribner, 1980; Badsey, Stephen. *Into the Reich: Battles on Germany's Western Front 1944–1945.* London: Osprey, 2002; Hechler, Ken. *The Bridge at Remagen.* Novato, Calif.: Presidio Press, 2005; Rawson, Andrew. *Bridge at Remagen: 27th Armoured Infantry Division.* London: Pen and Sword, 2004; Saunders, Tim.

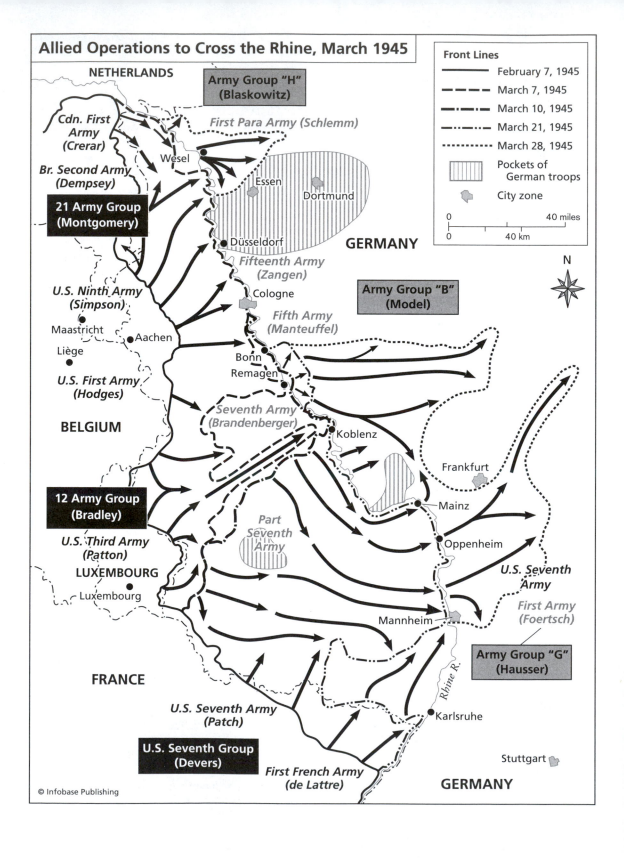

Allied Operations to Cross the Rhine, March 1945

NETHERLANDS

Army Group "H" (Blaskowitz)

First Para Army (Schlemm)

Cdn. First Army (Crerar)

Br. Second Army (Dempsey)

Wesel

Essen

Dortmund

21 Army Group (Montgomery)

Düsseldorf

GERMANY

Fifteenth Army (Zangen)

U.S. Ninth Army (Simpson)

Cologne

Army Group "B" (Model)

Fifth Army (Manteuffel)

Maastricht

Aachen

Liège

Bonn

Remagen

U.S. First Army (Hodges)

BELGIUM

Seventh Army (Brandenberger)

Koblenz

Frankfurt

12 Army Group (Bradley)

Mainz

U.S. Third Army (Patton)

Part Seventh Army

Oppenheim

LUXEMBOURG

Luxembourg

U.S. Seventh Army

First Army (Foertsch)

Mannheim

Army Group "G" (Hausser)

FRANCE

Rhine R.

U.S. Seventh Army (Patch)

Karlsruhe

U.S. Seventh Group (Devers)

First French Army (de Lattre)

Stuttgart

GERMANY

© Infobase Publishing

Front Lines

— February 7, 1945
– – – March 7, 1945
–·–·– March 10, 1945
–··–··– March 21, 1945
········· March 28, 1945

▦ Pockets of German troops

◆ City zone

0   40 miles
0   40 km

N

Operation Plunder and Varsity: The British and Canadian Rhine Crossing. London: Pen and Sword, 2006.

Ribbentrop, Joachim von (1893–1946)
Nazi German foreign minister (1933–1945)

Ribbentrop was born in Wesel, Germany, the son of an army officer. He was educated in Germany, Switzerland, France, and England, then lived for a time in Canada (1910–14), returning to Germany at the beginning of World War I, in which he fought on the eastern front before being attached to the German military mission in Turkey.

After the Armistice, Ribbentrop returned from Turkey to Germany and mustered out of the army, becoming a salesman of sparkling wine (*Sekt*). In 1920, he married the daughter of a wealthy producer of Sekt and thereby became financially independent. Seeking to rise in society, he prevailed upon a distant relative, who was ennobled, to adopt him so that he could add "von" to his own name.

In 1932, Ribbentrop met ADOLF HITLER and joined the NAZI PARTY. He rose rapidly in the party, entering Hitler's inner circle as his adviser on foreign affairs after Hitler became chancellor on January 30, 1933. In 1934, Ribbentrop was appointed Reich commissioner for disarmament at Geneva, where he negotiated (in June 1935) the Anglo-German Naval Agreement, which abrogated the TREATY OF VERSAILLES to the extent of allowing German naval rearmament.

Ribbentrop was named ambassador to Great Britain in 1936 and served until 1938. He encouraged Hitler's expansionist ambitions by reporting that the British were in no position to render military aid to Poland. While he was serving as ambassador to Britain, Ribbentrop also negotiated the ANTI-COMINTERN PACT with Japan in 1936, and after he became Reich minister of foreign affairs (February 1938), he negotiated the "PACT OF STEEL" with Italy (May 22, 1939), which allied Italy's fascist dictatorship with Germany's Nazi dictatorship. On August 23, 1939, Ribbentrop went on to negotiate the GERMAN-SOVIET NON-AGGRESSION PACT (August 23, 1939), which cleared from Hitler's path the final obstacle to war—the prospect of Soviet opposition—enabling him to carry out the INVASION OF POLAND on September 1, 1939.

The German-Soviet Non-Aggression Pact proved to be the high-water mark of Ribbentrop's influence with the government of the Third Reich. Although he signed the AXIS (TRIPARTITE) PACT with Japan and Italy on September 27, 1940, the role—or even pretense—of diplomacy necessarily faded into insignificance as the world was plunged more deeply into universal war. Thanks to the sufferance of Hitler, Ribbentrop maintained his post, but he exerted little actual influence. When some Foreign Office officials were implicated in the JULY PLOT (TO ASSASSINATE HITLER) (July 20, 1944), Ribbentrop was further marginalized.

The Allies arrested Ribbentrop in Hamburg on June 14, 1945, and bound him over to trial by the NUREMBERG WAR CRIMES TRIBUNAL. Convicted, he was hanged on October 16, 1946. Before his death, while in prison, he wrote a memoir entitled *Zwischen London und Moskau* (*Between London and Moscow*), which was published in 1953.

Further reading: Bloch, Michael. *Ribbentrop: A Biography.* New York: Crown, 1993; Weitz, John. *Hitler's Diplomat: The Life and Times of Joachim von Ribbentrop.* New York: Ticknor & Fields, 1992.

Ridgway, Matthew B. (1895–1993) *U.S. Army general who led the airborne assault on Sicily*

Ridgway was born at Fort Monroe, Virginia and enrolled in West Point, graduating in 1917. He served on the U.S.-Mexican border with the 3rd Infantry and in September 1918 returned to West Point as instructor in French and Spanish. He graduated from Infantry School in 1925 and, from 1925 to 1930, served in China, Texas, Nicaragua, the Canal Zone, and the Philippines. After returning to the United States, he graduated from the Infantry School advanced course in 1930, then from the Command and General Staff School in 1935.

Ridgway served on the staffs of VI Corps and Second Army, then attended the Army War College, graduating in 1937. After brief service with the Fourth Army based in San Francisco, he came to Washington, D.C., where he was attached to the War Plans Division of the War Department in September 1939. Following a series of promotions, he was appointed assistant division commander of the 82nd Infantry Division based in Louisiana in March 1942. He directed the 82nd's conversion to the 82nd Airborne Division, which was completed in August, and, promoted to temporary major general, he accompanied the division to the Mediterranean early in 1943, where he planned and executed the U.S. Army's first-ever airborne assault, parachuting a portion of the 82nd into Sicily during July 9–10, 1943. Later, during the ITALIAN CAMPAIGN, Ridgway led elements of the 82nd Airborne into combat in the Battle of SALERNO. He also parachuted with members of the 82nd into France in the airborne assault preceding the NORMANDY LANDINGS (D-DAY), before dawn on June 6, 1944. During breakout operations from Normandy, in August, his command was expanded to the XVIII Airborne Corps (the combined 82nd and 101st Airborne divisions), and he led the airborne contingent of the failed OPERATION MARKET-GARDEN in September.

At the Battle of the ARDENNES (BATTLE OF THE BULGE), the 101st Airborne held Bastogne against a massive German counterattack in the last great German offensive of the war during December 16, 1944–January 15, 1945.

From January to April 1945, Ridgway fought in the Rhineland and Ruhr, then was promoted to lieutenant general in June 1945 and given command of the Mediterranean region from November 1945 to January 1946, when he was appointed to the United Nations Military Staff Committee. From July 1948 to August 1949, Ridgway headed the Caribbean Defense Command, then accepted appointment as deputy chief of staff of the army.

During the Korean War, Ridgway took over command of the Eighth U.S. Army in Korea shortly after General Walton H. Walker was killed in an automobile accident. After President HARRY S. TRUMAN relieved General DOUGLAS MACARTHUR as UN commander and commander in chief Far East on April 11, 1951, Ridgway replaced him. In May 1952, Ridgway left Korea to succeed DWIGHT DAVID EISENHOWER as NATO supreme Allied commander Europe. He was promoted to general.

In 1953, Ridgway returned to the United States as army chief of staff, stepping down in June 1955 and retiring from the army. He subsequently worked in the private sector.

Further reading: Mitchell, George Charles. *Matthew B. Ridgway: Soldier, Statesman, Scholar, Citizen.* Mechanicsburg, Pa.: Stackpole Books, 2002; Ridgway, Matthew B., as told to Harold H. Martin. *Soldier: The Memoirs of Matthew B. Ridgway.* Westport, Conn.: Greenwood Publishing Group, 1974; Soffer, Jonathan M. *General Matthew B. Ridgway.* New York: Praeger, 1998.

Riefenstahl, Leni (1902–2003) *German director of Nazi propaganda films*

Born Berta Helene Amalie Riefenstahl in Berlin, Riefenstahl took the name Leni when she became an actress in German cinema. Before beginning her film career, she had studied painting and ballet and, during 1923–26, appeared as a dancer throughout Europe.

As a film actress, Riefenstahl specialized in "mountain films," a genre popular in Germany during the late 1920s and early 1930s, emphasizing the beauty of nature and "physical culture" (a cult of physical fitness). She moved on to become a director of such films and, in 1931, founded Leni Riefenstahl-Produktion. Her 1932 *Das blaue Licht* (*The Blue Light*) earned her a reputation as a fine director.

Riefenstahl's expertise in the mountain film genre drew the attention of the NAZI PARTY, which subsidized a series of movies celebrating physical culture and the superiority of the "Aryan" racial type. Most notable among these films were the 1933 *Sieg des Glaubens* (*Victory of the Faith*) and *Triumph des Willens* (*Triumph of the Will*), a 1935 documentary covering the 1934 Nazi Party convention at Nuremberg. *Triumph of the Will* was a masterpiece of propagandistic filmmaking and is still studied as an important milestone in the documentary genre. It played a key role in popularizing the Nazi Party, portraying it as an irresistible movement and introducing to the German people—and, to the rest of the world—the leaders of the party. Many film historians consider it one of the most important cinematic works of the 20th century.

In 1938, Riefenstahl released *Olympische Spiele* (*Olympia*) a documentary covering the Olympic Games held in Berlin in 1936 and incorporating highly sophisticated production techniques, including a magnificent score commissioned expressly for the film.

After the war, Riefenstahl was considered a controversial figure at best. Many frankly denounced her for the role she had played in promoting the Nazi Party and Nazi ideology. Allied authorities arrested and detained her, but she was subsequently cleared of involvement in war crimes and was never prosecuted. Despite this, no film studio would hire her—although she managed in 1954 to complete one project, *Tiefland* (*Lowland*), which she had started during the war.

With her film career ended, Riefenstahl turned to still photography, becoming especially well known for her underwater work. A final movie, *Impressionen unter Wasser* (*Impressions Under Water*), was released in 2002, the year before her death.

Further reading: Riefenstahl, Leni. *Leni Riefenstahl*. London: Picador, 1995; Rother, Rainer. *Leni Riefenstahl: The Seduction of Genius*. New York: Continuum International Publishing Group, 2002.

Rio Conference

Held in Rio de Janeiro, Brazil, during January 1942, the conference, sponsored by the United States, called together the foreign ministers of all American states (including the U.S. secretary of state) with the main purpose of obtaining a joint pledge to declare war against the Axis. Although many Latin American countries had already declared war, some had not. In the end, Chile and Argentina objected to the resolution, which was subsequently diluted to a joint pledge recommending that all nations sever relations with the Axis.

The Rio Conference also created the Inter-American Defense Board, which gave Latin America a voice in the defense of the hemisphere, and an Emergency Advisory Committee for Political Defense, which monitored pro-Axis activity in the hemisphere. This committee was probably the most effective agency to emerge from the conference, since its investigations compelled Chile to sever relations with the Axis in 1943.

Further reading: Friedman, Max Paul. *Nazis and Good Neighbors: The United States Campaign against the Germans of Latin America in World War II*. New York and London: Cambridge University Press, 2003; Humphreys, R. *Latin America and the Second World War: Nineteen Thirty-Nine to Nineteen Forty-Two*. London: Athlone Press, 1981.

Ritchie, Neil (1897–1983) *British general defeated by Erwin Rommel*

Educated at Lancing College and at the British military academy Sandhurst, Ritchie was commissioned in the Black Watch in 1914. He fought during World War I both on the Western Front and in Mesopotamia. He continued in service between the wars and, at the outbreak of World War II, was a brigadier general.

Ritchie served as a staff officer under Archibald Wavell, Alan Brooke (1st Viscount Alanbrooke), and Claude John Eyre Auchinleck, all of whom found him invaluable. Auchinleck assigned to him field command of the Eighth British Army in November 1941. The assignment was intended to be temporary until a permanent field commander could be found. As it turned out, Ritchie held the command when the Eighth Army and British forces in general were still undermanned and underequipped. At the time, the Eighth Army stood alone in North Africa against the German and Italian forces and, indeed, the Eighth was the only British land force fighting the Germans in any theater so early in the war.

Although the Eighth under Ritchie enjoyed some successes against Italian units, it was forced into retreat by the Afrika Korps under Erwin Rommel.

At the Battle of Gazala during May–June 1942, Ritchie was unable to exercise the kind of command that might have at least allowed Eighth Army to hold its own. Rommel scored a stunning victory, which resulted in the loss of the key port of Tobruk. In June 1942, Auchinleck removed Ritchie from command. Ritchie subsequently took over command of the 52nd Division and then, in 1944, XII Corps, which he led during the Normandy landings (D-day).

Ritchie did not retire after World War II, but served during the postwar years as commander in chief of British forces in the Far East. When he did leave the service, he accepted appointment as chairman of a Canadian insurance company and spent the remainder of his life in Toronto.

Further reading: Barnett, Correlli. *The Desert Generals.* London: Cassell, 1999; Keegan, John, ed. *Churchill's Generals.* New York: Grove Weidenfeld, 1991.

River Kwai Bridge

In 1939, even before Japan entered World War II, Japanese planners plotted a Thailand-Burma rail line to transport 3,000 tons of supplies daily in support of troops in remote Burma. Considering the formidable terrain and harsh tropical climate, the Japanese engineers projected that five years would be required to complete the 257-mile line. The biggest obstacles were the gorges and mountain cuts, which would require a multitude of bridges—some 600, total—most of them in Thailand.

Actual construction of the railroad was put off until September 16, 1942. Converging lines were begun, emanating from two existing terminals, at Thanbyuzayat, Burma, and at Nong Pladuk, Thailand (some 25 miles west of Bangkok). The lines were to be advanced toward one another. Construction crews consisted of about 61,000 Allied prisoners of war, among them 30,000 British prisoners, 18,000 Dutch, 13,000 Australian, and 700 U.S. soldiers. In addition, 250,000 Malays, Chinese, Tamils, and Burmese were used as slave labor. Of the POWs, it is estimated that 16,000 died, most of them from diseases endemic to the region and from malnutrition, abuse, and sheer exhaustion. In particular, beginning in January 1943, during an accelerated period of construction—which the labor camp authorities called the "speedo"—the prisoners were literally worked to death. Among the Asian slaves, mortality was even higher than among the POWs. It is believed that more than 80,000 died.

Work was completed on the railway not in five years, but in 16 months, the two lines meeting 23 miles south of Three Pagodas Pass in April 1943. The Japanese operated the line for 21 months before it was badly damaged by Allied air attacks, including those using a new type of radio-controlled "AZON" bomb. Except for 80 miles of track in Thailand between Nong Pladuk and Tha Sao, which operates today, the railroad was abandoned before the war ended.

The River Kwai Bridge is the most famous of the 600-plus bridges over which the tracks once ran. It spans 1,200 feet over the Kwai at a place the prisoners called Hellfire Pass because, at night, from the top of the mountain ridge, flickering torches along the construction site and camps looked like the fires of hell. The bridge took a full nine months to build, with prisoners and others working 18-hour shifts. Construction of the bridge was the subject of a famous 1957 film directed by David Lean and starring Alec Guinness, *The Bridge over the River Kwai.* Although the movie is considered a masterpiece of cinema, it has very little basis in the reality of the POW experience at Kwai or elsewhere along the Burma-Thailand Railway.

Further reading: Boulle, Pierre. *Bridge over the River Kwai.* London: Collins, 1968; Gordon, Ernest. *Through the Valley of the Kwai.* New York: Harper & Row, 1962; Kinvig, C. *River Kwai Railway.* London: Brassey's U.K., 2003; Searle, Ronald. *To the Kwai and Back: War Drawings 1939–1945.* New York: Atlantic Monthly Press, 1986.

River Plate, Battle of

This early naval battle of World War II was fought off the River Plate (Río de la Plata) on the south Atlantic coast of Uruguay and Argentina on December 13, 1939, between the German pocket

BATTLESHIP *Admiral Graf Spee* and an Allied naval task force.

Admiral Graf Spee (Captain Hans Langsdorff) was one of the German navy's most modern ships, mounting six 11-inch guns. By the time of the battle, the *Graf Spee* had sunk nine Allied ships in the Indian Ocean and South Atlantic. Engine trouble prompted its return to Germany, but Captain Langsdorff decided to return by an indirect route, via the River Plate, in order to intercept an Allied convoy known to be in the area. Commodore Henry Harwood, commanding British Force G (the British light cruisers *Ajax* and the New Zealand light cruiser *Achilles,* as well as the British cruiser *Exeter*—the *Cumberland,* another British cruiser, arrived after the battle), anticipated Langsdorff's intentions and set up an ambush.

When Langsdorff sighted Harwood's ships, he assumed they were the convoy and headed for them. The battle that developed as a result lasted one hour and 20 minutes. Harwood attacked from two directions, but instead of attempting to defend against both attacks, Langsdorff poured his formidable fire on *Exeter,* which was forced to withdraw to save itself. *Ajax* and *Achilles* also took heavy fire and were damaged, prompting Harwood to break off the attack. Apparently fearing for his malfunctioning engines, Langsdorff chose not to press the fight, but entered the port of Montevideo in neutral Uruguay.

The Uruguyan government gave him no more than 72 hours to leave the port or suffer internment for the duration. Although British reinforcements were dispatched, they were not due to arrive until December 19, which should have given *Graf Spee* an opportunity to escape. Langsdorff, however, was deceived by false British signals. Worse, his gunnery officer reported sighting the approach of the battle cruiser *Renown.* Assuming, then, that the British reinforcements had already arrived, and knowing that he was absolutely forbidden to accept internment, Langsdorff acted on orders he had been given to scuttle his ship if he believed he could not fight his way to Buenos Aires. On December 17, 1939, he scuttled the *Admiral Graf Spee,* then committed suicide.

The British celebrated the battle as a major victory—one they badly needed during the bleak early days of the war.

Further reading: Grove, Eric J. *The Price of Disobedience: The Battle of the River Plate Reconsidered.* Annapolis, Md.: Naval Institute Press, 2001; Grove, Mark. *The Battle of the River Plate 1939.* London: Osprey, 2006; Pope, Dudley. *The Battle of the River Plate: The Hunt for the German Pocket Battleship Graf Spee.* Ithaca, N.Y.: McBooks Press, 2005.

Rokossovsky, Konstantin (1896–1968) *one of Zhukov's most brilliant subordinate officers; like Zhukov, a marshal of the Soviet Union*

Rokossovsky rose rapidly in the Red Army through 1936, when he became a corps commander, but, like so many other officers of the period, he fell into disfavor with JOSEPH STALIN before World War II, and his career was effectively suspended. Rokossovsky was luckier than many, however, in that he was merely imprisoned and tortured for a time but was spared execution. Released in 1940, he was a corps commander during the German invasion of the SOVIET UNION in June 1941. In July, GEORGI KONSTANTINOVICH ZHUKOV raised him from corps to army command. Zhukov had once served under Rokossovsky and had great respect for him. He championed his former commander, and in September 1942 persuaded Stalin to turn over to him the Don front ("front" was the Red Army term for what the Western allies called an army group) between the Volga and Don Rivers during the Battle of STALINGRAD. Thus, in January 1943, Rokossovsky led the culminating operation against the "Stalingrad pocket" and had the honor of receiving the German surrender.

After Stalingrad, Rokossovsky transported his entire staff and a single army by rail to the Kursk sector. After receiving reinforcements, his force was redesignated the Central front and held the north face of the Kursk salient until after the conclusion of the Battle of KURSK in July.

After Kursk, Rokossovsky advanced toward the Dnieper, which he crossed during November 1944, having in the process amalgamated the Central and Briansk fronts to form the massive Belorussian front. Rokossovsky extended his lines westward through the Pripet marshes until his Belorussian front (later called the First Belorussian front) reached across all the southern half of the salient occupied by German Army Group Center. This allowed him to envelop and destroy that force in July.

Rokossovsky continued his advance, reaching the Vistula north and south of Warsaw by September 1944, whereupon Stalin promoted him to marshal of the Soviet Union. Despite this promotion, Stalin turned the First Belorussian front over to Zhukov and transferred Rokossovsky to the Second Belorussian front. Presumably, Stalin wanted to deny Rokossovsky—whom he had, after all, once purged—the honor of conquering Berlin.

As commander of the Second Belorussian front, Rokossovsky advanced across Poland in January 1945 and, after conducting various operations in West Prussia and Pomerania, supported Zhukov's advance to make contact with U.S. troops at Wismar, 124 miles west of the Oder River on May 2.

After the war, Rokossovsky, who had been born in Poland but had lived most of his life in the Soviet Union, remained in command of Soviet forces in northern Poland and Germany. In 1949, he was appointed Polish minister of national defense and marshal of Poland. In 1952, he became deputy chairman of the Council of Ministers of the People's Republic of Poland. After Poland was somewhat liberalized by reformers in 1956, Rokossovsky returned to the Soviet Union. In July 1957, he was named deputy minister of defense and commander of the Transcaucasian Military District. The following year he became chief inspector of the Ministry of Defense, the post he held until his retirement in April 1962.

Further reading: Glantz, David M., and Jonathan M. House. *When Titans Clashed: How the Red Army Stopped Hitler.* Lawrence: University Press of Kansas, 1998; Shukman, Harold, ed. *Stalin's Generals.* Charleston, S.C.: Phoenix Press, 2002.

Romania

"Greater Romania," a nation expanded to encompass virtually all Romanians in the Balkans, was created by the TREATY OF VERSAILLES, and it was strongly aligned with the West until the MUNICH CONFERENCE AND AGREEMENT, after which it fell increasingly into the German orbit. This realignment was formalized by a German-Romanian economic agreement of March 23, 1939, which gave Germany great influence over the Romanian economy. Out of this agreement grew another, signed on December 4, 1940, by which Germany effectively made Romania its economic puppet. What Germany most wanted from Romania was exclusive access to its rich oilfields—especially in the Ploeşti area—on which it came increasingly to rely. By 1941, Germany took in 47 percent of its crude oil supply from German-owned companies based in Romania.

In the years before the outbreak of World War II, Romania, suffering during the worldwide economic depression, increasingly gravitated toward right-wing, fascist political movements, the most important of which was the Iron Guard, which imitated the German NAZI PARTY in many particulars, especially in its highly organized anti-Semitism. By 1938, King Carol II abandoned all semblance of parliamentary monarchy and created a personal dictatorship, bolstered by growing connections with Germany. Carol was especially concerned about the military threat represented by the Soviet Union and Hungary; during the period of early German triumph in Europe, he and his ministers formally allied the nation with Germany on May 27, 1940. In June, Carol yielded to German "advice" that he cede Bessarabia and Northern Bukovina to the Soviet Union, which was at the time a German military ally by virtue of the GERMAN-SOVIET NON-AGGRESSION PACT. Next, in June, Germany prompted Romania to cede northern Transylvania to Hungary and, in September, to return Craiova (South Dobruja) to Bulgaria. In return for all these cessions, ADOLF HITLER pledged Germany's protection of Romanian sovereignty—or what was left of it. The cessions proved so unpopular with the Romanian people, however, that Carol abdicated on September 6, 1940, in favor of his son Michael. General ION ANTONESCU was named prime minister.

A German military mission was sent to Romania beginning on October 12, charged with the task of building up the Romanian army. Simultaneously, a German economic mission began work to ensure that the Romanian economy was tailored to serve Germany's wartime needs. When the Iron Guard, seeking ever more power, slipped the short leash on which he had kept it, Antonescu received Hitler's blessing to disarm the Iron Guard on the one hand and strengthen the army on the other. On January 21, 1941, this provoked the so-called Iron Guard Uprising against the Antonescu government. Antonescu responded by dissolving the Iron Guard completely and, on January 27, forming a new cabinet made up of military officers. Romania was now undeniably a military dictatorship. This was sufficient to persuade Hitler to permit Romania to enjoy nominal sovereignty within the Nazi orbit; Hitler's greatest concern was to preserve Romania's stability, so that its oil production would be unhindered and so that the country would be available to him as an advance base from which to mount operations against the Soviet Union.

Antonescu led Romania in a full military alliance with Germany beginning with the invasion of the SOVIET UNION in June 1941, a move that created much dissension within the Romanian government and general population. Great Britain declared war against Romania on December 7, 1941. On December 12, Romania followed Germany's lead and declared war on the United States.

Until the Red Army began to turn the tide against the German army at the Battle of STALINGRAD in January 1943, Antonescu stubbornly resisted calls from within his own government to withdraw from fighting in the Soviet Union. As the German situation deteriorated, however, he sent out peace feelers, proposing to BENITO MUSSOLINI that Italy and Romania jointly seek a separate peace with the Allies. Rebuffed by Mussolini, Antonescu made several attempts to contact the Allies directly. Each time, he stumbled against the Allied insistence on unconditional surrender. Antonescu believed that to surrender in this way

would ensure the ultimate absorption of Romania into the Soviet Union or, at least, its sphere of influence. At last, King Michael acted, arresting Antonescu on August 23, 1944, and ordering the surrender of all Romanian forces opposing the Red Army. Romania then concluded an armistice with the Soviet Union on September 12—a document that (as Antonescu had feared) gave the Soviets a dominant political and economic interest in the country.

Romania suffered mightily in World War II. Its casualties in the German invasion of the Soviet Union were estimated (in 1946) at 625,000; half this number were troops listed as missing. By the terms of the Soviet-Romanian armistice of September 12, 1944, Romania was obliged to provide at least 12 infantry divisions to fight in conjunction with Soviet forces. The Romanians actually provided significantly more than this number—perhaps the equivalent of 20 divisions—in aid of the Red Army's campaign to eject the Germans from Romanian territory and from Hungary and Czechoslovakia. During these campaigns, Romania contributed the fourth-largest Allied force in Europe (behind the Soviet Union, the United States, and Great Britain). Fighting for the Allies, the Romanian army suffered 160,000 casualties, including 111,000 killed or severely wounded.

See also PLOEŞTI RAID.

Further reading: Giurescu, Dinu C. *Romania in World War II.* New York: East European Monographs, 2000; Treptow, Kurt W., ed. *Romania and World War II.* Iasi, Romania: Center for Romanian Studies, 1996.

Rome-Berlin-Tokyo Axis   *See* AXIS (TRIPARTITE) PACT.

Rommel, Erwin Johannes Eugen (1891–1944) *Germany's legendary "Desert Fox," commander of the Afrika Korps and of the Atlantic Wall defenses*

Born in Heidenheim, Württemberg, Rommel was the son of a schoolteacher and joined the German

Erwin Rommel *(National Archives and Records Administration)*

Army in 1910 as an officer-aspirant. In January 1912, he was commissioned a second lieutenant and was assigned to a field artillery regiment in March 1914, shortly before the outbreak of World War I. He fought on the western front and was twice wounded. After recovering from his second wound, he transferred to the Württemberg Mountain Battalion and served in the Vosges, then on the Romanian and Italian fronts during 1917–18. He exhibited a marked talent for tactics, which he demonstrated by a bold infiltration during the Battle of Caporetto in the Italian campaign.

By the end of World War I, Rommel had risen to the position of staff officer, and in the much-reduced post–TREATY OF VERSAILLES army, he commanded an internal security company during 1919–21, then took charge of a company in the 13th Infantry Regiment headquartered at Stuttgart. In October 1929, Rommel was appointed an instructor at the Infantry School in Dresden; as a result of this assignment, he wrote what became the standard text on infantry tactics, *Infanterie Greiftan* (*Infantry Attacks*), which was published in 1937.

In October 1935, Rommel assumed command of a *Jaeger* ("hunter" or elite) battalion of the 17th Infantry Regiment, then in 1938 was assigned to command the War Academy at Wiener Neustadt. During 1938–39, Rommel was given the signal

honor of commanding the Führerbegleitbataillon, ADOLF HITLER's personal bodyguard. Hitler developed a high regard for Rommel, and during the invasion of POLAND he appointed him his chief for personal security.

In February 1940, Rommel assumed command of the 7th Panzer Division and was a key field commander during the Battle of FRANCE in May–June, 1940. Having demonstrated that he was one of Germany's leading exponents of armored warfare, Rommel was dispatched to Libya following the fall of France to command the Afrika Korps beginning in February 1941. In this command, he earned the sobriquet "Desert Fox" as he twice pushed British forces back across the Egyptian-Cyrenaican frontier in a spectacular series of large-scale armored battles. After the British surrendered at Tobruk in June 1942, Rommel was promoted to field marshal.

But even Rommel's genius could not compensate indefinitely for chronic problems of supply and general deficiencies of logistics. Moreover, in BERNARD LAW MONTGOMERY, he encountered an adversary far more skilled and determined than earlier British generals. In October–November 1942, Rommel suffered a severe defeat at the second of the two Battles of EL ALAMEIN and was recalled to Europe in March 1943. This was not to punish Rommel for his defeat, but to save him from further defeat. Hitler did not want the German people to see his favorite general in anything other than the context of victory.

Rommel was assigned to command Army Group B in northern Italy, then, in January 1944, was named to command of German forces in the Low Countries and northern France. In this role he oversaw the general rehabilitation and reinforcement of the "Atlantic Wall" defenses in anticipation of an Allied cross-Channel invasion. It would be Rommel's Army Group B that would bear the initial brunt of the NORMANDY LANDINGS (D-DAY) in June 1944.

Despite brilliant preparations for the invasion, Rommel proved unable to check the Allied onslaught; he was hampered in no small part by Hitler's refusal to allow him to deploy armored forces in the early stages of the fighting. Rommel mounted a fierce defense against the Allied break-out from Normandy, but failed here as well.

On July 17, 1944, Rommel was wounded in an Allied air attack, then, following the JULY PLOT (TO ASSASSINATE HITLER) three days later, he was implicated in the assassination conspiracy. Although Hitler arrested and executed some 5,000 persons suspected of complicity in the plot, he did not want the popular Rommel to be formally charged. Instead, the field marshal was given the option of ending his own life—and thereby saving his family from Nazi retribution. On October 14, 1944, he took cyanide. The Nazi propaganda machine reported that he had died a hero of the Reich, having succumbed to war wounds. Erwin Rommel was given a full state funeral.

See also TOBRUK, BATTLES OF.

Further reading: Fraser, David. *Knight's Cross: A Life of Field Marshal Erwin Rommel.* New York: Harper Perennial, 1995; Pimlott, John, ed. *Rommel and His Art of War.* London: Greenhill Books, 2003; Hart, Basil Henry Liddell, ed. *The Rommel Papers.* New York: Da Capo Press, 1982; Rommel, Erwin. *Attacks.* Provo, Utah: Athena Press, 1979.

Roosevelt, Franklin Delano (1882–1945)
America's wartime president and key Allied leader

Roosevelt was born to genteel privilege in Hyde Park, New York, and educated at Groton Preparatory School (Groton, Massachusetts) and at Harvard University. Although his academic record was undistinguished, Roosevelt was influenced during his college years by the Progressive political philosophy of his fifth cousin, President Theodore Roosevelt, and also fell in love with TR's niece, Eleanor Roosevelt, herself a passionate advocate for the poor. Franklin Roosevelt's marriage to Eleanor on March 17, 1905, increasingly developed in him an awareness of and concern for social issues.

Roosevelt attended Columbia University Law School but did not graduate, although he passed the New York bar and entered a Wall Street law firm. In 1910, he won election to the New York State Senate and was reelected in 1912. He left office to become assistant secretary of the navy in March 1913 under President Woodrow Wilson and, after the outbreak of World War I in Europe, was an eloquent advocate of U.S. military preparedness.

In 1920, Roosevelt was nominated as running mate to Democratic presidential candidate James M. Cox and vigorously campaigned for U.S. entry into the League of Nations, but, as expected, the pair lost in the Republican landslide that put Warren G. Harding and Calvin Coolidge into office. Roosevelt then pursued a business career, awaiting his next political opportunity. Polio struck him in August 1921, however, leaving him paralyzed from the waist down. The disability created by the disease seemed certain to end his political prospects. But thanks to the encouragement of his wife and of other close associates, Roosevelt remained politically active, and his 1924 and 1928 appearances at

President Franklin D. Roosevelt *(Franklin D. Roosevelt Presidential Library)*

the Democratic conventions to nominate Alfred E. Smith for president kept him before the public eye. At Smith's urging, he ran for governor of New York in 1928 and, a brilliant and charismatic campaigner, won. During his two gubernatorial terms, FDR introduced significant social reforms and, after the onset of the Great Depression, bold relief legislation. His performance as governor catapulted him to the Democratic presidential nomination in 1932.

In the depths of the Depression, FDR brought the hope and optimism of his sweeping New Deal program of social and economic legislation. Although the New Deal by no means succeeded in ending the Depression, it did offer urgently needed emergency relief to millions and renewed the American faith in democracy during an era when, in Europe, many nations (led by Italy and Germany) were becoming right-wing totalitarian dictatorships in opposition to the left-wing totalitarian dictatorship of the Soviet Union.

FDR was reelected in 1936 and to an unprecedented third term in 1940. As war threatened and then erupted in Europe and Asia, FDR aligned American neutrality increasingly to favor the Allies—the nations opposed to the Axis (chiefly Italy, Germany, and Japan). He established an especially strong personal relationship with British prime minister WINSTON CHURCHILL and created a partnership with Britain, which since the fall of France in 1940, stood alone against Nazi aggression, which was just short of a formal military alliance. Roosevelt pushed through Congress a massive budget for war preparedness and weapons production—he pledged to make the United States the "arsenal of democracy"—and ushered in the nation's first peacetime military draft. When the United States finally entered the war after the Japanese attack on Pearl Harbor (December 7, 1941), it did so better prepared for war than ever before in its history.

Like Churchill in Britain, FDR took an intense hands-on role in leading the nation through World War II. He acquired a strong and competent grasp of strategy, but most of all was a figure to whom the American people eagerly looked for leadership through a crisis unparalleled in U.S. or world history. Elected to a fourth term in 1944, he served only until April 12, 1945, when he was felled by a cerebral hemorrhage less than a month before victory came in Europe. He was succeeded by his vice president, HARRY S. TRUMAN.

See also PEARL HARBOR, BATTLE OF.

Further reading: Burns, James MacGregor. *Roosevelt: The Soldier of Freedom.* New York: Harcourt Brace Jovanovich, 1970; Dallek, Robert. *Franklin D. Roosevelt and American Foreign Policy, 1932–1945,* Oxford University Press, 1979; Davis, Kenneth S. *FDR: The War President, 1940–1943.* New York: Random House, 2000; Freidel, Frank. *Franklin D. Roosevelt: A Rendezvous with Destiny.* Boston: Little, Brown, 1990; Heinrichs, Waldo. *Threshold of War: Franklin D. Roosevelt and American Entry into World War II.* New York: Oxford University Press, 1988; Hunt, John Gabriel, ed. *The Essential Franklin Delano Roosevelt.* New York: Gramercy Books, 1995; Larrabee, Eric. *Commander in Chief: Franklin Delano Roosevelt, His Lieutenants, and Their War,* New York: Harper and Row, 1987.

Rosenberg, Alfred (1893–1946) *leading ideologist of Nazism*

Born into a shoemaker's family in Reval, Estonia (at the time a part of the Russian Empire), Rosenberg enrolled as a student of architecture in Moscow until the Russian Revolution of 1917 drove him out of the country. He settled in Munich in 1919, where he fell in with ADOLF HITLER, Ernst Roehm, and RUDOLF HESS and thereby became one of the creators of the NAZI PARTY (NSDAP).

Rosenberg edited the party newspaper, *Völkischer Beobachter,* and used its pages to define the Nazis as the valiant foes of a worldwide Jewish plot to dominate the world. In this way, he cemented in the public mind the role of anti-Semitism in Nazi doctrine. When Hitler was imprisoned after the Munich Beer Hall Putsch of November 1923, he named Rosenberg to lead the Nazi Party in his absence. In fact, Hitler counted on Rosenberg's complete incompetence as a politician and organizer to ensure that he would be nothing more than a caretaker of the party and would be both disinclined and unable to create for himself a power base by which he might wrest the party from his control. Hitler's instinct proved correct, and when he was released from prison, Rosenberg readily yielded leadership of the party back to him.

In the meantime, Rosenberg turned to his real talent, which was the formulation of party doctrine and the articulation of its ideology. In 1927, he published *Der Zukunftsweg einer deutschen Aussenpolitik* (*The Future Direction of a German Foreign Policy*), in which he set forth the German conquest of Poland and the USSR not only as military and political necessities, but as the moral and ideological means of saving the world from Bolshevism and Jewish domination. In 1934, Rosenberg published *Der Mythus des 20. Jahrhunderts* (*The Myth of the 20th Century*), an essay on German racial purity and the destiny of the German race—which Rosenberg theorized was descended from ancient Nordic ancestors—to dominate Europe and destroy the chief opposing races, the "Russian Tartars" and the "Semites" (Jews, Latin peoples, and even Christians—in the form of the Catholic Church). In that same year, his collected writings and speeches began to appear in a series titled *Blut und Ehre* (*Blood and Honour*), which culminated in a final volume published in 1941.

Beyond providing an expression of Nazi ideology, Rosenberg, early in World War II, also introduced Hitler to VIDKUN QUISLING, the Norwegian traitor who facilitated a Nazi coup in his native country. After this, however, Rosenberg receded into insignificance within the party and the German government. He was put in charge of transporting looted European artworks to Germany and, from July 1941, served in the largely honorific office of Reichsminister for the occupied eastern territories.

After the war, Rosenberg was convicted as a war criminal by the NUREMBERG WAR CRIMES TRIBUNAL and sentenced to death. He was hanged on October 16, 1946.

Further reading: Cecil, Robert. *The Myth of the Master Race: Alfred Rosenberg and Nazi Ideology.* New York:

Dodd, Mead, 1972; Nova, Fritz. *Alfred Rosenberg, Nazi Theorist of the Holocaust.* New York: Buccaneer Books, 1986; Rosenberg, Alfred. *Selected Writings.* London: Jonathan Cape, 1970.

Rotterdam air raid

The air raid on the Dutch port city of Rotterdam was carried out on May 14, 1940, to force the city into an immediate surrender during the invasion of the NETHERLANDS. A German AIRBORNE ASSAULT had deployed paratroops to seize and seal off all bridges into Rotterdam. In view of this and the imminence of an overwhelming invasion force, the Dutch agreed to discuss surrender terms; accordingly, the raid was cancelled—but the abort order arrived too late to stop 57 of 100 bombers launched from attacking. Although the bombs were aimed primarily at military targets, more than a square mile of Rotterdam's central city was flattened and nearly 1,000 civilians killed. Within hours of the raid, the Dutch government surrendered—having barely committed its army to combat.

The Allies used the Rotterdam raid as justification for their own STRATEGIC BOMBING policy, which targeted German cities and civilians. Indeed, the British RAF raided the Ruhr on the very day following the Rotterdam attack.

Further reading: Biddle, Tami David. *Rhetoric and Reality in Air Warfare: The Evolution of British and American Ideas about Strategic Bombing, 1914–1945.* Princeton, N.J.: Princeton University Press, 2004; Kennett, Lee B. *A History of Strategic Bombing.* New York: Scribner, 1982; Knell, Herman. *To Destroy a City: Strategic Bombing and Its Human Consequences in World War II.* New York: Da Capo, 2003.

Rudel, Hans Ulrich (1916–1982) *legendary German air ace of World War II*

Born in Konradswaldau, Germany, the son of a Protestant minister, Hans Ulrich Rudel left school before the outbreak of World War II to join the Luftwaffe. During the invasion of POLAND, he flew reconnaissance missions, earning on October 11,

Hans Ulrich Rudel wearing his Knight's Cross with Golden Oakleaves and Diamonds *(National Archives and Records Administration)*

1939, an Iron Cross 2nd Class. At his request, he was enrolled in Ju-87 Stuka dive-bombing training in May 1940 and participated in the AIRBORNE ASSAULT during the invasion of Crete in May 1941. Later in the year, he flew on the eastern front, providing close ground support in the invasion of the SOVIET UNION. He was awarded the Iron Cross 1st Class on July 18, 1941. In January 1945, Rudel was awarded the Golden Oakleaves and was promoted to colonel, having flown 2,530 sorties over the USSR, in which he claimed to have destroyed 519 Soviet tanks. In this hazardous work, he was shot down no fewer than 30 times by antiaircraft fire.

On February 9, Rudel, shot down yet again, was seriously injured. He returned to flight duty six weeks after his leg was amputated. When Germany surrendered on May 8, 1945, Rudel flew his Stuka to the American occupation zone to avoid capture by the Soviets. He moved to Argentina after the war and was employed there by the State Airplane Works. An unapologetic Nazi militarist, he wrote two books after the war, *We Frontline Soldiers* and *Our Opinion on the Rearmament of Germany,* in which he proposed a new war against the Soviet Union for the purpose of obtaining LEBENSRAUM. A third book, *Daggerthrust* (also called *Legend*), condemned all members of the German military who had failed to give ADOLF HITLER their full support and loyalty. Rudel left Argentina in 1953 to return to West Germany, where he became active in the neo-Nazi German Reich Party. His memoir, *Stuka Pilot,* appeared in 1958, and he enjoyed success as a prominent German businessman.

See also CRETE, ACTION ON.

Further reading: Just, Gunther. *Stuka-Pilot Hans-Ulrich Rudel: His Life Story in Words and Photographs.* Atglen, Pa.: Schiffer, 1990; Rudel, Hans-Ulrich. *Stuka Pilot.* New York: Ballantine Books, 1971.

Rundstedt, (Karl Rudolf) Gerd von (1875–1953) *one of Germany's most capable field marshals of World War II*

Rundstedt was born at Aschersleben, Germany, into a family with a Prussian military heritage. He was enrolled in the Oranienstein Cadet School from 1888 to 1891, then graduated from the Main Cadet School at Gross Lichterfelde in 1893 and was commissioned a second lieutenant that year in the 33rd Infantry Regiment. In 1902, he was sent to the prestigious Kriegsakademie, the German army's war college, from which he graduated with distinction, earning a promotion to captain and a slot on the General Staff in 1909.

At the outbreak of World War I, Rundstedt was chief operations officer of the 22d Reserve Division. He assumed command of the division after its regular commander was wounded at the battle of the Marne during September 5–10, 1914. Promoted to major in November 1914, Rundstedt was assigned to a number of staff posts in the course of the war, culminating in an appointment as chief of staff of the XV Corps in November 1918.

After the armistice, Rundstedt was among the elite cadre of 4,000 officers selected to lead the post–TREATY OF VERSAILLES army, the Reichwehr. He was promoted to lieutenant colonel and served as chief of staff of the 3rd Cavalry Division beginning in October 1920. In 1923, he was promoted to colonel and in 1922 commanded the 18th Infantry Regiment. Promoted to Generalmajor in November 1928, he assumed command of the 2nd Cavalry

Division. The following year, he was promoted to Generalleutnant, and in 1932 became General der Infanterie with command of First Army.

As a member of the Reichswehr's inner circle, Rundstedt was instrumental in the covert rearmament of Germany. He retired from active service with the rank of Generaloberst in October 1938, but was recalled to active duty on June 1, 1939 and assigned to command Army Group South during the Battle of FRANCE from May 10 to June 25, 1940. After his triumphal performance in this theater, he was promoted to field marshal on August 19, 1940, and commanded Army Group South in the invasion of the SOVIET UNION. Rundstedt led his army through the Ukraine, reaching the Don River on December 1, 1940.

Feeling the effects of age, he resigned his commission after the Ukraine campaign, only to be recalled yet again in March 1942 as commander in chief, west (OB West) and commander of Army Group B. His assignment was to make preparations against an anticipated Allied invasion of western Europe. In this mission, he fell into disagreement with ERWIN ROMMEL over how best to deploy the mobile reserve force, and a month after the NORMANDY LANDINGS (D-DAY), Rundstedt was relieved of command (on July 6, 1944). Nevertheless, ADOLF HITLER appointed him to the "Court of Honor" that tried the officers implicated in the JULY PLOT (TO ASSASSINATE HITLER).

As the western front continued to collapse, Rundstedt was recalled to duty for a third time, as commander of Army Group B, on September 5, 1944. He mounted the spectacular Ardennes offensive during September 16, 1944–January 16, 1945, the last-ditch German offensive of the war.

Rundstedt commanded the desperate defense of the Rhineland during January 1–March 10, 1945, and was personally dismissed from command by Hitler on March 9. Captured by U.S. forces in May, he was held in England from 1945 to 1948, then released to a quiet retirement in Hanover.

See also ARDENNES, BATTLE OF THE (BATTLE OF THE BULGE).

Further reading: Keegan, John. *Rundstedt.* New York: Ballantine, 1974; Messenger, Charles. *The Last Prussian: A Biography of Field Marshal Gerd Von Rundstedt, 1875–1953.* Dulles, Va.: Potomac Books, 1991.

Gerd von Rundstedt *(U.S. Army Command and General Staff College)*

Russian summer offensive of 1943

By the summer of 1943, the tide had clearly turned against the Germans on the Soviet front. ADOLF HITLER wanted at all costs to avoid retreat, but was willing to engage in what he called "strategic retrenchment," which, he hoped, would put his forces in a position to renew the offensive later, on a smaller scale. By 1943, Hitler had 3.07 million German troops in the Soviet Union, opposing 6.6 million Red Army troops. Moreover, he anticipated that the Western Allies would open up a second European front, which would call for the transfer of some troops from the east to the west.

Yet even as Hitler resolved to focus on defense on the Soviet front during the summer, German forces found themselves in a promising position at Kursk, where the Red Army bulge (or salient) was vulnerable to being pinched off by a timely attack. For their part, the Soviets also focused on this area. Instead of taking the initiative here, however, the Red Army waited for the Germans to act. In anticipation of possible German moves, Soviet planners prepared two operations: Operation Kutuzov, an assault against the German salient at Orel; and Operation Rumyantsev, an assault against the Belgorod-Kharkov salient. By the middle of May, the Soviets had five fronts (army groups) in readiness to carry out one of the two operations, depending on where the Germans made their move first. A sixth front was held in reserve in the Orel-Kursk-Kharkov sector.

On July 5, the Germans finally acted. WALTHER MODEL led his Ninth German Army in Operation Citadel, striking south while the Fourth Panzer Army advanced northward, toward Kursk. The Soviets moved quickly to contain these advances, narrowly preventing a Fourth Panzer breakthrough on July 12. On that date, Soviet Marshal GEORGI ZHUKOV launched Operation Kutuzov, attacking the north face of the Orel salient. Simultaneously, the Fifth Guards Tank Army engaged the Fourth Panzer Division.

Just as Operation Citadel was getting under way, Hitler was faced with a crisis in Sicily as U.S. and British forces began their advance from the beachheads they had established. On July 13, Hitler summarily canceled Operation Citadel, claiming that he needed the SS panzer divisions to hold Italy. He gave Model command of the Second Panzer Division as well as Ninth Army and ordered him to defend the Orel salient with the object of restoring the front there. When ERICH VON MANSTEIN protested that the sudden cancellation of Operation Citadel would appear to be a German defeat, Hitler authorized him to maintain the offensive long enough to claim some degree of victory. Four days later, however, he summarily ordered the SS panzer divisions out of the front.

Model in the meantime fought a fierce defense, which took a terrible toll on the Red Army. On July 25, however, Hitler, responding to the ouster and arrest of BENITO MUSSOLINI, warned Model that Army Group Center in the Soviet Union would have to yield no fewer than 24 divisions for redeployment in Italy. Model had no choice but to begin as orderly a withdrawal as possible. On August 5, Model abandoned Orel. At the same time, Belgorod was liberated by the Red Army. These events prompted JOSEPH STALIN to issue a "special order of the day" declaring an end to the "German legend" claiming that the Soviets were incapable of waging a summer campaign.

Stalin's "special order" notwithstanding, the Red Army had not yet mounted a full-scale summer offensive. The German withdrawal was orderly, and six entire Soviet fronts (army groups) were kept occupied defending against German units. An important Soviet breakthrough did come on August 23, when Manstein evacuated Kharkov, and at the end of the month eight Soviet fronts (army groups) began developing no fewer than 19 parallel advances toward the Dnieper River, the strongest being just west of Kursk and Kharkov. By September, Hitler reluctantly agreed to allow a limited withdrawal behind the Dnieper, but by this time the Red Army was able to force multiple crossings and pursue the retreating Germans. By December, the Soviets had gained substantial bridgeheads at key points on the river, dooming the Germans in the Ukraine.

See also KURSK, BATTLE OF.

Further reading: Bechtolsheim, Anton. *The Battle of Kharkov, 1942.* Leavenworth, Kans.: Historical Division, Headquarters, United States Army, Europe, Foreign Military Studies Branch, 1952; Fowler, William. *Kursk: The Vital 24 Hours.* Fort Myers, Fla.: Amber, 2005; Glantz, David M. *Kharkov 1942: Anatomy of a Military Disaster.* Rockville Centre, N.Y.: Sarpedon, 1998; Glantz, David M., and Jonathan M. House. *The Battle of Kursk.* Lawrence: University Press of Kansas, 1999; Nipe, George M. *Last Victory in Russia: The SS-Panzerkorps and Manstein's Kharkov Counteroffensive–February–March 1943.* Atglen, Pa.: Schiffer, 2000.

Russian winter counteroffensive of 1941–1942

On October 2, 1941, the German Army Group Center began Operation Typhoon in an effort to capture Moscow. Despite progress made, the Soviets resisted doggedly, and by November the German advance was bogged down in the mud of a wet winter. A freeze beginning on November 15 gave new impetus to Operation Typhoon, which regained mobility, and by November 24, German forces were on the outskirts of the Soviet capital, but were again halted by the end of the month. Now the winter came in earnest, as temperatures dropped as much as 30 degrees below zero. Soldiers as well as vehicles suffered—the men freezing, the machinery grinding to a halt when lubricants froze.

With the Germans stalled, Marshal Georgi Zhukov counterattacked on the morning of December 6. The Germans found it impossible to dig into the frozen ground, nor could they gain sufficient mobility to close the many gaps in their lines. German commanders predicted the total collapse of their lines. In response, Adolf Hitler ordered on December 18 what he termed "fanatical resistance," and on December 19 he relieved Walther von Brauchitsch as commander in chief of the German Army and assumed personal command of all German forces.

Despite the "fanatical resistance" order, German Army Group North withdrew from Tikhvin and Army Group Center from its positions near Moscow. In the meantime, to the north, German positions around Leningrad were eroding. Marshal Zhukov sought to exploit the growing vulnerability of the German position by a counteroffensive to drive Army Group Center to the line from which Operation Typhoon had been launched. At the same time, after Army Group South had finished its retreat from Rostov, the Soviet Black Sea Fleet landed three armies on the Kerch peninsula in east Crimea beginning on December 26. Still intent on resisting the counterattack by means of "fanatical resistance," Hitler shook up his high command in the Soviet Union, sending Field Marshal Fedor von Bock home and relieving both Heinz Guderian and Erich Hoepner. All had dared to challenge the "fanatical resistance" order.

In the meantime, Joseph Stalin announced a grand counteroffensive that pitted nine Red Army fronts (army groups) against the invaders all along a line stretching from Leningrad to the Crimea. Stalin intended to liberate Leningrad in the north, and the Donets basin and the Crimea in the south. The counteroffensive would also prevent the Germans from making a new attempt against Moscow.

Zhukov was tasked with enveloping and destroying Army Group Center, and he did force the Germans to spread themselves very thin, but his subordinate commanders were unable to achieve the level of coordination necessary to drive off the German army group. Field Marshal Günther von Kluge held his lines outside of Moscow, as did commanders to the north and south. By March, when the spring thaw halted all operations for weeks, the German lines had been pushed back in places, but German forces were also able to maintain a series of salients along a very broad front. Thus the Soviet counteroffensive halted the German advance—and even gained some ground—but it would not prevent the Germans from mounting a new summer offensive.

Stalin announced that the Red Army would conduct an active defense, but he also insisted on certain actions he characterized as "preemptive blows." These failed miserably, allowing the Germans to score a number of highly visible successes, which gave at least the illusion of continued victory. Nevertheless, the Red Army's progress was real, and by the end of the winter of 1941–42, it was becoming clear that the German position in the Soviet Union was increasingly vulnerable.

Further reading: Bergstrom, Christer, and Andrey Mikhailov. *Black Cross/Red Star: Operation Barbarossa 1941.* Pacifica, Calif.: Pacifica Press, 2000; Clark, Alan. *Barbarossa.* New York: Harper Perennial, 1985; Fugate, Bryan I. *Operation Barbarossa: Strategy and Tactics on the Eastern Front, 1941.* Novato, Calif.: Presidio Press, 1984; Glantz, David M., and Jonathan M. House. *When Titans Clashed: How the Red Army Stopped Hitler.* Lawrence: University Press of Kansas, 1998; Glantz, David M. *Before Stalingrad: Barbarossa—Hitler's Invasion of Russia 1941.* Stroud, U.K.: Tempus Publishing, 2003.

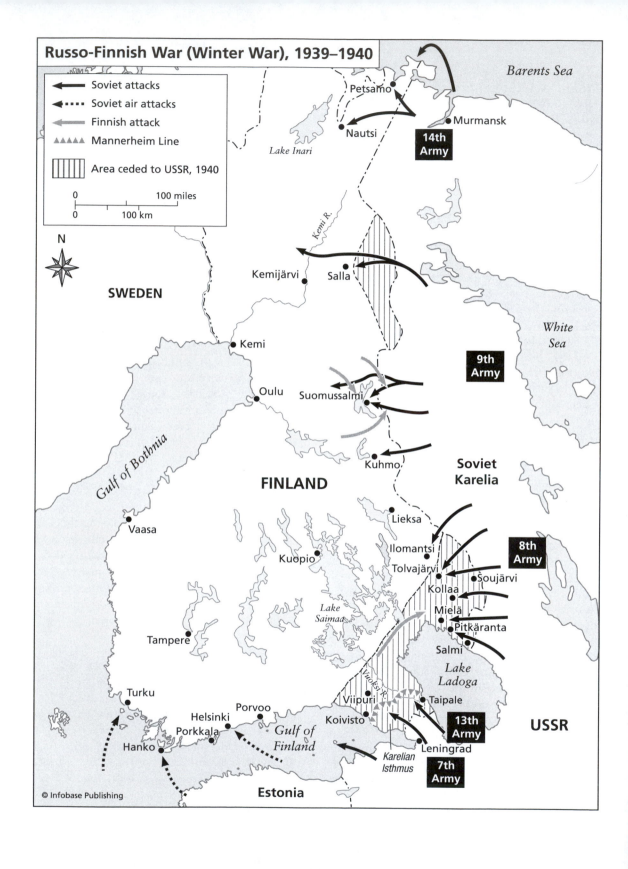

Russo-Finnish War (Winter War), 1939–1940

Legend:
- ⟵ Soviet attacks
- ◄┅┅ Soviet air attacks
- ⟵ Finnish attack
- ▲▲▲▲▲ Mannerheim Line
- ▦ Area ceded to USSR, 1940

0 — 100 miles
0 — 100 km

N

Barents Sea

Petsamo
Nautsi
Murmansk
14th Army

Lake Inari

Kemi R.

Kemijärvi
Salla
9th Army

White Sea

SWEDEN

Kemi

Oulu

Gulf of Bothnia

Suomussalmi

Kuhmo

FINLAND

Soviet Karelia

Vaasa

Lieksa

Kuopio

Ilomantsi
Tolvajärvi
8th Army
Soujärvi
Kollaa
Mielä
Pitkäranta
Salmi

Lake Saimaa

Tampere

Lake Ladoga

Vuoksi R.

Turku

Porvoo
Viipuri
Taipale
Helsinki
Koivisto
13th Army
USSR
Porkkala
Hanko
Gulf of Finland
Leningrad
Estonia
Karelian Isthmus
7th Army

© Infobase Publishing

Russo-Finnish War (Winter War)

The Russo-Finnish War coincided with the early months of World War II and began when the Soviet Union invaded Finland on November 30, 1939, without a declaration of war. The primary object of the invasion was to acquire Finland as a buffer zone against the eventuality of German aggression, which JOSEPH STALIN feared, despite having concluded the GERMAN-SOVIET NON-AGGRESSION PACT on August 23, 1939. By invading and annexing the eastern third of Poland, as well as territory in small Baltic and Balkan states, the Soviets believed they could protect their western frontier; however, the Russo-Finnish border was well within reach of Finnish artillery. Soviet planners believed that Germany might land in Finland and use it as a base from which to invade the Soviet Union. After trying unsuccessfully to conclude a military alliance with Finland—the Finns rejected it in the name of preserving their neutrality—Soviet-Finnish negotiations broke down on November 26, 1939, after four Soviet soldiers were killed and nine wounded by artillery fire near the Soviet village of Mainila. The Soviets claimed that the shells had been fired by the Finns; however, the Finnish artillery was actually stationed so far behind its border that this was impossible. Clearly, the incident had been staged by the Soviets as an excuse to go to war with Finland. These so-called Mainila shots were the pretext for the Red Army's invasion of Finland on November 30, 1939.

The Soviets bombed Helsinki on the first day of the war and simultaneously launched a ground attack along the MANNERHEIM LINE using seven Soviet divisions. Although the Finns were outgunned and outnumbered, they enjoyed the advantage of superior leadership and tactics, which exploited the snow and rugged terrain to advantage. At every point along the frontier, the Soviets were repulsed. As they withdrew, Colonel Paavo Talvela led a Finnish counterattack at Tolvajarvi. This effort faded by December 23, however, and was not decisive. Nevertheless, Soviet losses were heavy: 4,000 killed, 5,000 wounded. The Finns lost 630 killed and 1,320 wounded. The Red Air Force produced even more dismal results. Although aircraft flew more than 44,000 sorties and dropped 7,500 tons of ordnance, the bombardment produced no decisive effect.

Sensing that the Soviets had lost the initiative, the Finns staged a counterattack on the eastern border, where the 9th Finnish Division scored a great victory at Suomussalmi during December 11–January 8, destroying two entire Soviet divisions—killing some 27,500 Red Army soldiers. North of Lake Ladoga, separating the USSR and Finland, the Finns attacked at Kitela, destroying an entire Soviet division in January 1940 with "motti tactics." The Finnish word *motti* describes a pile of logs awaiting chopping or sawing. Finnish troops would surround the enemy column and block the road on which it advanced. They would then launch sharp attacks on the stalled enemy, splitting the column into isolated fragments, which would be starved, frozen, and finally "chopped" to death. The Finnish triumph at Kitela is often called the "Great Motti."

Despite their losses, the Soviets persisted. Whereas the Finns had better commanders and superior tactics, the Soviets had a virtually limitless supply of men, and Stalin was prepared to commit them to battle. Indeed, Soviet casualties were staggering: 126,875 killed out of 710,578 men ultimately deployed. Yet the Finns understood that they could not long hold out against such numbers. Finland sued for peace and on March 12, 1940, accepted installation of a Soviet-controlled puppet government. Finland also ceded the strategically valuable Karelian Isthmus and Viipuri.

Few in Finland were satisfied with the treaty of March 12, 1940, and, in June 1941, after Germany launched its invasion of the SOVIET UNION, Finland allied itself with Germany and participated in action on the Soviet front.

Further reading: Engle, Eloise. *The Winter War: The Soviet Attack on Finland, 1939–1940.* Mechanicsburg, Pa.: Stackpole Books, 1992; Trotter, William R. A *Frozen Hell: The Russo-Finnish Winter War of 1939–1940.* Chapel Hill, N.C.: Algonquin Books of Chapel Hill, 2000; Venvilainen, Olli. *Finland in the Second World War: Between Germany and Russia.* London: Palgrave Macmillan, 2002.

S

St. Nazaire Raid

On the night of March 27–28, 1942, the *Campbel-town* (one of the obsolescent U.S. destroyers Britain acquired through the U.S. LEND-LEASE program) boldly sailed past the defenses of the French port of St. Nazaire (St-Nazaire), deliberately rammed the outer caisson of the dock, then landed 268 British commandos, who destroyed dock machinery. The purpose of this daring raid was to destroy the only Atlantic dry dock available to the Germans that was big enough to accommodate the battleship *Tirpitz,* which could have been used to attack Allied convoys.

Many of the commandos were abandoned and were subsequently captured or killed. During the day on March 28, explosives in the *Campbeltown* were detonated, destroying the dock—and killing a number of German officers who were inspecting the ship. Two British commandos on board at the time remained silent about the explosion they knew to be imminent and therefore gave their lives to preserve the operation.

The raid was successful in that it destroyed the dry dock; however, its cost was great: 144 commandos and British naval personnel killed and more than 200 made prisoner.

Further reading: Dorrian, James. *St. Nazaire Raid: Operation CHARIOT—1942 French Coast.* London: Pen and Sword, 2006; Ford, Ken. *St. Nazaire 1942: The Great Commando Raid.* New York: Praeger, 2004; Mason, David. *Raid on St. Nazaire.* New York: Ballantine, 1970.

Saipan, Battle of

Saipan was the first island captured in the MARI-ANA ISLANDS CAMPAIGN and was a major American victory in the Pacific war, bringing Japan within range of U.S. B-29 bombers and precipitating the downfall of no less a figure than Japan's prime minister and military dictator, TOJO HEIDEKI.

Since the end of World War I, Saipan had been a Japanese mandate and was a major military and administrative base. The island was very well defended, offering high ground from which the western landing beaches would become killing fields. Moreover, Saipan was protected by coral reefs so formidable that U.S. Navy underwater demolition teams had to blast passages for the LANDING CRAFT that landed the 77,000 men of the 2nd and 4th U.S. Marine Divisions of Lt. Gen. HOLLAND "HOWLIN' MAD" SMITH's 5th Amphibious Corps on June 15, 1944. As it was, the landing phase did not go well. Prelanding naval and air bombardment had been neither sufficient nor sufficiently effective, which meant that the marines were instantly met by fierce resistance from the island's 32,000-man Japanese garrison (elements of the Thirty-First Japanese Army under Lt. Gen. Yoshitsugu Saito). In the first 48 hours of battle, 4,000 marines were killed or wounded. That the Japanese managed so effective a defense is the more remarkable in that Yoshitsugu had actually expected the landings to come elsewhere on the island, yet was able to shift his defenses quickly.

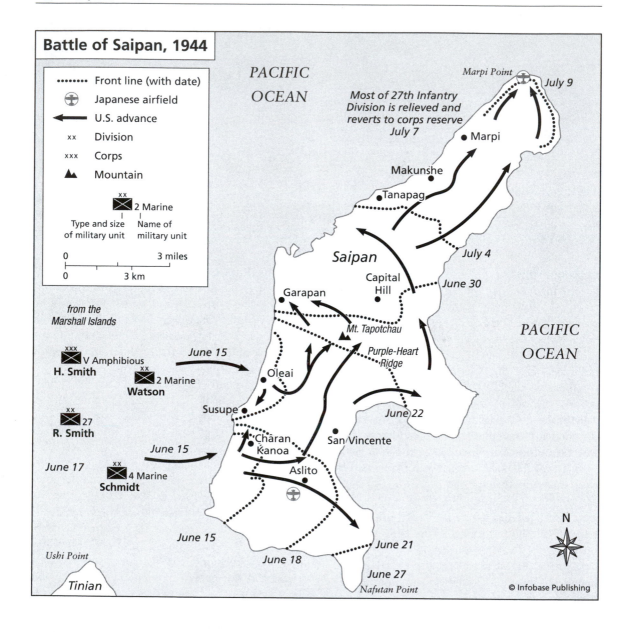

Battle of Saipan, 1944

Legend:
- Front line (with date)
- Japanese airfield
- U.S. advance
- xx   Division
- xxx   Corps
- ▲   Mountain

xx
2 Marine
Type and size | Name of
of military unit | military unit

0 ——— 3 miles
0 ——— 3 km

PACIFIC OCEAN

Marpi Point   July 9

Most of 27th Infantry Division is relieved and reverts to corps reserve July 7

Marpi

Makunshe

Tanapag

July 4

Saipan

June 30

Capital Hill

PACIFIC OCEAN

from the Marshall Islands

Garapan

Mt. Tapotchau

Purple-Heart Ridge

xxx
V Amphibious
H. Smith

June 15

xx
2 Marine
Watson

Oleai

xx
27
R. Smith

Susupe

June 22

June 17

xx
4 Marine
Schmidt

June 15

Charan Kanoa

San Vincente

Aslito

June 15

June 21

June 18

June 27

Ushi Point

Nafutan Point

Tinian

N

© Infobase Publishing

Yoshitsugu was confident that he would be able to pin the marines down on their beachhead, rendering them vulnerable to the Japanese Mobile Fleet, which would bombard the beachhead as well as destroy the marines' landing craft. This would, indeed, have been catastrophic for the American forces, but it never happened. The Mobile Fleet was defeated in the Battle of the PHILIPPINE SEA, leaving Yoshitsugu no choice but to pull back to the center of the 14-mile-long island and fight as costly a delaying action as possible. Whereas USMC commanders had estimated a three-day battle to take Saipan, Yoshitsugu managed to hold them off for three bloody weeks.

The first milestone objective attained was Aslito airfield on the south end of Saipan, which was captured on June 18. But an attempt to advance from this objective to the north was met by deadly resistance in the rugged terrain near Mount Tapotchau. The army's 27th Infantry Division, freshly landed, was sent into this sector and suffered severe casualties in a wooded patch dubbed Purple Heart Ridge. The advance of the 27th bogged down here until naval support fire battered Japanese defensive positions.

During the night of July 6–7, the Japanese mounted a desperate BANZAI CHARGE—the biggest and deadliest of the war—which nevertheless failed to throw back the U.S. soldiers. The charge, which cost the lives of at least 4,300 Japanese, was the last major Japanese operation on the island, although small bands of diehards continued to fight for months. The island was declared secure on July 9. On that day, many Japanese soldiers committed suicide rather than surrender, and even more civilians, who had been told that they would be raped, tortured, and even cannibalized by the Americans, also killed themselves, often by leaping to their deaths from Marpi Point.

Further reading: Leckie, Robert. *Strong Men Armed: The United States Marines against Japan.* New York: Da Capo Press, 1997; Petty, Bruce M., ed. *Saipan: Oral Histories of the Pacific War.* Jefferson, N.C.: McFarland, 2001; Rottman, Gordon. *Saipan and Tinian 1944: Piercing the Japanese Empire.* London: Osprey, 2004.

Salerno, Battle of

The principal Allied assault on mainland Italy during the ITALIAN CAMPAIGN was directed against Salerno on the west coast of Italy. From here, the Allies intended to take Naples, a major port city. Just before the September 9, 1943, landing, Marshal PIETRO BADOGLIO, who had become Italy's head of state after the removal and arrest of BENITO MUSSOLINI, surrendered to Allied supreme commander DWIGHT D. EISENHOWER, but Field Marshal ALBERT KESSELRING led German forces, which were deployed to all strategic points throughout Italy, in a determined resistance; the Germans rapidly moved south to engage the Allies.

The landing at Salerno, code-named Operation Avalanche, was carried out by the Fifth Army (MARK CLARK) at dawn on September 9. Landing on the right (southern flank) was the U.S. VI Corps (Ernest Dawley, subsequently relieved by JOHN LUCAS), whose 36th and 45th Infantry Divisions took Paestum within 72 hours and advanced inland 10 miles. Landing on the left (northern flank) was the British X Corps (56th and 46th divisions, Richard McCreery), which took Battipaglia and then Salerno itself.

On September 12, German forces counterattacked, recapturing Battipaglia and pushing back the Allies to within two miles of the coast in some places. To check the counterattack, Allied aircraft repeatedly struck at German positions on September 14. Aerial bombardment was supplemented by naval gunfire, and British general Sir HAROLD ALEXANDER, in overall command of Allied ground forces in Italy, sent the U.S. 82nd Airborne and the British 7th Armoured divisions to bolster the Fifth Army forces. This stopped the counterattack by nightfall on September 15, forcing Kesselring to retreat. On September 16, BERNARD LAW MONTGOMERY's British Eighth Army, up from southern Italy, joined the Fifth Army. With this, the Salerno landing was secured. Now reinforced by the U.S. 3rd Division, the Fifth Army broke out toward Naples, taking the city on October 1.

Further reading: Blaxland, Gregory. *Alexander's Generals: The Italian campaign, 1944–45.* London: W. Kimber, 1979; Botjer, George F. *Sideshow War: The Italian Campaign, 1943–1945.* College Station: Texas A&M University Press, 1996; Shepperd, G. A. *the Italian Campaign 1943–45: A Political and Military Reassessment.* London: Barker, 1968; Strawson, John. *The Italian Campaign.* New York: Carroll & Graf, 1988; Wallace, Robert. *The Italian Campaign.* Alexandria, Va.: Time Life Education, 1978.

Scapa Flow

Scapa Flow is a natural harbor located within the Orkney Islands off the northeast coast of Scotland. Its military significance has been recognized since the 13th century, and in World War I it was the northern base of the British Grand Fleet. During World War II, it was the base of the Home Fleet, which participated in ARCTIC CONVOY OPERATIONS as an escort.

Early in the war, in October 1939, German U-boat ace Günther Prien sailed U-47 into Scapa Flow and torpedoed HMS *Royal Oak,* which sank with the loss of 833 of its 1,400-man crew. The loss of *Royal Oak* prompted the British admiralty to set up an elaborate defense of Scapa Flow using anti-aircraft installations, minefields, and blockships. In 1940, by order of Prime Minister WINSTON CHURCHILL, concrete blocks were erected between the islands on the eastern side of Scapa Flow, creating four causeways today known as the Churchill Barriers. Most of the work was done by Italian prisoners of war. The base was not attacked again.

Further reading: McKee, Alexander. *Black Saturday: Tragedy at Scapa Flow.* London: Cerberus Publishing, 2005.

Schacht, Hjalmar (1877–1970) *Financial manager of the Third Reich*

Schacht was president of the Reichsbank from 1923 to 1930 and again from 1933 to 1939. He was ADOLF HITLER's architect of the Nazi war economy and held plenipotentiary authority from 1935 to 1937. Officially, he occupied the post of minister of economic affairs from August 1934 to November 1937; from 1937 until January 1943, he served the Reich as minister without portfolio.

Although Schacht was instrumental in much of Germany's economic planning during the 1930s, he increasingly opposed Hitler's rearmament policies because they exerted severe inflationary pressures. Schacht was held in such high regard, especially by the international community, that Hitler was loath to remove him, even when his opposition became increasingly strident. In 1937, however, under pressure from Hitler, Schacht resigned, although not before making clear his negative views on Nazi production and financial policy.

HERMANN GÖRING replaced Schacht, who quietly joined the resistance against Hitler. Following the JULY PLOT (TO ASSASSINATE HITLER) in 1944,

Schacht was arrested and spent the rest of the war in concentration camps. Tried by the NUREMBERG WAR CRIMES TRIBUNAL, he was acquitted of war crimes.

Further reading: Muhlen, Norbert. *Schacht: Hitler's Magician—The Life and Loans of Dr. Hjalmar Schacht.* New York: Alliance Book Corporation, 1939; Peterson, Edward N. *Hjalmar Schacht: For and against Hitler.* Boston: Christopher Publishing House, 1954; Schacht, Hjalmar Horace Greeley. *My First Seventy-Six Years.* New York: Wingate, 1955; Weitz, John. *Hitler's Banker: Hjalmar Horace Greeley Schacht.* Boston: Little, Brown, 1997.

Scheldt Estuary

During nearly three months, from September to November 1944, the Scheldt Estuary became the object of an Allied campaign to open a supply from the Belgian port of Antwerp to serve invasion forces.

BERNARD LAW MONTGOMERY's Twenty-First Army Group entered Antwerp on September 4, 1944. Montgomery's troops captured the port's extensive dock and lock systems intact. Now all that remained to be done was to connect these extraordinary port facilities via the Scheldt River with the Allied lines of advance through France and into Germany. The campaign for control of the estuary was critical to Allied logistics in its penetration of the countries occupied by Germany and Germany itself.

The fall of Antwerp to the Allies cut off the German Fifteenth Army (Lt. Gen. Gustav-Adolph von Zangen) on the west bank of the Scheldt. This afforded an opportunity for the Second U.S. Army (MILES DEMPSEY) to thrust between the German Fifteenth Army and the German forces defending the West Wall. Montgomery was absorbed in OPERATION MARKET-GARDEN, however, which he believed would expedite the Allied movement into Germany; he therefore initially neglected opening the Scheldt. The failure of Market-Garden denied the Allies the option of opening Rotterdam or Amsterdam as supply ports. Now Montgomery turned his attention to the Scheldt—but not before the German Fifteenth Army had begun making its escape from isolation. British Bomber Command began bombing German defenses on Walcheren Island, which dominated the mouth of the Scheldt, in mid-September, and Henry Crerar drew up plans for landing his Canadian 1st Corps on Walcheren after its dikes had been blasted by aerial bombardment and the inland German defenses largely flooded or isolated. Crerar was obliged to return to England for medical treatment on September 26, and turned over command of 2nd Corps to Lt. Gen. Guy Simonds, who in October led the 2nd Canadian Division toward the South Beveland isthmus, preparatory to an amphibious assault on Walcheren Island. Simultaneously, Operation Switchback attacked the German defenses around Breskens—what the Germans called Scheldt Fortress South. On October 16, Simonds was given clearance by Montgomery to employ the entire First Army to clear both banks of the Scheldt. Accordingly, the 2nd Canadian Division launched Operation Vitality along the isthmus to clear South Beveland and the eastern bank. Augmented by two brigades from 52nd (Lowland) Division, the Canadians overran South Beveland by the end of October.

The Canadians were now faced with traversing a 1,200-yard causeway to reach Walcheren Island. Three times they attacked along the causeway, and three times they were repulsed. At last relieved by the two brigades of 52nd (Lowland) Division, the Canadians withdrew. Elements of the 52nd bypassed the causeway and advanced across the Sloe Channel to the island.

While operations to land on Walcheren continued, the 3rd Canadian Division took Breskens on October 21, 1944. On November 1, British commandos launched two amphibious assaults on Walcheren. They faced extraordinary defenses, including PILLBOXES, concealed flamethrowers, and antipersonnel mines. The commandos called in naval and aerial bombardment to neutralize these defenses. More commandos landed at Flushing and were followed by the 155th Brigade of the 52nd (Lowland) Division. After two days of house-to-house combat, the Germans surrendered. Follow-

ing this, elements of the 155th Brigade made an amphibious crossing to Middleburg, Walcheren's capital, where the German commander capitulated on November 5. In the meantime, other commandos had captured all the batteries between Domburg and Flushing, which enabled MINESWEEPERS to begin clearing the Scheldt. All organized German resistance ended by November 8, 1944, and the Scheldt was pronounced clear of mines on November 26. On November 28, the first supply convoy arrived at Antwerp's docks.

Further reading: Moulton, J. L. *Battle for Antwerp: The Liberation of the City and the Opening of the Scheldt, 1944.* London: I. Allan, 1978; Rawson, Andrew. *Walcheren: Crossing the Scheldt.* London: Pen and Sword, 2003; Whitaker, Denis, and Shelagh Whitaker. *Tug of War: Eisenhower's Lost Opportunity: Allied Command and the Story Behind the Battle of the Scheldt.* Toronto: Stoddart, 2000.

Schellenberg, Walter (1910–1952) *head of the German Foreign Intelligence Service*

Born in Saarbrücken, Germany, Schellenberg grew up in Luxembourg, to which his family moved after World War I. He returned to Germany to attend the University of Marburg and then the University of Bonn. Initially enrolling as a medical student, he switched to law. Schellenberg joined the SCHUTZSTAFFEL (SS) in May 1933 and began working in counterintelligence. A meeting with REINHARD HEYDRICH brought him into the SS inner circle, and from 1939 to 1942 he served as aide to HEINRICH HIMMLER and was promoted to deputy leader of the Reich Central Security Office (Reichssicherheitshauptamt, RSHA). Himmler had sufficient confidence in Schellenberg to add a third brief to his portfolio: special plenipotentiary (Sonderbevollmächtigter). This position effectively made him Himmler's deputy, and since Himmler was general plenipotentiary to the entire Reich administration (Generalbevollmächtigter für die Verwaltung), Schellenberg came to occupy a position of great power and influence.

By 1939, Schellenberg was head of the RSHA's counterespionage section. In this capacity, in November, he orchestrated the so-called Venlo Incident in the Netherlands, which led to the capture of two important British secret agents. The captures gained Schellenberg promotion to SS colonel and earned him the important assignment in 1940 of compiling a list of 2,300 prominent Britons who were to be targeted for arrest after OPERATION SEALION, the planned invasion of Britain. Also in 1940, Schellenberg traveled to Spain to abduct the Duke and Duchess of Windsor, who had just fled France during the Battle of FRANCE. Schellenberg's mission was to persuade the couple to work for Germany; however, he failed even to intercept them.

By the end of 1941, Schellenberg had advanced to acting chief of the entire RSHA Foreign Intelligence Service (he became chief formally in 1943) and turned his attention to countering the Soviet spy ring known as the Red Orchestra. In this he enjoyed significant success and was promoted to major general in the WAFFEN-SS. In 1944, he replaced WILHELM CANARIS as head of the espionage organization known as the Abwehr.

As the war drew to its close in April 1945, Schellenberg talked Himmler into attempting to negotiate peace with the Western Allies through the Swedish count Folke Bernadotte. Schellenberg traveled to Stockholm to arrange the meeting between Bernadotte and Himmler and was in Denmark, attempting to arrange his own surrender, when Allied troops arrested him in June 1945. He was called on during the NUREMBERG WAR CRIMES TRIBUNAL proceedings to testify against fellow Nazis. In 1949, he himself was sentenced to six years' imprisonment. It was time he employed to write a memoir of his work in counterintelligence titled *The Labyrinth*. Released in 1951 because of an incurable liver ailment, he moved to Switzerland, then settled at Verbania Pallanza, Italy. He died the following year in Turin.

Further reading: Kahn, David. *Hitler's Spies: German Military Intelligence in World War II.* New York: Da Capo Press, 2000; Schellenberg, Walter. *The Labyrinth: Memoirs of Walter Schellenberg, Hitler's Chief of Counterintelligence.* New York: Da Capo Press, 2000.

Schindler, Oskar (1908–1974) *German industrialist who used his position to save some 1,300 Jews from certain death*

Schindler was an ethnic German of Catholic parentage born in Zwittau, Austria-Hungary (now part of the Czech Republic). Raised in wealth, he was a spoiled child and grew into a self-indulgent young man, notorious as a womanizer. Even after he married at the age of 19, he continued his multiple affairs and a life of general dissipation as a hard drinker and aggressive gambler. His financial recklessness destroyed his family's business, prompting him to exploit the exigencies of war after the invasion of POLAND to become a master of the black market. He moved readily between the underworld and the realm of the German administration in Poland, liberally bribing the GESTAPO and other officials. Using his influence, he acquired an enamelware factory in Poland, which he staffed with Jewish slave labor.

Up to this point, there was nothing especially unusual about Schindler, a corrupt war profiteer. Yet perhaps in spite of himself, he experienced an inner transformation and began to use his Emalia factory—producer of enamelware and munitions for the German army—to shelter his Jewish employees. The more he saw of the FINAL SOLUTION and the HOLOCAUST, the more Schindler became resolved to help as many Jews as possible, ultimately rescuing and protecting some 1,300 in a series of factories opened after the Emalia facility.

At the end of the war, Schindler fled to Argentina with his wife and a few of his workers. They lived together on a farm, which he left in 1958, abandoning his wife as well as his mistress to return to Germany. The rest of his life was spent shuttling between Germany and Israel, where some of the *"Schindlerjuden"* (Schindler's Jews, the men, women, and children he had saved) had gone to live. They cared for him and saw to it that the state of Israel officially recognized his heroic work during the war.

Schindler's story was told in 1982 by the Australian writer Thomas Keneally in his fact-based novel *Schindler's Ark* (published in the United States as *Schindler's List*), which was made into a successful and important motion picture by director Steven Spielberg in 1993.

Further reading: Fensch, Thomas, ed. *Oskar Schindler and His List: The Man, the Book, the Film, the Holocaust and Its Survivors.* Middlebury, Vt.: P.S. Eriksson, 1995; Keneally, Thomas. *Schindler's List.* New York: Touchstone, 1993.

Schlabrendorff, Fabian (1907–1980)
member of the German anti-Hitler resistance and would-be Hitler assassin

Fabian von Schlabrendorff was a lawyer who joined the German army during World War II and rose to the position of adjutant to HENNING VON TRESCKOW, a General Staff officer who also became a member of the anti-Hitler resistance. On March 13, 1943, Schlabrendorff planted a bomb on a plane carrying ADOLF HITLER to his eastern front headquarters at Smolensk. The detonator failed, and the bomb did not explode. Schlabrendorff was not arrested until after the collapse of the JULY PLOT (TO ASSASSINATE HITLER). Although he was not implicated in that attempt, GESTAPO agents tortured and interrogated him. When he refused to give any information, he was sent to DACHAU CONCENTRATION CAMP. In March 1945, shortly before the war in Europe ended, Schlabrendorff was acquitted of treason, but he was not released from the concentration camp until the German surrender in May.

After the war, Schlabrendorff resumed the practice of law and, from 1967 to 1975, served as a judge on the Constitutional Court of the Federal Republic of Germany.

Further reading: Schlabrendorff, Fabian von. *The Secret War against Hitler.* New York: Pitman, 1965.

Schuschnigg, Kurt von (1897–1977)
Austrian chancellor who tried unsuccessfully to prevent the Anschluss *in March 1938*

Born in Riva del Garda, Trento, Austria-Hungary (now in Italy), Schuschnigg became a lawyer in Innsbruck and a monarchist politician associated with the Christian Social Party. Schuschnigg was elected to the Nationalrat (lower house of parliament) in 1927 and then, in the administration of ENGELBERT DOLLFUSS during 1932–34, served as minister of justice (1932) and minister of education (1933). He became federal chancellor after Dollfuss was assassinated in 1934. Schuschnigg opposed the extreme right-wing Heimwehr, a paramilitary "defense" force, which he succeeded in dismantling in October 1936. Although his suppression of the Heimwehr was a triumph against right-wing extremism, Schuschnigg was forced to relinquish much of Austria's sovereignty following

Kurt von Schuschnigg *(Library of Congress)*

a meeting with ADOLF HITLER at Berchtesgaden in February 1938. Schuschnigg planned to reassert Austrian independence by means of a plebiscite scheduled for March 13, but the ANSCHLUSS of March 11–13 preempted this vote. Schuschnigg was forced into resignation on March 11. He was subsequently arrested and imprisoned by Nazi authorities and remained in custody until after the surrender of Germany to the Allies in May 1945.

After the war, Schuschnigg immigrated to the United States, where he lived from 1948 to 1967. He returned to Austria and wrote *Im Kampf Gegen Hitler* (1969; translated in 1971 as *The Brutal Takeover*).

Further reading: Bischof, Gunter, and Anton Pelinka, eds. *The Dollfuss/Schuschnigg Era in Austria: A Reassessment.* Somerset, N.J.: Transaction, 2003; Schuschnigg, Kurt. *The Brutal Takeover: The Austrian ex-Chancellor's Account of the Anschluss of Austria by Hitler.* London: Weidenfeld and Nicolson, 1971.

Schutzstaffel (SS)

No military organization was more feared in World War II than the Schutzstaffel, familiarly called the SS. Its name means "defense squadron," and it was created early in the history of the NAZI PARTY (NSDAP) as its paramilitary arm—the muscle behind its tactics of terror and intimidation. During the war, the WAFFEN SS—the fighting unit of the SS—became an elite army that operated outside of the regular German military (Wehrmacht) and sometimes at cross purposes with it.

Under the leadership of HEINRICH HIMMLER (beginning in 1929), the SS evolved into an elite guard animated by the powerful ideological and racial mythologies inculcated by Himmler. Personnel were selected for their fanatical loyalty to the party and to the person of ADOLF HITLER and (at least initially) for their racial purity as exemplars of German "Aryan" blood.

During the war, the Waffen SS fought as elite but essentially conventional soldiers, whereas the personnel of other SS classifications performed acts of outright atrocity on an organized and mas-

sive scale. The SICHERHEITSDIENST (SD)—Security Service—was a secret police force that terrorized occupied territories. The Einsatzgruppen—Special Action Groups—were principal agents of the FINAL SOLUTION, largely responsible for the mass execution of Jews and other civilians in the field, shooting perhaps a million noncombatants. The SS Totenkopfverbände (SS-TV)—Death's Head Formations—provided the personnel who ran the CONCENTRATION AND EXTERMINATION CAMPS. Through the Einsatzgruppen and SS-TV, Himmler was the chief manager of Final Solution operations and was, therefore, one of the chief architects of the HOLOCAUST. In addition to these units, which came directly under the control of the SS, the GESTAPO—Geheime Staatspolizei, or Secret State Police—and the Reichssicherheitshauptamt (RSHA)—Reich Main Security Office—were extensively staffed by SS members and therefore connected to the SS.

The direct predecessors of the SS were the STURMABTEILUNG (SA) (Assault Division) and Stabswache (Staff Guard), both formed in 1923. The SA was the Nazi Party's strong-arm force, and the smaller Stabswache had the mission of protecting Nazi leaders at rallies and other events. Both groups were forced into disbandment following the failure of the 1923 Beer Hall Putsch, but were reestablished in 1925—the Stabswache renamed the Stosstrupp. Before the year was out, the Stosstrupp was expanded as a national force and became the Schutzstaffel (SS). Its mission was to protect Nazi Party leaders everywhere in Germany, and, numbering no more than 280 persons, it was considered subordinate to the SA.

On January 6, 1929, Hitler appointed Heinrich Himmler to lead the SS. Himmler built the organization into a powerful rival to the SA. By the end of 1932, the SS enrolled 52,000 members. Within another year, there were 209,000. Himmler's most immediate models for the evolving organization were the contemporary Italian Fascist squads known as the Blackshirts, but he also reached back into history and mythology and borrowed ritual and organizational practices from the Knights Templar and even the Jesuits. Of course, the SS also drew on the existing SA for its organizational pattern and, until

1932, wore the SA uniform distinguished only by a black tie and a black cap with a *Totenkopf,* or death's head insignia. Beginning in 1933, the SS adopted its own distinctive black uniform, which was exchanged for a dove gray uniform just before the outbreak of the war. (Waffen SS units wore field gray uniforms like those of the regular army and in combat wore camouflage battle dress.)

Himmler and his chief lieutenant, REINHARD HEYDRICH, built the SS into the powerful organization it was at the outbreak of World War II. Heydrich was responsible for creating the SS intelligence, the Sicherheitsdienst (SD). The Waffen SS was formed in December 1940.

In 1934, an Austrian SS was formed covertly to prepare the way for the ANSCHLUSS, which occurred in 1938. Nominally, the Austrian SS was under Himmler's command, but was, in practice, independently led by Ernst Kaltenbrunner and ARTHUR SEYSS-INQUART. In contrast to the German SS, the Austrian branch was a covert organization until after the *Anschluss,* when it was simply incorporated into the German SS.

At the height of its development during World War II, the SS was a complex organization deemed by many to be a virtual "state within the state." The hierarchy flowed downward from Himmler to the Supreme Leaders, Higher Leaders, and Regular Leaders, all of whom reported directly to Himmler. Administratively, the SS was divided into a dozen principal offices, including the Personal Staff of the Reich Leader SS; the Main Administrative Office of the SS; the Administrative and Supply Department; the Office of SS Legal Matters; the Office of Race and Settlement; the Personnel Office; the Reich Central Security Office (RSHA); the Office of the Order Police; the Economics and Administration Office; the Education Office; the Main Office for Ethnic Germans (VOMI); and the Reich Commissioner for Germanic Resettlement. By 1944, the Gestapo, Sicherheitsdienst, Kriminalpolizei (Criminal Police), and the Einsatzgruppen were subordinate to the RSHA.

In terms of field organization the SS consisted of the following formations in Germany by the end of World War II:

Allgemeine SS: These were essentially part-time personnel who constituted a reserve force.

SS Cavalry Corps: This was mostly a ceremonial or honorific organization intended to draw the German upper class and nobility into the SS.

Germanic SS: This branch consisted of SS formations established in occupied countries as well as countries allied with Germany. Like the Allgemeine-SS, members were part-time.

Auxiliary SS: Created in 1945, the Auxiliary-SS consisted of conscripts who served as concentration camp guards and administrative personnel.

Waffen SS: This was the operational military component of the SS.

As already mentioned, the SS created a Totenkopfverbände (SS-TV) branch to administer the concentration and extermination camps and Einsatzgruppen to execute Jews and other targeted civilians in the field. Einsatzgruppen personnel followed close on the heels of the regular army as it invaded territory.

In 1936, the SS absorbed the regular German police forces and incorporated all local, state, and federal law enforcement agencies into the Ordnungspolizei, or Order Police, also known as the Orpo.

The SS created its own Medical Corps in 1930. Originally, the corps was a conventional medical service assigned to treat SS members; however, beginning in 1935, members of the SS Medical Corps served in the concentration camps and conducted human medical experiments, often of the most grotesque and sadistic nature. Doctor JOSEPH MENGELE, chief medical officer at the AUSCHWITZ EXTERMINATION CAMP, became the most infamous of the SS doctors. Not only did he perform the daily selections—designating which incoming camp inmates would be sent to the gas chambers and which would be put to work—he performed many medical experiments, including surgery without anesthesia and procedures that deliberately created disability or death.

During the 1930s, the SS was, by law, removed from the jurisdiction of the civilian courts, thereby giving SS personnel virtual carte blanche to act as they saw fit to carry out their mission. Even SS personnel were not entirely beyond the reach of the law, however; special SS and Police Courts were empowered to try SS personnel for criminal behavior.

The SS-Helferin Korps (Helper Corps) was an SS women's auxiliary. Personnel performed administrative and logistical functions. Most infamously, some served as female guards at concentration camps.

Further reading: Höhne, Heinz Zollin. *The Order of the Death's Head: The Story of Hitler's SS.* New York: Penguin, 2001; Reitlinger, Gerald. *The SS: Alibi of a Nation, 1922–1945.* New York: Da Capo Press, 1989; Rhodes, Richard. *Masters of Death: The SS-Einsatzgruppen and the Invention of the Holocaust.* New York: Vintage, 2003; Williamson, Gordon. *The SS: Hitler's Instrument of Terror.* Osceola, Wis.: Motorbooks International, 1994.

Schweinfurt raids

On August 17, 1943, and on October 14, 1943, the Eighth U.S. Air Force flew two bombing missions to destroy five ball-bearing plants in Schweinfurt, Germany. By destroying these plants, which made parts necessary to operate virtually every vehicle and piece of machinery, Allied air planners reasoned that they could significantly cripple German war production.

A total of 376 bombers were launched from bases in England during the first raid: 230 to Schweinfurt and 146 to nearby Regensburg (146 aircraft). Of these aircraft, 147 were lost. On the second raid, 60 out of 291 were lost—and 142 damaged. Although the raids hit their targets, war production was not greatly affected. The Germans moved some of the plants and rapidly rebuilt others.

In February and April 1944, the British Royal Air Force also raided Schweinfurt, suffering substantial losses while inflicting no strategically significant damage to German war production capacity.

Further reading: Coffey, Thomas M. *Decision over Schweinfurt: The U.S. 8th Air Force Battle for Daylight Bomb-*

ing. New York: D. McKay, 1977; Middlebrook, Martin. *The Schweinfurt-Regensburg Mission: American Raids on 17 August 1943.* London: Penguin U.K., 1995; Sweetman, John. *Schweinfurt: Disaster in the Skies.* New York: Ballantine Books, 1971.

Seeckt, Hans von (1866–1936) *German commander of the Reichswehr between the world wars*

Born in Schleswig the year before it became the capital of the Prussian province of Schleswig-Holstein, Seeckt began his military career in 1885 and rose rapidly, becoming an officer on the General Staff in 1889. During World War I, he served as chief of staff of the 11th Army and, subsequently, as chief of staff of the Turkish army.

Following the Armistice, he was appointed in November 1919 to head the Truppenamt (Troops Bureau), which succeeded the General Staff—outlawed by the TREATY OF VERSAILLES. Seeckt fashioned the diminutive army allowed by the treaty—a mere 100,000 men—into an elite force meant to serve as the core around which a very large army could be rapidly built. In this way, Seeckt made the most of the Versailles restrictions.

Seeckt recommended concluding the Treaty of Rapallo in 1922 to normalize relations between the Soviet Union and Germany. He believed that Germany should prepare the way for a Soviet-German alliance. In return for providing German training of the Soviet army and aid in heavy-industry construction, Seeckt was able to use Soviet territory for the covert training of tank and air crews and also to conduct weapons-development experiments. These expedients circumvented more of the Versailles restrictions.

Thanks to Seeckt, German military development was not greatly impeded by the Treaty of Versailles, and the small Reichswehr was readily transformed in the army with which Germany fought World War II. In the end, Seeckt did not overplay his hand with the Allied signatories of the Treaty of Versailles, but with the Weimar government of Germany. In 1926, the Prussian militarist approved and regularized dueling between officers, and he authorized the participation of a Hohenzollern prince in maneuvers. These acts, suited to imperial Germany but not the republic, forced his resignation on October 8, 1926. Seeckt then entered politics, serving in the Reichstag during 1930–32 and working as an adviser to the Chinese Nationalist Army in 1934–35.

Further reading: Corum, James S. *The Roots of Blitzkrieg: Hans von Seeckt and German Military Reform.* Lawrence: University Press of Kansas, 1994; Seeckt, Hans von. *Thoughts of a Soldier.* London: E. Benn, 1930.

Selassie, Haile (1892–1975) *emperor of Ethiopia who resisted Mussolini's 1935 invasion*

Haile Selassie was born Tafari Makonnen, the cousin of Emperor Menelik II. Menelik was succeeded in 1913 by his grandson Lij Yasu, who had been converted from Coptic Christianity to Islam and was now a zealous Muslim. In 1916, when he attempted to change the Coptic state religion of Ethiopia to Islam, Tafari Makonnen drove him from the throne and installed his aunt as Empress Zauditu, assuming for himself the regency as Ras Tafari and declaring himself heir to the throne. He was crowned King Ras Tafari in 1928 and, two years later, following the death of Zaudita (under suspicious circumstances), he became Emperor Haile Selassie I.

Haile Selassie was an absolute monarch but also a reformer who abolished slavery in his country. He came to be internationally respected as an early and heroic antifascist when he appeared before the League of Nations to seek aid against the Italian invasion of BENITO MUSSOLINI. The dignified emperor made a moving appeal, which, however, proved fruitless because the League lacked the military authority to intervene against the Italian aggression. Indeed, the Ethiopian episode demonstrated the ineffectualness of the League of Nations in preventing armed aggression.

After Italy invaded and then annexed Ethiopia, the emperor was forced into exile; in 1936, however, British forces liberated Ethiopia early in World War II, restoring Haile Selassie to the throne by 1941. He conducted himself throughout the war as an enlightened despot, refusing to relinquish any authority, but putting into operation long-range plans to modernize his nation. After the war, however, as Ethiopa emerged more fully into the modern world, resistance against the emperor's arbitrary autocracy grew. By the 1960s, he fended off a number of attempted coups d'état before he was finally deposed by the army in 1974.

Further reading: Gorham, Charles. *The Lion of Judah: A Life of Haile Selassie I, Emperor of Ethiopia.* New York: Ariel Books, 1966; Kapuscinski, Ryszard. *The Emperor.* New York: Vintage, 1989; Sbacchi, Alberto. *Legacy of Bitterness: Ethiopia and Fascist Italy, 1935–1941.* Lawrenceville, N.J.: Red Sea Press, 1997.

Sevastopol sieges

Sevastopol was the Soviet Union's principal Black Sea naval base and one of the most formidable fortresses in the world. Located on an eroded limestone promontory at the southwestern tip of the Crimea, the base was not readily approached by land. Lofty cliffs sheltered the anchorage in Severnaya Bay.

The forts at Sevastopol dated to the Crimean War of 1854–56 and were extensively modernized by the Soviet navy, which installed a dozen artillery batteries comprising a total of 42 guns in armored turrets and concrete emplacements. The fortress was garrisoned late in October 1941 by Major General I. Y. Petrov's Independent Maritime Army, 32,000 troops shipped in from Odessa. Petrov set up three lines of defense, the outermost extending in an arc some ten miles inland.

During September 26–November 16, the German Eleventh Army (with the Third Romanian Army subordinated to it) under ERICH VON MANSTEIN swept through the Crimea, clearing it of Soviet resistance except for Sevastopol. Manstein was impeded by the rugged terrain of Sevastopol and torrential rains. While he struggled to deploy his forces for a siege, Petrov continued to prepare defenses, then yielded overall command to Black

Sea Fleet commander in charge Vice Admiral F. S. Oktyabrsky.

Manstein finally launched his assault on Sevastopol on December 17, preempting Oktyabrsky's plan to disrupt the attack with amphibious landings along the coast. By December 22, Manstein's infantry breached the first and second lines of defense and were well on their way to penetrating the third line by December 26. With victory within his grasp, Manstein suffered a Soviet attack near Kerch on the 26th. German forces were thinly deployed here and vulnerable. On December 28 an even stronger Soviet force landed at Feodosiya and cut off the entire Kerch peninsula. This forced Manstein to withdraw two divisions from the Sevastopol siege to ward off a Soviet breakthrough.

In January 1942, the Soviet high command ordered Major General D. T. Kozlov to dispatch three armies on the Kerch peninsula. In May, Manstein deployed five German and two Romanian infantry divisions plus a panzer division (180 tanks) against Kozlov's 21 infantry divisions and 4 tank brigades (350 tanks). On May 8, Manstein launched an amphibious assault that dissolved Kozlov's front. The Germans gathered up more than 170,000 Red Army troops—JOSEPH STALIN having stubbornly forbidden their evacuation.

Now in a position to conduct a major offensive on the Crimean mainland, Manstein no longer needed to capture Sevastopol; he merely had to neutralize it by holding it under siege. Hitler, however, wanted to demonstrate the German army's heaviest artillery, and 33 pieces were brought up, ranging from 10.9 to 23 inches in caliber. The very largest, called Dora, was capable of hurling a 31-inch projectile 31 miles.

By this time, Oktyabrsky and Petrov had 106,000 troops and more than 80,000 naval personnel to garrison Sevastopol. Despite the massive German artillery bombardment, which began on June 2, four of Manstein's divisions attacking from the north on June 7 could not find a vulnerable point of entry. On June 11, he attempted an attack on the southeast, but was equally unsuccessful. Although the fort was badly damaged by the artillery, the many caves that sheltered the Soviet guns were not harmed.

The attack on the fortress stalled; however, on June 28, Manstein mounted a surprise attack by boat, which prompted Oktyabrsky to organize an evacuation on June 30. For the most part, however, the evacuation failed to take place, and on July 4, the Germans took the fortress and captured 90,000 prisoners.

The second siege of Sevastopol occurred in the spring of 1944—this time with the Red Army laying siege to German defenders—the Seventeenth German Army, in full retreat, which took refuge at the fortress. The army's commander, Lieutenant General Erwin Jaenecke, intended to use Sevastopol as a point from which he could organize an effective evacuation; however, Hitler demanded that he hold the fortress lest the Soviets seize control of the Black Sea. The Red Army made a mass assault on May 5, and, the next day, Hitler at last approved an evacuation. German ships took 38,000 troops off Cape Kherson; Soviet sources claim that 100,000 Germans had been killed or captured.

Further reading: Sweeting, C. G. *Blood and Iron: The German Conquest of Sevastopol.* Dulles, Va.: Potomac Books, 2004.

Seyss-Inquart, Arthur (1892–1946)
Austrian chancellor during the Anschluss

Seyss-Inquart was born at Stannern, near Iglau, Bohemia, in what was at the time Austria-Hungary and is now part of the Czech Republic. He fought during World War I in the Austro-Hungarian army, suffering a severe wound. He moved to Vienna after the armistice, where he began the practice of law in 1921. Seyss-Inquart was an early and ardent advocate of political union with Germany, and he formed an association with the Austrian Nazi Party, becoming a member and leader of the party's moderate branch, which, in contrast to the more radical faction, was tolerated by the Austrian government.

In June 1937, Seyss-Inquart was appointed to the Austrian Staatsrat (Federal Council of State) in the hope that he would integrate the Nazis into the mainstream and coax the Nazi Party into cooperating with the government. ADOLF HITLER used Seyss-Inquart as his inside man in the Austrian government and pressured Austria to appoint him minister of interior and security in February 1938. This put him in a position to replace the anti-Nazi, anti-*Anschluss* chancellor KURT VON SCHUSCHNIGG, which he did on March 11, 1938, just prior to the *Anschluss*.

Seyss-Inquart welcomed Germany's annexation of Austria, and the German government named him Reichsstatthalter (governor) of the Austrian provincial administration. He served until April 30, 1939, when he was named deputy governor of Poland and, later, Reichskommissar (commissioner) of the Netherlands. He served in that post until the surrender of Germany. Arrested by the Allies, he was tried by the NUREMBERG WAR CRIMES TRIBUNAL and sentenced to death. Seyss-Inquart was hanged at Nuremberg on October 16, 1946.

Further reading: Lehr, David. *Austria Before and After the Anschluss*. Pittsburgh: Dorrance, 2000; Low, Alfred D. *The Anschluss Movement 1931–1938 and the Great Powers*. Boulder, Colo.: East European Monographs, 1985; Schuschnigg, Kurt. *The Brutal Takeover: the Austrian Ex-chancellor's Account of the Anschluss of Austria by Hitler*. London: Weidenfeld and Nicolson, 1971.

Shibasaki Keiji (d. 1943) *Japanese commander during the Battle of Tarawa Island*

Rear Admiral Shibasaki Keiji commanded the Japanese garrison on the TARAWA ATOLL island of Beito during the Battle of Tarawa, November 20–23, 1943. He took command September 1943 and had under him 1,122 Imperial Marines of the 3rd Special Base Force, 1,497 Imperial Marines of the 7th Sasebo Special Landing Force, 1,427 Korean and Chinese laborers (111th Construction Unit), and 970 laborers of the 4th Fleet Construction Department.

Shibasaki, who, as a veteran of landings in China during the SINO-JAPANESE WAR, was thoroughly familiar with AMPHIBIOUS WARFARE, conducted a fiercely brilliant defense from behind extensive fortifications that he built in preparation for the invasion. His boast to his troops that it would take 1 million men 100 years to conquer the island proved unfounded, and he was probably killed on the very first day of the battle, presumably the victim of U.S. naval gunfire.

Further reading: Alexander, Joseph H. *Utmost Savagery: The Three Days of Tarawa*. Annapolis, Md.: Naval Institute Press, 1995; Hammel, Eric M., and John E. Lane. *Bloody Tarawa*. Pacifica, Calif.: Pacifica Press, 1999; Sherrod, Robert. *Tarawa: The Story of a Battle*. Fredricksburg, Tex.: Admiral Nimitz Foundation, 1993.

ships, British

As an island nation and the center of a vast empire, Great Britain had long depended on its navy for defense. Although post–World War I arms limitation agreements had capped the size of the Royal Navy and the maximum tonnage of its capital ships, the nation entered World War II with a large navy and a wide variety of ships. The most important British combatants are discussed in the following entries: AIRCRAFT CARRIER, BATTLESHIP, CORVETTE, CRUISER, DESTROYER, LANDING CRAFT, and SUBMARINE.

In addition to these major types of ships, the Royal Navy operated small, specialized aircraft carriers known as escort carriers, some built by British yards and some built in the United States. A typical British-built escort displaced 11,800 to 17,400 tons standard and was 512 to 594 feet in length. These ships accommodated about 15 aircraft and were crewed by 700 hands. The American-built escort carriers included the *Archer* Class (displacing 8,250 tons standard and accommodating 15 planes), the *Attacker* Class (11,400 tons standard, 18 aircraft), and the *Ruler* Class (11,400 tons standard and accommodating 22 aircraft).

In addition to large aircraft carriers and the small escort carriers, the Royal Navy operated CAM ships and MAC ships.

CAM ships were Catapult-Armed Merchantmen, merchant ships equipped with a catapult capable of launching a fighter aircraft to shoot down enemy planes or hunt for submarines. The ships had no means of recovering the aircraft after launch. The pilot would have to ditch near the ship and await rescue.

MAC ships—Merchant Aircraft Carriers—were merchant vessels—mainly grain transports and tankers—fitted with flight decks. They carried both cargo and aircraft. The ships of the *Empire Mac Dry Class* displaced 7,930 to 8,250 tons gross and were about 450 feet long. They were driven by a single diesel engine delivering 3,300 bhp and making no more than 12.5 knots. They were armed with a single 4-inch gun and two 40-mm AA guns as well as smaller guns, and they could accommodate four aircraft. The ships were crewed by 110 hands. The *Empire Mac* Tanker Class vessels displaced as much as 9,250 tons gross and were about 485 feet long. They had the same power plant as the dry class ships, the same armament, and could accommodate the same number of aircraft. A third type of MAC, the *Shell* Class, displaced 8,000 gross tons and made 13 knots with a 3,750-hp diesel. It accommodated four aircraft and was armed similarly to the ships of the other two classes.

Although the destroyer and the corvette were the principal British convoy escort craft, the Royal Navy fleet included a number of smaller escort craft, intended mainly to combat submarines.

Isle Class. These small ships (together with the similar *Tree, Shakespeare,* and *Dance* classes) were based on the design of commercial fishing trawlers. Together, the four classes included 218 vessels. The *Isle* Class ships displaced 545 tons standard and were 145 feet long with a beam of 27.5 feet and a draft of 10.5 feet. A single steam engine delivered 850 hp for a top speed of 12 knots. The vessels were armed with a single 12-pounder and three 20-mm AA guns as well as depth charges. Crew complement was 40 officers and men.

Black Swan Class. These submarine hunters were built in a quantity of 24, each displacing 1,300 tons standard. The ships were nearly 300 feet long, 37.5 feet in the beam, and had a draft of 8.5 feet. They were driven by a pair of steam turbines producing 3,600 shp for a speed of 19.5 knots. Arma-

ment consisted of three twin 4-inch guns, one quadruple 2-pounder AA gun, and six twin 20-mm AA guns, as well as depth charges. The ships were crewed by 180 officers and men.

Hunt Class. Officially designated "Fast Escort Vessels" (FEVB), this class consisted of 83 vessels designed primarily for antisubmarine duty. Three types, designated I, II, and III, were produced, the Type III displacing 1,015 tons standard and 1,090 under full load. The ships were 281.25 feet long, with a beam of 31.5 feet, and a shallow draft of just 7.75 feet. They were driven by a pair of steam turbines, which made 19,900 shp and yielded a top speed of 25 knots. Armament consisted of a pair of twin 4-inch guns, one quadruple 2-pounder AA gun, and a varying number of 20-mm AA guns, as well as two 21-inch torpedo tubes and a full load of depth charges. The ship's crew consisted of 170 officers and men.

Castle Class. The 44 ships of this class were slow, suited to escorting slow convoys. They displaced 1,060 tons standard and were 252 feet long, with a beam of 36.75 feet and a draft of 10 feet. A single steam engine produced 2,950 hp for a top speed of 16.5 knots. The ships carried a single 4-inch gun and two twin and six single 20-mm AA guns as well as a full load of depth charges. Additionally, the ships were a platform for the "Squid" system of antisubmarine mortars.

Bangor, Bathurst, and *Algerine* Classes. The vessels of these closely related classes were officially designated "minesweeping sloops"; however, they were used far more for escort duty than for clearing mines. The ships were produced in quantity: 173 *Bangor* Class vessels, 56 *Bathurst* Class, and 101 *Algerines.* The *Algerine* Class ships displaced 850 tons standard and 970 under load. They were 230 feet long, with a beam of 35.5 feet and a draft of 9.5 feet. Two steam turbines or two triple-expansion steam engines produced 2,000 hp, making a top speed of 16.5 knots. Armament consisted of a single 4-inch gun and four to eight 20-mm AA guns as well as more than 90 depth charges. The ships were crewed by 105 officers and men.

River Class. Variously called twin-screw corvettes or frigates, these ships were built in a quantity of 57 and displaced 1,370 tons standard. They were 301.5 feet long, with a beam of 36.5 feet and a draft of 12.83 feet. Two steam engines made 5,500 hp for a top speed of 20 knots. The ships were armed with two 4-inch guns, two 2-pounder AA guns, and two 20-mm AA guns. Antisubmarine armament consisted of a hedgehog and depth charges. The ship's complement was 107 officers and men.

Loch and *Bay* Classes. These frigates appeared late in the war as escorts. The *Bay* Class was very similar to the *Loch* Class and consisted of ships displacing 1,580 tons standard, with a length of 307.25 feet, a beam of 38.5 feet, and a draft of 9.5 feet. Two steam engines made 5,500 hp for a top speed of 19.5 knots. Armament consisted of two twin 4-inch guns, two twin 40-mm AA guns, two twin 20-mm AA guns, a hedgehog, and depth charges. The crew consisted of 157 officers and men.

COASTAL CRAFT

Smaller than the escort craft, coastal craft operated by the Royal Navy included 60-foot British power boats, 70-foot Vosper boats, Fairmile Motor Torpedo Boats (MTBs), steam gunboats, and harbor defense motor launches.

The 60-foot power boats and 70-foot Vosper boats were similar to the PT BOATS operated by the U.S. Navy. They were fast boats used as torpedo-launching platforms. In short, they were small combatants deployed against much larger vessels. The typical 60-foot boat displaced 22 tons and was propelled by a trio of gasoline engines that delivered 1,800 hp for a top speed of 33 knots. The boats carried two 18-inch torpedoes and had eight 7.7-mm machine guns. There was a crew of 9.

The longer Vospers were 72.5 feet in length, displacing 36 to 49 tons. Beam was 19.5 feet and draft 5.5 feet. Three gasoline engines delivered 4,000 bhp for a top speed of 40 knots. They carried a pair of 21-inch torpedoes and a variety of guns, typically a 6-pounder or 20-mm cannon and several machine guns. Twelve to 13 officers and men manned these craft.

The Fairmile MTBs were produced in four types: A, B, C, and D. All were intended for coastal patrol. The A and C types were quite similar, dis-

placing about 58 tons and measuring 110 feet in length, with a beam of 17.42 feet and a draft of six feet. Three gasoline engines made 1,800 bhp for a top speed of 22 knots. Armament consisted of a single 3-pounder gun and two 7.7-mm machine guns. Sixteen officers and men manned the craft.

B-type Fairmiles displaced 67 to 85 tons and were 112 feet long, with a beam of 18.25 feet and a five-foot draft. Their two gasoline engines produced 1,200 bhp for a top speed of 20 knots. Armament was a single 3-pounder and two 7.7-mm machine guns in addition to depth charges.

The D-type Fairmile craft were the heaviest, displacing 90 tons. Length was 110 feet, beam 21 feet, and draft 5.17 feet. Four gasoline engines delivered 5,000 bhp for a top speed of 29 knots. The craft carried two 6-pounder guns, one twin 20-mm cannon, two twin half-inch machine guns, and four 18-inch torpedoes. Crew complement was 30 officers and men.

The first of the British steam gunboats were launched in November 1941 and were produced in a small quantity of just seven. Displacing 165 tons, the boats were 145.75 feet long, had a 20-foot beam, and a 5.5-foot draft. Two steam turbines delivered 8,000 shp for a top speed of 35 knots. A three-inch gun, two 6-pounder guns, and two twin 20-mm cannon were the armament, and the boats were crewed by 27 officers and men.

The harbor defense launch was a humble craft used to defend the approaches to coastal ports. Displacing 54 tons, it was 72 feet long, with a beam of 15.83 feet and a draft of 5.5 feet. A pair of diesels made 320 bhp for a top speed of barely 12 knots. A single 3-pounder gun, one 20 mm cannon, and a pair of 7.7 mm machine guns constituted the armament. There was a crew of 10.

See also GREAT BRITAIN, NAVY OF.

Further reading: Colledge, J. J. *Ships of the Royal Navy.* Annapolis, Md.: Naval Institute Press, 1989; Jackson, Robert. *History of the Royal Navy in World War II.* Ramsburty, U.K.: Airlife, 1997; Ward, John. *Ships of World War II.* Osceola, Wis.: Motorbooks International, 2000; Young, John. *A Dictionary of Ships of the Royal Navy of the Second World War.* London: Stephens, 1975.

ships, French

At the outbreak of the war, France had the fourth-largest navy in the world, including many modern vessels.

SUBMARINES

Saphir Class. These small submarines, designed primarily as minelayers, consisted of a half-dozen boats launched between 1925 and 1929. Two of the submarines operated for the duration of the war under the flag of Free France. The *Saphir* boats displaced 761 tons surfaced and 925 tons submerged. They were 216.21 feet long, had a beam of 23.36 feet, and a draft of 14.11 feet. Propelled by a pair of diesels delivering 1,300 bhp for a top speed of 12 knots surfaced, they were also equipped with two electric motors for underwater propulsion. These delivered a total of 1,100 bhp for a submerged speed of 9 knots. The boats were armed with a single 75-mm gun and three 21.65-inch torpedo tubes. Minelaying capacity was 32 mines. It was crewed by 42 officers and men.

Surcouf Class. Ordered in 1926, the *Surcouf* was to be the first of a class of three large "cruiser submarines," capable of long endurance and providing a platform for heavy surface guns. The *Surcouf* was seized at Plymouth, England, in July 1940 and was operated by a Free French crew until it sank in February 1942 in the Caribbean following a collision. Its displacement of 3,270 tons surfaced and 4,250 submerged made it the heaviest submarine of the war. It was 360.89 feet long, 29.53 feet in the beam, and had a draft of 29.76 feet. Two diesels made 7,600 bhp for a top surface speed of 18 knots. Two electric motors delivered 3,400 bhp total for a submerged speed of 8.5 knots. Armament consisted of two 8-inch guns and an array of torpedo tubes: eight 21.65-inch tubes and four 15.75-inch tubes, some in trainable mountings. It was crewed by 118 officers and men.

BATTLESHIPS

The two most important battleships of the French navy were the *Richelieu* and *Jean Bart*. The *Richelieu* became part of the British Home Fleet during the war. Both ships had similar specifications, displacing approximately 41,000 tons standard and 47,500 under full load. They were more than 813 feet long, 108 feet 3 inches in the beam, with a draft of almost 32 feet. Four turbines delivered 150,000 shp for a top speed of 30 knots. Each carried eight 15-inch guns, nine 6-inch guns, twelve 100 mm AA guns, and sixteen 37 mm AA guns, plus eight 13.2 mm AA guns. The ships could launch three Loire-Nieuport floatplanes and were crewed by 1,500 officers and men.

CRUISERS

The most important class of French cruisers was the *La Galissonnière* Class, consisting of six ships. Built in the 1930s, these modern ships displaced 7,600 tons standard and 9,120 tons with full load. They were 586 feet 3 inches long and 57 feet 4 inches in the beam. Draft was 17 feet 5 inches. Geared turbines delivered 84,000 shp for a top speed of 35.7 knots. The ships were fitted with nine 6-inch guns, eight 3.-inch guns, and eight 13.2 mm AA guns. The ships carried four 21.7-inch torpedo tubes and could accommodate two floatplanes. Crew consisted of 540 officers and men. Three of the cruisers came into Allied control during the war. The others were scuttled, two of which were salvaged by the Italians, then sunk by Allied bombs in 1943.

Further reading: Le Masson, Henri. *The French Navy,* 2 vols. London: Macdonald, 1969; Auphan, Etienne. *The French Navy in World War II.* Westport, Conn.: Greenwood Press, 1976; Ward, John. *Ships of World War II.* Osceola, Wis.: Motorbooks International, 2000.

ships, German

The most important German combatants are discussed in the following entries: CRUISER, DESTROYER, and SUBMARINE. Of these, the most important German warship in World War II was the submarine. Other significant German naval combatants include battleships, escort craft (in addition to destroyers), and certain coastal craft.

BATTLESHIPS

The provisions of the TREATY OF VERSAILLES put severe tonnage limits on German naval vessels. For this reason, German naval architects developed the so-called POCKET BATTLESHIP, of which the *Scharnhorst* and *Gneisenau* were prime examples. By the provisions of the treaty, they were supposed to displace no more than 26,000 tons, although, as built, the ships actually displaced 32,000 tons standard and 38,900 tons under full load. Originally, four ships of the *Scharnhorst* Class were to be built, but only the *Gneisenau* was completed in addition to the *Scharnhorst*. The length of these vessels was 770 feet 8 inches, beam 98 feet 5 inches, and draft 29 feet 10 inches. Three steam turbines delivered 160,000 shp for a top speed of 32 knots. The ships were armed with nine 11-inch guns, twelve 150 mm guns, fourteen 105 mm AA guns, and sixteen 37 mm AA guns, as well as six 21-inch torpedo tubes. Two Arado floatplanes could be accommodated, and the ships were crewed by 1,840 officers and men.

Bismarck. One of the most famous—or infamous—ships of World War II, *Bismarck* was Germany's first post–World War I full-size battleship. It displaced 41,676 tons standard and 50,153 tons with full load. The ship was 823.5 feet long with a 118-foot beam. Draft was 30 feet 7 inches. Three steam turbines delivered 138,000 shp for a top speed of 29 knots. The ship had eight 15-inch guns, 12 150 mm guns, 16 105 mm AA guns, 16 37 mm AA guns, and 12 20 mm AA guns. It could accommodate two Arado floatplanes and carried a crew of 2,192. Launched early in 1939 and commissioned in August 1940, *Bismarck* sailed on its first combat mission in May 1941. On the 24th, it encountered the British battlecruiser *Hood* and battleship *Prince of Wales*. In the ensuing battle—the Battle of the Denmark Strait—*Hood* was sunk and the *Prince of Wales* seriously damaged. *Bismarck* was also damaged and was on its way to France for repair when it was sunk by a British task force on May 27 with the loss of all but 110 hands. The loss of *Bismarck* prompted ADOLF HITLER to curtail all operations of the German surface fleet.

Tirpitz. Launched in April 1939, *Tirpitz* was similar to its sister ship, *Bismarck*. It displaced 42,900 tons standard and 52,600 tons under load. She was 821 feet 10 inches in length, had a 118-foot beam, and a 36-foot draft. Three steam turbines delivered 138,000 shp for a top speed of 29 knots. It was armed with eight 15-inch guns, 12 150 mm guns, 16 105 mm AA guns, and eight 21-inch torpedo tubes. The *Tirpitz* could accommodate four Arado floatplanes and was crewed by 2,530 officers and men. It was sunk on November 12, 1944, in Norwegian waters by British air attack with the loss of 1,000 of its crew.

ESCORT CRAFT

Germany did not rely on convoys to the extent that Britain did, so it developed few escort vessels. The *Wolf* and *Möwe* classes were in effect light destroyers tasked with protecting Germany's coastal merchant traffic. The six *Wolf* Class ships displaced 933 tons standard and 1,320 under full load. They were 305 feet long with a beam of 28.5 feet and a draft of 9.2 feet. Two steam turbines delivered 23,000 shp for a top speed of 33 knots. Armament consisted of three 105 mm guns or three 5-inch guns and four single 20 mm AA guns as well as two triple 21-inch torpedo tubes. The ships were crewed by 129 officers and men.

Another type of coastal escort craft was the Geleitboote, of which 10 (F1 through F10) were built. In addition to performing escort duty, they were used as minelayers. The ships displaced 712 tons standard and 833 tons under full load. They were 249.3 feet long with a beam of 28.9 feet and a draft of 8.2 feet. Two steam turbines delivered 14,000 shp for a top speed of 28 knots. Each shp carried two single 105 mm guns and two twin 37 mm AA and four single 20 mm AA guns. Ship's complement was 121 officers and men.

COASTAL CRAFT

German light coastal craft included, most importantly, the *Leicht Schnellboat*—light fast boat, or LS; the *Raumboot* (R-Boot), a minesweeper, minelayer, and coastal escort; and the *Schnellboot* (S-Boot), which the British called an E-boat, used as a light, fast torpedo boat.

LS. These boats displaced 11.5 tons and were 41 feet long. They were 10.83 feet in the beam, with a draft of 2.5 feet. Equipped with an aircraft-type engine, they could attain a top speed of 42.5 knots. Armament consisted of a pair of 17.7-inch torpedoes and a 20 mm cannon. Complement was nine officers and men.

R-Boot. The standard R-Boot displaced 140 tons and was 131.23 feet long. Its beam was 18.37 feet, with a draft of 4.75 feet. Two diesel engines made 2,550 bhp for a top speed of 20.5 knots. Crewed by 38 officers and men, the boats were equipped with a 37 mm cannon and six 20 mm cannon.

S-Boot. These torpedo craft were speedy at 39.5 knots and carried two 21-inch torpedo tubes with four torpedoes. They were also equipped with a pair of 20 mm cannon. Displacement was 93 tons standard and 115 under full load. Length was 114.67 feet, beam 16.73 feet, and draft 4.6 feet. Three diesel engines produced 6,000 bhp. The crew complement was 21 officers and men.

Further reading: Jackson, Robert. *Kriegsmarine: The Illustrated History of the German Navy in World War II.* Osceola, Wis.: MBI Publishing, 2001; Showell, J. P. *German Navy in World War Two: An Illustrated Guide to the Kriegsmarine, 1920–1945.* Annapolis, Md.: Naval Institute Press, 1979; Showell, J. P. *The German Navy in World War Two: A Reference Guide to the Kriegsmarine, 1935–1945.* London: Arms and Armour Press, 1979; Stern, Robert C. *Kriegsmarine: A Pictorial History of the German Navy, 1935–1945.* Carrollton, Tex.: Squadron/Signal Publications, 1979; Tarrant, V. E. *The Last Year of the Kriegsmarine: May 1944–May 1945.* Annapolis, Md.: Naval Institute Press, 1994.

ships, Italian

Italy had a formidable modern navy at the outbreak of World War II. The nation's most important combatant ship types are discussed in CRUISER, DESTROYER, and SUBMARINE.

BATTLESHIPS

The pride of the Italian fleet were two modern battleships, the *Littoro* and *Vittorio Veneto,* completed in April and May 1940, respectively. Both ships, though badly battered, survived the war. *Vittorio Veneto* displaced 41,700 tons standard and 45,460 tons under full load. She was 780 feet long with a beam of 108 feet and a draft of 34 feet 5 inches. Four steam turbines delivered 128,000 shp for a top speed of 30 knots. It was armed with nine 15-inch guns, 12 6-inch guns, 12 3.5-inch AA guns, 20 37 mm AA guns, and 16 20 mm AA guns. The ship could accommodate three floatplanes and had a complement of 1,872 officers and men.

ESCORT CRAFT

In addition to destroyers for escort duty, the Italian fleet also included small escort vessels.

Spica Class. These 32 ships were small destroyers, often described as torpedo boats. They displaced just 795 tons standard and 1,020 tons under full load, and were nearly 274 feet long, 26.57 feet in the beam, and with a draft of 8.37 feet. Two steam turbines delivered 19,000 shp for a top speed of 34 knots. The *Spica* Class ships were armed with three 100 mm AA guns and four twin and two single 20 mm AA guns. There were also two single 13.2 mm AA guns. The ships carried four single or two twin 450 mm torpedo tubes and could lay up to 20 mines. Ship's complement consisted of 118 officers and men.

Gabbiano Class. The 60 ships of this class could be described as CORVETTES. They were designed expressly as submarine hunters and were unique in being equipped with two diesel engines for normal propulsion and two silent electric motors for stalking sonar- or hydrophone-equipped submarines. The diesels delivered a total of 4,300 shp and the electrics 150 shp. Top speed under diesel power was 18 knots. The ships displaced 670 tons standard and 740 under full load. They were 211.29 feet long and 28.54 feet in the beam, with an 8.3-foot draft. Armament consisted of a single 100 mm AA gun in addition to seven 20 mm AA guns. All carried a full load of depth charges, and some were equipped with two 450 mm torpedo tubes.

See also ITALY, NAVY OF.

Further reading: Bragadin, Marc'Antonio. *The Italian Navy in World War II.* New York: Arno, 1980; Sadkovich, James J. *The Italian Navy in World War II.* Westport, Conn.: Greenwood Press, 1994.

ships, Japanese

At the outbreak of World War II, Japan was the third-greatest naval power in the world. Some of its most important combatant ships are discussed in the following entries: AIRCRAFT CARRIERS, CRUISERS, DESTROYERS, and SUBMARINES. The Imperial Japanese Navy had the distinction of possessing the world's largest battleships, the *Yamato* and the *Musashi*.

BATTLESHIPS

Yamato Class. The *Yamato* and *Musashi* were ordered in 1937 and launched in 1941. The *Yamato* served as the flagship of Admiral YAMAMOTO ISOROKU. These were extraordinarily formidable vessels. The *Yamato* displaced 64,000 tons standard and 69,988 tons under full load. It was 863 feet long with a beam of 127.9 feet and a draft of 34 feet 3 inches. Four steam turbines delivered 150,000 shp for a top speed of 27 knots. The *Yamato* mounted nine 18.1-inch guns—the largest on any battleship in World War II—twelve 155 mm guns, 12 5-inch AA guns, 24 25 mm AA guns, and four 13 mm AA guns. It could accommodate six floatplanes and was crewed by 2,500 officers and men. Neither *Yamato* nor *Musashi* had much effect on the war at sea. *Yamato* never got within gun range during the pivotal BATTLE OF MIDWAY. Although it was present at the BATTLE OF THE PHILIPPINE SEA (June 1944), she did not fire its 18.1-inch guns for the first time until the BATTLE OF LEYTE GULF (October 1944). Bound for a spectacular KAMIKAZE mission during the BATTLE OF OKINAWA, it was sunk by U.S. aircraft on April 7, 1945, before it could get into action.

Kongo Class. These four ships were built between 1912 and 1915 and were modernized before World War II. Typical of the class was the *Kirishima*, which displaced 31,980 tons standard and 36,600 tons under full load. It was 728.5 feet long with a beam of 102 feet 4 inches and a draft of 31 feet 9 inches. Four steam turbines delivered 136,000 shp for a top speed of 30.5 knots. It was armed with eight 14-inch guns, 14 6-inch guns, eight 5-inch AA guns, and 20 1-inch AA guns. It accommodated three floatplanes and was crewed by 1,437 officers and men.

Nagato Class. The two ships of this class, *Nagato* (completed 1920) and *Mutsu* (1921), displaced 42,850 tons standard and were 725 feet 2 inches long. They were 113.5 feet in the beam and had a draft of 31 feet 2 inches. Top speed was 27 knots. Armament consisted of eight 16-inch guns, 20 5.5-inch guns, eight 5-inch dual-purpose guns, and up to 98 25 mm AA guns. The ships were crewed by 1,368 officers and men.

COASTAL CRAFT

The Imperial Japanese Navy was notoriously deficient in escort vessels (relying solely on destroyers for this function) and in coastal craft. Construction of small motor torpedo boats began only after the war was under way. The most numerous of these craft was the Type 14, which was built in a quantity of 49. These boats displaced 15 tons standard and were 49.2 feet long with a beam of 12 feet. Draft was 2.8 feet. A single gasoline engine made 920 bhp for a top speed of 33 knots in calm waters. The boats carried a single 25 mm cannon and two 18-inch torpedoes. The boats were crewed by seven officers and men.

See also JAPAN, NAVY OF.

Further reading: Atkinson, John. *Imperial Japanese Navy WWII.* Couldson, U.K.: Galago Books, 2003; Dull, Paul S. *A Battle History of the Imperial Japanese Navy, 1941–1945.* Annapolis, Md.: Naval Institute Press, 1978; Evans, David C. *Kaigun: Strategy, Tactics, and Technology in the Imperial Japanese Navy, 1887–1941.* Annapolis, Md.: Naval Institute Press, 1997; Skulski, Janusz. *The Battleship Yamato.* Annapolis, Md.: Naval Institute Press, 1989; Stille, Mark. *Imperial Japanese Navy Aircraft Carriers 1921–45.* London: Osprey, 2005; Yoshimura, Akira. *Battleship Musashi.* Tokyo: Kodansha International, 1999.

ships, Soviet

The Soviet navy was small compared with other Allied navies. It had three battleships and some 50 DESTROYERS, as well as a large submarine force of more than 200 boats. Coastal craft were important, and the Soviet fleet had about 300 torpedo boats.

Generally speaking, however, Soviet naval forces did not play a major role in the war.

SUBMARINES

Numerically, at the outbreak of World War II, the Soviet Union had the world's largest submarine fleet. But the boats were poorly commanded and inadequately crewed, most of the best officers having been purged by JOSEPH STALIN in 1937. The Soviet submarine fleet was also poorly armed, the Soviet navy never having developed a reliable torpedo. For this reason, the submarine fleet was used almost exclusively for defensive purposes. It is believed that the Soviet fleet lost one submarine for every enemy ship sunk.

K Class. This was the most important class of Soviet submarine. It displaced 2,095 tons submerged and could cruise at 18 knots surfaced and nine knots underwater. Armament consisted of six bow torpedo tubes and four stern torpedo tubes. These submarines had good endurance but were never deployed far from home because they were almost exclusively confined to defensive duty.

COASTAL CRAFT

The only truly distinctive vessels of the Soviet navy in World War II were the coastal craft, of which the most important and innovative was the G5 torpedo boat. Designed by famed aircraft designer A. N. Tupolev, the G5s were built in a quantity of nearly 300, of which 73 were lost in action. They displaced 16 tons and were 62.66 feet in length, with a beam of 11.15 feet and a draft of 3.28 feet. Two gasoline engines developed 2,000 bhp for a very fast top speed of 48 knots. The boats were armed with two 21-inch torpedoes and a pair of half-inch machine guns. The complement was seven officers and men.

See also SOVIET UNION, NAVY OF.

Further reading: Breyer, Siegfried. *Soviet Warship Development.* London: Conway Maritime Press, 1993; McLaughlin, Stephen. *Russian and Soviet Battleships.* Annapolis, Md.: Naval Institute Press, 2003; Polmar, Norman, and Jurrien Noot. *Submarines of the Russian and Soviet Navies, 1718–1990.* Annapolis, Md.: Naval Institute Press, 1991.

ships, United States

The principal U.S. Navy combatant ships of World War II are discussed in the following entries: AIRCRAFT CARRIERS, BATTLESHIPS, CORVETTES, CRUISERS, DESTROYERS, DESTROYER ESCORTS, LANDING CRAFT, MINESWEEPERS, PT BOATS, Q-SHIPS, and SUBMARINES. Two other significant combatant types were the Patrol Craft (PC) and Patrol Craft Escorts (PCE) classes. These were intended as escorts to protect coastal traffic and to hunt submarines. The PC Class ships were 174.9-foot-long craft, prototypes of which were completed before the United States entered the war. They were used to patrol the eastern seaboard, which was subject to a great deal of German U-boat activity. The PCE Class, developed from minesweeper designs, was larger and heavier, and was designed to work close to shore as well as to pursue submarines or escort convoys farther out to sea. The PCE ships displaced 795 tons standard and 850 tons under full load. They were 184.5 feet long, with a 33-foot beam and a draft of 9.5 feet. Two diesels supplied 1,900 bhp for a top speed of just 16 knots. The ships were armed with one 3-inch dual-purpose gun and two or three 40 mm AA guns as well as four single 20 mm AA guns. A hedgehog and depth charges were used for antisubmarine patrol. Ship's complement was 100 officers and men.

See also UNITED STATES, NAVY OF.

Further reading: Heiferman, Ronald. *U.S. Navy in World War II.* London: Chartwell Books, 1979; McGowen, Tom. *Carrier War: Aircraft Carriers in World War II.* Breckenridge, Colo.: 21st Century Books, 2001; Preston, Anthony. *Aircraft Carriers of World War II.* Rochester, U.K.: Grange Books, 1998; Reilly, Joseph. *U.S. Navy Destroyers of World War II.* New York: Sterling, 1984; Silverstone, Paul H. *U.S. Warships of World War II.* Garden City, N.Y.: Doubleday, 1966; Stern, Robert C. *U.S. Navy, 1942–1943.* London: Arms & Armour, 1990; Stern, Robert C. *U.S. Navy in World War Two, 1941–1942.* London: Arms & Armour, 1987; Terzibaschitsch, Stefan. *Battleships of the U.S. Navy in World War II.* New York: Bonanza Books, 1977.

Short, Walter Campbell (1880–1949)
general who commanded U.S. Army forces at Pearl Harbor on December 7, 1941

Born in Fillmore, Illinois, Short graduated from the University of Illinois in 1901 and was commissioned as an infantry second lieutenant in March 1902. Promoted to first lieutenant, he served in the Philippines in 1907, after which he was posted to Alaska. In 1913, he was an instructor at the Musketry School, Fort Sill, Oklahoma, and in 1916 participated in the Punitive Expedition against Pancho Villa under General John J. Pershing.

As a captain, Short was ordered to France with the 1st Division in June 1917, after the United States entered World War I. He served in Pershing's headquarters, then, as chief of staff of the Third Army, fought at Aisne-Marne during July 18–August 5, 1918, at Saint-Mihiel during September 12–16, and at Meuse-Argonne, September 26–November 11. Before the war was over, Short was promoted to temporary colonel, but reverted to captain when he returned to the United States. Promoted to major in 1920, he was assigned as an instructor at the General Staff School in Fort Leavenworth and wrote a textbook, *Employment of Machine Guns,* published in 1922. Promoted to lieutenant colonel in 1923, he graduated from the Army War College in 1925 and served with the 65th Infantry in Puerto Rico from 1925 to 1928. After another assignment as an instructor at Fort Leavenworth, he was assigned to the Bureau of Indian Affairs during 1930–34.

After promotion to colonel, Short was assigned to command the 6th Infantry at Jefferson Barracks in St. Louis. He left this post in 1936 to become assistant commandant of the Infantry School at Fort Benning, Georgia, and was promoted to brigadier general in December. He commanded a brigade of the 1st Division in New York in 1937, then the entire division from July 1938 to October 1940. He was assigned command of the Hawaiian Department in January 1941 and promoted to temporary lieutenant general the next month.

In retrospect, it is apparent that Short made many errors while commanding army forces at Pearl Harbor during the dangerous months pre-

Lieutenant General Walter Short *(U.S. Army)*

ceding the outbreak of war in the Pacific. He failed to establish close, routine communication with his navy counterpart, Admiral HUSBAND E. KIMMEL, and he failed to establish a system for evaluating and sharing intelligence. Most notorious was his decision to park the aircraft of his command wingtip to wingtip on Hickam Field. Fearing ground-based sabotage, he grouped the planes together to guard them more effectively, but he failed to anticipate air attack. By massing the aircraft together, he offered the Japanese fliers an ideal target.

Short was relieved of command almost immediately after the BATTLE OF PEARL HARBOR. He was retired on February 28, 1942, after a presidential commission—the Roberts Commission—concluded that he had been guilty of poor judgment and dereliction of duty. Subsequently, the joint Congressional Investigating Committee delivered a less harsh judgment, yet still cited Short for errors of judgment.

In civilian life, Short became an executive for the Ford Motor Company in 1942, but suffered ill health after the stress of Pearl Harbor and was forced to retire in 1946.

Further reading: Goldstein, Donald M., and Katherine V. Dillon, eds. *The Pearl Harbor Papers: Inside the Japanese Plans.* Dulles, Va.: Potomac Books, 1999; Lord, Walter. *Day of Infamy: Sixtieth-Anniversary Edition.* New York: Owl Books, 2001; Prange, Gordon W. *At Dawn We Slept: The Untold Story of Pearl Harbor,* revised edition. New York: Penguin, 1991; Prange, Gordon W., with Donald M. Goldstein and Katherine V. Dillon. *Dec. 7, 1941: The Day the Japanese Attacked Pearl Harbor.* New York: Warner Books, 1989; Prange, Gordon W., with Donald M. Goldstein and Katherine V. Dillon. *Pearl Harbor: The Verdict of History.* New York: Penguin, 2001.

Sicherheitsdienst (SD)

The Sicherheitsdienst (SD), "Security Service," was the intelligence service of the Nazi Schutzstaffel (SS). From 1933 to 1939, the SD was under the Sicherheitspolizei (Security Police), then was transferred to the Reichsicherheitshauptamt (Reich Security Service Office, RSHA).

The SD was created in 1932 by Reinhard Heydrich, who built it into a powerful organization that became the exclusive Nazi Party "information service" on June 9, 1934. In 1938, the SD was made the intelligence organization for the Reich as well as for the Nazi Party. It worked in parallel with the Gestapo, which it supported with intelligence information.

The mission of the SD was primarily to detect and eliminate those who would subvert or otherwise harm the Nazi Party and the Reich. The SD cultivated and managed a network of several hundred agents and thousands of informants throughout the Reich and, during the war, in the occupied territories as well. The SD was always primarily an intelligence-gathering agency serving the Gestapo, which was the executive agency. Ultimately, therefore, the SD came under the control of Heinrich Himmler, who, as chief of the German police, headed the Gestapo and was also the senior officer of the SS.

The SD developed out of an agency called the Ic-Dienst, which was established in 1931. In 1939, the SD was divided into the Inland-SD and Ausland-SD. The Inland-SD had charge of intelligence and security within Germany. The Ausland-SD was effectively the civilian foreign intelligence agency of the Third Reich. Separate offices within the Ausland-SD were devoted to espionage in the West; espionage in the Soviet Union and Japan; espionage "in the American sphere"; and espionage in Eastern Europe. The SD supplied most of the security forces personnel deployed in the occupied territories. SD battalions were assigned to SS and German police leaders. SD personnel also operated in all concentration camps and sometimes participated in SS Einsatzgruppen—the special units responsible for arresting and killing Jews and other "undesirables" in occupied countries. The SD was tasked with maintaining order and security in Poland's Jewish ghettos.

See also Final Solution and Holocaust, the.

Further reading: Barwick, James. *The Hangman's Crusade.* London: Macmillan U.K., 1980; Butler, Rupert. *The Gestapo: A History of Hitler's Secret Police 1933–45.* Phoenix, Ariz.: Amber Books, 2004; Calic, Edward. *Reinhard Heydrich: The Chilling Story of the Man Who Masterminded the Nazi Death Camps.* New York: Morrow, 1984; Whiting, Charles. *Heydrich: Henchman of Death.* Barnsely, U.K.: Leo Cooper, 1999; Williams, Max. *Reinhard Heydrich: Enigma.* Shropshire, U.K.: Ulric, 2002.

Sicily Campaign

Operation Husky was the code name for the Allied landings on Sicily, which were launched before dawn on July 10, 1943. This article covers the campaign that followed the landings.

Thanks to the Allies' skillfully executed program of decoys and deceptions (called Operation Mincemeat), only two German divisions were on site to oppose the landings on Sicily. Bernard Law Montgomery's two British Eighth Army corps, the X and XIII, landed between Pozallo and Syracuse on the east coast. XIII Corps took Syracuse on the very day of the landings. The three American divisions that landed between Cape Scaramia and Licata on the southwest coast experienced adverse weather and greater German opposition, but nevertheless were all ashore by the end of the day. When German armor counterattacked on July 11 at Gela, U.S. warships unleashed a naval artillery bombardment that saved the landings.

British general HAROLD ALEXANDER, in overall command of the invasion, ordered the American commander, GEORGE SMITH PATTON JR., to cover Montgomery's left flank as his British Eighth Army advanced against Catania (XIII Corps) and toward Leonforte and Enna (XXX Corps). This subordinate role frustrated U.S. Seventh Army Commander

Patton as well as OMAR BRADLEY, commanding the U.S. II Corps, who was in a position to trap the 15th Panzer Grenadier by cutting the island in half.

Eager for more positive action, Patton, on July 15, 1943, formed a provisional corps under Lt. Gen. Geoffrey Keyes to advance on Palermo. When Alexander ordered him to continue covering Montgomery's flank, Patton met with Alexander personally and persuaded him to allow Keyes to take Palermo, which fell on July 22. Although the capture of Sicily's biggest city had much psychological value—and although Patton collected a great many Italian prisoners of war as a result—the operation was not strictly necessary to conquer the island.

George S. Patton Jr. walks ashore on Sicily, July 11, 1943. Engineers have laid a steel mat on the sandy beach to facilitate motor transport. *(Patton Museum of Cavalry and Armor, Fort Knox, Kentucky)*

By July 17, the Germans had set up the first of three lines of defense, which extended from south of Catar across to San Stefano on the north coast. The mountainous Sicilian landscape greatly inhibited armored advance, which gave the defenders a great advantage. Montgomery soon bogged down. He did not take Catania until August 5.

In the meantime, on July 25, BENITO MUSSOLINI was removed from power. This prompted ADOLF HITLER to authorize preparations for a possible evacuation of German forces. On July 27, the Germans began withdrawing from the first defensive line, all the while continuing to exploit the terrain of Sicily to slow Allied progress. Nevertheless, the U.S. 1st Division emerged victorious from the five-day battle at Troina, and the British pushed the Germans back on Adrano. The fall of Troina and Adrana, both major strong points, prompted ALBERT KESSELRING, the German commander in charge, to begin an evacuation during the night of August 11–12. That the Allies allowed some 40,000 German and 62,000 Italian troops to withdraw intact was a major misstep in the conquest of Sicily. Belatedly, both the British and the Americans launched amphibious assaults in a hopeless effort to cut off the retreat.

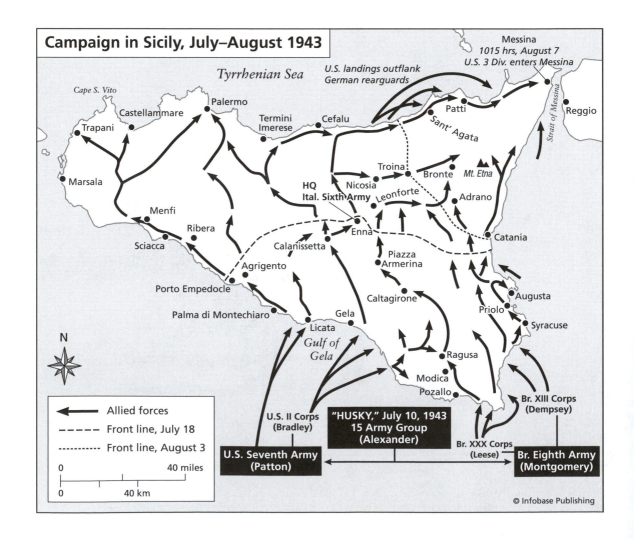

Campaign in Sicily, July–August 1943

General Harold Alexander (left) with George S. Patton Jr. and Rear Admiral Alan G. Kirk on a 1943 inspection tour during the Sicily Campaign (*National Archives and Records Administration*)

The failure to destroy more of the Axis army on Sicily was somewhat compensated for by Patton's spectacular liberation of Messina—stepping-off point to the Italian mainland—which he reached before Montgomery on August 16. This marked the end of the campaign, which was at best a deeply flawed Allied victory, since so many of Sicily's defenders lived to fight the Allies on the mainland.

Further reading: Birtle, Andrew J. *Sicily (U.S. Army Campaigns of World War II).* Washington, D.C.: Department of the Army, 1994; O'Neill, Herbert Charles. *Foothold in Europe: The Campaigns in Sicily, Italy, the Far East and Russia between July 1943 and May 1944.* London: Faber and Faber, 1945; Pack, S. W. C. *Operation, Husky: The Allied invasion of Sicily.* Newton Abbot, U.K.: David & Charles, 1977; Swanson, Jon M. *Operation Husky: A Case Study.* Carlisle, Pa.: U.S. Army War College, 1992; Shapiro, L. S. B. *They Left the Back Door Open: A Chronicle of the Allied Campaign in Sicily and Italy.* London: Jarrolds Ltd., 1944.

Sidi Rezegh, Battle of

The major action of the second British offensive in Libya, the Battle of Sidi Rezegh pitted British general ALAN CUNNINGHAM and the British Eighth Army (118,000 men) against an Axis Panzergruppe under ERWIN ROMMEL and including the three-division German Afrika Korps and eight Italian divisions, a total of 100,000 men.

The offensive, called Operation Crusader, was launched on November 18, 1941, by the British XIII Corps (infantry under A. R. Godwin-Austen) on the right along the Libyan coast, with XXX Corps (armor under Willoughby Norrie) making a wide swing on the left. XXX Corps occupied Sidi-Rezegh, which was the key to the relief of besieged Tobruk, on November 19. Rommel responded deftly, pushing back XXX Corps and thereby preventing its link-up with the Tobruk garrison. This accomplished, Rommel opened an intense counterattack on November 22, driving through to the British rear at the Egyptian frontier by November 25.

Cunningham asked for permission to withdraw to Mersa Matra, whereupon the theater commander in charge, CLAUDE JOHN AYRE AUCHINLECK, relieved him and appointed NEIL RITCHIE to command of the Eighth in his place. Under Ritchie for the next two weeks, the British units—though scattered—held against Rommel and even managed to open a corridor to Tobruk on November 29.

Rommel, always suffering from inadequate logistics, had no choice but to break off the attack. He fell back across Cyrenaica during the night of December 7–8, and, on the 15th, the British, in pursuit, occupied Gazala. They took Benghazi on December 25. The Eighth Army halted at El Agheila on January 6, having in the course of seven weeks of battle and pursuit killed more than 33,000 of the enemy for 17,700 Eighth Army losses.

Having achieved a magnificent victory, the British made the mistake of failing to follow up. This allowed Rommel to receive reinforcements, which he used to great advantage within two weeks.

Further reading: Carver, Michael. *Dilemmas of the Desert War: A New Look at the Libyan Campaign, 1940–1942.* Bloomington: Indiana University Press, 1986; Fielding, Sean. *They Sought Out Rommel: A Diary of the Libyan Campaign.* London: H. M. Stationery Office,

1942; Greene, Jack. *Rommel's North Africa Campaign: September 1940–November 1942.* New York: Da Capo Press, 1999.

Siegfried Line

The Siegfried Line, or West Wall, was the system of prepared defensive positions along Germany's western frontier in World War II. After the Normandy landings (D-day) and the Allied advance across France, the retreating German forces devoted time and effort to reinforcing and hardening the already formidable series of defensive positions.

As the Allies neared the Siegfried Line, they encountered increasingly fierce German resistance, even as the Allies suffered from shortages of fuel and other supplies due to their lines of communication and logistics having been stretched to their limits. By the fall of 1944, the Allies had seven armies arrayed along a line from the North Sea to Switzerland. These included, from north to south, the Twenty-First Army Group (Bernard Law Montgomery), which consisted of the Canadian First (Henry Crerar) and British Second (Miles Dempsey) Armies; the Twelfth Army Group (Omar Bradley), consisting of the Ninth U.S. (Henry Simpson), First U.S. (Courtney Hodges), and Third U.S. (George S. Patton Jr.) Armies; and the Sixth Army Group (Jacob Devers), consisting of the Seventh U.S. (Alexander Patch) and First French (Jean de Lattre de Tassigny). Opposing the Allies in the West were 63 German divisions (six armies) under Field Marshal Gerd von Rundstedt. The Fifteenth Army (Gustav Adolf von Zangen), First Parachute Army (Kurt Student), and the Seventh Army (Ernst Brandenberger) were all under the command of Field Marshal Walther Model. These forces held the line from the North Sea to the Moselle River. South of this, forward of the Siegfried Line in Alsace-Lorraine, were the First Army (Otto Knobelsdorff), Fifth Panzer Army (Hasso von Manteuffel), and the Nineteenth Army (Wiese), all under General Hermann Balck.

In the north, during the fall, with Operation Market-Garden, Montgomery attempted to establish a rapid bridgehead over the lower Rhine in order to flank the Siegfried Line at its northern end. The operation failed to establish the bridgehead, but was successful in taking South Beveland (October 30) and Walcheren Island (November 3) at the mouth of the Schelde River, which enabled the capture of the key port of Antwerp by November 26.

On the central sector of the front, the First U.S. Army reached the Siegfried Line at Aachen on September 12. The Battle of Aachen began on October 13 after the XIX and VII corps entered the city. This was the first German city to fall to the Allies. In November, the Ninth U.S. Army joined the First in an attack against the German defenses east of Aachen, an offensive that included the bloody fight for the Hürtgen Forest. By December 1, the First and Ninth Armies advanced to the small Roer River, 25 miles from Cologne. In the southern sector, the Third U.S. Army, having repulsed a counterattack by the German Fifth Panzer and First armies south of Metz (September 18–October 1), enveloped Metz on November 18, then pushed the Germans back to the Siegfired Line along the Saar River.

The Seventh U.S. Army drove to the Vosges Mountains, seized the Saverne Gap, then advanced into Strasbourg on November 23. After this, the army turned to the north, pushing against the Siegfried Line from Strasbourg past Karlsruhe, making contact with Third Army near Bitche. Simultaneously, the French First Army moved through Belfort and Mulhouse on November 22, reaching the Rhine River at the Swiss border. Despite this, the German Nineteenth Army continued to hold a salient known as the Colmar Pocket.

Despite advances all along the Siegfried Line front—and the capture of some 75,000 German prisoners by late fall—Allied progress had become frustratingly slow because of extremely tenacious and skillful German defense operations. Worse, the long offensive across so broad a front naturally left some weak points. The one at Ardennes the Germans would exploit with a massive offensive.

See also Ardennes, Battle of the (Battle of the Bulge).

Further reading: MacDonald, Charles Brown. *The Siegfried Line Campaign.* Washington, D.C.: Office of the Chief of Military History, Department of the Army, 1963; Short, Neil. *Germany's West Wall: The Siegfried Line.* London: Osprey, 2004; Short, Neil. *Hitler's Siegfried Line.* Stroud, U.K.: Sutton, 2003.

Singapore, fall of

Following the Fall of MALAYA, British general ARTHUR PERCIVAL led his troops in a withdrawal across the Johore Strait to the island of Singapore. On January 31, 1942, after the last of the British forces had cleared the causeway to the island, Percival ordered it destroyed—a job that was never fully completed.

With him on Singapore, Percival had some 85,000 British, Indian, and Australian troops—of whom only about 70,000 were armed combat soldiers. His formidable task was to defend a 30-mile perimeter. Moreover, although Singapore was a great naval fortress, its big guns were designed to be used against attacking ships. Capable only of firing at a flat trajectory, the guns could not be employed effectively against a land attack.

The conquest of Singapore was under the command of Japanese general YAMASHITA TOMOYUKI, fresh from the triumph of Malaya. He placed heavy siege guns at the southern tip of the Malay Peninsula and opened fire on Singapore beginning on February 5. Next, during the nights of February 8 and 9, Yamashita landed an amphibious force of about 5,000 men, who captured bridgeheads on the northwest and northern sides of the island. Japanese engineers made quick repairs to the causeway, sufficient to allow tanks and 25,000 more Japanese troops to invade.

While the Japanese ground forces advanced on Singapore City, artillery and aircraft continually attacked. On February 13, 3,000 British noncombatants were evacuated from Singapore in small boats, only to be intercepted by Japanese naval forces, which captured or killed the majority.

The unrelenting Japanese ground advance split and isolated the defenders, who were then defeated in detail. As the middle of February approached, the situation of the island, totally cut off, nearly without water, food, ammunition, or gasoline, seemed hopeless. Percival surrendered on February 15, 1942, yielding to the Japanese this strategically vital island, along with 32,000 Indian, 16,000 British, and 14,000 Australian troops as prisoners of war. Together, the defeats at Malaya and Singapore cost Great Britain 138,000 soldiers, of whom 130,000 became POWs.

Further reading: Barber, Noel. *Sinister Twilight: The Fall of Singapore.* London: Cassell, 2003; Bayly, Christopher, and Tim Harper. *Forgotten Armies: The Fall of British Asia, 1941–1945.* Cambridge, Mass.: Belknap Press, 2005; Farrell, Brian P. *The Defence and Fall of Singapore 1940–1942.* London: Tempus, 2005.

Sino-Japanese War

This conflict was one of the precipitating factors that propelled Japan into World War II. Since 1931, Japan had pursued a militant policy of imperial expansion at the expense of China, and in 1932 annexed Manchuria as Manchukuo. Japanese operations here erupted into a full-scale war on July 7, 1937, when Japanese troops stationed in north China fought with Chinese troops near the Marco Polo Bride at Lukouchiao, just outside of Peking (Beijing). Ostensibly, the Japanese troops were on night maneuvers, but it was clear the exchange was a deliberate Japanese provocation. What Japan called the "China Incident" became the pretext for a massive invasion.

The National Government Army of China, led by Generalissimo CHIANG KAI-SHEK (Jiang Jieshi), mustered some 2 million troops, who, despite their numbers, were ill equipped and poorly trained. A Communist guerrilla army of 150,000 supported the Nationalist forces, electing to suspend their struggle for control of China to fight the invaders. The Japanese invasion force numbered about 300,000 augmented by 150,000 Manchurians and Mongolians. In contrast to the defenders, the invaders were highly trained and equipped with the most modern weapons. They were led very ably. Even the Manchurian and

Portrait of Chiang Kai-shek *(Harry S. Truman Presidential Library)*

Mongolian auxiliaries, not nearly as well equipped or led, were nevertheless superior to the Nationalist Chinese forces. In addition, the militaristic government of Japan had a vast reserve to call upon if necessary, and it had developed a massive industrial capacity for war production.

On July 28, 1937, Japanese forces quickly captured Peking. Tientsin followed the next day, after which the invaders relentlessly marched west and south, brushing aside almost wholly ineffectual Chinese resistance. The westward-bound forces quickly seized the province of Chahar and part of Suiyuan. The southward-moving force menaced Nanking, Hankow, and Sian, but met more effective resistance from the Chinese regular army as well as from partisan forces. Even more critical than the resistance was the tenuous condition of supply lines, which were stretched very thin. Nevertheless, by December 27, 1937, Japanese troops

had taken Tsinan, capital of Shantung Province, which gave Japan control of the area north of the Yellow River.

While Japanese forces fought for the territory north of the Yellow River, an amphibious Japanese assault landed at Shanghai on August 8. Here Chinese defenders resisted with great tenacity, forcing Japan to pour in large numbers of reinforcements. Japanese aircraft heavily raided Shanghai, but the defenders nevertheless managed to pin the Japanese to their beachheads for two months—until the arrival of yet more reinforcements finally forced the fall of the city on November 8, 1937.

The Sino-Japanese War was largely an unbroken string of Chinese defeats, except for the September 25 Battle of P'ing-hsinkuan, in which the Japanese 5th Division was surprised and defeated in the Wutai Mountains, northern Shansi, by the Chinese 115th Division—a Communist unit of the Eighth Route Army. This was a signal victory against the Japanese, but it was of even greater value as political propaganda in that it allowed the Communists to take control of northwest China. Communist Chinese guerrillas established bases behind Japanese lines, which proved quite useful to the Allies during World War II.

Despite the defeat in Shansi, Japanese forces captured Nanking (Nanjing) on December 13 and embarked on an appalling orgy of murder, rape, and senseless destruction known to history as the RAPE OF NANKING.

A side event in the brutal invasion was the December 12, 1937, *Panay* Incident, in which Japanese aircraft attacked British and U.S. gunboats moored near Nanking. The *Panay*, a U.S. Navy gunboat, was sunk and a British boat severely damaged. Unwilling to provoke war with the United States, the Japanese apologized and paid an indemnity for the loss.

The second year of the Sino-Japanese War, 1938, began with a new offensive in northern China. The conquest of Shantung was complete before the end of January, and the Japanese continued to advance more forces toward Nanking and Hankow, slowed by attacks from the regular Chinese army and by guerrilla forces. By April, the Japanese had control of the rail lines. In April, at Taiercwang, Gen. Li Tsung-jen led regular and guerrilla forces exceeding 200,000 in an envelopment of a Japanese army of 60,000. The Japanese managed to break out, but only after losing one-third of their force. The invaders quickly recovered and, during May and June, renewed the assault from the north. Hsuchow fell on May 20, followed by Kaifeng on June 6. By the end of the month, the vital Peking-Nanking railroad was entirely in Japanese hands. In the meantime, Nationalist leader Chiang Kai-shek made another bargain with the Communists, agreeing to support another Communist army, the New Fourth Army, which was led in battle through east-central China under Yeh T'ing.

From Kaifeng, Japanese forces marched west to capture the rail junction at Chengchow to enable an advance down the railroad to Hankow. To forestall this action, the Chinese purposely destroyed the dikes holding back the waters of the Yellow River, flooding the countryside, drowning many Japanese troops, destroying great quantities of equipment, and bringing the advance to a halt during June and July. Almost immediately, however, the Japanese army shifted southward and resumed the advance on Hankow. Although resistance by Chinese ground forces was determined, Japanese air attacks forced the surrender of Hankow, temporary capital of Chiang's Nationalist government. Chiang himself fled the city and reestablished his capital and headquarters at Chungking (Chongqing) in mountainous Szechwan (Sichuan) Province. While this was taking place, a new Japanese amphibious force landed near Hong Kong on October 12 and quickly marched inland to take Canton, which fell on October 21. China's two major seaports were now controlled by Japanese forces.

By the beginning of 1939, despite the devastation visited by the invaders, the war was proving inconclusive. Although vast tracts of China were occupied by the Japanese, popular resistance continued to take a heavy toll on the invaders. The Japanese high command therefore modified its strategy, shifting from a program of rapid conquest to a war of attrition. Before the end of 1939, Japanese forces captured all of China's remaining seaports in an effort to strangle the nation into final submission. Before the beginning of 1940, only two tenuous supply routes fed into China: the tortuous Burma Road, winding up from British Burma to Kunming, and a narrow-gauge railroad running from Haiphong, French Indochina, also to Kunming.

Although Chiang Kai-shek and his tenuous allies, the Chinese Communists, continued their resistance, the Japanese set up a puppet government for occupied China at Nanking. It was headed by a well-respected Chinese politician, Wang Chingwei, who, despite his popularity, proved unable to prompt the defection of any of Chiang's supporters.

With much of China occupied, the Japanese moved against Indochina in June 1940. Having surrendered to Germany, France was in no position to resist Germany's ally Japan, and the Vichy administrators of French Indochina yielded permission to the Japanese to land forces. This closed the supply route from Haiphong to Kunming.

Next to close was the Burma Road. At this point, Japan and Great Britain were not yet at war, and the British, under threat of invasion from Germany, had no desire to start a war against Japan now, so when the Japanese demanded that the British in Burma close the Burma Road, Prime Minister WINSTON CHURCHILL agreed, thereby cutting off China from the rest of the world.

Despite this reversal, Chiang Kai-shek and Communist leader MAO ZEDONG refused to capitulate. Between August 20 and November 30, 1940, Mao led an intensive series of guerrilla raids in the provinces of Shensi, Chahar, Hubei, and Hunan, doing substantial damage to Japanese rear-echelon positions. Japan, in the meantime, occupied Indochina during September and established bases from which it could make additional air attacks on Chinese territory and pour in more land forces. Shortly after the occupation, on September 26, U.S. president FRANKLIN DELANO ROOSEVELT embargoed scrap iron and steel shipments to Japan, which precipitated a sharp decline in U.S.-Japanese relations, even as Japan formally concluded the AXIS (TRIPARTITE) PACT with Germany and Italy on September 27.

Beginning in 1941, Japanese forces conducted periodic punitive raids against Chinese Communist forces. Over the next three years, these raids would keep the Chinese Communist Eighth Route Army continually on the defensive and would cost it some 100,000 casualties. Worse, the Nationalist-Communist alliance began to disintegrate. When the Communist New Fourth Army, operating south of the Yangtze River in Anhwei (Anhvi), refused to cross the river to attack Japanese troops, Chiang Kai-shek moved Nationalist troops into the region. Responding to this, in late December 1940, the New Fourth Army began to cross the river, leaving only 10,000 troops and headquarters on the south bank. Nationalist forces attacked this element, destroying it and creating a crisis in relations with Mao and the Communists.

On April 13, 1941, Japan concluded a nonaggression treaty with the USSR. The United States froze Japanese assets in the United States on July 26, however, and in this hostile climate, the U.S. government quietly approved the formation of the American Volunteer Group, better known as the FLYING TIGERS, a mercenary air force of about 100 U.S. volunteer pilots led by retired U.S. Army captain CLAIRE L. CHENNAULT. The deployment of the Flying Tigers was complete by December 1941. In the meantime, in October, TOJO HIDEKI became Japan's premier, consummating the delivery of the Japanese government into the hands of the military. With the BATTLE OF PEARL HARBOR on December 7, 1941, the Sino-Japanese War merged into World War II.

Further Reading: Chang, K. Y. *Modern China and Japan, 1879–1952.* Hong Kong: Goofman, 1977; Dreyer, Edward L. *China at War, 1901–1949.* London: Longman, 1995.

Sittang River Bridge, Battle of

During the BURMA CAMPAIGN, the Japanese 33rd Division outflanked Major General John Smyth's 17th Indian Division, prompting him to order the demolition of the Sittang River Bridge in an effort to delay the Japanese advance on Rangoon. The demolition was accomplished on February 23,

1942, and cost the Japanese at least 10 days, but it also trapped two of Smyth's three brigades on the eastern bank of the Sittang. Some 5,000 men were taken prisoner by the Japanese, and all of the division's artillery and transport vehicles were lost.

Despite the time it bought, the Battle of the Sittang River Bridge was counted a British disaster at the time, and Lieutenant General Thomas Hutton, commander in charge of Burma, was relieved, as was Smyth—who was also compelled to accept early retirement. In subsequent years, Smyth found many defenders of his action, and his decision at Sittang River has long been a subject of heated argument.

Further reading: Astor, Gerald. *The Jungle War: Mavericks, Marauders and Madmen in the China-Burma-India Theater of World War II.* New York: Wiley, 2004; Dupuy, Trevor N. *Asiatic Land Battles: Allied Victories in China and Burma.* New York: Franklin Watts, 1963; Hogan, David W. *India-Burma (The U.S. Army Campaigns of World War II).* Carlisle, Pa.: Army Center of Military History, 1991; Webster, Donovan. *The Burma Road: The Epic Story of the China-Burma-India Theater in World War II.* New York: Farrar, Straus and Giroux, 2003.

Skorzeny, Otto (1908–1975) *commando leader*

Born in Austria, Skorzeny became a Nazi Party member in 1933 and served as a lieutenant colonel in the WAFFEN SS during World War II. He was commissioned to create special commando units in 1942 called the Friedenthal Hunting Groups (Friedenthaler Jadgverbände).

On September 12, 1943, he led 90 commandos in a glider and light-aircraft operation at Gran Sasso in the Abruzzi region of Italy. They snatched BENITO MUSSOLINI, who, having been ousted from power, was being held by order of the new Italian head of state, Marshal PIETRO BADOGLIO. Skorzeny's commandos transported Il Duce to Germany, and ADOLF HITLER set him up as the puppet ruler of northern Italy, which, at the time, was still occupied by the Germans.

The signal success of the Mussolini rescue earned Skorzeny a promotion and allowed him to expand his commando unit. In 1944, Hitler gave him the mission of rounding up and torturing those implicated in the JULY PLOT (TO ASSASSINATE HITLER). On October 17, 1944, he commanded the SS unit that arrested MIKLÓS HORTHY DE NAGY-BÁNYA and removed him from power in Hungary. During the battle of the ARDENNES (BATTLE OF THE BULGE), Skorzeny masterminded the infiltration behind American lines of hundreds of U.S.-uniformed English-speaking Germans.

After the war, in 1947, Skorzeny was tried by the NUREMBERG WAR CRIMES TRIBUNAL, which acquitted him of war crimes largely because a senior British officer testified that Skorzeny had done nothing that Allied commandos would not also have tried to do. Despite his acquittal at Nuremberg, Skorzeny was still subject to a West German denazification trial. Unwilling to chance the outcome of that proceeding, he escaped from Darmstadt prison in 1949 and fled to Spain, where he lived for the rest of his life.

Further reading: Skorzeny, Otto. *Skorzeny's Special Missions.* London: Greenhill Books, 1997; Whiting, Charles. *Skorzeny: "The Most Dangerous Man in Europe."* Conshohocken, Pa.: Combined Publishing, 1998.

Slim, Sir William Joseph (1891–1970)
British commander in Burma

Born near Bristol, England, Slim was educated at King Edward's School (Witley, Surrey) and was enrolled in the Officer Training Corps (OTC) there. After graduating, he taught school from 1909 to 1910, then worked as a bank clerk. In 1912, he continued OTC at Birmingham University and joined the army at the outbreak of World War I, serving as a second lieutenant in the 9th Battalion of the Royal Warwickshire Regiment. From July 13 to August 8, 1915, he fought in the disastrous Gallipoli campaign, suffering a severe wound on August 8, which laid him up until January 1916. He fought in France and in Mesopotamia, participating in the advance on Baghdad during December 10, 1916–March 11, 1917. He was then invalided to India (because he had never been officially certified as fit for duty after being wounded in Gallipoli), where he was appointed to the general staff and promoted to temporary major. At his own request, he was made a captain in the Indian army on May 31, 1919, and on March 27, 1920, he was assigned as captain of the 2/7 Gurkha Rifles, serving with them in the campaign against the Tochi Wazirs in October 1920.

After returning to England in 1924, Slim enrolled in the Staff College there, then returned to India in 1926, where he taught at the Staff College at Quetta. Returning again to England in 1929, he served at Army Headquarters until 1933 and was appointed an instructor at the Imperial Staff College, Camberley. In 1937, he taught at the Imperial Defense College and was promoted to lieutenant colonel the following year, when he also returned to India. He enrolled in the Senior Officer's School

Otto Skorzeny *(Library of Congress)*

at Belgaum and assumed command of the 2/7 Gurkhas in Assam during 1938–39. He returned to Belgaum as commandant of the Senior Officer's School and was promoted to the local rank of brigadier general.

At the outbreak of World War II, Slim was assigned to command the 10th Indian Brigade on September 23, 1939, which he prepared and trained for mechanized desert warfare. He led the brigade to East Africa as part of the 5th Indian Division, arriving at Port Sudan on August 2, 1940. Repulsed at Gallabat, Sudan, on November 6, 1940, due to poor air support and faulty reconnaissance, Slim was wounded late in January 1941 and was sent to India to recover.

Slim assumed command of the 10th Indian Division in Iraq on May 15, 1941. He captured Baghdad early in June, then pushed into Vichy-controlled Syria, where he captured Deir-es-Zor, using the slightest of resources. On August 25, Slim invaded Iran to open supply lines to the USSR. After this mission was accomplished, he returned to India in March 1942, where he took command of the newly created I Burma Corps (the 17th Indian and the Burma Divisions) on March 13 at Prome.

Fighting in a chronically undersupplied theater of the war, Slim conducted a determined delaying campaign against the Japanese, but was driven out of Burma by the end of April. He executed a skillful retreat across the Chindwin River, then directed the defense of India from June to December 1942. On April 14, 1943, he commanded the IV Corps as well I Burma Corps, which were pinned down at Arakan. After successfully extricating the corps, he was appointed to command the Eastern Army on October 16, 1943, transforming it into the Fourteenth Army and revitalizing its sunken morale. He led the Fourteenth in an operation that halted the Japanese offensives in Arakan during February 1944 and at Imphal-Kohima during March 6–July 15, then took charge of operations to liberate northern Burma during July–December 1944.

After northern Burma was cleared of Japanese, Slim commanded the British offensive of December–March 1945 that took Mandalay on March 20, 1945. He next advanced south along the Irrawaddy and Sittang valleys, taking Rangoon on May 2. After promotion to general on July 1, Slim was assigned command of Southeast Asian ground forces on August 16. He carried out pacification operations in Malaysia and Indonesia during August–November 1945—since, even after the Japanese surrender, diehards in these most remote corners of the war continued to fight.

Following World War II, Slim was appointed commandant of the Imperial Defense College, serving from 1946 to 1948. He then became chief of the Imperial General Staff on November 1, 1948, and was promoted to field marshal on January 4, 1949. In 1952, he was appointed governor-general of Australia, serving until 1960. Returning to England, he was named lieutenant governor deputy constable (1963–64), then governor and constable of Windsor Castle (1964–70).

Further reading: Lewin, Ronald. *Slim, the Standard-bearer: A Biography of Field-Marshal the Viscount Slim.* Conshohocken, Pa.: Combined Publishing, 1999; Slim, William. *Defeat Into Victory.* New York: Cooper Square Press, 2000; Slim, William. *Unofficial Victory.* London: Corgi, 1970.

small arms and rifles, British

PISTOLS

The most important British pistols of World War II were the Enfield No. 2 Mk. 1 and the Webley Mk 4. Both were 6-round revolvers, and both used the same 0.380 SAA 9.65 mm ball. The Enfield was 10.25 inches long, with a 5-inch barrel. It weighed 1.7 pounds and had a muzzle velocity of 600 feet per second. The Webley was slightly longer at 10.5 inches, but also had a 5-inch barrel and delivered its round at 600 feet per second. Its weight was identical to that of the Enfield weapon.

RIFLES

The most important British rifle of World War II was the Lee-Enfield No. 4 Mk 1. It was designed in

1939 and produced throughout and after the war, from 1939 to 1956, remaining in service as late as 1990. A bolt-action service rifle, its caliber was .303 inches and it fired a .303-inch SSA Ball Mk VI and Mk VII from a 10-round magazine. The rifle measured 44.4 inches in length, with a barrel length of 25.2 inches. It weighed 9 pounds, 3 ounces and could fire 15 to 30 rounds per minute. Muzzle velocity was 2,539 feet per second and effective range about 2,625 feet.

For jungle combat, the Lee-Enfield No. 4 Mk I was judged too long and heavy. In 1943, the No. 5, Mk I was produced. Like the No. 4 Mk I, it was .303 caliber, but it was only 39.5 inches in length, with a barrel of 18.75 inches. It weighed 7.15 pounds and had a muzzle velocity of about 2,400 feet per second.

British commandos often used the De Lisle carbine, designed in 1943 by an aircraft engineer, William Godfray De Lisle. The 0.45-inch caliber weapon was 35.25 inches long, with a short barrel of 7.25 inches. It weighed in at 8.25 pounds and could deliver seven rounds from its box magazine at a muzzle velocity of 830 feet per second.

Further reading: Hogg, Ian V. *The Encyclopedia of Infantry Weapons of World War II*. New York: Military Press, 1987; Petrillo, Alan M. *The Lee Enfield Number Four Rifles*. Latham, N.Y.: Excalibur Publications, 1992; Skennerton, Ian D. *British Small Arms of World War 2*. London: Greenhill Books, 1988; Stratton, Charles R. *British Enfield Rifles, Lee-Enfield No. 4 and No. 5 Rifles*. Tustin, Calif.: North Cape, 1990; Suermondt, Jan. *Infantry Weapons of World War II*. Willingdon Drove, U.K.: Gardners Books, 2004; Weeks, John. *Infantry Weapons*. London: Pan Macmillan, 1972.

small arms and rifles, French

PISTOLS

At the outbreak of World War II, the French were still issuing to officers the venerable pre–World War I Lebel Mle. 1892 revolver. The .275-caliber pistol held six rounds and had a barrel length of 9.37 inches. Muzzle velocity was 374 feet per sec-

ond. The French also issued a modern semiautomatic pistol, the Mle. 1935S—first produced in 1935—which was a 7.65 mm caliber weapon holding eight rounds. It was 7.4 inches long, with a 4.1-inch barrel and weighed 1.75 pounds unloaded. Muzzle velocity was 1,132 feet per second.

RIFLES

At the outbreak of World War II, the French army fought with a miscellaneous array of rifles, some as old in design as the 1866 Chassepot. Three rifles, however, were the most important:

Lebel Fusil d'infanterie mle 1886/93. First issued in 1886, this 8 mm rifle was updated in 1893 and used in both world wars. The rifle was 51.3 inches long, with a 31.4-inch barrel. It weighed 9.35 pounds and delivered a round at 2,380 feet per second. The tube magazine held eight rounds.

Berthier Fusil d'infanterie mle 07/15. The Berthier had begun to displace the Lebel by the outbreak of World War II. The 7.5 mm weapon was 42.7 inches long with a 22.8-inch barrel. It weighed only 7.85 pounds and delivered a muzzle velocity of 2,700 feet per second. The magazine was a five-round box.

Fusil MAS36. The latest of the French World War II weapons, the MAS36 was slow to reach production, so was issued only to front-line units. Caliber was 7.5 mm, length 40.13 inches, and barrel length 22.6 inches. The rifle weighed 8.09 pounds and could deliver a muzzle velocity of 2,700 feet per second. The box magazine held five rounds.

Further reading: Hogg, Ian V. *The Encyclopedia of Infantry Weapons of World War II*. New York: Military Press, 1987; Suermondt, Jan. *Infantry Weapons of World War II*. Willingdon Drove, U.K.: Gardners Books, 2004; Weeks, John. *Infantry Weapons*. London: Pan Macmillan, 1972.

small arms and rifles, German

German infantry weapons were some of the best of World War II, in terms of reliability as well as performance.

PISTOLS

Luger. The so-called Luger is one of the iconic weapons of World War II. The most familiar model was officially designated Pistole P08 and grew out of a design originally produced by Hugo Borchardt in 1893 and refined by George Luger. Some 35 variants of the Luger were used by the armies of many nations. The standard P08 had a barrel 4.055 inches long and an overall length of 8.75 inches. It fired a 9 mm Parabellum cartridge from an 8-round box magazine. The pistol weighed 1.92 pounds and produced a muzzle velocity of 1,250 feet per second.

Walther PP. Pistols by the Walther firm were more modern than the Lugers and began to replace them early in the war. The Walther PP was first manufactured in 1929 as a police weapon. It is considered one of the finest small arms of World War II. Some variants fired a 9 mm short round, others a 7.65 mm round. Still others fired a 6.35 mm and 5.56 mm long round (0.22 LR). The overall length of the weapon was just 6.8 inches. Barrel length was 2.9 inches. The pistol weighed 1.5 pounds and delivered a muzzle velocity of 950 feet per second. Its magazine held eight rounds.

Walther PPK. This was a short version of the PP. Variants fired the same types of ammunition as the PP, but the overall length of the weapon was just 6.1 inches, whereas the barrel length was stretched to 3.39 inches. Weight was 1.25 pounds, muzzle velocity 920 feet per second, and the magazine held seven rounds.

Walther P38. Second only to the P08 Luger in fame, this weapons was designed to replace that earlier pistol. It was a superb weapon, although costly. The P38 fired a 9 mm Parabellum round and was 8.58 inches in overall length, with a barrel of 4.88 inches. It weighed in at 2.12 pounds, delivered a muzzle velocity of 1,150 feet per second, and had an eight-round magazine.

RIFLES

Karabiner 98k. At the outbreak of World War II, many German units went into combat with this modification of the World War I Gewehr 98. The Gewehr was an 1898 design, which fired a 7.92 mm round and delivered a muzzle velocity of 2,100 feet per second. It weighed 9.26 pounds and had an overall length of 49.2 inches, which German infantry experts regarded as too long for front-line use. The Karabiner 98k modification shortened the length of the barrel from 29.1 inches to 23.6 and the overall length from 49.2 to 43.6 inches. Weight came down to 8.6 pounds, and muzzle velocity rose to 2,477 feet per second. Both weapons had a five-round box magazine.

Gewehr 41 (W). This self-loading weapon was first produced in 1941. It fired a 7.92 mm round from a 10-round box magazine. The rifle was 44.25 inches long, with a 21.5-inch barrel. Weight was 11.09 pounds. The weapon produced a muzzle velocity of 2,546 feet per second.

Gewehr 43. The self-loading system of the Gewehr 41 (W) proved cumbersome and complex in combat, and when Germans fighting on the Soviet front discovered the Soviet Tomarev automatic rifles, they copied the self-loading mechanism for the Gewehr 43. Like its predecessor, it fired a 7.92 mm round from a 10-round box magazine. It was 44 inches in overall length, with a 21.61-inch barrel. Weight was down to 9.7 pounds, and it delivered the same muzzle velocity—2,546 feet per second—as the earlier weapon.

Fallschirmjägergewehr 42. This infantry weapon was produced exclusively for the Luftwaffe, the German air force, to equip paratroops. It was an early example of the assault rifle. The weapon fired a 7.92 mm round from a 20-round box magazine. It was just 37 inches long, with a barrel length of 19.76 inches. Weight was 9.9 pounds and muzzle velocity 2,500 feet per second. Cyclic rate of fire was between 750 and 800 rounds per minute.

Sturmgewehr 44. Originally designated the Maschinenpistole 43, the Sturmgewehr 44 was an early assault weapon, which fired 7.92 mm ammunition from a 30-round box magazine at a cyclic rate of 500 rounds per minute. It was 37 inches in length overall, with a 16.5-inch barrel. The rifle weighed 11.5 pounds and delivered a muzzle velocity of 2,132 feet per second.

Further reading: Barker, A. J. *German Infantry Weapons of World War II.* London: Hippocrene Books, 1976;

Hogg, Ian V. *The Encyclopedia of Infantry Weapons of World War II*. New York: Military Press, 1987; Suermondt, Jan. *Infantry Weapons of World War II*. Willingdon Drove, U.K.: Gardners Books, 2004; Weeks, John. *Infantry Weapons*. London: Pan Macmillan, 1972.

small arms and rifles, Italian

Italy's principal rifle was the bolt-action Carcano M91, which fired 6.5 mm rounds from a six-round magazine. Muzzle velocity was 2,296.5 feet per second. The rifle was 50.59 inches long overall, with a 30.7-inch barrel. Unloaded weight was 8.38 pounds.

The most important pistols were the Pistola Automatica Glisenti modello 1910 and the Pistola Automatica Beretta modello 1934.

Pistola Automatica Glisenti modello 1910. Originally known as the Brizia, this pistol was adopted by the Italian army in 1910 and was cordially despised by most officers. Its action was sloppy and did not inspire confidence in the shooter. The cartridge was a 9 mm Glisenti fired from a seven-round box magazine, Overall length was 8.27 inches, with a barrel length of 4.02 inches. The Glisenti weighed two pounds and delivered a muzzle velocity of 1,050 feet per second.

Pistola Automatica Beretta modello 1934. This weapon made a welcome contrast with the 1910 pistol. Beautifully made and finished to an exacting standard, this pistol fired a 9 mm short round and had a seven-round magazine box. Overall length was six inches, and the barrel was 3.4 inches long. The pistol weighed 1.25 pounds and had a muzzle velocity of 950 feet per second.

Further reading: Hogg, Ian V. *The Encyclopedia of Infantry Weapons of World War II*. New York: Military Press, 1987; Suermondt, Jan. *Infantry Weapons of World War II*. Willingdon Drove, U.K.: Gardners Books, 2004; Weeks, John. *Infantry Weapons*. London: Pan Macmillan, 1972.

small arms and rifles, Japanese

Japanese infantry weapons were of generally mediocre quality, especially as the war in the Pacific got under way in earnest and speed of production took precedence over considerations of workmanship.

PISTOLS

During the 1930s, the Imperial Japanese Army generally used 8 mm Pistol Type 14 (called by Westerners the "Nambu" pistol), which was a good weapon. To meet the demands of wartime production, however, an attempt was made to simplify the service revolver, and the result, Pistol type 94 (94 Shiki Kenju), is generally considered the worst small arm of the war. Not only did it handle poorly, it was inherently unsafe because part of the trigger mechanism protruded from the left side of the weapon. This meant that it was easily discharged by accident. In addition, manufacturing standards were lax and the quality of the materials poor. The pistol fired an 8 mm Taisho 14 cartridge and had a muzzle velocity of 1,000 feet per second. Overall length was 7.2 inches, barrel length 3.78 inches, and weight 1.52 pounds. The box magazine held six shots.

RIFLES

The most important Japanese rifle was the Type 38, which fired a 6.5 mm round from a five-round box magazine. The weapon was 50.2 inches long overall and had a 31.4-inch barrel. It weighed 9.25 pounds and delivered a muzzle velocity of 2,400 feet per second.

The Type 99 was a version of the Type 38 raised to 7.7 caliber and incorporating a monopod for improved accuracy.

In addition to the Type 38 and Type 99, the Carbine Type 38 was widely used. Some models of this shortened version of the Type 38 featured a folding butt for use by airborne troops. The Parachutist's Rifle Type 2 was not a carbine, but a version of the Type 99 that could be broken down into halves. Yet another Type 38 modification was the Sniper Rifle Type 97, which incorporated a provision for a telescopic sight and a redesigned bolt handle.

Further reading: Hogg, Ian V. *The Encyclopedia of Infantry Weapons of World War II*. New York: Military Press,

1987; Suermondt, Jan. *Infantry Weapons of World War II.* Willingdon Drove, U.K.: Gardners Books, 2004; Weeks, John. *Infantry Weapons.* London: Pan Macmillan, 1972.

small arms and rifles, Soviet

Soviet small arms and rifles were not pretty, but they were durable, and the Tokarev rifles were among the best infantry weapons of the war.

PISTOLS

The Red Army entered World War II with the M1895 Nagant, a 7.65 mm weapon with a seven-round revolver magazine. The weapon was nine inches long overall with a barrel length of 4.5 inches. Unloaded weight was 1.65 pounds, and its muzzle velocity was 889 feet per second.

In the course of the war, the venerable Nagant was replaced—albeit not entirely—by the Tokarev TT-33, which had gone into production in 1933. This semiautomatic pistol fired a 7.62 mm cartridge Type P (M30) from an eight-round box magazine. It had a muzzle velocity of 1,380 feet per second. Overall length was 7.68 inches, barrel length 4.57 inches. The weapon weighed 1.83 pounds.

RIFLES

Two rifle types were widely used in the Red Army, the Mosin-Nagant rifles and the Tokarev rifles.

Mosin-Nagant rifles. The Mosin-Nagant Model 1891 was carried by the soldiers of the tsar's army in World War I. The old rifles were modernized beginning in 1930, and the Mosin-Nagant Model 1891/30 became a mainstay of the Red Army during World War II. It fired a 7.62 mm round from a five-round box magazine. Overall, it measured 48.5 inches long, with a 28.7-inch barrel. Weight was 8.8 pounds. The weapon delivered a muzzle velocity of 2,660 feet per second.

Model 1938 Carbine. The carbine version of the Mosin-Nagent Model 1891/30 fired the same 7.62-mm round, but was reduced in overall length to 40 inches, with a 20-inch barrel. Muzzle velocity rose to 2,514 feet per second.

Tokarev SVT 40. This semiautomatic rifle was one of the best small arms of the war. It fired 7.62 mm rounds from a 10-round box magazine, delivering a muzzle velocity of 2,723 feet per second for impressive penetrating power and accuracy. The weapon was 48.1 inches long overall, with a 24.6-inch barrel. It weighed 8.58 pounds.

Further reading: Hogg, Ian V. *The Encyclopedia of Infantry Weapons of World War II.* New York: Military Press, 1987; Suermondt, Jan. *Infantry Weapons of World War II.* Willingdon Drove, U.K.: Gardners Books, 2004; Weeks, John. *Infantry Weapons.* London: Pan Macmillan, 1972.

small arms and rifles, U.S.

U.S. history is intimately bound up with the development and manufacture of firearms, and the nation went to war with excellent small arms and rifles.

PISTOLS

Colt M1911A1 Automatic Pistol. The U.S. Army went to France in World War I with the Colt M1911, which had been accepted into service in 1911. Experience with the weapons resulted in a few design changes, resulting in the M1911A1, which was the American officer's weapon of World War II. It fired a .45 ball (M1911) out of a seven-round magazine box and developed a muzzle velocity of 825 feet per second. Overall length was 8.6 inches, with a 5.03-inch barrel. The weapon was hefty at three pounds.

Smith & Wesson 0.38/200 Revolver. This U.S. design was built for British and Commonwealth forces. It was a straightforward, highly dependable revolver, holding six rounds in its cylinder and delivering a muzzle velocity of 650 feet per second with an 0.380 SAA ball (a 9.65 mm round). Overall length was 10.125 inches, with a five-inch barrel. Weight was 1.94 pounds.

Smith & Wesson M1917. Produced during World War I, this was the standard U.S. Army service revolver. It fired a .45 ball M1911 at 830 feet per second. The chamber held six rounds. Overall length was 10.8 inches, with a 5.5-inch barrel. Weight was 2.25 pounds. Colt produced a very similar weapon for the army, the Revolver, Caliber .45, Colt New Service, M1917.

Liberator M1942. The most unusual pistol ever produced by the United States (the contractor was the Guide Lamp Division of General Motors!), the Liberator was an assassination weapon. Cheap and simple in the extreme, this little pistol was packed into a clear plastic bag together with 10 rounds and a set of instructions in illustrated, wordless comic-strip format. Thus packaged, it was parachute-dropped into occupied Europe and in the Far East theaters to be picked up and used by resistance fighters, partisans, and guerrillas. The Liberator fired a single shot, but had space in the handle to carry five rounds. Ammunition was a .45 ball M1911, which was fired at a muzzle velocity of 1,100 feet per second. The overall length of the weapon was just 5.55 inches, with a four-inch barrel. It weighed one pound.

RIFLES

Rifle, Caliber .30, Model of 1903. Known universally as the Springfield rifle, the weapon was adopted in 1903 and was manufactured in several variations. At the outbreak of World War II, with the new M1 Garand not yet available in sufficient numbers, the Springfield was issued to many troops. It was a highly accurate weapon, but was not self-loading. Nevertheless, it was highly favored by sharpshooters and snipers. The weapon fired a 7.62 mm (.30) round from a five-round box magazine. Muzzle velocity was 2,805 feet per second. Overall, the rifle was 43.5 inches in length, with a barrel of 24 inches. It weighed nine pounds.

Rifle, Caliber .30, M1 (Garand). The standard U.S. infantry rifle of World War I, the M1 was also the first self-loading rifle to be accepted for military service. Five and a half million were produced during the war. The rifle fired a 7.62 mm (.30) round from an eight-round box magazine. Muzzle velocity was 2,805 feet per second. Overall length was 43.6 inches, with a 24-inch barrel. The rifle weighed 9.5 pounds.

Carbine, Caliber .30, M1. For troops who required a lighter, smaller weapon than the M1 rifle, the Winchester-designed M1 carbine was the weapon of choice. It fired a 7.62 mm (.30) round from a box magazine that held 15 or 30 rounds. The overall length was 35.6 inches, and the barrel length was just 18 inches. The rifle weighed 5.2 pounds and delivered a muzzle velocity of 1,970 feet per second. An M2 version of the carbine incorporated an automatic fire feature, which delivered a cyclic rate of fire of 775 rounds per minute. An M3 version was designed for night fighting and included an infrared night sight. These weapons were highly favored by the marines, who welcomed the easy handling in tough jungle environments.

Further reading: Canfield, Bruce N. *Complete Guide to the M1 Garand and the M1 Carbine.* Lincoln, R.I.: Andrew Mowbray, 1998; Canfield, Bruce N. *U.S. Infantry Weapons of World War II.* Lincoln, R.I.: Andrew Mowbray, 1996; Hogg, Ian V. *The Encyclopedia of Infantry Weapons of World War II.* New York: Military Press, 1987; Suermondt, Jan. *Infantry Weapons of World War II.* Willingdon Drove, U.K.: Gardners Books, 2004; Weeks, John. *Infantry Weapons.* London: Pan Macmillan, 1972.

Smith, Holland M. "Howlin' Mad" (1882–1967) *U.S. Marine general commanding in the Pacific war, often called the father of modern amphibious warfare*

Born in Seale, Alabama, Smith graduated from Alabama Polytechnic Institute in 1901 and took a law degree at the University of Alabama in 1903. He practiced briefly in Montgomery, Alabama, before receiving a commission in the USMC in 1905. He served in the Philippines from 1906 to 1908, then, after a brief Stateside stint, he was posted to Panama. Returning to the United States in April 1910, he was stationed at Annapolis, Md.; Puget Sound, Washington; San Diego, California; and the Recruiting Station, Seattle, Washington. He rejoined the 1st Marine Brigade in the Philippines in 1912. In April 1914, he assumed command of the marine detachment aboard the USS *Galveston*, returned to the United States briefly, and was ordered to the Dominican Republic in June 1916, to fight against so-called "rebel bandits." He returned to the United States on May 30, 1917, and, within two weeks, was off to France as commander of the 8th Machine Gun Company, 5th Marines.

Holland M. "Howlin' Mad" Smith (United States Marine Corps)

On his arrival in France, Smith was detached from the 5th Marines and sent to the Army General Staff College at Langres, from which he graduated in February 1918. Appointed adjutant of the 4th Marine Brigade, he saw action in the Aisne-Marne Defensive, including at the Battle of Belleau Wood. After staff service during the Aisne-Marne, Oisne-Aisne, St-Mihiel, and Meuse-Argonne offensives, he served with the occupation forces following the Armistice. Smith was decorated with the Croix de Guerre with Palm by the French government and received a Meritorious Service Citation from the commander in chief, American Expeditionary Forces, for which he was subsequently awarded the Purple Heart medal.

Smith returned to the United States in April 1919 and enrolled in the Naval War College, Newport, Rhode Island, then served in the War Plans Section of the Office of Naval Operations, Washington, D.C. In May 1923, he served aboard the battleships Wyoming and Arkansas as fleet marine officer, U.S. Scouting Fleet. In February 1924, he was named chief of staff and officer in charge of operations and training for the Marine Brigade on expeditionary duty in Haiti. In 1925, he returned to the United States as chief of staff of the 1st Marine Brigade at Quantico, Virginia.

Smith enrolled in the Marine Corps Schools, Quantico, then was assigned as post quartermaster of the Marine Barracks, Philadelphia Navy Yard, from July 1927 to March 1931, when he served aboard the USS California as aide to the commander and force marine officer of the Battle Force, U.S. Fleet. In June 1933, he took command of the Marine Barracks at the Washington Navy Yard. Beginning in January 1935, he served two years at San Francisco as chief of staff, Department of the Pacific. In March 1937, he moved to Marine Corps Headquarters as director of the Division of Operations and Training. In April 1939, he was named assistant commandant of the Marine Corps under Major General Thomas Holcomb. He served until September.

On the brink of war, Smith directed extensive army, navy, and marine amphibious training, which proved crucial to U.S. landings during the war. Smith was also instrumental in preparing U.S. Army and Canadian troops for the Kiska and Attu landings in the ALEUTIANS ISLANDS CAMPAIGN. Smith then led the V Amphibious Corps in the assaults on the Gilberts and in MARSHALL ISLANDS CAMPAIGN, the BATTLE OF SAIPAN, and Tinian in the MARIANA ISLANDS CAMPAIGN. He had responsibility for all expeditionary troops in the Marianas. Following the Marianas campaign, Smith served as the first commanding general of Fleet Marine Force, Pacific, and headed Task Force 56 (Expeditionary Troops) at the BATTLE OF IWO JIMA.

Smith received the Distinguished Service Medal in recognition of this work in training America's amphibious forces. He received a Gold Star in lieu of a second Distinguished Service Medal for planning and executing the Gilbert and Marshall Islands operations, and another Gold Star for his service in the Marianas. Yet another Gold Star was awarded for his role in the invasion of Iwo Jima.

Smith returned to the United States in July 1945 to head the Marine Training and Replacement Command at Camp Pendleton, California. He retired on May 15, 1946, with the rank of lieutenant general, but was subsequently promoted to general on the retired list.

Further reading: Cooper, Norman V. *Fighting General: Biography of General Holland M. Smith.* Quantico, Va.: Marine Corps Association, 1987; Venzon, Anne Cipriano. *From Whaleboats to Amphibious Warfare: Lt. Gen. "Howling Mad" Smith and the U.S. Marine Corps.* New York: Praeger, 2003.

Smith, Walter Bedell (1895–1961) *Dwight D. Eisenhower's chief of staff for U.S. forces in Europe*

A native of Indianapolis, Smith enlisted in the Indiana National Guard in 1910 and served through 1915. When the United States entered World War I in April 1917, Smith was commissioned a second

Walter Bedell Smith *(Harry S. Truman Presidential Library)*

lieutenant of infantry in the regular army. He saw combat, then remained in the service after the Armistice, serving in several Stateside posts and in the Philippines. Smith was an instructor at the Infantry School.

In February 1942, shortly after the U.S. entry into World War II, Smith, promoted to brigadier general, was appointed secretary of the Joint Chiefs of Staff and U.S. secretary of the Combined Chiefs of Staff. In September 1943, he was named chief of staff, European theater of operations, and chief of staff to Dwight D. Eisenhower. He held these posts simultaneously until Eisenhower returned to the United States after the war in Europe ended. It was "Beetle" Smith who negotiated both the surrender of Italian (1943) and German armed forces (1945) and, on behalf of the Allies, accepted those surrenders.

After Smith returned to the United States in 1945, he was appointed chief of the Operations and Planning Division of the War Department General Staff. He retired from active duty in 1946 and became U.S. ambassador to the Soviet Union, serving until 1949. Returning to active duty, he commanded the First U.S. Army from 1949 to 1950, then served as head of the Central Intelligence Agency (CIA) from 1950 to 1953, having been promoted to general in 1951. He stepped down from the CIA and retired from the army in 1953 to accept an appointment as undersecretary of state, but resigned a year later to enter the private sector.

Further reading: Crosswell, D. K. R. *The Chief of Staff: The Military Career of General Walter Bedell Smith.* Westport, Conn.: Greenwood Press, 1991; Smith, Walter Bedell. *Eisenhower's Six Great Decisions: Europe, 1944–1945.* London: Longmans, Green, 1956.

Smuts, Jan Christiaan (1870–1950) *Afrikaner general and prime minister who eschewed South African neutrality in World War II*

Born near Riebeeck West (near Malmesbury), Cape Colony, Smuts grew up on a farm but was educated in England at Christ's College, Cambridge, from which he graduated in 1894. After passing the bar in 1895, he practiced in Capetown, South Africa. Smuts moved to Johannesburg in 1897 and became state's attorney for the Transvaal government in June 1898. After Pretoria fell to the British during the Second Boer War on June 5, 1900, Smuts was commissioned a general and fought at Diamond Hill during June 11–12. He then led the Boer offensive at Nooitgedacht/Magaliesburg on December 13, 1905, capturing Modderfontein in Transvaal on January 31, 1901.

On September 3, 1901, Smuts invaded the Cape Colony to stir up rebellion among the Cape Colony Boers. After defeating the 17th (British) Lancers at Elands River Poort on September 17, he was forced to withdraw in the face of British reinforcements, and his efforts to enlist the aid of the Cape Boers came to nothing.

Smuts was a principal at the peace conference at Vereeniging during May 15–31, 1902, and was instrumental in drawing up the Treaty of Vereeniging, which ended the war on May 31, 1902.

Smuts was appointed colonial secretary under Prime Minister Louis Botha in March 1907 and was one of the principal authors of the constitution of the Union of South Africa, enacted on May 31, 1910. During World War I, he sought accommodation with the British, and therefore suppressed Christian de Wet's anti-British Boer uprising during September–December 1914. Following this, he led South African forces in the conquest of German Southwest Africa (modern Namibia) from February to July 9, 1915. Smuts was put in command of East African operations during February 1916. After attending an Imperial war conference in London in 1917, Smuts was appointed a cabinet minister and privy councilor in March 1917. The British government invited him to sign the Treaty of Versailles, an honor he accepted although he believed the treaty too punitive.

On Botha's death in August 1919, Smuts became prime minister of South Africa. He never achieved popularity, and when his party lost the 1924 elections, he retired to private life for 10 years, reemerging in 1934 as deputy prime minis-

ter under J. B. M. Hertzog. Smuts differed sharply with Hertzog on the issue of South African neutrality in World War II. Hertzog favored it, Smuts did not, and Hertzog's government fell on September 5, 1939. Smuts again became prime minister and took command of the South African war effort, which was primarily directed at preventing Germany and Italy from conquering North Africa. British prime minister Winston Churchill regarded Smuts highly and frequently called on him for consultation. Smuts was promoted to field marshal in the British army in 1941—although he did not command in the field.

At the end of the war, Smuts participated in the San Francisco Conference and was among those who participated in drafting the United Nations charter in 1945. Despite his war service and international prestige, he was defeated in the 1948 elections and stepped down as prime minister, but retained a seat in parliament.

Further reading: Crafford, F. S. *Jan Smuts: A Biography.* Whitefish, Mont.: Kessinger, 2005; Smuts, J. C. *Jan Christian Smuts: A Biography.* New York: William Morrow, 1952.

Sobibór extermination camp

This camp, which the Germans opened near Chelm, Poland, in May 1942, is where 250,000 to 300,000 people were murdered.

On October 14, 1943, some of Sobibór's inmates revolted, killing several guards. About 600 prisoners escaped, of whom approximately half made it into the woods. There they found no succor from the local Poles, the overwhelming majority of whom were virulently anti-Semitic. Most of the escapees were apprehended by the locals and returned to face certain death.

The Germans closed Sobibór in November 1943, lest it inspire further acts of resistance there or elsewhere. All signs of its existence were obliterated.

See also concentration and extermination camps; Final Solution, the; and Holocaust, the.

Further reading: Arad, Yitzhak. *Belzec, Sobibor, Treblinka: The Operation Reinhard Death Camps.* Bloomington: Indiana University Press, 1999; Rashke, Richard. *Escape from Sobibor.* Urbana and Chicago: University of Illinois Press, 1995.

Somerville, James (1882–1949) *British admiral who worked closely with the U.S. Navy*

Born in Weybridge, Surrey, Somerville joined the Royal Navy as a cadet in 1898 and was serving as a lieutenant by 1904. Before World War I, he emerged as the Royal Navy's premier radio specialist. During the war, he served at Gallipoli and was decorated with the Distinguished Service Order.

Between the world wars, Somerville, promoted to captain in 1921, was director of Admiralty's Signal Department (1925–27) and served as an instructor at the Imperial Defence College (1929–31). Promoted to commodore in 1932, he was again promoted, to rear admiral, in 1933. He was assigned to command the Mediterranean Fleet destroyer flotillas from 1936 to 1938, and during the Spanish civil war helped protect Majorca from the Republicans. He served in the East Indies during 1938–39, then took a medical retirement—only to be recalled at the outbreak of World War II.

Somerville's early work during the war was in RADAR development. In May 1940, he served under Admiral Bertram Ramsay and was instrumental in organizing the DUNKIRK EVACUATION. After this, he was assigned to command HMS *Hood* and undertook the task of neutralizing the French fleet at the BATTLE OF MERS-EL-KÉBIR in French North Africa (now Algeria).

As commander of Force H, Somerville led a naval raid on Genoa on February 9, 1941, and took part in the sinking of the *BISMARCK* on May 26, 1941. Force H was also deployed to protect major convoys to Malta and Egypt. In March 1942, Sommerville was named to command the British Eastern Fleet, based at Ceylon (Sri Lanka), until the Japanese onslaught forced him to move his fleet to the Addu Atoll in the Maldives. He lost half of the fleet to Admiral NAGUMO CHUICHI in the successful Japanese Indian Ocean Raid of April 1942. In response, he attempted a counterattack, but was unable to intercept the Japanese fleet. This prompted him to withdraw to Kilindini, Kenya, and it was not until 1944 that, suitably reinforced, he was able to strike at Japanese-occupied Dutch East Indies.

In August 1944, Admiral Bruce Fraser replaced Somerville as commander of the Eastern Fleet. In October, Somerville was charged with leading the British Admiralty Delegation in Washington, D.C., which he did through December 1945. He worked extremely effectively with the Americans, especially Admiral ERNEST J. KING, despite King's reputation as an irascible man who was also an outspoken Anglophobe.

In May 1945, Somerville was promoted to admiral of the Fleet. He retired in December 1945 and was created lord lieutenant of Somerset in August 1946.

Further reading: Somerville, James. *The Somerville Papers: Selections from the Private and Official Correspondence of Admiral of the Fleet Sir James Somerville.* Aldershot, Hants, U.K.: Scolar Press for the Navy Records Society, 1995.

SONAR

SONAR—Sound-Navigation, Ranging—was developed by the U.S. Navy during World War I, at about the same time that British and French scientists developed the Allied Submarine Detection Investigation Committee (ASDIC) system. Both technologies used sound to detect submerged submarines. In 1943, the British Royal Navy began calling their ASDIC system by the American acronym SONAR.

SONAR systems in World War II were of two major types. Active SONAR systems used an acoustic projector to generate a sound wave into the water, which was reflected back by a target. The reflected waves were detected by a SONAR receiver, which analyzed the signal to determine the range, bearing, and relative motion of the target. Passive SONAR employed only receiving sensors, which detected the noise produced by the target—a submarine's engines, its rotating screw, or even the sound of its movement through the water. The received waveforms were analyzed for direction and distance.

Like RADAR, SONAR greatly extended the capability of combatants to detect the approach and movements of enemy forces. The technology was extremely important in antisubmarine warfare in all theaters of the war.

Further reading: Hackmann, Willem Dirk. *Seek and Strike: Sonar, Anti-submarine Warfare, and the Royal Navy, 1914–54.* London: H.M.S.O., 1984; Sternhell, Charles M., and Alan M. Thorndike. *Antisubmarine Warfare in World War II.* Walnut Creek, Calif.: Aegean Park Press, 1996.

Sonderkommando Elbe

The term *Sonderkommando* meant special detachment and was generally applied to units of the German SCHUTZSTAFFEL (SS) Einsatzgruppen assigned to murder Jews and other "undesirables" during German invasion operations. The term was also applied to squads of inmates at CONCENTRATION AND EXTERMINATION CAMPS who were used to dispose of the bodies of victims of the FINAL SOLUTION.

A special use of Sonderkommando was Sonderkommando Elbe, a unit of pilots and aircraft formed in April 1945 to ram incoming American bombers raiding German cities. The object was to inflict such high casualties on the bombers that the Americans would be forced at the very least to pause the bombing campaign, giving the Germans some time to recover and mount more effective antiaircraft defenses.

The ramming idea was, of course, the product of desperation. It was planned late in 1944 by Luftwaffe colonel Hans-Joachim Herrman, who proposed using some 800 high-altitude Bf-109G fighters entirely stripped of armor and armament to reduce weight sufficiently to enable them to operate at 36,000 feet. This would put them above the ceiling of American escort fighters and allow them to swoop down on the bombers. The ramming missions were not, strictly speaking, intended to be suicide attacks. Pilots were supposed to bail out immediately before impact. This was inherently impractical, however, and for all intents and purposes, the mission was perceived as one-way. Hermann predicted the loss of 300 pilots, which was no more than were lost in a typical month's combat.

Volunteers were recruited from training units, so as not to squander veteran pilots. Sonderkommando Elbe, formed in April 1945, was the first and last ramming unit. It consisted of 120 aircraft, flew a single mission, and managed to ram just 15 bombers, of which eight were destroyed.

Further reading: O'Neill, Richard. *Suicide Squads: Axis and Allied Special Attack Weapons of World War II.* London: New English Library, 1981.

South Africa

At the outbreak of World War II, South Africa—officially the Union of South Africa—was a British dominion. It encompassed the provinces of Cape of Good Hope, Natal, Orange Free State, Transvaal, and the mandated territory of South-West Africa.

South Africa was a rich source of gold, diamonds, coal, iron, and other important raw materials, but its industrial capacity was largely undeveloped, and its contribution to the Allied war effort limited. Moreover, the vast majority of South Africans were black, of mixed race, or Indian (designated by the white government as "African," "Colored," and "Indian"); these groups were essentially disenfranchised within the dominant white government and felt that they had little or no stake in the outcome of the war.

Thanks to the efforts of JAN CHRISTIAAN SMUTS, narrowly elected prime minister in 1939 over Barry Hertzog, an advocate of neutrality, South Africa rejected a neutral stance in the war; however, Smuts did not attempt to contribute a large army to the war effort, nor did he introduce conscription. He had to take care not to alienate certain Afrikaners, whose sympathies lay not with the English but with the Germans, and who might be pushed to rebel against his government. Nevertheless, Smuts did see to it that South Africa contributed raw materials and modest numbers of troops.

By September 1941, approximately 60,000 South African troops were serving in Egypt, including 16,000 blacks. This represented the peak of South Africa's manpower contribution to the ground war outside of South Africa's borders. At sea, the South African Naval Service patrolled the coast and was especially active in minesweeping. The South African Coastal Air Force augmented the efforts of the country's navy.

During the entire course of the war, 334,224 South Africans volunteered for service, a number that included 132,194 whites and 123,131 blacks. Casualties included some 9,000 killed, more than 8,000 wounded, and more than 14,000 made prisoner.

Further reading: Martin, H. J. *South Africa at War: Military and Industrial Organization and Operations in Connection with the Conduct of the War, 1939–1945.* Cape Town: Purnell, 1979; Mervis, Joel. *South Africa in World War II.* Cape Town: Times Media, 1989.

Soviet Union

In connection with World War II, Americans and Britons identified the Soviet Union as one of the gallant Allied nations united in the struggle against Nazi German aggression. Indeed, it was certainly this—but it was also one of the aggressors.

By virtue of the GERMAN-SOVIET NON-AGGRESSION PACT, the Soviet Union was a collaborator in the inception of World War II and participated in the September 1939 INVASION OF POLAND, which started the war. ADOLF HITLER betrayed the Soviets, when he launched the June 22, 1941, INVASION OF THE SOVIET UNION. At that point, JOSEPH STALIN and his propaganda machine transformed the conflict from World War II into the "Great Patriotic War of 1941–45." The other Allied nations—chiefly Great Britain and the United States—not only acquiesced in this transformation, they actively encouraged it to ensure that the war would continue to be interpreted unambiguously as a titanic contest between good and evil.

At the outbreak of World War II, the Soviet Union had a population of 170.5 million and a vast territory of 8.25 million square miles. Although the Soviet Union was under the brutally monolithic control of Stalin, it was, in theory, composed during the war of eleven major republics, the largest of which was the Russian Federation (RSFSR), which contained almost 64 percent of the Soviet population. Within the RSFSR were 14 "autonomous republics"—and this presence of subrepublics was typical of the other major Soviet republics as well.

In practice, none of the Soviet republics or subrepublics was in any real measure independent; however, their existence belied the image of a monolithic Soviet state. The nation actually encompassed a bewildering range of political divisions and was also ethnically diverse. Ethnic Russians—so called Great Russians—constituted the majority population of the USSR, amounting to 58.4 percent. When, as a result of the initial German-Soviet alliance, part of Poland, all of Moldavia, and the Baltic states were annexed to the Soviet Union, this percentage was effectively reduced to 52.7 percent. The largest minority in the Soviet Union at the outbreak of the war were Ukrainians, who constituted 16.6 percent of the population. White Russians, residents of Belorussia, made up 3.1 percent. In all, the USSR comprised about 14 nationalities that had a million or more members each. The diversity of languages was astounding. Some authorities report 80 mutually unintelligible languages as being spoken in the USSR in 1939; others report 120, and still others 170. It is not surprising, therefore, that even after the German invasion, the USSR was not entirely united against Hitler, and Stalin had to deal with entire populations that openly declared their allegiance to the invaders. Nevertheless, the war created, of necessity, much unity with the vast nation to an unprecedented degree.

POLITICAL BACKGROUND

The Soviet Union came into being as a result of two revolutions in 1917, the first of which overthrew

Tsar Nicholas II, ending the Romanov dynasty, and the second installed the Bolsheviks, Communists led principally by V. I. Lenin. The 1920s saw a bloody civil war between the Bolsheviks and those who opposed them. After the Bolsheviks prevailed, the regime of Stalin (Lenin's successor) instituted an accelerated program of industrialization, aimed at rapidly transforming the Soviet Union from a largely agricultural nation into a great industrial power. This program was driven by the forced collectivization of Soviet agriculture, which increased the urban population from 18 percent in 1929 to 33 percent by the outbreak of the war. The rapid expansion of the nation's industrial base was critical to ultimate victory in World War II; however, during the 1930s, the industrialization process was chaotic, and collectivization reduced agricultural output disastrously, creating privation and starvation on a massive scale. During the 1930s, at least 15 million peasants were swept away—killed—by famine.

In the meantime, Stalin ruled by a combination of brutal terror and the creation of a fanatical cult of personality. Moreover, the globalism of classic Marxism—as practiced by Lenin—was replaced by intense nationalism, in which Communist economic principles overlaid a return to a traditional Russian ethnic identity. As for the terror, Stalin institutionalized a kind of collective paranoia marked by periodic bloody purges of the Communist Party leadership. This included an extensive purge of the Red Army officer corps, which greatly weakened the military and made the country dangerously vulnerable to the German invasion that came in 1941.

SOVIET INDUSTRIAL MIGHT

Despite the famine and general hardship caused by forced collectivization and despite the weakening of the military by the purges of the 1930s, the rapid industrialization of the Soviet Union became the single greatest factor contributing to the Soviets' ability ultimately to turn the tide of the war against the German invaders.

Although industrialization was extensive by the outbreak of the war, industry was based dispropor-

tionately in the west. This made the sources of production especially vulnerable to destruction or capture by the invaders. Recognizing these dangers, on July 3, 1941, the State Committee of Defense created a Council for Evacuation, which executed the removal of much industry to the east in advance of the German invaders. Anywhere from 7.5 million to 25 million Soviet workers moved to new locations. A total of 2,593 industrial plants were evacuated in their entirety.

Evacuation proved critical in maintaining resistance against the German invaders. Despite this, the Soviets had to contend with major shortages of transport and fuel throughout the war, as well as shortages of iron and steel. Other strategic materials had to be mined as far east as possible. Remarkably, even with the disruption caused by evacuation and the necessity of exploiting new sources of many strategic raw materials, Soviet war production continuously grew and, even early in the war, outpaced German production. The Soviets produced 136,364 aircraft and nearly 100,000 tanks and other armored vehicles during 1941–45. The Soviets also benefited from the U.S. LEND-LEASE program, which shipped to the USSR 21,621 aircraft and 12,439 tanks and other armored vehicles during 1941–45. To accommodate war production, production for civilian needs was drastically reduced to a subsistence level.

WARTIME GOVERNMENT

Soviet government during the period of World War II was, on the one hand, intensely bureaucratic but, on the other, was subject to the absolute personal rule of Joseph Stalin. This bred a cult of personality around the dictator similar to those that grew up around Hitler and BENITO MUSSOLINI. Such a cult proved invaluable in rallying the Soviet people to follow Stalin as a war leader; however, the disadvantages of absolute rule were staggering. They included a general lack of initiative at all levels of Soviet government, administration, and the military.

In theory, the Soviet Union was not governed by Stalin, but by the Communist Party. In practice, Stalin administered the country through the party, which entered into every aspect of Soviet life, both in the civilian and military sectors. Membership in the Communist Party—the only political party permitted to exist—was voluntary; however, it was virtually impossible to pursue a career in any significant field without being a loyal member of the party. In this way, the party permeated every factory and every institution.

As the party provided ultimate control of the Soviet citizenry, the apparatus of state administration—the Soviet bureaucracy—regulated the day-to-day operations of virtually every institution of civil and military life. Production, city management, and all other aspects of administration were conducted through People's commissariats, many of which were highly specialized. Although a system of representative government was in place—in the two houses of the Supreme Soviet, which provided one deputy for every 300,000 citizens—there was no democracy. The Supreme Soviet was, in practice, entirely subordinate to Stalin and the party, as were the various commissariats.

Perhaps the only governmental organization within the Soviet system that wielded a high degree of genuinely autonomous power was the People's Commissariat for Internal Affairs, which included the NKVD, or secret police, and which was headed by the ruthless LAVRENTY BERIA. Stalin gave Beria wide latitude in arresting and imprisoning those perceived as threats to the regime; however, Stalin personally authorized all executions. An independent judiciary did not exist in the Soviet system.

Another important institution in the wartime USSR was the State Committee for Defense (GKO), chaired by Stalin with VYACHESLAV MOLOTOV as vice chair. The GKO had unlimited authority, could override any other department or official, and issued decrees and directives that had the full force of law. The GKO did not hold regular meetings, but convened whenever Stalin thought necessary. No minutes were kept of its sessions.

CIVIL DEFENSE

Civil defense was handled by Local Air Defense (Mestnoe PVO), which administered air raid shelters, fire fighting, and defense against chemical weapons. The Mestnoe PVO came under the direction of the NKVD and regional military headquarters, and it worked in cooperation with local and city soviets (administrative committees), which had responsibility for organizing all citizens between ages 16 and 60 as civil defense aides. The Mestnoe PVO built air raid shelters for some 20 million people, fought more than 90,000 fires, and defused countless bombs and mines.

In addition to civil defense forces, local citizens were recruited for the Narodnoe Opolchenie (NO), the Home Guards. These units, variously armed and trained, were organized on an ad hoc basis and only during emergencies. Home Guards proved quite effective in the BATTLE OF MOSCOW.

SOVIET LOSSES

Although Poland incurred a higher percentage rate of casualties in World War II, no nation suffered a higher toll in numbers killed than the Soviet Union. Nine million soldiers were killed or missing (and presumed killed). Twice this number was wounded. At least 20 million civilian deaths resulted directly from military action during the war; no one knows how many more died as a result of disease, starvation, and privation.

See also SOVIET UNION, AIR FORCE OF; SOVIET UNION, ARMY OF; SOVIET UNION, INVASION OF THE; and SOVIET UNION, NAVY OF.

Further reading: Gallagher, Matthew P. *The Soviet History of World War II.* Westport, Conn.: Greenwood Press, 1976; Linz, Susan J. *The Impact of World War II on the Soviet Union.* New York: Rowman & Littlefield, 1985; Roberts, Geoffrey K. *The Soviet Union and the Origins of the Second World War: Russo-German Relations and the Road to War 1933–1941.* New York and London: Palgrave Macmillan, 1995; Thurston, Robert W., and Bernd Bonwetsch, eds. *The People's War: Responses to World War II in the Soviet Union.* Urbana and London: University of Illinois Press, 2000.

Soviet Union, air force of

The Soviet military had three air arms, the Red Army Air Force, Long-Range Bomber Aviation, and the Naval Air Forces. The first two were administered by directorates of the People's Commissariat for Defense, and the last by the People's Commissariat of the Navy. In terms of operations, the land-based air forces were under the command of the relevant armies or fronts (army groups), and the naval air forces were subordinated to the relevant fleets.

At the time of the German INVASION OF THE SOVIET UNION, in June 1941, the Soviets had 8,105 combat aircraft, most of them obsolescent and outclassed by German planes, so that by the end of the year, their numbers had been decimated to 2,495. Production quickly made up these losses, however, and by January 1945, the Soviets had some 14,500 operational aircraft. Early catastrophic losses were due not only to poor equipment, but also to poor leadership and organization. In 1942, the Soviets introduced the "air army" system, which greatly streamlined command in the air force, so that one of 13 air armies had responsibility for supporting a particular front. Each air army typically consisted of a command staff, two or three fighter divisions, a "Shturmovik" (ground-attack) division, one or two night-bomber divisions, and reconnaissance and liaison units. The typical air army had 400 to 500 aircraft. Flexibility was built into the organization of the formation, which could, when necessary, draw on the Air Reserve for additional aircraft and pilots. By the end of the war, about 43 percent of all aircraft deployed by the Soviets belonged to the Air Reserve pool.

By the middle of the war, the Soviets were producing excellent fighters and well-trained pilots. Far less effective was Long-Range Bomber Aviation, which suffered catastrophic losses early in the war and never recovered as fully as the fighter and Shturmovik units did. In contrast to the American and British air arms, Soviet Long-Range Bomber Aviation did not engage in STRATEGIC BOMBING. Its missions were exclusively tactical, directed against Axis concentrations, railheads, depots, and the like.

Soviet naval air units were mainly equipped with conventional land-based aircraft and, although flown by naval officers, were used principally in support of land operations, typically guarding the flanks of large ground units. Nearly one-third of naval air sorties were flown on air defense missions. About a quarter of naval air missions were close ground support, and 14 percent of sorties were reconnaissance patrols. No more than 10 percent of naval air missions attacked Axis ships or naval bases.

See also AIRCRAFT, SOVIET; SOVIET UNION, ARMY OF; SOVIET UNION, INVASION OF THE; SOVIET UNION, NAVY OF; and SOVIET UNION.

Further reading: Green, William, and Gordon Swanborough. *Soviet Air Force Fighters.* New York: Arco, 1978; Polak, Tomas, and Christopher Shores. *Stalin's Falcons: The Aces of the Red Star: A Tribute to the Notable Fighter Pilots of the Soviet Air Forces 1918–1953.* London: Grub Street, 1999; Hardesty, Von. *Red Phoenix: The Rise of Soviet Air Power, 1941–1945.* Washington, D.C.: Smithsonian Books, 1991.

Soviet Union, army of

At the time of the German INVASION OF THE SOVIET UNION, the Red Army consisted of about 5.37 million officers and men. During the 10 days following the invasion, another 5 million were mobilized. Tanks and self-propelled guns in the Red Army numbered about 7,000 in June 1941 and reached a peak of 11,000 in January 1945. Artillery pieces numbered nearly 35,000 at the time of the German invasion and topped out at 98,700 in July 1943. Although these numbers are impressive, most forces were not fully equipped and few were adequately trained, especially in the opening months of the war. Vehicles and radio communications equipment were in especially short supply. Worst of all, in 1937 and 1938, JOSEPH STALIN conducted mass purges of Red Army officers, even though there was no evidence of disloyalty, let alone specific military plots against him. By 1938, about 35,000 officers out of an officer corps of 80,000 had been purged—many executed—including three of five marshals of the Soviet Union (the Red Army's most senior commanders), all 11 deputies of the commissar for war, 75 of 85 corps commanders, and 110 of 195 divisional commanders. The willful destruction of the Red Army senior officer corps left the force in large measure bereft of leaders, rendering it highly vulnerable to the enemy.

By the time of the invasion, the high command of the Red Army was the responsibility of the Stavka, which Stalin controlled personally. Administratively, the Commissariat of Defense divided Red Army management into 14 military districts covering the entire Soviet Union. Operationally, the largest units in the Red Army were the fronts, which were the equivalent of Western army groups, each consisting of a number of armies. Each Soviet army, in turn, consisted of two rifle corps, one mechanized corps, and one cavalry corps (or cavalry division). A rifle corps was made up of three rifle divisions, two artillery regiments, one antiaircraft battalion, and support units. A mechanized corps encompassed two tank divisions and a motorized rifle division. A rifle division was made up of three rifle regiments, two artillery regiments, one antitank battalion, one antiaircraft battalion, and support units. A tank division had two tank regiments, one motorized rifle regiment, one artillery regiment, and one antiaircraft regiment. A motorized rifle division consisted of two rifle regiments, one tank regiment, and one antiaircraft and antitank battalion. A rifle regiment—the basic unit of the Red Army—consisted of three infantry battalions, four 76 mm field guns, four 120 mm mortars, and six 45 mm antitank guns.

Throughout the war—even in victory—the Red Army absorbed spectacular losses, largely due to poor tactics, including a battle doctrine that called for attacking without tanks—which were generally held back until the infantry had achieved a breakthrough. Despite the high cost of this tactic, it was adhered to throughout most of the war. The latest and least controversial figures available (1990) concerning Red Army losses fix the total of those killed in action, missing in action, and prisoners who never returned at 8,668,400. Despite these losses, the Red Army always maintained a substantial numerical superiority over the German invading forces, and it was this more than anything

else that ultimately turned the tide against the invaders.

See also AIRCRAFT, SOVIET; SOVIET UNION, AIR FORCE OF; SOVIET UNION, INVASION OF THE; SOVIET UNION, NAVY OF; and SOVIET UNION.

Further reading: Kozhevnikov, M. N. *The Command and Staff of the Soviet Army in the Great Patriotic War 1941–1945: A Soviet View.* Honolulu: University Press of the Pacific, 2002; Larionov, V. V. *World War II: Decisive Battles of the Soviet Army.* Moscow: Progress Publishers, 1984; Shaw, John. *Red Army Resurgent.* Alexandria, Va.: Time Life, 1980.

Soviet Union, invasion of the

The German invasion of the Soviet Union was launched as OPERATION BARBAROSSA on June 22, 1941. The plans for the invasion and the circumstances of its launch are discussed in that article. This article discusses the course of the invasion itself.

The Germans invaded with a force of nearly 3.6 million troops, 3,600 tanks, and more than 2,700 aircraft. Red Army formations available on the western front included 140 divisions and 40 brigades—some 2.9 million men. Although about 15,000 tanks and 8,000 aircraft were available, the vast majority of both were obsolescent and certainly inferior to the German weapons.

ADOLF HITLER had hoped to crush the Soviet Union quickly, and the opening weeks of the invasion were a devastating example of BLITZKRIEG warfare with the added dimension of genocide committed against Jews and local Soviet political leaders; the latter were summarily executed by SCHUTZSTAFFEL (SS) Einsatzgruppen units pursuant to Hitler's infamous COMMISSAR ORDER. Both sides employed a scorched earth policy. The invaders sought to deprive Soviet defenders and civilians of all sustenance and sources of supply; the Soviets, in turn, sought to deprive the invaders of the same. Soviet troops attempted to disrupt German lines of supply and communication and to prevent the invaders from living off the Soviet land. The result was hardly the quick hit-and-run invasion Hitler

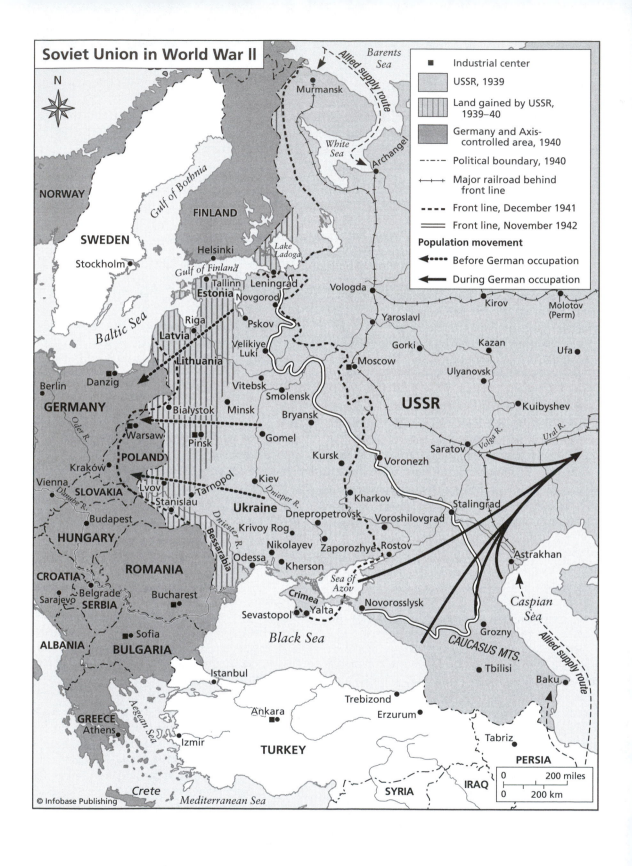

Soviet Union in World War II

N

Industrial center

USSR, 1939

Land gained by USSR, 1939–40

Germany and Axis-controlled area, 1940

Political boundary, 1940

Major railroad behind front line

Front line, December 1941

Front line, November 1942

Population movement

Before German occupation

During German occupation

NORWAY

SWEDEN

Stockholm

Gulf of Bothnia

FINLAND

Helsinki

Lake Ladoga

Gulf of Finland

Tallinn

Estonia

Leningrad

Novgorod

Barents Sea

Murmansk

White Sea

Archangel

Allied supply route

Vologda

Kirov

Molotov (Perm)

Yaroslavl

Gorki

Kazan

Ufa

Moscow

Ulyanovsk

Kuibyshev

Baltic Sea

Riga

Latvia

Lithuania

Pskov

Velikiye Luki

Vitebsk

Smolensk

Berlin

Danzig

GERMANY

Oder R.

Warsaw

POLAND

Bialystok

Minsk

Pinsk

Gomel

Bryansk

Kursk

USSR

Kraków

Vienna

SLOVAKIA

Lvov

Stanislau

Tarnopol

Kiev

Dnieper R.

Ukraine

Dnepropetrovsk

Voronezh

Saratov

Volga R.

Ural R.

Stalingrad

Dniester R.

Bessarabia

HUNGARY

Budapest

ROMANIA

Bucharest

Krivoy Rog

Nikolayev

Zaporozhye

Kharkov

Voroshilovgrad

Rostov

Astrakhan

Caspian Sea

CROATIA

Sarajevo

Belgrade

SERBIA

ALBANIA

Sofia

BULGARIA

Odessa

Kherson

Sea of Azov

Crimea

Sevastopol

Yalta

Novorosslysk

Black Sea

Grozny

Tbilisi

Baku

Allied supply route

CAUCASUS MTS.

GREECE

Athens

Izmir

Aegean Sea

Istanbul

Ankara

Trebizond

Erzurum

TURKEY

Tabriz

PERSIA

Crete

Mediterranean Sea

SYRIA

IRAQ

0   200 miles

0   200 km

© Infobase Publishing

had hoped for. The Red Army, initially overrun and extensively defeated, rallied and ultimately turned the tide against the Germans, whose defeat was partially due to the Soviet military and partially due to the vastness of the Soviet landscape and the infinite harshness of the country's climate. Like Napoleon before him, Hitler was effectively swallowed up by the land he sought to conquer.

JOSEPH STALIN was initially stunned into a kind of paralysis by the surprise invasion, which abrogated the GERMAN-SOVIET NON-AGGRESSION PACT. Yet he soon recovered and proved to be an effective and inspiring leader in rallying both the civilian population and the military to great sacrifices in resisting and defeating the invaders. Stalin took a personal hand in the military leadership of the defense. Many mistakes were made. Many thousands died. Yet the invasion was ultimately turned back and the Germans defeated. (However, Stalin by no means totally unified the ethnically and nationally diverse Soviet Union in opposition to the Germans; in some areas, significant minorities within the population aided the invaders in the hope of throwing off the Soviet yoke.)

On July 3, 1941, Stalin defined the struggle against the invaders as a "great patriotic war." He called for limitless sacrifice, including a scorched earth policy and partisan resistance behind the rapidly moving German lines. For his part, Hitler, reveling in his early successes, planned for a victory parade through Moscow by the end of August. This would be followed by the total destruction of Moscow and Leningrad (St. Petersburg) and the death or resettlement of the cities' populations. Ultimately, Hitler planned to resettle some 30 million Soviet citizens to the east. They would be replaced in the west by Germans and Germanic peoples. The plan was for vast portions of the Soviet Union to become German—permanently. Jews in the conquered territory would be subject to the FINAL SOLUTION and annihilated.

Despite early German successes at the battles of Białystok-Minsk and Smolensk, German field commanders began to realize that they had seriously underrated the Red Army, particularly its will to resist. Even when German commanders outgener-aled their Soviet counterparts, defeated Red Army forces withdrew, regrouped, and continued to fight. Moreover, the Red Army was rarely content to defend; even when battered, commanders ordered counterattacks, which took a steady toll on the invading forces. Worse for the invaders, who had intended quickly to wipe out Soviet industrial capacity, Stalin had overseen the mass evacuation of Soviet industry to the east of the Ural Mountains. War production proceeded at an astounding pace. Obsolescent equipment—especially aircraft—was largely destroyed in battle, only to be replaced by more modern and formidable equipment. Initially encountering mediocre aircraft and armor, the Germans were later stunned by the quality of new Soviet fighter aircraft and tanks.

The German plan called for the rapid occupation of Leningrad and Moscow, as well as the destruction of the industrial Donets Basin. Ultimately, the Red Army defeated all three objectives, albeit at a staggering cost.

After a devastating victory at the Battle of Smolensk during July 16–August 6, in which more than 100,000 Soviet troops were killed or captured, Hitler ordered his forces to divert from direct assaults on Moscow and Leningrad and concentrate instead on invading the Ukraine (in the south) and capturing the industrial and mining areas outside of Leningrad (in the north). Thus, the entire thrust of the invasion was shifted from the center to the wings—a most dubious change in plan. German Army Group Center, which was poised to take Moscow, now had to assume the defensive. This proved to be a fatal strategic blunder because it gave the Soviets time to organize effective counterattacks and to develop stronger defensive positions. Nevertheless, in the south, the Ukraine suffered badly and, by the end of September, Kiev had been totally encircled.

Hitler chose to disregard the problems at the center of the German invasion and to focus instead on his great success in Ukraine. Mistakenly concluding that the Soviet army had been bled white, he belatedly decided to authorize the advance on Moscow, so that it might be captured before winter. Because so many German resources had been diverted to the northern and southern wings of the invasion, however, the attack on Moscow, launched late in September by Army Group Center, could not be sustained. Despite early progress—culminating in the defeat of eight Soviet armies—which seemed to portend imminent victory, the Red Army redoubled its defensive positions and continuously found reinforcements. Its defensive efforts were greatly aided by the heavy autumn rains, which turned the battlefield into a muddy quagmire that neutralized the effectiveness of German tanks and transport vehicles. The attack on Moscow literally bogged down.

Proclaiming Moscow a fortress, Stalin refused to leave the city with the rest of the government and rallied soldiers and civilians to the defense of the capital. In November, the Germans staged an all-out attack and came to within 18 miles of the Kremlin. But German willpower was not matched by German logistics. Exhaustion of men and depletion of supplies stopped the advance, and by the beginning of December, the German panzer armies broke off their attack.

The German commanders hoped that the Soviet defenders were as depleted as their own forces. They had not planned for a lengthy invasion and were quite unprepared for a winter war. Their idea was to withdraw and regroup for a new attack in the spring. The Soviets, however, were not about to permit this. On December 5–6, the Red Army launched a devastating counterattack that punched through thinly stretched German lines. German field commanders sought Hitler's permission to withdraw to preserve their forces. Hitler refused; those commanders who objected were either dismissed or asked to be relieved. This defection of the military prompted Hitler to assume personal command of the invading forces on December 19, 1941—much to their detriment.

By the end of December, the Red Army had definitively repulsed the attempt to take Moscow. This marked the failure of Operation Barbarossa and shattered the myth of German invincibility. By January 31, 1942, the German army had lost approximately 918,000 men (killed, wounded, or captured) in the invasion—a staggering 28.7 percent of the invasion force. From these losses the army would never recover. The cost to the Red Army, however, was far more appalling: 3.35 million Soviet soldiers made prisoner and thousands more killed or wounded. Yet the German invasion had been thwarted, and the German army was set up for ultimate defeat by the Soviets.

Further reading: Bergstrom, Christer, and Andrey Mikhailov. *Black Cross/Red Star: Operation Barbarossa 1941*. Pacifica, Calif.: Pacifica Press, 2000; Clark, Alan. *Barbarossa*. New York: Harper Perennial, 1985; Fugate, Bryan I. *Operation Barbarossa: Strategy and Tactics on the Eastern Front, 1941*. Novato, Calif.: Presidio Press, 1984; Glantz, David M. *Before Stalingrad: Barbarossa—Hitler's Invasion of Russia 1941*. Stroud, U.K.: Tempus, 2003.

Soviet Union, navy of

The Soviet navy was under the command of Admiral Nikolai Kuznetsov as people's commissar of the navy. The navy consisted of four fleets: the Pacific Fleet, Polar Fleet, Red Banner Baltic Fleet, and Black Sea Fleet. In addition, there were the Pinsk River Flotilla and the Danube River Flotilla as well as a few smaller units. The major ocean fleets each had their own war councils, which commanded and coordinated ships, coastal artillery, marines, and the naval air force.

Before World War II, during the Soviet era, the navy had been largely neglected. It was regarded as a purely defensive force and therefore had few modern capital ships. On the eve of war, in 1939, the Soviets began a massive naval construction program, but they completed few ships before the war began. War production yielded two light cruisers, 19 destroyers, 54 submarines, and 900 torpedo boats, minesweepers, and other smaller craft; however, most of the navy's largest ships were obsolescent. In all, the navy had four battleships, one heavy cruiser, seven medium cruisers, five light cruisers, 78 destroyers, and more than 200 submarines. Only the submarines played a major role in the war. In addition, the navy had 2,800 aircraft—mostly obsolescent—and a force of about 100,000 marines. The navy was active mainly in the Baltic.

Further reading: Aselius, Gunnar. *The Rise and Fall of the Soviet Navy in the Baltic, 1921–1940.* London: Frank Cass, 2005; Meister, Jürg. *The Soviet Navy.* London: Macdonald, 1972; Polmar, Norman. *The Naval Institute Guide to the Soviet Navy.* Annapolis, Md.: Naval Institute Press, 1991.

Spaatz, General Carl A. "Tooey" (1891–1974) *principal combat commander of the U.S. Army Air Forces and architect of the buildup of the Eighth Air Force in England*

Spaatz was born in Boyertown, Pennsylvania, and graduated from the U.S. Military Academy in 1914. After flight training, he became a pilot assigned to the 1st Aero Squadron during the 1916 Punitive Expedition in Mexico against Pancho Villa. When the United States entered World War I in 1917, Spaatz was dispatched to France as commander of the 3rd Aviation Instruction Center at Issoudon. He flew combat missions during the last three weeks of the war and was credited with two victories in dogfights.

During the interwar years, Spaatz collaborated with controversial brigadier general and air power advocate William "Billy" Mitchell and commanded the successful 1929 "Question Mark" experiment in midair refueling. Spaatz was sent to England during the summer of 1940 to observe the Battle of Britain, and when the United States entered the war, he was named principal combat commander of the U.S. Army Air Forces, with primary responsibility for building up the Eighth Air Force, based in England. Spaatz also served directly under Gen. Dwight D. Eisenhower as air commander in the North African campaign, the Sicily campaign, and the Italian Campaign. He was instrumental in planning and executing air support for the Normandy landings (D-day).

Under Spaatz's overall command the Army Air Forces achieved air superiority over the German Luftwaffe. More controversially, Spaatz, an advocate of strategic bombing, championed raids that targeted the German oil industry, including the costly Ploeşti raid in Romania.

General Carl Spaatz (right) with Hoyt Vandenberg *(Dwight D. Eisenhower Presidential Library)*

Immediately after V-E Day, Spaatz transferred to the Pacific theater as overall commander of the B-29 strategic bombing campaign against Japan. He had the ultimate responsibility of directing the atomic bomb raids on Hiroshima and Nagasaki.

After the war, Spaatz became the first chief of staff of the independent U.S. Air Force in 1947. He retired the following year. With Harold H. "Hap" Arnold, he is justly considered a father of the independent air arm.

See also HIROSHIMA, ATOMIC BOMBING OF, and NAGASAKI, ATOMIC BOMBING OF.

Further reading: Mets, David R. *Master of Airpower: General Carl A. Spaatz.* Novato, Calif.: Presidio Press, 1988.

Spain

Spain's wartime leader, Generalissimo FRANCISCO FRANCO, owed much to fascist Italy's BENITO MUSSOLINI and Nazi Germany's ADOLF HITLER, both of whom had given Franco military support during the SPANISH CIVIL WAR, which put him and his fascist regime into power. Although Franco aligned Spain with the Axis during World War II and was a signatory of the ANTI-COMINTERN PACT before the war, he never joined the war on the Axis side. At the outbreak of war in September 1939, Franco proclaimed Spain neutral. When Italy joined the war on June 10, 1940, he upgraded this status to non-belligerency—favoring the Axis without participating militarily in the war. From then until 1944, Franco teased the Axis with vague promises of joining their cause. He never did, but Spain became a haven for Axis spies and saboteurs who freely used Spanish territory as an observation post. In addition, Italy's Tenth Light Flotilla attacked Gibraltar from southern Spain, Axis warships were allowed to use Spanish ports, and Axis aircrews who landed in Spain were repatriated rather than interned. The same held true for those escaped Axis POWs who found their way to Spanish soil.

Spain abandoned the Axis cause by early 1944, as the Allies pressured Franco to cut off exports to Germany of the strategic metal tungsten and to end the recruitment of soldiers for the Spanish Legion—a volunteer army in service to Germany. In October 1944, Spain recognized the Free French government under CHARLES DE GAULLE, and in April 1945 Franco severed diplomatic relations with Germany and Japan. These gestures were insufficient to produce an invitation from the founding members to join the UNITED NATIONS in May 1945, however, and Spain was not admitted until 1955.

Further reading: Beevor, Antony. *The Spanish Civil War.* New York: Peter Bedrick Books, 1983; Bolloten, Burnett. *The Spanish Civil War: Revolution and Counterrevolution.* Chapel Hill: University of North Carolina Press, 1991; Bowen, Wayne H. *Spain During World War II.* Columbia: University of Missouri Press, 2006; Burdick, Charles Burton. *Germany's Military Strategy and Spain in World War II.* Syracuse, N.Y.: Syracuse University Press, 1968.

Spanish civil war

During the 1930s, Spain was torn by political dissension, exacerbated by the hardships of the worldwide economic depression. In 1936, the left-wing Popular Front emerged victorious in the general elections. This sparked a coup d'état by the right-wing Falange, a fascist political party led by General FRANCISCO FRANCO.

The war began on July 18, 1936, when Franco took over the Spanish Foreign Legion garrison in Morocco and staged an army officers' revolt at Melilla. This touched off similar revolts in Spanish garrisons at Cádiz, Seville, Nourgos, Saragossa, Huesca, and elsewhere. While these were under way, Franco airlifted Foreign Legion units to Spain in late July. These troops were joined by other rebel soldiers as well as by insurgent "Nationalists." Together, they overwhelmed government forces and quickly seized control of southern and western Spain.

During late July and into August, Franco led a motorized advance on Madrid, the Spanish capital, but was repulsed by government forces during fighting in September and October. By this point, the country was bitterly divided into government territories and Nationalist territories. On September 29, 1936, the Nationalists proclaimed their own government, with Franco at its head. In April 1937, he was also named head of the fascist Falange Party.

The Spanish civil war developed virtually on the eve of World War II, as fascism and Nazism squared off against communism—with the Democratic nations looking on. The ideological nature of the conflict drew many outsiders into what was, after all, a civil conflict. The Falange was supported by Fascist Italy and Nazi Germany: some 40,000 to 60,000 Italian troops and about 20,000 Germans, including members of the Luftwaffe. The Spanish government (whose forces were generally called Loyalists) attracted volunteers from Britain, France, and the United States, despite official government policies of neutrality in the conflict. Only the Soviet Union gave its full and official support to the Loyalists. The volunteer brigades proved highly effective against the Falangists, but the outside support from Italy and Germany was also powerful, especially the German terror bombing of the villages of Guernica and Durango in 1937. German pilots regarded the Spanish civil war as an invaluable opportunity to practice their deadly craft.

In contrast to the Falangists, who enjoyed considerable unity, the Loyalists were torn by dissension, especially from the far left. When a bloody anarchist uprising broke out in Barcelona in May 1937, a new Loyalist government had to be formed, which moved far to the left and alienated many.

After an 80-day siege, Bilbao fell to the Falange on June 18, 1937. A Loyalist counteroffensive captured Teruel late in the year, but insurgents retook it in mid-February 1938. At this juncture, Joseph Stalin, no longer willing to antagonize Benito Mussolini or Adolf Hitler, suddenly withdrew Soviet aid to the communists fighting in Spain. This brought about the collapse of the leftists, which, in turn, fatally weakened government forces. On January 26, 1939, Franco took Barcelona, and Loyalist resistance throughout Spain folded. Madrid fell on March 28, 1939, ending the war and establishing Franco as dictator of Spain.

In the first great contest between fascism/Nazism and the democratically supported left, democracy lost. However, both Mussolini and Hitler were chagrined by Franco's refusal to abandon neutrality and join the Axis. Spain remained neutral throughout World War II.

Further reading: Beevor, Antony. *The Spanish Civil War.* New York: Peter Bedrick Books, 1983; Bolloten, Burnett. *The Spanish Civil War: Revolution and Counterrevolution.* Chapel Hill: University of North Carolina Press, 1991; Mitchell, David J. *The Spanish Civil War.* New York:

Franklin Watts, 1982; Payne, Robert. *The Civil War in Spain, 1936–1939.* New York: G. P. Putnam, 1962.

Special Air Service (SAS)

The Special Air Service (SAS) was a British special forces unit created in October 1941 by Lt. David Striding. Its members were recruited from Layforce, a British commando force under Lt. Col. Robert Laycock.

SAS was active in the North African Campaign and was employed to disrupt enemy desert airfields by means of airborne assault using small-group tactics. SAS was also active in the Sicily Campaign and the Italian Campaign.

SAS members implemented Operation Titanic, part of the Operation Fortitude campaign of deception during the Normandy landings (D-day). By simulating major airborne landings, SAS operatives drew some German attention away from heavily defended Omaha Beach on June 6, 1944. After this phase of operations, SAS personnel operated behind German lines to disrupt enemy communications and to transmit intelligence.

Further reading: Close, Roy. *In Action With the SAS: A Soldier's Odyssey from Dunkirk to Berlin.* Barnsley, South Yorkshire: Pen & Sword Military, 2005; Ely, Nigel. *For Queen and Country.* London: Blake, 2002; Ford, Roger. *Fire from the Forest: The SAS Brigade in France, 1944.* London: Cassell, 2004; Harrison, D. I. *These Men Are Dangerous: The Special Air Service at War.* London: Cassell, 1957.

Speer, Albert (1905–1981) *German minister for armaments and war production (1942–45)*

Born in Mannheim, Albert Speer studied architecture, graduating from technical schools in Karlsruhe, Munich, and Berlin. He was a practicing architect when, late in 1930, he heard Adolf Hitler speak at a Berlin rally and, fired with zeal, joined the Nazi Party in January 1931.

A young man of enthusiasm, intelligence, and great facility, he made a deep impression on Hitler, who hired him as his personal architect. Speer produced designs that satisfied Hitler's appetite for grandiose, vaguely classical structures, including major buildings as well as props for Nazi rallies. His most ambitious designs (never built) were for the complete rebuilding of Berlin and Linz, Austria.

During World War II, in 1942, Speer was appointed minister of armaments and munitions; in 1943, his brief was expanded, and he was named minister of armaments and war production. In this capacity, Speer had charge of the production, transportation, and placement of armaments of all kinds. His position was vertically integrated, so that he had authority over the production of raw materials as well as general industrial production. Speer substantially expanded the conscription and exploitation of slave labor, which was drawn from concentration camps and from conquered popula-

tions. It was this in particular for which he was tried after the war at the NUREMBERG WAR CRIMES TRIBUNAL. In contrast to many other top Nazi officials, Speer fully and freely confessed his guilt to the tribunal. He was sentenced to 20 years in Spandau prison and served the complete term.

Released in 1966, Speer became a highly successful author, chronicling the Nazi era. His *Erinnerungen* of 1969—published in English as *Inside the Third Reich* (1970)—was an international best seller. He also published *Spandau: The Secret Diaries* (1976) and *Infiltrator* (1981).

Further reading: Sereny, Gitta. *Albert Speer: His Battle with Truth*. New York: Vintage, 1996; Speer, Albert. *Inside the Third Reich*. New York: Simon & Schuster, 1997; Van der Vat, Dan. *The Good Nazi: The Life and Lies of Albert Speer*. New York: Houghton Mifflin, 1997.

Albert Speer *(University of California, Berkeley)*

Sperrle, Hugo (1885–1953) *Luftwaffe field marshal*

The son of a brewer in Ludwigsburg, Germany, Sperrle joined the Imperial German Army in 1903 as an infantry ensign. He transferred to the Army Air Service during World War I and flew as an observer throughout the entire war.

After the war, Sperrle was a zealous member of the FREIKORPS, then rejoined the German army. He eagerly entered the Luftwaffe when it was first created by HERMANN GÖRING and, immediately given the rank of major general (because of his World War I flying experience), he served in the SPANISH CIVIL WAR as commanding officer of the Kondor Legion, the Luftwaffe unit that fought on the side of the Spanish Falange. He emerged from the war a lieutenant general and took command of Luftfotte 3 (Air Fleet 3) in September 1939.

Sperrle did not serve in the INVASION OF POLAND, but he did provide air support for Army Group A (GERD VON RUNDSTEDT) during the BATTLE OF FRANCE in May–June 1940. The success of this campaign—and the brilliance of Sperrle's air support role—earned him a marshal's baton in July 1940.

During the BATTLE OF BRITAIN, Sperrle advocated concentrating on the destruction of the RAF, including its airfields, rather than conducting raids against London and other cities. He was overruled. Had his advice been heeded, it is likely that Germany, not Britain, would have prevailed in this key air battle.

Sperrle saw his Luftflotte 3 effectively cannibalized during the INVASION OF THE SOVIET UNION. He remained headquartered in Paris in 1941, presiding over four instead of 44 bomber groups. Discouraged by the course of the war, he led a life of considerable dissipation in Paris, but did continue to lead Luftflotte 3 in limited operations defending German positions in Belgium, France, and the Netherlands, and mounting a few operations during the NORMANDY LANDINGS (D-DAY). Lacking aircraft, however, he was able to do very little and was dismissed in August 1944. He did not receive another command.

Further reading: Bekker, Cajus. *The Luftwaffe War Diaries: The German Air Force in World War II.* New York: Da Capo Press, 1994; Corum, James S. *The Luftwaffe: Creating the Operational Air War, 1918–1940.* Lawrence: University Press of Kansas, 1997; Corum, James S., and Richard R. Muller. *The Luftwaffe's Way of War: German Air Force Doctrine, 1911–1945.* Baltimore: Nautical and Aviation Publishing Company of America, 1998.

Spruance, Raymond Ames (1886–1969)
deputy commander of the U.S. Pacific Fleet

Spruance was born in Baltimore and graduated from the United States Naval Academy in 1906. After sailing with Admiral George Dewey in the world voyage of the Great White Fleet, he served both at sea and on staff assignments during World War I. In 1939, he was promoted to rear admiral and assumed command of the 10th Naval District and the Caribbean Sea Frontier.

At the outbreak of World War II, Spruance commanded Cruiser Division 5 of the Pacific Fleet. When Admiral WILLIAM F. HALSEY fell ill in June 1942, Spruance was assigned temporary command of the Pacific Fleet and was instrumental in the turning-point American victory at the BATTLE OF MIDWAY.

Admiral Raymond Spruance *(U.S. Navy)*

After Midway, Spruance was named chief of staff under Adm. CHESTER NIMITZ and deputy commander of the Pacific fleet. He was promoted in 1943 to vice admiral and commanded the assaults at the BATTLE OF TARAWA ATOLL; in the MAKIN ISLAND RAID; at the BATTLE OF ENIWETOK ATOLL; at the BATTLE OF KWAJALEIN ATOLL; and at the BATTLE OF TRUK ISLAND. In February 1944, he was promoted to admiral and commanded navy forces in the BATTLE OF THE PHILIPPINE SEA during June 1944. In 1945, the final year of the war, Spruance was in command of naval operations at the BATTLE OF IWO JIMA and the OKINAWA CAMPAIGN.

After the war, Spruance was named president of the Naval War College, in which post he served until his retirement from the navy in 1948. President HARRY S. TRUMAN appointed him ambassador to the Philippines in 1952, where he served until 1955.

Further reading: Buell, Thomas B. *The Quiet Warrior: A Biography of Admiral Raymond A. Spruance.* Annapolis, Md.: Naval Institute Press, 1992.

Stalin, Joseph (1879–1953) *leader of the Soviet Union from 1929 until his death in 1953*

Born Joseph Vissarionovich Djugashvili in the Georgian hill town of Gori, Stalin grew up amid poverty and his father's brutality. After his father was killed in a brawl, 11-year-old Joseph was indulged by a doting mother, who groomed him for the Orthodox priesthood. At 14, he entered the Tiflis Theological Seminary, but was by this time a delinquent so incorrigible that he had earned the sobriquet Koba, after a legendary Georgian bandit and rebel. Rebelling against the harsh corporal discipline of the seminary, he became involved in antitsarist agitation and, in 1899, abruptly left the seminary to become a full-time revolutionary organizer. By 1901, he was a member of the Georgian branch of the Social Democratic Party, which sent him throughout the Caucasus to rally laborers and organize strikes.

In 1903, the Social Democrats fractured into Vladimir I. Lenin's Bolsheviks and the more moderate faction Lenin derisively called the Mensheviks. "Bolshevik" means majority, whereas Menshevik means minority—although, in fact, the moderates were the numerical majority and the radicals the minority. Stalin followed Lenin, with whom he became a close collaborator. He was a tireless organizer who also masterminded daring

Joseph Stalin first met his fellow Allied leaders, Franklin Roosevelt and Winston Churchill, at the Teheran Conference, November–December 1943. *(National Archives and Records Administration)*

robberies to finance the Bolsheviks. Arrested many times, he always managed to escape, and in 1912, Lenin elevated him to the Bolshevik Central Committee, the party's inner circle. In this capacity, Stalin became the first editor of *Pravda* (*Truth*), the official Bolshevik newspaper, and it was during this period of meteoric rise that he took the byname Stalin—"Man of Steel."

In 1913, Stalin's luck finally ran out. He was arrested, tried, and exiled to Siberia, enduring there for four years until the overthrow of Tsar Nicholas II in March 1917. After the failure of the first Bolshevik attempt to seize power during the summer of 1917—and in the absence of Leon Trotsky, who had been arrested, and Lenin, who had gone into hiding—Stalin worked vigorously to reconstitute and reorganize the party. He thereby played a major role in the party's rise to power during the November Revolution of 1917. When Lenin returned from his self-imposed exile in Switzerland, he gave Stalin a succession of commissar posts, and by 1922 he was general secretary of the party's Central Committee, a position from which he controlled the apparatus and official personnel of most of the party. With Lenin's death in 1924, Stalin was enabled to present himself as the leader's anointed successor. Moreover, as general secretary, he was in a position to eliminate anyone who dared to oppose him.

Whereas Lenin was the supreme ideologue, Stalin was the consummate pragmatist. He retreated from Lenin's ideal of world communist revolution by advocating nothing more than "socialism in one country." His economic program was far more moderate than Lenin's, and this provoked rebellion from Trotsky, Lev Kamenev, and Grigory Zinoviev, all party leftists. By 1928, however, Stalin had consolidated the party's right wing and managed to oust the leadership of the left. This achieved, he executed an abrupt about-face, instantly espousing radical leftist economic programs, including the forced collectivization of agriculture and a greatly accelerated program of industrialization. He turned now against the party's right wing, led by Nikolai Bukharin, so that, in the space of a single year, he managed to crush opposition on the left as well as

the right. As of 1929, Josef Stalin had become absolute dictator of the Soviet Union.

Stalin was determined to transform the Soviet Union from an agricultural nation into a modern industrial power. Toward this end, he was quite willing to sacrifice human life on a vast scale. Late in 1928, he expropriated the lands of the middle-class farmers (kulaks), "deporting" (to Siberia) or murdering those who resisted. He promulgated a series of five-year plans by which collectivization and industrialization were to be achieved. These plans became rigid gospel, and Stalin would order the export of grain and other produce to finance industrialization despite a devastating famine that swept the Soviet Union in 1932. Millions who resisted were executed, and millions more starved to death. It has been estimated that 25 million died as a direct result of forced collectivization during 1928–33.

During the period of the first five-year plan, opposition to Stalin mounted, exploding into a peasant revolt, which the dictator easily crushed. Next, when the 17th Party Congress indicated its support for Sergei Kirov, a moderate and a potential rival, Stalin had him assassinated in December 1934. He then used his murder as a pretext for arresting most of the party's highest-ranking officials as counterrevolutionary conspirators. From 1936 to 1938 Stalin conducted a series of show trials in which party officials and many in the senior officer corps of the Red Army were wrongly convicted of outrageous crimes or acts of treason. The results of this massive purge were devastating. By 1939, 98 of the 139 central committee members elected in 1934 had been executed, and 1,108 of the 1,966 delegates to the 17th party congress arrested. Under NKVD (secret police) chief LAVRENTY BERIA, millions of innocent Soviet citizens were arrested, executed, exiled, or imprisoned. By the eve of World War II, Stalin had destroyed all serious opposition and had terrorized the nation into submission even as he built it into an industrial giant and created about himself a cult of personality. A by-product of his purges, however, was the disastrous reduction of the Red Army officer corps. Senior leaders were exiled or killed, leaving the army weak and highly vulnerable.

As ADOLF HITLER rose to power and came to control more and more of Europe by the late 1930s, Stalin decided to come to a rapprochement with him to avoid a disastrous war based on ideology. With Hitler, he astonished and dismayed the world by concluding the GERMAN-SOVIET NON-AGGRESSION PACT of August 23, 1939. By this and other agreements, Stalin acquiesced in Hitler's plan to invade Poland, part of which, in fact, would fall to the USSR. For his part, Hitler agreed not to interfere in the Soviet invasion of Finland in the RUSSO-FINNISH WAR.

On June 22, 1941, Hitler abrogated the nonaggression pact with his INVASION OF THE SOVIET UNION. Stalin was stunned as the Germans rolled over a Red Army that had been purged of much of its senior officer corps. Yet soon overcoming his initial paralysis, Stalin rallied, took personal command of the Red Army, and organized an increasingly fierce and effective defense, which developed into a counteroffensive. Stalin moved vital war industries east, into Siberia and central Asia, just ahead of the advancing German armies, and he rallied the Soviet people to heights of patriotic fervor. He courted the Western allies, Britain and France, and in the interest of lifting the morale of the Soviet people, he officially rehabilitated the Orthodox Church.

By the middle of the war, as the tide in the USSR turned against the German invaders, Stalin earned a reputation as a military leader of considerable ability. As a valuable ally, he wielded much clout at the major Allied conferences conducted at Tehran, Yalta, and Potsdam. Millions of Soviet citizens consigned his former brutality to oblivion and now hailed Stalin as their savior.

No sooner was Hitler defeated and the war ended than Stalin instituted a new reign of terror at home, imposing more taxes on peasants, announcing new discoveries of counterrevolutionary conspiracies, and instituting a policy of aggressive Soviet expansion, especially throughout an eastern Europe devastated by the war. Before the decade was over, a Cold War developed between the Soviet Union and its growing orbit of "satellite" nations on the one hand and the democratic nations of the West (especially the United States) on the other.

Stalin became, if anything, increasingly paranoid during the last years of his regime. Shortly before he died in 1953, he declared his discovery of a plot among the Kremlin's physicians, and he seemed on the verge of yet another vast round of blood purges. Before this could begin, however, he succumbed to a cerebral hemorrhage on March 5, 1953.

Further reading: Bullock, Alan. *Hitler and Stalin: Parallel Lives,* 2d ed. London: Fontana Press, 1998; Deutscher, Isaac. *Stalin: A Political Biography,* 2d ed. New York: Oxford University Press, 1967; McNeal, Robert H. *Stalin: Man and Ruler.* New York: New York University Press, 1988.

Stalingrad, Battle of

After ADOLF HITLER decided to concentrate the INVASION OF THE SOVIET UNION on its northern and southern wings rather than in the center, Stalingrad became the focus of the German offensive in the south. The battle spanned June 22, 1942, to February 2, 1943. In the initial German attack, Field Marshal Fedor von Bock led Army Group B against Stalingrad, while, to the right (south) of Army Group B, Army Group A set as its objective the oil fields of the Caucasus.

Bock's attack came on June 22 from the line formed by the upper Donets River. His left wing advanced to the River Don at Voronezh on July 1, but he could not hold the city. This resulted in Bock's relief by Field Marshal Maximilian von Weichs on July 13. While the Voronezh attack failed, HERMANN HOTH led the Fourth Panzer Army in a 100-mile race to the Don, then turned southeast to drive between the Donets and the Don. This provided support for PAUL VON KLEIST to move his First Panzer Army across the lower Don as it advanced into the Caucasus and the oil fields there. At the same time, FRIEDRICH VON PAULUS led the Sixth Army eastward from the bend of the Don toward Stalingrad on the right (west) bank of the Volga. Thus, by August 24, German forces had reached the western margins of Stalingrad.

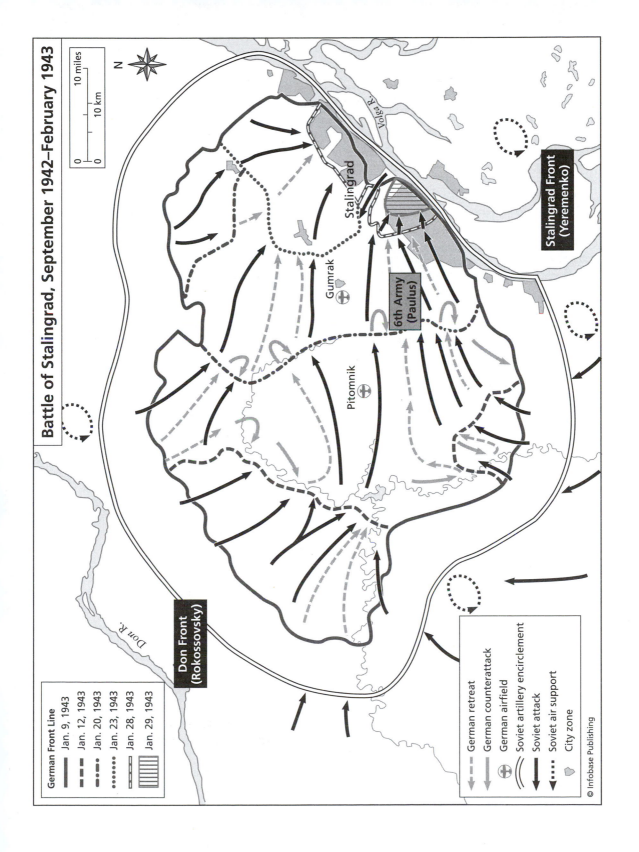

Battle of Stalingrad, September 1942–February 1943

N

10 miles

10 km

Volga R.

Stalingrad

Stalingrad Front
(Yeremenko)

Gumrak

6th Army
(Paulus)

Pitomnik

Don R.

Don Front
(Rokossovsky)

German Front Line

Jan. 9, 1943

Jan. 12, 1943

Jan. 20, 1943

Jan. 23, 1943

Jan. 28, 1943

Jan. 29, 1943

German retreat

German counterattack

German airfield

Soviet artillery encirclement

Soviet attack

Soviet air support

City zone

© Infobase Publishing

At this time, the Sixty-Second Red Army, amply reinforced by local civilian volunteers, mounted an urban warfare defense, fighting the Germans house by house. At great cost, the Germans advanced to central Stalingrad by September 22. It was by this time a city in ruins, leveled by incessant artillery fire.

Despite the destruction of the city, the Soviets were determined to prevent the Germans from capturing a place named after JOSEPH STALIN. The Soviet commander in charge, GEORGI ZHUKOV, cautiously reinforced the Stalingrad garrison to keep the Germans from reaching the Volga River. While this holding action unfolded, Zhukov built up his flanks both north and south of the city. On November 19, the Red Army mounted a counterattack under KONSTANTIN ROKOSSOVSKY. He descended from the north of Stalingrad, then, on November 21, crossed the Don at Kalach with his armor. This breached the German lines, allowing General Nikolai Vatutin to rout three armies: the Third Romanian, Eighth Italian, and Second Hungarian. The Germans responded with a counterattack from Panzer Corps H, but were repulsed.

While this exchange was fought north of the city, Gen. Andrei Yeremenko advanced from the south on November 20. Over the next five days, he scored total victories against the Fourth Romanian Army. This achieved, the two Soviet forces converged from north and south, linking up west of the city. Although the German Sixth Army was now in a hopeless position, ADOLF HITLER denied permission for a withdrawal. Thus, on November 23, the Red Army enveloped the Germans in the Soviet city—some 300,000 of the enemy, 22 divisions in all. German communication and supply were all but completely cut off. Luftwaffe chief HERMANN GÖRING pledged that the air force (Luftwaffe) would airlift 300 tons of supplies each day. The aircraft, however, were thwarted by terrible weather and stout Soviet air defenses. Cut off, the surrounded German army starved and froze.

At this point, Hitler gave permission for ERICH VON MANSTEIN to lead a relief force—designated Army Group Don—to break through the envelopment. From 60 miles southwest of Stalingrad,

Hoth's Fourth Panzer Army led the army group's attack beginning on December 12. Hoth was just 30 miles from Paulus's besieged troops by December 21. However, Soviet resistance was now so formidable that Hoth had to break off the attack. He withdrew on December 23, leaving Paulus to endure the Red Army offensive on his own.

On January 8, 1943, the Soviets issued a surrender demand. By this time, the German Sixth Army had lost 300,000 men, 2,000 tanks, and 4,000 guns. Once again, Hitler denied permission for the surrender, and on January 10, the Soviets launched a massive artillery attack, followed by an assault from three sides. By January 16, the German airfield had been captured.

On January 24, the Soviets again demanded surrender. Hitler responded with an order to fight to the last man. That hardly mattered. Part of the Sixth Army surrendered on January 31; the rest did so two days later. Only 91,000 men had survived to this point.

The Battle of Stalingrad was an epic German disaster; nevertheless, the long-delayed surrender had tied down so many Red Army troops that Kleist was able to withdraw from the Caucasus and thereby save Army Group A from suffering the fate of the Sixth Army. Despite this, Stalingrad was a turning point of the war on the eastern front. The Germans were never able to resume the offensive, and their defeat, especially after the subsequent BATTLE OF KURSK, became only a matter of time.

Further reading: Beevor, Antony. *Stalingrad: The Fateful Siege, 1942–1943.* New York: Penguin, 1999; Hoyt, Edwin P. *199 Days: The Battle for Stalingrad.* New York: Forge Books, 1999; Roberts, Geoffrey. *Victory at Stalingrad: The Battle That Changed History.* London: Longman, 2002.

Stark, Harold Rainsford (1880–1972) *U.S. chief of naval operations from 1939 to 1942*

Born in Wilkes-Barre, Pennsylvania, Stark graduated from the United States Naval Academy in 1903, 30th in a class of 50. He served on the cruiser

Harold Stark *(U.S. Navy)*

Hartford and was captain of the destroyer *Patterson* at the outbreak of World War I. In 1917, he was appointed aide to Admiral William S. Sims, commander in charge of U.S. naval forces in the war. Stationed in London, Stark assisted in coordinating U.S. and British naval operations.

After World War I, Stark served in a variety of ordnance commands and, in 1928, became chief of staff to the commander, Destroyer Squadrons, Battle Fleet. During 1933–34, he commanded the battleship *West Virginia* (BB47), from 1934 to 1937 was chief of the Bureau of Ordnance, and during 1937–38 commanded Cruiser Division, U.S. Fleet. During 1938–39, he commanded Cruisers, Battle Force, leaving this post in August 1939 to replace WILLIAM LEAHY as chief of naval operations. Believing that the United States would inevitably be drawn into World War II, he was instrumental in moving Congress to fund major ship construction.

Stark vigorously objected to President FRANKLIN D. ROOSEVELT's decision before the war to transfer the U.S. Pacific Fleet to Hawaii. Stark believed that Pearl Harbor was inadequate to the needs of the fleet, lacking adequate repair facilities, ammunition stocks, and fuel. He lobbied for the fleet to be returned to San Francisco. Although Stark was convinced that the Japanese would attack the United States—and initially believed that Pearl Harbor was vulnerable—he subsequently decided that the attack would most likely come in the Far East. Although he was not directly blamed for Pearl Harbor's unpreparedness in the BATTLE OF PEARL HARBOR, he was relieved as CNO shortly after the Japanese attack. President Roosevelt appointed him his personal representative in London, then named him to the post of ambassador to the Free French government. In October 1943, Stark was returned to a naval command, as commander of the 12th Fleet, with responsibility for the training of U.S. naval forces for the NORMANDY LANDINGS (D-DAY).

Stark retired from the navy shortly after the end of the war.

Further reading: Simpson, B. Mitchell. *Admiral Harold R. Stark: Architect of Victory, 1939–1945.* Columbia: University of South Carolina Press, 1989.

Stauffenberg, Claus von (1907–1944)
principal conspirator in the July Plot to assassinate Adolf Hitler

Born into a prosperous, noble family in Jettingen, Germany, Stauffenberg became an officer in the army in 1926 and earned official recognition as a panzer division staff officer during 1939–40 in the INVASION OF POLAND and the BATTLE OF FRANCE. He was then transferred to the Soviet front, where he witnessed firsthand the work of the SCHUTZSTAFFEL (SS) Einsatzgruppen, which followed the invasion forces and murdered civilians, especially Jews. Severely shaken, Stauffenberg requested and secured a transfer to the NORTH AFRICAN CAMPAIGN as a panzer staff officer. In April 1943, he was gravely wounded, losing his left eye, right arm, and two fingers of his left hand.

During a long convalescence in Germany, Stauffenberg decided that the survival of the nation depended on the removal of Hitler. The assassination plot he conceived was motivated in part by patriotism and a high moral sense, but it was also the product of a growing perception that Hitler intended to act against members of the old German aristocracy.

Stauffenberg quickly built an extensive conspiracy among fellow army officers, which became the July Plot to assassinate Adolf Hitler. Stauffenberg himself assumed the principal role of assassin, planting a brief-case bomb at Wolf's Lair, Hitler's military headquarters at Rastenburg, on July 20, 1944. The bomb was successfully placed, but failed to kill its intended victim—only slightly injuring Hitler—and a coup d'état in Berlin coordinated with the assassination instantly collapsed. The conspiracy likewise fell apart, and Stauffenberg as well as a handful of fellow conspirators were immediately arrested and executed without trial in Berlin on the very night of the assassination attempt, July 20. Eventually, some 5,000 individuals would be rounded up as conspirators; most were executed.

Further reading: Fest, Joachim. *Plotting Hitler's Death: The Story of German Resistance.* New York: Owl, 1997; Galante, Pierre. *Operation Valkyrie: The German Generals' Plot Against Hitler.* New York: Cooper Square, 2002.

Stavka (Soviet Supreme Command)

Stavka (*Shtab vierhvnogo komandovania*) was a generic term meaning "general headquarters" and was used in the tsarist army during World War I and the Red Army during World War II, when it was synonymous with the "Main Command of the Armed Forces of the Union of Soviet Socialist Republics." This specific version of the Stavka was created on June 23, 1941, by Joseph Stalin and consisted of his defense minister, Marshal Semyon Timoshenko (president); Marshal Georgi Zhukov (chief of the General Staff); Vyacheslav Molotov (Soviet foreign minister); and three other military officials, Marshals Kliment Voroshilov and Semyon Budenny and people's commissar of the navy admiral Nikolai Kuznetsov. Stalin served on the Stavka ex officio. In addition to the

principals, the Stavka included "permanent counselor," consisting of more top military officers, including representatives of the Red Air Force and Soviet air defense, and Lavrenty Beria, chief of the NKVD (Soviet secret police).

On July 10, 1941, Stavka became the Stavka of the Supreme Command, and on August 8, it was reorganized as the Supreme Chief Command.

Further reading: Ring, Dennis McManus. *Soviet Wartime Command and Control: Evolution of the State Defense Committee, the Stavka, Theaters of War, and Theaters of Military Operations.* Colorado Springs: U.S. Air University, Air War College, 1976.

Stettinius, Edward (1900–1949) *U.S. secretary of state during 1944–45 and a key figure in the creation of the United Nations*

Stettinius was born in Chicago and attended the University of Virginia, but left without graduating to enter business. In 1926, he was hired as assistant to a General Motors vice president and, in the space of five years, rose to a vice presidency himself. He joined United States Steel as an executive in 1934 and within four years was chairman of the board.

In 1939, Stettinius left the private sector to accept Franklin Delano Roosevelt's invitation to become chairman of the War Resources Board. The next year, he was appointed chairman of the National Defense Advisory Commission and in 1941 became director of priorities at the Office of Production Management (OPM). Later in 1941, he replaced Harry Hopkins as director of the Lend-Lease program.

President Roosevelt appointed Stettinius undersecretary of state in 1943, and the following year elevated him to secretary of state, after Cordell Hull resigned following FDR's 1944 reelection. Stettinius did not formulate original foreign policy, but he served the president well as adviser during the Yalta Conference, the last wartime conference the ailing Roosevelt attended. Although FDR himself would describe Hull as the "father of the

United Nations," Stettinius implemented much of the actual groundwork for the organization in 1945. He headed the U.S. delegation to the San Francisco Conference and played a key role in drafting the UN Charter.

After Roosevelt's death in April 1945, Stettinius served in the cabinet of HARRY S. TRUMAN for just two months, when he was replaced by JAMES F. BYRNES. Truman appointed Stettinius the first U.S. delegate to the United Nations. He retired in 1946.

Further reading: Stettinius, Edward R. *The Diaries of Edward R. Stettinius, Jr., 1943–1946.* New York: New Viewpoints, 1975; Stettinius, Edward R. *Roosevelt and the Russians: The Yalta Conference.* Garden City, N.Y.: Doubleday, 1949.

Stilwell, Joseph "Vinegar Joe" (1883– 1946) *U.S. general who fought on the China-Burma-India theater*

Born in Palatka, Florida, and raised in Yonkers, New York, Stilwell graduated from West Point in 1904 and joined the infantry as a second lieutenant. He requested duty in the Philippines and was assigned to the 12th Infantry Regiment, with which he saw action on Samar against the rebel Puljanes during February–April 1905. In 1906, he returned to West Point as a foreign language instructor and as professor of history and instructor in tactics. On January 11, 1911, he returned to the Philippines, then during November–December, visited China for the first time.

Stilwell returned again to West Point as a language instructor, teaching from 1913 to 1916 and was promoted to captain in September 1916. He became brigade adjutant in the 80th Division, was promoted to temporary major in July 1917, and shipped out to France in January 1918. He served during World War I as a staff intelligence officer and became deputy chief of staff for intelligence under General Joseph T. Dickman in IV Corps during the Meuse-Argonne offensive (September 26–November 11). Promoted to temporary lieutenant colonel on September 11, 1918, then temporary colonel in October, Stilwell remained in Germany after the Armistice as part of the army of occupation until May 1919.

In contrast to most of his colleagues, he did not want to return to the United States after the war and requested assignment to China as a language officer. He served there from August 6, 1919, to July 1923 and forged a friendship with the warlord Feng Yu-hsiang.

Stilwell returned to the States and attended Infantry School at Fort Benning from 1923 to 1924, then went on to the Command and General Staff School at Fort Leavenworth from 1925 to 1926. He returned to China to command a battalion of the 15th Infantry at Tientsin in August 1926. There he met GEORGE C. MARSHALL, thanks to whom he was promoted to lieutenant colonel in March 1928 and appointed head of the tactical section of the Infantry School in July 1929.

Stilwell left the Infantry School in 1933 to become training officer for the IX Corps reserves from 1933 to 1935. Promoted to colonel, he was assigned as military attaché to China on August 1, 1935. He closely observed the developing SINO-JAPANESE WAR before he returned to the United States in 1939, receiving promotion to brigadier general while en route.

"Vinegar Joe" Stilwell (right) with Ranger expert Frank Merrill *(National Archives and Records Administration)*

Assigned command of the 3d Brigade, 2nd Division in September 1939, Stilwell played a major role in prewar maneuvers, including the Louisiana-Texas maneuvers of May 1940. He gained the attention of his superiors for his deft ability to move troops quickly and unconventionally. On July 1, 1940, he was given command of the newly created 7th Division at Fort Ord, California, and, in September, was promoted to temporary major general. He was moved up to command of III Corps in July 1941.

After the BATTLE OF PEARL HARBOR and the U.S. entry into World War II, Stilwell was promoted to lieutenant general and appointed commanding general of U.S. Army forces in the China-Burma-India (CBI) Theater in January 1942. He set up a headquarters at Chungking (Chongqing), China, where he made an ally of CHIANG KAI-SHEK (Jiang Jieshi), who turned over to him command of Chinese forces in Burma on March 6, 1942. Stilwell arrived in Burma on March 11 with a single Chinese division and soon raised eight more.

Like his British CBI colleague General WILLIAM SLIM, Stilwell was forced to make do with chronic shortages of men, equipment, transportation, air power, and basic supplies. He was also afflicted by Chiang Kai-shek's mercurial temperament and continually changing orders. Because of a lack of reinforcements and other support, Stilwell was forced to withdraw from Burma to India during May 11–30, after which he turned his attention to training and equipping three Chinese divisions in India. He also became the architect of the HUMP, an airlift chain over the Himalayas to supply Kunming, China, during January–February 1943 after the Burma Road had been severed.

In July 1943, Stilwell was appointed deputy supreme Allied commander in the CBI under Lord LOUIS MOUNTBATTEN. Stilwell advocated the Salween-Mykikyina-Mogaung offensive of March–August 1944, which ended with the victorious BATTLE OF MYKIKYINA on August 3 and the subsequent liberation of all northern Burma. This triumph earned Stilwell promotion to temporary general; however, his always difficult relationship with Chiang broke down during this period and, at Chiang's request, he was recalled by President FRANKLIN D. ROOSEVELT on October 19, 1944.

Returned to the United States, Stilwell became commander of Army Ground Forces on January 23, 1945, and was decorated with the Legion of Merit and the Oak Leaf cluster of the DSM on February 10, 1945. He was then sent to Okinawa, where he took command of the Tenth Army on June 23 and was among the dignitaries invited to the Japanese surrender aboard the USS *Missouri* in Tokyo Bay on September 2, 1945.

Following the war, Stilwell was named president of the War Equipment Board and then commander of the Sixth Army and the Western Defense Command in January 1946. He died later that year of stomach cancer.

Further reading: Stilwell, Joseph. *The Stilwell Papers.* New York: Da Capo Press, 1991; Tuchman, Barbara. *Stilwell and the American Experience in China, 1911–45.* New York: Grove Press, 2001.

Stimson, Henry L. (1867–1950) *U.S. secretary of war during World War II*

Henry Stimson served with distinction five presidents since 1911, most notably as secretary of war in the cabinet of FRANKLIN D. ROOSEVELT. Born in New York City, Stimson studied law and was admitted to the New York bar in 1891. He was U.S. attorney for the southern district of New York from 1906 to 1909, then was appointed secretary of war by President William Howard Taft in 1911. He served until 1913. After the United States entered World War I in April 1917, Stimson served briefly in the field artillery in France.

In 1927, he returned to government service in the administration of President Calvin Coolidge, who named him special commissioner to Nicaragua and assigned him to mediate a civil war there, which bore on U.S. financial and political interests. Stimson was largely successful in this effort and earned a reputation as an able negotiator and statesman. He then served as governor-general of the Philippines.

In 1929, President Herbert Hoover appointed Stimson secretary of state, and in this capacity he served as leader of the U.S. delegation to the 1930 London Naval Conference, which sought to create a degree of global disarmament by setting limits on the tonnage of the naval fleets of the major powers.

When Japan occupied Manchuria in 1931 in a prelude to the SINO-JAPANESE WAR, Stimson dispatched stern notes to both Japan and China on January 7, 1932, articulating what became known as the Stimson Doctrine, declaring that the United States would refuse to acknowledge the legality of any treaty, agreement, or situation that infringed U.S. treaty rights or that had been created in violation of the 1919 Pact of Paris.

Stimson left the office of secretary of state after President Roosevelt entered the White House in 1933. When World War II began in Europe in September 1939, Stimson, in contrast to many of his Republican colleagues, was an eloquent advocate of U.S. intervention in the war on the side of the Allies, and he became a charter member of the Committee to Defend America by Aiding the Allies. This, combined with his long and distinguished service, moved FDR to appoint the lifelong Republican secretary of war in 1940. It was a bold act of bipartisanship and proved highly effective in creating Republican support for FDR's increasingly interventionist foreign policy. A vigorous advocate of preparedness, Stimson led the rearmament and training of the U.S. Army during the run-up to the BATTLE OF PEARL HARBOR, which brought the United States into the war in December 1941.

Stimson served as secretary of war throughout World War II and played an especially significant role in advising both FDR and his successor, HARRY S. TRUMAN, on atomic weapons policy. He was a strong advocate of using the new atomic weapons against Japan, advising that the bombs, when they became operational, should be dropped on Japanese cities of military importance. On the grounds of its great beauty and religious significance to the Japanese people, he successfully overrode a U.S. military recommendation that the city of Kyoto top the list of potential targets. After the war, Stimson defended the use of the atomic bombs, paradoxically enough, on humanitarian grounds,

earnestly arguing that only by these weapons had Japan been compelled to surrender and that they therefore saved countless Allied as well as Japanese lives that would have been lost in an invasion of the Japanese home islands.

After serving in the Truman administration for six months, Stimson resigned as secretary of state in September 1945. With the assistance of McGeorge Bundy, he wrote a memoir, *On Active Service in Peace and War,* published in 1948.

Further reading: Hodgson, Godfrey. *The Colonel: The Life and Wars of Henry Stimson, 1867–1950.* Boston: Northeastern University Press, 1992; Schmitz, David F. *Henry L. Stimson: The First Wise Man.* Lanham, Md.: SR Books, 2001; Stimson, Henry L., with McGeorge Bundy. *On Active Service in Peace and War.* New York: Octagon Books, 1971.

Strasser, Gregor (1892–1934) and Otto (1897–1974) *brothers who were early leaders of the Nazi Party*

Born in Geisenfeld, Gregor Strasser joined the Nazi Party virtually at its inception in 1920 and participated with ADOLF HITLER in the ill-fated Munich Beer Hall Putsch of 1923. While Hitler was incarcerated in Landsberg Prison, Gregor Strasser headed the party, boldly speaking and organizing, even though the party had been outlawed. When Hitler was released from prison, Strasser stepped down but was assigned to organize the party in northern Germany.

Strasser was elected to the Reichstag (parliament) and, in collaboration with his brother Otto and JOSEPH GOEBBELS, was instrumental in the explosive growth of the Nazi Party into a national mass movement. Despite their middle-class origin, both Strassers had immensely persuasive appeal for the working classes. Although this rapidly expanded the party's base, it did so by pushing the party leftward, in the direction of socialism—albeit always tinged with conventional Nazi racism and nationalism. Hitler was pleased by the party's showing in the 1928 elections, but he was distressed by its new direction. For his part, Otto was also increasingly displeased with Hitler, who, he now understood, was not interested in making the Nazi Party a worker's party. When Hitler began forging ties with Germany's power elite, including industrialists and financiers, Otto left the party in 1930 and founded the Schwarze Front (Black Front) in opposition to it.

Gregor parted company with his brother and remained loyal to Hitler, advancing by the early 1930s to the number-two position in the party leadership, just below Hitler. Despite his loyalty, however, he remained a partisan of the left and opposed Hitler's affiliation with the capitalists. He also discouraged the emphasis on anti-Semitism and hoped that he could steer the party onto a radical socialist track. As he came to loggerheads with Hitler, he finally quit the party in 1932. Strasser had hoped that many party members would follow him, but this hope proved to be unfounded. Hitler's appeal by this point was so great that few left the party, and Hitler went on the following year to assume the post of German chancellor. In 1934, he had Gregor Strasser killed on June 30 as part of the "Long Knives" purge of the Sturmabteilung (SA).

Otto Strasser was more fortunate. He left Germany and found refuge in Canada. He did not return to his native country until 1955, when he made an abortive attempt to reenter politics.

Further reading: McDonough, Frank. *Hitler and the Rise of the Nazi Party.* London: Longman, 2003; Orlow, Dietrich. *The History of the Nazi Party, 1933–1945.* Pittsburgh: University of Pittsburgh Press, 1973.

strategic bombing of Germany

World War I had seen experiments in the long-range bombing of strategic targets, including London, but it was in World War II that the strategic bombing concept was most thoroughly developed. Adolf Hitler extensively bombed civilian targets, especially during The Blitz of London and other English cities; yet these attacks are best defined as terrorism on a large scale rather than part of a fully developed program of strategic bombing. True strategic bombing targets cities, but does so mainly

U.S. B-17s drop bombs over a German city. *(National Archives and Records Administration)*

to destroy industrial production and transportation networks, then only secondarily to terrorize the civilian population and undermine a nation's will to continue to fight the war. Strategic bombing is a form of economic warfare, which directly attacks war production and other industrial and transportation enterprises.

Among British as well as American air officers were many who believed that a large-scale program of strategic bombing could create a devastating and therefore decisive economic effect, including, ultimately, the complete destruction of the enemy's war economy. Despite significant political resistance in Britain and the United States during the 1930s, advocates of strategic bombing managed to persuade their governments to fund the design and construction of heavy four-engine bombers (including, in Britain, the Wellington, Whitley, and Hampden; and in the United States, the B-17, B-24, and B-29), which were the necessary platforms from which heavy, long-range bombing could be executed.

German advocates of strategic bombing failed notably to prevail on Hitler, who focused production on fighters, fighter-bombers, and medium bombers—none of which constituted an adequate platform for strategic bombing. Unequipped for strategic bombing, the Germans entered World War II without a strategic bombing doctrine. For their part, however, the British avoided implementing strategic bombing early in the war, lest they provoke the Germans. What finally drove the launch of the strategic campaign was the desperate situation created by the BATTLE OF FRANCE and subsequently the BATTLE OF BRITAIN. In 1940, strategic bombing was Britain's only option for striking back at Germany.

The British conducted strategic bombing under cover of night. This had the advantage of making the bombers difficult to intercept with fighters or to hit with ground-based antiaircraft artillery. Early in the war, long-range fighters were unavailable to escort the bombers deep into enemy territory; this made the bombers especially vulnerable. Yet night bombing had the distinct disadvantage of rendering targets all but invisible; precision bombing was therefore out of the question; therefore, the British employed carpet-bombing (also called area-bombing) techniques. Instead of targeting particular industrial plants or transportation hubs, for example, the British would

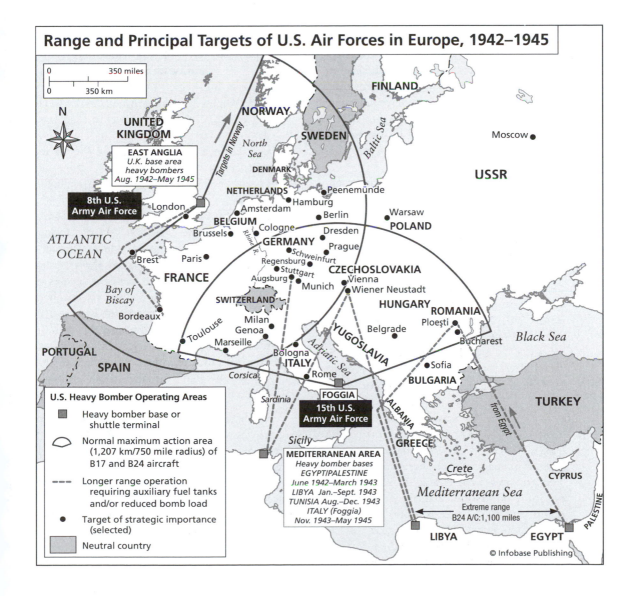

Range and Principal Targets of U.S. Air Forces in Europe, 1942–1945

U.S. Heavy Bomber Operating Areas
- ■ Heavy bomber base or shuttle terminal
- ◠ Normal maximum action area (1,207 km/750 mile radius) of B17 and B24 aircraft
- --- Longer range operation requiring auxiliary fuel tanks and/or reduced bomb load
- ● Target of strategic importance (selected)
- Neutral country

© Infobase Publishing

bomb an entire urban area, hoping to hit valuable industrial targets in the process. This was a highly destructive approach, but there was no guarantee that a raid would hit anything of real strategic value.

When the United States entered the air offensive in 1942—with the U.S. Eighth Army Air Force flying out of bases in England—American air planners decided to risk precision bombing in daylight. Thus, the Allied strategic bombing program against Germany became a day and night affair. The Americans would bomb carefully chosen targets by day, and the British would employ carpet bombing by night. As the war progressed, long-range fighters (such as the P-51 Mustang) became available to escort bombers all the way to their targets and back. Despite this welcome boon, casualties among Allied airmen—especially the Americans—were extremely heavy. Some 50,000 British and American airmen died in the process of inflicting somewhat less than a million fatal German casualties.

The major Allied strategic raids against Germany included the following:

May 30–31, 1942: A British raid on Cologne destroyed most of the center city at a cost of 41 bombers.

July 24, 1943: A combined British and American incendiary raid against Hamburg created a firestorm in which some 50,000 civilians were killed. (Bomber losses are unknown.)

August 1, 1943: The PLOEŞTI RAID targeted refineries in this Romanian city. The U.S. Army Air Force (Eighth and Ninth Air Forces) lost 50 planes, but did inflict major damage—which, however, was soon repaired.

August 17, 1943: The SCHWEINFURT RAIDS targeted German ball-bearing production. The U.S. raid on this day also targeted Regensburg, a major center of aircraft production. The factories were damaged, but not put out of commission, and the loss to U.S. Eighth Army Air Force bombers was heavy: 60 bombers lost, 122 badly damaged.

August 17, 1943: The British raid on PEENE-MÜNDE (V-2 BASE) caused serious damage to

missile launch facilities, but these were soon repaired. The RAF lost 69 heavy bombers.

October 14, 1943: In another U.S. Eighth Army Air Force raid on Schweinfurt, 60 bombers were lost and 138 damaged; however, the ball-bearing plants were destroyed—only to be quickly rebuilt.

November 18, 1943–March 31, 1944: The British RAF conducted some 35 raids against Berlin during this period, each raid consisting of more than 500 aircraft. Damage to the city was extensive, but 1,047 bombers were lost during the offensive.

February 20–26, 1944: Known as "Big Week," this U.S. offensive targeted German aircraft factories and wiped out about half of Germany's fighter production capacity. Losses to the Eighth, Ninth, and Fifteenth U.S. Army Air Forces were 226 bombers.

March 11, 1944: A British raid on the oil and railroad facilities at Essen was highly successful and was carried out with negligible losses.

February 13–14, 1945: U.S. and British bombers targeted the medieval city of Dresden with heavy incendiaries, which created a massive firestorm that razed the city and killed 135,000 German civilians. Losses to the Allies were no more than six bombers. Given its high cost in civilian lives and its occurrence so late in the war, this was the most controversial strategic raid of the war's European theater. Allied critics charged that it was motivated by nothing more "strategic" than a thirst for vengeance.

As the list of major strategic bombing missions suggests, the cost in equipment and the lives of aircrews was high. The effectiveness of strategic bombing was bitterly debated both during the war and after it. Proponents claimed that it significantly reduced the German capacity to make war. Critics contended that strategic bombing wasted the lives of aircrews and, because it targeted civilians, was inherently immoral. Most likely, an accurate assessment of strategic bombing lies between the extremes of "decisive factor" and "marginally effective adjunct."

See also AIRCRAFT, BRITISH; AIRCRAFT, UNITED STATES; BOMBER AIRCRAFT; GREAT BRITAIN, AIR FORCE OF; UNITED STATES ARMY AIR FORCES; and STRATEGIC BOMBING OF JAPAN.

Further reading: Biddle, Tami Davis. *Rhetoric and Reality in Air Warfare: The Evolution of British and American Ideas about Strategic Bombing, 1914–1945.* Princeton, N.J.: Princeton University Press, 2004; Knell, Hermann. *To Destroy a City: Strategic Bombing and Its Human Consequences in World War II.* New York: Da Capo Press, 2003; Ross, Stewart Halsey. *Strategic Bombing by the United States in World War II: The Myths and the Facts.* Jefferson, N.C.: McFarland, 2002.

strategic bombing of Japan

For a definition of strategic bombing, see STRATEGIC BOMBING OF GERMANY.

Although the DOOLITTLE TOKYO RAID took place early in the war, on April 18, 1942, the United States was not in a position to launch the full strategic bombing of Japan until June 15, 1944, when 50 B-29 bombers of the Twentieth U.S. Army Air Force bombed steel mills at Yawata, Kyushu. The B-29, the largest bomber of the war, with the greatest payload and longest range, was used exclusively in the Pacific theater. Once the Mariana Islands campaign had been successfully concluded, the United States came into possession of air bases that put the Japanese home islands within B-29 range. Before this, the bombers had to operate from bases in India and stage through China—a long and hazardous route that precluded routine strategic bombing runs.

The Marianas were secured on June 15, 1944 (coincidentally, the day of the Yawata raid), and the first raid staged from them came on November 24, against Tokyo's Nakajima aircraft factory. Under Brig. Gen. Haywood S. Hansell, the B-29s conducted a series of high-altitude daylight raids, mainly against aircraft factories. The raids were only marginally successful due to mechanical problems with the new bombers and, even more, due to the inherent inaccuracy of bombing from high altitude. Air Force commander in charge HAROLD "HAP" ARNOLD ordered Hansell (an advocate of precision bombing) to try a new approach, abandoning daylight precision raids for night attacks at low altitude using incendiary bombs. The first such raid, on Nagoya, January 3, 1945, was not a spectacular success, whereas a daylight precision raid on Kobe in mid January was highly effective. Although Hansell may have thought of this as a vindication of his advocacy of precision bombing, Arnold nevertheless relieved him and put in his place Maj. Gen. CURTIS E. LEMAY, a far bolder innovator.

At first, LeMay combined high-altitude precision missions with incendiary raids—also conducted at high altitude during daytime. The incendiary raids looked promising, and Arnold ordered them to be increased. On February 25, 150 B-29s firebombed Tokyo, razing a square mile of the city. Successful though this was, LeMay decided to increase its effectiveness by bombing at low altitude during the night. Moreover, LeMay stripped the bombers of their many (heavy) defensive guns. The combination of low altitude and the absence of extra weight allowed the aircraft to carry bigger bomb loads. On March 9–10, 1945, at night, some 300 B-29s dropped 2,000 tons of incendiary bombs on Tokyo from a low altitude of 5,000 to 9,000 feet. The resulting firestorm killed about 85,000 inhabitants of the city and destroyed many industrial targets.

Throughout the rest of March, LeMay ordered incendiary attacks against Nagoya, Kobe, and Osaka, as well as new raids against Tokyo and Kawasaki—all with devastating results. More incendiary raids followed, then the bombers of the Twenty-first Air Force were diverted to the OKINAWA CAMPAIGN until mid-May, when raids targeted Tokyo, Nagoya, Kobe, Osaka, Yokohama, and Kawasaki. When Japanese fighters attempted to ward off daylight attacks, the P-51 Mustang fighters escorting the B-29s decimated them, so that, by June, the Japanese were no longer able to offer fighter defense. At this time, LeMay decided to begin attacking some 60 lesser Japanese cities. He also targeted the Japanese oil industry and succeeded in all but totally destroying it.

Strategic bombing was extremely effective in Japan, and by July there were virtually no targets left to hit. Yet, effective as the bombing campaign was, it did not end the war. Combat continued until the atomic bombing of Hiroshima and Nagasaki in August.

See also AIRCRAFT, UNITED STATES; BOMBER AIRCRAFT; HIROSHIMA, ATOMIC BOMBING OF; NAGASAKI, ATOMIC BOMBING OF; and UNITED STATES ARMY AIR FORCES.

Further reading: Biddle, Tami Davis. *Rhetoric and Reality in Air Warfare: The Evolution of British and American Ideas about Strategic Bombing, 1914–1945.* Princeton, N.J.: Princeton University Press, 2004; Greer, Ron, and Mike Wicks. *Fire from the Sky: A Diary over Japan.* Jacksonville, Ark.: Greer, 2005; Knell, Hermann. *To Destroy a City: Strategic Bombing and Its Human Consequences in World War II.* New York: Da Capo Press, 2003; Ross, Stewart Halsey. *Strategic Bombing by the United States in World War II: The Myths and the Facts.* Jefferson, N.C.: McFarland, 2002.

Streicher, Julius (1885–1946) *Nazi Party's leading spokesman for and advocate of the persecution of the Jews*

Born in Fleinhausen, Germany, Streicher saw action during World War I, then became an elementary schoolteacher. He joined the NAZI PARTY virtually at its inception in 1921 and became a close associate and personal friend of ADOLF HITLER. In 1923, Streicher founded *Der Stürmer,* which became the leading anti-Semitic mouthpiece of the party. Sales of the newspaper made Streicher a wealthy man, and its rhetoric formed the basis of the campaign of Jewish persecution that, during the 1930s, culminated in the passage of the 1935 NUREMBERG LAWS, which institutionalized anti-Semitic persecution. Hitler appointed Streicher Gauleiter (district leader) of Franconia in 1925.

As he became increasingly wealthy and influential, Streicher behaved more erratically and carelessly, embezzling funds and indulging sadistic sexual perversions, which he made little effort to hide. In 1940, the Nazi Party sanctioned him by stripping him of all of his party offices. Nevertheless, under Hitler's protection, he continued to edit *Der Stürmer* throughout the entire war.

After Germany surrendered in May 1945, Streicher attempted to evade Allied capture by disguising himself as a painter. He was nevertheless captured on May 23, 1945, by American forces near Waldring, Bavaria. He was tried by the NUREMBERG WAR CRIMES TRIBUNAL and found guilty on October 1, 1946, of crimes against humanity. He was hanged on October 16.

Further reading: Bytwerk, Randall L. *Julius Streicher: Nazi Editor of the Notorious Anti-Semitic Newspaper Der Stürmer.* New York: Cooper Square Press, 2001.

Student, Kurt (1890–1978) *German airborne assault innovator and commander*

Kurt Student joined the German Air Force just before World War I, in 1913. At the outbreak of the war, he served on the Galician front but was transferred in October 1916 to the western front, where he served as a pilot in the AOK 3 and Jasta 9 squadrons (from October 1916), scoring six kills against French pilots during 1916–17.

Between the world wars, Student began developing techniques of airborne assault and was the German pioneer of paratroop operations. Student's paratroopers achieved the spectacular victory against the great Belgian FORTRESS EBEN-EMAEL during the BLITZKRIEG through the Low Countries. His next major airborne operation was in 1941, when he oversaw ACTION ON CRETE that resulted in the capture of the island. This operation was something of a Pyrrhic victory, however, proving so costly that ADOLF HITLER personally barred further major airborne assaults.

Student next masterminded *Unternehmen Eiche* in 1943—the daring commando operation to rescue BENITO MUSSOLINI after he had been deposed as Italy's premier. Commanded in the field by

OTTO SKORZENY, the operation used gliders and light aircraft to land on the hilltop compound in which Mussolini was being held. It was a remarkable success.

Student participated in the defense against the NORMANDY LANDINGS (D-DAY) in 1944, then, as commanding officer of the First Paratroop Army, fought successfully against BERNARD LAW MONTGOMERY's attempt to secure a bridgehead over the Rhine at Arnhem in OPERATION MARKET-GARDEN.

Student ended the war on the eastern front, in Mecklenburg. He was captured by British forces in Schleswig-Holstein in April 1945 and, cleared of war crimes, was freed in 1948.

Further reading: Quarrie, Bruce. *German Airborne Divisions: Blitzkrieg 1940–41.* London: Osprey, 2004; Quarrie, Bruce. *German Airborne Troops, 1939–45.* Osprey, 1983.

Sturmabteilung (SA)

The Sturmabteilung (Assault Division) was founded in Munich by ADOLF HITLER as the paramilitary arm of the fledgling NAZI PARTY. SA members were commonly referred to as storm troopers or, after the uniforms, as Brownshirts. They were in reality little more than uniformed thugs, largely drawn from the FREIKORPS, the unauthorized militia units that sprang into being throughout Germany in the years following the punitive TREATY OF VERSAILLES. Because the Freikorps consisted chiefly of disaffected World War I veterans, the SA was mainly an organization of veterans. Hitler self-consciously modeled the SA after BENITO MUSSOLINI's paramilitary fascist strongarm unit, the Blackshirts.

The mission of the SA was to provide protection during Nazi rallies and to engage in street brawls with party opponents, mainly leftists. In addition, the SA served as an instrument of physical intimidation of would-be opponents.

The SA was effectively suspended following the collapse of Hitler's Munich Beer Hall Putsch of 1923, but was quickly reconstituted in 1925. In January 1931, Ernst Röhm assumed command of the SA and built it into a large and formidable force, much more

along traditional military lines. His ultimate intention was to fashion the storm troopers into the principal military force of Germany. Röhm exploited the Great Depression to recruit large numbers of troopers from the ranks of the unemployed and desperate. By 1932, there were some 400,000 storm troopers. By the following year, when Hitler became chancellor of Germany, it is estimated that SA membership may have reached 2 million. At this time, the post-Versailles German regular army consisted of just 100,000 officers and men.

Hitler used the SA to wage a street-level war against political opponents as well as Jews; however, Röhm increasingly opposed the upper classes, capitalists, financiers, and industrialists—all groups that Hitler had begun courting in his rise to power. The army, too, looked upon the SA as a menace. Finally, Hitler himself saw in Röhm a potential rival. When Röhm threatened to lead his SA in what he called a "second Nazi revolution"—essentially a socialist revolt against the moneyed classes—and when he talked openly of merging the SA and the army (under his overall leadership, of course), Hitler struck back. On June 30, 1934, he led a blood purge against the SA leadership in what became known as the Night of the Long Knives. SCHUTZSTAFFEL (SS) men raided an SA meeting and summarily murdered most of the SA leadership, including Röhm. This effectively muzzled the SA, which, greatly reduced in numbers, continued to exist but was of little political significance. Beginning in 1939, its chief function was to train citizen Home Guard units.

Further reading: Evans, Richard J. *The Coming of the Third Reich.* New York: Penguin, 2004; Littlejohn, David. *The SA 1921–45: Hitler's Stormtroopers.* London: Osprey, 1990; Maracin, Paul R. *The Night of the Long Knives: Forty-Eight Hours That Changed the History of the World.* Guilford, Conn.: Lyons Press, 2004.

submarines

World War I demonstrated the effectiveness of submarines as a naval weapon for use against enemy combatant ships and, even more, against enemy

View through the periscope of a U.S. submarine after torpedoing a Japanese transport *(National Archives and Records Administration)*

merchant and troop convoys. In the Atlantic, the German submarine fleet during World War II preyed upon Allied shipping, which plied the long convoy routes between the United States and Europe and the United States and the Soviet Union. In the Pacific, American submarines targeted the Japanese troop and cargo convoys that were essential to communications among that nation's far-flung island conquests.

BRITISH SUBMARINES

O Class (later designated *Oberon* Class). These craft were developed in the decade following World War I to replace the L Class boats of that war. They were early examples of truly long-range submarines, built with a prescient eye toward a possible future conflict with far-off Japan. The first of the O Class submarines, HMS *Oberon*, was launched in 1924 and two sister subs followed. Slow and awkward, the original O Class submarines were replaced by the *Odin* Class (six boats) in 1928–29. These achieved greater speed and were capable of more maneuverability. The *Odin* Class submarines displaced 1,781 tons surfaced and 2,038 submerged. They were 283.5 feet long with a beam of almost 30 feet and a draft of 13.67 feet. Two diesels produced 4,400 bhp on the surface, and two electric motors

produced a total of 1,320 hp submerged. Top surface speed was 17.5 knots. Submerged, the boats could make nine knots. Maximum surface range was 13,125 miles. Underwater endurance was 60 miles. The boats carried a single 4-inch gun and eight 21-inch torpedoes. Crews consisted of 53 men.

P and R Classes. These two classes were similar to the *Odin* boats, except for minor details. They were built during 1929–30.

Porpoise Class. The submarines of this class were developed from the P-Class submarines, but were purpose-built as minelayers and included a tack mechanism on deck to deploy the mines. Launched between 1932 and 1938, the class consisted of six vessels. Early in the war, mines capable of being laid through torpedo tubes rendered the dedicated submarine minelayers obsolete; however, the *Porpoise* boats continued to lay mines, especially in the Mediterranean. The boats displaced 1,768 tons surfaced and 2,053 submerged. Their length was 289 feet, their beam 29.83 feet, and draft 16 feet. A pair of diesels produced 3,300 bhp on the surface, and two electric motors made 1,630 bhp submerged. Top surfaced speed was just 15.5 knots. Submerged maximum was nine knots. The submarines had a range of 13,240 miles and an underwater endurance of 76 miles. They were armed with a single 4-inch gun and six 21-inch torpedo tubes. Each was capable of deploying a load of 50 mines. Crew complement was 59 men.

Thames Class. Built between 1932 and 1934, the three submarines of this class were designed to maintain a speed adequate to keep up with the operations of the surface fleet. Although they were large submarines for their time—displacing 2,166 tons surfaced and 2,680 submerged, with a length of 345 feet, a beam of 28.25 feet, and a draft of 15.67 feet—the *Thames* Class boats topped out at 22.5 knots surface and 10.5 knots submerged. Range was 11,515 miles with a 136-mile submerged endurance. Two diesels delivered 10,000 bhp, and two electric motors made a total of 2,500 bhp. There was one 4-inch gun and six 21-inch torpedo tubes. The crew consisted of 61 hands.

S Class. This was the most numerous class of British World War II submarines and consisted of two subclasses, the *Swordfish*-type boats—submarines launched between 1931 and 1933—and the *Shark*-type boats, consisting of eight launched between 1934 and 1937. These small submarines performed well against the enemy. They displaced just 860 tons surfaced and 990 submerged. With a length of 217 feet, a beam of 23.5 feet, and a draft of 10.5 feet, they were driven by two diesels making a total of 1,900 bhp on the surface, with two electric motors making 1,300 bhp. Surface speed was 15 knots, submerged speed 9 knots. The boats had a range of 8,635 miles and were armed with either a single 4-inch gun and six torpedo tubes or one 3-inch gun and seven 21-inch tubes. A total of 62 S Class boats were produced.

T Class. The standard Royal Navy patrol submarine, the T-Class boats were produced in a quantity of 54, beginning in 1937. They were relatively slow at 15.25 knots surfaced and nine knots submerged, and they were small, displacing 1,325 tons surfaced and 1,570 submerged. The T-Class boats were 275 feet long, had a beam of 26.58 feet, and a draft of 14.75 feet. A pair of diesels made 2,500 bhp, with electric motors delivering 1,450 bhp. The range of the boats was 12,665 miles. The T-Class boats carried one 4-inch gun and 10 or 11 21-inch torpedo tubes. They were crewed by 56 to 61 hands.

U and V Classes. These small submarines were used in shallow and confined waters, including the Mediterranean and the North Sea. The V Class was an updated version of the U Class and was similar to it in most respects. V-Class boats displaced 670 tons surfaced and 740 submerged. They were 62.79 feet long, had a beam of 16 feet, and a draft of 15.5 feet. Two diesels made a total of just 800 bhp, and a pair of electric motors churned out 760 bhp. Surface speed was a slow 12.5 knots. Submerged speed was nine knots. The boats mounted a single 3-inch gun and four 21-inch torpedo tubes. They were used mainly for coastal operations.

FRENCH SUBMARINES

Two French submarine classes were of particular interest, the minelaying *Saphir* Class and the class of what were in effect submersible cruisers designated the *Surcouf* Class.

Saphir Class. Six boats of this class were completed between 1925 and 1929. They were designed to deploy mines stored in the space between widely separated double hulls. During the war, three of these submarines were captured by the Axis, one was scuttled, and two operated under the Free French flag for most of the war. The *Saphir* Class boats displaced 761 tons surfaced and 925 submerged. They were 216.21 feet long, with a beam of 23.36 feet and a draft of 14.11 feet. Two diesels provided propulsion on the surface, developing 1,300 bhp. Submerged, two electric motors delivered 1,100 bhp. Top speed surfaced was 12 knots; submerged, nine knots. The submarines were armed with one 75-mm gun, three 21.65-inch torpedo tubes, two 15.75-inch torpedo tubes (in trainable mounts), and 32 mines.

Surcouf Class. These four submarines were the heaviest in the world, displacing 3,270 tons surfaced and 4,250 tons submerged. They were intended to function as submersible cruisers, with good endurance (11,515 miles, surfaced) and heavy armament: two 8-inch guns, two 37 mm guns, eight 21.65-inch torpedo tubes, and four 15.75-inch torpedo tubes (in trainable mounts). The *Surcouf* boats were 360.89 feet long, with a beam of 29.53 feet and a draft of 29.76 feet. Two diesels delivered 7,600 bhp on the surface, and two electric motors delivered 3,400 hp submerged. Top speed surfaced was 10 knots; submerged top speed was five knots. The speed limitation of these submarine behemoths limited their usefulness; however, *Surcouf* was operated by a Free French crew until it sank in 1942 following a collision.

U.S. SUBMARINES

The U.S. Navy had a large submarine fleet, which, at the beginning of the war included some aging boats, but also newly developed designs.

"Old" S Class. The "Old" S class ("Sugar" boats) were of late World War I to post–World War I vintage and were considered obsolescent at the outbreak of World War II—even though the U.S. Navy still operated about 64 of them. They were

committed to combat early in World War II, but enjoyed little success against superior craft of the Axis. The boats were built in four groups, the first launched between 1918 and 1922, the other three groups soon afterward—with slight improvements. The S Class boats of Group 1 displaced 854 tons surfaced and 1,065 tons submerged. They were 219.25 feet long with a beam of 20.67 feet and a draft of 15.5 feet. Two diesels provided surface propulsion, delivering 1,200 bhp; two electric motors made 1,500 hp submerged. Top speed was 14.5 knots surfaced and 11 knots submerged. The boats were armed with one 4-inch or 3-inch gun and four to five 21-inch torpedo tubes. The boats were crewed by 42 officers and men.

Narwhal Class. The three submarines of this class were built during the 1920s and were modeled after the French *Surcouf* class, intended to serve as a kind of submarine cruiser, capable of significant endurance. The *Narwhal*-class subs could cruise 20,725 miles without refueling. They displaced 2,730 tons surfaced and 3,900 tons submerged. Their length was 370.58 feet, beam 33.25 feet, and draft 15.75 feet. Four diesels delivered 5,400 bhp on the surface, and two electric motors delivered 2,540 hp submerged. Top speed on the surface was

At the periscope *(U.S. Navy)*

17 knots, but only eight knots submerged—which was considered dangerously slow. They were used mainly for the clandestine transport of personnel—and landed select forces near Tarawa, Makin Island, and Attu in the Aleutians. Armament of the *Narwhal*-class boats included two 6-inch guns and six 21-inch torpedo tubes; later modifications increased the number of tubes to 10. A crew of 89 officers and men manned the boats.

"New" S Class. These 16 craft were built in the late 1930s and early 1940s. They were designed with double hulls for enhanced survivability and proved to be very durable boats. The submarines displaced 1,440 tons surfaced and 2,200 tons submerged. They were 308 feet long, with a beam of 26.17 feet and a draft of 14.25 feet. Four diesels delivered 5,500 bhp in a composite drive system, whereby two of the diesels were directly geared to shafts and two drove generators, which powered the electric motors. Four electric motors made 2,660 hp submerged. Top speed surfaced was 21 knots; submerged, the boats made nine knots. The boats were armed with a 3-inch gun (later upgraded to a 4-inch gun) and eight 21-inch torpedo tubes. Their crew was 75 officers and men.

Gato and *Balao* Class. The T class followed the "New" S class in 1940 and introduced improved armament. The *Gato* class, in turn, improved on the T class in terms of endurance, and 73 boats were produced. Improvements to the hull were incorporated into the *Balao* class, of which 122 were completed before the end of the war. The *Gato* and *Balao* class boats served mainly in the Pacific. The *Gato* class boats displaced 1,525 tons surfaced and 2,415 tons submerged. They were 311.75 feet long, 27.25 feet in the beam, and drew 15.25 feet. Four diesels delivered 5,400 bhp, and four electric motors made 2,740 hp. Top speed was 20 knots surfaced and 8.5 knots submerged. These submarines carried one 5-inch gun and ten 21-inch torpedo tubes. They were crewed by 80 officers and men.

Tench Class. These were the last U.S. submarines of World War II, with 33 completed between 1944 and 1946. They were similar to the *Balao* class, displacing 1,570 tons surfaced and 2,415 tons submerged. They were 311.67 feet long, 27.25 feet in the beam, and had a draft of 15.25 feet. Four diesels produced 5,400 bhp, and two electric motors delivered 2,740 hp. Surface speed was 20 knots; submerged top speed was nine knots. The submarines had excellent endurance at 13,245 miles. They were armed with two 5-inch guns and had ten 21-inch torpedo tubes.

GERMAN SUBMARINES

The German navy in World War II was largely a submarine fleet, especially after KARL DÖNITZ took over naval command from ERICH RAEDER. Although the TREATY OF VERSAILLES barred Germany from producing or operating submarines, in 1935 the nation defied the treaty by building the Type II, of which a total of 50 (Type IIA through Type IID) were built before production was ceased in 1941. The Type II was a coastal submarine, intended mainly for short-range defense. In the IID configuration, it displaced only 314 tons surfaced and 364 tons submerged. It was 144 feet long, with a beam of 16 feet and a draft of 12 feet 9 inches. Two diesels delivered 700 bhp and two electric motors delivered 410 hp. Surfaced speed was 13 knots, submerged a very slow four knots. The boats were armed with one to four 20-mm AA guns and three 21-inch torpedo tubes. They were crewed by 25 officers and men.

Type VII. The Type VII was originally built for Germany by Finland during the 1930s. Five iterations were produced: Type VIIA through Type VIIF. (A Type VIIE was planned but never produced.) In contrast to the Type II, the Type VII was designed as a seagoing submarine—although it was still small by World War II standards. It displaced 769 tons surfaced and 871 tons submerged, was 218 feet long, with a beam of 20 feet 4 inches and a draft of 15 feet 7 inches. Two diesels delivered 2,800 bhp, and two electric motors made 750 hp. Surface speed was 17.5 knots, submerged speed 7.5 knots. Armament consisted of one 88 mm gun, one 37 mm AA gun, and two (later eight) 20 mm AA guns. The boat had five 21-inch torpedo tubes and was crewed by 44 officers and men.

Type IX. The Type IX was available at the outbreak of the war and was a long-range (15,535-mile) submarine displacing 1,120 tons surfaced and 1,232 tons submerged. It was 251 feet long with a beam of 22 feet 2 inches and a draft of 15 feet 5 inches. Two diesels delivered 4,400 bhp, and two electric motors made 1,000 hp. Surface speed was 18.2 knots; submerged top speed was 7.5 knots. The submarine was armed with one 105 mm gun, one 37 mm AA gun, one 20 mm AA gun, and six 21-inch torpedo tubes. The ship's complement was 48 officers and men.

Type XB. This was the German navy's mine-laying submarine. It displaced 1,763 tons surfaced and 2,177 tons submerged. The Type XB was 294 feet long with a beam of 30 feet 2 inches and a draft of 13 feet 6 inches. Two diesels delivered 4,200 bhp, and two electrics 1,100 hp. Top surface speed was 16.5 knots; submerged speed was 7 knots. The minelayer had a long range of 21,375 miles. It was armed with a single 105 mm gun, a 37 mm AA gun, and as many as four 20 mm AA guns. It carried two 21-inch torpedo tubes and 66 mines.

Type XVII. This small coastal submarine was a daring experiment in high-speed underwater propulsion. As Allied antisubmarine air operations became increasingly sophisticated, it was becoming too risky for submarines to use their high surface speeds for attack. To get around this limitation, the Germans experimented with the Walter closed-cycle propulsion system, which used volatile hydrogen peroxide to produce a combination of steam and free hydrogen, which drove a turbine at very high speed. The Type XVII was able to cruise at nine knots on the surface and to blast away at 21.5 knots underwater, using its Walter engine. The only drawback was that the hydrogen peroxide-hydrogen mix was extremely unstable and explosive, making these vessels inherently unsafe.

The Type XVII displaced just 312 tons surfaced and 357 tons submerged. It was 136 feet long with a beam of 11 feet 2 inches and a draft of 14 feet. A 210 bhp diesel was used on the surface. A 77 hp electric motor could push the boat along at five knots underwater when the Walter engine was not being used. The Walter delivered 2,500 hp for the top speed of 21.5 knots. Armament consisted of two 21-inch torpedo tubes. The boat was crewed by 19 officers and men.

Type XXI. This highly advanced design was double-hulled and had three different engines: diesels for surface propulsion, electric turbines for high-speed submerged propulsion, and small electric motors for creeping propulsion underwater. The submarine displaced 1,621 tons surfaced and 1,819 tons submerged. It was 251 feet 8 inches long, with a beam of 21 feet 9 inches and a draft of 20 feet 4 inches. The diesels delivered 4,000 bhp for a top speed of 15.5 knots. The turbine electrics delivered 5,000 hp for a 16-knot submerged speed. The smaller electrics made just 226 hp and produced a top speed of 3.5 knots. Armament consisted of four 30 mm or 20 mm AA guns and six 21-inch torpedo tubes. The submarine was crewed by 57 officers and men.

ITALIAN SUBMARINES

The Italian navy had a substantial submarine fleet, most of which were small, highly maneuverable, and with limited range—all suitable for service in the Mediterranean, their principal theater of operations.

Sirena Class. This was typical of the Mediterranean boats. Twelve were built, and they were similar to the 10 submarines of *Perla* class, the 17 of the *Adua* class, and the 13 of the *Acciaio* class. The *Sirena* class boats displaced about 700 tons surfaced and as much as 860 tons submerged. They were 197 feet long, with a beam of 21 feet 2 inches and a draft of 15 feet 5 inches. Propulsion was provided by two diesel engines delivering 1,200 bhp and electric motors making 800 hp. Top speed on the surface was 14 knots; submerged, 8 knots. The submarines were armed with a 100 mm gun and two to four 13.2 mm machine guns. There were six 21-inch torpedo tubes, and the crew consisted of 45 officers and men.

Cagni Class. These four boats were large submarines—suitable for service on the Atlantic. They displaced 1,680 tons surfaced and 2,170 tons submerged. They were 288 feet 5 inches long, with a beam of 25.5 feet, and a draft of 18 feet 9 inches. Two diesels delivered 4,370 bhp, and two electric

motors made 1,800 hp. Top speed on the surface was 17 knots; submerged, the submarine made 8.5 knots. It was armed with two 100 mm guns and four 13.2 mm machine guns. There were fourteen 17.7-inch torpedo tubes, and the complement was 82 officers and men.

Archimede Class. The four submarines of this class were products of the 1930s and were used extensively in the SPANISH CIVIL WAR. They were also used in the Red Sea waters off the Ethiopian coast. Displacement was 985 tons surfaced and 1,259 tons submerged. The submarines were 231 feet long, with a beam of 22 feet 5 inches and a draft of 13.5 feet. Diesels delivered 3,000 bhp on the surface, and electric motors made 1,300 hp submerged. Top surface speed was 17 knots surfaced and eight knots submerged. The *Archimede* class had two 100 mm guns, two 13.2 mm machine guns, and eight 21-inch torpedo tubes. They were crewed by 55 officers and men.

JAPANESE SUBMARINES

In contrast to the Germans—and to the Americans—the Japanese adhered to an inflexible submarine warfare doctrine that targeted warships rather than merchant vessels. This limited their effectiveness. Japanese submarines ranged widely in size, from very large vessels to medium vessels, to small craft—and even midget submarines.

I-15 Class. These boats were typical of the large oceangoing Japanese submarines. They displaced 2,590 tons surfaced and 3,655 tons submerged. They were 356 feet long, with a 30.5-inch beam and a draft of 16 feet 9 inches. Diesels made 12,400 bhp on the surface, and electric motors delivered 2,000 hp submerged. Surfaced, the boats moved swiftly at 23.5 knots, but were fairly slow underwater at eight knots maximum. They were capable of a range of 16,155 miles. The I-15 boats were armed with a single 5.5-inch gun, two 25-mm AA guns, and six 21-inch torpedo tubes. The I-15 class had a low, horizontal structure that protruded from the conning tower and accommodated a single, folding-wing Yokosuka E14Y1 aircraft. A folding crane on deck was used to recover the plane. The submarine was crewed by 100 officers and men.

RO-100 Class. These boats were typical of the medium Japanese submarines. They were intended mainly for coastal operations, with a range of just over 4,000 miles. The submarines displaced 601 tons surfaced and 782 tons submerged. They were 199 feet long, with a 20-foot beam and a draft of 11.5 feet. On the surface, diesels produced 1,100 bhp; submerged, electric motors made 760 hp. Top surface speed was 14 knots; submerged top speed was 8 knots. The boats were armed with a single 3-inch gun (often stripped from the boats, however) and four 21-inch torpedo tubes. The RO-100 class was crewed by 38 officers and men.

Ha-201 Class. These small coastal submarines were developed late in the war for close-in defense. They were fast underwater at 13 knots, though rather slow on the surface at 10.5 knots. Surfaced displacement was 377 tons; 440 tons submerged. The boats were 173 feet long, with a beam of 13 feet 1 inch and a draft of 11 feet 2 inches. Armament consisted of one 7.7 mm machine gun and two 21-inch torpedo tubes. The boats were crewed by 22 officers and men.

"Midget submarines." The Imperial Japanese Navy became well known for its use of so-called midget submarines, small vessels crewed by one or two men and launched from mother ships—sometimes larger submarines.

The Japanese used five *Ko-hyoteki* class midget submarines in the BATTLE OF PEARL HARBOR on December 7, 1941, none of which accomplished anything of military value and one of which was sunk by the destroyer USS *Ward*.

Some midget submarines were intended for close-in covert attacks; others were KAMIKAZE, or suicide, weapons. These one-way midget submarines were of the *Kaiten* and *Kairyu* class. They were armed only with a fixed warhead and were, in fact, human-guided torpedoes. Another midget submarine, the *Kohyoteki* class, also had a fixed explosive charge; but this was intended to be used as a self-destruction measure to avoid capture, not as a true kamikaze device. These submarines were armed with two light torpedoes in muzzle-loaded 17.7-inch tubes.

Although the Japanese midget submarines were objects of interest and inspired some fear among the Allies, they were never operationally very successful.

Further reading: Blair, Clay. *Hitler's U-Boat War: The Hunted, 1942–1945.* New York: Modern Library, 2000; Blair, Clay. *Hitler's U-Boat War: The Hunters, 1939–1942.* New York: Modern Library, 2000; Boyd, Carl, and Akihiko Yoshida. *The Japanese Submarine Force and World War II.* Annapolis, Md.: Naval Institute Press, 2002; Chant, Christopher. *An Illustrated Data Guide to Submarines of World War II.* New York: Chelsea House, 1997; Lowder, Hughston E. *Silent Service: U.S. Submarines in World War II.* Baltimore, Md.: Silent Service Books, 1987; Rohwer, Jürgen. *Axis Submarine Successes of World War Two: German, Italian, and Japanese Submarine Successes, 1939–1945.* Annapolis, Md.: Naval Institute Press, 1999; Ward, John. *Submarines of World War II.* Osceola, Wis.: Motorbooks International, 2001.

Sudetenland

Strictly speaking, the Sudetenland consisted of northeastern Bohemia and northern Moravia, which, although part of Czechoslovakia, was overwhelmingly German-speaking. ADOLF HITLER defined the Sudetenland more broadly, declaring that it consisted of all ethnically German areas of Czechoslovakia contiguous with Germany and Austria.

Czechoslovakia had gained the Sudetenland as a result of the TREATY OF VERSAILLES, which brought some 3 million Germans under Czech jurisdiction. The Germans were treated well by the Czech government, but a Sudeten nationalist leader, Konrad Henlein, called on Hitler for support in recovering the Sudetenland for Germany. Hitler demanded annexation of the Sudentenland and threatened war to achieve it. This, in turn, led to the APPEASEMENT POLICY advocated by British prime minister NEVILLE CHAMBERLAIN in the MUNICH CONFERENCE AND AGREEMENT.

Further reading: Adams, R. J. Q. *British Politics and Foreign Policy in the Age of Appeasement, 1935–39.* Palo Alto, Calif.: Stanford University Press, 1994; McDonough, Frank. *Hitler, Chamberlain and Appeasement.* Cambridge: Cambridge University Press, 2002; Schmitz,

David F., and Richard D. Challener, eds. *Appeasement in Europe: A Reassessment of U.S. Policies.* Westport, Conn.: Greenwood Publishing Group, 1990.

Sun Li-jen (1899–1990) *Nationalist Chinese (Kuomintang) general called the "Rommel of the East"*

Born in Anhui Province, Sun Li-jen studied civil engineering at Tsinghua University in 1920 then completed his senior year at Purdue University, Indiana, graduating in 1925. While he was in the United States, Sun Li-jen decided he could best serve his country not as an engineer but as a military officer; for at this time, China, torn by civil war, seemed about to be overrun by both the Soviets and the Japanese. Lying about his age—so as to be eligible for admission as a cadet—he enrolled at Virginia Military Institute and graduated in 1927. He then returned to China and joined CHIANG KAI-SHEK (Jiang Jieshi) and the Nationalist Army in its Northern Expedition against the warlord generals of the Beiyang Army. Sun rapidly rose through the ranks as a field commander and became one of Chiang's top lieutenants.

During World War II, Sun commanded the New 38th Division in Burma. Although he was unable to prevent the Japanese from severing the Burma Road, his outstanding leadership earned the attention and praise of British general WILLIAM SLIM, who incorporated Sun and his 38th Division into X Force, the Chinese forces under the command of U.S. general JOSEPH STILWELL. Stilwell put Sun in the vanguard of his 1943 drive to retake North Burma and open an alternative land route into China via the Ledo Road.

Sun ended the war in command of the New First Army, which was considered the best Chinese force employed against the Japanese. It is generally credited with more victories against Japanese forces than any other Chinese unit.

In August 1955, Sun was arrested and charged with attempting a coup d'état against Chiang Kai-shek in Taiwan. He spent the next 33 years under house arrest, but was exonerated on March 20, 1988.

Further reading: Fong, Nina. *Burma War and General Sun Li-jen.* Taipei, Taiwan: Tai Yuan, 1965.

surrender documents of 1943–1945

This article discusses the documents that brought an end to hostilities in World War II. The treaties that formally ended the war and reestablished peaceful relations among the belligerents are discussed in TREATIES ENDING THE WAR.

ITALIAN SURRENDER DOCUMENTS

The first of the surrender documents culminating in the Allied victory in World War II was the Armistice with Italy, signed on September 3, 1943, at Fairfield Camp, Sicily, between the provisional government of Italy (under Marshal PIETRO BADOGLIO) and the United States and Great Britain, represented by General DWIGHT D. EISENHOWER, in his capacity as commander in chief of Allied Forces.

The armistice laid down 12 conditions:

1. Immediate cessation of all hostile activity by the Italian armed forces.
2. Italy will use its best endeavors to deny, to the Germans, facilities that might be used against the United Nations.
3. All prisoners or internees of the United Nations to be immediately turned over to the Allied Commander in Chief, and none of these may now or at any time be evacuated to Germany.
4. Immediate transfer of the Italian Fleet and Italian aircraft to such points as may be designated by the Allied Commander in Chief, with details of disarmament to be prescribed by him.
5. Italian merchant shipping may be requisitioned by the Allied Commander in Chief to meet the needs of his military-naval program.
6. Immediate surrender of Corsica and of all Italian territory, both islands and mainland, to the Allies, for such use as operational bases and other purposes as the Allies may see fit.
7. Immediate guarantee of the free use by the Allies of all airfields and naval ports in Italian territory, regardless of the rate of evacuation of the Italian territory by the German forces.

These ports and fields to be protected by Italian armed forces until this function is taken over by the Allies.

8. Immediate withdrawal to Italy of Italian armed forces from all participation in the current war from whatever areas in which they may be now engaged.

9. Guarantee by the Italian Government that if necessary it will employ all its available armed forces to insure prompt and exact compliance with all the provisions of this armistice.

10. The Commander in Chief of the Allied Forces reserves to himself the right to take any measure which in his opinion may be necessary for the protection of the interests of the Allied Forces for the prosecution of the war, and the Italian Government binds itself to take such administrative or other action as the Commander in Chief may require, and in particular the Commander in Chief will establish Allied Military Government over such parts of Italian territory as he may deem necessary in the military interests of the Allied Nations.

11. The Commander in Chief of the Allied Forces will have a full right to impose measures of disarmament, demobilization, and demilitarization.

12. Other conditions of a political, economic, and financial nature with which Italy will be bound to comply will be transmitted at a later date.

On September 23, 1943, the Cunningham-de Courten Agreement (officially titled the "Armistice with Italy: Employment and Disposition of Italian Fleet and Merchant Marine") was signed at Taranto, Italy, by the Allied Naval Commander in Chief, Mediterranean, and the Italian Minister of Marine. This was an amendment to the September 3 Armistice, which specified how "the [Italian naval] Fleet and the Italian Mercantile Marine should be employed in the Allied effort to assist in the prosecution of the war against the Axis powers." The agreement stipulated:

(A) Such ships as can be employed to assist actively in the Allied effort will be kept in commission and will be used under the orders of the Commander in Chief, Mediterranean, as may

be arranged between the Allied Commander in Chief and the Italian Government.

(B) Ships that cannot be so employed will be reduced to a care and maintenance basis and be placed in designated ports, measures of disarmament being undertaken as may be necessary.

(C) The Government of Italy will declare the names and whereabouts of
   (i) Warships
   (ii) Merchant ships now in their possession that previously belonged to any of the United Nations. These vessels are to be returned forthwith as may be directed by the Allied Commander in Chief. This will be without prejudice to negotiations between the governments that may subsequently be made in connection with replacing losses of ships of the United Nations caused by Italian action.

(D) The Allied Naval Commander in Chief will act as the agent of the Allied Commander in Chief in all matters concerning the employment of the Italian Fleet or Merchant Navy, their disposition, and related matters.

(E) It should be clearly understood that the extent to which the terms of the Armistice are modified to allow of the arrangements outlined above and that follow are dependent upon the extent and effectiveness of Italian cooperation.

2. Method of Operation. The Commander in Chief, Mediterranean will place at the disposal of the Italian Ministry of Marine a high-ranking Naval officer with the appropriate staff who will be responsible to the Commander in Chief, Mediterranean, for all matters in connection with the operation of the Italian Fleet, and be the medium through which dealings will be carried out in connection with the Italian Mercantile Marine. The Flag Officer acting for these duties (Flag Officer Liaison) will keep the Italian Ministry of Marine informed of the requirements of the Commander in Chief, Mediterranean, and will act in close cooperation as regards issue of all orders to the Italian Fleet.

3. Proposed disposition of the Italian Fleet.
   (a) Battleships. All battleships will be placed on a care and maintenance basis in ports to

be designated and will have such measures of disarmament applied as may be directed. These measures of disarmament will be such that the ships can be brought into operation again if it so seems desirable. Each ship will have on board a proportion of Italian Naval personnel to keep the ships in proper condition and the Commander in Chief, Mediterranean, will have the right of inspection at any time.

(b) Cruisers. Such cruisers as can be of immediate assistance will be kept in commission. At present it is visualised that one squadron of four cruisers will suffice and the remainder will be kept in care and maintenance as for the battleships but at a rather greater degree of readiness to be brought into service if required.

(c) Destroyers and Torpedo Boats. It is proposed to keep these in commission and to use them on escort and similar duties as may be requisite. It is proposed that they should be divided into escort groups working as units and that they should be based on Italian ports.

(d) Small Craft. M.A.S., Minesweepers, auxiliaries and similar small craft will be employed to the full, detailed arrangements being made with the Flag Officer (Liaison) by the Italian Ministry of Marine for their best employment.

(e) Submarines. In the first instance submarines will be immobilised in ports to be designated and at a later date these may be brought into service as may be required to assist the Allied effort.

4. Status of Italian Navy. Under this modification of the armistice terms, all the Italian ships will continue to fly their flags. A large proportion of the Italian Navy will thus remain in active commission operating their own ships and fighting alongside the forces of the United Nations against the Axis Powers.

The requisite Liaison officers will be supplied to facilitate the working of the Italian ships in cooperation with allied forces. A small Italian liaison mission will be attached to the Headquarters of the Commander in Chief, Mediterranean, to deal with matters affecting the Italian Fleet.

5. Mercantile Marine. It is the intention that the Italian Mercantile Marine should operate under the same conditions as the merchant ships of the Allied Nations. . . .

On September 29, 1943, the formal Instrument of Surrender of Italy was signed at Malta by Marshal Badoglio of Italy and Dwight Eisenhower on behalf of the United States and Britain. The surrender was unconditional and embodied the terms of the Armistice. It was amended on November 9, 1943, to include the Soviet Union and to modify Article 29 of the Instrument. That article originally stipulated: "Benito Mussolini, his Chief Fascist associates and all persons suspected of having committed war crimes or analogous offenses whose names appear on lists to be communicated by the United Nations will forthwith be apprehended and surrendered into the hands of the United Nations. Any instructions given by the United Nations for this purpose will be complied with." It was modified as follows: "Benito Mussolini, his chief Fascist associates, and all persons suspected of having committed war crimes or analogous offenses whose names appear on lists to be communicated by the United Nations and who now or in the future are on territory controlled by the Allied Military Command or by the Italian Government, will forthwith be apprehended and surrendered into the hands of the United Nations. Any instructions given by the United Nations to this purpose will be complied with." Both the original article and the amendment were mooted when Mussolini and his mistress, Clara Petacci, were captured by Italian partisans, who executed them on April 28, 1945.

On November 17, 1943, the Cunningham–de Courten Agreement was amended to satisfy Italian national pride and sovereignty by stipulating that Italian vessels employed by the Allies in the war effort shall "be manned so far as possible by crews provided by Italian Ministry of Marine and will fly the Italian flag."

ARMISTICE AGREEMENT WITH ROMANIA

An Armistice Agreement with Romania was signed on September 12, 1944, at Moscow by representatives of Romania, on the one hand, and the United States, Great Britain, and the Soviet Union, on the other. Romania agreed that, as of August 24, 1944, at 4 A.M., it had entirely discontinued military operations against the Soviet Union and had withdrawn from the war against the United Nations. Romania also stipulated that it has broken off relations with Germany and its satellites and has "entered the war on the side of the Allied Powers against Germany and Hungary for the purpose of restoring Romanian independence and sovereignty, for which purpose she provides not less than twelve infantry divisions with corps troops." Military operations would be "conducted under the general leadership of the Allied (Soviet) High Command." In addition, Romania agreed to the immediate restoration of its border with the Soviet Union per an agreement of June 8, 1940. Romanian officials agreed to take steps to disarm and intern German and Hungarian armed forces on Romanian territory. German and Hungarian citizens living in Romania would likewise be interned. The document specifically excluded German and Hungarian Jews from internment.

ARMISTICE AGREEMENT WITH BULGARIA

The Armistice Agreement with Bulgaria was signed on October 28, 1944, at Moscow by representatives of Bulgaria, on the one hand, and Britain, the United States, and the Soviet Union, on the other. The document included standard clauses concerning cessation of hostilities, severance of relations with Germany, and submission to Allied occupation and control, as well as a stipulation that Bulgaria would return "to the Soviet Union, to Greece and Yugoslavia and to the other United Nations, by the dates specified by the Allied Control Commission and in a good state of preservation, all valuables and materials removed during the war by Germany or Bulgaria from United Nations territory and belonging to state, public or cooperative organizations, enterprises, institutions or individual citizens, such as factory and works equipment, locomotives, rolling-stock, tractors, motor vehicles, historic monuments, museum treasures and any other property." Article 12 obligated Bulgaria "to hand over as booty to the Allied (Soviet) High Command all war material of Germany and her satellites located on Bulgarian territory, including vessels of the fleets of Germany and her satellites located in Bulgarian waters."

ARMISTICE AGREEMENT WITH HUNGARY

The Armistice Agreement with Hungary was signed on January 20, 1945, at Moscow by representatives of Hungary, on the one hand, and the Soviet Union, Britain, and the United States, on the other. In addition to such standard conditions of armistice as immediate cessation of hostilities, severance of relations with Germany, disarming of all Axis soldiers within Hungary, and so on, the armistice specified the following in Article 5:

> The Government of Hungary will immediately release, regardless of citizenship and nationality, all persons held in confinement in connection with their activities in favor of the United Nations or because of their sympathies with the United Nations' cause or for racial or religious reasons, and will repeal all discriminatory legislation and disabilities arising therefrom.

> The Government of Hungary will take all necessary measures to ensure that all displaced persons or refugees within the limits of Hungarian territory, including Jews and stateless persons, are accorded at least the same measure of protection and security as its own nationals.

GERMAN SURRENDER DOCUMENTS

On May 4, 1945, the "Instrument of Surrender of All German Armed Forces in Holland, in Northwest Germany Including All Islands, and in Denmark" was signed at Reims, France, by British field marshal BERNARD LAW MONTGOMERY, on behalf of the Allies, and by a group of German commanders on behalf of Germany, having been authorized by Admiral KARL DÖNITZ, who had been designated by ADOLF HITLER as head of state immediately before Hitler committed suicide. The text of the surrender instrument follows:

> 1. The German Command agrees to the surrender of all armed forces in HOLLAND, in northwest GERMANY including the FRISIAN ISLANDS and HELIGOLAND and all islands, in SCHLESWIG-HOLSTEIN, and in DENMARK, to the C. in C. 22 Army Group.

> This to include all naval ships in these areas

> These forces to lay down their arms and to surrender unconditionally.

2. All hostilities on land, on sea, or in the air by German forces in the above areas to cease at 0800 hrs. British Double Summer Time on Saturday 5 May 1945.

3. The German command to carry out at once, and without argument or comment, all further orders that will be issued by the Allied Powers on any subject.

4. Disobedience of orders, or failure to comply with them, will be regarded as a breach of these surrender terms and will be dealt with by the Allies in accordance with the laws and usages of war.

5. This instrument of surrender is independent of, without prejudice to, and will be superseded by any general instrument of surrender imposed by or on behalf of the Allied Powers and applicable to Germany and the German armed forces as a whole.

6. This instrument of surrender is written in English and in German.

The English version is the authentic text.

7. The decision of the Allied Powers will be final if any doubt or dispute arise as to the meaning or interpretation of the surrender terms.

On May 7, at Reims, details regarding the surrender and disposition of German military assets were issued by the supreme allied commander and acknowledged by the German high command. Most significantly, a message was dispatched to all U-Boats at sea:

Carry out the following instructions forthwith which have been given by the Allied Representatives

(A) Surface immediately and remain surfaced.

(B) Report immediately in P/L your position in latitude and longitude and number of your "U" Boat to nearest British, US, Canadian or Soviet coast W/T station on 500 kc/s (600 metres) and to call sign GZZ 10 on one of the following high frequencies: 16845-12685 or 5970 kc/s.

(C) Fly a large black or blue flag by day.

(D) Burn navigation lights by night.

(E) Jettison all ammunition, remove breach-blocks from guns and render torpedos safe by removing pistols.

All mines are to be rendered safe.

(F) Make all signals in P/L.

(G) Follow strictly the instructions for proceeding to Allied ports from your present area given in immediately following message.

(H) Observe strictly the orders of Allied Representatives to refrain from scuttling or in any way damaging your "U" Boat.

2. These instructions will be repeated at two-hour intervals until further notice.

Also on May 7, 1945, at Reims, an Act of Military Surrender was concluded by the supreme allied commander (with U.S. and Soviet commanders present and a Free French commander witnessing) and signed by the German high command. The principal sentence ran, simply: "We the undersigned, acting by authority of the German High Command, hereby surrender unconditionally to the Supreme Commander, Allied Expeditionary Forces and simultaneously to the Soviet High Command all forces on land, sea and in the air who are at this date under German control." The document continued:

2. The German High Command will at once issue orders to all German military, naval and air authorities and to all forces under German control to cease active operations at '2301' hours Central European time on '8 May' and to remain in the positions occupied at that time. No ship, vessel, or aircraft is to be scuttled, or any damage done to their hull, machinery or equipment.

3. The German High Command will at once issue to the appropriate commander, and ensure the carrying out of any further orders issued by the Supreme Commander, Allied Expeditionary Force and by the Soviet High Command.

4. This act of military surrender is without prejudice to, and will be superseded by any general instrument of surrender imposed by, or on behalf of the United Nations and applicable to GERMANY and the German armed forces as a whole.

5. In the event of the German High Command or any of the forces under their control failing to act in accordance with this Act of Surrender, the Supreme Commander, Allied Expeditionary Force and the Soviet High Command will take such punitive or other action as they deem appropriate.

The Reims document was followed on May 8, at the insistence of JOSEPH STALIN, by a definitive Act of Surrender, signed at Berlin. Signatories included the supreme commander, Allied Expeditionary Forces, and Supreme High Command of the Red Army, on the one side, and the German High Command on the other:

1. We the undersigned, acting by authority of the German High Command, hereby surrender unconditionally to the Supreme Commander, Allied Expeditionary Force and simultaneously to the Supreme High Command of the Red Army all forces on land, at sea, and in the air who are at this date under German control.

2. The German High Command will at once issue order to all German military, naval and air authorities and to all forces under German control to cease active operations at 2301 hours Central European time on 8th May 1945, to remain in all positions occupied at that time and to disarm completely, handing over their weapons and equipment to the local allied commanders or officers designated by Representatives of the Allied Supreme Commands. No ship, vessel, or aircraft is to be scuttled, or any damage done to their hull, machinery or equipment, and also to machines of all kinds, armament, apparatus, and all the technical means of prosecution of war in general.

3. The German High Command will at once issue to the appropriate commanders, and ensure the carrying out of any further orders issued by the Supreme Commander, Allied Expeditionary Force and by the Supreme Command of the Red Army.

4. This act of military surrender is without prejudice to, and will be superseded by any general instrument of surrender imposed by, or on behalf of the United Nations and applicable to GERMANY and the German armed forces as a whole.

5. In the event of the German High Command or any of the forces under their control failing to act in accordance with this Act of Surrender, the Supreme Commander, Allied Expeditionary Force and the Supreme High Command of the Red Army will take such punitive or other action as they deem appropriate.

6. This Act is drawn up in the English, Russian and German languages. The English and Russian are the only authentic texts.

On June 5, 1945, at Berlin, representatives of the Provisional Government of France, the Soviet Union, Britain, and the United States issued an "Allied Declaration on Control of Germany," which was the official instrument by which the Allies assumed control of the German government after Germany's unconditional surrender:

The German armed forces on land, at sea and in the air have been completely defeated and have surrendered unconditionally and Germany, which bears responsibility for the war, is no longer capable of resisting the will of the victorious Power. The unconditional surrender of Germany has thereby been effected, and Germany has become subject to such requirements as may now or hereafter be imposed upon her . . .

ARTICLE 1

Germany, and all German military, naval and air authorities and all forces under German control shall immediately cease hostilities in all theatres of war against the forces of the United Nations on land, at sea and in the air.

ARTICLE 2

(a) All armed forces of Germany or under German control, wherever they may be situated, including land, air, anti-aircraft and naval forces, the S.S., S.A. and Gestapo, and all other forces of auxiliary organisations equipped with weapons, shall be completely disarmed, handing over their weapons and equipment to local Allied Commanders or to officers designated by the Allied Representatives

(b) The personnel of the formations and units of all the forces referred to in paragraph (a) above shall, at the discretion of the Commander-in-Chief of the Armed Forces of the Allied State concerned, be declared to be prisoners of war, pending further decisions, and shall be subject to such conditions and directions as may be prescribed by the respective Allied Representatives.

(c) All forces referred to in paragraph (a) above, wherever they may be, will remain in their present positions pending instructions from the Allied Representatives.

(d) Evacuation by the said forces of all territories outside the frontiers of Germany as they existed on the 31st December, 1937, will proceed according to instructions to be given by the Allied Representatives.

(e) Detachments of civil police to be armed with small arms only, for the maintenance of order and for guard duties, will be designated by the Allied Representatives.

ARTICLE 3

(a) All aircraft of any kind or nationality in Germany or German-occupied or controlled territories or waters, military, naval or civil, other than aircraft in the service of the Allies, will remain on the ground, on the water or aboard ships pending further instructions.

(b) All German or German-controlled aircraft in or over territories or waters not occupied or controlled by Germany will proceed to Germany or to such other place or places as may be specified by the Allied Representatives.

ARTICLE 4

(a) All German or German-controlled naval vessels, surface and submarine, auxiliary naval craft, and merchant and other shipping, wherever such vessels may be at the time of this Declaration, and all other merchant ships of whatever nationality in German ports, will remain in or proceed immediately to ports and bases as specified by the Allied Representatives. The crews of such vessels will remain on board pending further instructions.

(b) All ships and vessels of the United Nations, whether or not title has been transferred as the result of prize court or other proceedings, which are at the disposal of Germany or under German control at the time of this Declaration, will proceed at the dates and to the ports or bases specified by the Allied Representatives.

ARTICLE 5

(a) All or any of the following articles in the possession of the German armed forces or under German control or at German disposal will be held intact and in good condition at the disposal of the Allied Representatives, for such purposes and at such times and places as they may prescribe:

(i) all arms, ammunition, explosives, military equipment, stores and supplies and other implements of war of all kinds and all other war materials;

(ii) all naval vessels of all classes, both surface and submarine, auxiliary naval craft and all merchant shipping, whether afloat, under repair or construction, built or building;

(iii) all aircraft of all kinds, aviation and anti-aircraft equipment and devices;

(iv) all transportation and communications facilities and equipment, by land, water or air;

(v) all military installations and establishments, including airfields, seaplane bases, ports and naval bases, storage depots, permanent and temporary land and coast fortifications, fortresses and other fortified areas, together with plans and drawings of all such fortifications, installations and establishments;

(vi) all factories, plants, shops, research institutions, laboratories, testing stations, technical data, patents, plans, drawings and inventions, designed or intended to produce or to facilitate the production or use of the articles, materials, and facilities referred to in sub-paragraphs (i), (ii), (iii), (iv) and (v) above or otherwise to further the conduct of war.

(b) At the demand of the Allied Representatives the following will be furnished:

(i) the labour, services and plant required for the maintenance or operation of any of the six categories mentioned in paragraph (a) above; and

(ii) any information or records that may be required by the Allied Representatives in connection with the same.

(c) At the demand of the Allied Representatives all facilities will be provided for the movement of Allied troops and agencies, their equipment and supplies, on the railways, roads and other land communications or by sea, river or air. All means of transportation will be maintained in good order and repair, and the labour, services and plant necessary therefor will be furnished.

ARTICLE 6

(a) The German authorities will release to the Allied Representatives, in accordance with the procedure to be laid down by them, all prisoners of war at present in their power, belonging to the forces of the United Nations, and will furnish full lists of these persons, indicating the places of their detention in Germany or territory occupied by Germany. Pending the release of such prisoners of war, the German authorities and people will protect them in their persons and property and provide them with adequate food, clothing, shelter, medical attention and money in accordance with their rank or official position.

(b) The German authorities and people will in like manner provide for and release all other nationals of the United Nations who are confined, interned or otherwise under restraint, and all other persons who may be confined, interned or otherwise under restraint for political reasons or as a result of any Nazi action, law or regulation which discriminates on the ground of race, colour, creed or political belief.

(c) The German authorities will, at the demand of the Allied Representatives, hand over control of places of detention to such officers as may be designated for the purpose by the Allied Representatives.

ARTICLE 7

The German authorities concerned will furnish to the Allied Representatives:

(a) full information regarding the forces referred to in Article 2 (a), and, in particular, will furnish forthwith all information which the Allied Representatives may require concerning the numbers, locations and dispositions of such forces, whether located inside or outside Germany;

(b) complete and detailed information concerning mines, minefields and other obstacles to movement by land, sea or air, and the safety lanes in connection therewith. All such safety lanes will be kept open and clearly marked; all mines, minefields and other dangerous obstacles will as far as possible be rendered safe, and all aids to navigation will be reinstated. Unarmed

German military and civilian personnel with the necessary equipment will be made available and utilized for the above purposes and for the removal of mines, minefields and other obstacles as directed by the Allied Representatives.

ARTICLE 8

There shall be no destruction, removal, concealment, transfer or scuttling of, or damage to, any military, naval, air, shipping, port, industrial and other like property and facilities and all records and archives, wherever they may be situated, except as may be directed by the Allied Representatives.

ARTICLE 9

Pending the institution of control by the Allied Representatives over all means of communication, all radio and telecommunication installations and other forms of wire or wireless communications, whether ashore or afloat, under German control, will cease transmission except as directed by the Allied Representatives.

ARTICLE 10

The forces, ships, aircraft, military equipment, and other property in Germany or in German control or service or at German disposal, of any other country at war with any of the Allies, will be subject to the provisions of this Declaration and of any proclamations, orders, ordinances or instructions issued thereunder.

ARTICLE 11

(a) The principal Nazi leaders as specified by the Allied Representatives, and all persons from time to time named or designated by rank, office or employment by the Allied Representatives as being suspected of having committed, ordered or abetted war crimes or analogous offences, will be apprehended and surrendered to the Allied Representatives.

(b) The same will apply in the case of any national of any of the United Nations who is alleged to have committed an offence against his national law, and who may at any time be named or designated by rank, office or employment by the Allied Representatives.

(c) The German authorities and people will comply with any instructions given by the Allied Representatives for the apprehension and surrender of such persons.

ARTICLE 12

The Allied Representatives will station forces and civil agencies in any or all parts of Germany as they may determine.

ARTICLE 13

(a) In the exercise of the supreme authority with respect to Germany assumed by the Governments of the United States of America, the Union of Soviet Socialist Republics and the United Kingdom, and the Provisional Government of the French Republic, the four Allied Governments will take such steps, including the complete disarmament and demilitarization of Germany, as they deem requisite for future peace and security.

(b) The Allied Representatives will impose on Germany additional political, administrative, economic, financial, military and other requirements arising from the complete defeat of Germany. The Allied Representatives, or persons or agencies duly designated to act on their authority, will issue proclamations, orders, ordinances and instructions for the purpose of laying down such additional requirements, and of giving effect to the other provisions of this Declaration. All German authorities and the German people shall carry out unconditionally the requirements of the Allied Representatives, and shall fully comply with all such proclamations, orders, ordinances and instructions.

ARTICLE 14

This Declaration enters into force and effect at the date and hour set forth below. In the event of failure on the part of the German authorities or people promptly and completely to fulfill their obligations hereby or hereafter imposed, the Allied Representatives will take whatever action may be deemed by them to be appropriate under the circumstances.

JAPANESE SURRENDER DOCUMENTS

On September 2, 1945, representatives of the empire of Japan boarded the United States battleship *Missouri* anchored in Tokyo Bay to sign an Instrument of Surrender. The Allies included representatives from Australia, Canada, China, France (Provisional Government of the French Republic), Netherlands, New Zealand, Union of Soviet Social-

General Douglas MacArthur witnesses the signatures of the Japanese representatives on the surrender instrument concluded aboard the battleship *Missouri* in Tokyo Bay on September 2, 1945. *(National Archives and Records Administration)*

ist Republics, Great Britain, and the United States. Presiding over the surrender ceremony was General DOUGLAS MACARTHUR, supreme allied commander, Pacific.

The surrender documents included the emperor's presentation of the credentials of his representatives, a foreign minister and a general:

HIROHITO,

By the Grace of Heaven, Emperor of Japan, seated on the Throne occupied by the same Dynasty changeless through ages eternal,

To all who these Presents shall come, Greeting!

We do hereby authorise Mamoru Shigemitsu, Zyosanmi, First Class of the Imperial Order of the Rising Sun to attach his signature by command and in behalf of Ourselves and Our Government unto the Instrument of Surrender which is required by the Supreme Commander for the Allied Powers to be signed. In witness whereof, We have hereunto set Our signature and caused the Great Seal of the Empire to be affixed. Given at Our Palace in Tokyo, this first day of the ninth month of the twentieth year of Syowa, being the two thousand six hundred and fifth year from the Accession of the Emperor Zinmu.

HIROHITO,

By the Grace of Heaven, Emperor of Japan, seated on the Throne occupied by the same Dynasty changeless through ages eternal,

To all who these Presents shall come, Greeting!

We do hereby authorise Yoshijiro Umezu, Zyosanmi, First Class of the Imperial Order of the Rising Sun to attach his signature by command and in behalf of Ourselves and Our Government unto the Instrument of Surrender which is required by the Supreme Commander for the Allied Powers to be signed. In witness whereof, We have hereunto set Our signature and caused the Great Seal of the Empire to be affixed. Given at Our Palace in Tokyo, this first day of the ninth month of the twentieth year of Syowa, being the two thousand six hundred and fifth year from the Accession of the Emperor Zinmu.

The Instrument of Surrender itself was a brief document, beginning with the Japanese acceptance of the provisions of the POTSDAM DECLARATION and concluding with the relinquishment to the supreme commander for the Allied powers all government authority:

We, acting by command of and in behalf of the Emperor of Japan, the Japanese Government and the Japanese Imperial General Headquarters, hereby accept the provisions set forth in the declaration issued by the heads of the Governments of the United States, China, and Great Britain on 26 July 1945 at Potsdam, and subsequently adhered to by the Union of Soviet Socialist Republics, which four powers are hereafter referred to as the Allied Powers.

We hereby proclaim the unconditional surrender to the Allied Powers of the Japanese Imperial General Headquarters and of all Japanese armed forces and all armed forces under the Japanese control wherever situated.

We hereby command all Japanese forces wherever situated and the Japanese people to cease hostilities forthwith, to preserve and save from damage all ships, aircraft, and military and civil property and to comply with all requirements which may be imposed by the Supreme Commander for the Allied Powers or by agencies of the Japanese Government at his direction.

We hereby command the Japanese Imperial Headquarters to issue at once orders to the Commanders of all Japanese forces and all forces under Japanese control wherever situated to surrender unconditionally themselves and all forces under their control. We hereby command all civil, military and naval officials to obey and enforce all proclamations, and orders and directives deemed by the Supreme Commander for the Allied Powers to be proper to effectuate this surrender and issued by him or under his authority and we direct all such officials to remain at their posts and to continue to perform their non-combatant duties unless specifically relieved by him or under his authority.

We hereby undertake for the Emperor, the Japanese Government and their successors to carry out the provisions of the Potsdam Declaration in good faith, and to issue whatever orders and take whatever actions may be required by the Supreme Commander for the Allied Powers or by any other designated representative of the Allied Powers for the purpose of giving effect to that Declaration.

We hereby command the Japanese Imperial Government and the Japanese Imperial General Headquarters at once to liberate all allied prisoners of war and civilian internees now under Japanese control and to provide for their protection, care, maintenance and immediate transportation to places as directed.

The authority of the Emperor and the Japanese Government to rule the state shall be subject to the Supreme Commander for the Allied Powers who will take such steps as he deems proper to effectuate these terms of surrender.

On the same day that the Instrument of Surrender was signed, Hirohito issued a proclamation on receipt of the surrender documents:

Accepting the terms set forth in the Declaration issued by the heads of the Governments of the United States, Great Britain, and China on July 26th, 1945 at Potsdam and subsequently adhered to by the Union of Soviet Socialist Republics, We have commanded the Japanese Imperial Government and the Japanese Imperial General Headquarters to sign on Our behalf the Instrument of Surrender presented by the Supreme Commander for the Allied Powers and to issue General Orders to the Military and Naval Forces in accordance with the direction of the Supreme Commander for the Allied Powers. We command all Our people forthwith to cease hostilities, to lay down their arms and faithfully to carry out all the provisions of Instrument of Surrender and the General Orders issued by the Japanese Imperial General Headquarters hereunder. This second day of the ninth month of the twentieth year of Syowa.

On September 3, 1945, General YAMASHITA TOMOYUKI, commanding the Imperial Japanese Army in the Philippines, and Vice Adm. Denhici Okochi, commanding the Imperial Japanese Navy in the Philippines, signed "Surrender of the Japanese and Japanese-Controlled Armed Forces in the Philippine Islands to the Commanding General United States Army Forces, Western Pacific" at Camp John Hay, Baguio, Mountain Province, Luzon, Philippine Islands. Like the document signed on the *Missouri,* the instrument by which the Japanese commanders surrendered their forces in the Philippines was based on Emperor Hirohito's acceptance of the terms for unconditional surrender laid down in the Potsdam Declaration. The text of the document was brief:

Pursuant to and in accordance with the proclamation of the Emperor of Japan accepting the terms set forth in the declaration issued by the heads of the Governments of the United States, Great Britain, and China on 26 July 1945; at Potsdam and subsequently adhered to by the Union of Soviet Socialist Republics; and to the formal instrument of surrender of the Japanese Imperial Government and the Japanese Imperial General Headquarters signed at Tokyo Bay at 0908 on 2 September 1945:

1. Acting by command of and in behalf of the Emperor of Japan, the Japanese Imperial Government and the Japanese Imperial General Headquarters, We hereby surrender unconditionally to the Commanding General, United States Army Forces, Western Pacific, all Japanese and Japanese-controlled armed forces, air, sea, ground and auxiliary, in the Philippine Islands.

2. We hereby command all Japanese forces wherever situated in the Philippine Islands to cease hostilities forthwith, to preserve and save from damage all ships, aircraft, and military and civil property, and to comply with all requirements which may be imposed by the Commanding General, United States Army Forces, Western Pacific, or his authorized representatives.

3. We hereby direct the commanders of all Japanese forces in the Philippine Islands to issue at once to all forces under their command to surrender unconditionally themselves and all forces under their control, as prisoners of war, to the nearest United States Force Commander.

4. We hereby direct the commanders of all Japanese forces in the Philippine Islands to surrender intact and in good order to the nearest United States Army Force Commander, at times and at places directed by him, all equipment and supplies of whatever nature under their control.

5. We hereby direct the commanders of all Japanese forces in the Philippine Islands at once to liberate all Allied prisoners of war and civilian internees under their control, and to provide for their protection, care, maintenance and immediate transportation to places as directed by the nearest United States Army Force Commander.

6. We hereby undertake to transmit the directives given in Paragraphs 1 through 5, above, to all Japanese forces in the Philippine Islands immediately by all means within our power, and further to furnish to the Commanding General, United States Army Forces, Western Pacific, all necessary Japanese emissaries fully empowered to bring about the surrender of Japanese forces in the Philippine Islands with whom we are not in contact.

7. We hereby undertake to furnish immediately to the Commanding General, United States Army Forces, Western Pacific, a statement of the designation, numbers, locations, and commanders of all Japanese armed forces, ground, sea, or air, in the Philippine Islands.

8. We hereby undertake faithfully to obey all further proclamations, orders and directives deemed by the Commanding General, United States Armed Forces, Western Pacific, to be

proper to effectuate this surrender. Signed at Camp John Hay, Baguio, Mountain Province, Luzon, Philippine Islands, at 1210 hours 3 September 1945.

On September 9, 1945, at Seoul, Korea, commanders of Japanese ground, air, and naval forces in Korea, north and south of 38 degrees north latitude and commanders of United States forces in Korea signed "Formal Surrender by the Senior Japanese Ground, Sea, Air and Auxiliary Forces Commands Within Korea South of 38 North Latitude to the Commanding General, United States Army Forces in Korea, for and in Behalf of the Commander-in-Chief United States Army Forces, Pacific." The Japanese governor-general of Korea signed a separate acknowledgment of the document.

The document surrendered Japanese forces south of the 38th parallel to the United States Army Forces in Korea; although territory north of the 38th parallel lay outside of U.S. Army authority—and under Soviet control—the Japanese commander of forces in that region also signed the surrender document. The text is as follows:

WHEREAS an Instrument of Surrender was on the 2d day of September 1945 by command of and behalf of the Emperor of Japan, the Japanese Government and the Japanese Imperial Headquarters signed by Foreign Minister Mamouru Shigemitsu by command and in behalf of the Emperor of Japan, the Japanese Government and by Yoshijiro Umezu by command of and in behalf of the Japanese Imperial Headquarters and

WHEREAS the terms of the Instrument of Surrender were subsequently as follows:

"1. We, acting by command of and in behalf of the Emperor of Japan, the Japanese Government and the Japanese Imperial General Headquarters, hereby accept the provisions set forth in the declaration issued by the heads of the Governments of the United States, China, and Great Britain on 26 July 1945 at Potsdam, and subsequently adhered to by the Union of Soviet Socialist Republics, which four powers are hereafter referred to as the Allied Powers.

"2. We hereby proclaim the unconditional surrender to the Allied Powers of the Japanese Imperial General Headquarters and of all Japanese armed forces and all armed forces under the Japanese control wherever situated.

"3. We hereby command all Japanese forces wherever situated and the Japanese people to cease hostilities forthwith, to preserve and save from damage all ships, aircraft, and military and civil property and to comply with all requirements which my be imposed by the Supreme Commander for the Allied Powers or by agencies of the Japanese Government at his direction.

"4. We hereby command the Japanese Imperial Headquarters to issue at once orders to the Commanders of all Japanese forces and all forces under Japanese control wherever situated to surrender unconditionally themselves and all forces under their control.

"5. We hereby command all civil, military and naval officials to obey and enforce all proclamations, and orders and directives deemed by the Supreme Commander for the Allied Powers to be proper to effectuate this surrender and issued by him or under his authority and we direct all such officials to remain at their posts and to continue to perform their non-combatant duties unless specifically relieved by him or under his authority.

"6. We hereby undertake for the Emperor, the Japanese Government and their successors to carry out the provisions of the Potsdam Declaration in good faith, and to issue whatever orders and take whatever actions may be required by the Supreme Commander for the Allied Powers or by any other designated representative of the Allied Powers for the purpose of giving effect to that Declaration.

"7. We hereby command the Japanese Imperial Government and the Japanese Imperial General Headquarters at once to liberate all allied prisoners of war and civilian internees now under Japanese control and to provide for their protection, care, maintenance and immediate transportation to places as directed.

"8. The authority of the Emperor and the Japanese Government to rule the state shall be subject to the Supreme Commander for the Allied Powers who will take such steps as he deems proper to effectuate these terms of surrender."

WHEREAS the terms of surrender were, on the 2d day of September 1945 as given by the United States, the Republic of China, the United Kingdom, the Soviet Union of Socialist Republics and other allied powers, accepted by the Imperial Japanese Government, and

WHEREAS on the 2d day of September 1945 the Imperial General Headquarters by direction of the Emperor has ordered all its commanders in Japan and abroad to cause the Japanese Armed Forces and Japanese controlled forces under their command to cease hostilities at once, to lay down their arms and remain in their present locations and to surrender unconditionally to commanders acting in behalf of the United States, the Republic of China, the United Kingdom, the British Empire and the Union of Socialist Republics, and

WHEREAS the Imperial General Headquarters, its senior commanders and all ground, sea, air and auxiliary forces in the main islands of Japan, minor islands adjacent thereto, Korea south of 38 north latitude and the Philippines were directed to surrender to the Commander-in-Chief of the United States Army Forces, Pacific and

WHEREAS the Commander-in-Chief of the United States Army Forces, Pacific has appointed the Commanding General, XXIV Corps as the Command General, United States Army Forces in Korea, and has directed him as such to act for the Commander-in-Chief United States Army Forces, Pacific in the reception of the surrender of the senior Japanese commanders of all Japanese ground, sea, air and auxiliary forces in Korea south of 38 north latitude and all islands adjacent thereto. Now therefor

We, the undersigned, senior Japanese commanders of all Japanese ground, sea, air and auxiliary forces in Korea south of 38 north latitude, do hereby acknowledge:

a. That we have been duly advised and fully informed of the contents of the Proclamation by the Emperor of Japan, the Instrument of Surrender and the orders herein above referred to.

b. That we accept our duties and obligations under said instruments and orders and recognize

the necessity for our strict compliance therewith and adherence thereto.

c. That the Commanding General, United States Army Forces in Korea, is the duly authorized representative of the Commander-in-Chief United States Army Forces, Pacific and that we will completely and immediately carry out and put into effect his instructions.

Finally, we do hereby formally and unconditionally surrender to the Commanding General, United States Army Forces in Korea, all persons in Korea south of 38 degrees North Latitude who are in the Armed Forces of Japan, and all military installations, ordnance, ships, aircraft, and other military equipment or property of every kind or description in Korea, including all islands adjacent thereto, south of 38 degrees North Latitude over which we exercise jurisdiction or control.

In case of conflict or ambiguity between the English text of this document and any translation thereof, the English shall prevail. Signed at SEOUL, KOREA at 1630 hours on the 9th day of September 1945.

On September 12, 1945, at Singapore, the supreme allied commander, Southeast Asia (Lord LOUIS MOUNTBATTEN) and the supreme commander, Japanese Expeditionary Forces, Southern Regions concluded the "Instrument of Surrender of Japanese Forces under the Command or Control of the Supreme Commander, Japanese Expeditionary Forces, Southern Regions, Within the Operational Theatre of the Supreme Allied Commander, South East Asia." The text of the document was straightforward:

1. In pursuance of and in compliance with:

   (a) the Instrument of Surrender signed by the Japanese plenipotentiaries by command and on behalf of the Emperor of Japan, the Japanese Government and the Japanese Imperial General Headquarters at Tokyo on 2 September, 1945;

   (b) General Order No. 1, promulgated at the same place and on the same date;

   (c) the Local Agreement made by the Supreme Commander, Japanese Expeditionary Forces, Southern Regions, with the Supreme Allied Commander, South East Asia at Rangoon on 27 August, 1945; to all of which Instrument of Surrender, General Order and Local Agreement this present Instrument is complementary and which it in no way supersedes, the Supreme Commander, Japanese Expeditionary Forces, Southern Regions (Field Marshall Count Terauchi) does hereby surrender unconditionally to the Supreme Allied Commander, South East Asia (Admiral The Lord Louis Mountbatten) himself and all Japanese sea, ground, air and auxiliary forces under his command or control and within the operational theatre of the Supreme Allied Commander, South East Asia.

2. The Supreme Commander, Japanese Expeditionary Forces, Southern Regions, undertakes to ensure that all orders and instructions that may be issued from time to time by the Supreme Allied Commander, South East Asia, or by any of his subordinate Naval, Military, or Air-Force Commanders of whatever rank acting in his name, are scrupulously and promptly obeyed by all Japanese sea, ground, air and auxiliary forces under the command or control of the Supreme Commander, Japanese Expeditionary Forces, Southern Regions, and within the operational theatre of the Supreme Allied Commander, South East Asia.

3. Any disobedience of, or delay or failure to comply with, orders or instructions issued by the Supreme Allied Commander, South East Asia, or issued on his behalf by any of his subordinate Naval, Military, or Air Force Commanders of whatever rank, and any action which the Supreme Allied Commander, South East Asia, or his subordinate Commanders action on his behalf, may determine to be detrimental to the Allied Powers, will be dealt with as the Supreme Allied Commander, South East Asia may decide.

4. This Instrument takes effect from the time and date of signing.

5. This Instrument is drawn up in the English Language, which is the only authentic version. In any case of doubt to intention or meaning, the decision of the Supreme Allied Commander, South East Asia is final. It is the responsibility of the Supreme Commander, Japanese Expeditionary Forces, Southern Regions, to make such translations into Japanese as he may require.

With the Japanese instruments of surrender, World War II came to an end. Definitive treaties were later concluded with all of the Axis powers.

Further reading: Leiss, Amelia C., ed. *European Peace Treaties after World War II: Negotiations and Texts of Treaties with Italy, Bulgaria, Hungary, Rumania, and Finland.* Boston: World Peace Foundation, 1954; United Nations. *Surrender by Japan: Terms Between the United States of America and the Other Allied Powers and Japan, Signed at Tokyo Bay September 2, 1945, Effective September 2, 1945, Together with Proclamation by the Emperor of Japan.* Washington, D.C.: U.S. Government Printing Office, 1946; United Nations. *Surrender of Italy, Germany and Japan, World War II: Instruments of Surrender, Public Papers and Addresses of the President and of the Supreme Commanders.* Washington, D.C.: U.S. Government Printing Office, 1946.

Suzuki Kantaro (1867–1948) *Japanese privy councilor who formed Japan's last wartime government*

Suzuki was a retired admiral who, late in life, earned a wide political following in Japan. He was a moderate, who, in its last desperate months, sought an end to the war. His position on the privy council was not sufficiently powerful for him to attack, let alone overcome, the militarists, but when Prime Minister Kuniaki Koiso stepped down in April 1945, Suzuki made his move. At age 78, he became prime minister and began sending out peace feelers through various intermediaries. However, when the Allies issued the POTSDAM DECLARATION demanding unconditional surrender, Suzuki responded with apparently noncommittal ambiguity, which prompted the United States to proceed with atomic attacks on Hiroshima and Nagasaki on August 6 and 9, 1945. Nevertheless, it was Suzuki who outlined for Emperor HIROHITO the terms by which he could use his imperial power to end the war. In this, Suzuki directly opposed the militarists within the cabinet.

Suzuki resigned on August 15, after he had achieved his goal—the emperor's announcement of Japan's surrender. On the next morning, militarists

Suzuki Kantaro *(Japanese National Diet Library)*

made two assassination attempts against him, but failed. He lived quietly for three years after the war.

Further reading: Frank, Richard B. *Downfall: The End of the Imperial Japanese Empire.* New York: Penguin, 2001; Toland, John. *The Rising Sun: The Decline and Fall of the Japanese Empire, 1936–1945.* New York: Modern Library, 2003.

Sweden

At the outbreak of World War II, Sweden had a population of about 6.5 million. With a democratic government, it was a longtime neutral power and had not fought a war since 1814. The nation was militarily weak, possessing an army of 403,000 men and no tanks. The Swedish air force consisted of 596 aircraft, and the country's navy had just 47 ships in service as of September 1939. The Swedish

economy was heavily dependent on foreign trade. Although highly vulnerable, Sweden's remote northern location and its position among buffer states—Norway, Denmark, and Finland—afforded some protection. Its greatest natural resource, from the standpoint of strategic materiel, was iron ore, which it possessed in abundance. Before and during the war, Sweden was a major supplier of iron to Germany.

In spring 1939, ADOLF HITLER proposed a non-aggression pact with Sweden. The Swedish government spurned the proposal and, fearing Hitler, attempted to form a Nordic defense union. When that failed, it proposed a Swedish-Finnish alliance, which came to nothing after the Soviet Union objected. When the war began in September 1939, Sweden declared itself neutral. With the outbreak of the RUSSO-FINNISH WAR, Sweden supplied Finland with strategic materials and permitted the recruitment of a volunteer corps for Finnish service. But when the Allies called on Sweden for permission to transit its territory, they were refused. After Germany occupied Denmark and Norway in 1940, however, Sweden yielded to menacing German demands for right of transit. Sweden revoked this permission in 1943, by which time Germany had been sufficiently weakened that it was no longer in a position to intimidate Sweden into compliance with its wishes.

From early in the war, Sweden beckoned to many oppressed and endangered people as a safe haven. Large numbers of Norwegians and Danes sought refuge in Sweden, using the country as a staging point in a flight to Britain.

Further reading: Packard, Jerrold M. *Neither Friend Nor Foe: The European Neutrals in World War II.* Portland, Ore.: Fireword, 2000; Scott, Franklin D. *Sweden: The Nation's History.* Carbondale: Southern Illinois University Press, 1989.

Switzerland

At the outbreak of World War II, Switzerland was a democratic country of 4.2 million with a long tradition of absolute neutrality. Its population spoke

German, Italian, or French and it was located geographically and culturally among Italy, Germany, and France; these factors made the maintenance of neutrality difficult. Switzerland's mountainous topography presented a formidable objective for any potential invader, and the Swiss army was large—450,000 men—and well trained, although not mechanized. The Swiss air force was very small, with 150 obsolescent Swiss fighters and just 50 state-of-the-art German Messerschmidt Me-109s. Swiss military planners resolved to adopt a wholly defensive strategy, which called for French aid in the event of a German invasion. After the BATTLE OF FRANCE, Swiss planners decided that, in the event of invasion by Italy or Germany, the Swiss army would abandon most of Switzerland and concentrate its defense in the southern Alps as a "National Redoubt."

While the war on the western front raged in May 1940, the Swiss believed invasion to be imminent. French and German aircraft regularly fought within Swiss air space—and were sometimes shot down by Swiss antiaircraft artillery. Later, British aircraft flew over Switzerland en route to Germany and Italy. The Germans demanded that the Swiss black out their cities at night because the lights were being used by British airmen as navigational aids. Reluctantly, the Swiss government complied—and on several occasions Swiss cities were accidentally bombed by Allied aircraft.

Despite its neutrality, Switzerland was obliged by treaty to permit the transit of nonwar materials between Italy and Germany. This function, including the maintenance of the Simplon and Gotthard tunnels and the Brenner Pass, gave the Swiss a valuable negotiating chip in dealing with Germany. The landlocked Swiss, for their part, needed Germany, which was a source of much fuel and food.

Switzerland served as a haven for escaped prisoners of war, French Resistance agents, and Italian partisans. For refugees, Switzerland was a most unreliable destination. The country admitted some refugees and turned others away—most notoriously some 170,000 Jews who had fled France after the VICHY GOVERNMENT declared them undesirable. By the end of the war, about 400,000 refugees had been received by or had traveled through Switzerland, many under the auspices of the International Red Cross, which was headquartered in Geneva.

Like many other neutral countries, Switzerland unwillingly functioned as a center of espionage operations, most notably those of ALLEN DULLES, head of the OFFICE OF STRATEGIC SERVICES facility in Berne.

The celebrated Swiss banks prospered during World War II as repositories of money, securities, bullion, and other valuables of both the Allies and the Axis, governments as well as individuals. Despite protestations of ethical neutrality, a number of Swiss banking firms accepted funds and other loot stolen by the Nazis—including much that had been stolen from Jews—and thereby became defendants in a number of postwar lawsuits brought by survivors of the HOLOCAUST, their families, and others.

Further reading: Braillard, Philippe. *Switzerland and the Crisis of Dormant Assets and Nazi Gold.* London: Kegan Paul, 2000; Codevilla, Angelo M. *Between the Alps and a Hard Place: Switzerland in World War II.* Chicago: Regnery, 2000; Gautsch, Willi. *General Henri Guisan: Commander-in-Chief of the Swiss Army in World War II.* Asheville, N.C.: Front Street Press, 2003; Tanner, Stephen. *Refuge from the Reich: American Airmen and Switzerland during World War II.* New York: Perseus, 2000; Wylie, Neville. *Britain, Switzerland, and the Second World War.* New York: Oxford University Press, 2003.

Syria

At the outbreak of World War II, Syria, formerly part of the Ottoman Empire, was a French mandate. After French defeat in the BATTLE OF FRANCE in June 1940, Syria sided with the VICHY GOVERNMENT and, in December 1940, General Henri-Fernand Dentz was named Vichy high commissioner for Syria.

Dentz allowed German aircraft to land in Syria in May 1941, acting in accordance with protocols agreed to by the Vichy government. This triggered an Allied (Australian, British, Free French) invasion on June 8, which ended the following month in an armistice and the proclamation of an independent Syrian republic in September 1941. Free elections in 1943 supported the nationalist agenda; nevertheless, the country remained under Anglo–Free French occupation. When V-E Day ended the war in Europe, anticolonial rioting erupted in Damascus, the capital, prompting the French to bomb the city. In April 1946, both the French and the British withdrew from Syria.

Further reading: Hitti, Philip Khuri. *History of Syria Including Lebanon and Palestine,* vol. 2. Piscataway, N.J.: Gorgias Press, 2002.

Szilard, Leo (1898–1964) *Hungarian-born physicist who may be regarded as the godfather of the Manhattan Project*

Born in Budapest, Hungary, Szilard received a doctorate in physics from the University of Berlin in 1922 and joined the faculty of Berlin's Institute of Theoretical Physics. With the rise of the Nazis in 1933, Szilard, a Jew, sought refuge in Vienna and, the following year, immigrated to England, where he joined the physics faculty of the medical college of St. Bartholomew's Hospital in London. At St. Bartholomew's, Szilard collaborated with the British physicist T. A. Chalmers to create the first successful method of separating isotopes of artificial radioactive elements. This breakthrough prompted an offer of a faculty position from Columbia University in New York, which Szilard accepted in 1937.

Szilard became increasingly aware of research being conducted in Nazi Germany—led by the brilliant physicist WERNER HEISENBERG—to harness the energy of an atomic chain reaction to create a military weapon of unprecedented explosive power. With fellow physicists—and European émigrés—EDWARD TELLER and Eugene Wigner, Szilard persuaded the most celebrated German-born scientist living in America, ALBERT EINSTEIN, to endorse a letter Szilard himself composed to President FRANKLIN D. ROOSEVELT, urging that the United States immediately begin work on developing an atomic bomb. This was the origin of the Manhattan Project.

Beginning in 1942, Szilard worked in nuclear physics at the University of Chicago. He collaborated with ENRICO FERMI on the construction of the world's first nuclear reactor, in which the first controlled chain reaction took place—the necessary initial step toward creation of the atomic bomb.

Late in the war, after the defeat of Germany, Szilard led a group of fellow Manhattan Project scientists in petitioning President HARRY S. TRUMAN not to use the atomic bomb. This effort proved in vain, and in 1946 Szilard, appalled by the weapons he had helped bring into being, abruptly abandoned nuclear physics for biology, securing an appointment as professor of biophysics at the University of Chicago. He also became a passionate public proponent of the peaceful uses of atomic energy, nuclear disarmament, and close international control of nuclear weapons. To promote what he considered sane nuclear policies, he founded the Council for a Livable World.

Further reading: Lanouette, William, with Bela Szilard. *Genius in the Shadows: A Biography of Leo Szilard, the Man Behind the Bomb.* Chicago: University Of Chicago Press, 1994; Szilard, Leo. *Leo Szilard: His Version of the Facts.* Cambridge, Mass.: MIT Press, 1980; Szilard, Leo. *Toward a Livable World: Leo Szilard and the Crusade for Nuclear Arms Control.* Cambridge, Mass.: MIT Press, 1987.

T

Tanaka Raizo (1892–1969) *Japanese destroyer commander who fought many Pacific actions*

Tanaka was a brilliant destroyer commander who played key roles in the Battle of the Java Sea, the BATTLE OF MIDWAY, and the GUADALCANAL CAMPAIGN, in which he defeated a superior U.S. naval force at the Battle of Tassafaronga, a nighttime encounter off the Guadalcanal coast on November 30, 1942. Tanaka's torpedo attack severely damaged three U.S. cruisers and sank a fourth.

During the NEW GEORGIA CAMPAIGN in July 1943, Tanaka's flagship was sunk. He protested to higher command that using his destroyers to reinforce troops was a waste of resources. For this, he was dismissed and never reassigned to sea duty. In this way, the Japanese command wasted one of its most brilliant tacticians—a naval commander universally feared and admired by his Allied opponents.

Tanaka ended the war as naval commander in Burma, a sideline job.

Further reading: Fuchida, Misuo, and Masatake Okumiya. *Midway: The Battle That Doomed Japan, the Japanese Navy's Story.* Annapolis, Md.: Bluejacket Books, 2001; Parshall, Jonathan B., and Anthony Tully. *Shattered Sword: The Untold Story of the Battle of Midway.* Dulles, Va.: Potomac Books, 2005.

Tanaka Raizo *(National Archives and Records Administration)*

tank destroyers

During World War II, several combatant armies felt the need for a self-propelled antitank gun, known in the U.S. Army as a tank destroyer. Tank destroyers were less versatile than tanks and were not designed to be used against infantry; however, they were less expensive to manufacture than tanks and easier to maintain in the field.

Vehicles specifically designed for the antitank role made their debut in World War II. Some tank destroyers were designed to be lighter, faster, and cheaper than medium tanks, yet still capable of destroying heavy tanks at long range. Another type of tank destroyer was actually more heavily armored than the tanks it was intended to destroy. This latter class of vehicles was designed to fight close in and be more survivable than a conventional tank in a duel.

The German army was equipped with a tank destroyer known as the *Panzerjäger,* or "tank hunter." This was an expedient design that simply took an existing antitank gun and mounted it on an available chassis for mobility. The Germans recycled the chassis of their obsolescent Panzer I light tank as the Panzerjäger I self-propelled 47 mm antitank gun. Later, during the INVASION OF THE SOVIET UNION, they similarly adapted Panzer II by putting captured Soviet 76.2 mm antitank guns on Panzer II chassis. The result was the Marder II mobile antitank gun. The most numerous German tank destroyer type was the Marder III, which mounted a German 75 mm antitank gun on a Czech-built Panzer 38(t) chassis. The most powerful Panzerjäger was the Nashorn (Rhinoceros), which had an 88 mm gun.

The vulnerability of the Panzerjäger was its open top and thin armor. Later in the war, these deficiencies were addressed by the Jagdpanzers (hunting tanks), which provided better armor protection and superior gun mountings.

Soviet designers also created tank destroyers by mounting antitank guns on hulls without turrets. These vehicles could carry large guns, but training the gun required movement of the vehicle itself. The Soviets mounted an 85 mm gun to produce the SU-85 and a 100 mm gun for the SU-100. In both cases, the chassis was the same as that used on the celebrated T-34 tank. The Soviets mounted even heavier guns—a 122 mm gun on the ISU-122 and a 152 mm gun on the ISU-152—on an IS-2 heavy tank chassis. These heavy tank destroyers were christened *Zveroboy* (beast killer) and were highly effective against the heaviest German armor.

American tank destroyer designs (as well as those the British derived from them) were radically different from those of the Germans and the Sovi-

ets. American tank destroyers were designed for mobility and were heavily armed. In contrast to the German and Soviet designs, the American tank destroyers usually retained the conventional tank turret, albeit with an open top to save weight and to accommodate a larger gun.

The first World War II U.S. tank destroyer mounted a 75 mm gun on an M-3 half-track chassis. Later, 3-inch guns and 90 mm guns were used. Still later came the 76 mm Gun Motor Carriage M-18, which was relatively small, quite fast, and flexible—its gun fully trainable in a turret; however, the gun proved ineffective against large German tanks and was replaced by the 90 mm M-36.

The British started making tank destroyers in 1944 by converting U.S. Sherman tanks with the addition of a QF 17-pounder gun. Next, this gun was also mounted on the U.S. M-10 Wolverine, creating the Achilles. Similarly modified, the U.S. Valentine tank became the British Archer. The British also mounted the gun on a British tank chassis, the Cromwell, which resulted in the A-30 Challenger (A30).

Tank destroyers never proved as successful as tanks, mainly because of their vulnerability to counterattack and the reduced flexibility of their turretless designs. They were used almost exclusively in the defensive role.

See also ARMOR, BRITISH; ARMOR, FRENCH; ARMOR, GERMAN; ARMOR, ITALIAN; ARMOR, JAPANESE; ARMOR, SOVIET; and ARMOR, UNITED STATES.

Further reading: Yeide, Harry. *The Tank Killers: A History of America's World War II Tank Destroyer Force.* Drexel Hill, Pa.: Casemate, 2005; Zaloga, Steven. *U.S. Tank and Tank Destroyer Battalions in the ETO 1944–45.* London: Osprey, 2005; Zaloga, Steven. *M10 and M36 Tank Destroyers 1942–53.* London: Osprey, 2002; Zaloga, Steven. *M18 Hellcat Tank Destroyer 1943–97 (New Vanguard).* London: Osprey, 2004.

tanks   *See* ARMOR, BRITISH; ARMOR, FRENCH; ARMOR, GERMAN; ARMOR, ITALIAN; ARMOR, JAPANESE; ARMOR, SOVIET; ARMOR, UNITED STATES; and TANK DESTROYERS.

Taranto, Battle of

The Battle of Taranto was a raid (dubbed Operation Judgment) launched on November 11, 1940, by elements of the British Mediterranean Fleet (Admiral ANDREW CUNNINGHAM) against the Taranto naval base in southern Italy. Twenty-one obsolescent Swordfish biplane torpedo bombers were launched from the aircraft carrier *Illustrious* and attacked Taranto in two waves spaced one hour apart. Each wave was led by two pathfinder aircraft, which deployed flares to illuminate the targets, then flew toward the inner harbor in a bid to draw antiaircraft fire away from the rest of the attackers. The raid achieved total surprise, and the British aircraft managed to hit two older battleships and a cruiser, and also to damage the dockyard. The raid prompted the Italian ships to evacuate Taranto for Italy's west coast. This relieved a major threat to British convoys. British losses were light: just two aircraft.

Historically, the Taranto raid is often cited as the end of the age of the battleship and the rise of the aircraft carrier, because carrier-launched airplanes defeated two battleships in the space of two hours. More immediately, the raid was studied closely by the Japanese, who used it as a model for the tactics they employed in the BATTLE OF PEARL HARBOR. Like Taranto, Pearl Harbor was shallow, yet as the Japanese were quick to learn, airplane-launched torpedoes could still be effective in these shallow waters if they were properly modified and skillfully launched.

Further reading: Wragg, David. *Swordfish: The Story of the Taranto Raid.* London: Weidenfeld & Nicolson, 2004.

Tarawa Atoll, Battle of

The capture of the Pacific Atoll of Tarawa in November 1943 launched the MARSHALL ISLANDS CAMPAIGN, which initiated the U.S. drive across the central Pacific.

Tarawa is an atoll in the Gilbert Islands consisting of small islands, the largest of which, Betio, is no more than 2.5 miles in length. The main Japanese garrison of 4,500 troops was located on this island, extremely well dug into defensive positions. As garrison commander SHIBASAKI KEIJI boasted to his men, the island could not be taken by a million soldiers in a hundred years. Indeed, the U.S. Navy unleashed huge amounts of ordnance in preparation for the landings, including naval gun bombardment and aerial bombardment, yet made distressingly little impact on the defenses—although the preparatory attacks did disrupt Japanese communications, thereby preventing a counterattack on the first night after the landings.

The Tarawa landings on November 20, 1943, used landing vehicles, tracked (LVTs) for the first time in AMPHIBIOUS WARFARE. These were true armored amphibians, which could be deployed from landing ships into the water, then driven directly up to the beach and driven well inland, so that troops did not have to wade or walk ashore. Unfortunately, a shortage of LVTs meant that second-wave assault troops had to be carried in conventionally on LANDING CRAFT. Worse because of faulty calculation of tides, many of the landing craft ran up on coral reefs, obliging the marines to wade long distances ashore. This exposed them to enemy fire and created heavy casualties that greatly imperiled the landings on the first day. Nevertheless, under Maj. Gen. Julian Smith, the 2nd Marine Division managed to occupy positions on the southern shore of the island as well as on the western end, thereby forcing the Japanese garrison to divide. This ultimately proved fatal to the defenders, and although the enemy counterattacked with suicidal BANZAI CHARGES, the marines held their positions and, by November 23, had overrun the small island.

The victory was extremely hard-won: 1,009 marines killed and 2,101 wounded. These numbers created universal shock among the American public, who would soon discover, however, that Tarawa—"Terrible Tarawa," as marines called it—was nothing more than a baptism of fire in the central Pacific. There would be victories even more hard-won.

Further reading: Alexander, Joseph H. *Utmost Savagery: The Three Days of Tarawa.* Annapolis, Md.: Naval Institute Press, 1995; Hammel, Eric. *Bloody Tarawa: The 2d Marine Division, November 20–23, 1943.* Osceola, Wis.: Zenith Press, 2006; Sherrod, Robert. *Tarawa: The Story of a Battle.* Fredericksburg, Tex.: Admiral Nimitz Foundation, 1993.

Tedder, Arthur (1890–1967) *British air marshal who played a major role in planning the Normandy Landings (D-day)*

Born in Glenguin, Scotland, the son of a civil servant, Tedder was educated at Magdalene College, Cambridge, where he won the Prince Consort Prize for History in 1913. Instead of going on to an academic career, he was commissioned in the Special Reserve of the Dorset Regiment during World War I, then joined the Royal Flying Corps in 1916. He proved to be a superb pilot and flew bombing and reconnaissance missions before he was given command of 70 Squadron.

After World War I, Tedder was commissioned in the Royal Air Force (RAF) and in 1929 became an instructor at the RAF Staff College, Cranston. He served as head of the Air Armament School during 1934–36, was appointed director of training at the Air Ministry (1936–38), and was assigned simultaneously as air officer commander in Singapore.

British air marshal Arthur Tedder (right) and Dwight D. Eisenhower at SHAEF Headquarters, Reims, France, on the occasion of the German surrender, May 7, 1945 *(Dwight D. Eisenhower Presidential Library)*

In 1938, Tedder was promoted to vice air marshal and named director general of Research and Development in the Air Ministry. He held this post at the outbreak of World War II until 1940, when he was named air commander in the Middle East. In this post he played a key role in the NORTH AFRICAN CAMPAIGN, both before and after the United States joined the British on this front. He worked directly under General DWIGHT DAVID EISENHOWER in Africa, Sicily, and then in London, where he was a key architect of the Normandy landings in June 1944. Tedder had charge of planning and providing all-important tactical air support for the Normandy operation. He strongly advocated vigorous bombardment of the rail and communications network in France to disrupt German troop movements. His advocacy of such bombing—even at the cost of many French civilian casualties—put him at odds with other British air officers as well as with the American Eighth Air Force commander, CARL SPAATZ. Prime Minister WINSTON CHURCHILL was also deeply disturbed by the prospect of inflicting so many French civilian casualties, and he feared that Tedder allowed himself to be overly influenced by some American officers who likewise championed the extensive pre-invasion bombing. Nevertheless, it was Tedder's strategy that prevailed prior to and during the D-day operation.

Whatever Churchill's reservations about Tedder, he delegated him in January 1945 to meet with JOSEPH STALIN to outline plans for the conclusion of the war against Germany. It was Tedder who, on May 8, 1945, led the Allied delegation sent to Berlin to accept the surrender of the German government.

After the war, in 1946, Tedder was named chief of the Air Staff. He held this post until his retirement from the RAF in 1950. Created First Baron of Glenquin, he was made chair of the British Joint Services Commission, based in Washington, D.C., then returned to Britain as chancellor of his alma mater, Cambridge University.

Further reading: Tedder, Arthur. *Air Power in War*. Westport, Conn.: Greenwood Press, 1975; Tedder, Arthur.

With Prejudice: The War Memoirs of Marshal of the Royal Air Force, Lord Tedder. Boston: Little, Brown, 1967.

Teller, Edward (1908–2003) *One of the key scientists of the Manhattan Project*

Born in Budapest, Hungary, into a prosperous Jewish family, Teller was educated in Budapest, then enrolled in the Institute of Technology at Karlsruhe, Germany, where he earned a degree in chemical engineering. After graduation, he went to Munich and Leipzig, where, in 1930, he took a Ph.D. in physical chemistry. Teller became a pioneering researcher and theorist in the field of atomic physics and worked closely with the world's foremost atomic physicist, Niels Bohr, in Copenhagen. During this period he also taught at the University of Göttingen (1931–33).

With the rise of ADOLF HITLER and the NAZI PARTY, Teller recognized that, as a Jew, his career prospects in Germany were virtually ended. In 1935, at the invitation of George Washington University in Washington, D.C., he and his wife, Augusta Harkanyi (whom he had just married), came to the United States. With the atomic physicist and cosmologist George Gamow (who developed the "Big Bang" theory of the creation of the universe), Teller studied the ways in which subatomic particles may escape the nucleus of the atom during radioactive decay. While deeply immersed in atomic physics and chemistry, Teller was stunned in 1939 by a report from his early mentor, Bohr, on the successful experimental fission ("splitting") of the uranium atom. This news, together with an appeal by President FRANKLIN D. ROOSEVELT for scientists to aid in the defense of the United States against the growing dangers of Nazi aggression, led Teller to devote himself to the problem of developing nuclear weapons. Becoming a U.S. citizen in 1941, Teller joined the Italian expatriate nuclear physicist Enrico Fermi at the University of Chicago and collaborated in producing the first self-sustaining nuclear chain reaction in the world's first nuclear reactor. After this work, in 1943, J. ROBERT OPPENHEIMER, scientific director of the Manhattan Project, the massive U.S.-

Edward Teller, 1958 *(U.S. Department of Energy, Lawrence Livermore Laboratory)*

British effort to create an atomic bomb, invited Teller to become one of the first members of the team working at the top-secret Los Alamos Laboratory in New Mexico.

The task of the Los Alamos scientists was to design and build—as quickly as possible—a fission bomb, which would create an explosion by liberating the energy of a uranium-based chain reaction. Teller nevertheless became increasingly intrigued by the prospects of a thermonuclear hydrogen fusion bomb, which would use the energy liberated by the fusion of hydrogen atoms to create a bomb far more powerful than the fission weapon. Thus, although Teller played an important role in creating the atomic bombs that were used against Japan in 1945, his greater role was in leading atomic

weapons research after the war in the development of the hydrogen bomb.

In 1946, Teller joined the Institute for Nuclear Studies at the University of Chicago, even as he continued to work as a consultant at Los Alamos. When, in 1949, the Soviet Union detonated its first atomic bomb (far sooner than most American experts had thought technologically possible for that country), Teller became an increasingly passionate advocate of the new fusion bomb, which he referred to as "the Super." In this he was opposed by Oppenheimer, who chaired the U.S. Atomic Energy Commission's general advisory committee. However, President HARRY S. TRUMAN overrode the committee's recommendation, and Teller was put in charge of the development of a hydrogen bomb. In 1951, Teller collaborated with the physicist Stanislaw Marcin Ulam on a trigger mechanism for the new weapon. This resulted in a breakthrough that produced the first "H-bomb" detonation at Eniwetok Atoll in the Pacific on November 1, 1952. Ulam's role in the creation of the weapon was soon overshadowed by Teller, who was identified in the public mind as "the father of the H-bomb."

Teller's zeal in the creation of thermonuclear weapons earned the enmity of many American scientists. Worse, when he testified against his former chief, Oppenheimer, at 1954 U.S. government hearings on Oppenheimer as a potential security risk, many fellow scientists simply turned their backs on him. Despite this, Teller went on to create the nation's second nuclear weapons laboratory, the Lawrence Livermore Laboratory, in Livermore, California, in 1952. This facility became the center of U.S. thermonuclear weapon design and fabrication throughout the long Cold War period. Teller served as associate director of Livermore from 1954 to 1958 and from 1960 to 1975. He was director during 1958–60. During much of this time, he was also professor of physics at the University of California, Berkeley. A prominent and outspoken anticommunist, he continued to advocate research and production programs aimed at keeping the United States ahead of the Soviet Union in nuclear and thermonuclear arms.

Further reading: Goodchild, Peter. *Edward Teller: The Real Dr. Strangelove.* Cambridge, Mass.: Harvard University Press, 2004; Teller, Edward, with Judith Shoolery. *Memoirs: A Twentieth-Century Journey in Science and Politics.* New York: Perseus, 2002.

Ter Poorten, Hein (1887–1968) *Royal Netherlands Army commander in the Pacific theater*

Ter Poorten was born on Java, Dutch East Indies, and became an artillery officer in the Dutch army in 1911. He was one of the founding officers of the Dutch army air force, and in 1919 enrolled at the Hogere Krijgsschool staff college, then returned to the East Indies, where he rose in the officer corps.

On the eve of World War II, in July 1939, Ter Poorten was chief of the General Staff of the Koninklijk Nederlands Indisch Leger (Royal Netherlands Indies Army, KNIL), and in October 1941, after the death of Lt. Gen. Gerardus Johannes Berenschot in an airplane crash, Ter Poorten became commander in chief of the KNIL. In January 1942, with the Pacific war now under way, Ter Poorten became commander of land forces in the American-British-Dutch-Australian Command (ABDACOM), the short-lived unified command of all Allied forces in Southeast Asia. In March, after ABDACOM was dissolved, he became de facto commander of all Allied forces on Java. Outnumbered and overwhelmed by the general Japanese advance, he surrendered Java to the Japanese and spent the rest of the war as a prisoner of war. Liberated in 1945, he returned to the Netherlands.

See also NETHERLANDS EAST INDIES, ACTION IN.

Further reading: Krancher, Jan A., ed. *The Defining Years of the Dutch East Indies, 1942–1949: Survivors' Accounts of Japanese Invasion and Enslavement of Europeans and the Revolution That Created Free Indonesia.* Jefferson, N.C.: McFarland, 2003; Rees, Laurence. *Horror in the East: Japan and the Atrocities of World War II.* New York: Da Capo, 2002; Rottman, Gordon. *Japanese Army in World War II: Conquest of the Pacific 1941–42.* London: Osprey, 2005.

Terauchi Hisaichi (1879–1946) *commander of the Japanese Imperial Army's Southern Expeditionary Army Group*

The son of a Japanese field marshal and former war minister and prime minister, Terauchi inherited the title of count on the death of his father in 1919. A coup d'état in February 1936 resulted in a purge of the military from which he emerged as Japan's senior general. In March he was named minister of war under Prime Minister Hirota Koki. After Hirota's government fell early the next year, Terauchi became inspector general of military training in February 1937. In August of that year, he was assigned as commander of the North China Area Army in the SINO-JAPANESE WAR.

After Japan entered World War II as a member of the Axis, Terauchi became commander of the Southern Expeditionary Army and set up his Saigon headquarters on December 4, 1941. After the FALL OF SINGAPORE in February 1942, he moved his headquarters there.

Terauchi presided over the conquest of the southern area, including the Malay states, Thailand, and the Philippines. He was not a brilliant strategist, but he was an extraordinarily able manager and coordinator of operations. In a Japanese military rife with jealousies and back-stabbing, he was the rarest of men: an officer universally respected, who enjoyed almost universal loyalty and cooperation.

Terauchi was stricken with a cerebral hemorrhage in 1945 and was therefore unable to surrender his command in the official ceremony in Singapore on September 12, 1945. Lord LOUIS MOUNTBATTEN personally accepted his surrender on November 30, 1945, in Saigon. Mountbatten provided the ailing Terauchi with a bungalow in Rengam, Malaya, where he died in June 1946.

Further reading: Pfannes, Charles E. *The Great Commanders of World War II: The Japanese.* New York: Zebra Books, 1982.

Thailand

During World War II, Thailand was ostensibly ruled by a council of regency, governing in place of

King Ananta Mahidol, who waited out the war in Switzerland; in practical terms, however, the country was governed by a military dictator, Field Marshal Pibul Songgram, who favored the Japanese, in whom he saw the possibility of resisting Western colonial influence.

Pibul commanded an army of 50,000 men, an air force of 150 combat aircraft (many obsolete or obsolescent), and a navy consisting of a British-built World War I destroyer, nine Italian-built torpedo boats, and various small craft. Before the war, Pibul had ordered two light cruisers from an Italian shipyard, but the Italian navy preemptively commandeered these before they were launched.

Shortly after the outbreak of the war, in 1940, Britain and France concluded nonaggression pacts with Thailand, which declared itself neutral. Despite the pacts and the declaration of neutrality, Pibul attacked two neighboring French protectorates, Laos and Cambodia, in an effort to regain disputed border territory. Pibul prevailed on land, but lost at sea, and both the French and the Thais turned to Japan to mediate the dispute. In accordance with the Japanese decision, the VICHY GOVERNMENT of France ceded the disputed territory to Thailand in May 1941.

On December 8, 1941, the day after war began in the Pacific, Japan used French Indochina and Thailand as staging areas from which to launch operations against Malaya. The Thais resisted both the Japanese military activity on their territory and a British advance from Malaya through Thai land; however, on December 9, Pibul ordered an end to all resistance. On January 25, Pibul declared war on Britain and the United States (but not China). Britain reciprocated, but the United States, preferring to consider Thailand an enemy-occupied country rather than an enemy country, did not. Nevertheless, Thailand officially collaborated with the Japanese and thereby gained considerable surrounding territory by way of reward. Unofficially, a nationalist movement developed that was anti-Japanese and pro-Allies. Nai Pridi Bhanomyong's Free Thai Movement (together with at least one other resistance movement) cooperated both with the SPECIAL OPERATIONS EXECUTIVE and the OFFICE OF STRATEGIC SERVICES—respectively the British and American guerrilla and partisan coordinating agencies—to become XO Group, which fomented and organized resistance in Thailand. Thanks to Allied successes and the Free Thai Movement, Pibul fell from power in July 1944, and guerrillas wrested control of northern Thailand from the Japanese well before Japan's general surrender in September 1945.

See also MALAYA, FALL OF.

Further reading: Baker, Chris, and Pasuk Phongpaichit. *A History of Thailand.* Cambridge and New York: Cambridge University Press, 2005; Terwiel, B. J. *A History of Modern Thailand, 1767–1942.* Queensland, Australia: University of Queensland Press, 1984; Wright, Joseph J. *The Balancing Act: A History of Modern Thailand.* Bangkok, Thailand: Asia Books, 1991.

theaters of World War II

World War II was the biggest armed conflict in human history and engulfed virtually the entire globe. Historians as well as those who fought the war generally divide the conflict into geographical "theaters." These include:

Africa and the Mediterranean theater: The scene of combat from 1940 to 1943, this theater included North Africa and the Middle East.

Atlantic theater: The Atlantic Ocean and its coastal rim saw fighting from the very beginning of the war in 1939 until the very end. The Allies used the Atlantic sea lanes as a vital route for convoys, which were preyed upon by German U-boats.

China-Burma-India theater: The "C-B-I" encompassed China, Burma, and India. Here, the Japanese sought to control China and southern Asia, which was rich in many of the raw materials (especially rubber) Japan needed for its war effort. The Allies—mostly Anglo-Indian, Chinese, and American forces—had precious few military assets to devote to the theater, which made combat here especially grim.

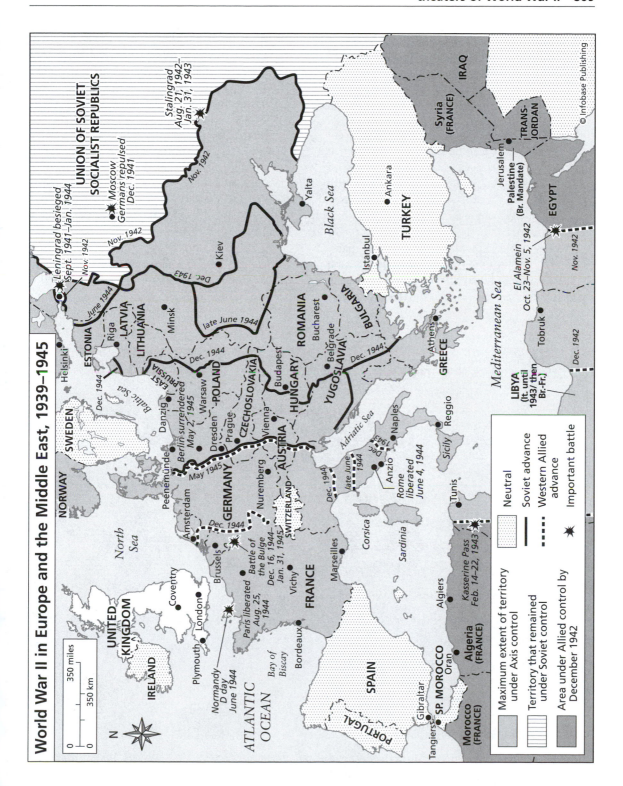

World War II in Europe and the Middle East, 1939–1945

UNION OF SOVIET SOCIALIST REPUBLICS

Stalingrad
Aug. 21, 1942–
Jan. 31, 1943

Moscow
Germans repulsed
Dec. 1941

Nov. 1942

Leningrad besieged
Sept. 1941–Jan. 1944

Nov. 1942

June 1944

Kiev

Dec. 1943

late June 1944

ESTONIA

LATVIA

LITHUANIA

Minsk

Riga

Dec. 1944

Helsinki

Black Sea

Yalta

TURKEY

Ankara

Istanbul

IRAQ

Syria
(FRANCE)

TRANS-
JORDAN

Jerusalem

Palestine
(Br. Mandate)

EGYPT

El Alamein
Oct. 23–Nov. 5, 1942

Nov. 1942

Tobruk

Dec. 1942

LIBYA
(It. until
1943; then
Br.-Fr.)

Mediterranean Sea

ROMANIA

Bucharest

BULGARIA

Belgrade

Dec. 1944

YUGOSLAVIA

HUNGARY

Budapest

Dec. 1944

Athens

GREECE

Adriatic Sea

POLAND

Warsaw

CZECHOSLOVAKIA

Prague

Dresden

EAST
PRUSSIA

Danzig

Baltic Sea

SWEDEN

NORWAY

Peenemünde

Berlin surrendered
May 2, 1945

GERMANY

Nuremberg

Amsterdam

Dec. 1944

May 1945

Vienna

AUSTRIA

SWITZERLAND

Dec. 1944

late June
1944

Rome
liberated
June 4, 1944

Anzio

Naples

Reggio

Sicily

Dec. 1943

Sardinia

Corsica

Tunis

Kasserine Pass
Feb. 14–22, 1943

Algiers

Marseilles

FRANCE

Vichy

Bordeaux

Bay of
Biscay

Brussels

Battle of
the Bulge
Dec. 16, 1944–
Jan. 31, 1945

Paris liberated
Aug. 25,
1944

Normandy
D day
June 1944

ATLANTIC
OCEAN

North
Sea

UNITED
KINGDOM

London

Coventry

Plymouth

IRELAND

N

350 miles

350 km

0

0

SPAIN

PORTUGAL

Gibraltar

Tangiers

SP. MOROCCO

Oran

Algeria
(FRANCE)

Morocco
(FRANCE)

© Infobase Publishing

Neutral

Soviet advance

Western Allied
advance

Important battle

Maximum extent of territory
under Axis control

Territory that remained
under Soviet control

Area under Allied control by
December 1942

Greece and the Balkans theater: This theater was active mainly early in the war, from 1939 to 1941, and involved initially Italy, Germany, and the Soviet Union against Greece which was assisted by the British and Romania. Fighting took place mainly in Greece including Crete, Yugoslavia, and the adjacent waters of the Mediterranean. Seized early in the war, Greece, Yugoslavia, and the rest of the Balkans remained in German hands until the end of the war—despite much partisan activity against the occupiers.

Italian theater: Active from 1943—after the Allies invaded Sicily and the Italian mainland, prompting the downfall of BENITO MUSSOLINI—until the end of the war in Europe, Italy saw some of the bloodiest fighting of the conflict in a bitter contest between Anglo-American forces and extremely determined German defenders.

Pacific Theater: A vast theater, combat encompassed the Aleutians in the north to the tropical islands below the equator in the south. The fighting spanned 1941 to 1945, beginning with the BATTLE OF PEARL HARBOR on December 7, 1941, and ending with the atomic bomb attacks on Hiroshima and Nagasaki, Japan, on August 6 and 9, 1945. The principal combatants were the United States (with British, British Commonwealth, and Philippine allies) and the empire of Japan. Fighting here was chiefly naval and amphibious, culminating, however, in the STRATEGIC BOMBING OF JAPAN.

Burials at sea were frequent events in the Pacific theater. *(National Archives and Records Administration)*

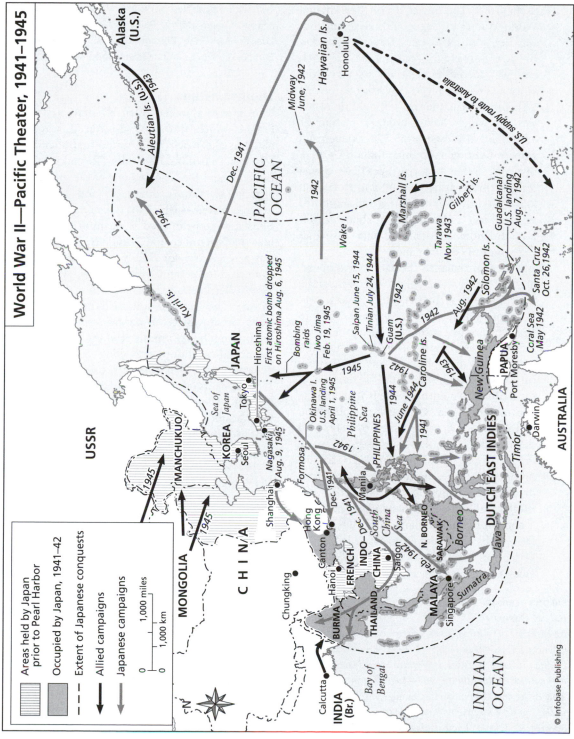

World War II—Pacific Theater, 1941–1945

Alaska (U.S.)

Aleutian Is. (U.S.) 1943

1942

Dec. 1941

PACIFIC OCEAN

Midway June, 1942

Hawaiian Is.

Honolulu

U.S. supply route to Australia

1942

Wake I.

Marshall Is.

Gilbert Is.

Tarawa Nov. 1943

Kuril Is.

Solomon Is.

Guadalcanal I. U.S. landing Aug. 7, 1942

Santa Cruz Oct. 26, 1942

Aug. 1942

1942

USSR

Sea of Japan

Hiroshima

First atomic bomb dropped on Hiroshima Aug. 6, 1945

Bombing raids

Iwo Jima Feb. 19, 1945

Saipan June 15, 1944

Tinian July 24, 1944

Guam (U.S.)

Caroline Is.

1942

1943

Coral Sea May 1942

New Guinea

PAPUA

Port Moresby

JAPAN

Tokyo

KOREA

Seoul

Nagasaki Aug. 9, 1945

Shanghai

Okinawa I. U.S. landing April 1, 1945

Formosa

Philippine Sea

1942

1945

June 1944

1944

1941

PHILIPPINES

Manila

Darwin

AUSTRALIA

Timor

MANCHUKUO

1945

1945

MONGOLIA

C H I N A

Chungking

Hong Kong

Canton

Dec. 1941

South China Sea

N. BORNEO

SARAWAK

Borneo

Java

DUTCH EAST INDIES

INDO-CHINA

Hanoi

Saigon

FRENCH

THAILAND

Feb. 1942

BURMA

MALAYA

Singapore

Sumatra

Calcutta

INDIA (Br.)

Bay of Bengal

INDIAN OCEAN

© Infobase Publishing

Legend:
- Areas held by Japan prior to Pearl Harbor
- Occupied by Japan, 1941–42
- Extent of Japanese conquests
- Allied campaigns
- Japanese campaigns

0   1,000 miles
0   1,000 km

N

Russian front: The Soviet Union had entered World War II in league with Germany, but was betrayed by ADOLF HITLER'S INVASION OF THE SOVIET UNION on June 22, 1941, and was forced to fight for its very existence against the biggest invasion in history. This theater saw the costliest fighting of the war, in which Soviet military manpower amounted to as many as 39,574,900 men and women fighting about nine million German invaders. Some historians calculate Soviet military losses at between 10 and 29 million killed, wounded, and missing, and combined military and civilian deaths at about 27 million or more. German military casualties were in excess of six million.

Western (European) theater: Encompassing Britain (air war only), France, Belgium, Luxembourg, Netherlands, Germany, and Czechoslovakia, combat spanned 1940 to 1945, beginning with the German advance into the west and with its early culmination in the BATTLE OF FRANCE and the BATTLE OF BRITAIN, followed by the occupation of most of western Europe (save Britain and the neutral nations) by Germany. The liberation of these lands began on June 6, 1944, with the Allied NORMANDY LANDINGS (D-DAY), the principal Allied invasion of German-occupied Europe. In addition to the hundreds of thousands of soldiers killed in this theater, millions of civilians died, including a portion of the 6 million Jews killed in the HOLOCAUST and many citizens killed by the aerial bombardment of cities, especially the STRATEGIC BOMBING OF GERMANY.

Further reading: Botjer, George F. *Sideshow War: The Italian Campaign, 1943–1945.* College Station: Texas A&M University Press, 1996; Carruthers, Bob, and John Erickson. *Russian Front, 1941–1945.* London: Cassell, 1999; Dunmore, Spencer. *In Great Waters: The Epic Story of the Battle of the Atlantic, 1939–1945.* Toronto: McClelland & Stewart, 1999; Sandler, Stanley, ed. *World War II in the Pacific: An Encyclopedia.* New York: Garland, 2001; Spector, Ronald H. *Eagle against the Sun: The American War with Japan.* New York: Free Press, 1985; Time-Life editors. *Conquest of the Balkans.* Alexandria, Va.: Time-Life Books, 1990; Wilmot, Chester. *The Struggle for Europe.* Westport, Conn.: Greenwood Press, 1972.

Theresienstadt

Terezin was a walled town 35 miles outside of Prague, which, during World War II, was designated as the Reich Protectorate of Bohemia and Moravia. REINHARD HEYDRICH, Reich Protector of Bohemia and Moravia and one of the prime architects of the FINAL SOLUTION and HOLOCAUST, ordered Terezin—which the Germans called Theresienstadt—to be opened as a camp (or ghetto) for Jews in November 1941. Initially, Theresienstadt was a repository for elderly Jews unfit for forced labor and for certain "privileged" Jews (including World War I veterans, former senior servants, and so on). The German administrators used it as a front, or showplace, to deceive representatives of the International Committee of the Red Cross as to the actual conditions prevailing in German CONCENTRATION AND EXTERMINATION CAMPS.

Despite its outward cleanliness and serenity, the reality of Theresienstadt was that it functioned as a transit camp for Jews (and others) ultimately bound for slave labor or death in other camps. Of 141,162 Jews consigned to Theresienstadt during the war, 88,162 were eventually sent to death camps. In 1945, 1,623 Jews were released as refugees to Sweden or Switzerland, and 16,382 were alive in the camp at the end of the war. During the war, a total of 33,456 persons, mostly Jews, died there.

Further reading: Berkley, George E. *Hitler's Gift: The Story of Theresienstadt.* Boston: Branden Books, 2002; Schiff, Vera. *Theresienstadt.* Tornoto: Lugas, 1996; Troller, Norbert. *Theresienstadt: Hitler's Gift to the Jews.* Chapel Hill: University of North Carolina Press, 2004.

Tibbets, Paul (1915–   ) *pilot of the* Enola Gay, *which dropped an atomic bomb on Hiroshima, Japan*

Paul Warfield Tibbets Jr. was born in Quincy, Illinois, and joined the Army Air Corps as a flying

Colonel Paul Tibbets about to take off for Hiroshima *(National Archives and Records Administration)*

next morning, he and his crew flew the *Enola Gay* from Tinian to Hiroshima. It was loaded with a single weapon, an atomic bomb, which Tibbets's bombardier dropped over the city at 8:15 A.M. local time.

Tibbets was decorated for his action and was widely regarded as a hero—although reviled by some as a mass murderer. Tibbets himself never professed feelings of guilt, but believed that he had performed his duty in an important military operation. He remained in the air force after the war and, in 1959, was promoted to brigadier general. His assignment in the 1960s as military attaché in India met with local political protest, and he was recalled. Tibbets retired from the U.S. Air Force on August 31, 1966 and went to work for Executive Jet Aviation in Columbus, Ohio, retiring as its president in 1987.

See also HIROSHIMA, ATOMIC BOMBING OF, and NAGASAKI, ATOMIC BOMBING OF.

Further reading: Greene, Bob. *Duty: A Father, His Son, and the Man Who Won the War.* New York: William Morrow, 2000; "Pilot: Brig. Gen. Paul W. Tibbets (USAF Ret.)," official Tibbets Web site, http://www.theenolagay.com/index.html.

cadet in 1937 at Fort Thomas, Kentucky. Commissioned a second lieutenant in 1938, he rose to command of the 340th Bomb Squadron, 97th Heavy Bomb Group, in March 1942, flying B-17 heavy bombers. Tibbets piloted the lead B-17 out of RAF Polebrook Field, England, on the U.S. Eighth Air Force's first bombing mission in Europe on August 17, 1942. He later flew in the Mediterranean theater, then was recalled to the United States to test-fly the newly developed B-29 Superfortress. In November 1944, as a colonel, he was named to command the 509th Composite Group at Wendover Army Air Field, Utah, a special bomber group that was being trained to deliver and deploy the atomic bomb under development by the MANHATTAN PROJECT.

Tibbets was responsible for developing appropriate bombing tactics and for overseeing the training of the 509th. He was deployed with his command to the Pacific island of Tinian, where, on August 5, 1945, he formally named B-29 serial number 44-86292 *Enola Gay,* after his mother. At 2:45 on the

Timoshenko, Semyon (1895–1970) *rival of Marshal Georgi Zhukov in the defense against the German invasion of the Soviet Union*

Semyon Konstantinovich Timoshenko was the son of peasant stock, born at Frumanka, near Odessa in southern Ukraine. During World War I, in 1915, he was conscripted into the tsarist army and served in the cavalry. With the outbreak of the Russian Revolution in 1917, he joined the Bolsheviks, becoming a Red Army officer in 1918 and a member of the Bolshevik Party the following year. Timoshenko saw action against the Whites during the civil war in the 1920s and, while fighting at Tsaritsyn (later renamed Stalingrad), he became a friend and associate of JOSEPH STALIN. Stalin rapidly promoted his friend in the officer corps, and by the end of the 1920s Timoshenko was given command of all Red

Army cavalry. His rise continued during the 1930s: to Red Army commander in the Byelorussian SSR (today Belarus) in 1933, then in Kiev (1935), and in the northern Caucasus and Kharkov (1937). After again serving as overall commander in Kiev in 1938, he was assigned command of the entire western border region in 1939. By this time, Timoshenko became a member of the Central Committee of the Communist Party and was so personally trusted by Stalin that he escaped the great purge of the Red Army during the 1930s, to be its senior officer.

In January 1940, during the Russo-Finnish War, Timoshenko took over command of Soviet forces, which had faltered badly under Kliment Voroshilov. Timoshenko broke through the Mannerheim Line, thereby prompting Finland to sue for peace. This victory resulted in Timoshenko's elevation to People's Commissar for Defense, which included promotion to marshal of the Soviet Union.

Timoshenko was a highly competent professional who, in contrast to many of his hidebound fellow officers, urged the rapid modernization of the Red Army. Thanks to him, a crash program of tank production was begun. However, he also reintroduced many of the harsher aspects of military discipline as practiced in the old tsarist army. This earned him a number of significant enemies.

After the Soviet Union was invaded in June 1941, Stalin assumed personal command of the Red Army and took over from Timoshenko the position of defense commissar. He assigned Timoshenko to the central front to carry out a fighting retreat from the border to Smolensk in the hope of preserving as much of the army intact as possible. Casualties were heavy, but Timoshenko nevertheless saved most of his forces, which were then deployed in the defense of Moscow.

In September, Timoshenko was transferred to the Ukraine, where the Red Army had suffered catastrophic casualties topping 1.5 million. Timoshenko's leadership did not bring victory, but he did avert further disaster by stabilizing the front. Next, in May 1942, Timoshenko led 640,000 men in a counteroffensive at Kharkov. It was a bold attempt to turn the tide of the invasion, and

although Timoshenko enjoyed some initial success, a German counter-counteroffensive soon brought his advance to a bloody halt. While he had slowed the German advance against Stalingrad, Timoshenko had failed to turn it back. This failure followed (and contrasted with) Georgi Zhukov's successful defense of Moscow in December 1941, persuading Stalin that Zhukov was the superior commander. He summarily removed his old friend from front-line command and assigned him supporting roles at the Stalingrad (June 1942), Leningrad (June 1943), Caucasus (June 1944), and Baltic (August 1944) fronts.

Now overshadowed by Zhukov, Timoshenko nevertheless continued to perform well in lesser roles and was lavishly decorated, being twice named Hero of the Soviet Union (1940 and 1965) and earning the highest Order of Victory (1945) as well as the Order of Lenin (five times), the Order of the October Revolution, the Order of the Red Banner (five times), and the Order of Suvorov (three times). After the war, he was reappointed Soviet army commander in Belarus (March 1946), the southern Urals (June 1946), and, again, Belorussian SSR (March 1949). In 1960, he was elevated to the largely honorific post of inspector-general of the Defense Ministry.

Further reading: Glantz, David M., and Jonathan M. House. *When Titans Clashed: How the Red Army Stopped Hitler.* Lawrence: University Press of Kansas, 1998; Shukman, Harold, ed. *Stalin's Generals.* New York: Grove Press, 1993.

Tito (Josip Broz) (1892–1980) *secretary-general of the Communist Party of Yugoslavia*

Born Josip Broz in Kumrovec, near Zagreb, Croatia (then part of the Austro-Hungarian Empire), Tito was one of 15 children in a peasant family. When he was 13 years old, he moved to Sisak and apprenticed himself to a locksmith. At the conclusion of his apprenticeship, he became an itinerant metalworker and joined the metalworkers' trade union. This led him to membership in the Social Democratic Party of Croatia. His socialist activism was disrupted by the outbreak of World War I in 1914. He voluntarily enlisted in the 25th Regiment of Zagreb, which marched against the Serbs in August 1914. Soon accused of disseminating antiwar propaganda, however, Broz was imprisoned but released in January 1915 after the charges were dropped. He was sent back to his regiment on the Carpathian front and was decorated for bravery. The 25th Regiment was subsequently transferred to the Bukovina front, where Broz was seriously wounded and taken prisoner by the Russians.

Broz was a POW in the Ural Mountains when the Bolshevik Revolution broke out in 1917. During the resulting chaos, he traveled to Siberia and joined the Bolsheviks, enlisting in the Red Guard during the Russian civil war. He returned to Yugoslavia in 1920 a communist—yet of a distinctly moderate stripe.

Broz joined the Communist Party of Yugoslavia (CPY) and was arrested by the government in 1923. Acquitted of sedition after a trial, he began working in a Croatian shipyard, only to be rearrested in 1925, tried, and sentenced to seven months' probation. Such harassment by government authorities strengthened Broz's resolve, and he found himself rising in the hierarchy of the CPY. By 1928, he was a deputy of the Politburo of the CPY Central Committee and secretary-general of the Croatian and Slovenian committees. Arrested yet again in August 1928, Broz was sentenced to five years' imprisonment and was not released until 1934. No sooner had he gained his freedom than he set off on a tour of Europe to promote the Communist cause. To protect his identity during these travels, he adopted the code name Tito, which became his byname from then on.

Tito went to Moscow in 1935 and worked in the Balkan section of the Comintern, the organization of international communism. In August 1936, he was named organizational secretary of the CPY Politburo; however, in 1937, JOSEPH STALIN began his infamous purges, which included the liquidation of prominent Yugoslav Communists—some 800 in all. Tito escaped the purge and was even named secretary-general of the Comintern in 1937.

He then returned to Yugoslavia to reorganize the CPY, of which he became secretary-general in October 1940.

Like the rest of the international Communist movement, Tito was stunned by the GERMAN-SOVIET NON-AGGRESSION PACT Stalin concluded with ADOLF HITLER. At the outbreak of World War II, Yugoslavia declared itself neutral, but after the pro-Axis leader Prince Paul was overthrown in a coup d'état, Hitler took preemptive action by the INVASION OF YUGOSLAVIA.

Initially, the occupation met with widespread passivity from the Yugoslavs, but when Hitler launched the INVASION OF THE SOVIET UNION on June 22, 1941, abrogating the nonaggression pact, Tito seized the initiative and led a well-coordinated partisan campaign of sabotage and resistance.

Tito proved to be a brilliant partisan leader. He was so successful that, by the summer of 1942, he was able to go beyond sabotage and organize a full-scale offensive in Bosnia and Croatia. These actions forced the Germans to take substantial numbers of troops out of the front lines facing the Soviets to

Josip Broz Tito *(National Archives and Records Administration)*

suppress the partisans. Despite a counteroffensive against them, Tito's partisans held their ground, so that, in December 1943, Tito announced the creation of a provisional government in Yugoslavia, with himself as president, secretary of defense, and marshal of the armed forces. The Western Allies greeted this warmly, and Tito continued to lead Yugoslav partisans through the end of the war.

After the defeat of Germany in May 1945, Tito set about transforming his provisional government into a permanent one. He received strong support because of his nearly universal popularity as a war hero and patriot. Although he unmistakably steered Yugoslavia on a Communist course, he stoutly resisted falling into Stalin's orbit as another Soviet satellite. Tito remained independent of—yet cooperative with—both the Soviets and the Western democracies. He ruled Yugoslavia as an enlightened despot, and while he insisted on one-party Communist government, he permitted a high degree of free enterprise in Yugoslavia, which made the nation one of the most prosperous in Eastern Europe.

Tito's death just before his 88th birthday spelled an end to Yugoslav unity, and the constituent states fell into brutal civil war, which became most intense during the late 1980s and 1990s.

Further reading: Barnett, Neil. *Tito.* Dulles, Va.: Haus Publishers Ltd., 2006; Djilas, Milovan. *Tito: The Story from Inside.* New York: Harcourt Brace Jovanovich, 1980.

Tobruk, Battles of

Three battles took place in and around the eastern Libyan harbor and port of Tobruk, long an important naval, air, and general military base.

The first battle began on January 7, 1941, when Gen. Sir RICHARD O'CONNOR's British XIII Corps, having advanced west from Bardia, laid siege to Tobruk, which, at the time was held by Italian forces. On January 21, the 6th Australian Division and the 7th (British) Armoured Division attacked the Tobruk fortress, which was garrisoned by 32,000 Italian troops of Rodolpho Graziani's Tenth

Army under Gen. Petassi Manella. This attack divided the perimeter defenses, and by nightfall on January 22, Tobruk had fallen to the British, whose losses were minimal. Manella and 25,000 of his men were made prisoners of war.

The second battle was the result of Gen. ERWIN ROMMEL's first Axis offensive in North Africa, which began on March 24, 1941, at El Agheila, Libya. Rommel rolled over spotty British resistance to recapture Benghazi on April 4. He reached Tobruk on April 8. The fortress there was now garrisoned mainly by the 9th Australian Division. Rommel did not lay siege, but instead led a relentless storming attack during April 10–14. Repulsed, he regrouped and tried again on April 30. Once again he was driven back. Rommel now settled into a siege, which spanned 240 days. During this period, the British Royal Navy managed to resupply the garrison and also replaced the Australians with the 70th (British) Infantry. It was November 29 before the British Eighth Army, victorious at the BATTLE OF SIDI-REZEGH, broke through to Tobruk and relieved the garrison.

The Third Battle of Tobruk was fought during Rommel's second Libyan Offensive in June 1942. After Rommel's Panzerarmee Afrika, including his vaunted Afrika Korps, rolled over British defenses at the BATTLE OF GAZALA, then pushed the British Eighth Army back across the Egyptian border, Rommel turned to Tobruk. Prime Minister WINSTON CHURCHILL, unwilling to relinquish the fortress, strongly urged Gen. NEIL RITCHIE to leave behind a 35,000-man garrison (2nd South African Division) to hold Tobruk after the rest of the British had withdrawn from Libya. On June 17, Rommel captured Sidi-Rezegh, then immediately attacked Tobruk. On June 19, after a two-day battle, the South Africans surrendered to the 15th and 21st Panzer divisions. It was a stunning defeat, which threw open the door for Rommel to drive into Egypt. Ritchie was relieved as Eighth Army commander.

Further reading: Harrison, Frank. *Tobruk: The Birth of a Legend.* London: Cassell, 2003; Heckstall-Smith, Anthony. *Tobruk: The Story of a Siege.* London: Cerberus, 2005; Latimer, Jon. *Tobruk 1941: Rommel's Opening Move.* London: Osprey, 2001; Mitcham, Samuel. *Rommel's Greatest Victory: The Desert Fox and the Fall of Tobruk, Spring 1942.* Novato, Calif.: Presidio Press, 1998.

Todt, Fritz (1891–1942) *German engineer*

Todt was born in Pforzheim, the son of the owner of a minor factory. After studying engineering in Karlsruhe and at the School for Advanced Technical Studies in Munich, Todt fought in World War I as an infantryman and then as an aerial observer. He was decorated with the Iron Cross.

After the war, he returned to Munich to complete his engineering studies and, in 1920, was hired by Sager & Woerner, a civil engineering firm. He became an early member of the NAZI PARTY, joining on January 5, 1922, and rose to the rank of Oberführer (brigadier general) in the STURMABTEILUNG (SA). At this time, he earned a doctorate in engineering, writing a dissertation on road surfaces.

After ADOLF HITLER became Reich chancellor in 1933, Todt was appointed inspector general for German roadways and was instrumental in founding a construction company to build the Reichsautobahnen, the new system of German superhighways. Todt went on to become director of the Head Office for Engineering in the Administration of the Reich and general commissioner for the regulation of the construction industry. These were powerful positions, which gave Todt considerable autonomy and freedom of action apart from the usual Reich bureaucracy. In addition to his civilian offices, Todt was made a major general in the Luftwaffe in March 1935.

In 1938, Todt created Organization Todt (OT), which united various government firms and private companies with the Reichsarbeitsdienst (Reich Labor Service) for the purpose of building the SIEGFRIED LINE (also known as the West Wall), the massive system of fixed defenses intended to protect the western border of Germany. On March 17, 1940, Todt was named Reich minister for armaments and munitions and personally directed the work of Organization Todt in occupied France and the Low Countries. Following the INVASION OF THE SOVIET UNION in June 1941, Todt was transferred to the eastern front to oversee the rebuilding of the ruined Soviet infrastructure.

Organization Todt carried out what has been described as the most extensive national building program since the days of the Roman Empire. Approximately 1.4 million workers (many of them slave laborers from occupied countries) were employed by OT. OT was responsible for the Siegfried Line, for much of the Atlantic Wall (which defended the Atlantic approaches to the occupied West), oil storage facilities, various air force bases, massive U-boat bunkers, industrial plants, and various specialized structures, including those associated with the operation of the V-1 BUZZ BOMB and V-2 ROCKET.

Within the Nazi hierarchy, Todt was the object of both enormous admiration and great fear, suspicion, and outright envy. For his part, he held himself aloof from the high command of the Wehrmacht as well as from the likes of HERMANN GÖRING, for whose Luftwaffe he did a great deal of construction. On February 8, 1942, Todt was returning from a meeting with Hitler at the Führer's Rastenburg headquarters (Wolf's Lair) when his aircraft mysteriously exploded. Many suspected that he was a victim of assassination. He was succeeded as Reich minister for armaments and munitions by the powerful ALBERT SPEER.

Further reading: Jaskot, Paul. *The Architecture of Oppression: The SS, Forced Labor and the Nazi Monumental Building Economy.* London: Spon Press, 1999; Kaufmann, J. E. *Fortress Third Reich: German Fortifications and Defense Systems in World War II.* New York: Da Capo Press, 2003; Short, Neil. *Germany's West Wall: The Siegfried Line.* London: Osprey, 2004; Witt, Alan F. *The Atlantic Wall: Hitler's Defenses for D-Day 1941–1944.* London: Enigma Books, 2004.

Togo Shigenori (1882–1950) *Japan's minister of foreign affairs during World War II*

Togo began his career as a university professor before joining the Japanese diplomatic corps in

Togo Shigenori *(National Archives and Records Administration)*

Togo was in an impossible position after the Potsdam Declaration. He could not openly advocate defeatism, yet he wanted to signal to the Allies the possibility of surrender. Toward this end, he withheld official response to the Potsdam Declaration in the hope of securing mediation from the Soviets. Allied leaders tended to interpret Togo's silence as a defiant rejection of the Potsdam Declaration, and therefore stepped up the STRATEGIC BOMBING OF JAPAN, culminating in the nuclear attacks against Hiroshima and Nagasaki.

Togo was in many ways a tragic figure. Driven by a sense of duty, he personally signed the declaration of war against the United States—even though he opposed the war. His signature resulted in his being tried at the TOKYO WAR CRIMES TRIALS after the war. He was sentenced as a war criminal to 20 years, and he died in prison.

Further reading: Butow, Robert J. C. *Japan's Decision to Surrender.* Palo Alto, Calif.: Stanford University Press, 1954; Ike, Nobutaka, ed. *Japan's Decision for War: Records of the 1941 Policy Conferences.* Palo Alto, Calif.: Stanford University Press, 1961; Togo, Shigenori. *The Cause of Japan.* Westport, Conn.: Greenwood Press, 1977.

Tojo Hideki (1884–1948) *Japanese prime minister and generalissimo during most of World War II*

Among the public of the Western Allies, Tojo Hideki was seen as the Japanese counterpart of ADOLF HITLER. Yet whereas Hitler was a genuine popular political leader, Tojo was actually no more than a military bureaucrat whose Japanese sobriquet, "The Razor," was intended to characterize his skill at slicing through bureaucratic matters with the utmost efficiency.

Tojo was born on December 30, 1884, in Iwate prefecture, to a military family. Tojo Eikyo, his father, was a general, and Tojo Hideki attended the Imperial Military Academy, graduated in 1905, and entered the army. He was a good officer and an even better administrator. His combat experience was limited to his direction of operations against the Chinese in Chahar—near Zhangjiakou—in

1912, which culminated in his appointment as ambassador to Germany in 1937. An opponent of the ANTI-COMINTERN PACT of 1936, he became ambassador to the Soviet Union in 1938.

Togo believed that Japan could not win a war against the United States, and, as foreign minister on the eve of the BATTLE OF PEARL HARBOR, he tried earnestly to negotiate with the United States a means of avoiding war. Even after the war was under way, Togo remained convinced that Japan would suffer inevitable defeat and so looked for possibilities to negotiate a favorable peace. When the Allies presented the POTSDAM DECLARATION in 1945, which was essentially a demand for unconditional surrender, Togo favored accepting it and ending the war. He also hoped to avoid war with the Soviet Union.

August 1937 during the SINO-JAPANESE WAR. Up to this point, he held regimental staff assignments, then graduated from the Army Staff College in 1915. From 1919 to 1921, he was stationed in Berlin as assistant military attaché. Promoted to major, he was appointed a resident officer in Germany during 1921–22. Tojo's diplomatic service drew him into the inner circles of government, and he became part of Japanese army efforts to wrest control of national policy and administration from civilian hands.

Promoted to lieutenant colonel in 1924, Tojo was named chief of the Army Ministry's Mobilization Plans Bureau, a position that put him at the nexus of Japan's war preparation efforts. He was promoted to colonel in 1929, given a regimental command, then made chief of the Organization and Mobilization Section of the Army General Staff. After serving in this post from 1931 to 1933, he was promoted to major general and made deputy commandant of the Military Academy. His next position was as commander of an infantry brigade in 1934–35, then of the Kwantung Army Gendarmerie, a post in which military leaders of the highest rank were traditionally groomed. He held this position until 1937, gaining promotion to lieutenant general in 1936 and serving as chief of staff of the Kwantung Army from 1937 to 1938.

Returned to Japan, Tojo was named vice minister of the army and chief of Army Air Headquarters. While World War II erupted in Europe, Tojo became increasingly well known as a spokesman for the army's most aggressively pro-Axis faction. By the time this faction gained control of the government, Tojo was a general and, in 1941, was named prime minister. Even members of the government who objected to military domination welcomed Tojo's selection because they believed that only by giving him the post could a military coup d'état be avoided. On the eve of its entry into World War II, the Japanese government was highly unstable.

Predictably as prime minister, Tojo did all he could to propel Japan into war. Once war broke out, he was an aggressive advocate of expanding the scope of the conflict. He functioned during the war as a generalissimo, with dictatorial powers in foreign as well as domestic affairs. For most of the war, he served as prime minister as well as chief of the Army General Staff, formulating military strategy and directing military operations with ruthlessness yet with little imagination. His greatest failure was in neglecting to develop a long-term strategy for the conflict. Everything depended on rapid, overwhelming victory—and when that did not occur, Tojo's Japan was without alternatives and found itself doomed to defeat.

After Japan's defeat in the BATTLE OF SAIPAN on July 12, 1944, a coalition of Japanese statesmen felt emboldened to force Tojo's removal as head of the military and, ultimately, as prime minister as well. He was removed as chief of staff on July 16, 1944. Two days later, his cabinet resigned en masse. Tojo

Tojo Hideki *(National Archives and Records Administration)*

offered no objection or resistance to his sudden loss of position, and when Japan surrendered in September 1945, he shot himself in a suicide attempt. He recovered and was tried as a war criminal at the Tokyo War Crimes Trials. Found guilty, he was hanged on December 23, 1948.

Further reading: Browne, Courtney. *Tojo: The Last Banzai.* New York: Da Capo, 1998; Hoyt, Edwin. *Warlord: Tojo against the World.* New York: Cooper Square Press, 2001.

Tokyo fire bombing

As with the strategic bombing of Germany, the U.S. Army Air Forces attempted daylight precision bombing in the strategic bombing of Japan. The results, however, were poor, largely because of the prevailing wind conditions over Japan, which tended to make high-altitude bombing inaccurate. This led Twentieth Air Force commander in charge Curtis E. Lemay to try carpet bombing at night from low level, using incendiaries. The fire bombing proved highly devastating.

The first fire-bombing raid was against Kobe on February 3, 1945. Next, during the night of February 23–24, Tokyo was targeted with incendiaries, and a square mile of the city was razed. This prompted a more massive raid during the night of March 9–10 by 334 Marianas-based B-29s. The aircraft dropped incendiaries for some two hours, producing a firestorm—the mass movement of air created by a large fire which in turn, creates a fire of even more intense heat and greater destructiveness over a very wide area. Most of the city was engulfed. An estimated 100,000 Tokyo residents were killed, and about 16 square miles of the capital were consumed. A third raid was carried out against Tokyo on May 26.

The Tokyo fire bombing of March 9–10, 1945, was more destructive than the atomic raids on Hiroshima and Nagasaki. Like the atomic raids, the fire bombing was (and remains) controversial, as some historians classify it as a war crime.

See also Dresden air raid; Hiroshima, atomic bombing of; and Nagasaki, atomic bombing of.

Further reading: Greer, Ron, and Mike Wicks. *Fire from the Sky: A Diary over Japan.* Jacksonville, Ark.: Greer, 2005.

Tokyo war crimes trials

From May 3, 1946, to November 12, 1948, Japanese Class A war criminals—civilian and former military officers who had either killed prisoners or had been indicted for roles in instigating the war—were tried by the International Military Tribunal for the Far East (IMTFE) in Tokyo. Those tried in Tokyo were the first of some 20,000 Japanese who would eventually be tried. Many of those tried later were tried in the countries of their victims. Some convictions resulted in prison terms; 900 individuals were executed.

In the Tokyo trials, the prosecution team consisted of justices from 11 Allied nations: Australia, Canada, China, France, Great Britain, India, the Netherlands, New Zealand, the Philippines, the Soviet Union, and the United States. The American public paid little attention to the Tokyo trials and even less to the other trials elsewhere in Asia. Except for Tojo Hideki, the Western public was largely unfamiliar with the Japanese leadership, and whereas Allied leaders liberally demonized Adolf Hitler and other top German leaders, they wanted to avoid doing the same to Hirohito, since he was to remain on the Japanese throne. (Hirohito was not indicted by the tribunal.)

Of 80 Class A war criminal suspects detained after 1945, 28 were brought to trial in Tokyo. The accused included nine civilians and 19 military officers, including four wartime prime ministers (Tojo preeminent among them), three former foreign ministers (Togo Shigenori being the most important), four former war ministers, two former navy ministers, six former generals, two former ambassadors, three former economic and financial leaders, one adviser to the emperor, one political theorist, one admiral, and one colonel.

Although the particulars of the indictments varied, all defendants were accused of promoting a scheme of conquest that "contemplated and carried out … murdering, maiming and ill-treating prisoners of war [and] civilian internees . . . forcing them to labor under inhumane conditions . . . plundering public and private property, wantonly destroying cities, towns and villages beyond any justification of military necessity; [perpetrating] mass murder, rape, pillage, brigandage, torture and other barbaric cruelties upon the helpless civilian population of the overrun countries." Issues raised in the trials included the NANKING MASSACRE and Japanese unconventional warfare practices such as opium trafficking designed to weaken the will of the Chinese people to resist, and bacteriological warfare.

Two of the original 28 defendants died of natural causes during the trials; one suffered a total mental collapse and was confined to a psychiatric hospital, then was released in 1948 without standing trial. All other defendants were found guilty. Of these, seven were sentenced to death by hanging, 16 to life imprisonment, and two to lesser terms. Those sentenced to death were found guilty of inciting or participating in mass atrocities.

Three of the 16 defendants sentenced to life imprisonment died between 1949 and 1950 in prison; the rest were paroled between 1954 and 1956. Two former ambassadors were sentenced to seven and 20 years in prison, respectively. One died after two years in prison; the other, Shigemitsu Mamoru, was paroled in 1950 and, in 1954, was appointed foreign minister.

Further reading: Maga, Timothy P. *Judgment at Tokyo: The Japanese War Crimes Trials.* Lexington: University Press of Kentucky, 2001; Minear, Richard R. *Victors' Justice: The Tokyo War Crimes Trial.* Ann Arbor: University of Michigan Press, Center for Japanese Studies, 2001.

Toyoda Soemu (1885–1957) *Commander in charge of the Japanese Combined Fleet, from March 1944 to the end of World War II*

Toyoda Soemu graduated from the Naval Academy in 1905. At the outbreak of World War II in the Pacific, he held the rank of admiral and commanded the Kure Naval Station. He was elevated to the Supreme War Council in November 1942 and in May 1943 was assigned to command the Yokosuka Naval Base.

Following the death of Admiral KOGA MINEICHI, Toyoda became commander in charge of the Combined Fleet on May 3, 1944. He authorized Operation A-Go, an all-out naval offensive that led to the BATTLE OF THE PHILIPPINE SEA in June at which Ozawa Jisaburo was disastrously defeated.

Despite the failure of A-Go, Toyoda was appointed chief of the Naval General Staff in May 1945. As a member of the Supreme War Council, Toyoda argued passionately against Emperor HIROHITO's desire to negotiate an end to the war after the atomic attacks on Hiroshima and Nagasaki in August 1945. After the war, his hard-line stance earned him an indictment and trial before an Allied tribunal, but he was acquitted.

Further reading: Atkinson, John. *Imperial Japanese Navy WWII.* Couldson, U.K.: Galago Books, 2003; Dull, Paul S. *A Battle History of the Imperial Japanese Navy, 1941–1945.* Annapolis, Md.: Naval Institute Press, 1978; Evans, David C. *Kaigun: Strategy, Tactics, and Technology in the Imperial Japanese Navy, 1887–1941.* Annapolis, Md.: Naval Institute Press, 1997.

transport aircraft

World War II was the first war in which aircraft were used to transport significant numbers of troops and weapons. Converted bombers and specialized, purpose-built aircraft—both powered and gliders—greatly increased the mobility of forces during the war.

UNITED STATES

The United States produced some of the most successful purpose-built transport aircraft and did so in unprecedented numbers.

C-47: By far the most famous (and most numerous) transport aircraft of World War II was the celebrated Douglas C-47 Skytrain, the military version of the DC-3 airliner introduced to commercial aviation in 1935. Wartime military production of this aircraft reached 10,048, and another

2,700 or more were produced in the Soviet Union (as the Lisunov Li-2). The British called their C-47s Dakotas. The aircraft was used in every theater of the war for troop and cargo transport and for the deployment of paratroops in AIRBORNE ASSAULT.

The C-47 was crewed by three and could transport 27 troops with equipment. A twin-engine craft, it was powered by two 1,200-hp Pratt & Whitney 14-cylinder radials. Top speed was 230 miles per hour and service ceiling was 24,000 feet. Its range was 1,600 miles. Maximum takeoff weight for the C-47 was 26,000 pounds. The plane had a wingspan of 95.5 feet and was 63 feet 9 inches long.

C-46: Less famous than the C-47, the C-46 Curtiss Commando was also originally designed for the commercial aviation market. It outperformed the C-47 and was therefore used more extensively in the Pacific theater, where its greater range and ceiling were key assets.

A total of 3,180 C-46s were built during the war. They were used for general transport as well as airborne assault and were powered by twin 2,000-hp Pratt & Whitney 18-cylinder radial engines. Top speed was 264 miles per hour, service ceiling was 27,600 feet, and range was 2,300 miles. The aircraft had a maximum takeoff weight of 48,000 pounds, a wingspan of 108 feet, and a length of 76 feet 4 inches.

C-87: The Consolidated B-24 Liberator was one of the great four-engine bombers of World War II. The C-87, also called a Liberator, was the cargo and troop transport version of the bomber. It could hold 38 men with their equipment and was powered by four 1,200-hp Pratt & Whitney Twin Wasp 14-cylinder radial engines. Top speed was 270 miles per hour, service ceiling 32,000 feet, and range 2,290 miles. The maximum takeoff weight of the aircraft was 62,000 pounds. It had a wingspan of 110 feet and was 67 feet 1 inch long.

CG-4A: The Waco CG-4A Haig (called Hadrian by the British) was the only American glider to see combat service in World War II. A total of 12,393 of these gliders were delivered, and they were used extensively for airborne assault.

The CG-4A had a maximum towing speed of 125 miles per hour. Its maximum takeoff weight was 9,000 pounds; it had a wingspan of 83 feet 8 inches and a length of 48 feet, 3.75 inches. It could carry 15 fully equipped troops or a jeep, or a 75 mm howitzer (with crew). The glider was typically towed by C-46s or C-47s.

GREAT BRITAIN

Armstrong Whitworth Albemarle. This transport version of the Bristol bomber was used both as a transport and as a glider tug. Built mainly of wood, it was powered by two 1,590-hp Bristol Hercules 14-cylinder radials and had a top speed of 256 miles per hour. Service ceiling was 10,500 feet, and range was 1,350 miles. The Albemarle's maximum takeoff weight was 36,500 pounds. Wingspan was 77 feet, length 59 feet, 11 inches. Unlike most transports, the Albemarle was armed—albeit lightly—with two 7.7 mm Vickers machine guns.

Armstrong Whitworth Whitley. These aircraft were used for paratroop transport and, sometimes, for towing gliders. The plane was a modification of a British medium bomber design. It was powered by a pair of 1,145-hp Rolls-Royce Merlin X 12-cylinder engines for a top speed of 222 miles per hour to a service ceiling of 17,600 feet. Range was 1,650 miles, and maximum takeoff weight was 33,500 pounds. The Whitley had a wingspan of 84 feet and was 70.5 feet long.

Handley Page Halifax. Yet another bomber modified as a transport and glider tug, the Halifax was powered by four 1,615-hp Bristol Hercules engines and had a top speed of 282 miles per hour and service ceiling of 20,000 feet. Maximum takeoff weight was 54,400 pounds, wingspan was 98 feet 10 inches, and length 71 feet 7 inches.

Short Stirling. This heavy bomber design was used for tugging gliders and for general transport, including airborne assault. It had four 1,650-hp Bristol Hercules 14-cylinder engines and could make 280 miles per hour. Service ceiling was 17,000 feet and range 3,000 miles. The Stirling had a wingspan of 99 feet 1 inch and was 87 feet 3 inches long. Maximum takeoff weight was 70,000 pounds.

Airspeed Horsa. The British used gliders more extensively than the Americans. The most numerous British glider was the Horsa, which could transport 20 men and had a top towing speed of 100 miles per hour. Maximum takeoff weight was 15,250 pounds, wingspan was 88 feet, and length was 67 feet.

General Aircraft Hamilcar. The largest and heaviest RAF glider, the Hamilcar had a maximum takeoff weight of 37,000 pounds. It was towed at 150 miles per hour and had a wingspan of 110 feet. The glider was 68 feet long. The Hamilcar was the only Allied glider capable of delivering a tank into combat.

ITALY

The single Italian air transport of note was the tri-motor Savoia-Marchetti S.M.81/T, which could carry 18 fully equipped troops or paratroops into battle. It was powered by a trio of 670-hp Piaggo 9-cylinder radials to a top speed of 211 miles per hour. Service ceiling was 22,966 feet and range was 1,234 miles. Maximum takeoff weight was 23,149 pounds. The aircraft had a wingspan of 78 feet 9 inches and was 58 feet 5 inches long. It was armed with five 7.7 mm machine guns.

GERMANY

The Germans built several innovative transports and glider transports.

Gotha Go 244B. This twin-engine transport could carry 21 troops with their equipment and was powered by two 1,140-hp Gnome-Rhone 14-cylinder radial engines to a top speed of 180 miles per hour. Service ceiling was 24,607 feet, but range was just 460 miles. The wingspan was 80 feet 4.6 inches, length 51 feet. This transport was a powered version of the Gotha Go 242 glider and was machine-gun equipped.

Messerschmidt Me323. Another powered glider, the Me 323 added six 1,140-hp Gnome-Rhone engines to the giant Me 321 glider to produce an aircraft capable of transporting an entire company (130 men) or the equivalent amount of cargo. Top speed was 177 miles per hour and range was 684 miles. Maximum takeoff weight was a staggering 94,799 pounds. Wingspan was 180 feet, and length

92 feet, 4.3 inches. The aircraft was sometimes armed with machine guns. Fewer than 200 were built. Lumbering giants, they were highly vulnerable to fighters and antiaircraft fire, so they were not used near the front lines—a limitation that significantly reduced their usefulness.

Heinkel He 111Z. This oddity consisted of two He 111 bombers (also used individually as transports) joined together at the wing to create a twin-fuselage five-engine giant, which was used as a glider tug and paratroop transport. As a tug, it towed Germany's largest gliders, such as the Go 242.

The He 111Z had five 1,350-hp Junkers Jumor 12-cylinder liquid-cooled engines and could make a top speed of 249 miles per hour. Service ceiling was 21,982 feet and range was 1,212 miles. Its takeoff weight was 30,856 pounds.

DFS 230. This was the main troop glider used by German forces. It could carry 10 troops and 606 pounds of equipment. Towing speed was 130 miles per hour, and maximum takeoff weight was 4,630 pounds. The glider had a wingspan of 68 feet 5.7 inches and was 36 feet 10.5 inches long. These were the gliders that made the spectacular assault on Fort Eben-Emael in Belgium near the start of the German invasion of western Europe.

Further reading: Gunston, Bill. *Illustrated Directory of Fighting Aircraft of World War II.* London: Zenith Press, 1999; Wilson, Stewart. *Aircraft of WWII.* Fishwyck, Australia: Australian Aviation, 1999; Winchester, Jim, ed. *Aircraft of World War II.* Berkeley, Calif.: Thunder Bay Press, 2004.

Treaties Ending the War

This article discusses the formal documents (to which the United States was a party) establishing peace among the belligerent nations. For the documents that immediately ended the fighting, see SURRENDER DOCUMENTS OF 1943–1945.

PEACE TREATY BETWEEN THE ALLIES AND ITALY

The first peace treaty concluded between the Allies and a former Axis nation was with Italy. It was signed in Paris on February 10, 1947, by representatives from Albania, Australia, Belgium, Brazil, Canada, China, Czechoslovakia, Ethiopia, France, Great Britain, Greece, India, Iraq, Mexico, the Netherlands, New Zealand, Pakistan, Poland, Slovak Republic, South Africa, the Soviet Union, the United States, Yugoslavia, and Italy.

The treaty stipulated that Italian fascism was overturned as a result of Allied victory, but "with the assistance of the democratic elements of the Italian people." This fact gave Italy privileged status among the defeated nations of the former Axis, the Allies explicitly recognizing that while the government of Benito Mussolini bore responsibility as an aggressor, a significant portion of the Italian people opposed the government and its war.

Part I of the treaty reestablished Italy's frontiers as they existed on January 1, 1938, except that the prewar conquest of Ethiopia and the wartime acquisitions in Albania were annulled. Also, the Dodecanese was ceded to Greece, and certain Adriatic islands were likewise ceded to Greece or Albania. The boundary between Italy and France was also subject to further adjustment, as were some lesser territories.

Part II of the treaty consisted of "Political Clauses," including provisions to enforce human rights and eliminate all vestiges of fascism:

> Article 15
>
> Italy shall take all measures necessary to secure to all persons under Italian jurisdiction ... the enjoyment of human rights and of the fundamental freedoms, including freedom of expression, of press and publication, of religious worship, of political opinion, and of public meeting.
>
> Article 17
>
> Italy ... shall not permit the resurgence on Italian territory of [Fascist] organizations, whether political, military, or semi-military, whose purpose it is to deprive the people of their democratic rights.

The treaty imposed limits on Italian armed forces, but specified that these limitations were subject to modification "by agreement between the Allied and Associated Powers and Italy or, after Italy becomes a member of the United Nations, by agreement between the Security Council and Italy." Finally, a schedule for the withdrawal of Allied troops was established and reparations were fixed:

- The Soviet Union, $100 million
- Yugoslavia, $125 million
- Greece, $105 million
- Ethiopia, $25 million
- Albania, $5 million

France, Britain, and the United States renounced reparations claims.

JAPAN

The first treaty concerning Japan was a Trusteeship Agreement for the Former Japanese Mandated Islands, signed on April 2, 1947, in New York by the former Japanese Mandate Islands, the United Nations, and the United States. The agreement transferred the Japanese Mandate Islands to a Trusteeship System of the United Nations under the administering authority of the United States. The treaty stipulated that the Pacific islands north of the equator held by Germany before World War I and assigned to Japanese mandate by Article 22 of the Covenant of the League of Nations (considered part of the Treaty of Versailles, which ended World War I) were no longer under Japanese control. By virtue of its defeat, Japan had "ceased to exercise any authority in these islands"; therefore, the United Nations placed them under the Trusteeship System, designating them the Trust Territory and assigning to the United States "administering authority" over the islands.

The United States was given full powers of administration of the Trust Territory and was authorized to establish a military presence on the islands. In addition, the United States was obligated to "foster the development of such political institutions as are suited to the Trust Territory" and to promote "self-government or independence as may be appropriate to the particular circumstances of the Trust Territory." The United States also accepted responsibility for promoting economic advancement and self-sufficiency, social advancement, and educational advancement.

The definitive Treaty of Peace with Japan was signed on September 8, 1951, in San Francisco by Argentina, Australia, Belgium, Bolivia, Brazil, Cambodia, Canada, Chile, Costa Rica, Cuba, Dominican Republic, Ecuador, Egypt, El Salvador, Ethiopia, France, Great Britain, Greece, Guatemala, Haiti, Honduras, Iran, Iraq, Laos, Lebanon, Liberia, Mexico, the Netherlands, New Zealand, Nicaragua, Norway, Pakistan, Panama, Paraguay, Peru, Philippines, Saudi Arabia, South Africa, Sri Lanka, Syrian Arab Republic, Turkey, the United States, Uruguay, Venezuela, Vietnam, and Japan. Among the Allied and Associated powers, however, the Soviet Union, the People's Republic of China, and Taiwan declined to sign the treaty.

The treaty recapitulated the terms outlined in the 1945 surrender document, including Japanese affirmation of its renunciation of rights to all territories surrendered by the armistice. Additionally, the 1951 treaty included Japanese renunciation of any special rights with regard to China; however, because the treaty failed to convey to the Soviet Union special title to the Kuril Islands or to southern Sakhalin—territories promised to the Soviet Union by the YALTA AGREEMENT—the Soviets refused to sign. The treaty also did not confer Taiwan—the sole remaining bastion of pro-Western Nationalist China—on the People's Republic of China. For that reason, neither Taiwan nor the People's Republic signed. Inasmuch as all the rest of the Allies and Associated Powers did sign, however, the treaty was considered universally valid.

Other key treaty provisions included these:

- A stipulation that Japan should pay reparations, the amounts of which were deferred to bilateral negotiation
- A stipulation that Japan would adhere to the principles of the United Nations Charter
- A stipulation that Japan would adhere to internationally accepted fair trade and commerce practices

The treaty provided for a transition from a government of military occupation to full civil sovereignty within 90 days of the date on which the treaty came into force. Significantly, the treaty contained no military clauses reducing and restricting armed forces in Japan. These were considered unnecessary by the Japanese constitution adopted in 1946, which strictly forbade the maintenance of *any* Japanese armed forces. (Ultimately, the United States would insist that Japan create a small defense force.)

On the same day that the peace treaty was signed, Japan also concluded the Japanese–United States Security Treaty, by which the United States was permitted to maintain military forces in Japan for mutual defense. (This treaty was supplemented in 1954 by a Mutual Defense Assistance Agreement with Japan and superseded in 1960 by the Treaty of Mutual Cooperation and Security between the United States and Japan.)

On April 22, 1953, at Tokyo, Japanese representatives received a U.S. "Note by which the Government of the United States of America, in Pursuance of Article 7 of the Treaty of Peace with Japan, signed at San Francisco on 8 September 1951, Notified the Japanese Government of those Pre-War Bilateral Treaties between the Two Countries which the United States of America Desires to Keep in Force or Revive. This was essentially a list of those pre–World War II U.S.-Japanese treaties that the United States wished to continue or reinstate. Included in the list were treaties relating to extradition, narcotic drug conventions, postal conventions, an "Arrangement Relating to Perpetual Leaseholds (1937)," a liquor-smuggling convention, and a reciprocal exemption from taxation of merchant vessels.

GERMANY

Germany presented a special case with regard to treaty making because the Third Reich, the government that had declared war on the Allies, had ceased to exist, and its former leaders were either dead or had been removed from office and, in many cases, convicted as war criminals. Therefore, the postwar agreements relating to Germany concerned the administration of the occupied territories.

On June 5, 1945, at Berlin, representatives of the Provisional Government of France, the Soviet

Union, Britain, and the United States issued an "Allied Declaration on Control of Germany," which was the official instrument by which the Allies assumed control of the German government after Germany's unconditional surrender. This document is discussed in SURRENDER DOCUMENTS OF 1945. In addition to the "Allied Declaration on Control of Germany," the United States, Great Britain, the Soviet Union, and the Provisional Government of the French Republic issued between June 5 and November 30, 1945, a series of Statements on the Occupation of Germany. These documents address matters beyond Germany's immediate surrender, and so are discussed here.

The Allied statements contracted Germany's frontiers to their extent as of December 31, 1937, before the ANSCHLUSS (the annexation of Austria), the acquisition of the SUDETENLAND, and the INVASION OF POLAND. This reduced territory was then divided "for the purposes of occupation . . . into four zones, one to be allotted to each Power as follows: an eastern zone to the Union of Soviet Socialist Republics; a north-western zone to the United Kingdom; a south-western zone to the United States of America; a western zone to France." The Allies agreed that each of the four occupying nations was to designate a commander in chief with responsibility for its zone; however, Berlin was treated as a special case. Despite its location deep within the Soviet zone, it was also to be divided into four zones of occupation: "An Inter-Allied Governing Authority (in Russian, *Komandatura*) consisting of four Commandants, appointed by their respective Commanders-in-Chief, will be established to direct jointly its administration."

The occupying Allies created a "control machinery" for Germany during the "period when Germany is carrying out the basic requirements of unconditional surrender." This machinery consisted of the assignment of supreme authority in Germany to be exercised "by the British, United States, Soviet and French Commanders-in-Chief, each in his own zone of occupation, and also jointly, in matters affecting Germany as a whole," each commander to act on instructions from his

government. In Berlin, administration was directed by an Inter-Allied Governing Authority, which operated under the general direction of the Allied Control Council. The authority was to consist of four commandants, "each of whom will serve in rotation as Chief Commandant. They will be assisted by a technical staff which will supervise and control the activities of the local German organs." Because Berlin was an enclave within the Soviet zone of occupation, three air corridors into the city were established.

The cooperation mandated by the Allied Statements soon dissolved in the cold war era. The temporary dividing lines between the Soviet zone in the east and the British, French, and U.S. zones became a permanent boundary, culminating on June 7, 1948, when the Western nations announced their intention to create West Germany as a separate capitalist nation. The Soviets responded two weeks later with a blockade of West Berlin, protesting that Berlin, deep within Soviet-occupied territory, could not serve as the capital of West Germany. The United States kept West Berlin supplied via the Berlin Airlift until the Soviets relented and reopened access to West Berlin on May 12, 1949. Later that month, East and West Germany became separate nations, and, beginning in 1961, Soviet authorities built a wall dividing East and West Berlin. The wall endured for more than 40 years as an icon of Soviet oppression. The fall of the Berlin Wall, beginning in 1989, marked the end of the cold war and was a prelude to the collapse of the Soviet Union itself.

After the political division of Germany, France, Great Britain, and the United States concluded a series of Agreements on Germany. Signed on April 8, 1949, at Washington, D.C., these documents defined the three nations' powers and responsibilities following establishment of the German Federal Republic—West Germany.

The Agreed Memorandum Regarding the Principles Governing Exercise of Powers and Responsibilities of U.S.-U.K.-French Governments following the Establishment of the German Federal Republic asserted the retention of "supreme authority" by the three nations, including the "right to revoke or

Post–World War II Occupation Zones of Germany

Legend:
- U.S. zone
- British zone
- French zone
- Soviet zone
- Taken over by Poland
- O Under Four Power control

© Infobase Publishing

Division of Berlin after World War II

alter any legislative or administrative decisions in the three western zones of Germany." But the memorandum also gave the German governing authorities the right to take administrative and legislative action, which would "have validity if not vetoed by the Allied Authority." The memorandum stipulated that "military government will disappear, and that the function of the Allies shall be mainly supervisory." The three nations declared their "major objective" to be the encouragement and facilitation of "the closest integration, on a mutually beneficial basis, of the German people under a democratic federal state within the framework of a European association."

An Occupation Statute Defining the Powers to be Retained by the Occupation Authorities precisely defined the ongoing role of the United States, France, and Britain in the government of the newly created Federal Republic of Germany (West Germany), reserving to the three nations authority in disarmament and demilitarization issues; controls with regard to the Ruhr River, restitution, reparations, claims against Germany; authority in foreign affairs; authority in matters relating to displaced persons and refugees; authority in matters relating to the Allied forces; respect for the Basic Law (German federal constitution) and the constitutions of the German Länder (states); control over foreign trade; and control of persons charged with war crimes. Control over internal matters would be restricted "to the minimum extent necessary to ensure use of funds, food and other supplies in such manner as to reduce to a minimum the need for external assistance to Germany."

An Agreement as to Tripartite Controls created the machinery by which France, Britain, and the United States consolidated their occupation of western Germany into a single Western Zone governed by a single authoritative body, the Allied high commission, composed of one high commissioner from each occupying power. The most important provisions of the Agreement as to Tripartite Controls included a stipulation that personnel of the Allied High Commission were to be kept to a minimum so as to facilitate German federal exercise of responsibility for government; a stipulation that approval of amendments to the Basic Law (federal constitution) required unanimous agreement among the high commissioners; an agreement that the authority of each of the three occupying powers would be, in part, proportional to the funding provided by that power; the creation of an apparatus for appeal of High Commission decisions; a stipulation that High Commission be addressed to German government authorities rather than directly to the German people.

An Agreed Minute Respecting Berlin specifically applied tripartite controls to the "western sectors of Berlin."

In their Agreed Minute on Claims against Germany, the three occupying powers pledged "to develop proposals for the settlement of financial claims against Germany."

The Agreed Minute on Württemberg-Baden Plebiscite authorized the establishment of the German Land (state) of Baden-Württemberg.

The Agreement Regarding Kehl provided for interim control of the Rhine port city of Kehl, which was subject to dispute between Germany and France. The Agreement Regarding Kehl was intended to avoid a conflict that threatened to delay the creation of the West German state.

In its Message to the Military Governors from the Foreign Ministers of the United States, United Kingdom, and France, the Allied authorities provided guidelines for military governors of the western sectors of occupied Germany for policies on the eve of the creation of the German Federal Republic.

The Message to the Bonn Parliamentary Council from the foreign ministers of the United States, United Kingdom, and France expressed to the Bonn Parliamentary Council—the German body that was the core of the new Federal Republic—the consensus of the foreign ministers on the role of the Western allies in the government of West Germany. Essentially this was an expression of the Memorandum Regarding Germany.

Further reading: Army Library. *Pacific Islands and Trust Territories; A Select Bibliography.* Washington, D.C.: U.S. Government Printing Office, 1971; Butow, R. C. *Japan's Decision to Surrender.* Palo Alto, Calif.: Stanford University Press, 1954; Finn, Richard B. *Winners in Peace: MacArthur, Yoshida, and Postwar Japan.* Berkeley: University of California Press, 1992; Frederiksen, Oliver Jul. *The American Military Occupation of Germany, 1945–1953.* Darmstadt, West Germany: Historical Division, Headquarters, U.S. Army, Europe, 1953; Giangreco, D. M., and Robert E. Griffin. *Airbridge to Berlin: The Berlin Crisis of 1948.* Novato, Calif.: Presidio Press, 1988; Haydock, Michael D. *City Under Siege: The Berlin Blockade and Airlift, 1948–49.* Washington, D.C.: Brasseys, 1999; Ruhm von Oppen, Beate. *Documents on Germany under Occupation, 1945–1954.* London and New York: Oxford University Press, 1955.

Treblinka extermination camp

Treblinka was one of Germany's network of CONCENTRATION AND EXTERMINATION CAMPS. It was located on the Bug River in Poland, about 45 miles northeast of Warsaw. The camp opened in July 1942 and received the inhabitants of the WARSAW GHETTO for extermination in the FINAL SOLUTION. It is believed that 900,000 Jews were killed in Treblinka alone.

In August 1943, some 700 prisoners staged an uprising in which 15 guards were killed. Out of the 700 who attempted to escape, only 12 succeeded;

however, the camp was razed in November 1943, largely to wipe out any trace of the uprising to prevent its example from inspiring others to attempt escape.

See also HOLOCAUST, THE.

Further reading: Arad, Yitzhak. *Belzec, Sobibor, Treblinka: The Operation Reinhard Death Camps.* Bloomington: Indiana University Press, 1999; Steiner, Jean-Francois. *Treblinka.* New York: Plume, 1994.

Tresckow, Henning von (1901–1944) *anti-Hitler conspirator*

Born in Magdeburg, Germany, Henning von Tresckow enlisted in the German army during World War I and was commissioned an officer before the Armistice of 1918. He left military service after the war and pursued a successful career as a stockbroker, only to return to the army in 1924. By the outbreak of war in 1939, he was a lieutenant colonel on the staff of Fedor von Bock, his uncle.

Tresckow played a planning role in Germany's invasion of CZECHOSLOVAKIA and the INVASION OF POLAND. In the latter operation, he was profoundly shocked by the actions of the Einsatzgruppen—attached to the SCHUTZSTAFFEL (SS)—which murdered Jews and other "undesirables" during the course of the invasion. The brutality of the GESTAPO in administering the occupied territories also appalled him. In this frame of mind, Tresckow became an eyewitness to the murder of Red Army prisoners of war during Germany's 1941 INVASION OF THE SOVIET UNION. This persuaded him that the Nazi regime was so incorrigibly evil that it had to be overthrown.

Tresckow became a general staff officer in 1942 and began slowly to recruit senior army officers into a conspiracy to carry out a coup d'état. He approached the likes of von Bock, GÜNTHER VON KLUGE, ERICH VON MANSTEIN, and GERD VON RUNDSTEDT, all of whom declined to join—yet also refrained from informing on Tresckow. This alone was a measure of the growing disaffection within the German officer corps.

On March 14, 1943, Tresckow and his adjutant, Fabian Schlabrendorff, planted a bomb on a plane carrying ADOLF HITLER to Smolensk. The detonator malfunctioned and the bomb failed to explode. The sabotage was not traced to Tresckow, who, the following September, was appointed chief of staff to the Second Army.

Undaunted, he turned to CLAUS VON STAUFFENBERG, an officer he had managed to recruit into his conspiracy in 1942. With Stauffenberg, he planned the JULY PLOT (TO ASSASSINATE HITLER) in 1944. This time, the bomb, planted at Wolf's Lair, Hitler's Rastenberg headquarters, did explode, but Hitler escaped with relatively minor injuries. Learning that the plot had miscarried and the coup d'état had collapsed, Tresckow bade farewell to his fellow conspirators, drove to the eastern front, and committed suicide by detonating a hand grenade near his head.

Further reading: Fest, Joachim. *Plotting Hitler's Death: The Story of German Resistance.* New York: Owl, 1997; Galante, Pierre. *Operation Valkyrie: The German Generals' Plot Against Hitler.* New York: Cooper Square, 2002.

Trier, Walter (1890–1951) *early anti-Nazi activist who became an Allied propagandist*

Walter Trier was born in Prague in 1890 and moved to Munich in 1909. He gathered a devoted following with his political cartoons, which were published in the popular magazines *Kladderadatsch* and *Simplicissimus.* During the early rise of the NAZI PARTY in the 1920s, Trier lampooned ADOLF HITLER and the party with a series of cartoons in *Simplicissimus.* Despite threats, Trier continued to draw cartoons, which *Simplicissimus* continued to publish; however, in 1933, when Hitler was named chancellor of Germany, *Simplicissimus* was forced to back off. As Trier saw more and more anti-Nazi artists and writers being arrested, he and fellow cartoonist Thomas Heine fled the country. Trier settled in England, where he worked for the magazine *Lilliput.* In addition, he drew cartoons for the London-based German-language daily *Die Zeitung* and for *The New Yorker,* creating more than 80 of that magazine's most memorable covers during the 1930s and the war period.

During World War II, Trier volunteered his services to the British Ministry of Information, creating anti-Nazi leaflets and political propaganda drawings. After the war, Trier settled in Canada.

Further reading: Art Gallery of Toronto. *Humorist Walter Trier: Selections from the Trier-Fodor Foundation Gift.* Toronto: Art Gallery of Toronto, 1980; Trier, Walter. *Walter Trier.* Berlin: Eulenspiegel Verlag, 1971.

Trott, Adam von (1909–1944) *German anti-Nazi activist and anti-Hitler conspirator*

Born in Germany, Trott was educated at Oxford University—he was a Rhodes scholar—then returned to Germany and trained as a lawyer. Trott was an early opponent of ADOLF HITLER and the NAZI PARTY. He nevertheless secured a government position in the Third Reich as a legation counselor in the German Foreign Office, a position that gave him the opportunity to travel abroad. Covertly, he made contact with various German politicians in exile as well as with the governments of Britain and the United States, all in an attempt to undermine the Hitler regime.

Trott was among the approximately 5,000 individuals arrested after the collapse of the 1944 JULY PLOT (TO ASSASSINATE HITLER). He was executed at Plötzewnsee Prison on August 15, 1944.

Further reading: Klemperer, Klemens von, ed. *Noble Combat: The Letters of Shiela Grant Duff and Adam von Trott zu Solz 1932–1939.* New York: Oxford University Press, 1988; MacDonogh, Giles. *A Good German: A Biography of Adam von Trott Zu Solz.* New York: Overlook, 1993.

Truk Island, Battles of

This major Japanese naval and air base on the island of Truk in the Carolines, 1,500 miles west of

Tarawa and 800 miles north of Rabaul, was twice targeted by U.S. admiral CHESTER NIMITZ during his advance across the central Pacific.

On February 17–18, 1944, Adm. RAYMOND SPRUANCE led his Fifth Fleet into the Carolines. The battleships *New Jersey* and *Iowa,* the cruisers *Minneapolis* and *New Orleans,* and four destroyers bombarded Japanese ships outside the Truk lagoon, while Task Froce 58 under Adm. MARC MITSCHER launched 72 Hellcats from five carriers to attack inside the protected anchorage of the Truk lagoon. The result of this first engagement was the sinking of two light cruisers, four destroyers, nine smaller naval vessels, and 24 merchant ships. The attack damaged or destroyed virtually all of the 365 Japanese planes at Truk. The cost to the Americans was 25 aircraft and serious damage to the aircraft carrier *Intrepid.*

Mitscher's Task Force 58 returned to Truk on April 28 and 29 with the intention of finishing off Truk, an installation of such strategic importance that it was often called the "Gibraltar of the Pacific." Mitscher launched fighters and bombers against the base, sinking ships and destroying 93 aircraft. Although 46 U.S. pilots were shot down, most were rescued.

A U.S. Navy OS2U floatplane is recovered after rescuing downed pilot Lt. JG. G. M. Blair during the Battle of Truk. *(National Archives and Records Administration)*

Together, the two battles entirely neutralized Truk, opening the way for the U.S. offensive to move beyond the Carolines and on to the MARIANA ISLANDS CAMPAIGN.

Further reading: Lindemann, Klaus. *Hailstorm over Truk Lagoon: Operations against Truk by Carrier Task Force 58, 17 and 18 February 1944, and the Shipwrecks of World War II.* Singapore: Maruzen Asia, 1982; Stewart, William Herman. *Ghost Fleet of the Truk Lagoon: An Account of "Operation Hailstone," February, 1944.* Missoula, Mont.: Pictorial Histories, 1986.

Truman, Harry S. (1884–1972) *thirty-third president of the United States, succeeding Franklin D. Roosevelt*

Born in, Lamar, Missouri, and raised in Independence, Truman was the son of a farmer. After graduating from high school, he worked as a bank clerk in Kansas City, Missouri, then returned to the family farm near Grandview in 1906 and took over its management following the death of his father in 1914. When the United States entered World War I in 1917, Truman—at 33 well beyond draft age—volunteered and served in France as the captain of a field artillery battery. He returned to the United States in 1919, married his childhood sweetheart, Elizabeth ("Bess") Wallace, and started a haberdashery with an army buddy. The business went bankrupt a short time later, and in 1922, supported by the powerful Kansas City Democratic machine of Thomas "Boss" Pendergast, Truman was elected to a county judgeship (in Missouri, the equivalent of county commissioner). Although he failed to gain reelection in 1924, he was elected presiding judge of the county court in 1926 and served two four-year terms, during which he built a reputation for honesty and efficiency—which made him popular with his constituents, but also alarmed Pendergast, fearful that he might be unable to control his protégé.

Despite Pendergast's misgivings, he tapped Truman as a candidate for the U.S. Senate—after everyone else he had approached turned him down. Truman was elected and entered the Senate in

Harry S. Truman *(Harry S. Truman Presidential Library)*

1935. His first term was undistinguished, especially because his colleagues were suspicious of his origins and typically referred to him as the "Senator from Pendergast." He was nevertheless reelected, and during his second term he created the Special Committee Investigating National Defense, soon better known as the Truman Committee. Truman and the committee quickly earned national recognition for their investigations of graft, fraud, and deficiencies in defense and war production. The Truman Committee not only saved the government significant amounts of money, it also ensured a high degree of efficiency and reliability in America's war industries.

In 1944, President FRANKLIN D. ROOSEVELT chose Truman, now a nationally recognized figure, as his running mate in his fourth-term candidacy. During his 82 days as vice president, Truman met only once with the president—and that briefly. When FDR died suddenly on April 12, 1945,

Truman assumed office with virtually no preparation. Although the war in Europe was near victory, the war against Japan was still raging. Truman had the burden of catching up on all the president had failed to tell him (including the imminence of an atomic bomb), on continuing to prosecute a titanic two-front war, and on trying to govern in the footsteps of a political giant.

Truman quickly took up his task and saw the nation through to victory. It was his decision to use atomic weapons against Japan, and it was he who handled the difficult negotiations with the Soviets at the end of the war. After the war, Truman became the architect of America's cold war strategy of the "containment" of communism. He championed the MARSHALL PLAN for the postwar recovery of Europe and a subsequent aid program for the countries of Asia.

Against all predictions, Truman was reelected in 1948, defeating Republican candidate Thomas E. Dewey. During his second term, he introduced an extension of FDR's New Deal, called the Fair Deal, which included ambitious social welfare programs—most of which were defeated or diluted. Truman scored a new cold war victory in 1948 with his management of the Berlin crisis by using the Berlin Airlift, and he led the United States in the creation of the North Atlantic Treaty Organization (NATO). The most critical test of the so-called Truman Doctrine—as the containment policy came to be called—came in June 1950 with the start of the Korean War. Truman navigated a difficult course, setting as his objective the defeat of the Communist forces that had invaded South Korea without touching off a larger war—quite possibly a third world war.

The frustrations of the Korean War—and especially his firing of General DOUGLAS MACARTHUR as supreme commander of U.S. and UN forces in Korea—made Truman a most unpopular president during his second term. He chose not to run again and was succeeded by DWIGHT DAVID EISENHOWER.

Truman enjoyed a long and productive retirement in his beloved Missouri after leaving the White House, writing two memoirs and devoting much of his time to his favorite pursuit, reading history. He also lived long enough to see his reputation rise in the eye of history. By the time of his death, he knew that many Americans regarded him as a great president—in the 20th century perhaps second only to FDR.

Further reading: Ferrell, Robert H., ed. *The Autobiography of Harry S. Truman.* Boulder: Colorado Associated University Press, 1980; Ferrell, Robert H., ed. *Dear Bess: The Letters from Harry to Bess Truman, 1910–1959.* New York: Norton, 1983; Ferrell, Robert H., ed. *Harry S. Truman: A Life.* Columbia: University of Missouri Press, 1994; Ferrell, Robert H., ed. *Off the Record: The Private Papers of Harry S. Truman.* 1980; reprint ed., Columbia: University of Missouri Press, 1997; McCullough, David. *Truman.* New York: Simon and Schuster, 1992; Truman, Harry S. *Memoirs, Volume 1: Year of Decisions.* Garden City, N.Y.: Doubleday, 1955; Truman, Harry S. *Memoirs, Volume 2: Years of Trial and Hope.* Garden City, N.Y.: Doubleday, 1956.

Truscott, Lucian (1895–1965) *U.S. general who commanded (successively) 3rd Infantry Division, VI Corps, Fifteenth Army, and Fifth Army*

A native of Chatfield, Texas, Truscott enlisted in the army after the United States entered World War I in 1917. He was chosen for officer training and received his commission in the cavalry as a second lieutenant. He did not see action in World War I, but, between the wars, served in the cavalry as well as staff posts.

In 1942, Colonel Truscott developed an American commando unit modeled after the British commandos. Promoted to brigadier general, Truscott took command of the unit—designated as the 1st Ranger Battalion—on June 19, 1942, and served under William O. Darby. Little less than a year later, Truscott was promoted to major general and assigned command of the 3rd Infantry Division in April 1943. He was instrumental in planning OPERATION HUSKY, the invasion of Sicily, and he led his division in the operation during July 1943. Truscott next participated in the ITALIAN CAMPAIGN, landing at Salerno in September 1943. In January 1944, during the Anzio campaign, after VI Corps under Lieutenant General John P. Lucas failed to break out of the beachhead, Truscott was ordered to relieve him. It was Truscott who finally managed the breakthrough.

After Anzio, Truscott continued to command VI Corps in Italy until August 1944, when he and his corps were transferred to the western front as part of Operation Anvil/Dragoon, the Allied landings on the French Riviera, which followed up the Normandy landings (D-day) to the north. VI Corps landed on August 15, 1944. Two months later, in October, he was given command of the newly formed Fifteenth Army. This was followed in December by a return to Italy and command of the Fifth Army, after Lieutenant General Mark Clark was promoted to command of 15th Army Group. Truscott had command of the Fifth during the difficult winter of 1944–45, by which time most of his army was fighting in the rugged mountains of Italy's north. Truscott saw the Fifth Army through to the end of the Italian Campaign and the war.

On October 8, 1945, Truscott relieved General George S. Patton Jr. as commander of Third U.S. Army and served as military governor of occupied Bavaria. When the Seventh Army was deactivated in March 1946, Truscott and the Third Army also assumed administration of the Western Military District, which included parts of Baden, Württemberg, and Hesse-Darmstadt. Truscott was a courageous and vigorous leader in some of the most difficult sectors of the European war.

See also Rangers.

Further reading: Truscott, Lucian. *Command Missions: A Personal Story.* Novato, Calif.: Presidio, 1990.

Turing, Alan (1912–1954) *mathematician who developed early computer theory and was instrumental in British cryptography and code breaking during World War II*

Alan Mathison Turing was born in London, the son of a civil servant in the Indian service. He graduated from King's College, Cambridge, with a degree in mathematics in 1934 and was elected to a fellowship at the college for his research in probability theory. Two years later, he published "On Computable Numbers, with an Application to the *Entscheidungsproblem* [Decision Problem]." This paper is widely viewed as the modern foundation of computer theory.

In the same year that "On Computable Numbers" appeared, Turing enrolled at Princeton University and earned a Ph.D. in mathematical logic in 1938.

Turing returned to England and King's College in 1938 and, at the outbreak of World War II in September 1939, volunteered his services at the headquarters of the Government Code and Cipher School at Bletchley Park, Buckinghamshire. Turing was part of a team dedicated to breaking the "unbreakable" German Enigma cipher and machine. Turing and the others elaborated on the

Alan Turing, as commemorated on a postage stamp *(Author's collection)*

work of a team of Polish mathematician-cryptanalysts to create, during 1939 and the spring of 1940, a radically new code-breaking machine called the Bombe—after the Polish-built Bomba (an earlier, now outmoded decryption machine, that was named after a Polish ice cream).

Turing's ever-evolving Bombes were early computers, which allowed the Bletchley Park cryptanalysts to decode some 39,000 intercepted messages each month by 1942; later in the war, this volume rose to an astounding 84,000 messages. Thanks to Turing's work, a great many German military, naval, and diplomatic radio messages were routinely decoded. At the end of the war, Turing was made an officer of the Order of the British Empire in recognition of his work.

After the war, Turing joined the National Physical Laboratory (NPL) in 1945 and began to design an electronic computer. His design for the Automatic Computing Engine (ACE) was a nearly complete plan for an electronic stored-program general-purpose digital computer, but the machine, which his colleagues considered too complex, was never built. Discouraged, Turing left NPL and became deputy director of the Computing Machine Laboratory in Manchester. He designed the programming system for the Mark I, the world's first commercially available electronic digital computer. In 1951, Turing was elected a fellow of the Royal Society, but a year later, in March 1952, he was tried on charges of homosexuality—then a crime under British law—and sentenced to a year of hormone therapy. In the depths of the cold war, the British government judged him to be a security risk, and he withdrew to the University of Manchester in May 1953 as the first reader in the Theory of Computing.

Turing had embarked in 1951 on research into the extraordinary field of artificial life—using the Mark I to model chemical mechanisms by which genes could control the development of anatomical structure in plants and animals—and despite his conviction for homosexuality and the loss of his security clearance, he seemed healthy and happy. He was found on June 7, 1954, dead in his bed. The cause was cyanide poisoning. Police investigators found a homemade device for silver-plating teaspoons, which included a cyanide reservoir, in Turing's house. Officially, the mysterious death was declared a suicide.

Further reading: Hodges, Andrew. *Alan Turing: The Enigma.* New York: Simon and Schuster, 1983; Newton, David E. *Alan Turing: A Study in Light and Shadow.* Philadelphia: Xlibris, 2003; Turing, Alan Mathison. *The Essential Turing: Seminal Writings in Computing, Logic, Philosophy, Artificial Intelligence, and Artificial Life, Plus the Secrets of Enigma.* New York: Oxford University Press, 2004.

Turkey

Turkey had thrown in its lot with Germany and the other Central Powers during World War I and suffered mightily for it. Most of the Turkish leaders of the World War II era had lived through the first war, and they were determined to keep their nation out of the second world conflagration. Moreover, the Turks were well aware that their armed forces were inadequate in strength and equipped with obsolescent vehicles and weaponry. They had no desire to assume a war footing. Ismet Inönü, successor to President Kemal Atatürk, enjoyed dictatorial power and decreed absolute neutrality. No other Turkish politician challenged this position.

It was one thing to declare neutrality, however, and another to maintain it. Turkey and the USSR had long been enemies, but the Turks relied on a 1925 Treaty of Friendship—renewed in 1935—to avoid hostility with their northern neighbor. Italy was seen as a more serious threat, and in May 1939, Turkey and Great Britain issued a joint declaration proclaiming that they would aid each other if an act of aggression should lead to war in the Mediterranean. The language was sufficiently vague that Turkey believed it had guaranteed aid to itself if attacked but had not incurred a reciprocal obligation to aid Britain. In June 1939, France and Turkey issued a similar declaration.

Turkey's feeling of security did not last long. The GERMAN-SOVIET NON-AGGRESSION PACT of August 1939 strongly suggested that Germany and the USSR might well combine to attack Turkey. The Turkish foreign minister made a preemptive trip to Moscow in the hope of negotiating a mutual security pact, but the effort came to nothing; therefore, Turkey signed a tripartite treaty in October 1939 with the British and French, who promised to come to Turkey's aid if it were attacked by another European power. In return, Turkey would aid France and Britain if there were an act of aggression leading to war in the Mediterranean. The treaty exempted Turkey from giving such aid if the Soviet Union were involved.

The outbreak and early course of the war rendered these agreements essentially moot and placed Turkey at grave risk. The fall of France in the BATTLE OF FRANCE meant that it could not help Turkey—but neither could beleaguered Great Britain. On the other hand, Britain was not about to prevail upon Turkey for aid, since it recognized that doing so would invite German or Italian conquest of the country. The German occupation of the Balkans by April 1941 brought the war to the very frontiers of Turkey, prompting that nation to conclude a Treaty of Territorial Integrity and Friendship with Germany on June 18, 1941. This brought some relief—but not as much as the INVASION OF THE SOVIET UNION, which occurred just four days later. Now it seemed highly unlikely that either the Soviets or the Germans would invade Turkey. Nevertheless, Germany's ambassador to Turkey, FRANZ VON PAPEN, repeatedly pressured Inönü to join the war on Germany's side. The Turkish leader unwaveringly refused.

The gradual turning of the tide against the Axis in the fall of 1942 prompted WINSTON CHURCHILL to apply pressure of his own, urging Turkey to join the war on the side of the Allies. Toward this end, the Allies provided the Turks with significant quantities of military supplies and hardware, but Turkey continually dodged commitment until the defeat of Germany was a foregone conclusion. At last, on February 23, 1945, the nation declared war against Germany—doing so mainly to establish itself as a founding member of the UNITED NATIONS.

No sooner had the war in Europe ended than JOSEPH STALIN threatened Turkey by warning that he would not renew the Treaty of Friendship and Territorial Integrity unless the Turks permitted the establishment of Soviet bases in the Dardanelles straits and unless Kars and Ardahan, provinces on Turkey's eastern border, were ceded to the Soviets. Turkey, having survived World War II unscathed, now faced the Soviets at the start of the cold war.

Further reading: Deringil, Selim. *Turkish Foreign Policy during the Second World War: An "Active" Neutrality.* Cambridge and New York: Cambridge University Press, 2004; Weber, Frak G. *The Evasive Neutral: Germany, Britain and the Quest for a Turkish Alliance in the Second World War.* Columbia: University of Missouri Press, 1985.

Turner, Richmond (1885–1961) *American admiral, architect of amphibious warfare in the Pacific*

Richmond Kelly Turner was born in Portland, Oregon, and graduated from the U.S. Naval Academy at Annapolis in 1908. Over the next four years, he served in a variety of assignments on various ships and in 1913 Lt. (j.g.) Turner was given command of the destroyer *Stewart*. He then was transferred to ordnance engineering training, served briefly on the gunboat *Marietta*, and was assigned to the battleships *Pennsylvania, Michigan,* and *Mississippi* during 1916–19.

Promoted to lieutenant commander, Turner served from 1919 to 1922 as ordnance officer at the Naval Gun Factory, Washington, D.C., then transferred to sea duty as gunnery officer aboard the battleship *California.* He also served as fleet gunnery officer on the Staff of Commander Scouting Fleet and was commanding officer of the destroyer *Mervine.*

In 1925, Turner was promoted to commander and was assigned to the Bureau of Ordnance at the Navy Department. In 1927, he took flight training at Pensacola, Florida, and in 1928 assumed command of the seaplane tender *Jason.* He served concurrently as commander, Aircraft Squadrons, Asiatic Fleet. During 1933–34, he was executive officer of the aircraft carrier *Saratoga.*

Rear Admiral Richmond Turner confers with marine general Alexander Vandegraft. *(National Archives and Records Administration)*

Now a captain, Turner enrolled in the Naval War College, then was appointed to the faculty of the college, serving in this capacity during 1935–38. His next sea duty was as commander of the heavy cruiser *Astoria,* which he sailed on a diplomatic mission to Japan in 1939.

Turner returned to shore duty in 1940 as director of the War Plans Division in Washington, D.C. In 1941 he was promoted to rear admiral and in December 1941 was named assistant chief of staff to the commander in chief, U.S. Fleet. He left this post in June 1942 to take command of the Amphibious Force, South Pacific Force. In this capacity, Turner (subsequently promoted to vice admiral) planned and executed amphibious assaults on enemy positions in the south, central, and western Pacific. Turner became the chief architect of U.S. Pacific amphibious strategy. He was promoted to admiral and assigned the task of commanding the amphibious component of the invasion of Japan. That nation's surrender after the atomic attacks on Hiroshima and Nagasaki made this last posting of the war unnecessary.

After the war, Turner served on the Navy Department's General Board and was named U.S. naval representative to the United Nations Military Staff Committee. He retired in July 1947.

Further reading: Dyer, George Carroll. *The Amphibians Came to Conquer: The Story of Admiral Richmond Kelly Turner.* Washington, D.C.: U.S. Government Printing Office, 1971.

Tuskegee Airmen

In May 1939, two pilots of the National Airman's Association, an organization of African-American aviators, met with Missouri senator HARRY S. TRUMAN, who agreed to sponsor a bill to allow black pilots to serve in the Civilian Pilot Training Program of the U.S. Army Air Corps (USAAC), which was then an all-white force. In December 1940, under pressure from the administration of FRANKLIN D. ROOSEVELT, the USAAC submitted a plan to the War Department for creating an "experimental" all-black fighter squadron consisting of 33 pilots. On January 16, 1941, the 99th Pursuit Squadron was created, to be trained at Tuskegee Army Air Field in Tuskegee, Alabama. A few months later, on July 19, 1941, the air corps—now redesignated the U.S. Army Air Forces—instituted a program to train African Americans as military pilots, with primary flight training to be conducted by the Division of Aeronautics of Tuskegee Institute, the celebrated black institution of higher education first led by Booker T. Washington in 1881. After completing primary training at Moton Field on the Tuskegee campus, each pilot was to be sent to the neighboring Tuskegee Army Air Field for advanced flight training, including transition to combat aircraft.

The first class of Tuskegee airmen graduated on March 7, 1942, and was assigned to the 99th Fighter Squadron, under the command of Lt. Col. Benjamin Davis Jr., one of a handful of African-American officers in the segregated U.S. Army Air Force of the period. On April 15, 1943, the 99th was shipped out to North Africa to fly fighter escort for bombers. On July 2, 1943, a Tuskegee pilot, Capt. Charles B. Hall, became the first of the airmen to score a victory, shooting down a German FW-190 fighter.

Later in 1943, the 322d Fighter Group was organized, consisting of three all-black fighter squadrons, and, with the 99th Squadron, relocated to bases in Italy as part of the Twelfth Air Force.

The Tuskegee airmen met with initial prejudice from many white pilots; however, the black aviators soon amassed a superb record and were so skilled at bomber escort that Twelfth Air Force bomber crews specifically requested fighter escorts to be drawn from the black units. Four Tuskegee airmen were decorated with the Distinguished Flying Cross, the most coveted pilot decoration in the Army Air Force.

In September 1943, the Army Air Force began a twin-engine training program at Tuskegee to train black bomber pilots. The war ended before any of the bomber pilots saw combat. By war's end, 992 pilots had graduated from Tuskegee training, of whom 450 served in combat. Some 150 Tuskegee airmen died in training or in action. The Tuskegee program also trained other black personnel for aircrew and ground-crew duties, including flight engineers, gunners, mechanics, and so on. The Army Air Force set up other segregated schools in Texas and New Mexico to train black airmen as navigators and bombardiers.

The all-black 477th Bombardment Group was created late in the war and was stationed first at Godman Field, Kentucky, then at Freeman Field, Indiana. The Tuskegee airmen of the 477th protested the particularly stringent segregationist policies of Freeman Field commander Col. Robert Selway, and on April 5, 1945, black pilots tried to enter the segregated officer's club. Four days later, Col. Selway ordered the black officers to sign a statement that they had read and accepted "Regulation 85-2," which stated the segregation policy. One hundred one officers refused, and the refusal was noted negatively in their service records. It was not until August 12, 1995, that the U.S. Air Force officially cleared the service records of the so-called Freeman Field Mutineers.

Further reading: Bucholtz, Chirs. *332nd Fighter Group: Tuskegee Airmen.* London: Osprey, 2007; Homan, Lynn M., and Thomas Reilly. *Tuskegee Airmen.* Charleston, S.C.: Arcadia Tempus, 1998.

U

Ukraine campaign

Nowhere was the German INVASION OF THE SOVIET UNION more successful or devastating than in Ukraine, which offered little effective resistance to the invaders until after the spring of 1943 and the Soviet victory at the BATTLE OF STALINGRAD. With this, the Soviets were in a position to begin a campaign to drive southwest into the German-occupied Ukraine along a 500-mile front between the Pripet Marshes on the north and the Black Sea on the south.

Generals Markian Popov, KONSTANTIN ROKOSSOVSKY, Nikolai Vatutin, Ivan Konev, Rodion Malinovsky, Fedor Tolbukhin, and Ivan Petrov led the Soviet forces south from Orel beginning on July 23, 1943. The tactic used can best be described as a steamroller, with tremendously powerful massed attacks by armor (including the famed Soviet T-34 tank, generally considered the finest all-around tank of the war), ground-support aircraft, and heavy artillery, with the liberal application of rockets. The German defenders steadily fell back before the onslaught. Popov took Orel on August 5, and Vatutin captured Belgorod (200 miles to the south) on the same day. This accomplished, he advanced to the southwest to reinforce Konev's attack on Kharkov. Kharkov was a key city, used by both armies as a hub of communications and supply. It had already changed hands twice. Konev was determined to retake it and, with Vatutin, enveloped the German positions in Kharkov, which fell on August 23.

After this third and final Battle of Kharkov, Vatutin withdrew to the northwest to join forces with Rokossovsky. In September, the two led their combined armies in a breakthrough to Konotop, deep inside the Ukraine. While this was developing, Tolbukhin, 200 miles south of Kharkov, attacked German positions between Stalino and the Sea of Azov beginning on August 22. Soviet tanks made short work of second-line German troops (mainly militia forces) and advanced into Taganrog on August 30. On September 7, Malinovsky captured Stalino.

To the south of these operations, Petrov attacked the final German bridgehead into the Caucasus, which stretched from the Taman Peninsula south to Novorossisk, a city the Soviets had held under siege for nearly a year. Now, on September 15, Petrov finally broke through, forcing the remnants of eight German divisions to retreat across the Kerch Strait into the Crimea by September 28. The German Seventeenth Army offered stiff resistance and held in position in the Crimea until the spring of 1944.

The great Soviet drive inexorably forced the Germans toward the vast Pripet Marshes. These were largely impassable, and the German commanders realized the marshes would force the retreating armies to divide and probably suffer defeat in detail. The only alternative to this was to fight rearguard actions aimed at rescuing major units by allowing them to move north into Belarus and south into other parts of the Ukraine. Next, Field Marshals GÜNTHER VON KLUGE and ERICH VON MANSTEIN were ordered to hold the line of the Dnieper River. This would stabilize the front during the winter, buying time for the withdrawal of the armies intact. Anticipating this, the Red Army commanders advanced rapidly on four fronts. In the north (the First Ukrainian Front), on September 23, Rokossovsky captured Chernigov, 75 miles northeast of Kiev. To his left, Vatutin crossed the Dnieper early in October, positioning his forces north and south of Kiev. As Vatutin held his position on either side of the city, Rokossovsky, on November 6, entered and retook Kiev from the east. Vatutin then advanced rapidly westward, but was stopped by panzers under HASSO VON MANTEUFFEL.

On the Second Ukrainian Front, located on the Dnieper downstream from the First Front, Konev established a bridgehead on the river across from Kremenchug early in October. He then advanced to the southwest, opening the Third Ukrainian Front, which Malinovsky exploited by crossing the Dnieper to capture Dnepropetrovsk on October 25, defeating the forces of Field Marshal PAUL VON KLEIST.

South of this newly opened front, the Fourth Ukrainian Front was only thinly held by the Germans. They yielded to the advance of Tolbukhin as he marched all the way to the Dnieper's Black Sea mouth. This cut off all the German forces in the Crimea.

The year 1943 ended without a clearly defined German line left to attack; therefore, the Soviets simply swept en masse across the western half of the Ukraine. Vatutin thrust out of Kiev in a great winter offensive beginning on December 24, 1943. Before January, he had recaptured Korosten and Zhitomir. On January 4, Vatutin crossed the 1939 Polish frontier. Coordinated with this westward advance, a northern force sped 100 miles forward to capture Lutsk on February 5, and a southern force reinforced Konev's right wing, allowing the envelopment of 10 German divisions on February 3. ADOLF HITLER personally ordered these surrounded forces to hold their position on the Dnieper near Cherkassy. Manstein attempted to relieve the trapped soldiers but only incurred 20,000 casualties in the process. On February 7, 18,000 German troops surrendered to the Red Army. Nikopol, in the eastern bend of the Dnieper, fell to Tolbukhin on February 8. While Tolbukhin proceeded with mop-up operations, Malinovsky advanced the Third Ukrainian Front to Krivoi Rog by February 22.

Early the next month, Vatutin was mortally wounded. His First Ukrainian Army was taken over by GEORGI ZHUKOV, who launched an offensive beginning on March 4, 1944. Within five days, he was outside of Tarnopol. In the meantime, Konev attacked from the south on March 6, routing a panzer force near Uman, then crossing the Bug River on March 15. He rushed beyond this point another 70 miles to take the German pontoon bridge over the Dniester River at Mogilev. In the course of this advance, Vinnitsa, former headquarters of Adolf Hitler in the Ukraine, fell on March 20.

Farther south, Malinovsky raced across the mouths of the Dnieper and the Bug to take Kherson on March 13 and Nikolayev on March 28. By the end of the month, Zhukov occupied what had been prewar Romania. At the same time, Konev reached the Carpathian foothills. Zhukov kept moving westward, marching through Jablonica Pass, which opened the Hungarian Plain to the Red Army.

Hitler responded to the Soviet invasion of Hungary by occupying that country. Additionally, he ordered a strong counterattack (led by WALTHER MODEL) from Lvov, Ukraine, which blunted Zhukov's thrust. At this time, Konev, thwarted along the northern Romanian frontier, turned his left flank south along the Dniester, menacing the rear of the Germans opposing Malinovsky's drive along the north shore of the Black Sea. This effectively squeezed the Germans out of Odessa on April 10.

By July, when the Red Army renewed its offensive, Lvov was the only Ukrainian city still held by the Germans. It was recaptured on July 27, even as masses of Red Army troops were storming through the Balkans and Poland. The Ukraine campaign was at an end.

See also KHARKOV, BATTLES OF.

Further reading: Bergstrom, Christer, and Andrey Mikhailov. *Black Cross/Red Star: Operation Barbarossa 1941.* Pacifica, Calif.: Pacifica Press, 2000; Clark, Alan. *Barbarossa.* New York: Harper Perennial, 1985; Fugate, Bryan I. *Operation Barbarossa: Strategy and Tactics on the Eastern Front, 1941.* Novato, Calif.: Presidio Press, 1984; Glantz, David M., and Harold S. Orenstein. *The Battle for the Ukraine: The Red Army's Korsun'-Shevchenkovskii Operation, 1944.* London: Frank Cass, 2003.

Ultra

Ultra was the name that the British intelligence service initially applied to its decrypts of German communications in World War II. Before the war ended, the United States also used the term, which was applied to all intelligence derived from any important cryptanalytic sources. The origin of the name is in the designation of code breaking as a secret beyond "top secret"—that is, an *ultra secret.*

The looseness with which the term *Ultra* was applied by the end of the war has led to some confusion, especially because "Ultra" was often used synonymously and specifically with decrypts of messages coded by the ENIGMA CIPHER AND MACHINE. This need not cause undo confusion since most Ultra decrypts were derived from German traffic generated by Enigma.

Ultra decrypts were tremendously valuable to the Allies, but they had to be exploited sparingly, lest the enemy become aware that his ciphers had been compromised. (Indeed, the decrypted information was used with such care that neither the Germans nor the Japanese ever discovered that their major codes had been broken and that their radio communication was being routinely intercepted and read.) Often, Ultra intelligence was deliberately withheld from commanders in the field. When information relating to the location of U-boats was received, for instance, the information was not disseminated without a cover story. The commanders of vessels hunting U-boats might be told that a search plane had "accidentally" discovered the location of a boat.

Although Ultra intelligence came too late to be of help during the BATTLE OF BRITAIN, it was valu-able in almost every encounter after this period. In the Pacific, "Ultra" was often applied to PURPLE (JAPANESE DIPLOMATIC CIPHER) decrypts.

Prime Minister WINSTON CHURCHILL once declared, "It was thanks to Ultra that we won the war." Churchill believed that the Ultra intelligence was most valuable in tracking U-boats, which preyed upon Allied convoys and continually threatened to strangle the British lifeline from America.

See also MAGIC (JAPANESE CODE) and ORANGE (JAPANESE CODE).

Further reading: Aldrich, Richard J. *Intelligence and the War against Japan: Britain, America and the Politics of Secret Service.* New York: Cambridge University Press, 2000; Hodges, Alan. *Alan Turing: The Enigma.* New York: Walker, 2000; Kozaczuk, Wladyslaw, and Jerzy Straszak. *Enigma: How the Poles Broke the Nazi Code.* London: Hippocrene, 2004; Lewin, Ronald. *The American Magic: Codes, Ciphers, and the Defeat of Japan.* New York: Penguin, 1983; Sebag-Montefiore, Hugh. *Enigma: The Battle for the Code.* New York: Wiley, 2001; Winton, John. *Ultra in the Pacific: How Breaking Japanese Codes and Ciphers Affected Naval Operations against Japan 1941–45.* London: Leo Cooper, 1993.

United Nations

The League of Nations, created by the TREATY OF VERSAILLES (which was never ratified by the United States) proved utterly incapable of averting World War II. Despite this fact, both President FRANKLIN D. ROOSEVELT and Prime Minister WINSTON CHURCHILL believed that the basic concept of the League of Nations had been valid and that the world required a new, more effective deliberative body and forum to manage global affairs and to avert future wars. This concept was adumbrated in the ATLANTIC CHARTER, signed by Roosevelt and Churchill in August 1941, before the United States entered the war. During the early phases of the war, following America's entry, the term "United Nations" was used synonymously with "Allies," denoting those countries united in opposition to the Axis. Twenty-six "United Nations" subscribed to the UNITED NATIONS DECLARATION of January 1, 1942, a document that stated Allied war aims.

As for planning the "United Nations" as an international body to replace the defunct League of Nations, Roosevelt, Churchill, and the Soviet Union's JOSEPH STALIN took the lead. The first concrete step in the creation of the organization came in during August 21–October 7, 1944, at the Dumbarton Oaks Conference, in Washington, D.C., at the Dumbarton Oaks Estate. Here diplomats and international scholars from the United States, Great Britain, the Soviet Union, and China hammered out the contours of the United Nations. They agreed on its purpose, its general structure, and, in principle, its function, but had serious disagreements over membership and voting—mainly because the Soviets insisted that each constituent republic of the USSR be given an individual membership and a vote—something that would have yielded to the Soviets' disproportionate control over the decisions of the UN. At the YALTA CONFERENCE, held in the Crimean Black Sea resort town of Yalta during February 1945, Roosevelt, Churchill, and Stalin laid out the nature and authority of the Security Council and also reached a tentative compromise on the number of Soviet republics to be granted independent memberships in the UN. They also agreed that the UN would include a trusteeship system to succeed the League of Nations mandate system. The Yalta decisions were combined with the Dumbarton Oaks proposals as the basis for discussion at the United Nations Conference on International Organization (UNCIO), which convened—even before World War II had ended—at San Francisco on April 25, 1945.

Attended by representatives of 50 countries, the conference produced the final Charter of the United Nations. That document was signed on June 26 and promulgated on October 24, 1945, a little more than a month after the Japanese surrender ended the war.

Further reading: Eichelberger, Clark M. *Organizing for Peace: A Personal History of the Founding of the United Nations.* New York: Harper & Row, 1977; Schlesinger,

Stephen C. *Act of Creation—The Founding of the United Nations: A Story of Superpowers, Secret Agents, Wartime Allies and Enemies, and Their Quest for a Peaceful World.* Denver: Westview Press, 2004.

United Nations Declaration

In a meeting at Washington. D.C., the 26 principal nations united against the Axis powers in World War II signed the United Nations Declaration on January 1, 1942, pledging their resources to achieving complete victory in accordance with the principles of the ATLANTIC CHARTER. The original signatories included the United States, Great Britain, the Soviet Union, China, Australia, Belgium, Canada, Costa Rica, Cuba, Czechoslovakia, Dominican Republic, El Salvador, Greece, Guatemala, Haiti, Honduras, India, Luxembourg, the Netherlands, New Zealand, Nicaragua, Norway, Panama, Poland, South Africa, and Yugoslavia. In addition, a number of nations subsequently communicated adherence to the declaration: Mexico (June 5, 1942), Philippines (June 10, 1942), Ethiopia (July 28, 1942), Iraq (Jan. 16, 1943), Brazil (Feb. 8, 1943), Bolivia (Apr. 27, 1943), Iran (Sept. 10, 1943), Colombia (Dec. 22, 1943), Liberia (Feb. 26, 1944), France (Dec. 26, 1944), Ecuador (Feb. 7, 1945), Peru (Feb. 11, 1945), Chile (Feb. 12, 1945), Paraguay (Feb. 12, 1945), Venezuela (Feb. 16, 1945), Uruguay (Feb. 23, 1945), Turkey (Feb. 24, 1945), Egypt (Feb. 27, 1945), and Saudi Arabia (Mar. 1, 1945).

The United Nations Declaration was a brief, straightforward document:

> The Governments signatory hereto,
>
> Having subscribed to a common program of purposes and principles embodied in the Joint Declaration of the President of United States of America and the Prime Minister of the United Kingdom of Great Britain and Northern Ireland dated August 14, 1941, known as the Atlantic Charter.
>
> Being convinced that complete victory over their enemies is essential to defend life, liberty, independence and religious freedom, and to preserve

human rights and justice in their own lands as well as in other lands, and that they are now engaged in a common struggle against savage and brutal forces seeking to subjugate the world,

DECLARE:

(1) Each Government pledges itself to employ its full resources, military or economic, against those members of the Tripartite Pact and its adherents with which such government is at war.

(2) Each Government pledges itself to cooperate with the Governments signatory hereto and not to make a separate armistice or peace with the enemies.

The foregoing declaration may be adhered to by other nations which are, or which may be, rendering material assistance and contributions in the struggle for victory over Hitlerism.

The principles of the Atlantic Charter, to which the signatories of the United Nations Declaration subscribed, included the renunciation of territorial aggression; prohibition of territorial changes without consent of the peoples concerned; restoration of sovereign rights and self-government; access to essential raw materials for all nations; world economic cooperation; freedom from fear; freedom from want; freedom of the seas; and disarmament of aggressors.

In much the same way as Woodrow Wilson's famous Fourteen Points of 1918 had been the basis of the Covenant of the League of Nations, the Atlantic Charter's principles, as confirmed by the United Nations Declaration would serve as the philosophical foundation for the establishment of the UNITED NATIONS as the war came to an end.

Further reading: Armstrong, David, Lorna Lloyd, and John Redmond. *From Versailles to Maastricht: International Organizations in the Twentieth Century.* New York: St. Martin's Press, 1996; Army Information School. *Pillars of Peace: Documents Pertaining to American Interest in Establishing a Lasting World Peace.* Carlisle Barracks, Pa.: Book Department, Army Information School, 1946; Hoopes, Townsend, and Douglas Brinkley. *FDR and the Creation of the U.N.* New Haven, Conn.: Yale University Press, 1997; Patterson, Charles. *The Oxford 50th Anniversary Book of the United Nations.* New York: Oxford University Press, 1995.

United States

Except for a relatively brief period of imperialist expansion at the end of the 19th century and beginning of the 20th—the period of the Spanish-American War, the annexation of the Philippines, and the acquisition of other Pacific territories—the United States had been largely isolationist in popular sentiment. This was the case at the time of the outbreak of World War II in Europe, although foreign policy under FRANKLIN D. ROOSEVELT inexorably moved the nation closer to international engagement.

President Woodrow Wilson had taken the nation into World War I to "make the world safe for democracy"—really, to remold the world in the democratic image of the United States—but this foray into an interventionist foreign policy, although it defeated the Central Powers in the war, did not bring about the millennial change in world affairs Wilson had promised and hoped for. After World War I, Congress and the American public repudiated Wilson's internationalism by rejecting both the TREATY OF VERSAILLES and the League of

Women flocked to war factories during World War II. Here a woman assembles part of a plexiglass turret for a bomber. *(National Archives and Records Administration)*

U.S. Manufacturing during World War II

Legend:
- ■ Principal location of munitions manufacture
- ▼ Naval shipyard
- ▽ Merchant shipyard
- ⬡ Automobile companies making tanks and trucks
- ✈ Center of aircraft production
- ☢ Main Manhattan Project site

- Norfolk — Major center of war production
- ▮ Center of oil production
- — Main oil pipeline

© Infobase Publishing

Nations, and, under Wilson's successor, Warren G. Harding, the United States retreated into an isolationism that was more determined than ever. In addition to rejecting Versailles and the League, the U.S. Senate readily ratified the agreements produced by the Washington Naval Armament Conference of 1922, which mandated the scrapping of many warships and put severe limitations on the construction of new vessels. Moreover, the United States agreed that it would refrain from fortifying its Pacific possessions west of Hawaii—including Guam and the Philippines.

In the interwar years, the U.S. Army and Navy were greatly reduced in strength. During the period, the average strength of the regular army was about 135,000 men. The navy's average strength was 100,000. As war clouds gathered in Europe during the late 1930s—and when war began in September 1939—President Roosevelt successfully coaxed

Congress into war preparations at an accelerating tempo, greatly increasing defense production, instituting the first peacetime draft in American history, and successively modifying the NEUTRALITY ACTS to allow for furnishing arms and other materiel to the Allies.

While it is true that the United States entered World War II—on December 8, 1941—better prepared than it had ever been for any earlier war, the army of 1940 consisted of only 260,023 men, the navy of 160,997, and the marines just 28,345. By the time of the BATTLE OF PEARL HARBOR, these numbers were much higher—1,657,157 personnel in the army, 383,150 in the navy, and 75,346 in the marines—but the small force that existed in the years immediately leading up to the war meant that the United States had a disproportionately weak hand when it came to diplomacy. Although the nation's tremendous production capacity made it a major player economically, the United States was in no position to make military threats to powers that had already geared up for war. All the worse for the United States—and the world—these powers were well aware of America's military weakness and tended to dismiss the country as an inconsiderable force.

AMERICA STIRS

By no means did the start of World War II with the INVASION OF POLAND in September 1939 suddenly rouse America to war preparedness—although it was clear that Roosevelt and his advisers were more persuaded than most that war would inevitably come to America. However, the fall of France in the BATTLE OF FRANCE in June 1940 did galvanize Congress, if not the general public. Encouraged by FDR, before the summer was out Congress voted $78 billion for war spending—a fantastic sum in a nation with a gross national product of just $101 billion in 1940. Shortly after this, the National Guard was federalized—a reserve of about 300,000 men—and the peacetime draft commenced, aiming at conscripting 2 million men within a year. The LEND-LEASE ACT of March 11, 1941, authorized the president to send material aid to any nation whose interests he deemed vital to those of the United States.

AMERICA PRODUCES

A workforce that had suffered through a decade of the Great Depression was pressed into eager service in defense and war production. In 1940, FDR had pledged America to produce 50,000 aircraft—which seemed to many an impossibility. By the end of the war, 300,000 had been built—the United States supplied planes not only to its own forces, but also to those of Britain, the Soviet Union, Canada, Australia, and New Zealand. U.S. shipyards launched 14 millions tons of shipping, including 88,000 landing craft, 215 submarines, 147 aircraft carriers (of varying sizes), and 952 other warships of all kinds. Just as important were the 5,200 merchant ships built during the war—most of them the famed LIBERTY SHIPS, produced using U.S. methods of factory prefabrication. Dur-

ing five years of war, U.S. industry turned out $181 billion in munitions of all kinds. Nearly 9 million Americans were employed in war industry by 1944 (the peak production year), of whom 29 percent were women and 8 percent African Americans.

LIFE ON THE HOME FRONT

In contrast to the nations of Europe and Asia, the United States was not directly visited by the ravages of war. Nevertheless, Americans made sacrifices in the form of accepting rationing of certain food items (especially meats), gasoline, tires, and other strategic materials given a high priority for the military forces. Housing during the war, especially in and around centers of industry, was scarce and costly. The encroachment on the traditional American freedom to consume at will (if one could afford it) caused some grumbling, but most Americans saw such sacrifice as a patriotic duty—especially because it directly supported "our boys" overseas. The fact was that while most Americans perceived that they were making sacrifices, wartime economic prosperity meant that most actually lived better than during the Depression.

As they had during World War I, Americans eagerly answered the nation's call to fund the struggle. The income tax rates skyrocketed, but despite this, Americans routinely bought U.S. war bonds and stamps. They also accepted—although they were vaguely amused and puzzled by—the mass recruitment of women into war production. Industries that had barred married women from employment—or had simply refused to hire *any* women, married or single—now welcomed them. "Rosie the Riveter"—the image of an overalls-clad woman grasping a rivet gun—became a national patriotic icon. Women also served in unprecedented numbers in the armed forces in support roles—some of which, however, were quite hazardous and demanding, including military nursing in combat zones and ferrying combat aircraft from factories to domestic air bases.

Racial and ethnic prejudice in America was generally ameliorated during the war years, as more African Americans were admitted into the workforce, anti-Semitism notably declined, and prejudices against most immigrant groups dissolved in a general sentiment of egalitarianism born of a feeling that "we're all in this together." The egregious exception to this was the attitude toward Americans (including American citizens) of Japanese descent, who, in large numbers, were interned in camps created for them.

The prevailing sentiment on the home front during World War II differed from that of World War I. Whereas the emotions of 1917–18 tended to be idealistic and crusading, the feeling in World War II was a consciousness of necessity—grim necessity approached with optimism. Americans believed they had an important job to do, and they were determined to do it.

AMERICAN GOVERNMENT

President Roosevelt always portrayed the war as a struggle of democratic values against those of totalitarian tyranny, and he made the same personal, always genial and optimistic appeal to his fellow Americans as he had made during the long crisis of the Depression. Americans personally identified with Roosevelt—and even with WINSTON CHURCHILL—as avatars of democratic values, even as they demonized the likes of ADOLF HITLER, BENITO MUSSOLINI, and TOJO HIDEKI as the embodiment of totalitarian evil. The values of World War II were generally perceived less abstractly than those of World War I.

Roosevelt and other war leaders gave American government an intensely human face; nevertheless, a complex bureaucracy was rapidly installed at all levels of government in order to administer the war and war-related programs. Most of the welter of new agencies dealt with economic and technological matters. The major offices and agencies included the Board of Economic Warfare (later called the Office of Economic Warfare); the National Defense Advisory Commission; the National Housing Agency; the National War Labor Board; the Office of Civilian Defense (OCD); the Office of Defense Transportation; the Office of Emergency Management; the Office of Economic Stabilization; Office of Lend-Lease Management; Office of Price Administration; Office of Production Management; Office of Scientific Research and Development; OFFICE OF STRATEGIC SERVICES (OSS); Office of War Information; Office of War Mobilization (later called Office of War Mobilization and Reconversion); Petroleum Administrator for War; Rubber Administration; Smaller War Plants Corporation; War Food Administration; War Manpower Commission; War Labor Board; War Production Board; War Relocation Authority; and the War Shipping Administration. The face of government may have been Roosevelt's, but, each in its own area, the new agencies wielded the most immediate authority.

CIVIL DEFENSE

Civil defense was active in the United States, although the nation was not subject to the kind of aerial bombardment that battered cities in Asia and Europe. Nevertheless, German U-boat attacks on Allied shipping off the East Coast were common, and the Japanese did manage a small number of inconsequential (but frightening) air attacks on the U.S. West Coast during September 1942 by an aircraft launched from a Japanese submarine. The OCD, under New York mayor Fiorello LaGuardia, managed a relatively minor program of air raid drills, blackout enforcement (coastal lights silhouetted shipping, making it easy for German U-boats to target vessels), first aid training, and the like. More effective than the OCD in organizing civilian volunteers for civil defense work were private agencies, paramount among them the American Red Cross.

See also INTERNMENT, JAPANESE-AMERICAN; WOMEN IN WORLD WAR II; UNITED STATES ARMY; UNITED STATES ARMY AIR CORPS; UNITED STATES ARMY AIR FORCES; UNITED STATES COAST GUARD; UNITED STATES MARINE CORPS; UNITED STATES MERCHANT MARINE; and UNITED STATES NAVY.

Further reading: Colman, Penny. *Rosie the Riveter: Women Working on the Home Front in World War II*. New York: Crown, 1998; Cooke, Alistair. *The American Home Front: 1941–1942*. New York: Atlantic Monthly Press, 2006; Lingeman, Richard R. *Don't You Know There's a War On? The American Home Front, 1941–1945*. New York: Nation Books, 2003; MacDonnell, Francis. *Insidious Foes:*

The Axis Fifth Column and the American Home. New York: Oxford University Press, 1995; Smith, David C. *American Women in a World at War: Contemporary Accounts from World War II.* Lanham, Md.: SR Books, 1996; Winkler, Allan M. *Home Front U.S.A.: America During World War II.* Wheeling, Ill.: Harlan Davidson, 1986.

United States Army

As mentioned in the UNITED STATES entry, the U.S. Army grew from an average prewar strength of 135,000 to a force of 1,657,157 personnel by December 31, 1941. Its peak World War II strength was reached on March 31, 1945: 8,157,386 men and women.

The U.S. army, like the other armed forces, was under civilian control: the president of the United States served as commander in chief, and the chief administrator was the secretary of war. Throughout the conflict, this cabinet post was filled by HENRY STIMSON.

The U.S. Army consisted of the Regular Army, the National Guard, and the Organized Reserves—plus the UNITED STATES ARMY AIR CORPS, which was renamed the UNITED STATES ARMY AIR FORCES on June 20, 1941. Early in the war, in March 1942, the overall operational administration of the army was divided into Army Ground Forces, under Gen. LESLEY McNAIR, which had charge of all training functions and controlled all ground combat troops within the United States; the Army Air Forces; and the Services of Supply (SOS), under Maj. Gen. Brehon Somervell, which was responsible for logistics and procurement. It fell to McNair to oversee the development of a fully trained army prepared for victorious global combat. With the administration of the army divided in these three ways, the U.S. Army chief of staff, General GEORGE C. MARSHALL, the most senior U.S. Army officer, was free to devote himself solely to operations and plans—actually prosecuting the war. Answering directly to him were his major field commanders, which included DWIGHT D. EISENHOWER, supreme Allied commander, Europe, and DOUGLAS MacARTHUR, supreme Allied commander for much of the

Colonel George S. Patton Jr. and Brigadier General Maxwell Murray review the troops of 16th Field Artillery, Ft. Myer, Virginia, during a ceremony honoring Murray in 1940. *(Virginia Military Institute Archives)*

George S. Patton Jr., commander, 2nd Armored Division, and Lieutenant Colonel R. W. Grow confer at Manchester, Tennessee, June 19, 1941. *(Patton Museum of Cavalry and Armor, Fort Knox, Kentucky)*

Pacific theater. Operationally, the U.S. Army consisted of armies, which were often gathered together in army groups—some of which included the armies of Allied nations in addition to U.S. armies. During World War II, the U.S. Army deployed 11 field armies: the First, Second, Third, and Fourth—all of which existed before the war—to which were added during the war the Fifth, Sixth, Seventh, Eighth, Ninth, Tenth, and Fifteenth.

By quite early in the war, the U.S. Army was perhaps the best-trained and best-equipped army in World War II. In categories where equipment might have fallen short of the enemy's—for example, it was a fact that American tanks were inferior to those of Germany—sheer numbers generally made up for any deficiency; American tankers learned to attack German tanks only if the American tanks substantially outnumbered the Germans. The U.S. Army was the beneficiary of American industrial might and delivered the products of U.S. war industries against the enemy in tremendous volume and with great skill.

Of a total of 11,260,000 U.S. Army personnel mobilized during World War II, 234,874 were killed in action and 83,400 died of other causes. A total of 565,861 were wounded in action.

Further reading: Axelrod, Alan. *Encyclopedia of the U.S. Army.* New York: Checkmark, 2006; Center of Military History. *U.S. Army in World War II, Pictorial Record, The War Against Germany: Europe and Adjacent Areas.* Washington, D.C.: Dept. of the Army, 2006; Dzwonchyk, Wayne M., and John Ray Skates. *Brief History of the U.S. Army in World War II.* Washington, D.C.: United States Government Printing Office, 1992; Ethell, Jeffrey L., and David C. Isby. *G.I. Victory: The U.S. Army in World War II Color.* London: Greenhill, 1995; Stanton, Shelby L. *World War II Order of Battle: An Encyclopedic Reference to U.S. Army Ground Forces from Battalion through Division, 1939–1946.* Mechanicsburg, Pa.: Stackpole Books, 2006.

United States Army Air Corps

The U.S. Army Air Corps (USAAC) was the designation of the air arm of the UNITED STATES ARMY from July 2, 1926—when it was created by the Air Corps Act of 1926 to replace the U.S. Army Air Service (USAAS)—until June 20, 1941, when it, in turn, was replaced by the UNITED STATES ARMY AIR FORCES.

In contrast to the USAAS, the USAAC had its own assistant secretary of war for air and air sections on the General Staff. The USAAC consisted of five agencies: Training Center, for flight training; Technical School; Balloon and Airship School; Tactical School; and Materiel Division (which included an Engineering School, Depots, Procurement Plan-

The P-40 began life as the XP-40, an experimental pursuit plane tested by the Army Air Corps in the 1930s. *(United States Air Force History Center)*

ning Representatives, and Plant Representatives). On the eve of World War II, before becoming the USAAF, the Air Corps had 23,455 enlisted men. In 1939, its inventory of aircraft numbered 2,177 planes. This was small in comparison to most of the great European powers and Japan, but the aircraft were generally modern.

The USAAC worked hard to develop air power strategy and doctrine and to establish a significant degree of independence from ground forces by creating, in 1935, the General Headquarters Air Force (GHQ Air Force), which centralized organization. In 1939, GHQ Air Force was transferred from control by the army chief of staff to the chief of the Air Corps.

Further reading: Axelrod, Alan. *Encyclopedia of the U.S. Air Force.* New York: Checkmark, 2006; Maurer, Maurer. *Aviation in the Army: The Official Pictorial History of the AAF.* Washington, D.C.: Air Force History Support Office, 1987.

United States Army Air Forces

Between 1940 and 1941, during the period of the German BLITZKRIEG of Europe and the BATTLE OF BRITAIN but before U.S. entry into World War II, the U.S. Congress funded the expansion of the UNITED STATES ARMY AIR CORPS so that it tripled in size. USAAC planners anticipated creating an air arm that would eventually number 2,165,000 men—a veritable army unto itself. Such an organization required a new, enlarged status. Therefore, on June 20, 1941, Army Regulation 95-5 created the United States Army Air Forces (USAAF), which replaced the USAAC and took its place alongside the UNITED STATES ARMY's three other major divisions: Army Ground Forces, Army Service Forces, and Defense and Theater Commands; this arrangement was modified in March 1942, so that the army was apportioned into just three main divisions: Army Ground Forces, Services of Supply (SOS), and the USAAF.

Internally the USAAF was divided into Combat Command (responsible for air operations), which was the successor organization to the USAAC's

Charles Hall and Lemuel Custis were two of the USAAF's celebrated Tuskegee Airmen. *(USAF History Center)*

General Headquarters Air Force (GHQ Air Force) and the Air Corps (AC). The AC encompassed two subcommands: Materiel, and Training and Operations. In turn, Training and Operations had four subordinate organizations—Technical Schools, Southwest Training, Gulf Training, and Southeast Training—designed to build a credible air force as quickly as possible.

The USAAF was just six months old when the BATTLE OF PEARL HARBOR thrust the United States into World War II. In its first year of operations, the USAAF quintupled to 764,000, and in its second year tripled this number. By 1944, it reached a staggering 2,372,292, representing 31 percent of U.S. Army strength at the time. By the middle of 1944, the USAAF inventory boasted 78,757 aircraft, of which 445 were very heavy bombers and 11,720 were heavy bombers. By this year, the USAAF was organized into 10 major commands in the continental United States: Training, Troop Carrier, Air Transport, Materiel, Air Service, and Proving Ground Commands, in addition to the numbered air forces, which included First Air Force, Second Air Force, Third Air Force, and Fourth Air Force. There were also eight USAAF agencies: AAF Board, Tactical and Redistribution Centers, Army Airways Communications System and Weather Wings, School of Aviation Medicine, First Motion Picture Unit, and Aeronautical Chart Plant. Overseas, the numbered air forces were subordinated to theater of operations command and included Eighth Air Force, Eleventh Air Force, Twelfth Air Force, Fifteenth Air Force, and Twentieth Air Force.

The USAAF rapidly demobilized after the war. By May 1947, the USAAF mustered only 303,000 men and 25,000 aircraft (most of the surplus aircraft were summarily scrapped). Just two forces remained outside the continental United States, in occupied Germany and Japan. Despite this reduction, the USAAF was restructured after the war into an entirely independent service, the United States Air Force, which was created on September 18, 1947, pursuant to the National Security Act of 1947 and Executive Order 9877.

Further reading: Axelrod, Alan. *Encyclopedia of the U.S. Air Force.* New York: Checkmark, 2006; Maurer, Maurer. *Aviation in the Army: The Official Pictorial History of the AAF.* Washington, D.C.: Air Force History Support Office, 1987).

United States Coast Guard

At the time of World War II, the United States Coast Guard was under the peacetime jurisdiction of the U.S. Department of the Treasury. On July 1, 1940, it had 13,766 officers and men. In November 1941, the Coast Guard was incorporated under the overall command of the UNITED STATES NAVY—although some Coast Guard units and cutters had been assigned to the navy before then. By December 31, 1943, the Coast Guard reached its peak wartime strength of 171,939 officers and men.

Even before the United States entered the war, President FRANKLIN D. ROOSEVELT assigned the Coast Guard, beginning in 1939, to patrol coastal areas to enforce the NEUTRALITY ACTS. The Coast Guard also had responsibility for port security beginning on June 20, 1940, under provisions of the Espionage Act of 1917. Later in 1940, the Dangerous Cargo Act gave the Coast Guard jurisdiction over ships carrying high explosives and other dangerous cargoes.

On April 9, 1941, pursuant to the ATLANTIC CHARTER, the defense of Greenland (a Danish possession) was assigned to U.S. responsibility, and the Coast Guard was tasked as the primary military service to carry out cold-weather operations. The Greenland coastal patrol continued throughout the war.

Beginning in the spring of 1941, some cutters and units were assigned to the navy. On November 1, 1941, the rest of the Coast Guard was put under the operational control of the navy. In addition to the Greenland patrol, the Coast Guard operated antisubmarine warfare escorts, participated in AMPHIBIOUS WARFARE operations (Coast Guardsmen were typically expert small boat handlers), search and rescue, beach patrol, and port security. During the war, Coast Guard–manned ships sank at least 11 enemy submarines. Coast Guard–manned LANDING CRAFT landed army and marine forces in North Africa, Italy, France, and the Pacific. Coast Guardsmen also helped train members of the other military services in handling small amphibious craft.

Of a total of 231,000 men and 10,000 women who served in the Coast Guard during World War II, 1,918 were killed—about one-third of this number dying in combat. The Coast Guard was returned to the Department of the Treasury on January 1, 1946.

Further reading: Scheina, Robert L. *U.S. Coast Guard Cutters and Craft of World War II.* Annapolis, Md.: Naval Institute Press, 1982; Willoughby, Malcolm F. *U.S. Coast Guard in World War II.* Annapolis, Md.: Naval Institute Press, 1989.

United States Marine Corps

The USMC is a separate service within the Department of the Navy. It went into World War II with a reputation as an elite cadre of troops specially trained in AMPHIBIOUS WARFARE and in small-group tactics, and it proved itself, mainly in the Pacific theater, fighting extremely fierce battles on many Japanese-held islands. Typically, the marines were the first troops landed on an island objective; often, their assault was followed by larger UNITED STATES ARMY contingents.

On the eve of war, as of July 1, 1940, the marines consisted of 28,364 officers and men. On December 31, 1941, their numbers had risen to 75,346. Peak strength was reached at the end of the war, August 31, 1945, at 485,833 officers and men.

Despite its operation under the aegis of the Navy Department—and (until 1947) without representation on the Joint Chiefs of Staff—the marines enjoyed considerable autonomy, even operating their own aviation units. The corps was commanded by the Corps Commandant (Thomas Holcomb, 1936–43; ALEXANDER VANDEGRIFT, 1944–47), who maintained his own headquarters.

The basic World War II–era operational organization of the marines was laid down in 1933 when the Fleet Marine Force (FMF) was established for the purpose of amphibious operations. The FMF consisted of two brigades, each supported by a Marine Aviation Group (AVG). One brigade was stationed at Quantico, Virginia, the other in San Diego, California. Most of the rest of the Marine Corps was stationed on garrison duty in various locations worldwide. Before U.S. entry into the war, the two FMF brigades were redesignated in February 1941 as the 1st and 2nd Marine Divisions. Each of these consisted of three infantry regiments, one artillery regiment, support organizations, and aviation support—called the 1st and 2nd Marine Aircraft Wings, respectively. During the war, a total of six marine divisions were activated, in addition to raider battalions, paramarines (parachute-trained marines), and glider groups, in addition to special defensive garrisons.

In September 1943, to support Admiral CHESTER NIMITZ's massive central Pacific campaign, the V Amphibious Corps was created, which would land at the BATTLE OF TARAWA ATOLL and in the MARSHALL ISLANDS CAMPAIGN.

V Amphibious Corps was part of the FMF, which was redesignated the Fleet Marine Force, Pacific in 1944. FMFPac was under the command of HOLLAND M. "HOWLIN' MAD" SMITH until October 1944, when Major General Harry Schmidt took over.

The marines earned a grim reputation for getting the job done by absorbing heavy casualties. Total USMC casualties in the war were 91,718, including 24,511 killed in action or died of wounds.

Further reading: Alexander, Joseph H. *Battle History of the U.S. Marines.* New York: Harper Perennial, 1999; Axelrod, Alan. *Encyclopedia of the U.S. Marines.* New York: Checkmark, 2006; Gailey, Harry A. *Historical Dictionary of the United States Marine Corps.* Lanham, Md.: Scarecrow, 1998.

Small and elite, the U.S. Marines maintained their own aviation section, flying aircraft such as this Corsair, which prepares to take off before dawn. *(National Archives and Records Administration)*

United States Marine Corps Women's Reserve

The Marine Corps was the last of the services to create a women's force in World War II. Approved

Women in military service: Shown here is the first contingent of 253 female marines who reported for duty at U.S. Marine headquarters, 1943. *(Library of Congress)*

in November 1942, the United States Marine Corps Women's Reserve had an initial authorized strength of 1,000 officers and 18,000 enlisted women. The Reserve was commanded by Maj. Ruth Streeter. The first recruits were trained at Hunter College, New York City, and officers were trained at Mount Holyoke College (South Hadley, Massachusetts). Within months, however, all training was transferred to facilities at Marine Corps Base Camp Lejeune in South Carolina. The Women Reservists were not combat marines, but were assigned as clerks and stenographers. By the beginning of 1944, 85 percent of enlisted personnel at Marine Headquarters in Washington were women reservists.

The organization had been formed on the understanding that it would be disbanded after the war and all personnel discharged; however, a small cadre of "Women Reservists" was retained after the war, and in June 1948, the secretary of the navy ordered the integration of women into the regular Marine Corps.

Further reading: Soderbergh, Peter A. *Women Marines: The World War II Era.* New York: Praeger, 1992.

United States Merchant Marine

No service in World War II was more important than the Merchant Marine, which operated the thousands of convoy vessels that kept supplies and matériel flowing to Europe (especially Britain) and the Soviet Union. It is also true that no service was more hazardous.

On the eve of war, the U.S. Merchant Marine consisted of 55,000 experienced mariners. Through U.S. Maritime Service training programs, this was increased to more than 215,000 before the end of the war. Merchant vessels were targeted by submarines, surface raiders, destroyers, aircraft, and KAMIKAZE attack, and were also endangered by mines and the customary hazards of the sea. The U.S. Merchant Marine suffered the highest rate of casualties of any service in World War II. Officially, 1,554 U.S. merchant ships were sunk by enemy attack, including 733 ships of over 1,000 gross tons. Many more ships were damaged. Some 8,300 merchant mariners were killed at sea and another 12,000 wounded (of whom at least 1,100 died from their wounds). A total of 663 men and women were taken prisoner. The grim fact was that 1 in 26 merchant mariners was killed in action.

The Merchant Marine was a civilian organization—although, on larger ships, U.S. Navy personnel typically manned defense antiaircraft guns—under the jurisdiction of the War Shipping Administration.

See also CONVOY SYSTEM and LIBERTY SHIPS.

Further reading: Bunker, John. *Heroes in Dungarees: The Story of the American Merchant Marine in World War II.* Pensacola, Fl.: Naval Aviation Museum Foundation, 2006; Felknor, Bruce L., ed. *The U.S. Merchant Marine at War, 1775–1945.* Annapolis, Md.: Naval Institute Press, 1999; Reminick, Gerald, and Bill Harris, eds. *Patriots and Heroes: True Stories of the U.S. Merchant Marine in World War II.* 2 vols. El Cerrito, Calif.: Glencannon Press, 2003; Rosen, Herman E. *Gallant Ship, Brave Men: The Heroic Story of a World War II Liberty Ship.* Philadelphia: Xlibris, 2003.

United States Navy

At the time of World War II, the U.S. Navy was under the civilian control of the president, as commander in chief, and of the Department of the Navy, represented in the cabinet by the secretary of the navy. Charles Edison was secretary on the eve of U.S. entry into the war, but was replaced in July 1940 by (William) Franklin Knox, who served until his death in May 1944, when he was replaced by JAMES FORRESTAL, who had been undersecretary of the navy.

As of 1939, the U.S. Navy had 15 battleships—some quite old—five aircraft carriers, 18 heavy cruisers, 19 light cruisers, 61 submarines, and many smaller craft. The navy operated its own aviation section, which included carrier-launched aircraft, seaplanes, and land-based aircraft. Like the other services, the navy greatly expanded during the war, growing from 160,997 officers and men on July 1, 1940 to a peak of 3,408,347 by the end of the war, August 31, 1945. As of June 30, 1940, the navy inventory consisted of 1,099 ships of all types. By June 30, 1945, that inventory had exploded to 67,952. The number of ships built or acquired between 1940 and the end of the war, August 31, 1945, was staggering and included 10 battleships, 27 large aircraft carriers, 111 escort carriers, 47 cruisers, 370 destroyers, 504 destroyer escorts, 217 submarines, and 66,055 landing craft.

Crewmen of the submarine USS *Barb* display their battle flag, showing Japanese shipping sunk. *(National Archives and Records Administration)*

Although the navy entered the war in the belief that the battleship was the supreme seaborne weapon, it soon became apparent (as is clear from the foregoing list) that the aircraft carrier had assumed the major combat role. Between 1940 and 1945, some 75,000 aircraft were delivered to the navy, and its air personnel grew from 10,923 (including 2,965 pilots) in mid-1940 to 437,524 (60,747 pilots) by the end of the war.

The senior naval commander during World War II was the Chief of Naval Operations (CNO). Although the navy was a two-ocean force, its greatest strength was in the Pacific Fleet. Early in 1941, before the United States entered the war, the Atlantic Fleet was put under the command of Vice Admiral ERNEST KING and the Pacific Fleet under HUSBAND E. KIMMEL. After war broke out, King was redesignated commander in charge, U.S. Fleet. King insisted that this position not be abbreviated (as would be customary) CINCUS (pronounced *sink-us!*), but COMINCH. As COMINCH, King was given extraordinary powers, which largely bypassed the secretary of the navy and allowed him to report directly to President FRANKLIN D. ROOSEVELT. After the BATTLE OF PEARL HARBOR, Kimmel was relieved as commander of the Pacific Fleet and replaced by Admiral CHESTER NIMITZ.

By the middle of the war, 1943, the naval forces assigned to the Southwest Pacific were designated the Seventh Fleet. Those in the South Pacific became the Third Fleet, and the Central Pacific forces were designated the Fifth Fleet. The South Atlantic forces became the Fourth Fleet, and Naval Forces, Northwest African Waters was designated the Eighth Fleet, while Naval Forces, Europe became the Twelfth Fleet. The Tenth Fleet was a shore-based antisubmarine command established in May 1943. Operationally, the fleets formed offensive units as needed, which were designated as task forces—or as task groups made up of two or more task forces. Task Force 38, of the Third Fleet, was the most powerful, built around the Pacific Fleet's fast aircraft carriers.

During World War II, the navy controlled and administered the UNITED STATES COAST GUARD.

U.S. Navy casualties in World War II included 36,950 killed in battle and 25,664 dead from other causes; 37,778 were wounded.

See also SHIPS, UNITED STATES.

Further reading: Axelrod, Alan. *Encyclopedia of the U.S. Navy.* New York: Checkmark, 2006; Henry, Mark. *The US Navy in World War II.* London: Osprey, 2002; Morison, Samuel Eliot. *History of United States Naval Operations in World War II.* 15 vols. London: Book Sales, 2001; Morison, Samuel Eliot. *The Two-Ocean War: The Definitive Short History of the United States Navy in World War II.* New York: Ballantine Books, 1972; Smith, S. E. *The United States Navy in World War II.* New York: William Morrow, 1986.

Ushijima Mitsuru (1887–1945) *Principal Japanese commander in the Okinawa Campaign*

Ushijima was a career officer in the Imperial Japanese Army. He commanded 1st Regiment during 1936–37 and 36th Brigade from 1937 to 1938 during the SINO-JAPANESE WAR. From 1938 to 1939, he served as commandant of the Military Preparation School, then briefly served as commandant of the Infantry School in 1939. That same year, he was promoted to general and given command of the 11th Division. During 1941–42, Ushijima was commandant of the Noncommissioned Officers School and from 1942 to 1944 commanded the Japanese Military Academy.

During 1944–45, Ushijima was general officer commanding 32nd Army, Ryukyu Islands. He led this force—100,000 strong—during the Okinawa Campaign and at the culminating battle directed the primary resistance in the south. Defeated after a fierce resistance, Ushijima committed suicide rather than surrender on June 22, 1945.

Further reading: Astor, Gerald. *Operation Iceberg: The Invasion and Conquest of Okinawa in World War II.* New York: Dell, 1996; Feifer, George. *The Battle of Okinawa: The Blood and the Bomb.* Guilford, Conn.: Lyons Press, 2001; Leckie, Robert. *Okinawa: The Last Battle of World War II.* New York: Penguin, 1996; Yahrara, Hiromichi. *The Battle for Okinawa.* New York: Wiley, 1997.

V

V-1 buzz bomb

The V-1 was a German flying bomb, a winged rocket designed for level flight that was a precursor of the modern cruise missile. The Allies called it a "buzz bomb" and also a "doodlebug." Officially it was the Fieseler Fi 103/FZG-76, also designated the Vergeltungswaffe-1—meaning "vengeance weapon" or "reprisal weapon." It was from this name, coined by German propaganda minister JOSEPH GOEBBELS, that the "V" designation came. The vengeance or reprisal in question was for the Allied STRATEGIC BOMBING OF GERMANY.

The V-1 was used between June 1944 and March 1945 against targets in southeastern England and Belgium, especially the cities of London and Antwerp. Generally, the V-1s were launched from rails resembling ski jumps, which were placed along the French Pas-de-Calais coast and parts of the Dutch coast. Experimentally, a few V-1s were launched from German aircraft over the North Sea.

The V-1 was an unmanned cruise-type missile with a large warhead. It was very inaccurate, capable of being aimed at a city-size target, but nothing smaller—a particular factory, say, or an airfield. The V-1 guidance system was very rudimentary. It flew by an autopilot, which regulated altitude and speed by means of a pendulum system that obtained fore and aft feedback (to adjust attitude and pitch). A gyromagnetic compass controlled the interaction between yaw and roll.

A small propeller mounted on the nose of the V-1 turned a long screw inside the missile. As the missile flew, airflow turned the propeller and threaded shaft, pushing a washer on the shaft, which, at a distance set by the launch crew, would close an electric circuit, thereby activating a solenoid attached to a guillotine device. The guillotine cut the elevator control cable, so that the V-1 would be sent into a steep dive over the target. The system was highly inventive, but quite faulty. Many V-1s failed to dive and therefore detonated with less than the intended effect, or they dived prematurely or too late.

The V-1 was designed by Robert Lusser of the Fieseler aircraft company. Fritz Gosslau, an engineer employed by the Argus engine works, designed

V-1s captured by the Allies *(Library of Congress)*

855

the pulse jet engine, which propelled the V-1 to a top speed of 390 miles per hour. Initially, its range was limited—just 150 miles—but later versions could fly 250 miles. The V-1 was 25.5 feet long with a wingspan of 17.5 feet. It weighed 4,800 pounds. The missile flew low, at an altitude of between 300 to 3,000 feet. Its warhead was a 1,832-pound load of Amatol high explosive. Once the missile had been developed, production was cheap. It was made of sheet metal and plywood and took a mere 50 man-hours to assemble.

Nearly 30,000 V-1s were manufactured, of which about 10,000 were fired at England from June 12, 1944, to March 29, 1945. Of these, 2,419 reached metropolitan London. Casualties in the capital were about 5,500 killed and 16,000 injured. Allied fighters and antiaircraft fire shot down 4,261 V-1s.

See also Blitz, the; Peenemünde (V-1 and V-2 base); and V-2 rocket.

Further reading: Irons, Roy. *Hitler's Terror Weapons: The Price of Vengeance.* New York: HarperSport, 2003; Zaloga, Steven. *V-1 Flying Bomb 1942–52: Hitler's Infamous "Doodlebug."* London: Osprey, 2005.

V-2 rocket

As with the V-1 buzz bomb, the "V" designation for this weapon was an abbreviation for *Vergeltungswaffe,* "vengeance weapon" or "reprisal weapon." Whereas the V-1 was a pulse-jet-driven cruise-type missile, the V-2 was a genuine ballistic missile, the direct predecessor of the rockets that are used to explore space and send satellites into orbit.

As a weapon, the V-2 was used against targets in Britain and Belgium. Although the V-2 was more advanced than the V-1, the V-2 did not replace the V-1; the two weapons were used simultaneously during the latter part of the war.

The German military took an early interest in rockets as weapons. In 1932 the Reichswehr (the post–Treaty of Versailles German army) began studying the feasibility of rockets as artillery weapons. General Walter Dornberger, in charge of army rocket development, was impressed by a design

A V-2 being readied for launch *(German Museum, Munich)*

and demonstration by Wernher von Braun, who soon became the leading German rocket scientist.

In 1934, von Braun successfully test flew the A2 rocket, which used ethanol and liquid oxygen for fuel. From the A2, an A3 and A4 were developed—the latter being a full-sized rocket (A1 through A3 were little more than models), which had a range of 110 miles and could loft a ton beyond the earth's atmosphere. At this time, General Dornberger moved the rocket development team from relatively cramped quarters at Kummersdorf (near Berlin) to Peenemünde, on the island of Usedom on Germany's Baltic coast.

By October 1942, von Braun had largely perfected the A4 design, which became the first artificial object to fly beyond the earth's atmosphere. Further improved, the A4 was designated the V-2, and production began early the following year. German secrecy was compromised, however, when Polish resistance workers recovered a V-2 test fired at Blizna, Poland, and transmitted technical information to British intelligence. This prompted British bomber command to launch extensive raids against Peenemünde, which failed to stop either experimentation or production, but did retard both.

Technically, the V-2 was an unmanned, internally guided ballistic missile. It was launched vertically, achieving a trajectory that took it into space, then, its fuel exhausted, it would go into a free-fall (ballistic) trajectory. Its range was about 200 miles, and it could carry a 2,200-pound warhead. Because of its ballistic trajectory, it was virtually impossible to shoot down, either with aircraft or antiaircraft artillery. Like the V-1, the V-2 was very inaccurate. It was capable of hitting a target the size of a city, but the rocketeer could not designate a specific target within the city.

The V-2 was fueled by an ethanol and water mixture, which burned in the presence of liquid oxygen as an oxidizer. The fuel and oxidizer were pumped at high speed by turbines that ran on steam produced by concentrated hydrogen peroxide with potassium permanganate catalyst. Ignition of the fuel-oxidizer mixture produced intense heat and high-pressure exhaust, which provided the thrust.

Guidance of the V-2 was by a gyroscopic inertial navigation system, which controlled four rudders on the tail fins and four internal rudders to guide thrust at the exit of the motor. Some later incarnations of the V-2 were guided by radio signals transmitted from the ground, but this system was never perfected.

More than 6,000 V-2s were built, of which about 3,500 were launched against Allied targets. The remainder were grabbed up by the victorious Allies and became the basis for both the U.S. and the Soviet postwar space programs. Although Dornberger advocated the development and use of mobile launch platforms, ADOLF HITLER insisted on the construction of fixed facilities with underground blockhouses. His idea was to produce V-2s in several factories, which would be linked to launch sites by railroads, thereby enabling virtually continuous launches. The fixed sites, however, became frequent targets for air raids, and nothing approaching a continuous launch schedule was ever achieved. The first launch site was built at Éperlecques, near St. Omer in the Pas-de-Calais area of France in 1943. Later sites were built near Cherbourg. After Allied bombing raids took a toll on all the sites, Hitler relented and authorized the construction of large truck-towed trailers to transport the missiles to various quickly erected launch

sites. From arrival at a site to firing took no more than 90 minutes. Another 30 minutes was required to pack up and leave the site. This arrangement allowed the Germans to launch about 10 V-2s per day between September 1944 and March 1945 without much fear of air strikes.

The V-2s were mass produced by slave labor at the Mittelwerk tunnel system under the Kohnstein mountain, near Nordhausen, Germany. Working conditions were appalling, and more than 10,500 slaves died by October 1943. Ultimately, the death rate among V-2 workers reached 100 a day.

The V-2 claimed the lives of about 7,000 Londoners, an average of two deaths per launching. This figure takes into account the fact that many of the rockets exploded in midair or missed their targets; a direct hit could produce many deaths, as it did for the 567 citizens of Antwerp who were killed when a V-2 struck a movie theater.

Further reading: Dornberger, Walter. *V-2.* New York: Ballantine Books, 1954; Dungan, T. D. *V-2: A Combat History of the First Ballistic Missile.* Yardley, Pa.: Westholme, 2005; Huzel, Dieter K. *Peenemunde to Canaveral.* Englewood Cliffs, N.J.: Prentice Hall, 1965; King, Benjamin, and Timothy J. Kutta. *Impact: The History of Germany's V-Weapons in World War II.* New York: Da Capo Press, 2003.

Vandegrift, Alexander (1887–1973)
eighteenth commandant of the United States Marine Corps

Born in Charlottesville, Virginia, Vandegrift attended the University of Virginia for two years before entering the Marine Corps with a commission as a second lieutenant in 1909. During 1912–23, he served in the Caribbean and Central America and took part in action in Nicaragua, in the invasion and occupation of Veracruz, Mexico, in 1914, and the pacification of Haiti in 1915.

From 1923 to 1926, Major Vandegrift commanded a battalion at Marine Corps Base Quantico, Virginia, then was appointed assistant chief of staff at Marine Corps Base San Diego. During 1927–28, he served in China. Promoted to lieutenant colonel in 1934, Vandegrift returned to China in 1935 and was promoted to colonel in 1936. During 1937–41, he was stationed at Marine Corps Headquarters in Washington. Promoted to brigadier general in 1940, he was assistant commander of 1st Marine Division by 1941 and, early in 1942, was made commanding general of the division.

Major General Vandegrift led the division to the south Pacific in May 1942 and commanded it during the GUADALCANAL CAMPAIGN (August–December 1942), an action for which he received the Medal of Honor. Promoted to lieutenant general, Vandegrift commanded the First Marine Amphibious Corps during the opening of the BOUGAINVILLE CAMPAIGN. He then returned to the United States, late in 1943, to accept appointment as commandant of the Marine Corps, effective January 1, 1944.

Vandegrift presided over the continued explosive wartime expansion of the marines. After the war, it fell to him to direct the orderly reduction of the Corps, which meant fighting to prevent its total dissolution by a parsimonious Congress eager to demobilize. Promoted to general in March 1945, Vandegrift was the first marine officer to attain that rank while on active duty. He stepped down as commandant on January 1, 1948, and retired from the Corps the following year.

Further reading: Foster, John. *Guadalcanal General: The Story of A. A. Vandegrift USMC.* New York: William Morrow, 1966; Vandegrift, Alexander. *Once a Marine: The Memoirs of General A. A. Vandegrift Commandant of the U.S. Marines in WW II.* Quantico, Va.: Marine Corps Association, 1982.

Vasilevsky, Aleksandr Mikhailovich
(1895–1977) *Soviet commander in operations against Japan*

Born to the family of an Orthodox priest in a village east of Moscow, Vasilevsky briefly enrolled at the Alexander Military Law Academy in 1915 before being commissioned a staff captain in the tsarist army during World War I. He resigned after the Russian Revolution of 1917, then joined the Red Army in April 1919 and fought in the civil war. Although he had a good record as a combat officer, his training and talent lay in administrative and staff work; however, he was soon elevated to brigade and divisional commands.

During the 1920s, Vasilevsky became closely connected with JOSEPH STALIN and VYACHESLAV MOLOTOV, both of whom greatly aided the advancement of his career, so that by 1931 he was commanding officer of the Volga Military District. In contrast to many other senior officers, Vasilevsky survived Stalin's purge of the Red Army during 1937–38. He was appointed to the General Staff in October 1937 and was advanced to lieutenant general in October 1941, after the German INVASION OF THE SOVIET UNION. This put him in a position in April 1942 to succeed Boris Shaposhnikov as chief of the General Staff, and he worked closely with Marshal GEORGI ZHUKOV to plan operations at the BATTLE OF STALINGRAD, which proved to be the turning point of the war. Some historians believe that the Soviet victory here owed more to Vasilevsky's strategic planning and administration than it did to Zhukov's more visible role in the field. Certainly Stalin recognized Vasilevsky's achievement, elevating him to general on February 16, 1943 (he already held the title of marshal of the Soviet Union).

During the rest of 1943 and throughout 1944, Vasilievsky continued as the chief administrator of the Red Army. Early in 1945, he took a field command, leading the Northwestern Front in its advance through Poland and into East Prussia. Immediately after Germany surrendered in May 1945, Vasilevsky was transferred to the Far East Front, where he assumed command of Red Army forces after the Soviet Union's declaration of war on Japan in August. He led the advance into China and Korea (Operation August Storm), which resulted in the defeat of the Japanese Kwantung Army.

After the war, Vasilievsky continued in command of the Far East until 1948, when he returned to Moscow as deputy minister for defense. In March 1949, he was appointed minister for defense. In 1952, he became a member of the Central Committee of the Communist Party, but, after Stalin's death in March 1953, he was replaced as minister of defense by Nikolai Bulganin and, in the post-Stalinist era, held no important posts for the rest of his life.

Further reading: Kozhevnikov, M. N. *The Command and Staff of the Soviet Army in the Great Patriotic War 1941–1945: A Soviet View.* Honolulu: University Press of the Pacific, 2002; Larionov, V. V. *World War II: Decisive Battles of the Soviet Army.* Moscow: Progress Publishers, 1984; Shaw, John. *Red Army Resurgent.* Alexandria, Va.: Time Life, 1980; Vasilevsky, A. M. *A Lifelong Cause.* Moscow: Progress, 1981.

V-E Day

V-E Day, Victory in Europe Day, was officially designated as May 8, 1945, the date on which the German government—under the authority of KARL DÖNITZ, who became head of state after the suicide of ADOLF HITLER—surrendered to the Allies in Berlin. A surrender had taken place the day before in Reims, France, but was rejected by JOSEPH STALIN, who insisted on a definitive capitulation at Soviet-held Berlin.

The Allies' proclamation of V-E Day touched off celebrations in London and throughout the United States, where President HARRY S. TRUMAN, in announcing the final triumph over the Germans, dedicated the victory to the late FRANKLIN D. ROOSEVELT, who had died the month before.

German chief of staff General ALFRED JODL signed surrender documents at SHAEF headquarters in Reims at 02:41 on the morning of May 7, 1945. The terms of the surrender set 23:01 Central European Time on May 8, 1945, as the precise moment at which all active military operations would cease. By British reckoning, using British Double Summer Time, the time in London was 00:01 May 9. The Soviets—and, today, the Russians—celebrate May 9 as Victory Day. In 1985, West German President Richard von Weizsdcker, on the occasion of the 40th anniversary of V-E day, hailed it as "the day of liberation" from the Nazi regime.

See also V-J DAY.

Further reading: Hastings, Max. *Victory in Europe: D-Day to V-E Day.* Boston: Little, Brown, 1992.

Vella Lavella, Battle of

The battle began on August 15, 1943, during the NEW GEORGIA CAMPAIGN, with the landing of U.S. troops on Vella Lavella. Their objective was to hop over and cut off the very strong Japanese garrison on Kolombangara Island; however, Vella Lavella proved a stubborn objective in itself. The battle ground on for more than a month, when, on September 18, the 3rd New Zealand Division landed to replace the U.S. forces on the island.

Even fiercer than the ground battle was the action in the air and at sea. The Japanese continually staged air raids against the U.S. troops on the island—108 raids in a month. The sea Battle of Vella Lavella was fought on the night of October 6–7, 1943, and resulted in the sinking of a Japanese and an American destroyer (as well as damage to two other U.S. destroyers). The U.S. Navy tried unsuccessfully to interdict the evacuation of Japanese troops from the island. That evacuation ended the battle.

Further reading: Horton, Dick Crofton. *New Georgia: Pattern for Victory.* New York: Ballantine Books, 1971.

Versailles, Treaty of

One of the most momentous treaties in history, the Treaty of Versailles ended World War I and, through the subjoined Covenant of the League of Nations, founded that international body. The treaty, however, levied excessively punitive conditions against Germany, which created the economic and cultural climate in which the outbreak of another world war was virtually assured.

The Treaty of Versailles was signed on June 28, 1919, at Versailles, France, and was largely the work of the so-called Big Four, U.S. president Woodrow Wilson, French premier Georges Clemenceau, British prime minister David Lloyd George, and Italy's

Europe after World War I, 1919

New and reconstituted nations

Demilitarized and Allied occupation zones

premier Vittorio Orlando. None of the Central Powers, including Germany, was permitted to negotiate the terms. Signatories included the United States, the British Empire, France, Italy, and Japan (called the "Principal Allied and Associated Powers"), Belgium, Bolivia, Brazil, China, Cuba, Ecuador, Greece, Guatemala, Haiti, the Hedjaz, Honduras, Liberia, Nicaragua, Panama, Peru, Poland, Portugal, Romania, Serb-Croat-Slovene State, Siam, Czechoslovakia, and Uruguay (called "The Allied and Associated Powers") and Germany. Neither the treaty nor the Covenant of the League of Nations was ratified by the U.S. Senate, so America, swept by a wave of postwar isolationism, did not subscribe to the treaty, even though so much of

it had been the work of the American head of state.

President Wilson had championed a conciliatory settlement of the war, based on his famous Fourteen Points, which he had enumerated before a joint session of Congress on January 8, 1918, as the basis for a just peace:

- Point one called for "open covenants, openly arrived at," mandating an end to the kind of secret treaties and alliances that had historically dragged Europe into war.
- Point two, freedom of the seas
- Point three, removal of economic barriers to international trade

- Point four, radical reduction of armaments to the lowest point consistent with domestic security
- Point five, modification of all colonial claims on the basis of the self-determination of peoples

The eight points that followed these addressed specific postwar territorial settlements, and, most important, the 14th point called for the creation of a league of nations, an international body that would guarantee political independence and territorial integrity for all nations and would provide a forum for the peaceful resolution of conflict.

Opposing Wilson's idealistically conciliatory position was French premier Georges Clemenceau, whose country had made the greatest sacrifices in the war. Clemenceau was determined not only to secure France against future German attack by permanently destroying Germany's ability to make war, but also to exact vengeance. He called for a harshly punitive treaty. British prime minister David Lloyd George personally favored a more moderate treaty, but he had been elected on his promise that Germany would be punished. Additionally, he was concerned that Wilson's Fourteen Points would interfere with British colonial policy. As for Italy's Vittorio Orlando, his chief concern was neither ideological nor punitive, but merely to ensure that Italy would receive the territories it had been promised in 1915 as inducement to join the Allied cause.

After much rancorous debate among the Big Four, Clemenceau was persuaded to abandon his chief demand, that the left bank of the Rhine be detached from Germany and put under French military control, in exchange for British and American promises of future alliance and support. Nevertheless, most of the treaty fell far short of the idealism of the Fourteen Points and was punitive as well as humiliating to Germany and its allies, collectively called the Central Powers.

The Treaty of Versailles is a complex document, the size of a small book. Its chief provisions include German territorial cessions, German admission of guilt for having started the war, German disarmament, and an assessment against Germany (and

other Central Powers) of catastrophically large monetary reparations (not yet calculated at the time of the treaty's signing). More specifically, the treaty called for:

- The reduction of the population and territory of Germany by about 10 percent
- The return of Alsace and Lorraine to France
- Placement of the Saarland under the supervision of the League of Nations until 1935
- Cession to Belgium of three small northern areas of Germany
- Pursuant to a plebiscite in Schleswig, return of northern Schleswig to Denmark
- The drawing of new Polish borders, giving most of formerly German West Prussia and Poznań (Posen) to Poland, in addition to creating a "corridor" to the Baltic Sea; pursuant to a plebiscite, Poland also gained part of Upper Silesia
- Declaration of Danzig (Gdańsk) as a free city
- Relinquishment of Germany's overseas colonies in China, the Pacific, and Africa to Britain, France, Japan, and other Allied nations under "mandates" administered by the League of Nations
- Endorsement by Germany of a "war guilt clause," deeming itself the aggressor; this was not only spiritually debilitating, it made Germany liable for all reparations to the Allied nations
- Accusation that the German emperor, Wilhelm II, had committed war crimes; he was guaranteed a fair trial, and the Allies reserved the right to bring unspecified others before war crimes tribunals. (Ultimately, neither the kaiser nor anyone else was tried for war crimes following World War I.)
- Call for reparations; these had not been computed by the time the treaty was signed but in 1921 were fixed at $33,000,000,000. (All signatories understood that payment of such a sum would permanently destroy the German economy. They also understood that this would have a negative impact not just on Germany, but on international finance. Nevertheless, the

Allies insisted that Germany pay, and the treaty allowed for punitive actions if Germany failed to make the payments according to a specified schedule.)

- Limitation of the German army to 100,000 men and abolishment of the general staff
- Prohibition of the manufacture of armored cars, tanks, submarines, airplanes, and poison gas; drastic curtailment of all munitions production
- Declaration of Germany west of the Rhine and up to 30 miles east of that river as a demilitarized zone.
- Allied occupation of the Rhineland to continue for at least fifteen years, and possibly longer

President Wilson was dismayed by much of the treaty, but he persuaded himself that it was the best he could obtain and that, in any case, its many inequities would eventually be resolved by the League of Nations. Moreover, he believed that the disarmament of Germany would inspire voluntary disarmament by other nations. And, Wilson comforted himself, he did prevail on his fourteenth point: the Treaty of Versailles included the Covenant of the League of Nations.

On May 7, 1919, the treaty was presented to a German delegation headed by Foreign Minister Ulrich Graf von Brockdorff-Rantzau. The delegation denounced it, protesting that it abrogated the Fourteen Points, which had been the basis of the armistice on November 11, 1918. Brockdorff-Rantzau further declared that Germany was unable to pay the reparations demanded. Germany's chancellor, Philipp Scheidemann, likewise denounced the treaty when it was presented to him. In response, the Allies initiated a naval blockade of Germany. Scheidemann and Brockdorff-Rantzau resigned in protest on June 21, and that same day at Scapa Flow, German sailors scuttled all 50 warships of High Seas Fleet to keep the vessels from becoming Allied prizes. A new German chancellor, Gustav Bauer, sent another delegation to Versailles and, on June 28, signed the document under protest, informing the Allies that the treaty was being accepted only to end the hardships (mostly severe food shortages) caused by the "inhuman" naval blockade.

The Treaty of Versailles is one of history's most profoundly tragic documents. It created the political, economic, and emotional climate that promoted the rise of ADOLF HITLER and the NAZI PARTY, making a second world war virtually inevitable. Almost immediately Germany flouted the treaty and began to rearm. The 100,000-man limitation put on the army was used by German military planners to create an elite, all-volunteer *Führerheer,* an "army of leaders," which would become the core of the formidable army with which Hitler fought World War II. After Hitler assumed the office of chancellor in 1933, rearmament became progressively more blatant, and the timid, war-weary former Allies did nothing to enforce the provisions of the Treaty of Versailles.

Further reading: Boemeke, Manfred F., ed. *The Treaty of Versailles: A Reassessment after 75 Years.* New York: Cambridge University Press, 1998; Kleine-Ahlbrandt, W. Laird. *The Burden of Victory: France, Britain, and the Enforcement of the Versailles Peace, 1919–1925.* Lanham, Md.: University Press of America, 1995.

Vichy government

On June 10, as the BATTLE OF FRANCE was coming to its climax with the Germans closing in on Paris, the French government fled to Tours, declaring Paris an open city. France's prime minister, PAUL REYNAUD, wanted to continue to resist the Germans, perhaps from exile in French North Africa, but most of his cabinet, guided by HENRI-PHILIPPE PÉTAIN, favored an armistice. On June 14 the cabinet left Tours for Bordeaux. In a last-ditch effort to keep France from capitulating, British prime minister WINSTON CHURCHILL proposed a full political union of France and Britain, the better to fight Germany. The cabinet, however, now wholly under the influence of Pétain, spurned the proposal, and Reynaud resigned. Pétain was appointed premier and immediately sought surrender terms from Germany. The result was the armistice of June 22, 1940, signed near Compiègne, in the very railway car in which the Germans had signed the armistice ending World War I.

The June 22 armistice allowed France a show of semisovereignty, but divided the country into an unoccupied southern zone (with a capital at Vichy—and therefore known as Vichy France) and an occupied northern and western coastal zone. France itself was to bear the monetary costs of occupation. Its army was restricted to 100,000 men, and its navy was disarmed and restricted to its home ports.

About 30 French leaders, including ÉDOUARD DALADIER, fled to North Africa to set up a government in exile there. Pétain outflanked them, however, ordering their arrest on arrival in Morocco. However, Brigadier General CHARLES DE GAULLE, undersecretary of war in the now defunct Reynaud cabinet, had previously flown to London. He was determined to rally "Free French" resistance, with himself as leader. He broadcast his first radio appeal from London on June 18, 1940, calling on French patriots to continue the fight. It was—at least at first—to no avail. The majority of the French people, wishing to avoid the horrors of a second world war, pledged their allegiance to Pétain and Vichy.

On July 9–10, the French parliament convened at Vichy. PIERRE LAVAL, Pétain's ambitious vice premier, was certain that Germany had already won the war and would inevitably come to control all of Europe. Hoping to claim for France a viable place in this new order, he persuaded parliament to vote itself and the Third Republic out of existence and to authorize Pétain to write a new constitution (which was never completed). France was reformed into a kind of decentralized, corporate state in which government was centered in the traditional provinces. However, it soon became apparent that Pétain and his closest adherents were relatively moderate. Those who were genuinely dedicated fascists broke with Pétain and cooperated with German authorities in undermining the Vichy regime in an effort to make France a kind of German satellite or even ally.

To retain his authority, Pétain dismissed Laval in December 1940 and confined him briefly to house arrest. Laval and Pétain subsequently met with ADOLF HITLER at Montoire on October 24, 1940, and thereafter presented a publicly united front advocating Franco-German "collaboration."

The actual fact was that Hitler felt no need for collaboration with France. He merely allowed the Vichy government to exist as a temporary measure to make occupation easier; by using French authorities to police the country, fewer Germans were required for the job. Under Pétain, Laval was succeeded by Pierre-Étienne Flandin, who was soon succeeded by Admiral FRANÇOIS DARLAN. Darlan revived efforts to achieve outright collaboration with the Germans, but Hitler continued to keep Darlan and other collaborationists at arm's length as he exploited France for labor and raw materials.

Yielding to German pressure, Pétain restored Laval to power in April 1942. Laval remained vice premier until the Vichy government collapsed in 1944. Laval found himself caving in to increasingly onerous German demands, especially for forced labor. He also set about suppressing the French resistance. By the fall of 1942, it was apparent that Vichy had no real authority and was a German puppet regime. The last vestige of autonomy was ended by the Anglo-American landings in North Africa and the commencement of the NORTH AFRICAN CAMPAIGN. Although Vichy forces in French-held Morocco and Algeria did briefly resist the American landings, they capitulated when DWIGHT DAVID EISENHOWER negotiated an armistice with Darlan. This prompted Hitler on November 11 to send troops from occupied France into Vichy France to seize the entire country. Even in wholly occupied France, the Vichy government continued to function but only as an administrative shell.

Further reading: Jackson, Julian. *France: The Dark Years, 1940–1944.* New York: Oxford University Press, 2003; Ousby, Ian. *Occupation.* New York: Cooper Square Press, 2000; Paxton, Robert O. *Vichy France.* New York: Columbia University Press, 2001.

Victor Emmanuel III (1869–1947) *Italian king during World War II*

Born in Naples, Victor Emmanuel was given a military education before coming unexpectedly to the throne following the 1900 assassination of his father, King Umberto I. Of liberal inclination, he accepted a fully constitutional monarchy and generally followed the wishes of his Liberal cabinet. World War I—in which Victor Emmanuel III had willingly acquiesced, siding with the Allies—brought economic hardship to Italy and, after the war, great political instability. In this chaotic climate, BENITO MUSSOLINI rapidly rose to power, and, despite his liberal leanings, Victor Emmanuel did nothing to interfere with the rapid development of fascism. Mussolini's ascension to the premiership in 1922 immediately reduced the king to a figurehead, and so he remained through the long lead-up to Italy's entrance into World War II.

The war went badly for Italy from the start, and, in 1943, after the Allied invasion of Sicily, Victor Emmanuel stunned his subjects and most of the rest of the world by ordering the removal of Mussolini; the Fascist Council complied, and, following his removal, Mussolini was arrested. The king then endorsed the installation of Marshal PIETRO BADOGLIO as Italian premier on the understanding that Badoglio would immediately seek an armistice with the Allies.

Victor Emmanuel's bold action did not get Italy out of the war. Germany continued to occupy the country and set up Mussolini as a puppet in the north. Nevertheless, the king did buy Italy a privileged place, as a former Axis power, with regard to treatment by the Allies. On June 5, 1944, when the Allies liberated Rome, Victor Emanuel named his son, Crown Prince Umberto, lieutenant general of Italy. He renounced all authority for himself, but did retain the title of king.

After the war, in 1946, the Italian people voted in a plebiscite to decide whether Italy would continue as a monarchy or become a republic. Victor Emmanuel III abdicated in favor of Umberto on May 9, 1946, in the hope that this might persuade the people to maintain the monarchy. It did not. After Italians voted for a republic, Victor Emmanuel and his family left the country and lived out the rest of their lives in exile in Alexandria, Egypt.

Further reading: Cassels, Alan. *Fascist Italy.* Wheeling, Ill.: Harlan Davidson, 1985; Lyttelton, Adrian, ed. *Liberal and Fascist Italy: 1900–1945.* New York: Oxford University Press, 2002.

V-J Day

August 15, 1945, was proclaimed among the Allied nations Victory over Japan Day—V-J Day—a designation intended to parallel V-E DAY, which had already taken place on May 8, 1945. The Japanese commemorate this day as Shusen-kinenbi (Memorial Day for the End of the War). In Korea and many other Asian nations occupied by Japan during the war, August 15 is celebrated as Liberation Day.

Although the surrender of Japan was not signed until September 2, 1945, it was on August 15 that Emperor HIROHITO announced his acceptance on behalf of the nation of the terms of the POTSDAM DECLARATION and, therefore, accepted unconditional surrender. The announcement came via a recorded radio broadcast and was the first time the Japanese people had ever heard their emperor speak. Just before the broadcast, the Japanese government cabled U.S. President HARRY S. TRUMAN by way of the Swiss diplomatic mission in Washington, announcing that it accepted the Potsdam Declaration. With Japan's surrender, World War II came to an end; so V-J Day marks the end of the war.

V-J Day celebrated on a U.S. city street *(National Archives and Records Administration)*

Although Truman subsequently proclaimed September 2 as VJ-Day, in the United States August 14 was generally accepted as V-J Day—because, in U.S. time zones, news of the surrender broke on this day.

In the name of political correctness, there has been a recent tendency among some historians to call V-J Day V-P Day (Victory in the Pacific Day). (Australia has celebrated V-P Day from the beginning.) Only in Rhode Island is V-J Day celebrated as a legal state holiday, called "Victory Day" and observed on the second Monday of August.

Further reading:: Knauer, Kelly, ed. *V-J Day*. New York: Time-Warner, 2005; Fields, Alan. *V-J Day*. New York: Dell, 1978.

Voroshilov, Kliment (1881–1969) *Red Army commander*

Born in Verkhneye, Ukraine, Voroshilov joined the Bolsheviks in 1903, and after the 1917 Russian Revolution became a member of the Ukrainian provisional government and commissar for internal affairs. He became a close associate of JOSEPH STALIN and helped him triumph over Leon Trotsky in Stalin's climb to power.

Elected to the Central Committee of the Communist Party in 1921, Voroshilov remained a member until 1961. After the death of Mikhail Frunze in 1925, Voroshilov was appointed people's commissar for military and navy affairs and chairman of the Military Revolutionary Council of the USSR. He became a full member of the party's Politburo in 1926 and actively collaborated with Stalin in the purges of the late 1930s. He encouraged Stalin to remove and execute Marshal Mikhail Tukhachevsky, whose death cleared the way for his own appointment as people's commissar for defense in 1934. The following year he was named a marshal of the Soviet Union. The purges that removed so many senior military officers from the Red Army cleared Voroshilov's career path, but also removed (and in many cases murdered) officers far more qualified than he for top command.

At the outbreak of World War II, Voroshilov was a member of the State Defense Committee and commanded Soviet troops during the FINNISH-SOVIET WAR from November 1939 to January 1940. This was a catastrophe for the Red Army. Despite its vast superiority in numbers, the army suffered heavy casualties and was unable to break through the MANNERHEIM LINE. SEMYON TIMOSHENKO replaced Voroshilov in Finland and won the war.

Following the German INVASION OF THE SOVIET UNION on June 22, 1941, Voroshilov was put in command of the armies in the northwest. He led them gallantly, exhibiting great personal courage in the field, but he was unable to prevent the invaders from enveloping Leningrad and was therefore relieved of field command. He sat out the rest of the war but maintained his nominal titles and military offices.

After the war, during 1945–47, Voroshilov was put in charge of establishing the Communist government of Hungary. He was appointed to the Presidium of the Central Committee in 1952 and, after Stalin's death in March 1953, became chairman of the Presidium of the Supreme Soviet, effectively president of the Soviet Union, with NIKITA KHRUSHCHEV as first secretary of the Communist Party and Georgy Malenkov as premier. When Khrushchev denounced Stalin in 1956, Voroshilov reacted by joining the "Anti-Party Group" opposed to Khrushchev, but, after June 1957, he instead decided to support Khrushchev.

Voroshilov officially retired as Presidium chairman and president on May 7, 1960, and was replaced by Leonid Brezhnev. After Khrushchev's own downfall, Brezhnev restored Voroshilov to the Central Committee in 1966 as a figurehead of the conservative regime. He was, for a second time, named a Hero of the Soviet Union in 1968.

Further reading: Kozhevnikov, M. N. *The Command and Staff of the Soviet Army in the Great Patriotic War 1941–1945: A Soviet View.* Honolulu: University Press of the Pacific, 2002; Larionov, V. V. *World War II: Decisive Battles of the Soviet Army.* Moscow: Progress, 1984; Shaw, John. *Red Army Resurgent.* Alexandria, Va.: Time Life, 1980.

W

Waffen SS

The Waffen SS—the "Armed SS"—was the combat arm of the SCHUTZSTAFFEL (SS). During World War II, it often functioned as an elite combat force, fighting independently of but in cooperation with the regular German military, the WEHRMACHT. Like the SS as a whole, the Waffen SS was headed by HEINRICH HIMMLER, who, however, did not exercise field military command until very late in the war—then did so with poor results.

The Waffen SS began as a small bodyguard or protection unit for the NAZI PARTY leadership. By the end of World War II, it had expanded into a force of nearly a million combat soldiers, 38 divisions, a number of them elite units. In contrast to the Wehrmacht, the Waffen SS was condemned after the war by the NUREMBERG WAR CRIMES TRIBUNAL as a criminal organization. As a result, most Waffen SS veterans (except for SS conscripts) were denied the benefits accorded veterans of the regular army, and many Waffen SS officers were found guilty of war crimes.

In the early 1920s, ADOLF HITLER was becoming wary of the growing strength and size of the Storm Troopers, or STURMABTEILUNG (SA), and created a unit of 200 handpicked men to serve as his personal bodyguard—in part to protect him against the SA. This unit developed into the Schutzstaffel (SS), or protection squad. In January 1929 Hitler appointed Himmler to lead the SS. By 1933, Hitler had authorized Himmler to increase the size of the SS, which Himmler wanted to form into an elite army of soldiers within the party. SS membership was 52,000 by the end of 1933; at this time, the SA numbered as many as 2 million men. In 1934, on June 30, in what became known as the "Night of the Long Knives," Hitler turned the SS against the SA, executing thousands of SA officers. This freed Himmler to expand the SS in various ways, including the creation of the SS Verfügungstruppe, which encompassed Hitler's new bodyguard, the Stabwache. From the Verfügungstruppe, the Waffen SS would develop, and from the Stabwache, the elite 1st SS Panzer Division, called Leibstandarte SS Adolf Hitler, would be formed. This SS unit swore a personal loyalty oath directly to Hitler.

In 1935, in defiance of the TREATY OF VERSAILLES, Hitler reintroduced conscription—mandatory military service—in Germany. At the same time, he officially transformed the SS Verfügungstruppen into a full-scale military unit and authorized the creation of special training schools for the officers and men of what would become the Waffen SS. In addition to the 1st SS Panzer Division, the Deutschland and Germania battalions were formed; they became elements of the 2nd SS Panzer Division Das Reich and the 5th SS Panzer Division Wiking. After the ANSCHLUSS—the annexation of Austria in 1938—a new Waffen SS regiment, consisting of Austrians, was created and named Der Führer.

The Waffen SS quickly evolved after the outbreak of the war and officially received its title,

Waffen SS, in March 1940. The Waffen SS fought in almost every major battle of the war. Its units were sent from one front to another, in response to the need for elite troops.

The Waffen SS compiled a mixed battle record. Some units exhibited great courage, audacity, training, and skill, often combined with a ruthlessness that produced war crimes and atrocities. Other units were mediocre and unexceptional. The Allies learned both to respect the best units of the Waffen SS as a formidable military enemy, but also generally to revile the troops as war criminals.

Most Waffen SS soldiers were given special intensive combat training, which included three elements: the creation of a high degree of physical fitness, the acquisition of small-arms proficiency, and—of great importance—thorough political indoctrination. One in three Waffen SS candidates failed to graduate from basic training. After basic training, recruits were given advanced training in a combat specialty. Officers were also given special training, which emphasized developing a strong bond with the men they commanded, almost a relationship among equals—which was very different from the policy that prevailed in the Wehrmacht.

Initially, the Waffen SS performed poorly, probably due to an overemphasis on political indoctrination at the expense of full military training. Before long, however, the best Waffen SS units evolved into a highly effective elite force.

Originally, Waffen SS members were chosen—like other SS members—from among German citizens, especially those deemed to possess highly desirable "Aryan" racial characteristics and heritage. As the war progressed, however, Himmler acted on his idea of expanding the Waffen SS to include SS-controlled foreign legions. Absorbed in Germanic mythology and lore, which figured in the creation of the original SS, Himmler now conceived of a Europe united by an SS crusade to save the continent from the racially inferior "Bolshevik hordes." Thus, through a combination of political ideology and vaguely medieval mythology, Himmler recruited Danish, French, Azeri, Armenian, Flemish, Norwegian, Finnish, and Dutch Waffen SS formations. By 1942–43, Bosnians, Latvians, Estonians, and Ukrainians had also joined the Waffen SS.

Eventually, even the foreign Waffen SS units were subject to recruitment by conscription to supplement those who volunteered. Many foreign volunteers were prosecuted by their home countries after the war; significant numbers were executed for treason.

The most enduring legacy of the Waffen SS was not the skill of some of the organization's most elite units, but the overall taint of war crimes and atrocities. In some cases, the conduct of the Waffen SS was sufficiently egregious to prompt complaints from regular army commanders. After the war, the Nuremberg tribunal made no effort to discriminate among Waffen SS units that functioned purely as military organizations and those that committed war crimes. Instead, the tribunal indicted the entire SS—and, with it, the Waffen SS—as a criminal organization. Its leaders were accordingly subject to prosecution.

Further reading: Quarrie, Bruce. *Hitler's Samurai: The Waffen-SS in Action.* New York: Arco, 1983; Stein, George H. *The Waffen-SS: Hitler's Elite Guard at War 1939–1945.* Ithaca, N.Y.: Cornell University Press, 1966; Williamson, Gordon. *Loyalty Is My Honor.* Osceola, Wis.: Motorbooks International, 1995.

Wainwright, Jonathan (1883–1953) *U.S. general who fought a valiant but hopeless defense of the Philippines and endured as a POW throughout virtually all of World War II*

Born in Walla Walla, Washington, Wainwright graduated from West Point in 1906 and saw service with the 1st Cavalry in Texas, then went with the 1st to the Philippines, where he participated in a campaign against Moro pirates on Job Island during 1908–10. Promoted to first lieutenant in 1912, he graduated from the Mounted Service School in 1916, was promoted to captain, and when the United States entered World War I in April 1917, he was made a temporary major of field artillery. Wainwright served as an instructor at the officers training camp in Plattsburgh, New York, then shipped out for

France with the 76th Division in February 1918. He served on detached service with the British near Ypres, Belgium, before being posted as assistant chief of staff for operations (G-3) in the U.S. 82nd Division. He served with the unit in the Saint-Mihiel offensive of September 12–16 and at Meuse-Argonne during September 26–November 11.

Wainwright remained in Germany with Third Army on occupation duty after the armistice until October 1920. On his return to the United States, he reverted to his peacetime rank of captain, but was soon promoted to major and assigned as an instructor at the Cavalry School, Fort Riley, Kansas. In 1921, he became a general staff officer with 3rd Infantry Division. From 1921 to 1923, he served in the War Department, then was assigned to the 3rd Cavalry until 1925, when he returned to the War Department. Promoted to lieutenant colonel in 1929, he graduated from the Command and General Staff School at Fort Leavenworth in 1931, then went on to the Army War College, from which he graduated in 1934. The following year, promoted to colonel, he served as commandant of the Cavalry School. He left the school in 1936 to assume command of the 3rd Cavalry. In 1938, promoted to the temporary rank of brigadier general, he was assigned to command the 1st Cavalry Brigade.

In September 1940, Wainwright was promoted to major general and shipped out to the Philippines to command the Philippine Division. He served as senior field commander under General Douglas MacArthur. When the Japanese attacked and invaded the Philippines at the start of World War II in the Pacific, the brunt of the defense fell on Wainwright. His mission, as commander of the Northern Luzon Force (11th, 21st, 71st, and 91st Filipino Divisions, and the U.S. 26th Cavalry Regiment), was to delay the Japanese, who had landed at Lingayen Gulf during December 22–31, so that the American and Filipino forces could fall back to Bataan and take a stand there in the hope of being reinforced. The defense of northern Bataan withdrew under a first assault during January 10–25, and Wainwright and MacArthur repulsed a second assault during January 26–February 23.

In the thick of combat, Wainwright was promoted to lieutenant general and made commander of U.S. Forces in the Philippines after President Franklin D. Roosevelt ordered MacArthur to evacuate to Australia in March 1942. Reinforcements were never sent, and Wainwright was left to conduct a defense as best he could entirely on his own. He did so through early April 1942, forcing the Japanese to pay dearly for the conquest of the islands. The Bataan-based U.S. and Filipino forces surrendered on April 9, and a massive Japanese assault on Corregidor forced Wainwright to surrender all forces on May 6. The general and his men were sent to POW camps in the Philippines, Taiwan, and finally Manchuria, and were treated with appalling brutality by their Japanese captors. Wainwright did much to sustain the morale and honor not only of himself but of his imprisoned command.

Whereas a Japanese commander in Wainwright's situation would have been disgraced by surrender, Wainwright, after his liberation by Soviet troops in Manchuria in August 1945, was hailed as a war hero. The emaciated Wainwright was accorded the honor of attending the Japanese surrender ceremonies in Tokyo Bay aboard the USS *Missouri* on September 2. He commented with characteristic reserve, good humor, and self-irony: "The last surrender I attended the shoe was on the other foot."

Wainwright was awarded the Medal of Honor and assigned to command the Fourth Army in Texas in January 1946, but retired the following year.

See also Bataan Death March.

Further reading: Wainwright, Jonathan. *General Wainwright's Story: The Account of Four Years of Humiliating Defeat, Surrender, and Captivity.* Westport, Conn.: Greenwood Press, 1970.

Wake Island, Battle of

The name "Wake Island" is misleading, because it denotes not a single body of land, but a group of three remote coral islets in the Pacific, 2,300 miles west of Hawaii. Claimed by the United States after the Spanish-American War, Wake Island was defended by the 1st Defense Battalion—just 449 marines—at the outbreak of World War II. In addition to the ground troops, there were a dozen marine F4F Wildcat fighter aircraft based on Wake. Also present were 69 sailors, five army signalmen, and 1,216 civilians, most of them construction workers building fortifications on the islands. The marines were under the command of Major James Devereux, with U.S. Navy Commander WINFIELD CUNNINGHAM in overall command.

On December 8, 34 Japanese carrier-based bombers raided Wake, destroying eight of the Wildcats on the ground. The first Japanese landing attempt came on December 11, 1941, but was repulsed by the small marine garrison. The outnumbered defenders took a spectacular toll on the attackers. Firing five-inch guns, they sank two destroyers, damaged a third, and also damaged two Japanese cruisers.

No reinforcements or relief came from the United States, and the marines and others were left to their fate. The Japanese returned on December 22, with 2,000 specially trained men and overwhelmed the marine garrison. Cunningham surrendered that day to General Sadamichi Kajioka.

The taking of this tiny outpost was, to the Japanese, stunning in its cost. In addition to the ships lost, 820 of the invaders were killed and 335 wounded. The marines lost 50 killed; 70 civilians also died. All others were taken prisoner. Many survived the war.

Further reading: Alexander, Joseph H. *The Battle History of the U.S. Marines.* New York: HarperPerennial, 1999; Millett, Allan R. *Semper Fidelis: The History of the United States Marine Corps,* revised and expanded. New York: Free Press, 1991; Sloan, Bill. *Given Up for Dead: America's Heroic Stand at Wake Island.* New York: Bantam, 2003; Wukovits, John. *Pacific Alamo: The Battle for Wake Island.* New York: NAL Trade, 2003.

Wannsee Conference

Held on January 20, 1942, at Wannsee, a villa on Lake Wannsee in southwestern Berlin, the conference was a meeting called by REINHARD HEYDRICH between officials of the SCHUTZSTAFFEL (SS) and administrators of the German civilian government to secure the cooperation of the SS and the civilians in carrying out the FINAL SOLUTION, the genocide of the Jews of Europe in what historians came to call the HOLOCAUST.

By the time of the meeting, the Final Solution was already under way; SS Einsatzgruppen murder squads were executing Jews in the occupied territories of eastern Europe and the Soviet Union. The conference was called to lay out policy and plans for extermination on an even more massive and systematic scale. More important, Heydrich wanted to impress on the civilian administrators that the elimination of European Jewry was of the highest priority: a major war aim.

Heydrich and his assistant, ADOLF EICHMANN, prepared minutes of the conference, which historians refer to as the Wannsee Protocol. This document summarizes the shift in policy from removing Jews by coaxing or forcing emigration to deportation, forced labor, and outright genocide. Deportation was synonymous with confinement to concentration camps. Forced labor was both a means of extracting labor useful to the Reich and the war effort and, because the labor was especially grueling, of bringing about the eventual death of the laborers. Genocide—outright execution—however, would increasingly become the fate of Europe's Jews under the Nazi regime.

The Wannsee Conference demonstrates that complicity in the Holocaust reached virtually all German government agencies. Present at the meeting were SS Obergruppenführer Reinhard Heydrich, Chief of the Reichsicherheitshauptamt (RSHA), the Reich Main Security Office and Reichsprotektor of Bohemia-Moravia; Gauleiter Dr. Alfred Meyer, Reich Ministry for the Occupied Eastern territories; Reichsamtleiter Dr. Georg Leibbrandt, Reich Ministry for the Occupied Eastern territories; Dr. Wilhelm Stuckart, Reich Ministry for the Interior; Dr. Erich Neumann, Director, Office of the Four Year Plan; Dr. Roland Freisler, Reich Ministry of Justice; Josef Bühler, Government of the General Government (occupied Poland); Dr. Martin Luther, Foreign Office; SA

Oberführer Gerhard Klopfer, Party Chancellery; Ministerialdirektor Friedrich Wilhelm Kritzinger, Reich Chancellery; SS Gruppenführer Otto Hofmann, Race and Settlement Main Office; SS Gruppenführer Heinrich Müller, Chief of Amt IV (Gestapo), RSHA; SS Obersturmbannführer Adolf Eichmann, Reich Security Main Office (Gestapo); SS Oberführer Dr. Karl Eberhard Schöngarth, SD (assigned to the General Government); and SS Sturmbannführer Dr. Rudolf Lange, Commander of the SD for Latvia.

Further reading: Lehrer, Steven. *Wannsee House and the Holocaust.* Jefferson, N.C.: McFarland, 2000; Roseman, Mark. *The Wannsee Conference and the Final Solution: A Reconsideration.* London: Picador, 2003.

Warsaw Ghetto Uprising

Part of the FINAL SOLUTION—the genocide of Europe's Jews in the HOLOCAUST—involved the establishment of ghettos in German-occupied territories in which Jews were confined until they could be dispatched to CONCENTRATION AND EXTERMINATION CAMPS. The Warsaw Ghetto, within the city's old Jewish quarter, was enclosed first by barbed wire and later by a brick wall. By summer 1942, about half a million Jews were crowded into the 840 acres of the ghetto. Starvation, privation, and epidemic disease killed thousands monthly.

Starting on July 22, 1942, 5,000 Jews per day were transferred from the ghetto to the TREBLINKA EXTERMINATION CAMP. By September, only about 55,000 Jews remained in the Warsaw Ghetto. Realizing that their situation was desperate, those who remained decided to resist. They had no hope for a military victory, but decided that it was better to fight than to submit passively to extermination. The Jewish Fighting Organization (Żydowska Organizacja Bojowa, ŻOB) was formed and covertly took control of the ghetto. On January 9, 1943, SCHUTZSTAFFEL (SS) head HEINRICH HIMMLER ordered the deportation of 8,000 Jews. The order was met by resistance, as many refused to report as ordered, and ZOB fighters began sniping

at German troops. Under fire, the deportation proceedings were called off, and, greatly encouraged, ZOB organized an even more widespread resistance effort, fortifying hideouts, scrounging weapons, and improvising explosives for the battle all knew was coming.

On April 19, 1943, about 3,000 German troops under SS Brigadier General Jürgen Stroop, including 2,600 SS troops as well as regular army soldiers and police, attacked the ghetto with tanks and other armored vehicles, as well as machine guns and artillery. Opposing them were some 600 ZOB fighters and 400 from another group, the Jewish Military Union (ZZW). From well-prepared positions, the Jews fought with one machine gun, pistols, hand grenades, and Molotov cocktails. Stroop was shocked at the ferocity and organization of the resistance. He was obliged to fight in the ghetto streets daily, finally declaring the ghetto secure on May 16—even though resistance continued.

Polish Home Army and other Polish resistance fighters tried unsuccessfully to breach the ghetto's walls in the hope of providing an exit route for the Jews. Those Jewish fighters who were not killed in combat committed suicide or were captured; however, 50 ZOB fighters escaped through the sewers. The uprising killed 14,000 Jews, many the victims of arson fires. Seven thousand survivors were murdered at Treblinka. Others were sent to the Majdanek camp, where they met the same fate. German casualties were not officially calculated, but probably included 400 killed and 1,000 wounded.

See also WARSAW RISING.

Further reading: Gutman, Israel. *Resistance: The Warsaw Ghetto Uprising.* New York: Mariner Books, 1998; Kurzman, Dan. *The Bravest Battle: The Twenty-Eight Days of the Warsaw Ghetto Uprising.* New York: Da Capo, 1993.

Warsaw Rising

The Warsaw Rising, sometimes called the Second Warsaw Uprising to distinguish it from the earlier WARSAW GHETTO UPRISING, was part of Operation Tempest, a planned resistance by the Polish Home Army against the German occupiers. The rising began on August 1, 1944, and was projected as a 10-day action, but it endured for 63 days. The hope was not only to defeat the Germans in the capital city, but also to obtain control of Warsaw to prevent the Soviets from seizing the city when they "liberated" it.

The rising was commanded by Home Army general Antoni Chrusciel and involved about 37,600 Polish insurgents, most of whom were Polish Home Army troops. In the initial stage of the uprising, fewer than 14 percent of the insurgents were armed (equipment included 20 heavy machine guns, 98 light machine guns, 844 submachine guns, 1,386 rifles, and 2,665 handguns), but more arms and ammunition came from western Allied and Soviet air drops or were captured from the Germans. In any case, much of the combat took place with hand grenades and Molotov cocktails.

Initially, most of the city quickly fell to the insurgents, although they failed to capture the principal arteries and railway stations. The insurgents continued to fight, however, in the expectation of reinforcements from the Western Allies or the Soviets. There was also a strong possibility, they felt, that Germany would soon collapse. This hope was dashed on August 20, when 21,300 German troops (including Oskar Dirlewanger's so-called Police Brigade, a unit of convicted Polish criminals in the German service) stormed through the city streets. HEINRICH HIMMLER had ordered the soldiers to shoot all Poles on sight, whether insurgents or not. In this way, 40,000 citizens of Warsaw were cut down before Lt. Gen. Erich von dem Bach-Zelewski, commander in charge of the operation, ordered the indiscriminate killings to cease. On August 25, Bach-Zelewski began his organized counterattack. It was a bitter street-by-street battle. In the meantime, the Red Army was stopped by a German counteroffensive just outside of Warsaw, and JOSEPH STALIN refused to order a renewal of the Soviet offensive; therefore, no relief would come to the fighters in the city. Almost certainly, Stalin intended for the Germans to kill as many members of the Home Army as possible, because he saw these men as obstacles to ultimate Soviet control of Poland.

Under siege, the insurgents organized soup kitchens, dug wells, and provided shelter and medical care for Warsaw's residents during the fighting. But slowly, the Germans regained control of the city. On October 1, Polish Home Army general Tadeusz Komorowski surrendered, having secured from the Germans a pledge that the insurgents would be treated as regular combatants and that all surviving civilians would be evacuated from Warsaw.

The toll of the Warsaw Rising was 15,000 insurgents killed, along with 250,000 civilians—out of a total population of 1,000,000. German losses may have been as high as 17,000 dead and missing. After the evacuation, the Germans deliberately and systematically leveled more than 80 percent of Warsaw.

Further reading: Ciechanowski, Jan M. *The Warsaw Rising of 1944.* New York: Cambridge University Press, 2002; Davies, Norman. *Rising '44: The Battle for Warsaw.* New York: Viking, 2004.

Wavell, Archibald (1883–1950) *British field marshal who defeated the Italians in the Middle East, but was in turn defeated by the Germans*

Born in Colchester, Wavell grew up in India, where his father was a general officer in the British army. After graduating from Winchester College, Wavell enrolled at Sandhurst, then was commissioned in the Black Watch in 1900 and fought in the Second ("Great") Boer War. In 1903, he was transferred to India, and in 1908 fought in the Bazar Valley campaign. He was transferred again, in 1911, this time to Russia as an observer attached to the Russian army.

Wavell was serving as a staff officer in 1914 at the outbreak of World War I and, at his request, was transferred into a combat unit. In 1915, he was wounded at Ypres, Belgium, and lost an eye. After his recovery in 1916, he served as a liaison officer to the Russian army in Turkey, then was transferred in 1918 to the staff of Edmund Allenby in Palestine.

During the interwar period Wavell served in various posts before he was posted once again in Palestine. He was appointed to head the Middle

East Command in July 1939 and held that post at the outbreak of World War II.

Little happened in this theater until Italy declared war on France in June 1940. Italian forces in North Africa were large, and Wavell, outnumbered, nevertheless conducted a highly successful defense against each Italian attack. He then counterattacked and occupied the Italian colonies in Ethiopia and Somaliland. By February 1941, Wavell seemed about to sweep away the last Italian forces remaining in Libya; however, he was ordered to halt his advance against Libya so that he could send troops to Greece to defend against a German and Italian invasion. Wavell objected but obeyed. This gave the Germans a golden opportunity to reinforce the Italians in North Africa—a circumstance that prevented the British from making a credible defense in Greece. Wavell's troops had to withdraw to Crete. To complicate matters further, a pro-Axis faction took control of Iraq, which ignited a brief Anglo-Iraqi war.

Although the dilution of his forces was not his fault, Wavell was relieved as commander of British forces in the Middle East by Sir CLAUDE AUCHINLECK in July 1941. He was transferred to India as commander in charge yet again of inadequate forces. When Japan declared war on Great Britain in December 1941, Wavell was given command of the short-lived American-British-Dutch-Australian (ABDA) Command. He was soon forced to evacuate his headquarters from Java.

Wavell was never given resources commensurate with his talents as a leader. As a result, he presided over the early British disasters in the Middle East, Singapore, Malaya, and Burma. Nevertheless, in 1943, he was created a viscount and named viceroy of India. He administered India during the rest of the war and was replaced by Lord LOUIS MOUNTBATTEN in 1947. Wavell's final honor came in 1947, when he was made high steward of Colchester.

Further reading: Connell, John. *Wavell, Supreme Commander, 1941–1943.* London: Collins, 1969; Lewin, Ronald. *The Chief: Field Marshall Lord Wavell, Commander-in-Chief and Viceroy, 1939–1947.* New York: Farrar, Straus and Giroux, 1980; Pitt, Barrie. *The Crucible of War—Wavell's Command: The Definitive History of the Desert War.* London: Cassell, 2001.

Wehrmacht

Wehrmacht was the name correctly applied to all of the armed forces of Germany from 1935 to 1945. During World War II, the Wehrmacht included the army (Heer), the navy (Kriegsmarine), and the air force (Luftwaffe). It is not incorrect to add the WAFFEN SS and STURMABTEILUNG (SA) under the Wehrmacht rubric, but in customary usage, these were not included. Moreover, as commonly used, "Wehrmacht" referred to regular army land forces rather than to the navy and air force or the SA and SS.

Before 1935, the Wehrmacht was called the Reichswehr. After the war—when Germany was remilitarized in 1955—the term was abandoned in favor of Bundeswehr. For this reason, "Wehrmacht" is virtually synonymous with the German army during World War II.

Between 1935 and 1945, some 18.2 million officers and men served in the Wehrmacht. Of this number, 5.3 million were killed and 11 million were made prisoners of war.

See also GERMANY, AIR FORCE OF; GERMANY, ARMY OF; and GERMANY, NAVY OF.

Further reading: Buchner, Alex. *The German Infantry Handbook.* Atglen, Pa.: Schiffer, 1991; Davies, W. J. K. *German Army Handbook.* New York: Arco, 1984; Mitcham, Samuel W. *Hitler's Legions: The German Army Order Battle, World War II.* Chelsea, Mich.: Scarborough House, 1985; Pimlot, John. *Wehrmacht: The Illustrated History of the German Army in World War II.* Osceola, Wis.: Motorbooks International, 1997; Thomas, Nigel. *German Army 1939–1945: Blitzkrieg.* London: Osprey, 1998; Thomas, Nigel. *German Army 1939–45: Eastern Front 1943–1945.* London: Osprey, 1999; Thomas, Nigel. *The German Army in World War II.* London: Osprey, 2002; Williamson, Gordon. *German Army Elite Units 1939–45.* London: Osprey, 2002.

Wei Li-huang (1897–1955) *Nationalist Chinese general*

Wei Li-huang joined the Nationalist—or Kuomintang (Guomindag, KMT)—faction in the 1920s and distinguished himself in the Northern

Expedition, CHIANG KAI-SHEK's (Jiang Jieshi) two-year campaign to unify China under the Nationalist banner. He then went on to success during the Bandit (Communist) Suppression Campaigns of 1930–34 and earned the epithet "Hundred Victories Wei."

At the outbreak of the SINO-JAPANESE WAR, Wei commanded the First War Area, then was transferred during World War II to southern China, relieving Ch'en Ch'eng as commander of Y-Force, 100,000 soldiers supporting General JOSEPH W. STILWELL's BURMA CAMPAIGN. Wei led an offensive into southern Yunnan beginning on May 11, 1944, and captured Tengchung on September 15. He then fought through heavy Japanese resistance to link up with Chinese divisions in Wanting (Wandingzhen), Burma, on January 27, 1945.

After the war, Wei fought against Communist forces in the revolution that created the People's Republic of China.

Further reading: Bagby, Wesley M. *The Eagle-Dragon Alliance: America's Relations With China in World War II.* Newark: University of Delaware Press, 1992; Dorn, Frank. *The Sino-Japanese War, 1937–41: From Marco Polo Bridge to Pearl Harbor.* New York: Macmillan, 1974; Dupuy, Trevor N. *Asiatic Land Battles: Allied Victories in China and Burma.* New York: Franklin Watts, 1963; Puyu Hu. *A Brief History of the Sino-Japanese War (1937–1945).* Tapei, Taiwan: Chung Wu, 1974.

Weil, Simone (1909–1943) *French philosopher who was a key figure in the French resistance*

A brilliant writer and social philosopher, Weil taught philosophy in various schools for girls during 1931–38. She was radical in many of her views and demonstrated her commitment to social justice by refusing to eat more than those who lived on the government dole or by attempting to live in the manner of the unskilled working class. In 1936, she trained with an anarchist unit to fight in the SPANISH CIVIL WAR, but severe burns caused by boiling cooking oil forced her to convalesce in Portugal. Her long convalescence gave rise to a number of spiritual or mystical experiences, which made her more introspective and prompted her to retreat from her social activism.

After the French collapse following the BATTLE OF FRANCE, Weill left occupied Paris for the south of France, where she labored as a farm servant. With her parents, she fled to the United States in 1942, but then went to London, where she worked with the French resistance. Her former impulse to social activism reemerged, and by way of identifying with the French under German occupation, she refused to eat more than the official ration in occupied France. The combination of overwork and malnutrition sent her to the hospital, where it was discovered that she had tuberculosis. She died in a sanatorium.

Weil's most important writings on war and resistance were published with her other works after her death: *L'Enracinement* (1949; translated as *The Need for Roots*), concerning the relation of the individual to the state, and *Oppression et Liberté* (1955; *Oppression and Liberty*), essays on war and other subjects.

Further reading: Pétrement, Simone. *Simone Weil: A Life.* New York: Pantheon Books, 1976; Weil, Simone. *The Simone Weil Reader.* London: Moyer Bell, 1985.

Western Desert Campaigns

The Western Desert Campaigns were fought in Libya and Egypt from June 1940 to January 1943, mainly by British and Commonwealth forces in an effort to prevent the Axis (German and Italian forces) from taking control of the Suez Canal, which the Allies depended on for supply and communications.

There were two major campaigns, the first against the Italians, and the second against the Germans and Italians, led by ERWIN ROMMEL.

The campaign against the Italians was a mostly one-sided affair. Despite enjoying a substantial superiority of numbers over British and Commonwealth forces, the Italians were driven out of most of their positions and were nearly ejected from Libya. The campaign against the Germans was an epic struggle ranging over a vast amount of desert, some 1,500 square miles, and included land, air, and sea (Mediterranean) components. Whereas the Italian army in the Western Desert was generally poorly trained and poorly led, Rommel's forces—usually numerically inferior to their British and Commonwealth adversaries—were superbly trained and led. British troops and commanders learned the lessons of desert warfare haltingly. In the end, British persistence and access to superior logistics prevailed over Rommel's brilliance as a tactician.

In addition to facing each other, the armies had to contend with harsh desert conditions and vast spaces. Logistics was always a critical issue, as was exhaustion and endemic illness. It was above all a war of mobility, in which armor played the key role, supported by aircraft.

Although Italy declared war on June 10, 1940, BENITO MUSSOLINI was slow to order his marshal in Libya, Rodolfo Graziani, to invade British-held Egypt with his Tenth Army (commanded in the field by General Mario Berti). Opposing this was the British Western Desert Force, which had just two divisions to Berti's five (later nine). The British commander, ARCHIBALD WAVELL, nevertheless attacked on December 9, 1940, achieving total surprise and inflicting heavy losses on the Italians. In January, Bardia fell to the British, prompting the Italians to withdraw to Tripolitania, whereupon ADOLF HITLER authorized the German 5th Light Division (part of the Afrika Korps) to assist them. Despite this, British general RICHARD O'CONNOR took Tobruk at the first of the BATTLES OF TOBRUK on January 22. This accomplished, he advanced across the desert to cut off the retreat of the Tenth Army at Beda Fomm. Wavell and O'Connor were then poised to drive the Italians completely out of Libya when the order came to send troops to Greece to confront a combined German-Italian invasion there. This gave Rommel an opening to counterattack, and he captured El Agheila on March 24, 1941, and Mersa Brega on April 1. He managed to capture O'Connor himself and lay siege to Tobruk, continuing his advance all the way to Sollum, thereby rolling back every gain made by Wavell and O'Connor. Worse, Rommel had captured airfields from which the Germans were able to launch raids in support of the SIEGE OF MALTA, the key British stronghold in the Mediterranean theater.

Fortunately for the British, Rommel received little support from the German high command, which was focused on the INVASION OF THE SOVIET UNION and wanted Rommel to do no more than defend in the Western Desert. The lack of support—especially logistics—would fatally cripple Rommel. In contrast, WINSTON CHURCHILL grasped the importance of prevailing in North Africa. He saw it as the opening to the entire Mediterranean and what he repeatedly called the "soft underbelly of Europe" itself. He rushed tanks and fighter planes to Wavell and urged him to go on the offensive—prematurely, as it turned out. Wavell's defeat led to his replacement by CLAUDE JOHN AYRE AUCHINLECK on July 1. Recognizing that Wavell had fallen victim to Churchill's zeal, Auchinleck bided his time until he had a sufficient force to conduct a successful offensive. Under him was Lt. General ALAN CUNNINGHAM and the newly formed Eighth Army, which was composed of XIII Corps (the Western Desert Force) and XXX Corps. On November 18, Auchinleck launched Operation Crusader against Rommel's Panzer Group Afrika (consisting of the Afrika Korps and 21st Italian Corps), which stopped Rommel from attempting a new assault on Tobruk and therefore kept him out of Egypt. In the middle of the BATTLE OF SIDI REZEGH, Cunningham asked Auchinleck to decide whether he should withdraw. This prompted Auchinleck to relieve Cunningham and replace him with Maj. Gen. NEIL RITCHIE, who inflicted such heavy losses on Rommel that, on December 8, he withdrew toward Cyrenaica.

Resupplied in January, Rommel attacked Mersa Brega on January 21, 1942, preventing Auchinleck from invading Tripolitania. On January 22, Rommel forced a British retreat, then rushed on to capture Benghazi. After much jockeying and maneuvering, Rommel defeated Ritchie at the BATTLE OF GAZALA (May 26–June 17, 1942), which put him in a position to recapture Tobruk.

Auchinleck responded by dismissing Ritchie and assuming personal command of the Eighth Army, which withdrew to Mersa Matruh—only to be bested by Rommel again at the end of June. This was the low point of the Western Desert Campaign. The Eighth Army withdrew all the way to partially prepared defenses at El Alamein and awaited the arrival of reserves from Syria and Egypt.

On July 1, the first of the BATTLES OF EL ALAMEIN began. Rommel was uncharacteristically impulsive, whereas Auchinleck responded methodically, holding the advance of the Axis—but gaining nothing decisive.

Early in August, Auchinleck was replaced by HAROLD ALEXANDER, and BERNARD LAW MONTGOMERY was given command of the Eighth Army. It was Montgomery who did the most to inject Auchinleck's cautiously defensive approach with boldness. The result was a British victory at Alain Haifa at the end of August. This achieved, Montgomery trained and conditioned the Eighth Army to prepare it for Operation Lightfoot, a new offensive launched on October 23 and culminating in the 12-day second Battle of El Alamein. Rommel was soundly defeated, but Montgomery failed to exploit this fully, and Rommel's forces retired battered but intact—than some 30,000 taken as prisoners of war.

Montgomery now chased Rommel across Libya, failing to destroy his army but taking Tripoli on January 23, 1943, and forcing the Desert Fox to withdraw into Tunisia, thereby ending the Western Desert Campaign.

Further reading: Bierman, John, and Colin Smith. *War without Hate: The Desert Campaign of 1940–43*. New York: Penguin, 2004; Moorehead, Alan. *Desert War: The North African Campaign 1940–1943*. New York: Penguin, 2001; Pitt, Barrie. *The Crucible of War: Western Desert 1941*. New York: Paragon House, 1989.

Western Front Campaign of 1940 *See* BATTLE OF FRANCE.

Weygand, Maxime (1867–1965) *defeatist French commander in chief of the Allied armies in France during the Battle of France*

Weygand was born in Belgium and educated in France. He graduated with distinction from the French military academy, Saint-Cyr, in 1888, then enrolled at the prestigious Saumur cavalry school, where he subsequently served as an instructor. At the outbreak of World War I in 1914, Ferdinand Foch appointed Weygand his chief of staff.

During the interwar years, in 1920, Weygand served as adviser to the Polish army in its fight against the Bolshevik Red Army. He served as French high commissioner in Syria during 1923–24 and as vice president of the Superior War Council of France and inspector general of the army during 1931–35. He retired on January 21, 1935, but was recalled—at age 73—on May 20, 1940, to take command of the French armies during the BATTLE OF FRANCE, which had already turned very much against the French. The old man entered into a situation that seemed to him hopeless, and the best advice he could give was to capitulate. That is precisely what the French did.

Weygand retired in December 1941 to his country villa at Grasse, near Cannes. When the Allies invaded North Africa in 1942, he attempted to fly to Algiers—to assist the Allies—but was intercepted by the Germans and held at Schloss Itter, in Austria. He remained a prisoner until U.S. troops liberated him on May 5, 1945. No sooner was he released than he was transported to Paris by plane and, on the order of CHARLES DE GAULLE, arrested. Despite this, his reputation was officially rehabilitated and restored, de Gaulle later admitting that, by the time Weygand assumed command, the Battle of France had indeed been lost.

Further reading: Bloch, Marc. *Strange Defeat*. New York: Norton, 1999; Jackson, Julian. *The Fall of France: The Nazi Invasion of 1940*. New York: Oxford University

Press, 2003; Pallud, Jean-Paul. *Blitzkrieg in the West.* London: After the Battle, 1991.

Whittle, Frank (1907–1996) *British inventor of the jet engine*

Whittle was born in Coventry, the son of a mechanic. Passionately attracted to flying, he joined the Royal Air Force (RAF) as a "boy apprentice," but soon earned his wings at RAF College, Cranwell, and served in a fighter squadron from 1928 to 1931. In 1931, he became a test pilot, then left the cockpit the following year to study aeronautical engineering at the RAF engineering school and at Cambridge, which he attended from 1934 to 1937.

Whittle was interested in developing aircraft that could fly faster and higher. He recognized that conventional piston engines driving propellers were limited in reaching these goals, and, in 1928, he proposed the concept of jet propulsion in his senior thesis at the RAF College. The British Air Ministry reviewed the thesis and rejected the notion of jet propulsion as unworkable. Although unable to get government or industry support, Whittle continued to pursue jet technology and patented a design for a turbo jet engine in 1930. Six years later, he found partners with whom he established Power Jets Ltd. for manufacturing engines. He tested his first actual prototype—in a static, ground-based test—in 1937.

Whittle's static test is usually considered the birth of the jet engine; however, it was a German, Hans Pabst von Ohain, who first demonstrated jet engine in flight, on August 27, 1939. Impressed by this, the British government began supporting Whittle's work after the outbreak of World War II in September 1939. On May 15, 1941, a Gloster E.28/39 was fitted with a Whittle engine and flew successfully. Power Jets Ltd. was taken over by the British government in 1944. During that year, the RAF Gloster Meteor, powered by a jet engine, intercepted German V-1 BUZZ BOMB missiles; however, the British neither developed nor used jets as extensively in World War II as the Germans did— and, at that, the Germans produced too few jets too

late in the war to have a significant impact on air combat in Europe.

Whittle retired from the RAF in 1948 and was knighted. Belatedly grateful, the British government granted him a tax-free gift of £100,000. He moved to the United States in 1977 to accept an appointment as a research professor at the U.S. Naval Academy, Annapolis, Maryland, and in 1986 the British government awarded him the Order of Merit.

Further reading: Golley, John. *Genesis: Frank Whittle and the Invention of the Jet Engine.* Ramsbury, Wiltshire, U.K.: Crowood Press, 1997; Nahum, Andrew. *Frank Whittle: Invention of the Jet.* Kallista, Victoria, Australia: Totem Books, 2006.

Wilson, Henry Maitland "Jumbo" (1881–1964) *British field marshal in the Middle East and Mediterranean*

Wilson was born to the landed gentry of Suffolk and educated at Eton College, then at the British military academy, Sandhurst. He joined the Rifle Brigade in 1900 and was dispatched to South Africa, where he fought in the Second ("Great") Boer War. He was decorated with the Queen's and King's medals for his service in that conflict and, in 1908, was promoted to captain. After a posting in Ireland, he was appointed adjutant of the Oxford Officers Training Corps in 1911.

At the outbreak of World War I in 1914, he was a brigade major in the 16th Irish Division and fought in France. In 1915, he was made a staff officer of the 41st Division and then, in October 1917, was appointed general staff officer of the New Zealand Division. He was selected after the war for enrollment in the staff course at Camberley and at Sandhurst, then returned to his regiment.

In the 1930s, Wilson became an instructor at Camberley and worked on the development of mechanized infantry and armor. From this emerged the pattern for the standard British motor battalion of World War II.

In June 1939, Wilson was put in command of British and Commonwealth forces defending Egypt and the Sudan. He established his headquarters at Cairo and presided over the build up of forces in Egypt on the eve of World War II. When, at the outbreak of war, the Germans attempted to turn the Egyptians against the British, Wilson exercised considerable diplomatic skill to retain Egyptian cooperation.

When BENITO MUSSOLINI declared war against France on June 10, 1940, Wilson invaded Libya. He was repulsed, however, after France withdrew from the war, thereby freeing up more Italian troops to oppose his advance. The Italians invaded Egypt in September 1940. Badly outnumbered—31,000 troops versus 80,000, 120 tanks versus 275—Wilson acted quickly and unconventionally to divide the Italian forces on December 7, 1940, and drove them out of Sidi Barani and Egypt.

Wilson was in command as the British forces (under Sir RICHARD O'CONNOR) advanced to Libya and successfully captured Tobruk. After this, in April 1941, he was named military governor of Cyrenaica, then was tapped to lead two infantry divisions and an armored brigade to Greece to help defend against what was first an Italian invasion and then an invasion augmented by the Germans. Thinly spread, Wilson's forces were inadequate, and he was compelled to withdraw to Crete.

After the Greek expedition, Wilson returned to the Middle East and fought in Syria to prevent both Syria and Lebanon from falling into Axis hands. Promoted to general, he assumed command of the Ninth Army in Syria and Palestine in December 1941. In the summer of the following year, he took charge of a newly created independent Persia-Iraq command to block a potential German thrust into these countries.

Wilson was a capable officer and tremendously popular, both with his men and with fellow commanders. He was much in the running to succeed CLAUDE JOHN AYRE AUCHINLECK as commander of the Eighth Army in the winter of 1942, but was passed over in favor of BERNARD LAW MONTGOMERY. Wilson was appointed commander in chief of the Middle East and, under orders from WINSTON CHURCHILL, mounted an expedition to occupy the

small Greek islands of Kos, Leros, and Samos in September 1943 with the object of creating a diversion during the ITALIAN CAMPAIGN. The expedition was a bad idea, and Wilson's forces sustained heavy casualties, for which Wilson was widely blamed. Nevertheless, when DWIGHT D. EISENHOWER was named supreme Allied commander, Europe, it was Wilson who took over as supreme Allied commander in the Mediterranean in January 1944 and oversaw the Italian Campaign until December 1944, when he was dispatched to Washington, D.C., as chief of the British Joint Staff Mission.

Promoted to field marshal on December 29, 1944, he served as head of the British Joint Staff Mission until well after the end of the war, in 1947. Back in Britain, Wilson served as constable of the Tower of London from 1955 to 1960.

Further reading: Wilson, Henry Maitland. *Eight Years Overseas, 1939–1947.* London: Hutchinson, 1948.

Wingate, Orde (1903–1944) *British commander of the famed Chindits— legendary Burmese guerrillas*

Born in India and educated at the Charterhouse and Royal Military Academy, Woolwich, Wingate entered the Royal Artillery in 1923 and was dispatched to service in the Sudan and Libya during 1928–33. He was an intelligence officer in Palestine during 1936–39 and used this assignment to develop guerrilla and small-unit tactics by mounting night patrols to repel Arab raids on Jewish communities along the Mosul-Haifa oil pipeline. Wingate's specialty became penetrating the enemy lines and attacking from the rear with light infantry raiders.

During World War II, from January to May 1941, he commanded the Ethiopian-Sudanese force that captured Addis Ababa, Ethiopia, from the Italians. After this, he was dispatched to India, where he organized the Chindits (elite "Long Range Penetration" troops) and worked with U.S. commander FRANK MERRILL to create the raider force dubbed "Merrill's Marauders."

Wingate led his Chindits during February–May 1943 into Japanese-held Burma, crossed the Chindwin River, and—deep behind enemy lines, relying entirely on air drops for supply—he operated against the Japanese, penetrating as far as the Irrawaddy and Salween Rivers before returning to India.

In March 1944, Wingate assumed command of an AIRBORNE ASSAULT into central Burma. He managed to interdict the Mandalay-Myitkyinā railway—a key Japanese communications and supply artery—before he was killed in an airplane crash on March 24. With his death, the Allies lost one of their few great experts in unconventional warfare.

Further reading: Bierman, John, and Colin Smith. *Fire in the Night: Wingate of Burma, Ethiopia, and Zion*. New York: Random House, 1999; Royle, Trevor. *Orde Wingate: Irregular Soldier*. London: Trafalgar Square, 1996.

Wolf pack U-boat tactics

Germany's top naval commander, KARL DÖNITZ, developed the *Rudeltaktik*—which the Allies called the wolf pack—as a devastatingly effective way to conduct submarine warfare against Allied convoys.

The wolf pack idea may be traced to U-boat tactics of World War I, which were specifically designed to defeat the CONVOY SYSTEM, introduced by the British during that war. Escorted convoys prevented individual U-boats from picking off isolated ships. By forming U-boats into a "wolf pack," then delaying the attack until all submarines in the pack were assembled and in position for a massed, coordinated assault, the attackers could overwhelm convoy escorts and thereby disrupt defense of the transport ships. Wolf pack tactics required one submarine to act as the "shadower," making contact with a convoy, shadowing it, and reporting its position to the other boats as they rendezvoused and gathered into a pack for the coordinated attack.

After wolf pack tactics were reintroduced early in World War II, the Allies sustained heavy losses until they developed commensurately effective antisubmarine warfare tactics.

Further reading: Mallman-Showell, Jack P. *U-Boat Warfare: The Evolution of the Wolf Pack*. Annapolis, Md.: Naval Institute Press, 2002; Williamson, Gordon. *Wolf Pack: The Story of the U-Boat in World War II*. London: Osprey, 2005.

Women Accepted for Voluntary Emergency Service (WAVES)

The WAVES—Women Accepted for Voluntary Emergency Service—was established on July 30, 1942, under the command of Lieutenant Commander Mildred H. McAfee (appointed August 2). WAVES personnel filled clerical positions ashore, thereby freeing men for sea and combat duty. It was not until October 1944 that the navy began accepting African-American women for the WAVES.

During the war, more than 100,000 women served in the WAVES before the service was disbanded in 1945. No women were allowed to serve on sea duty.

Further reading: Godson, Susan H. *Serving Proudly: A History of Women in the U.S. Navy*. Annapolis, Md.: Naval Institute Press, 2001.

Women Airforce Service Pilots (WASP)

Acting on an earlier suggestion by famed aviator Jacqueline Cochran, Lt. Gen. HENRY H. "HAP" ARNOLD, chief of staff of the UNITED STATES ARMY AIR FORCES, authorized on October 7, 1942, a training program for 500 women ferry pilots, which became the Women Airforce Service Pilots (WASP) on August 5, 1943.

From 1942 until it was deactivated in December 1944, WASP attracted more than 33,000 applicants, of whom 1,074 graduated from the rigorous training program to become WASPs. These pilots delivered a wide range of planes from manufacturers to air base destinations in the continental United States. The unit flew some 75 million miles, with each pilot averaging 14 flying hours each month. Former WASPs were belatedly recognized by Congress as veterans, entitled to veteran's benefits, in 1978.

These three female pilots leaving their ship at the four engine school at Lockbourne are members of a group of WASPs who have been trained to ferry the B-17 Flying Fortresses. *(U.S. Air Force)*

See also WOMEN'S AUXILIARY FERRYING SQUADRON (WAFS).

Further reading: Johnson, Ann R. "The WASP of World War II," *Aerospace Historian* (Summer–Fall, 1970), 76–82.

MARINE CORPS WOMEN'S RESERVE; WOMEN'S ARMY CORPS; WOMEN'S AUXILIARY FERRYING SQUADRON; WOMEN AIRFORCE SERVICE PILOTS; WOMEN ACCEPTED FOR VOLUNTARY EMERGENCY SERVICE.

women in World War II, United States

World War II saw increased employment opportunities for women on the home front in war production, in resistance movements and espionage operations, and in the conventional military organizations of all the combatants.

The role of women in the war is discussed in the following articles: ESPIONAGE AND COUNTERESPIONAGE; UNITED STATES (see "America Produces" and "Life on the Home Front"); UNITED STATES

Women's Army Corps (WAC)

The Women's Army Corps (WAC) was established as the Women's Army Auxiliary Corps (WAAC) by Congress on May 14, 1941, primarily to furnish the U.S. Army with clerks, typists, switchboard operators, and the like, thereby freeing up men for combat and other service. Oveta Culp Hobby was appointed as the first director of the WAAC, which soon recruited its authorized limit of 150,000 women, of whom 35,000 were trained as officers.

Initially, most auxiliaries (as the WAACs were called) worked as file clerks, typists, stenographers, or motor pool drivers. Later, positions became more diverse, especially in the U.S. Army Air Forces, where WAACs worked as weather observers and forecasters, cryptographers, radio operators and repairers, sheet metal workers, parachute riggers, Link trainer instructors, bombsight maintenance specialists, aerial photograph analysts, and control tower operators. More than a thousand women ran the tabulating machines used to keep track of personnel records.

On July 3, 1943, the Women's Army Auxiliary Corps became the Women's Army Corps, and the personnel were no longer considered auxiliaries but members of the Regular Army. During this same month, the first battalion of WACs to reach the European theater of operations arrived in London—557 enlisted women and 19 officers assigned to duty with the Eighth Air Force. A second battalion arrived during September and October. Most of the women worked as telephone switchboard operators, clerks, typists, secretaries, and motor pool drivers, while WAC officers served as executive secretaries, cryptographers, and photo interpreters. A detachment of 300 WACs served with Supreme Headquarters, Allied Expeditionary Force (SHAEF), often handling highly classified materials. In February 1945, a battalion of 800 African-American WACs, the 6888th Central Postal Battalion, were sent to Europe and were responsible for the redirection of mail to all U.S. personnel in the European theater of operations (USA, USN, USMC, civilians, and Red Cross workers). WACs were also assigned extensively to the Pacific theater.

Most of the WACs were demobilized after V-J Day in August 1945. But early in 1946, the U.S. Army asked Congress for the authority to establish the Women's Army Corps as a permanent part of the Regular Army. Authorization came by act of Congress on June 12, 1948. The WAC became a separate corps of the Regular Army and remained part of the USA organization until 1978, when women were fully assimilated into all but the combat branches of the service.

Further reading: Earley, Charity Adams. *One Woman's Army: A Black Officer Remembers the WAC.* College Station: Texas A&M University Press, 1989; Treadwell, Mattie E. *The Women's Army Corps.* Washington, D.C.: U.S. Government Printing Office, 1954.

Women's Auxiliary Ferrying Squadron (WAFS)

Nancy Harkness Love was one of two prominent female aviators of the 1930s who proposed the use of women in noncombat flying roles. But whereas Jacqueline Cochran proposed training women as pilots, Love wanted to recruit women who already held commercial pilot's licenses, had logged 500 hours of flying time, and were rated to fly 200 horsepower craft. At first, Maj. Gen. HENRY H. "HAP" ARNOLD, chief of the UNITED STATES ARMY AIR FORCE, rejected Love's proposal, but in September 1942, he approved the creation of a women's ferrying squadron. The Women's Auxiliary Ferrying Squadron (WAFS) was founded the same month.

Although the WAFS was established as the Second Ferrying Group, New Castle Army Air Base, near Wilmington, Delaware, with Love as its director, the organization was never formally activated as a USAAF squadron and was actually a civil auxiliary. By the beginning of 1943, there were only 23 WAFS performing ferry duties, albeit performing them with a high degree of proficiency. Arnold decided to authorize a training school at Avenger Field, Sweetwater, Texas, and the WAFS were merged with the new women pilots. In August 1943, all women pilots serving with the USAAF became WASP (Women Airforce Service Pilots).

Further reading: Kosier, Edwin J. "Women in the Air Force," *Aerospace Historian* (Summer 1968): 18–23.

"wonder weapons"

As the fortunes of war turned against Germany, ADOLF HITLER made frequent reference to *Wunderwaffen,* "wonder weapons" under development by German scientists that would suddenly and inevitably turn the tide against the Allies. By the final months of the war, fewer and fewer Germans believed in either the existence or the efficacy of *Wunderwaffen* and mocked the idea by abbreviating the word to "Wuwa"—in effect the nonsense syllables *voo-vah.*

In fact, German weapons designers did rush to create a number of wonder weapons, including early jet aircraft and the V-1 BUZZ BOMB and V-2 ROCKET. The Reich also funded the development of an atomic bomb, which, however, never came close to becoming a usable weapon. Although some wonder weapons were produced and proved effective, they were not decisive, mainly because they could not be deployed in sufficient quantity.

Further reading: Ford, Roger. *Germany's Secret Weapons in World War II.* London: Zenith Press, 2000; Georg, Friedrich. *Hitler's Miracle Weapons: The Secret History of the Rockets and Flying Craft of the Third Reich.* Solihull, West Midlands, U.K.: Helion, 2005; Rose, Paul Lawrence. *Heisenberg and the Nazi Atomic Bomb Project, 1939–1945: A Study in German Culture.* Berkeley: University of California Press, 2001.

Yalta Conference and Agreement

The Yalta Conference took place in February 1945 at the Soviet Black Sea resort of Yalta, among the Big Three: FRANKLIN D. ROOSEVELT, WINSTON CHURCHILL, and JOSEPH STALIN. As the war against Germany was coming to a close, the United States and Great Britain sought to bring the Soviet Union into the still-unfinished war against Japan. The contest there was no longer seriously in doubt; the Japanese had been virtually defeated militarily. Nevertheless, they continued to fight, inflicting terrible casualties on the Americans and, to a lesser extent, on British and Commonwealth troops. Indeed, more Americans were being killed—by a defeated enemy no less—in this closing phase of the Pacific war than in all the combat between December 7, 1941, and the beginning of 1945.

Up to this point, with his hands more than full fighting the German INVASION OF THE SOVIET UNION then prosecuting an offensive against Germany, Stalin had avoided war with Japan. At Yalta, however, Roosevelt persuaded him to agree to declare war against Japan "two or three months" after the surrender of Germany. In return, the Soviet Union would acquire part of Sakhalin Island and the Kuril Islands—territories that Russia had lost to Japan in the 1905 Russo-Japanese War. Stalin was also assured of postwar Soviet dominance in Outer Mongolia and Manchuria. All of these terms were set down in the "Yalta Agreement on the Kuriles and Entry of the Soviet Union in the War against Japan," signed on February 11, 1945.

The Yalta Agreement was an excellent bargain for the Soviets. The successful use by the United States of atomic bombs against HIROSHIMA and NAGASAKI made a costly invasion of Japan unnecessary and ended the war much sooner than anticipated. Biding his time, Stalin had delayed declaring war well beyond the time frame specified in the Yalta Agreement, but he finally did so on August 8, 1945, two days after the atomic bombing of Hiroshima. By this expedient, the Soviets reaped the rewards of the agreement without having had to commit to a long battle.

The "Big Three" at Yalta: Churchill, Roosevelt, and Stalin *(Library of Congress)*

Further reading: Phillips, Charles, and Alan Axelrod. "Yalta Agreement," in *Encyclopedia of Historical Treaties and Alliances,* 2nd ed. New York: Facts On File, 2006, II: 606–607.

Yamada Otozo (1881–1965) *Japanese captain general of the Kwantung Army in Manchuria*

Yamada Otozo was a career military officer in the Imperial Japanese Army. From 1922 to 1926, he was commanding officer of the 26th Cavalry Regiment, then served in Korea during 1926–27 as chief of staff of the Chosen Army. He held positions on the Japanese General Staff from 1928 to 1930, when he was named head of the Training Branch Cavalry School. After two years as commanding officer of the 4th Cavalry Brigade, he was appointed commandant of the Army Signal School, serving from 1933 to 1934, when he returned to high-level staff duty until his appointment in 1937 as commandant of the Military Academy.

In 1938, Yamada was installed as general officer commanding the 12th Division in Manchuria. Soon after, he was elevated to command of the Third Army there, then served as commander in chief of the Central China Expeditionary Army during part of the Sino-Japanese War and most of World War II. He was also inspector-general of military training and, for a time, commander in chief of the General Defense Command and a member of the Supreme War Council. During 1944–45, he was commander in chief of the Kwantung Army in Manchuria.

Captured by the Red Army at the very end of the war, he was accused of having authorized human medical experimentation on Chinese citizens in Manchuria. The 1949 Khavbarosk Trial, conducted by Soviet authorities, convicted Yamada and 11 other military officers, doctors, and veterinarian officers, handing down sentences ranging from five to 25 years' imprisonment. Yamada received a 25-year sentence but was released in 1956 after Japan and the Soviet Union reestablished diplomatic relations.

Further reading: Harris, Sheldon. *Factories of Death: Japanese Biological Warfare, 1932–45 and the American Cover-Up.* London and New York: Routledge, 2001; Rees, Laurence. *Horror in the East: Japan and the Atrocities of World War II.* New York: Da Capo Press, 2002; Tanaka, Yuki. *Hidden Horrors: Japanese War Crimes in World War II.* Denver: Westview Press, 1998.

Yamamoto Isoroku (1884–1943) *Japanese admiral who planned and executed the Battle of Pearl Harbor*

Born Takano Isoroku in Nugata prefecture, the future Japanese supreme naval commander was adopted by the Yamamoto family, whose name he subsequently took. He graduated from the naval academy in 1904 and first saw action at the epoch-making Battle of Tsushima during the Russo-Japanese War. He was wounded in that war on May 26, 1905, losing two fingers from his left hand—an injury that nearly caused his dismissal from the navy.

In 1906, Yamamoto served aboard a variety of ships, then graduated from the U.S. Navy Torpedo School in 1908. He enrolled in the Naval Staff College, from which he graduated in 1911 and, the same year, graduated from the Naval Gunnery School. Appointed an instructor there, he was promoted to lieutenant commander in 1915. He graduated from the senior course at the Naval Staff College in 1916.

As a staff officer with the Second Fleet, Yamamoto was sent to the United States to study at Harvard University from 1919 to 1921. He acquired an admiration and respect for the country while he was a student and became aware of its potential as an industrial giant. This impression would weigh heavily on him as Japan prepared to enter World War II against America.

After leaving Harvard, Yamamoto returned to Japan as an instructor at the Naval War College, serving in this post from 1921 to 1923, when he was promoted captain and sent on a tour of inspection and observation to the United States and Europe as an admiral's aide. Named deputy commander of Kasumiga Ura Naval Air Station in 1924, he came to the United States again in 1925, this time as naval attaché in Washington, D.C., returning to Japan in 1928 as captain of the aircraft carrier *Akagi*.

In 1929, Yamamoto was promoted to rear admiral and in 1930 became chief of the Technological Division of the Navy Technological Department. In 1933, he was assigned to command the 1st Naval Air Division, then, promoted vice admiral in 1934, he became head of the Japanese delegation to the London Naval Conference of 1934–35.

Yamamoto was personally opposed to official Japanese insistence on naval parity with Britain and the United States, but, acting on orders, took a hard line in treaty negotiations and rejected any further extension of the tonnage ratios established by the Washington Naval Treaty of 1922. This freed Japan to accelerate its naval expansion.

Named chief of Naval Aviation Headquarters in 1935, Yamamoto presciently championed the use of the aircraft carrier as the principal offensive weapon of the navy. He then served as navy minister from 1936 to 1939, using his position in an attempt to moderate the extreme militarism of a government on the verge of a war he believed Japan could not win. In the meantime, Yamamoto accepted in 1938 a concurrent reappointment as chief of Naval Aviation Headquarters. He left both this position and the naval ministry to become commander of the Combined Fleet in 1939 and, in 1940, commander of First Fleet as well.

Yamamoto was tasked with making preparations for war against Britain and the United States. He went about this work fatalistically, in the belief that American industrial power and population would doom Japan to defeat, especially if the war dragged on. When it became clear to him that he could not stop his nation's rush toward conflict, he planned a surprise attack on the American fleet and naval base at Pearl Harbor in the hope that a sufficiently devastating blow would bring a quick negotiated peace with the United States.

Although the Pearl Harbor operation achieved the object of surprise and was indeed devastating, it proved to be a strategic blunder of fatal consequences, instantly galvanizing American resolve to defeat Japan.

Yamamoto Isoroku *(National Archives and Records Administration)*

Yamamoto followed up the Pearl Harbor attack with a series of lightning naval campaigns that captured the East Indies during January–March 1942 and that achieved success in the Indian Ocean during April 2–9, 1942. However, he met defeat against the U.S. Navy at the BATTLE OF MIDWAY on June 4, 1942, which he had hoped would be a showdown that would destroy the American fleet. Instead, the battle turned the tide of the Pacific war against the Japanese. Defeat at Midway deeply undermined Yamamoto's confidence, making him relatively timid in his leadership of the various battles of the Solomon Islands.

Unknown to Yamamoto and other Japanese war leaders, the United States, which had broken the chief Japanese military and diplomatic codes even before the war began, intercepted a radio message that revealed Yamamoto was to fly to a tour of Japanese bases on Shortland Island on April 18, 1943. U.S. fighter aircraft were dispatched to intercept and shoot down his plane. Yamamoto was killed near Bougainville. It was a blow from which the Imperial Japanese Navy did not recover.

Further reading: Agawa, Hiroyuki. *The Reluctant Admiral: Yamamoto and the Imperial Navy*. Tokyo: Kodansha International, 2000; Hoyt, Edwin P. *Yamamoto: The Man Who Planned the Attack on Pearl Harbor*. Guilford, Conn.: Lyons Press, 2001.

Yamashita Tomoyuki (1885–1946)
Japanese general associated with war crimes committed in the Philippines

Born in Kochi prefecture, Yamashita graduated from the Japanese Imperial Military Academy in 1906 and was commissioned as an infantry officer. He graduated from the Staff College in 1916 and was assigned to the German Section of the Intelligence Division of the Army General Staff two years later. During 1919–1921, he served as resident officer in Berne, Switzerland, then occupied the same position in Germany during 1921–1922.

Promoted to major in 1922 and to lieutenant colonel in 1925, Yamashita became military attaché in Vienna and, concurrently, in Budapest during 1927–1929. He returned to Japan in 1929 as a colonel assigned to the Military Research Division, Central Ordnance Bureau. The following year he assumed regimental command, then, in 1932, was appointed chief of the Military Affairs Section in the Army Ministry. He was elevated to chief of the Military Research Section in the Army Ministry's Military Research Bureau in 1935.

Like many other senior army officers, Yamashita was politically active. He was an ardent member of General Sadao Araki's hyper-nationalist Kodo-ha (Imperial Way) faction and initially supported the revolt of young Koda-ha officers on February 21, 1936, acting as liaison between them and the army central command. However, he soon turned against the faction and thereby saved his career. During 1936–1937, he commanded a brigade in Korea and was promoted to lieutenant general in 1937.

Yamashita was named chief of staff for the North China Area Army in 1937, serving in this post until 1939, when he took command of the 4th Division. In 1940, he became inspector general of army aviation and chief of the Military Aviation Observation Mission to Germany and Italy. He was assigned to command the Kwantung Defense Army in 1941, then transferred to command of 25th Army in November. It was at the head of this force that he led the invasion of Malaya during December 8–10 and directed the Japanese campaign down the Malay Peninsula, which swept away the British and Commonwealth defenders. Outnumbered by a factor of two, the "Tiger of Malaya" drove the British back to Singapore, where they surrendered on February 15, 1942.

Despite Yamashita's triumphs, his longtime rival, Prime Minister Tojo Hideki ordered Yamashita to be transferred to command of the First Area Army in Manchuria, by July 1942 a backwater in the war. This consignment to the sidelines proved only temporary and, in 1943, promoted to general, Yamashita was returned to the principal theater of the war as commander of the Fourteenth Area Army, assigned to defend the Philippines and northern Luzon. He reached Manila barely a week before U.S. forces landed on Leyte on October 20, 1944, so had little effect on the landings, but he did mount a fierce and well-executed defense of Luzon. Nevertheless, by February–April, his army had withdrawn into the mountains of northeastern Luzon, and in September 1945, he surrendered.

Yamashita was tried for the atrocities and other war crimes of Japanese troops who defended Manila in early 1945. Although he bore no direct responsibility for his troops' actions in the Philippine capital, he was judged at the Tokyo War Crimes Trials to bear responsibility nevertheless by virtue of his status as overall commander. Convicted, he was executed on February 23, 1946.

See also Malaya, fall of; Philippines, fall and reconquest of; and Singapore, fall of.

Further reading: Barker, A. J. *Yamashita*. New York: Ballantine Books, 1973; Reel, A. Frank. *The Case of General Yamashita*. New York: Octagon Books, 1971.

Yugoslavia

Yugoslavia was created on December 1, 1918, after World War I, as the Kingdom of the Serbs, Croats, and Slovenes, uniting disparate southern Slav lands that had been under the control of the Austro-Hungarian Empire with the already independent Serbia and Montenegro. As Yugoslavia (from 1929), the country had a population of nearly 16 million and covered a little over 95,000 square miles. Between the world wars, the unity of Yugoslavia was always tenuous, with friction especially strong between the country's Catholic Croat and Orthodox Serb populations.

At the outbreak of World War II in September 1939, Yugoslavia declared itself neutral; however, the divisions between Croat and Serb was aggravated by the war. The Serbs (who dominated the armed forces) were pro-Allied, whereas the Croats, although not enthusiastically pro-German, were unwilling to antagonize the Axis. In any case, Yugoslav neutrality became something of a moot point because Germany dominated the country's foreign trade and also owned a major share of its important mines of nonferrous metals. The government of Yugoslavia, headed by Prince Paul (as regent to the underage King Peter), increasingly yielded to German demands for agricultural produce and raw materials. Yugoslavia also yielded to Germany on the matter of anti-Semitic policy. More immediately menacing to the country was the entry of Yugoslavia's neighbors—Hungary, Romania, and Bulgaria—into the Axis orbit. The fact was that the Allies, reeling from one defeat after another at this early stage of the war, were in no position to help Yugoslavia resist German influence or intimidation. As for the Soviet Union, JOSEPH STALIN had no desire to alienate Hitler, with whom he had signed the GERMAN-SOVIET NON-AGGRESSION PACT. Thus Yugoslavia lay surrounded by Axis powers and at the mercy of both Italy and Germany.

Hitler was interested in Yugoslavia for its agricultural produce and raw materials, and also as a means of readily traversing the Balkans. At length, he pressured Prince Paul into signing the AXIS (TRIPARTITE) PACT. This unleashed anti-Axis demonstrations among Serbian nationalists, and on March 27, 1941, Serbs, together with various elements of the military, staged a coup d'état in which Prince Paul was overthrown (his regency over young King Peter was abolished), and a government was established under the presidency of General Dušan Simović. Croat elements within the new government insisted on continued adherence to the Axis Pact, to which the Serbs, suddenly fearful of German invasion, agreed. This did not appease Hitler, however, who immediately issued "Directive 25," which decreed the obliteration of Yugoslavia. The German invasion of Yugoslavia, which began on April 6, 1941, took place simultaneously with the German assault on Greece.

The invasion began with the bombing of Belgrade and was followed by ground operations. Yugoslav resistance rapidly crumbled, and a capitulation was signed on April 17.

Hitler installed a puppet regime under the ostensible leadership of General Milan Nedić, then instituted a policy of "Germanizing" Yugoslavia and, to this end, authorized what many Croats were all too willing to carry out: a campaign of genocide against Croatia's Serb minority (along with Jews, Gypsies, and other "undesirables"). Besides its moral reprehensibility, this proved to be a colossal mistake on Hitler's part, since it galvanized Serbian resolve to resist the Axis, thereby triggering a Serb rebellion that became a highly effective partisan resistance against the German occupation.

While Yugoslavia roiled under occupation, King Peter (now free of Prince Paul's regency) arrived in London in June 1941 and established a government in exile, around which military forces coalesced. As usual in Yugoslav affairs, however, many cracks and divisions rapidly developed, and the Allies threw their support behind the most dynamic leader, the Communist partisan TITO (JOSIP BROZ). Through the intervention of British prime minister WINSTON CHURCHILL, Tito agreed to work with King Peter. Churchill broadly hinted that this would put Tito in a position to assume control of most of the country once the Germans had been forced to withdraw. This is precisely what happened in 1944. In the meantime, Tito proved to be a highly effective partisan leader. By the end of 1943, Tito's forces—perhaps 200,000 strong—had not only survived but were pinning down no fewer than 35 Axis divisions (about 750,000 men), who would otherwise be deployed against the Western Allies in the Italian Campaign or against the Soviets on the eastern front. For the Western Allies, the price of this cooperation was a Communist Yugoslavia after the war; however, Tito proved to be no Stalinist puppet, and his Yugoslavia maintained genuine independence both from the West and the Soviet Union.

Further reading: Barnett, Neil. *Tito*. Dulles, Va.: Haus, 2006; Djilas, Milovan. *Tito: The Story from Inside*. New York: Harcourt Brace Jovanovich, 1980; Thomas, Nigel. *Axis Forces in Yugoslavia 1941–45*. London: Osprey, 1995; Thomas, Nigel. *Partisan Warfare 1941–45*. London: Osprey, 1992.

Z

Zhukov, Georgi Konstantinovich (1896–1974) *Marshal of the Soviet Union and the most celebrated Red Army commander of World War II*

Zhukov was born to a peasant family in Strelkovka, about 60 miles east of Moscow. He was apprenticed to a fur trader in 1908 and worked in this profession until 1915, when he was drafted into the tsarist army. He was rapidly promoted from private to noncommissioned officer and served in various cavalry units, including, most notably, the Novgorod Dragoons. He distinguished himself at the front and was awarded two Orders of St. George for bravery.

With the outbreak of the Russian civil war in 1918, Zhukov joined the Red Army in October 1918 and was given command of a cavalry squadron in the First Cavalry Army. He graduated from a junior officers military school in 1920, then after the civil war, enrolled in an intermediate-level cavalry officer course, which he completed in 1925. Following this, he studied advanced military science in a clandestine Kriegsakademie (war college) in Germany as part of the secret military collaboration that took place between the Soviet Union and the Weimar Republic in the late 1920s, owing to Germany's successful effort to circumvent the rearmament restrictions imposed by the TREATY OF VERSAILLES.

Returning to the Soviet Union, Zhukov studied at the Frunze Military Academy from 1928 to 1931. In 1938, he was made deputy commander of the Byelorussian Military District. Zhukov was almost immediately caught up in JOSEPH STALIN's purges and managed to escape relief from command, imprisonment, and even execution by virtue of an administrative error.

On the eve of World War II, Zhukov led the the Soviet First Army Group, which defeated the

Marshal Georgi Konstantinovich Zhukov *(Library of Congress)*

889

Japanese Sixth Army at the Khalka River near Nomonhan, Mongolia, during July–August 1939 in the Second Russo-Japanese War. He was then appointed deputy commander (1939) and commander (1940) of the Kiev Military District, and during the German INVASION OF THE SOVIET UNION in June 1941, he was rushed to the front to help with the defense of Smolensk in August. After the collapse of that defense, he organized the defense of Leningrad (present-day St. Petersburg) as commander of the Leningrad Front (army group) during September–October 1941. He transferred next to the Western Front, which defeated the German assault on Moscow during 1941–42.

Zhukov was a leading Red Army officer throughout the rest of the war, participating in every major operation, including the decisive defense of Stalingrad during 1942–43. He also directed the BATTLE OF KURSK in July 1943, the Byelorussian offensive during the summer of 1944, and the advance into Germany and BATTLE OF BERLIN in 1945. It was Zhukov who accepted the surrender of Nazi Germany on behalf of the Soviet Union on May 8, 1945, and it was he who headed the military administration of the Soviet zone of occupied Germany from May 1945 to March 1946.

Following World War II, the immensely popular Zhukov was assigned by a wary and envious Stalin a series of obscure regional commands—most notably the Odessa Military District. On Stalin's death in 1953, Zhukov was immediately elevated to deputy minister of defense and supported NIKITA KHRUSHCHEV in his opposition to the chairman of the Council of Ministers, Georgi Malenkov, who sought a reduction in military spending. After Khrushchev forced Malenkov to resign and replaced him with Nikolay Bulganin in February 1955, Zhukov succeeded Bulganin as minister of defense. He was also elected an alternate member of the Communist Party's Presidium.

In the postwar years, Zhukov undertook vigorous programs to introduce greater professionalism into the Soviet armed forces. Because this meant reducing the Communist Party's role in military affairs and promoting nonpolitical but militarily qualified officers to positions of greater power, friction developed with Khrushchev, who was now Soviet premier. Zhukov, however, managed to redeem himself in Khrushchev's estimation by his efforts to keep the premier in power when a majority of the Presidium (the so-called anti-party group) tried to oust Khrushchev. Zhukov ordered aircraft to transport members of the Central Committee from far-flung regions of the country to Moscow to restore the political balance in Khrushchev's favor in June 1957. Khrushchev responded by promoting Zhukov to full membership in the Presidium in July—though he still disagreed over his movement to replace party officials with military officers in the administration of the armed forces. The disagreement grew in intensity and, on October 26, 1957, Zhukov was dismissed as minister of defense. A week later, he was removed from his party posts and retired into obscurity. When Khrushchev himself fell from power in October 1964, Zhukov was awarded the Order of Lenin (1966) and was authorized to publish his autobiography (1969).

Further reading: Chaney, Otto Preston. *Zhukov.* Norman: University of Oklahoma Press, 1996; Zhukov, Georgi. *Memoirs of Marshal G. Zhukov.* New York: Delacorte Press, 1971.

Zog I (1895–1961) *king of Albania on the eve of World War II*

Born Ahmed Bey Zogu at Castle Burgajet, Albania, Zog, a commoner, was a supporter of Austria during World War I and, after the war, led the reformist Popular Party. He served in various ministerial posts from 1920 until he was briefly forced into exile by political rivals in June 1924. He returned to Albania in December and was elected president on February 1, 1925, then proclaimed king on September 1, 1928.

Zog was welcomed by a majority of Albanians as a strong leader who brought relative stability to turbulent postwar Albania. His rightist tendencies drew him toward Italian dictator BENITO MUSSOLINI, with who he made an association in 1925, securing from Italy a substantial loan followed in 1926 by a treaty of friendship and security. In 1927, Zog concluded a 20-year defensive military alliance. For his part, Mussolini was interested only in using Albania as a steppingstone into the Balkans, and, using financial manipulation and military threat, Mussolini came to control Albania's finances and armed forces by the eve of World War II in 1939. Throughout the 1930s, Zog tried to pry Albania from the Italian's grasp, but could not. At last, on April 7, 1939, all pretense was dropped and Mussolini made Albania into a protectorate. Victor Emmanuel III became king of Italy, forcing Zog to step down and enter into exile. Zog entertained a hope of returning after the war, but was barred by the immediate postwar establishment of Communist rule under ENVER HOXHA. Zog formally abdicated on January 2, 1946.

Further reading: Fischer, Bernd Jurgen. *Albania at War, 1939–1945.* Lafayette, Ind.: Purdue University Press, 1999; Tomes, Jason. *King Zog of Albania: Europe's Self-Made Muslim Monarch.* New York: New York University Press, 2004; Vickers, Miranda, and James Pettifer. *Albania: From Anarchy to Balkan Identity.* New York: New York University Press, 2000.

Bibliography

The following are general reference and narrative works on World War II. For books on specific subjects, see the "Further reading" section of the *Encyclopedia* article of interest.

Adams, Michael C. C. *The Best War Ever: America and World War II.* Baltimore: Johns Hopkins University Press, 1994.

Ambrose, Stephen E. *Citizen Soldiers: The U.S. Army from the Normandy Beaches to the Bulge to the Surrender of Germany, June 7, 1944–May 7, 1945.* New York: Simon & Schuster, 1997.

Bartov, Omer. *Hitler's Army: Soldiers, Nazis, and War in the Third Reich.* New York: Oxford University Press, 1991.

Bergerund, Eric M. *Fire in the Sky: The Air War in the South Pacific.* Denver, Colo.: Westview Press, 1999.

Bergerund, Eric M. *Touched with Fire: The Land War in the South Pacific.* New York: Viking, 1996.

Beschloss, Michael. *The Conquerors: Roosevelt, Truman and the Destruction of Hitler's Germany, 1941–1945.* New York: Simon & Schuster, 2002.

Bookman, John T., and Stephen T. Powers. *The March to Victory: A Guide to World War II Battles and Battlefields from London to the Rhine.* New York: Harper & Row, 1986.

Brinkley, Douglas, and Michael E. Haskew, eds. *The World War II Desk Reference.* New York: HarperCollins, 2004.

Buchanan, Albert Russell. *The United States and World War II.* New York: Harper & Row, 1964.

Bullock, Alan. *Hitler and Stalin: Parallel Lives.* New York: Knopf, 1992.

Burleigh, Michael. *The Third Reich: A New History.* New York: Hill and Wang, 2000.

Calvocoressi, Peter. *Total War: The Story of World War II.* New York: Pantheon Books, 1972.

Chambers, John W., and David Culbert, eds. *World War II, Film, and History.* New York: Oxford University Press, 1996.

Craven, Wesley Frank, and James Lea Cate, eds. *The Army Air Forces in World War II,* 7 vols. Chicago: University of Chicago Press, 1948–58.

Dear, I. C. B., ed. *The Oxford Companion to World War II.* Oxford: Oxford University Press, 2001.

Denfeld, Duane. *World War II Museums and Relics of Europe.* Manhattan, Kans.: Military Affairs/Aerospace Historian Publications, 1980.

Flower, Desmond, and James Reeves, eds. *The War, 1939–1945.* London: Cassell, 1960.

Franks, Clifton R., ed. *The Second World War.* West Point Military History Series. Wayne, N.J.: Avery, 1984.

Gantenbein, James Watson, comp. and ed. *Documentary Background of World War II, 1931 to 1941.* New York: Columbia University Press, 1948.

Goldhagen, Daniel J. *Hitler's Willing Executioners: Ordinary Germans and the Holocaust.* New York: Knopf, 1996.

Goodwin, Doris Kearns. *No Ordinary Time: Franklin and Eleanor Roosevelt: The Home Front in World War II.* New York: Simon & Schuster, 1994.

Hart, Liddel, ed. *History of the Second World War.* New York: Exeter Books, 1980.

Hess, Gary R. *The United States at War, 1941–1945.* Arlington Heights, Ill.: H. Davidson, 1986.

Jacobsen, Hans-Adolf, and Arthur L. Smith Jr., comps. and eds. *World War II, Policy and Strategy: Selected Documents with Commentary.* Santa Barbara, Calif.: Clio Books, 1979.

Keegan, John. *Encyclopedia of World War II.* London and New York: Hamlyn, 1977.

————. *The Second World War.* London: Hutchinson, 1989.

————, ed. *The Times Atlas of the Second World War.* New York: Harper & Row, 1989.

————, ed. *Who Was Who in World War II.* London: Arms and Armour Press, 1978.

Lamb, Richard. *War in Italy, 1943–1945: A Brutal Story.* New York: St. Martin's Press, 1993.

Langsam, Walter Consuelo, ed. *Historic Documents of World War II.* Princeton, N.J.: Van Nostrand, 1958.

Macdonald, John. *Great Battles of World War II.* New York: Macmillan, 1986.

Michel, Henri. *The Second World War.* London: Deutsch, 1975.

Miller, Nathan. *War at Sea: A Naval History of World War II.* New York: Scribner, 1995.

Morison, Samuel Eliot. *History of United States Naval Operations in World War II,* 15 vols. Boston: Little, Brown, 1947–1962.

Murray, Williamson, and Allan R. Millett. *A War to Be Won: Fighting the Second World War, 1937–1945.* Cambridge, Mass.: Belknap Press of Harvard University, 2000.

Neillands, Robin. *The Bomber War: The Allied Air Offensive against Nazi Germany.* New York: Overlook Press, 2001.

Noakes, J., and G. Pridham. *Nazism, 1919–1945.* Atlantic Highlands, N.J.: Humanities Press, 1983–1988.

Overy, R. J. *Russia's War.* New York: Penguin Books, 1998.

Perret, Geoffrey. *There's a War to Be Won: The United States Army in World War II.* New York: Random House, 1991.

Shachtman, Tom. *Terrors and Marvels: How Science and Technology Changed the Character and Outcome of World War II.* New York: William Morrow, 2002.

Shirer, William L. *The Rise and Fall of the Third Reich; A History of Nazi Germany.* New York: Simon and Schuster, 1960.

Snyder, Louis Leo. *Louis L. Snyder's Historical Guide to World War II.* Westport, Conn.: Greenwood Press, 1982.

————. *Encyclopedia of the Third Reich.* New York: McGraw-Hill, 1976.

————. *The War: A Concise History, 1939–1945.* New York: Simon & Schuster, 1960.

Spector, Ronald H. *Eagle against the Sun: The American War with Japan.* New York: Free Press, 1985.

Stanton, Shelby L. *Order of Battle, U.S. Army, World War II.* Novato, Calif.: Presidio, 1984.

Taylor, A. J. P. *The Origins of the Second World War.* New York: Atheneum, 1961.

Terkel, Studs. *The Good War: An Oral History of World War Two.* New York: Pantheon Books, 1984.

Toland, John. *The Rising Sun; The Decline and Fall of the Japanese Empire, 1936–1945.* New York: Random House, 1970.

Van Creveld, Martin. *Fighting Power: German and U.S. Army Performance, 1939–1945.* Westport, Conn.: Greenwood Press, 1982.

Weinberg, Gerhard L. *A World at Arms: A Global History of World War II.* New York: Cambridge University Press, 1994.

Wheeler, Richard. *A Special Valor: The U.S. Marines and the Pacific War.* New York: Harper & Row, 1983.

Young, Peter, ed. *Atlas of the Second World War.* New York: G. P. Putnam's Sons, 1974.

Index

Page numbers in **boldface** indicate primary discussions. Page numbers in *italic* indicate illustrations.